Unwritten Rome

In *Unwritten Rome*, T.P. Wiseman continues to rethink the history of Rome and Roman literature. He presents us with an imaginative and appealing picture of the early society of pre-literary Rome—as a free and uninhibited world in which the arts and popular entertainments flourished. His original angle allows the voice of the Roman people to be retrieved from contemporary artefacts and figured monuments, and from selected passages of later literature.

> *"This book will be essential reading for every serious student of the history of Roman literature; it will be quite impossible to ignore it. As Wiseman cast brilliant light on Roman myth in his recent book* [The Myths of Rome], *here he does the same for the broader literary tradition... This is a feast of a book that you dive into and just keep going..."*
>
> Barry B. Powell, Professor of Classics Emeritus,
> University of Wisconsin–Madison

> *"Wiseman has a gift for combining different kinds of evidence, over which he has an unrivalled mastery, into new and provocative arguments... The book will be an indispensable companion to Wiseman's much acclaimed* The Myths of Rome..."
> Professor Tim Cornell, Department of Classics and Ancient History,
> University of Manchester

T.P. Wiseman is Emeritus Professor of Classics at Exeter University and a Fellow of the British Academy. In 2005, he won the American Philological Association's Goodwin Award of Merit for his most recent book, *The Myths of Rome*.

T.P. Wiseman's books, all with University of Exeter Press
except where indicated, include:

Clio's Cosmetics: Three Studies in Greco-Roman Literature
(1979, reprinted 2004 by Bristol Phoenix Press, UEP's sister imprint)
Death of an Emperor: Flavius Josephus (1991)
Talking to Virgil: A Miscellany (1992)
Historiography and Imagination: Eight essays on Roman culture (1994)
Remus: A Roman myth (1995, CUP)
Roman Drama and Roman History (1998)
The Myths of Rome (2004, paperback, 2008)
Remembering the Roman People (forthcoming, OUP)

Unwritten Rome

T.P. WISEMAN

UNIVERSITY
of
EXETER
PRESS

Cover illustration: Silenus-head terracotta antefix, early fifth century BC, from below the Basilica Iulia in the Roman Forum. Reproduced by permission of the Soprintendenza per i Beni Archeologici di Roma.

First published in 2008 by
University of Exeter Press
Reed Hall, Streatham Drive
Exeter EX4 4QR
UK
www.exeterpress.co.uk

British Library Cataloguing in Publication Data
A catalogue record for this book is available from the British Library.

Hardback ISBN: 978 0 85989 822 5
Paperback ISBN: 978 0 85989 823 2

Typeset in Bembo and Gill Sans
by XL Publishing Services, Tiverton

Printed in Great Britain by Cromwell Press, Trowbridge

For
Michael Crawford
William Harris
David Ridgway
(British School at Rome, 1962–3)

Contents

Illustrations

Acknowledgements

I am very grateful for permission to reprint the following chapters:

3: *Arethusa* 39.3 (2006), 513–29

4: *Journal of Roman Studies* 85 (1995), 1–22

5: Christer Bruun (ed.), *The Roman Middle Republic: Politics, Religion and Historiography c.400–133 BC* (Acta Instituti Romani Finlandiae 23, Rome 2000), 265–99

6: W.V. Harris and E. Lo Cascio (eds), *Noctes Campanae: Studi di storia antica ed archeologia dell'Italia preromana e romana in memoria di Martin W. Frederiksen* (Itala Tellus 1, Luciano, Naples 2005), 227–43

8: Kathryn Welch and T.W. Hillard (eds), *Roman Crossings: Theory and Practice in the Roman Republic* (Classical Press of Wales, Swansea 2005), 49–58

9: Bettina Bergmann and Christine Kondoleon (eds), *The Art of Ancient Spectacle* (Studies in the History of Art 56, Washington D.C. 1999), 194–203: reprinted by permission of the National Gallery of Art, Washington; all rights reserved

10: Edward Bispham and Christopher Smith (eds), *Religion in Archaic and Republican Rome and Italy: Evidence and Experience* (Edinburgh 2000), 108–14

11: *Symbolae Osloenses* 77 (2002), 82–8: by permission of Taylor and Francis AS (www.tandf.no/symbolae)

12: *Ancient History Bulletin* 19.1–2 (2005), 59–69

13. Geraldine Herbert-Brown (ed.), *Ovid's Fasti: Historical Readings at its Bimillennium* (Oxford 2002), 275–99: by permission of Oxford University Press

14: John Marincola (ed.), *The Blackwell Companion to Greek and Roman Historiography* (Blackwell, Oxford 2007), 67–75

15: D.S. Levene and D.P. Nelis (eds), *Clio and the Poets: Augustan Poets and the Traditions of Ancient Historiography* (*Mnemosyne* Supplement 224, Brill, Leiden 2002), 331–62

17: Mario Citroni (ed.), *Memoria e identità* (Studi e testi 21, Florence 2003), 21–38

18: *Greece and Rome* 45 (1998), 19–26: copyright the Classical Association, with permission

In all these chapters, additional material is included in square brackets. Chapters 1, 2, 7 and 16, and the Afterword to chapter 18, are previously unpublished.

CHAPTER ONE

Unwritten Rome

Brave men lived before Agamemnon,
Plenty of them—but they're all unmournable,
Buried unknown in the long night
Because they lack the sacred bard.

Horace *Odes* 4.9.25–8

I

Brave men lived before Romulus, too. Rome dates from at least the thirteenth century BC,[1] a thousand years before the sacred bard first wrote heroic verse in Latin. When it was first called 'Rome', nobody knows; but the archaeological record reveals a substantial community already in the ninth century BC.[2]

Its size and expansion can be inferred from the first major stage in its development, when the burial-ground in the low-lying area north of the Palatine was abandoned, and a new one created nearly a mile away on the plateau of the Esquiline.[3] The archaeological context of that is *Cultura laziale* IIA1, about 875 BC on the conventional dating.[4] The Esquiline cemetery remained in use for more than eight centuries, until Augustus' friend Maecenas redeveloped it for his suburban park,[5] and it was already more than two hundred years old when the people who used it began to scratch names on the vases that were buried with the deceased. These graffiti are the earliest known writing in Rome—an Etruscan *snu*[. . .] on a fragment of an 'Italo-geometric' plate [fig.

---

1   The terracing on the Capitol in the late Bronze Age (say 1300–1200 BC) may have removed the trace of Middle Bronze-Age occupation, for which only sporadic and unstratified material survives: see Lugli and Rosa 2001 (esp. 285), Baroni 2001.
2   Or the tenth, if the proposed recalibration of *Cultura laziale* II A–B is correct: see Bettelli 1997.191–8, Nijboer *et al.* 1999/2000. See Cornell 1995.48–57 for an accessible summary of the archaeological data.
3   Summary in Holloway 1994.20–36.
4   Bettelli 1997.215–16; on the revised dating (n. 2 above) it would be about a century earlier.
5   Horace *Satires* 1.8.8–16; Bodel 1994.38–54.

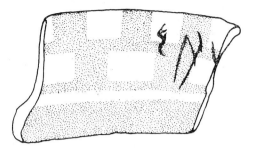

Fig. 1 'Perhaps the earliest inscription from Rome' (Colonna 1987.58): graffito on an Italo-geometric plate from the Esquiline cemetery at Rome, first half of the seventh century BC.

1], and a Greek *ktektos* or *kleiklos* on a Corinthian oil-flask, both in the seventh century BC.[6]

That was about the time when the Romans (as we can now safely call them) undertook a huge public-works project. By depositing up to 20,000 cubic metres of fill, they raised the ground level of the basin between the Palatine and the Capitol, to minimise flooding and provide the foundation for a pebble-paved public area, the Roman Forum.[7] Rectangular public buildings in stone soon began to replace thatch-and-timber huts, and by the middle of the sixth century BC they were being decorated with terracotta panels and friezes. One fragment that happens to survive, probably from the third phase of the 'king's house' (*regia*) at the east end of the Forum,[8] gives us our first glimpse into the imaginary world of archaic Rome [fig. 2]. What we see is quite mysterious: panthers and a minotaur. The image must have a meaning, but it was probably never written down.

Writing was, however, in public use by this time. The most spectacular evidence for that comes from a sixth-century cult site now identified as the Volcanal, close to the Comitium.[9] It consists of the lower part of a square-cut pillar, covered on all four sides with a long inscription [fig. 3]. About half the text survives, enough to allow the conjecture that it consisted of regulations and prohibitions connected with the sacred site. However, since it runs both vertically and '*boustrophedon*' (i.e. reading alternately left to right and right to

---

6   Colonna 1987.57–8, Poucet 1989.287–8. See respectively Bagnasco Gianni 1996.305 and Solin 1983 (illustration at Holloway 1994.25).
7   Ammerman 1990; cf. Ammerman 1998 and 2006.303–7 for the 'Velabrum' valley.
8   Cristofani 1990.61 (item 3.2.13), Holloway 1994.60–4.
9   Holloway 1994.81–7, Cornell 1995.94–5; full details in Cristofani 1990.58–9 (item 3.1.39). Volcanal: Coarelli 1983.161–78.

Fig. 2 Fragment of terracotta frieze, found in the 1950s and attributed to the *regia*: mid–sixth century BC.

Fig. 3 Archaic inscription from the Volcanal, discovered by Giacomo Boni in 1901. Starting at the top right, it reads: [. . .]*m kalato* | *rem ha*[. . .]*od iouxmen* | *ta kapia dotau*[. . .]*m i te ri*[. . .]*m quoi ha* | *uelod nequ*[. . .]*od iouestod.* . .

left, or in this case alternately up and down), it is hard to imagine that it was meant for direct communication with the citizens.[10] The rules were cut in stone to make them permanent, but I doubt if one Roman in a hundred could have read them for himself. It was the priest, through his crier, the *kalator*, who told the People what to do and what not to do.[11]

What mattered in practice was not written documents but the winged word:[12]

> ... *uerbum saepe unum perciet auris*
> *omnibus in populo, missum praeconis ab ore.*

> A single word often makes attentive the ears of everyone in the assembly, when it is shot from the crier's mouth.

Even the Twelve Tables, the Roman law code, supposedly set up in bronze or ivory on the Rostra in 449 BC, were communicated through oral means, taught as a 'compulsory recitation' to young Romans in school.[13] Public inscriptions were symbolic monuments, not information media.

Another use of writing in early Rome came to light in the 1870s, when the city was being redeveloped as the capital of united Italy. Up on the high ground where the new railway station was built, substantial lengths of the city wall of republican Rome were discovered [fig. 4]. The wall was built in the 370s BC. Seven miles long and forty feet high, it was a huge undertaking. Hundreds of thousands of tufa blocks were cut from the quarries of newly-conquered Veii, marked by the masons with code-letters on the side that didn't show.[14]

Bitter experience had made it necessary. In 387/6 BC (perhaps the first reliably dated event in Roman history),[15] Rome was captured and sacked by a marauding army of Gauls. New defences were necessary to make sure that would not happen again—and it didn't, for nearly 800 years. As well as the great walls, Rome also created a new and more open political system, with power shared between 'patricians' and 'plebeians' (as later Roman idiom described them). It is likely that these new conditions made Rome attractive to ambitious immigrants from other parts of Italy, including areas like Campania

---

10 So Cristofani 1990.58, rightly. Cf. Harris 1989.50–1 on public inscriptions in archaic Greece.
11 E.g. Varro *De lingua Latina* 6.27 (*pontifices*), Ovid *Fasti* 2.527–8 (*curio maximus*). *Kalatores*: *CIL* 6.36840.c.1 (= fig. 3, bottom right); cf. 2184–90, 36932, 37167.
12 Lucretius 4.563–4. Winged words: Homer *Iliad* 1.201 etc.
13 Cicero *De legibus* 2.59 (*ut carmen necessarium*), cf. 2.9; Harris 1989.151–3, not refuted by Cornell 1991.31–2. Bronze tablets: Diodorus 12.26.1, Livy 3.57.10, Dionysius of Halicarnassus 10.57.7. Ivory tablets: Pomponius in *Digest* 1.2.2.4.
14 Säflund 1932.109–11.
15 Polybius 1.6.1–2 (from Timaeus?), cf. 2.18–20; Diodorus Siculus 14.110.1, 14.115, Justin 6.6.5.

Fig. 4 Remains of the fourth-century BC city wall near Roma Termini station. In this photograph, taken soon after excavation, the masons' marks are clearly visible.

and Etruria where the art of writing may have been more widely practised.[16] One such, no doubt, was the fourth-century master craftsman Novius Plautius, who made the 'Ficoroni *cista*' [fig. 31, p. 104 below]. His *praenomen* suggests a Campanian origin, and the inscription he attached to his work reveals a confident mastery of the medium [fig. 5].[17]

What else was writing used for in Rome at this time? Unlike the Greek-speaking world (Novius Plautius was a contemporary of Aristotle), there is no sign here that the poet's song, the actors' performance or the story-teller's narrative was yet thought worthy to be 'committed to letters' and preserved for ever like laws and treaties.[18] Another fine fourth-century *cista* from Latium [fig. 22, p. 94 below] shows Agamemnon in a scene unknown to Greek literature, and identifies him as *Acmemeno*;[19] evidently the artist, and no doubt his patron too, knew the name not from written texts but from hearing it spoken.

The earliest certain evidence for narrative writing in Rome comes from the

---

16 For Etruria, see Colonna 1976, Torelli 1996.

17 *CIL* 1².561 = *ILLRP* 1197.

18 *Litteris mandare*: e.g. Sisenna fr. 127P (Aulus Gellius 12.15.2), Caesar *De bello Gallico* 6.14.3. Early treaty inscriptions: Dionysius of Halicarnassus 4.58.4 (Rome and Gabii), Polybius 3.22.1–3 and 26.1 (Rome and Carthage), Cicero *Pro Balbo* 53 (Rome and Latins), Livy 4.7.10 (Rome and Ardea).

19 Battaglia and Emiliozzi 1976.146–50 (no. 45), tav. cxcii.

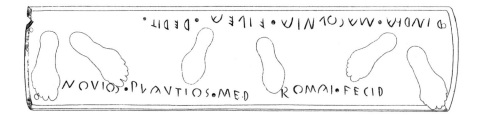

Fig. 5 Signature plate attached to the lid of the 'Ficoroni *cista*', in the Villa Giulia Museum, Rome. The footprints are of the figures of Liber Pater flanked by two satyrs which formed the handle. The front inscription reads 'Novios Plautios made me in Rome', the rear one 'Dindia Macolnia gave [me] to her daughter'. About 340 BC.

tomb of the Scipios on the Via Latina. The two earliest sarcophagi are those of L. Scipio 'Barbatus', consul in 298 BC, and his son L. Scipio, consul in 259 BC. They carry the following inscriptions in 'Saturnian' verse:[20]

1. *Cornelius Lucius   Scipio Barbatus*
    Gnaiuod patre prognatus   fortis uir sapiensque
    quoius forma uirtutei   parisuma fuit
    consol censor aidilis   quei fuit apud uos
    Taurasia Cisauna   Samnio cepit
    subigit omne Loucanam   opsidesque abdoucit
    Cornelius Lucius Scipio Barbatus
    father Gnaeus' offspring, a brave and educated man,
    whose beauty matched his character.
    He was consul, censor, aedile among you,
    Taurasia, Cisauna, Samnium he conquered,
    he subjugated all Lucania and brought back captives.

2. *honc oino ploirume   consentiont R[omane]*
    duonoro optumo   fuise uiro
    Luciom Scipione   filios Barbati
    consol censor aidilis   hic fuet a[pud uos]
    hec cepit Corsica   Aleriaque urbe
    dedet Tempestatebus   aide merito[d]
    This man most Romans agree
    was the very best of good men,

---

20 *ILLRP* 309–10, illustrated in Coarelli 1996.219–20. Translation: Goldberg 1995. 62–3, very slightly adapted.

> Lucius Scipio, the son of Barbatus.
> He was consul, censor, aedile among you,
> he captured Corsica and the city of Aleria,
> he fittingly dedicated a temple to the Weather.

The second-person-plural address (*apud uos*) can hardly have been meant in the first instance for a group reading by lamplight in an underground burial chamber. In the context, 'you' ought to be the Roman People, and the inference is surely right that the texts were first composed for delivery at the two men's funerals, about 270 and 230 BC.[21] The spelling and the letter-forms show that the inscription on Barbatus' coffin was cut much later than that on his son's (one might guess about 190 BC);[22] so there was evidently a written version of the funeral poem about his achievements which could be quoted two generations later, when his descendants wanted to make his sarcophagus as impressive as his son's.

Those were the two generations that saw the creation and first flowering of Latin literature.[23] We can know of that development only anachronistically, through the works of authors two centuries later who took literature as much for granted as the air they breathed. Because they had no notion of it themselves, they cannot convey to us what was involved for the pioneering cultural entrepreneurs who first wrote plays and epic poems in Latin—Andronicus from Greek Tarentum, known by his Roman-citizen name as Livius;[24] Gnaeus Naevius, from Campania and proud of it;[25] and Quintus Ennius from Rudiae in the heel of Italy, trilingual in Oscan, Greek and Latin.[26]

At the same time, Romans were now writing history in prose. But these authors were senators—Quintus Fabius Pictor, from an ancient patrician family, and Lucius Cincius Alimentus—and they wrote in Greek.[27] Fabius' history was evidently translated into Latin, but we do not know when; Latin historiography proper began in the mid-second century, with Cato and Cassius Hemina.[28] By

---

21 Zevi 1968. See Polybius 6.53–4 for Roman aristocratic funerals.

22 Coarelli 1996.217–23.

23 Brilliantly analysed by Feeney 2005, esp. 232–3 on 'the differences between artistic and textual production in Rome in, say, 260 BCE and in, say, 200 BCE', and 236–7 on the *semigraeci* (Suetonius *De grammaticis* 1.2) who created it.

24 Cicero *Brutus* 72 for his origin (from Accius, who evidently misdated his arrival in Rome); Gruen 1990.80–3.

25 Aulus Gellius 1.24.2 (*plenum superbiae Campanae*); Gruen 1990.92–3.

26 Aulus Gellius 17.17.1 on his 'three hearts'; see ch. 3 below.

27 Dionysius of Halicarnassus 1.6.2 (date), 1.74.1 (Cincius a senator); Appian *Hannibalic War* 27.116 (Fabius a senator).

28 Pictor in Latin: Varro in Quintilian 1.6.12, Aulus Gellius 5.4.3, Nonius 835L, Servius *auctus* on *Aeneid* 8.630. Cato: Cicero *De senectute* 38 (at work on the final book in 150 BC). Cassius Hemina: Censorinus *De die natali* 17.11 (146 BC); Rawson 1991.246.

that time, Ennius' great epic *Annales* had already given the Romans the whole story of their city, from Aeneas and Romulus right down to the wars they had fought in themselves.

It is very easy, when following a summary narrative like the one we have just constructed, to lose track of the passing of time. It is only when we set it out in visual form [fig. 6] that the problem of 'unwritten Rome' becomes apparent. Every century represents a period well beyond the range of living memory, at the limit even of what can be learned from the memories of grand-parents. So when the Roman past was first written down by the poets, playwrights and historians of the late third century BC, how much of it was accurately remembered?

II

Historians writing in Greek must have been aware of the principles of Greek historiography, as set out by the great masters of the genre. For Herodotus, it was not enough to accept or reject existing stories; the historian must take responsibility for his own narrative.[29] Thucydides insisted on first-hand knowl-edge, or the careful interviewing of eye-witnesses; for periods where that was not possible, the historian must make rational inferences from the evidence (τεκμήρια, 'indications').[30] It seems that Fabius Pictor and Cincius Alimentus acted on these principles. 'Each of them,' wrote Dionysius,[31] 'related the events at which he himself had been present with great exactness, as being well acquainted with them, but touched only in a summary way upon the early events that followed the foundation of the city.'

In fact, 'indications' did exist which could have allowed Thucydidean inferences about early Rome; but there were not many of them, and they were not easy to use.

In the Treasury of the Aediles, next to the temple of Jupiter Optimus Maximus on the Capitol, was a bronze tablet preserving the first treaty between Rome and Carthage. Polybius believed it was made in the first year of the Republic by the consuls L. Iunius Brutus and M. Horatius. He provided a translation for his Greek readers, but warned them that 'the modern language has developed so many differences from the ancient Roman tongue that the

---

29 Herodotus 1.5.3: 'So this is what the Persians and Phoenicians say. I am not going to come down in favour of this or that account of events, but I will talk about the man who, to my certain knowledge, first undertook criminal acts against the Greeks. I will show who it was who did this, and then proceed with the rest of my account.' Translation by Robin Water-field (World's Classics).

30 Thucydides 1.1.1 (τεκμαιρόμενος), 1.20.1, 1.21.1 (τεκμήρια); 1.22.2–3 (eye-witnesses).

31 Dionysius of Halicarnassus 1.6.2 (trans. E. Cary, Loeb); 'exactness' is the Thucydidean concept of ἀκρίβεια.

	1400	
Middle Bronze Age occupation?		
	1300	
Late Bronze Age: terracing on Capitol		
	1200	
	1100	
	1000	
	900	
Creation of Esquiline cemetery		
	800	
	700	
First graffiti on pots [fig. 1];	600	
Forum valley developed		
Terracotta decoration [fig. 2]		
Volcanal inscription [fig. 3]		'House of Tarquin', ch. 16
	500	Tarquins expelled, ch. 17
'Twelve Tables' law code		
	400	
city wall [fig. 4]		
'Ficoroni *cista*' [fig. 5]		Marsyas statue, ch. 5
	300	Q. Fabius and Lupercalia, ch. 4
Scipio tombs		
Livius Andronicus; Naevius		*ludi Florales*, ch. 9
Fabius Pictor; Cincius Alimentus	200	
Ennius; Cato		
Cassius Hemina		
	100	
		Sulla, ch. 10; Varro, ch. 15
		Livy, Dionysius
	BC/AD	Ovid
		Valerius Maximus, ch. 15
		Octavia, ch. 12
	100	
		Plutarch
	200	
	300	
	400	Augustine
	500	

Fig. 6 Time chart of Roman history, from the first evidence of occupation to the end of the Roman empire in the West. Latin literature began in the twelfth of these nineteen centuries. *Left:* developments mentioned in this chapter. *Right:* a selection of dates relevant to later chapters.

best scholars among the Romans themselves have great difficulty in inter-preting certain points, even after much study'.[32]

At the temple of Diana on the Aventine there was a bronze pillar with an ancient inscription 'in the letters used long ago in Greece', naming the cities of the Latin league. In the temple of Semo Sancus on the Quirinal there was a wooden shield covered in ox-hide with an inscription 'in ancient characters' recording Rome's treaty with Gabii.[33] Dionysius dates both inscriptions to the sixth century BC, but it is unlikely that either he or his source could read them.

Dionysius also reports that Romulus, after his second triumph, put up a statue to himself at the Volcanal, with an inscription 'in Greek letters' recording his achievements. Elsewhere, following a different source, he inter-prets the same ancient inscription as reporting the deeds of Romulus' right-hand man Hostus Hostilius.[34] This is, in fact, the very inscription found in 1901 [fig. 3 above].[35] Broken and covered over in the repaving of the Forum in the late Republic,[36] it was still complete and visible in the second century BC when the authors Dionysius used were writing. 'What is disturbing,' observes Tim Cornell,[37] 'is that Dionysius' sources should have been so grossly mistaken in their interpretation of the text and its monumental setting.' I think it is just what we should expect.

Livy reports an outbreak of plague in 363 BC, as a result of which the Senate revived the ancient custom of 'hammering a nail'. He explains in a digression:[38]

lex uetusta est, priscis litteris uerbisque scripta, ut qui praetor maximus sit idibus Septem-bribus clauum pangat; fixa fuit dextro lateri aedis Iouis optimi maximi, ex qua parte Mineruae templum est. eum clauum, quia rarae per ea tempora litterae erant, notam numeri annorum fuisse ferunt eoque Mineruae templo dicatam legem quia numerus Mineruae inuentum sit. Volsiniis quoque clauos indices numeri annorum fixos in templo Nortiae, Etruscae deae, comparere diligens talium monumentorum auctor Cincius adfirmat.

There is an ancient law, written in archaic letters and phraseology, that he who is *praetor maximus* should hammer a nail on the Ides of September. The text was fastened up on the right side of the temple of Jupiter Optimus Maximus, where the sanctuary of Minerva is. It is said that this nail marked the number of the

---

32 Polybius 3.22.1 (date), 22.3 (trans. Ian Scott-Kilvert, Penguin Classics), 26.1 (aediles' treasury); see now Serrati 2006.114–18. For the consuls in Year One, see ch. 18 below.

33 Dionysius of Halicarnassus 4.26.5, 4.58.4.

34 Dionysius of Halicarnassus 2.54.2, 3.1.2 (cf. 1.87.2, tomb of Faustulus); Festus 184L shows that it was the same site.

35 Coarelli 1983.166–9, Cornell 1991.27–9.

36 Festus 416L (*postquam id Cotta strauit*), with Coarelli 1985.196–7.

37 Cornell 1991.28–9.

38 Livy 7.3.5–7; detailed discussion in Oakley 1998.73–81.

years, since letters were little known at that time, and that the law was assigned to Minerva's shrine because numbers are her invention. Cincius, a scrupulous authority on records of this kind, asserts that at Volsinii too nails as markers of the number of the years may be seen in the temple of the Etruscan goddess Nortia.

Livy's source L. Cincius (not to be confused with Cincius Alimentus the historian) was an antiquarian, like those learned Romans Polybius had consulted about the Carthage treaty. Livy cites him not as a fellow-historian but as a specialist in esoteric lore, and it seems that Cincius himself thought of his scholarship in those terms. Besides the merely informative titles—On the Calendar, On Archaic Words, etc.—he also wrote a substantial work called Mystagogica, as if by interpreting such ancient documents he was leading his readers to a level of arcane knowledge denied to the uninitiated.[39]

Similar learned commentaries were applied to two texts in particular that were proverbial for archaic phraseology: the Twelve Tables law code and the hymn of the Salian priests.[40] But even the experts were often baffled. The Salii themselves hardly understood their own hymn,[41] and when Cicero reports commentators admitting that they didn't understand a particular point in the Twelve Tables, we need not suppose his example was unique.[42] Of one thing we can be certain: when the commentators met a difficulty, they tried to solve it from what they already knew. Whenever their guess was wrong, another difference between archaic Rome and their own times was lost for ever.

To be fair to the Roman antiquarians, they did know that the distant past might be very unfamiliar, and sometimes they succeeded in preserving evidence of a lost world. Consider for instance this passage from the elder Pliny on the wearing of crowns (coronae):[43]

semper tamen auctoritas uel ludicro quaesitarum fuit. namque ad certamina in circum per ludos et ipsi descendebant et seruos suos equosque mittebant. inde illa xii tabularum lex:

---

39 Festus 498L, citing book 2 of the Mystagogica on an inscription dated to 380 BC. Cf. Macrobius Saturnalia 1.12.12 (De fastis), Festus 236L etc (De uerbis priscis).

40 Fortunatianus Ars rhetorica 3.6 (124 Helm) on antiqua uerba . . . abolita, ut sunt in xii tabulis et Saliari carmine. Cf. Horace Epistles 2.1.86–7 on the unintelligibility of the Salian hymn. For jurists as antiquarians, see Harries 2006.176–82.

41 Quintilian 1.6.40. Commentaries on carmen Saliare: Aelius Stilo (Varro De lingua Latina 7.2, Festus 124L, 132L), Cincius (Macrobius Saturnalia 1.12.12), Sabidius (Schol. Veronensis on Aeneid 10.241).

42 Cicero De legibus 2.59 on lessum (Crawford 1996.706–7): hoc ueteres interpretes Sex. Aelius L. Acilius non satis se intellegere dixerunt. Sex. Aelius Paetus was consul in 198 BC (see Pomponius in Digest 1.2.2.38 for his text and interpretation of the Twelve Tables); L. Acilius was writing in the mid-second century BC (cf. Cicero De amicitia 6); Cicero also cites the opinion of L. Aelius Stilo (late second century). For the Twelve Tables in the late Republic, see Watson 1974.111–22.

43 Pliny Nat. Hist. 21.7 (Crawford 1996.708–10).

'qui coronam parit ipse pecuniaue eius uirtutisque suae ergo duitur ei.' quam serui equiue *meruissent pecunia partam lege dici nemo dubitauit. quis ergo honos? ut ipsi mortuo parentibusque eius, dum intus positus esset forisue ferretur, sine fraude esset imposita.*

There was always distinction in the winning [of *coronae*], even in sporting competitions. For they used to go down to the circus themselves to compete at the games, as well as entering their slaves and horses. Whence that law in the Twelve Tables: 'Whoever wins a crown, either himself or his property, or it be given him for his bravery...' Nobody has ever doubted that by 'won by his property' the law means that [*corona*] which his slaves or horses had earned. So what was the honour? That at his death and that of his parents [the *corona*] might legally be placed on the body while it lay in the house or was carried out [for burial].

Rightly or wrongly, Pliny infers from the law that in the early Republic charioteers at the games might be Roman citizens competing in person, rather than professionals employed by the four teams who raced in the Circus in the late Republic and under the emperors.[44]

Such insights are not common. Perhaps the best example is in Macrobius, where Furius Albinus demonstrates that dancing and singing were acceptable among the Roman elite in the time of the elder Cato, and not in the time of Cicero.[45] But there the contrasting social *mores* were only a century apart, and the evidence for the earlier situation came from literary texts that offered no interpretative problems. Evidence for the distant past was much less easy to handle.

One method of enquiry much favoured by Roman antiquarians was via the etymology of place-names. 'Velabrum', for instance, was a place in the low-lying valley between the Palatine and the Capitol, reached by going from the Forum down the Vicus Tuscus to what is now the church of S. Giorgio in Velabro.[46] Varro believed the whole valley had been a lake or marsh (*palus*) crossed by ferry-boats, with Velabrum as the landing-stage.[47] Although his derivation of the name from *uehere*, 'to convey', is far-fetched—other authors derived it from *uela*, 'sails'[48]—the idea of a waterlogged valley seemed plausible

44 See Rawson 1991.389–407, esp. 392–3 on this passage. For the four *factiones*, and their unattested but early origin, see Cameron 1976.56–60.

45 Macrobius *Saturnalia* 3.13.4–15, citing speeches by Cato and Scipio Aemilianus (respectively frr. 114–15 and fr. 30 Malcovati).

46 Porphyrio on Horace *Satires* 2.3.228 (*Tuscus dicitur uicus quo itur ad Velabrum*); cf. Livy 27.37.14–15.

47 Varro *De lingua Latina* 5.43–4, 5.156; Solinus 1.14 (cf. Varro *Antiquitates humanae* fr. 10.4 Mirsch); Dionysius of Halicarnassus 2.50.2 (λίμνη); Tibullus 2.5.33–4 (*per uada*), Propertius 4.9.5–6 (*Velabra . . . stagnabant*), Ovid *Fasti* 6.405–8 (*per undas*).

48 Ps.Acro on Horace *Ars poetica* 67 (*Velabrum dictum quod uelis transiretur*); cf. Propertius 4.9.6.

enough as a genuine memory of the conditions of very early Rome.[49] But it turns out that Varro's inference was false: deep-core analysis now reveals that the valley had not been a marsh at all.[50]

Like Cincius the 'mystagogue', Varro too thought of his studies as a mystery.[51] That was appropriate, since the ancient texts they sought out were quasi-religious relics, carefully preserved in temples and cult sites.[52] Even the documents of the magistrates of the Republic were thought of in those terms, as Dionysius shows in his discussion of chronology:[53]

> δηλοῦται δὲ ἐξ ἄλλων τε πολλῶν καὶ τῶν καλουμένων τιμητικῶν ὑπομνημάτων, ἃ διαδέχεται παῖς παρὰ πατρὸς καὶ περὶ πολλοῦ ποιεῖται τοῖς μεθ᾽ ἑαυτὸν ἐσομένοις ὥσπερ ἱερὰ πατρῷα παραδιδόναι· πολλοὶ δ᾽ εἰσὶν ἀπὸ τῶν τιμητικῶν οἴκων ἄνδρες ἐπιφανεῖς οἱ διαφυλάττοντες αὐτά.

> This is demonstrated by (among other sources) the so-called 'censorial commentaries', which a son receives from his father and takes great care to hand on to those who come after him as if they were ancestral holy relics. Many are the distinguished men from censorial houses who preserve them.

Early Rome had no public records office. The outgoing magistrate evidently took his writing-tablets with him, and kept them as private property.[54] One wonders how many can have survived from the fourth century or before, and whether archaic Latin was any more intelligible when written on wax in cursive script than when cut into bronze or stone in a monumental inscription.

Roman aristocratic houses also contained family trees in the *atrium*, the ancestors' named portraits linked by lines that might go right back to kings or gods.[55] Not surprisingly, the portrait captions (*imaginum tituli*) were notoriously

---

49 E.g. Coarelli 1983.229: 'Questa situazione è quella originaria, prima dei lavori di bonifica dell'area.'

50 Ammerman 2006.306–7: 'While the valley bottom was from time to time seasonally wet in the winter months, especially when the Tiber was in flood for a few days, it was essentially a dry zone in the other months of the year.'

51 Varro *De lingua Latina* 5.8 (*adytum et initia*); cf. n. 39 above. A book by Varro evidently entitled *Mystagogi* is cited by Fulgentius in the fifth century AD (*Expositio sermonum antiquorum* 11).

52 Dionysius of Halicarnassus 1.73.1: the Roman historians took their material ἐκ παλαιῶν λόγων ἐν ἱεραῖς δέλτοις σωζομένων.

53 Dionysius of Halicarnassus 1.74.5, seeking to establish the date of the Gallic sack as 120 years after the expulsion of the Tarquins.

54 See Culham 1991.124–8, inferring from documents of 73 BC (Sherk 1969.135, lines 58–9) and 39 BC (Reynolds 1982.57, lines 1–3) that the same applied in the late Republic; the records are described as δέλτοι and κηρώματα, waxed wooden tablets. Cf. Pliny *Nat. Hist.* 35.7 on *codices et monimenta rerum in magistratu gestarum*.

55 Pliny *Nat. Hist.* 35.6 (*stemmata uero lineis discurrebant ad imagines pictas*), Statius *Siluae* 2.6.11 (*stemma iunctum*). Kings: Plutarch *Numa* 1.1. Gods: Suetonius *Galba* 2.

unreliable as historical evidence;[56] no doubt they were regularly repainted, with the chance every time of new material being added to flatter the family. However, a more interesting objection is offered by a Roman author cited by Plutarch:[57]

> ἔστι δὲ καὶ περὶ τῶν Νομᾶ τοῦ βασιλέως χρόνων, καθ' οὓς γέγονε, νεανικὴ διαφορά, καίπερ ἐξ ἀρχῆς εἰς τοῦτον κατάγεσθαι τῶν στεμμάτων ἀκριβῶς δοκούντων. ἀλλὰ Κλώδιός τις ἐν ἐλέγχῳ χρόνων (οὕτω γάρ πως ἐπιγέγραπται τὸ βιβλίον) ἰσχυρίζεται τὰς μὲν ἀρχαίας ἐκείνας ἀναγραφὰς ἐν τοῖς Κελτικοῖς πάθεσι τῆς πόλεως ἠφανίσθαι, τὰς δὲ νῦν φαινομένας οὐκ ἀληθῶς συγκεῖσθαι δι' ἀνδρῶν χαριζομένων τισὶν εἰς τὰ πρῶτα γένη καὶ τοὺς ἐπιφανεστάτους οἴκους ἐξ οὗ προσηκόντων εἰσβιαζομένοις.

> There is also a vigorous dispute about the time at which king Numa lived, even though the family trees appear to have been traced down accurately to him from the starting-point. But a certain Clodius in his *Critical Enquiry into Chronology* (which is roughly how the book is titled) forcefully maintains that those ancient records were lost in the sack of the city by the Gauls, and that the ones presented nowadays are put together untruthfully by men who wish to gratify certain individuals by thrusting them into the leading families and the most distinguished houses when they have no right to be there.

The implication is that the owners of the great houses of Clodius' time (whenever that was) claimed that their family trees were authentic right back to Numa; and that Clodius denied the validity of their pretensions by insisting that the walls that carried the family trees could not be older than 387 BC.

The Romans believed (wrongly) that the Gauls had destroyed the actual fabric of the city, which therefore had to be rebuilt from the ground up.[58] The reason for that belief was the rarity of authentic early texts. We may be sure that Clodius' critical enquiry did not restrict itself to family trees, for if the very walls were destroyed, what chance was there for wax tablets? As Livy succinctly put it, 'any written records there were in public and private documents mostly perished in the burning city'.[59] Although there is no sign in the archaeological record of any general conflagration in the early fourth century, the reason for the Romans' firm belief in it only makes sense if there really were very few early texts surviving. It may be that only very few had ever existed.

---

56 Livy 4.16.4, 8.40.4.
57 Plutarch *Numa* 1.1, cf. 21.2 on οὐκ ἀληθῆ στέμματα. See Crawford 1998, who points out that *stemmata* began at the bottom of the wall.
58 Livy 5.55.3–5, 6.1.3 (*uelut ab stirpibus . . . renatae urbis*); Tacitus *Annals* 15.43.1.
59 Livy 6.1.2: *si quae [litterae] in commentariis pontificum aliisque publicis priuatisque erant monumentis, incensa urbe pleraeque interiere* (see pp. 263–70 below for the chronicle of the *pontifices*); Plutarch *Camillus* 22.1 (accurate chronology therefore impossible).

How then was it possible for Livy, Dionysius and Plutarch to provide their vivid and detailed political history of sixth- and fifth-century Rome? The answer must be that by their time the gap in knowledge had been filled by conjecture.

If the author of that 'critical enquiry into chronology' had been able to see Augustus' triumphal arch decorated with lists of every yearly magistracy from Lucius Brutus, and every triumph from Romulus, all dated in years from the foundation of the city, he might well have wondered where the information had been found. Some of the names and dates will have come from genuine research by men like Cincius, others perhaps from a combination of aristocratic pride (those portrait captions) and a patriotic determination to achieve a continuous history of the Republic, year by year. Once there was a list of names, a natural predisposition to suppose that the past was like the present would allow historians (the second- and first-century writers whom Livy and Dionysius used as sources) to populate the early Republic with *optimates* and *populares*, *nobiles* and *noui homines*, operating in a wholly recognisable political and military world.[60]

Livy knew from his reading in the antiquarians that there were no public records surviving from the early Republic, and that one rare piece of evidence attested *praetor maximus* as the title of Rome's chief magistrate in (presumably) the fifth century.[61] But he was not going to allow that knowledge to impugn the narrative structure provided by his predecessors, which he could turn into a great moral story of triumph and tragedy.

III

If we are right to infer, firstly that very little documentary evidence survived from the pre-fourth-century world, secondly that what there was could be read and understood only with the greatest difficulty, and thirdly that the narrative historians of the late Republic felt free to ignore it anyway, the problem of 'unwritten Rome' remains unsolved.

Indeed it becomes ever more acute, with even Romulus and Remus now claimed as historical figures.[62] The eighth-century wall discovered below the northern slope of the Palatine by Andrea Carandini in 1988 is roughly on the line of the '*pomerium* of Romulus' described by Tacitus in a famous digression.[63]

---

60 See Badian 1966.18–23; Wiseman 1987a.257–8; Gabba 1991.80–5.

61 Livy 6.1.2, 7.3.5 (on which see pp. 306 and 310 below).

62 On the 'historicity' of the foundation legend, see for instance Grandazzi 1991, Carandini and Cappelli 2000, Fraschetti 2002, Carandini 2003, Carandini 2006.

63 Tacitus *Annals* 12.24.1–2. Cf. Carandini 1997.497 and 580 on 'la ricostruzione di Tacito, basata sul ricordo recente delle porte e di tratti delle mura del Palatino, conservatisi fino all'età di Augusto [. . .] la descrizione di Tacito, redatta poco dopo l'età augustea, durante la quale porte e tratti delle mura erano ancora in vista.'

Carandini assumes that the Varronian date for the foundation of the city is historical, and that our literary sources preserve the 'living memory' of oral tradition.[64] Others disagree, of course, but he defies his critics with a fine disdain:[65]

> Chi è che interpreta le mura in termini di fondazione di un primo re chiamato o meno Romolo: Andrea Carandini o oltre venti generazioni di Romani senza soluzione di continuità nella loro memoria?

Those twenty generations represent the five and a half centuries back from Fabius Pictor's narrative of Romulus to the supposed date of the foundation of Rome.[66]

Much the same length of time separated Geoffrey of Monmouth's detailed history of King Arthur from the date of his supposed reign in the sixth century AD.[67] Many scholars have wanted to believe in Arthur as at least a powerful warlord,[68] but of course no one supposes that Geoffrey's conqueror of Norway, Denmark, Gaul and Rome was ever anything but a fantasy. The latest defender of the historicity of the reign of Arthur goes as far as he dares in appealing to oral tradition:[69]

> Working on the supposition of a historian writing down the words of the oldest person available, recording what they had been told by, for example, a grand-parent when they were a child, [. . .] 200 years is the maximum time one can reasonably expect oral tradition to survive without serious distortion.

(That would bring us within range of a hypothetical eighth-century written source of the extant ninth-century *Historia Brittonum*, which calls Arthur a war-leader, *dux bellorum*. QED. . .) But even that, deeply implausible as it is, pales in comparison with Carandini's vision of twenty generations 'with no break in the continuity of their memory'.

Five or six centuries are also what separate the composition of Homer's *Iliad* from the destruction of Troy VI (conventionally dated to about 1280 BC). Notoriously, Heinrich Schliemann believed that the Homeric epics were literally true, and even after more than a century of debate on the historicity of the Trojan War it is still possible to argue, in all seriousness, that 'Homer's *Iliad*

---

64 E.g. Carandini 1997.37: 'La tradizione orale, raccolta e trammandata nei testi, è spesso l'unica vivente memoria che si giunge dall'interno di quel lontano passato.'
65 Carandini 2003.11–12. See Wiseman 2006a for a detailed discussion of Carandini's method.
66 Fabius dated the foundation to 747 BC (Dionysius of Halicarnassus 1.74.1). Narrative: Fabius Pictor *FGrH* 809 F4 = Dionysius of Halicarnassus 1.79.4–83.3, Plutarch *Romulus* 3.1–6.7.
67 Geoffrey dated the death of Arthur to AD 542. Narrative: *Historia regum Britanniae* 8.19–11.2 (completed about 1136).
68 Excellent summary and discussion in Hutton 2003.39–58. For the written sources on fifth- and sixth-century Britain, see Dark 2000.32–48, esp. 43–5 on 'inadmissible evidence'.
69 Gidlow 2004.91, going well beyond his stated source (Dark 2000.43).

[has] the status of a source text'.[70] However, not even Joachim Latacz wants to make Achilles and Agamemnon historical figures like Carandini's Romulus.

Everything depends on the reliability of 'oral tradition'—or 'cultural memory', in the more fashionable recent term. We might appeal to modern anthropological evidence,[71] but perhaps it is more appropriate to listen to a great historian writing in Rome in the second century BC. Polybius notes that in beginning his main narrative in 220 BC he is dealing with events 'in our own time and that of our fathers'; either he himself had taken part in them or he had heard about them from eye-witnesses. Then he goes on:[72]

> τὸ γὰρ ἀνωτέρω προσλαμβάνειν τοῖς χρόνοις, ὡς ἀκοὴν ἐξ ἀκοῆς γράφειν, οὐκ ἐφαίνεθ' ἡμῖν ἀσφαλεῖς ἔχειν οὔτε τὰς διαλήψεις οὔτε τὰς ἀποφάσεις.
>
> For to include material further back in time, so as to write hearsay on hearsay, did not seem to me to be safe for either judgements or assertions.

Cultural memory, or hearsay on hearsay? Twenty generations, or two at the most?

As Moses Finley pointed out many years ago, wherever independent evidence allows the comparison, traditional oral narrative about events in the past ends up by distorting those events in a quite fundamental way.[73] Every time the tale was told, it was told to a particular audience on a particular occasion, and their expectations and preconceptions changed over time with the changing circumstances of the community. Oral tradition does not transmit what has become obsolete or irrelevant. It is also hospitable to creative fiction, as the Greeks and Romans understood very well.[74] The will to believe is always strong, and a good story-teller can easily activate it.[75]

---

70 Latacz 2004.91, 138—on the basis of *Wilusa* (*Ilios*) and *Achchiyawa* (*Achaioi*) in the Hittite texts, and *Danaya* (*Danaoi*) in an Egyptian inscription of the fourteenth century BC.

71 As do the two best discussions of oral tradition known to me, Davies 1984 and Hutton 2003.18–27.

72 Polybius 4.2.3.

73 Finley 1964.2–3, citing the *Song of Roland*, the *Nibelungenlied*, and the South Slav tradition on the battle of Kosovo.

74 See for instance Hesiod *Theogony* 27 and Polybius 3.33.17 on 'lies like the truth'; Thucydides 1.21.1 and Tacitus *Annals* 3.19.2 on the achievement of instant myth; Seneca *Apocolocyntosis* 1.2, Quintilian 1.8.21 and Lucian *On Writing History* 32 on saying whatever comes into your head.

75 See Finley 1964.2 on classicists' 'will to believe' in the Trojan War; Hutton 2003.12 on fiction's 'capacity to overpower virtually *any* facts given sufficient time'. Remember Mopsa and Autolycus in *The Winter's Tale* (act 4 scene 3): 'Is it true, think you?' 'Very true, and but a month old. Here's the midwife's name on't, one Mistress Taleporter, and five or six honest wives who were present. Why should I carry lies abroad?'

Livy, like Homer and Geoffrey of Monmouth, was a good story-teller. But the fact remains that he knew hardly anything about the real conditions of archaic Rome, and what little he did know he ignored.

IV

In their attempts to evade the consequences of this unwelcome conclusion, some modern scholars appeal to one particular category of data as impervious to change. They take it as axiomatic that cults and rituals remain the same over long periods of time, and therefore that reports of them in late authors are valid as evidence for early Rome.[76] Moreover, it is only a step from that to accepting as necessarily ancient the aetiological stories offered by our sources to explain those cults and rituals.[77]

But is this escape clause really valid? Even for the most obviously ancient of Roman cults, as we shall see in chapter 4, the sources seem to imply a sequence of developing rituals and interpretations reflecting the changing needs of Roman society.[78] And if the *Lupercalia* are too controversial an example, we can take the new evidence about Anna Perenna,[79] whose cult underwent substantial changes in the first century AD.

Ovid gives a detailed account of Anna Perenna's festival on the Ides of March. It took place, he says, in an open field by the river bank, which a contemporary calendar places at the first milestone on the Via Flaminia.[80] Eighty years later, Martial refers to Anna's cult site as a sacred grove, evidently not far from the Milvian Bridge, which was at the third milestone on the Flaminia.[81] Not only that, but he describes the grove as 'delighting in the blood of virgins', which seems to imply some kind of pre-wedding initiation for young girls. Scholars infer an archaic rite unchanged for centuries,[82] but Ovid knows nothing about that; his celebrants dance and make love with girls who are clearly sexually experienced. A further anomaly is that a calendar of AD 354

---

76 See for instance Coarelli 2005.32 on 'una delle costanti più note di ogni rito religioso, il suo carattere stabile e conservatore'; Carandini 2006.412 on 'le istituzioni sacre, come i culti, quanto di più durevole e congelato possa esistere nel mondo umano e pertanto una delle chiavi per intendere la storia dei primordi'; and Schultz 2006.12 on the Romans as 'a people who prided themselves on their scrupulous maintenance of ancient forms, [and] are very likely to have tried to preserve the details of ritual observance for centuries'.

77 Carandini 2006.412 (my emphasis): 'I Romani, in particolare, cancellavano quasi nulla del loro passato religioso e *leggendario*, conservandolo piamente attraverso secoli.'

78 See pp. 52–83 below on the *Lupercalia*; *pace* Coarelli 2005.30 on 'le ragioni intrinseche, strutturali, che collegano in un insieme coerente un rito di purificazione della città con un rito di fertilità'.

79 Piranomonte 2002, on which see now Wiseman 2006b.

80 Ovid *Fasti* 3.523–30; *Fasti Vaticani* on 15 March (Degrassi 1963.172–3).

81 Martial 4.64.16–17 (cf. 23–4 on the proximity of *Muluius*).

82 E.g. Torelli 1984.57–66; Boëls-Janssen 1993.23–39.

dates Anna's festival not to the Ides of March but to 18 June. Ovid knows nothing of that either.[83]

We now know that during the first century AD the cult site was moved to a sacred spring complex on the north side of the Monti Parioli [fig. 7], no longer by the river and no longer on the Via Flaminia.[84] We also know from the inscriptions that at least by the second century AD it was the scene of mime competitions [fig. 8].[85] It seems beyond doubt that the place, date and nature of Anna Perenna's festival had all been changed.[86]

Fig. 7 Anna Perenna cult site at Piazza Euclide, Rome: the remains of a rectangular basin with second-century AD inscriptions inserted into the wall.

The virgins' rite of passage inferred from Martial recalls the custom that so horrified Christian polemicists, of Roman brides surrendering their virginity on the phallic image of the god Priapus.[87] The only direct evidence for this ritual defloration seems to be a marble relief once in Naples [fig. 9]; however,

83 *Fasti Filocaliani* (Degrassi 1963.248–9); not in Ovid *Fasti* 6.
84 Piranomonte 2002.34–7 for the date: coins in the basin from Augustus to the late fourth century AD.
85 Piranomonte 2002.26–33; Slater 2005.319–20; Wiseman 2006b.55–9.
86 Anna's myth was changed too: see Ovid *Fasti* 3.647–55, Silius Italicus 8.178–83, and Wiseman 2006b.58–9 on the differences between them.
87 Lactantius *Divine Institutes* 1.20.36, Augustine *City of God* 6.9 and 7.24 (CSEL 40.292, 337).

Fig. 8 Inscription from Anna Perenna's cult site (on the left in fig. 7): 'The vow [which] once I had made to the consecrated nymphs, who deserved it because of the victory of my good patron C. Acilius Eutyches, we pay; and we attest in verses that they are sacred, and we dedicated an altar to the welcome springs. Eutychides, freedman.' The metre is iambic *senarii*. An *archimimus* L. Acilius Eutyches, clearly a relative, is attested in AD 169 (*CIL* 14.2408 = *ILS* 5196).

Fig. 9 Nineteenth-century drawing of a marble relief showing a girl about to be prepared for marriage by Priapus. The stone was once in the *gabinetto segreto* of Naples Museum; present whereabouts evidently unknown.

the best-omened time for Roman weddings was after the Ides of June,[88] and according to Martial it was in June that Priapus was 'received by proud Venus' (whatever that means) in a ceremony unknown to Ovid.[89] Since Anna Perenna shared her new cult site with the nymphs,[90] and since from the first century AD onwards Priapus is described as the nymphs' companion,[91] the conclusion is inevitable that Anna's grove, 'delighting in the blood of virgins', and Anna's festival, now on 18 June at the auspicious time for weddings, were the setting for Priapus' initiation of young girls into matrimony by *droit de seigneur*.

It is important to understand what this new information implies. If one puts one's trust in comparative anthropology and the history of religions 'understood as an autonomous discipline',[92] with data from various times and various societies synchronically juxtaposed, it is natural to see Martial's description of Anna Perenna's sacred grove as evidence for an archaic initiation rite, and thence to conclude, in a circular argument, that ancient rites survived unchanged because the Romans were particularly conservative in religious matters. The discovery of the Anna Perenna inscriptions reveals how precarious that method is. The outcome is just the opposite of the 'history of religions' model: since the Romans were evidently quite happy to reorganise an ancient cult in the first century AD, we have no reason to doubt that they

88 Ovid *Fasti* 6.219–34, cf. 713–14.
89 Martial 3.68.7–10; not in Ovid *Fasti* 6.
90 Piranomonte 2002.26–30 for the *nymphae sacratae* (see fig. 8); Wiseman 2006b.55–9.
91 Petronius *Satyricon* 133.3, *Corpus Priapeorum* 33.1–4, *CIL* 14.3565.13–32 (Courtney 1995.148–9).
92 I borrow the phrase from Coarelli 2005.30.

did so periodically throughout their history. Cult and ritual change, like everything else in society.

What matters is not just what the new texts themselves say, but how they
have led to the explanation of otherwise baffling references in the literature. Of
course I may be prejudiced, but this example seems to me to vindicate the classicists' traditionally empirical method—close reading of the sources, careful
consideration of what they may or may not presuppose, and the avoidance of
unexamined preconceptions.

V

There are no short cuts, there are no magic wands, there is no time machine to
take us back to unwritten Rome. All we have is evidence and argument—
what survives from the ancient world, and what we can make it tell us about
what we want to know.

'What survives from the ancient world' includes above all a huge and varied
corpus of literary texts, the writings of poets, playwrights, statesmen, scholars,
historians, satirists, novelists, theologians. The narratives such authors provide
of what they believed was early Roman history are of very little direct use to
us, since they could have had no knowledge of the reality of Roman experience before (say) the late fourth century BC. But the texts also tell us a great
many things about which their authors were uniquely well informed, and even
the most unhistorical narrative may sometimes reveal information the author
was not aware he was giving.

What the modern historian has to do was well described by R.G. Collingwood sixty years ago:[93]

> As natural science finds its proper method when the scientist, in Bacon's
> metaphor, puts nature to the question, tortures her by experiment in order to
> wring from her answers to his own questions, so history finds its proper method
> when the historian puts his authorities in the witness-box, and by cross-ques-
> tioning extorts from them information which in their original statements they
> have withheld, either because they did not wish to give it or because they did
> not possess it. [...] Where the scissors-and-paste historian said quite confi-
> dently 'There is nothing in such-and-such an author about such-and-such a
> subject', the scientific or Baconian historian will reply, 'Oh, isn't there? Do you
> not see that in this passage about a totally different matter it is implied that the
> author took such-and-such a view of the subject about which he says nothing?'

---

93 Collingwood 1946.237, 270. Francis Bacon's empiricism is rightly perceived as inimical to
    the idea of 'cultural memory': see Carandini 2006.15 ('Per i Baconiani la cultura, al fondo, è
    solo uno svantaggio nell'osservazione, perché moltiplicherebbe i preconcetti'), cf. 413 on
    my own *Baconismo*.

This book is a sequence of such enquiries, to see whether it is possible to extract usable evidence about pre-literary Rome.

We begin with the cross-questioning of two witnesses, Livy and Ennius; then follow four studies (chapters 4–7) on Roman cults and rituals, and three more (chapters 8–10) on a particular type of religious festival, the 'games' (*ludi*) put on in honour of the gods; that in turn leads to three chapters (11–13) on the nature of Roman theatre performances; two studies on the origin and nature of Roman historiography (chapters 14–15) are followed by a discussion of the interpretation of archaeological evidence (chapter 16); and the final two chapters test the evidence for a defining moment in early Roman history, the expulsion of the Tarquins and the establishment of a republic.

CHAPTER TWO

What Can Livy Tell Us?

I

When Titus Livius began his great history of Rome, some time around 30 BC, Roman literature was more than two centuries old. Its history was already a subject of learned controversy, and the earliest text that the scholars of his time had been able to identify was a play by his namesake Livius Andronicus, evidently datable to 240 BC.[1] The first historians of Rome, Fabius Pictor and Cincius Alimentus, were writing at least a generation after that,[2] so even through his earliest sources Livy could hardly have had any sense of what Roman culture was like in its pre-literary phase.

However, we need not assume automatically that Livy can tell us nothing about 'unwritten Rome'. If we read him carefully enough, it may be possible to use the material he transmits, and even the phraseology he uses, to infer something about that lost world. For instance, how did *he* deal with the idea of an oral culture and the origins of literature? His treatment of 240 BC is lost, but we do have his reaction to the work of Livius Andronicus in a later context.

In 207 the aged poet was asked to compose a hymn to Juno, for a ceremony in expiation of alarming prodigies:[3]

> *decreuere item pontifices ut uirgines ter nouenae per urbem euntes carmen canerent. id cum in Iouis Statoris aede discerent conditum ab Liuio poeta carmen, tacta de caelo aedis in Auentino Iunonis Reginae ... tum septem et uiginti uirgines, longam indutae uestem, carmen in Iunonem Reginam canentes ibant, illa tempestate forsitan laudabile rudibus ingeniis, nunc abhorrens et inconditum si referatur.*

The pontiffs also decreed that three bands of maidens, each consisting of nine, should go through the city singing a hymn. This hymn was composed by the poet Livius, and while they were practising it in the temple of Jupiter Stator,

---

1 Cicero *Brutus* 72–3 (from Atticus), *Tusculan Disputations* 1.3; Aulus Gellius 17.21.42 (from Varro?). The coincidence of the names *Titus Livius/Livius Andronicus* may be of interest to Shakespearean scholars.

2 Livy 1.44.2 (*scriptorum antiquissimus Fabius Pictor*), 21.38.3 and 22.7.4 (Cincius and Fabius as contemporary witnesses, 218–217 BC); cf. Dionysius of Halicarnassus 1.6.2 on Roman historians, ὧν εἰσι πρεσβύτατοι Κόιντός τε Φάβιος καί Λεύκιος Κίγκιος.

3 Livy 27.37.7 and 13 (trans. Roberts, Everyman Library, slightly adapted).

the shrine of Queen Juno on the Aventine was struck by lightning. [. . .] Then twenty-seven maidens, vested in long robes, walked in procession singing a hymn in honour of Queen Juno, which was perhaps admired in those rude days but would be considered very uncouth and unpleasing if it were recited now.

The hymn was 'composed' (*conditum*). That means it was written down, for *condere*—'to store, put away, preserve'—is a regular word for literary composition, especially of poetry.[4] The act of writing stores the poet's words. However, Livy comments that if it were repeated in his day it would seem *inconditum*, evidently meaning something like 'artless'.

There are 29 other places in the extant text where Livy uses the adjective *inconditus*. In 21 of them it means 'disorderly, unstructured', to describe a crowd, an undisciplined army, or a city under mob rule.[5] The other eight passages, however, offer better parallels for what Livy says about Livius Andronicus' hymn. For instance, he reports that the priests at the Apollo temple at Hieracome in Caria deliver the oracular responses *uersibus haud inconditis*.[6] English translations render the phrase 'in smooth and graceful verses' (Everyman), 'in verses not without polish' (Loeb), 'in verses of some literary quality' (Penguin), all indicating by contrast what *uersus inconditi* would have been.

A more direct indication comes in the excursus on the origin of drama in book 7, where Livy reports that Etruscan dancers were brought to Rome to perform in the year 364 BC:[7]

> *imitari deinde eos iuuentus, simul* **inconditis** *inter se iocularia fundentes* **uersibus,** *coepere.*
> Afterwards the young men [of Rome] began to imitate them, exercising their wit on each other in burlesque verses.

That is the Everyman translation; the Loeb has 'in uncouth verses', the Penguin 'in crude improvised verse'. The essential point is evidently that the young men's banter was not only unsophisticated but unscripted as well.

That sense also fits the remaining six examples of *inconditus* in Livy, all of which describe the songs and jokes of Roman soldiers in the triumphal proces-

---

4   E.g. Cicero *Ad Atticum* 1.16.5, Lucretius 5.2, Virgil *Eclogues* 6.7, Horace *Epistles* 1.3.24, Propertius 2.1.14; full references at *TLL* 4.153.74–154.29. The usage may go back to the Twelve Tables: Crawford 1996.677–9.

5   *Turba*: 21.57.12, 22.45.3, 25.1.4, 25.13.10, 25.15.13, 29.1.22, 36.33.4. *Multitudo*: 24.29.1, 26.40.16, 27.32.8, 32.13.14, 43.10.5, 44.45.6. Army: 29.34.11, 30.11.5, 30.28.3, 35.28.3, 42.66.8, 44.39.1. Revolutionary Syracuse, 214–12 BC: 24.24.2, 26.40.1.

6   38.13.1.

7   7.2.5. Cf. 7.2.7, *non, sicut ante, Fescennino uersu similem incompositum temere ac rudem alternis iaciebant*; Servius *auctus* on *Eclogues* 6.7 defines *inconditus* as *incompositus*.

sion.[8] As Stephen Oakley rightly observes, 'these *incondita* or *inconditi uersus* exercised a curious fascination upon L[ivy], who often alludes to them'.[9] In fact, there are eight such episodes, all in the first ten books, and since they purport to be just what we are looking for, namely evidence for the oral culture of the early Republic, a close comparison of them may be useful for our theme.

II

1: The battle of Algidus, 458 BC. Rome makes war on the Aequi after their leader Cloelius Gracchus treats her ambassadors with contempt; the consul L. Minucius and his army are surrounded and besieged; Cincinnatus is called from the plough to be dictator; the Aequi are defeated and sent beneath the yoke. At the dictator's triumph, tables are spread with food for the soldiers before all the houses:[10]

> *epulantesque cum carmine triumphali et sollemnibus iocis comisantium modo currum secuti sunt.*
> They regaled themselves and followed the chariot in the manner of revellers, with triumph-songs and the joking appropriate to the occasion.

2: A. Cornelius Cossus, 437 BC. Rome makes war on the Veientes after their king Lars Tolumnius has had Roman ambassadors murdered; Cossus, a handsome cavalry officer, kills Tolumnius in single combat. The dictator, Mamercus Aemilius, holds a triumph:[11]

> *longe maximum triumphi spectaculum fuit Cossus, spolia opima regis interfecti gerens; in eum milites* **carmina incondita** *aequantes eum Romulo canere.*
> By far the most prominent sight in the triumphal procession was Cossus, carrying the 'spoils of honour' of the king he had slain, while the troops sang impromptu songs comparing him to Romulus.

In the procession all the citizens look not at the dictator's chariot but at Cossus, who hangs his spoils in a *sollemnis dedicatio* next to those of Romulus in the Jupiter Feretrius temple. By order of the people, the dictator offers a gold crown to Jupiter.[12]

---

8   4.20.2 (*carmina*), 4.53.11 (*uersus*), 5.49.7 (*ioci*), 7.38.3 (*iocus*); 7.10.13, 10.30.9 (*incondita* as a substantive, as at Varro *Menippean Satires* fr. 363B and Virgil *Ecogues* 2.4).
9   Oakley 1998.361.
10 3.25.7–8 (contempt), 3.26.7–10 (plough scene); quotation from 3.29.5.
11 4.17.1–6 (murder); quotation from 4.20.2.
12 4.20.3 (procession and dedication), 4.20.4 (crown).

3: M. Menenius, 410 BC. The plebeians complain about the illegal occupation of *ager publicus*; Menenius as tribune of the *plebs* proposes an agrarian law and blocks the consul's levy of troops, but a dangerous incursion by the Aequi allows the consul to prevail. Though the Aequi are defeated, the *plebs* and the soldiers are still resentful when the consul holds his *ouatio*:[13]

> *alternis* **inconditi uersus** *militari licentia iactati quibus consul increpitus, Meneni celebre nomen fuit, cum ad omnem mentionem tribuni fauor circumstantis populi cum uocibus militum certaret.*
>
> Impromptu songs were shouted in turns with soldiers' freedom of speech, in which the consul was abused but Menenius' name was glorified, while at every mention of the tribune the applause of the people standing by competed with the soldiers' voices.

The patricians are concerned less about the people than about the outspokenness of the soldiers, which Livy describes as *prope sollemnis*.[14]

4: Camillus and the Gauls, 390 BC. During the siege of the Capitol, both sides suffer from famine and a truce is arranged; terms are agreed for the Gauls to withdraw, but Brennus contemptuously throws his sword on to the scale. Then Camillus arrives, and with the help of the gods defeats the Gauls in two battles:[15]

> *triumphans in urbem redit, interque* **iocos** *militares quos* **inconditos** *iaciunt, Romulus ac parens patriae conditorque alter urbis haud uanis laudibus appellabatur.*
>
> He returned to the city in triumph, and amid the impromptu jokes shouted by the soldiers he was called 'Romulus', 'father of his country', 'the second founder'—no empty praise.

5: Manlius and the Gaul, 361 BC. The Romans face a Gallic war-band at the Anio bridge on the Via Salaria; a huge Gaul issues a challenge to single combat; young Titus Manlius fights and kills him with the help of the gods, and takes his torque; the Gauls are rooted to the spot by fear and astonishment. The Romans joyfully escort Manlius to the dictator:[16]

> *inter carminum prope <in> modum* **incondita** *quaedam militariter ioculantes Torquati cognomen auditum; celebratum deinde posteris etiam familiae honori fuit.*

---

13 4.53.2 (*lex agraria*), 4.53.6 (*ager publicus*); quotation from 4.53.11–12.
14 4.53.13: Menenius was prevented from obtaining the post of *trib. mil. cos. pot.*
15 5.48.4 (truce), 5.48.8–9 (Brennus), 5.49.1 and 5 (gods); quotation from 5.49.7.
16 7.10.4 (gods), 7.10.12 (fear and astonishment); quotation from 7.10.13 (Oakley 1998.147 for the text).

Amid the soldiers' impromptu joking, almost like songs, the name 'Torquatus' was heard, which from then on was a mark of honour to the family's descendants too.

The dictator gives a speech in his praise at an assembly (*contio*), and rewards him with a gold crown.[17]

6: Faliscans and Tarquinians, 356 BC. Rome makes war on Falerii and Tarquinii; the Roman soldiers are at first terror-struck by the enemy priests advancing like Furies with blazing torches, brandishing snakes. But then they rout them and capture their camp:[18]

> *praeda ingenti parta uictores reuerterunt, militaribus iocis cum apparatum hostium tum suum increpantes pauorem.*
> They captured a huge amount of booty and returned victorious, mocking in their soldiers' jokes both the enemy's paraphernalia and their own fear.

7: The elder Decius Mus, 343 BC. A Roman army advancing into Samnium is trapped in a narrow valley; Decius, a military tribune, sees a high point unoccupied by the enemy and takes a group of picked men to hold it; the Samnites are dumb-struck, the main army escapes and Decius and his men, with the help of Fortuna, fight their way back to it; the consul holds an assembly (*contio*) in his honour, but Decius urges an attack while the enemy are paralysed with fear (*pauore attoniti*); the Samnites are routed.[19] Decius is awarded a gold crown and other decorations:[20]

> *consules ambo de Samnitibus triumpharunt sequente Decio insigni cum laude donisque, cum **incondito** militari **ioco** haud minus tribuni celebre nomen quam consul esset.*
> Both consuls held a triumph over the Samnites, with Decius following, conspicuous by praise and decorations, since in the soldiers' impromptu jokes the tribune's name was no less celebrated than a consul.

8: The battle of Sentinum, 295 BC. On the Roman left wing the consul Decius Mus (son of the hero of the last item) attacks the Gauls, but his cavalry are panic-stricken; facing defeat, he utters the *deuotio* prayer and formally sacrifices himself; the Gauls in turn are paralysed by dread; his colleague Fabius

---

17 7.10.14 (*mirisque pro contione eam pugnam laudibus tulit*).
18 7.17.3 (*uelut lymphati*), 7.17.4 (*uana miracula*); quotation from 7.17.5.
19 7.34.1–37.3, elaborate narrative: 7.34.6 (Fortuna), 7.34.8 (*admiratione pauentibus*), 7.35.5, 8 and 12 (Fortuna), 7.36.10 (*pauore attonitos*); *pauor* also at 7.36.3 and 13.
20 7.37.1–2 (including *corona obsidialis*); quotation from 7.38.3.

Rullianus defeats the Samnites on the other wing and takes the Gauls in the rear. Fabius triumphs alone:[21]

> *milites triumphantem secuti sunt. celebrata **inconditis** militaribus non magis uictoria Q. Fabi quam mors praeclara P. Deci est excitataque memoria parentis, aequata euentu publico priuatoque, filii laudibus.*
>
> The soldiers followed his triumph. In their impromptus the glorious death of Publius Decius was celebrated no less than the victory of Quintus Fabius, and the memory of the elder Decius, equaled by the outcome both privately and publicly, was recalled by the praises of the younger.

The first point to make about these eight passages is an elementary one: Livy's sources were not reporting the soldiers' songs at first hand. This is not evidence like that of Suetonius and Velleius Paterculus on the soldiers' triumph songs in 46 and 43 BC.[22] It is true that Fabius Pictor or Cincius Alimentus could have talked to old men whose grandfathers had told them what the soldiers sang at the triumph in 295 BC; but item 8 is only the last in a coherent sequence which has to be interpreted as a whole. The phenomenon must be, in some sense, a literary one.

One of the group (item 3) stands out for its unusual context, political rather than military. The combination of tribunician resistance to the levy and agrarian legislation against illegal occupiers of *ager publicus* is powerfully reminiscent of the years 151–133 BC,[23] and it is not unlikely that the episode was elaborated, or even created, in the second century BC. But it is far from clear why the elaboration should have taken the form of soldiers' songs.

By definition, *incondita carmina* are not written down. But at some point in the development of the historiographical tradition on the early Republic—between, say, 210 BC and 20 BC (from Fabius Pictor to Livy's first decade)—the content of the soldiers' extempore songs on at least eight occasions became 'known', and thus available as data for Roman history. The question is: how?

---

21 10.28.10 (*uelut lymphaticus pauor*), 10.28.13–18 (*deuotio*), 10.29.1 (*uix humanae opis*), 10.29.2 (*uelut alienata mente*), 10.29.4 (Furies and *formido*), 10.29.7 (*attoniti*); quotation from 10.30.9, referring to the elder Decius Mus' *deuotio* in 340 BC.

22 Suetonius *Diuus Iulius* 49.4, 51, 82; Velleius 2.67.3; Courtney 1993.483–5.

23 Levy: Livy *Periochae* 48 and 55 (consuls imprisoned by tribunes, 151 and 138 BC); Taylor 1962.19–27. *Ager publicus*: Plutarch *Tiberius Gracchus* 8.1–4 (C. Laelius, 140 BC?), Appian *Civil Wars* 1.7–11 (*lex Sempronia*, 133 BC); on Laelius, see Astin 1967.307–10.

III

Let us look more closely at what these stories have in common. All but two of them explicitly celebrate the name of a particular hero, whether that of the triumphant commander (item 4), his fallen colleague (item 8), a particularly heroic soldier (items 2, 5, 7), or a champion of the *plebs* (item 3). One of the two exceptions (item 1) is probably not an exception at all, since praise of Cincinnatus is implicit in the story. (The other is item 6, where the soldiers mock the enemy's flummery and their own previous fear.) The phraseology is consistent: praise, of course (*laus* and *laudare*),[24] but also celebration (*celeber* and *celebrare*), especially of the hero's name.[25]

Where the hero is a junior officer, there may be an assembly (*contio*) in which the commander praises and decorates him;[26] direct speech may characterise his fearlessness, initiative or good discipline.[27] Direct speech is in any case a very conspicuous characteristic of these episodes, from '*satin salue?*' and '*uae uictis!*' (Cincinnatus at the plough, Brennus at the scales) to Decius' nocturnal lecture to the soldiers on Fortune and necessity.[28] Speeches by the protagonists frequently establish the moral parameters of the story, as in the Romans' response to Cloelius Gracchus' insult (item 1), Cossus' reaction at the sight of the impious Tolumnius (item 2), the Gaul's challenge at the Anio bridge (item 5), and Decius' recognition of his inherited fate (item 8).[29]

Particularly interesting are the speeches Livy does *not* give us, but which mark a dramatic turn of events. In item 3, Menenius' defiant harangue to the people is interrupted by a messenger with news of a military disaster; in item 4, the action is precipitated by *conloquia* between Gauls and Romans; in item 6, the contemptuous speech of the consul and officers turns the soldiers from panic to blind rage; in item 7, Decius interrupts the consul's speech in his praise by pointing out the opportunity for a decisive attack; and in item 8, the speech of the *pontifex* M. Livius makes the consul's self-sought death a Roman victory.[30] These speeches are an integral part of the action.

---

24 4.53.11; 5.49.7; 7.10.12 and 14; 7.36.7 and 9, 7.37.1, 7.38.3; 10.29.20, 10.30.9.

25 4.20.3 (*celebritas*); 4.53.11 (*celebre nomen*); 7.10.13 (*cognomen celebratum*); 7.38.3 (*celebre nomen*); 10.30.9 (*celebrata*). Honorific comparisons: 4.20.2, 5.49.7 (Romulus); 10.30.9 (father).

26 *Contio*: 7.10.14 (*corona aurea*); 7.36.9, 7.37.1 (*corona aurea*, etc); cf. 3.29.3 (*corona aurea* voted to Cincinnatus by Minucius' army), and 4.20.4 (*corona aurea* dedicated to Jupiter), where *populi iussu* may imply a *contio*.

27 4.19.3; 7.10.2–4; 7.34.4–7 and 13–14, 7.35.2–12, 7.36.5–6. ('*Macte uirtute*' at 7.10.4, 7.36.5.)

28 3.26.9, 5.48.9; 7.35.2–12. Two other two-word speeches at 3.27.7 ('*adcelera, signifer!*', '*sequere, miles!*').

29 3.25.8 ('*deorum hominumque simul uiolata iura*'); 4.19.1 ('*hicine est ruptor foederis humani uiolatorque gentium iuris?*'); 7.9.8 ('*quem nunc Roma uirum fortissimum habet. . .*'); 10.28.12–13 ('*quid ultra moror familiare fatum?*').

30 4.53.2–3; 5.48.4 and 8; 7.17.4; 7.36.9–10; 10.29.3–4. Another example may be 3.25.9 (item 1), if the news of the Sabine raid interrupted the tribunes.

Equally pervasive is the role of the gods. The action of item 1 begins when the Aequian leader tells the Roman ambassadors to address their complaints to a nearby oak-tree, and they take him at his word:

'*et haec sacrata quercus et quidquid deorum est audiant. . .*'
'May this holy oak and whatever gods there are hear . . .'

Similarly, what Cossus avenges in item 2 is Tolumnius' sacrilegious murder of ambassadors:

'*iam ego hanc mactatam uictimam, si modo sancti quicquam in terris di uolunt, legatorum manibus dabo.*'
'If it is the gods' will that there should be anything sacred in the world, I shall give him to the shades of the ambassadors as a sacrificial victim.'

The Romans' piety will be rewarded.[31] In item 4, Camillus' intervention is attributed explicitly to divine help, in a very conspicuous ring construction:[32]

sed dique et homines prohibuere redemptos uiuere Romanos . . . iam uerterat fortuna, iam deorum opes humanaque consilia rem Romanam adiuuabant.
But both gods and men forbade the lives of Romans to be paid for . . . Now fortune had turned, and the gods' help and human strategy aided the Roman cause.

In item 5, Manlius' commanding officer commends his *pietas* as well as his bravery:[33]

'*perge et nomen Romanum inuictum iuuantibus dis praesta.*'
'Proceed—and with the gods' help prove the Roman name to be invincible.'

For Decius in item 7 it is a particular divinity, Fortuna Populi Romani, who favours his exploit.[34] For his son, the *deuotus* of item 8, the gods who matter are Tellus, the Di Manes, and the addressees of the pontiff's archaic prayer to activate the anger of *caelestes* and *inferi*.[35]

The *sollemnes precationes* of the self-sacrifice recall the *sollemnis dedicatio* of Cossus' 'spoils of honour' in item 2. Even the soldiers' shouting, paradoxically

---

31 3.25.8, 4.19.1.
32 5.49.1 and 5. Ogilvie 1965.737: 'At that juncture divine intervention brings Camillus on to the stage (49.1, cf. 49.5), and L. stresses that the Romans have earned their reprieve by their piety.'
33 7.10.4.
34 7.34.6 (cf. 1.46.5)—also known as Fortuna Publica (*ILLRP* 112, Ovid *Fasti* 4.375–6, *Fasti Praenestini* on 5 April), Fortuna Publica Populi Romani (*Fasti Esquilini* on 25 May), or Fortuna Publica Populi Romani Quiritium (*Fasti Caeretani* and *magistrorum uici* on 25 May).
35 10.28.13–17, with a reference back from 10.28.15 to 8.9.6 ('*Iane, Iuppiter, Mars pater, Quirine, Bellona, Lares, Diui Nouensiles, Di Indigetes. . .*'); 10.29.1 (*uix humanae opis*).

at first sight, is twice described as *sollemnis* (items 1 and 3); the point is that the triumphal procession is a religious ritual, and the soldiers' freedom of speech is a part of it.[36]

After the consul's self-immolation in item 8, the *pontifex* does what a *pontifex* has to do, namely teach the people.[37] Marcus Livius explains to the soldiers that the Gauls and Samnites are in the power of the chthonic deities, summoned and dragged down after the consul himself:[38]

> '*Furiarum ac formidinis plena omnia ad hostes esse.*'
> 'Everything on the enemy side is filled with the Furies' terror.'

The Furies appear also in item 6, where the situation is reversed; there it is Etruscan priests who destroy Roman morale as they come on 'like Furies' (*incessu furiali*) with their snakes and torches,[39] but the soldiers are told not to fear their empty show.

You know the gods are on your side when the enemy is dumbfounded, thunderstruck, afflicted with irrational terror. Here too the vocabulary is consistent. The Gauls in item 5 and the Samnites in item 7 are transfixed by *pauor* and *admiratio*; the Samnites in item 7 and the Gauls in item 8 are *attoniti*, the latter having been sent almost out of their minds (*uelut alienata mente*) after Decius' self-immolation.[40] A similar paralysis afflicts the Romans in the early stages of items 6 (*uelut lymphati et attoniti*) and 8 (*uelut lymphaticus pauor*)—but the repeated 'as if' (*uelut*) shows that it wasn't the real thing.[41] These are not stories in which the gods are hostile to Rome.

How did Camillus arrive at the Capitol in item 4? Livy refers to the gods' involvement, and then blandly goes on: 'For by some chance the Dictator arrived'. But the truce had only been to allow negotiations; it would hardly extend to allowing Camillus and his relief force to pass through the besiegers' lines. One can only assume that the Gauls were *attoniti*, as they had been when Fabius Dorsuo, trusting in his gods, walked through their lines to make his sacrifice on the Quirinal, and walked back again.[42] It may be worth noting that

---

36 10.28.16, 4.20.3; 3.29.5, 4.53.13.
37 1.20.6–7 (*ut . . . edoceret*), Plut. *Numa* 9.4 (διδάσκων), Cicero *De oratore* 2.52.
38 10.29.4; cf. 8.9.7 for the *deuotio* prayer ('*hostesque populi Romani Quiritium terrore formidine morteque adficiatis*'), 8.9.10 for the effect of the *deuotus* on the enemy (*quacumque equo inuectus est, ibi haud secus quam pestifero sideri icti pauebant*).
39 7.17.3; for Furies with snakes and torches, cf. (e.g.) Virgil *Aeneid* 4.472–3, 7.447 and 456–7, Ovid *Metamorphoses* 10.349–50.
40 7.10.12; 7.34.8, 7.36.10; 10.29.7, 10.29.2. Compare 2.10.5 on Horatius Cocles at the bridge: *ipso miraculo audaciae obstupefecit hostes*. The Horatius story also celebrates one particular hero (2.10.2, *unus uir*), features vivid dialogue (2.10.3–4, 7–8) and a pious prayer in direct speech (2.10.11), and implies an internal audience (2.10.10, *clamor Romanorum*).
41 7.17.3, 10.28.10.
42 5.49.1 (*nam forte quadam . . . dictator interuenit*); cf. 5.48.4 (truce), 5.48.5 (relief forces); 5.46.2–3.

Fabius' walk and the arrival of Camillus are two of four stories in Livy's fifth book where siege conditions seem to be arbitrarily suspended. The others are the Roman soldier's conversation with the soothsayer at the siege of Veii, and the Faliscan schoolmaster's walk to the besiegers' camp with the children of the local aristocracy.[43] The question is not, I think, how strictly sieges were actually conducted in Italy in the early fourth century BC, but what type of narrative could present such stories with any appearance of credibility.

Another recurring feature of these episodes is the presence of spectators within the story. This is a device to produce *enargeia*, the vividness that presents a scene as if it were before our eyes.[44] The classic example is Thucydides' account of the battle in the harbour at Syracuse, with its focus on the emotions of the two armies watching from the shore. As Plutarch observed, the historian seems to make his hearers into spectators; listening to the text is like watching the action yourself.[45] It was a famous passage, imitated in characteristically long-winded fashion by Dionysius of Halicarnassus to describe the 'battle of the triplets' that decided the fate of Alba Longa.[46] Livy does it much more economically in his description of Titus Manlius' duel in item 5:[47]

> *ubi constitere inter duas acies tot circa mortalium animis spe metuque pendentibus. . .*
>
> When they took up their stand between the two armies, the hearts of the many men standing round them were on tenterhooks of hope and fear.

There are similar 'internal spectators' in the other episodes: the crowd receiving Cincinnatus in item 1;[48] the women and children watching Camillus' battle against the Gauls in item 4;[49] the frightened Roman soldiers in item 6;[50] the Samnite army, and then the main Roman army, in item 7.[51] And in all eight cases the soldiers' shouting at the triumph implies a crowd of spectators, necessarily present even when Livy does not refer to them.[52]

---

43 5.15.6–7; 5.27.1–2.

44 *Est enim haec pars orationis quae rem constituat paene ante oculos* (Cicero *Partitiones oratoriae* 20); *rerum, quasi gerantur, sub aspectum paene subiectio* (Cicero *De oratore* 3.202); cf. Quint. *Inst.* 6.2.32 (*enargeia*), 9.2.40 (*sub oculos subiectio*). For *enargeia* in Livy, see Feldherr 1998.4–12.

45 Thucydides 7.71.1–4; Plutarch *Moralia* 347a (οἷον θεατὴν ποιῆσαι τὸν ἀκροατήν).

46 Dionysius of Halicarnassus 3.18–20, esp. 3.18.2 (θεαταί), 3.19.1–3 (Thucydides pastiche); see Walker 1993.

47 7.10.9 (trans. Betty Radice, Penguin Classics); cf. 7.10.6 (*uisu ac specie aestimantibus*).

48 3.26.11–12 (*ea frequentia . . . plebis concursus ingens*).

49 5.48.3 (*in conspectu habentes . . . coniuges et liberos*).

50 7.17.3 (*insueta . . . specie*); cf. 7.10.6 (n. 47 above) for *species*.

51 7.34.8 (*cum omnium in se uertisset oculos*), 7.36.7–8 (*coniectis in eum omnium oculis*).

52 As he does at 4.20.3 (*ciuium ora*), 4.53.12 (*fauor circumstantis populi*).

IV

Putting these common elements together—celebration of a particular protagonist, dramatic speech and dialogue, participation by the gods, the presence of an audience—we may now come back to our question (p. 29 above) about the transmission of the *incondita carmina*.

When Livy describes Manlius' single combat as 'more in the manner of a spectacle than by the rules of war', he is describing a scene within his story, not commenting, as he does elsewhere, on the nature of the story itself.[53] Nevertheless, it may be significant that the theatre is in his mind.[54] Similarly, when in item 6 he refers to the paraphernalia of the Etruscan priests, he twice uses a word (*apparatus*) which frequently refers to theatrical productions,[55] and he applies it to a spectacle often seen on the Roman stage, that of Furies with blazing torches.[56]

Little is known about the *fabulae praetextae*, Roman plays on Roman subjects.[57] The classic titles were Naevius' *Clastidium* (on M. Marcellus in 222 BC), Naevius' *Romulus* and *Lupus* (perhaps alternative titles for the same play), Ennius' *Ambracia* and *Sabinae*, Pacuvius' *Paulus* (probably on Aemilius Paulus in 168 BC), Accius' *Aeneadae* or *Decius*, and Accius' *Brutus*.[58] Of these, *Aeneadae* or *Decius* dealt with our item 8, while the action of *Clastidium* was a single combat resulting in 'spoils of honour' (*spolia opima*), as in our item 2; Plutarch's account makes much of the triumphal procession, with due mention of the soldiers' songs.[59]

Ancient theorists of drama likened the *praetexta* to tragedy,[60] but it is clear that the known plots were not 'tragic' in the modern sense of the word. Even Decius' self-sacrifice, and Brutus' execution of his sons and heroic death, were exemplary acts in plays that ended well for the Romans; the other plots do not have even that much 'tragedy' in them. The reason for the theorists' categori-

---

53 7.10.6 (*spectaculi magis more quam lege belli*). For narrative itself as theatrical, see 5.21.9 (*haec ad ostentationem scaenae gaudentis miraculis aptiora*); Dionysius of Halicarnassus 3.18.1, 9.22.3; Plutarch *Romulus* 8.7.

54 Cf. Feldherr 1998.101: 'he explicitly draws attention to the "theatricality" of the scene in a manner that gives the question of spectacle a thematic importance within the episode.'

55 7.17.5. Stage: 27.6.19, 27.31.1, 31.49.4, 31.50.2, 32.7.14, 40.45.6, 45.32.8; cf. also Cicero *Ad Atticum* 15.2.3, 15.12.1, *Ad familiares* 7.1.2, *De officiis* 2.56, *Tusculan Disputations* 5.9; Valerius Maximus 2.4.2; Ulpian in *Digest* 7.1.15.5; Tertullian *De spectaculis* 4.4.

56 Cicero *Pro Roscio Amerino* 66–7 (*quem ad modum in fabulis saepenumero uidetis*), *In Pisonem* 46 (*ut in scaena uidetis*), *De legibus* 1.40 (*sicut in fabulis*).

57 The surviving evidence is presented with very thorough discussion in Manuwald 2001. See below, pp. 194–9, 206–7.

58 Fragments in Manuwald 2001.134, 141–3, 162, 172, 180–1, 196–8, 220–1.

59 Plutarch *Marcellus* 6.4–8.5 (soldiers' songs at 8.2); Livy's treatment in book 20 may have been similar, to judge by Eutropius 3.6.1–2.

60 Texts and discussion in Manuwald 2001.29–51.

sation was that the *praetexta*, like tragedy, dealt with the deeds of quasi-historical kings and heroes; the criterion was merely 'the dignity of the characters' (*personarum dignitas*).[61]

Polybius, who belonged to the generation between Pacuvius and Accius, used 'tragedy' as a disparaging metaphor in discussing the Romans' use of the fear of the gods as an instrument of social control. The context is Polybius' observation of how 'the constant renewal of the good report of brave men' inspired young Romans to sacrifice even life for the safety of the Republic; the example he gives is Horatius Cocles at the bridge, in a version of the story where Cocles does not survive.[62] Polybius' choice of the word *tragoidia* here was pointed out nearly forty years ago by Santo Mazzarino, who also noted that even the wretchedly few surviving fragments of *praetextae* include some conspicuous prayers to the gods.[63]

He might also have mentioned the comment of 'Mercury' to the audience in the prologue to Plautus' *Amphitruo*:[64]

> . . .*ut alios in tragoediis*
> *uidi, Neptunum Virtutem Victoriam*
> *Martem Bellonam, commemorare quae bona*
> *uobis fecissent*. . .

. . .as I've seen other gods in tragedies—Neptune, Virtus, Victoria, Mars, Bellona—remind you of what good things they've done for you.

The 'tragedies' where the gods of Rome reminded the Roman people of their benefits to them were probably plays on Roman subjects; and no doubt the good things they had done included the divine assistance implicit in most of our Livian episodes.

The sudden appearance of Camillus in item 4—the *peripateia*, as Ogilvie aptly calls it—is easier to imagine on the stage than in real siege conditions; and the same may be said of the soothsayer at Veii, the Faliscan schoolmaster, and

---

61 Diomedes in *Grammatici Latini* 1.489K (Manuwald 2001.31): *in quibus imperatorum negotia agebantur et publica et reges Romani uel duces inducuntur, personarum dignitate et sublimitate tragoediis similes.* Euanthius *De fabula* 4.1 (Manuwald 2001.37): *praetextatas* [*sic*] *a dignitate personarum tragicarum* . . .
62 Polybius 6.54.2–6 (inspiration), 6.55 (Cocles), 6.56.6–7 (δεισιδαιμονία), 6.56.8 (ἐκτετραγῴδηται), 6.56.11 (τῇ τοιαύτῃ τραγῳδίᾳ). Translation of 6.54.2 by Ian Scott-Kilvert (Penguin Classics).
63 Pacuvius *Paulus* fr. 1 Manuwald ('*pater supreme nostrae progenii patris*. . .'); Accius *Aeneadae* or *Decius* fr. 4 Manuwald ('*te sancte uenerans precibus, inuicte, inuoco,* | *portenta ut populo patriae uerruncent bene*'). See Mazzarino 1966.63–4, in a chapter entitled 'Society and historical thought in the age of the *praetexta*'.
64 Plautus *Amphitruo* 41–5; Wiseman 1998.19–20. Cf. also Phaedrus 2.7.23–4 (*di sunt locuti more translaticio*).

Fabius Dorsuo.[65] But any idea of stage performances influencing Livy's narrative method must be abandoned if Andrew Feldherr is to be believed:

> [F]ar from claiming the drama as a model for the way he presents Roman
> history, Livy consistently depicts the theatre as antithetical to his narrative in its
> aims and effects . . . Livy exploits Roman cultural constructions of the drama as
> a socially pernicious and fundamentally alien form of spectacle to highlight by
> contrast the salutary potential of his own history and its direct link to the
> centers of Roman power.

According to this view, the theatre was 'an institution isolated from the normal
conduct of civic life', foreign and anomalous, quite inconsistent with Livy's
patriotic purpose.[66]

It is a paradoxical view, as Feldherr admits: dramatic productions, as he
points out, took place 'within the context of official civic festivals', and 'consti-
tuted part of the cult practices of the state religion'.[67] Much depends on two
assumptions, that the *praetexta* was not an important dramatic form, and that
the action of plays seen in Rome, 'in the vast majority of cases, took place
outside Rome, usually in a markedly Greek milieu'.[68] That seems to infer
much too much from the surviving texts of Plautus and Terence. It is true that
Livy disapproved of the luxury and violence of the *ludi scaenici* in his own time,
as did Valerius Maximus a generation later, but he would surely have agreed
with Valerius that the theatre was one of 'the ancient and memorable institutions of our city'.[69] For the Romans' attitude to their public games—'especially
holy, solemn and sacred in their usages and institutions'—the language of
Cicero's speeches is surely decisive.[70]

So there need be no *a priori* objection to the hypothesis that some or all of
our Livian passages originated as performance scenarios. And if that hypothesis
is available, it may account for the *incondita carmina*.

---

65 See above, nn. 42–3. Ogilvie 1965.737; cf. Dionysius of Halicarnassus 3.18.1 for theatrical
    peripeteiai in Roman history.
66 Feldherr 1998.165–87; quotations from 165–6 and 170, cf. 181 ('anomalous'). The argu-
    ment about alienness (178–87) relies heavily on 7.2.4, *ceterum parua quoque, ut ferme principia
    omnia, et ea ipsa peregrina res fuit*. But when Livy says 'then it was new, small and alien', he
    surely implies '*now* it is familiar, huge, and part of Roman experience'.
67 Feldherr 1998.169, 174.
68 Feldherr 1998.176, with 172 on the *praetexta* as 'a not entirely successful experiment'.
69 7.2.13 (*hanc uix opulentis regnis tolerabilem insaniam*); Valerius Maximus 2.4.1 (violence), 2.4.6
    (luxury), and his preface to book 2 (*iniciam stilum . . . nostrae urbis . . . priscis et memorabilibus
    institutis*). Rioting fans: Dio Cassius 54.17.4–5 (*stasis*, before 18 BC), Tacitus *Annals* 1.54.2
    (*discordia*, AD 14), 1.77.1–2 (*seditio*, AD 15).
70 Cicero *De haruspicum responso* 24 (on the *ludi Megalenses*): *more institutisque maxime casti,
    sollemnes, religiosi*. Cf. *In Verrem* 5.36 on the *ludi Ceriales* and *plebeii* (respectively *sanctissimi*
    and *antiquissimi*).

Horace, writing about 12 BC, complains that the theatre of his time is obsessed with mere spectacle, and the example he gives is of a play on the capture of Corinth in 146 BC, featuring an interminable triumphal procession with wagon-loads of captured booty.[71] In five of our eight Livy passages—and in Plutarch's account of Marcellus' triumph, which may owe something indirectly to Naevius' play—specific mention is made of the amount of booty carried at the triumph.[72] Perhaps the procession was a traditional joyful conclusion to historical plays about Roman victories, rather like the closing revel (*komos*) in Aristophanes;[73] at Cincinnatus' triumph, we are told that the soldiers acted like revellers (*comisantes*).[74]

That does at least offer a solution to the problem of extemporised verses surviving into the much later literary tradition of historiography. Livy and his predecessors may have heard those *incondita carmina*, and seen the exemplary episodes they celebrated, in patriotic performances at the theatre games (*ludi scaenici*). If so, it seems that Livy has given us some good evidence after all, not so much in the stories he tells as in what can be inferred from his manner of telling them.

V

It may even be possible to support this hypothesis from a non-Livian source. In the section 'On miracles' of his collection of exemplary tales from history, Valerius Maximus tells the story of C. Fabricius' defence of Thurii against the Lucanians and Bruttians in 282 BC. When the Romans were nervous about attacking the besiegers, a young man of huge physique exhorted them, then seized a scaling ladder and made his way through the enemy lines to their camp; he climbed the rampart and shouted back to the Romans that the way to victory was achieved. The Romans attacked the camp and thus drew the Lucanians and Bruttians away from the siege; in the desperate battle that followed, the heroic young man defeated the enemy single-handed; twenty thousand were killed, five thousand taken prisoner, including the commander, and twenty-three standards captured.

The following day Fabricius held an assembly, and announced that the young man had won the 'siege crown' decoration (*corona uallaris*); but he was nowhere to be found. The Romans recognised that Mars himself had been

---

71 Horace *Epistles* 2.1.187–92; Brink 1982.432 on *captiua Corinthos* (cf. Cicero *De officiis* 2.28, *Philippics* 8.18; Livy 5.30.2, 38.43.10).

72 3.28.4, 4.19.6, 4.53.10, 7.17.5, 10.30.10; Plutarch *Marcellus* 8.1, cf. Eutropius 3.6.2 (n. 59 above).

73 Aristophanes *Acharnians* 1190–1233 (triumphal); *Peace* 1316–57, *Birds* 1720–65 (hymenaeal). Was there a wedding κῶμος at the end of Ennius' *Sabinae*?

74 3.29.5, *comisantium modo*.

among them, and Fabricius proclaimed a festival of thanksgiving (*supplicatio*) to the god:[75]

> *a laureatis militibus magna cum animorum laetitia oblati auxilii testimonium ei est redditum.*
>
> Wearing laurel wreaths and in great happiness of mind, the soldiers bore witness to Mars of the help he had provided.

Although this concluding scene is not a triumph, the structure of the narrative is very like that of the Livian passages.

It was probably not taken from Livy, who distances himself from miracle stories and conspicuously omits the very similar epiphany of the Dioscuri at the battle of Lake Regillus.[76] Other historians, however, were more hospitable to such material,[77] and I think we are entitled to take Valerius' unknown source as confirmation that our eight episodes reflect not just one historian's way of working but a real aspect of Roman life—a way of presenting exemplary actions to the public—that had a more general influence on Roman historiography.

I think we can also infer that these dramatised episodes from ancient history were put on regularly at the theatrical festivals. That seems to be implied by Horace's experience, since the fall of Corinth was hardly a topical subject in his day. It may also be implied by two apparently puzzling comments by Cicero—that the stage was a source of information, and that ordinary working people were fascinated by history.[78] That was surely one of the main purposes of the Roman games, to educate and inspire the citizen body by 'the constant renewal [as Polybius put it] of the good report of brave men'.[79]

What Livy can tell us is not (of course) how Roman heroism was celebrated in the early Republic, but how the heroism of the early Republic was celebrated in his own time. It is easy to imagine how the experience of seeing such exemplary deeds of bravery and piety recycled in stage performances year after year may have conditioned the way historians constructed their narratives. Not only that, but Polybius' evidence takes us back to the middle of the second century BC; even then, the Roman custom of representing the great deeds of the past was a *traditional* one. We cannot be sure that it went right back to the early Republic, but it is more likely than not that it predates Roman literature. And if that is the case, then perhaps even Livy's sophisticated literary history may have preserved some flavour of the culture of pre-literary Rome.

---

75 Valerius Maximus 1.8.6; the reference to the *gradus uictoriae* was no doubt an allusion to Gradiuus, one of the names of Mars.

76 2.19–20; cf. Levene 1993.18–20, 152–3.

77 See below, pp. 247–62.

78 Cicero *De legibus* 1.47, *De finibus* 5.51–2 (on the latter passage cf. Wiseman 1987a.252–6).

79 Polybius 6.54.2; the Roman phrase would be *res bene gestae*.

CHAPTER THREE

Fauns, Prophets, and Ennius' Annales

I

The invention of Latin epic is attributed to Ennius by the grammarian Diomedes in the fourth century AD:[1]

> *epos dicitur Graece carmine hexametro diuinarum rerum et heroicarum humanarumque comprehensio... Latine paulo communius carmen auditur. epos Latinum primus digne scripsit is qui res Romanorum decem et octo complexus est libris, qui et annales <in>scribuntur, quod singulorum fere annorum actus contineant, sicut publici annales quos pontifices scribaeque conficiunt, uel Romais, quod Romanorum res gestas declarant.*

> Epos in Greek means the composition of the deeds of gods, heroes and mortals in a hexameter poem... In Latin it is more often called *carmen*. The first Latin *epos* worthy of the name was written by the poet who encompassed the deeds of the Romans in eighteen books, which are entitled *Annales* because they contain the events of practically each year, like the public annals composed by the priests and scribes, or 'the *Romaid*' because they make manifest the achievements of the Romans.

Ennius himself expressed his primacy in a famous passage, one of the most frequently cited of all the surviving fragments of the *Annals*:[2]

> scripsere alii rem
> uorsibus quos olim Faunei uatesque canebant.

> Others have written of the matter [the first Punic War] in the verses which of old the Fauns and prophets chanted.

The reference is to Gnaeus Naevius.[3] Although Ennius thinks of him as a fellow *writer*, it seems that Naevius doesn't count as a proper 'literary author' because he used a metre appropriate to the pre-literary world.[4]

---

1 Diomedes *Ars grammatica* book 3, in *Grammatici Latini* 1.483–4 Keil; I follow Skutsch 1985.46 in reading *Romais* for the MSS' *romanis*.
2 Ennius *Annales* 206–7 Sk.
3 Stated explicitly by Cicero (*Brutus* 75–6), and obvious anyway.
4 Cicero *Brutus* 71: '*nec dicti studiosus quisquam erat ante hunc*' ait [Ennius] *ipse de se nec mentitur in gloriando.*

That at least is my reading of the lines. But it is important to remember how little we know about the culture and society of third-century Rome—despite the confident assumptions of some recent scholarship. For instance, Enrica Sciarrino argues that the audience for early Roman epic was not the same as for drama, and that Livius Andronicus' *Odyssey* translation 'opened the way to the encroachment of poets . . . on more exclusive sites of social interaction'.[5] Perhaps so: but Homeric bards like Demodocus performed for the games in the *agora* as well as for the 'elite' at the palace;[6] and Oliver Taplin has very plausibly argued that only a festival context can explain the length and complexity of the Homeric epics themselves.[7] Can we really be sure that conditions were radically different in Rome? Why not imagine the *ludi Romani*—or the *ludi plebeii*, for that matter—as the primary performance context of oral narrative poetry, and then of Naevius' and Ennius' epics?

As for the 'elite' itself, the use of sociological models may be misleading if it implies that Roman society was necessarily as hierarchical in the third century BC as it was in the first. There was no differential seating at the *ludi* until 194 BC, when privileged seats were provided for the senators, and the sources for that innovation (contradictory as they are) show clearly how controversial and unpopular it was.[8] Equally clearly, Pliny's account of the equestrian insignia implies a proliferation of hierarchical indicators from the Gracchan period onwards; but not before.[9]

I am much more in sympathy with Sander Goldberg's sense of how little is really known about the world of Naevius and Ennius. But here too I have a reservation. Is it really true, as he asserts,[10] that 'whatever archaic tradition preceded [Ennius' poem] remains beyond recovery'? If it is, then there is no point trying to understand what Ennius meant when he called Naevius' metre 'the verses which of old the Fauns and prophets chanted'. I hope to show that it may be possible, after all, to say something useful about the 'pre-literary' world of third-century Rome.

Glimpses into that world, from people close enough to it to be well informed, are hard to interpret but disproportionately precious. The most famous of them is the elder Cato's evocation of the custom, long obsolete in his own time, of guests at a banquet rising in turn to sing the praises of the men

5   Sciarrino 2006.458.
6   Homer *Odyssey* 8.12, 16, 109, 254–65 (*agora*); 40–45, 62–70, 104–7 (palace).
7   Taplin 2000.23–32.
8   Asconius 69–70C (citing Cicero's *Pro Cornelio* and Valerius Antias fr. 37P), Cicero *De haruspicum responso* 24, Livy 34.44.5 and 54.4–8.
9   Pliny *Nat. Hist.* 33.29–36.
10 Goldberg 2006.446.

of old.[11] Cato also knew of professional praise singers at banquets, and claimed that the *maiores* despised them.[12] Then there is Fabius Pictor's account of the procession at the *ludi Romani*, with its dancing choruses of Sileni in hairy tunics and satyrs in goatskin loincloths, mocking the serious participants in a manner that was literally satirical.[13] Perhaps Ennius' line can give us a similar insight into this unfamiliar world?

II

Vorsibus quos olim Faunei uatesque canebant is quoted six times in our extant texts. Cicero (twice) uses it as evidence for progress in the literary arts, and Quintilian to prove that poetry existed before the laws of metre.[14] But it is the other three citations that are more interesting for our purposes.

First, Varro, in his discussion of 'words which have been put down by the poets'.[15] He quotes the line, and then offers his exposition:[16]

> *Fauni dei Latinorum, ita ut Faunus et Fauna sit; hos uersibus quos uocant Saturnios in siluestribus locis traditum est solitos fari <futura, a> quo fando Faunos dictos. antiqui poetas uates appellabant a uersibus uiendis, ut <de> poematis cum scribam ostendam.*
>
> *Fauni* are gods of the Latins, in this sense, that there are both Faunus and Fauna. It has been handed down that they are accustomed to speak the future in wooded places, using the verses known as 'Saturnian', and called *Fauni* from

---

11 Cicero *Disp. Tusc.* 4.3: *grauissimus auctor in originibus dixit Cato, morem apud maiores hunc epularum fuisse, ut deinceps qui accumberent canerent ad tibiam clarorum uirorum laudes atque uirtutes.* Cicero *Brutus* 75: *atque utinam exstarent illa carmina, quae multis saeclis ante suam aetatem in epulis esse cantitata a singulis conuiuis de clarorum uirorum laudibus in originibus scriptum reliquit Cato.* Cf. also Cicero *Disp. Tusc.* 1.3, Horace *Odes* 4.15.29–32, Valerius Maximus 2.1.10, Quintilian 1.10.20. Varro has a different version, in which praises are sung by *pueri modesti* (*De uita populi Romani* fr. 84 Riposati = Nonius 107–8L). For the background, see Rösler 1990 and Zorzetti 1990; but also Horsfall 1994.70–73, a reminder that the Cato passage may be no more than a calque of Greek scholarship on the *symposion* (e.g. Dicaearchus fr. 88), and Goldberg 2006.431.

12 Aulus Gellius 11.2.5: *praeterea ex eodem libro Catonis haec etiam sparsim et intercise commeminimus: . . . 'poeticae artis honos non erat. si quis in ea re studebat aut sese ad conuiuia adplicabat crassator uocabatur'.* For the background, see Peruzzi 1998.157–64, and Goldberg 2006.431–4, with n. 9.

13 Dionysius of Halicarnassus 7.72.10 (*FGrH* 809 F13, p. 867), cf. 7.71.1 on Q. Fabius: παλαιότατος γὰρ ἀνὴρ τῶν τὰ Ῥωμαϊκὰ συνταξαμένων, καὶ πίστιν οὐκ ἐξ ὧν ἤκουσε μόνον, ἀλλὰ καὶ ἐξ ὧν αὐτὸς ἔγνω παρεχόμενος. For the background, see Szilágyi 1981.

14 Cicero *Brutus* 71 (cf. 75), *Orator* 171; Quintilian 9.4.115.

15 Varro *De lingua Latina* 7.5: *dicam in hoc libro de uerbis quae a poetis sunt posita.*

16 Ibid. 7.36 (repeated in Servius *auctus* on *Georgics* 1,11, who alone has *futura* after *fari*); I follow R.G. Kent's Loeb text. See Aronen 1999 on 'Saturnian verses', and Pasco-Pranger 2002.306–10 for an adventurous association of this passage with the story of Numa, Picus and Faunus at Ovid *Fasti* 3.285–328.

that 'speaking'. The ancients called poets *uates* from 'weaving verses', as I shall show when I write about poems.

Fauna was one of the names of the Bona Dea in the records of the *pontifices*; another was Fatua, also derived from *fari*, to speak.[17] She was thought of as a prophetess, just as Faunus was thought of as a prophet.[18] Some said she was a Dryad, just as some said Faunus was Pan.[19] Naturally, as divinities of the wild, they 'spoke' in woods and groves.[20]

Prophecy is also the context of Cicero's quotation of the Ennius line in *De diuinatione*. Quintus is discussing the phenomenon of directly inspired divination, when a kind of *furor* in the soul enables certain individuals to prophesy the future:[21]

> *eodem enim modo multa a uaticinantibus saepe praedicta sunt, neque solum uerbis sed etiam 'uersibus quos olim Fauni uatesque canebant'. similiter Marcius et Publicius uates cecinisse dicuntur; quo de genere Apollinis operta prolata sunt.*
>
> For in that way many things have been predicted by those who chant prophecies, not only in prose but also 'in the verses which of old the Fauns and prophets chanted'. The prophets Marcius and Publicius are said to have chanted in the same way, and the secrets of Apollo were brought forth in that style too.

What matters here is the equivalence of *uerba* and *uersus*, speaking in prose and chanting in verse. Though Faunus is 'the speaker', his prophecies can equally be described as chanted *carmina*.[22] So Ennius' *Fauni . . . canebant* is in no way paradoxical.

But who, or what, were the *Fauni*? It's clear that Cicero did not share Varro's interpretation of the plural as referring to two individual deities,

---

17 Macrobius *Saturnalia* 1.12.21–22: *hanc* [sc. Maiam] *eandem Bonam Faunamque, Opem et Fatuam pontificum libris indigitari: Bonam quod omnium nobis ad uictum bonorum causa est, Faunam quod omni usui animantium fauet, Opem quod ipsius auxilio uita constat, Fatuam a fando. . .*

18 Justin 43.1.8: *Fauno uxor fuit nomine Fatua, quae adsidue diuino spiritu inpleta ueluti per furorem futura praemonebat.* Plutarch *Moralia* 268D (*Quaestiones Romanae* 20, on the Bona Dea): ὡς οἱ μυθολογοῦντες ἱστοροῦσι, Φαύνου μὲν ἦν γυνὴ τοῦ μάντεως. . .

19 Plutarch *Caesar* 9.3 (Dryad); Horace *Odes* 1.17.1–2, Ovid *Fasti* 2.267–80, 2.424, etc (Pan Lykaios).

20 For instance in the first year of the Republic: Dionysius of Halicarnassus 5.16.2–3, explaining that the Romans attribute φωναὶ δαιμόνιοι to Faunus; cf. Servius on *Aeneid* 7.81 for Faunus named ἀπὸ τοῦ φωνῆς, *quod uoce non signis ostendit futura.* Calpurnius Siculus (*Eclogues* 1.8–32) offers a literary version of the idea, with Faunus' prophecy inscribed on a beech tree in the grove.

21 Cicero *De diuinatione* 1.114–15 (cf. 1.4 on *furor*).

22 E.g. Festus 432L on Saturnians, *quibus Faunus fata* **cecinisse** *hominibus uidetur*; Calpurnius Siculus *Ecl.* 1.29 and 34 (*canere*), 1.32, 35, 92 (*carmen*); cf. Ovid *Fasti* 3.323 on Faunus and Picus (*quae carmina dicant. . .*). The equivalence of *fari* and *canere* in prophecy is shown by Catullus 64.382–3 on the Fates: *talia* **praefantes** *quondam felicia Pelei* **carmina** *diuino* **cecinerunt** *pectore Parcae.*

Faunus and Fauna. A little earlier in the *De diuinatione* he makes Quintus point out that *Fauni* have often been heard in battles, clearly implying a particular category of divinity.[23] These *Fauni* were 'half-gods', dwellers in the country-side, the companions of nymphs and satyrs;[24] but they were still prophetic, both in their own right and as the inspirers of prophecy in mortals.[25]

It is also clear that Cicero did not share Varro's interpretation of *uates* as meaning poets. Nothing more is known of Publicius, dismissed as *nescio quis* by the sceptical Marcus in book 2 of the dialogue;[26] but Gnaeus Marcius was a well-known prophet, famous in Ennius' time for having foretold the disaster at Cannae.[27] Such prophets were active throughout the history of the republic, and we know from Livy and Horace that their oracular predictions were collected in volume form.[28]

The final quotation of the Ennius line is in the anonymous *Origo gentis Romanae*, a treatise probably of the fourth century AD but based on much earlier material. (None of the thirty or so authorities cited is demonstrably post-Augustan.) The author reports the successive reigns in Italy of Janus, Saturnus and Picus, and then goes on:[29]

post Picum regnauit in Italia Faunus, quem a fando dictum uolunt, quod is solet futura praecinere uersibus quos Saturnios dicimus; quod genus metri in uaticatione Saturniae primum proditum est. eius rei Ennius testis est, cum ait 'uersibus quos olim Fauni uatesque canebant'.

After Picus Faunus reigned in Italy. They derive his name from 'speaking', because he is accustomed to prophesy the future in the verses we call Saturnian, a type of metre first used in the prophecy of Saturnia [*or* in a prophecy at

---

23 Cicero *De diuinatione* 1.101: *saepe etiam et in proeliis Fauni auditi . . . esse dicuntur*. So too in *De natura deorum* 2.6 (*saepe Faunorum uoces auditae*), though the sceptic's answer at 3.15 uses the singular.

24 *Semidei*: Ovid *Metamorphoses* 1.192–3. See for instance Lucretius 4.580–1; Virgil *Eclogues* 6.27, *Georgics* 1.10–11, *Aeneid* 8.314; Horace *Epistles* 1.19.4, *Ars poetica* 244; Ovid *Metamorphoses* 6.392–3.

25 Nemesianus *Eclogues* 2.73 (*Fauni uates*); Fronto *De eloquentia* 2.12, Teubner p. 141 (*Fauni uaticinantium incitatores*). Cf. Martianus Capella 2.167 on the *longaeuorum chori qui habitant siluas, nemora, lucos, lacus, fontes ac fluuios, appellanturque Panes, Fauni, Fones, Satyri, Siluani, Nymphae, Fatui Fatuaeque uel Fantuae uel etiam Fanae, a quibus fana dicta, quod soleant diuinare*.

26 Cicero *De diuinatione* 2.113. It may be relevant that C. Marcius and T. 'Publius' (Publicius?) were among the first plebeian augurs, elected in 300 BC: Livy 10.9.2, with Wiseman 1998.103–4.

27 Livy 25.12.1–8 (prophecy discovered in 212 BC); cf. Cicero *De diuinatione* 1.89 (*Marcios quondam fratres, nobile loco ortos*), Festus 162L (*in carmine Cn. Marci uatis*).

28 Livy 25.1.12, 25.12.3 (*libri uaticini*); Horace *Epistles* 2.1.26 (*annosa uolumina uatum*). Prophets active: nn. 47–8 below, discussion in Wiseman 1994.49–67.

29 *Origo gentis Romanae* 4.4–5 (omitting a sentence condemned as a gloss since Gruner's edition in 1757). I think this passage disproves *e silentio* the attempt by Aronen (1999.63–9) to make Saturnus, as well as Faunus, an oracular deity.

Saturnia]. Ennius is our witness for that, when he says 'in the verses which of old the Fauns and prophets chanted'.

Saturnia was the stronghold on the Capitol founded by Saturnus,[30] and it is possible that there existed a supposed prophecy of its foundation. In this Euhemerised telling of the myth, exploited by Virgil in *Aeneid* 7, Faunus is part of a prehistoric dynasty of Latin monarchs; it was he who received Evander and his Arcadian colonists.[31] But he is a prophet in this guise too, providing dream-oracles in his sacred grove to his son and successor Latinus.[32]

III

Prophecy was primarily an oral mode; the words used of it were 'song' and 'singing', *carmen* and *canere*.[33] The same words defined the Camenae, those 'cultural signifiers of pre-poetic song' who inspired the oral poet's performance.[34] But listening to a prophet was probably not like listening to a poet.

What did a prophet *sound* like? Ovid sets the scene, where he describes the inspiration of the prophetess whose name was formed from *carmen*:[35]

> *parua mora est, caelum uates ac numina sumit*
> *fitque sui toto pectore plena dei;*
> *uix illam subito posses cognoscere, tanto*
> *sanctior et tanto quam modo maior erat.*

There is a moment's pause. Then the prophetess assumes the powers of heaven, and is filled with her god to the depths of her heart. Suddenly you could hardly recognise her, so much holier she was, and so much taller than before.

That was for a message of good news ('*laeta canam*'), but often the prophet's demeanour was fierce and threatening,[36] a far cry from the song of the poet.

---

30 Saturnia: *Origo gentis Romanae* 3.1 and 3.7, citing Virgil *Aeneid* 8.357–8; see also Ovid *Fasti* 6.31, Pliny *Nat. Hist.* 3.68, Festus 430L. Placed in 1300–1200 BC ('Bronzo recente, fase prima') by Carandini 1997.120.

31 Virgil *Aeneid* 7.47–9; Dionysius of Halicarnassus 1.31.2, Justin 43.1.6, *Origo gentis Romanae* 5.1–3.

32 Virgil *Aeneid* 7.81–103, esp. 82 (*fatidici genitoris*).

33 *Canere*: e.g. Livy 1.45.5, 1.55.6, 5.15.4; see n. 22 above. *Carmina*: e.g. Livy 25.12.2–8, Festus 162L (Cn. Marcius). Primarily oral: Cicero *De diuinatione* 2.149 (*siue tu uatem . . . audieris*). For 'song and memory' in general see Horsfall 2003.11–17, 36–47.

34 Festus (Paulus) 38L: *Camenae musae a carminibus sunt dictae, uel quod canunt antiquorum laudes. . .*; cf. Varro *De lingua Latina* 7.26–7 (*Casmenae>Carmenae>Camenae*), Servius on *Ecl.* 3.59 (*a cantu*), Macrobius *Commentary on Somnium Scipionis* 2.3.4 (*a canendo*). 'Cultural signifier': Sciarrino 2006.454.

35 Ovid *Fasti* 6.537–40 (cf. 1.503–6, also on Carmentis).

36 Lucretius 1.102–3 (*uatum terriloquis . . . dictis*), 1.109 (*minis . . . uatum*); Ovid *Fasti* 1.504 (*torua*).

(My use of the word 'chant' to translate Ennius' *canebant* is a crude attempt to register the difference.)

Different sorts of *carmina* sounded different because they had different things to say. In the pre-literary world (to put it in a modern idiom), the manner and the message were inseparable. But once they were written down and collected in books, *carmina* from widely different sources lost their distinctiveness.

Such collections of *carmina antiqua* are attested by Varro, Festus and Macrobius, who use them to cite (respectively) a description of a shepherds' festival,[37] a quasi-Homeric narrative of dawn,[38] and a piece of father-to-son advice on agriculture.[39] A religious precept cited by Nigidius Figulus may be a fourth example.[40] The variety and unpredictability of these haphazardly surviving items are a salutary warning of how little we understand pre-literary culture.

For instance, we have no idea where, when or why the *carmina* of the Salii were written down.[41] Nor do we know how Dionysius of Halicarnassus found his information about 'songs' in honour of Faunus, the twin founders and Marcius 'Coriolanus',[42] or whether the narrative *carmen Priami* and *carmen Nelei* existed independently or could be cited only from a general collection.[43] But the fact that no authors are named may allow one inference, at least—that these *carmina* were first composed in an oral culture and only later preserved in writing.[44] There is a clear contrast with Naevius' poem: though often cited as the *carmen belli Punici*, it always has the author's name attached.[45]

---

37 Varro *De uita populi Romani* fr. 23 Riposati (Nonius 31L), Horsfall 2003.46: *etiam pellis bubulus oleo perfusas percurrebant ibique cernuabant. a quo **ille uersus uetus** est **in carminibus**: 'ibi pastores ludos faciunt coriis Consualia'*.

38 Festus 214L: *obstinet dicebant antiqui, quod nunc ostendit; ut **in ueteribus carminibus**: 'sed iam se caelo cedens Aurora obstinet suum patrem'*.

39 Macrobius *Saturnalia* 5.20.18 (on *Georgics* 1.101), Horsfall 2003.45: **in libro** enim **uetustissimorum carminum**, *qui ante omnia quae a Latinis scripta sunt compositus ferebatur, inuenitur hoc rusticum **uetus canticum**: 'hiberno puluere, uerno luto, grandia farra, camille, metes'*. Also in Festus (Paulus) 82L: **in antiquo carmine**, *cum pater filio de agricultura praeciperet*.

40 Aulus Gellius 4.9.1: *Nigidius Figulus . . . in undecimo commentariorum grammaticorum uersum **ex antiquo carmine** refert memoria hercle dignum: 'religentem esse oportet, religiosus ne fuas'*.

41 Plural in Varro *De lingua Latina* 9.61, Festus (Paulus) 3L, Festus 124L, Macrobius *Saturnalia* 1.9.14 (*Saliorum quoque antiquissimis carminibus . . . canitur*), 1.15.14 (*ut Salii in carminibus canunt*). Singular (*carmen Saliorum* or *carmen Saliare*) in Varro *De lingua Latina* 5.110, 7.26–7, Festus (or Paulus) 109L, 222L, 224L, 230L, 231L, Terentius Scaurus in *Grammatici Latini* 7.28 Keil.

42 Dionysius of Halicarnassus 1.31.2 on Faunus (καὶ αὐτὸν ὡς τῶν ἐπιχωρίων τινὰ Ῥωμαῖοι δαιμόνων θυσίαις καὶ ᾠδαῖς γεραίρουσιν), 1.79.10 on Romulus and Remus (ὡς ἐν τοῖς πατρίοις ὕμνοις ὑπὸ Ῥωμαίων ἔτι καὶ νῦν ᾄδεται), 8.62.3 on Coriolanus (ᾄδεται καὶ ὑμνεῖται πρὸς πάντων ὡς εὐσεβὴς καὶ δίκαιος ἀνήρ).

43 Varro *De lingua Latina* 7.28 (*in carmine Priami*); Festus 418L, 482L, Charisius in *Grammatici Latini* 1.84 Keil (*in Nelei carmine*).

44 As an analogy, cf. Varro *De lingua Latina* 6.18 on the *togata praetexta data †eis† Apollinaribus ludis*, identified by the occasion, not the playwright.

45 Festus 306L, Nonius 290L, Priscian in *Grammatici Latini* 2.198, 234, 242, 351 Keil; cf. Aulus Gellius 17.21.45.

These 'old songs' may have been hymns or narratives sung to the lyre, or precepts to be given in a speaking voice. What the Fauns and prophets chanted (in a metre that Ennius thought an epic poet shouldn't use) was something quite different, a phenomenon that persisted long into the fully literate society of the late Republic and early Empire. The next section explores its later manifestations, which turn out to be unexpectedly relevant to Ennius' own poem.

IV

Among the omens and portents associated with the outbreak of civil war in 49 BC, Dio reports that 'certain oracles were chanted, purporting to be those of the Sibyl, and some people became inspired and prophesied many things'.[46] The prophecies Dio describes were no doubt like those delivered in earlier crises: in 87 BC, for instance, the Senate took note of the 'inspired predictions' (*furibundae praedictiones*) of the prophet Cornelius Culleolus,[47] and we happen to know of similar warnings in 78 and 63.[48]

Attributing a particular oracle to the Sibyl was probably easier after 83 BC, when the original *carmina Sibyllae* were destroyed with the temple of Capitoline Jupiter. In 76 an embassy was sent to Erythrae to replace them; it came back with about 1000 verses collected from individuals, and others were found from other sources. But it must have been easy for professional prophets to claim knowledge of items the embassy had missed.[49] The official collection had only limited authority, as Augustus showed when as *pontifex maximus* he purged it of unsuitable items.[50]

What exactly the prophets foretold in 49 BC is not recorded, but it is unlikely that it was encouraging. For the Romans had defied the Sibyl's warning by restoring king Ptolemy six years earlier, and Dio records that the citizens were afraid of the anger of the gods.[51]

In AD 19, at a time when the fear of civil war had returned,[52] a quasi-

---

46 Dio Cassius 41.14.4: λόγιά τινα ὡς καὶ τῆς Σιβύλλης ὄντα ᾔδετο, κάτοχοί τέ τινες γιγνόμενοι συχνὰ ἐθείαζον. The Loeb translation takes ᾔδετο as from εἴδω/οἶδα ('some oracles ... were made known'), but Dio's usage in similar passages elsewhere (nn. 53–5 below) suggests that it was from ᾄδω, perhaps reproducing *canebantur* in a Latin source.

47 Cicero *De diuinatione* 1.4; cf. Plutarch *Marius* 42.4.

48 Sallust *Histories* 1.67.3M (*uatum carmina*), Cicero *De consulatu suo* 10.28–9 Courtney (*uates oracla furenti pectore fundebant*). [Cf. also Appian *Civil Wars* 1.121.563 on the θεόληπτοί τινες who brought about the reconciliation of Pompey and Crassus in 71 BC.]

49 Dionysius of Halicarnassus 4.62.5–6 (from Varro), Lactantius *Diuinae institutiones* 1.6.11 and 14 (citing Varro and Fenestella).

50 Suetonius *Diuus Augustus* 31.1: *solos retinuit Sibyllinos* [libros], *hos quoque dilectu habito*.

51 Dio Cassius 39.15.1–16.2 (Sibyl's warning); 39.55.3, 56.4, 59.3, 60.4 (defiance); 39.61.1–4 (citizens' fear, 54 BC).

52 Tacitus *Annals* 1.4.2, 1.16.1, 1.31.1, 1.35.3–4 (AD 14), 2.39.1 (AD 16), 2.59.2–3, 2.78.1 (AD 19); Suetonius *Tiberius* 25.1–2 (AD 14); *SC de Pisone patre* 45–9 (AD 19).

Sibylline oracle was chanted again, and this time Dio quotes it verbatim:

'When thrice three hundred years have come and gone,
Then civil conflict shall destroy the Romans. . .'

Tiberius tried to calm the People's fears by insisting that the oracle was false, and he repeated Augustus' purging of all books of prophecy.[53] But that could not stop oral circulation, and the same oracle was remembered in AD 64, when the fire of Rome was taken as its fulfilment.[54] Nero assured the populace that these lines could not be found in any collection of oracles, but in vain: they simply chanted another, more specific, 'Sibylline' prophecy instead.[55]

What is interesting about these passages is not only the continued importance of oral prophecy for the Roman People as late as the first century AD, but also the content of the Sibyl's alarming forecast. Why should the citizens have been afraid of the nine hundredth year of Rome? Surely they knew that AD 19 was *ab urbe condita* 771? All they had to do was go to Augustus' arch in the Forum and look at the list of consuls and triumphs; the AUC date was given for every triumph and for every tenth set of consuls.[56] Why did the Roman People not believe so authoritative a source of information?

I think the point is this, that all *human* knowledge is fallible. Only the gods know the truth, and only the *uates*—prophet or poet—is divinely inspired to reveal it. That's not how we see it, or how Cicero and Tacitus saw it, but to most ordinary Romans it was probably self-evident.

Lines from the great poets could attain quasi-oracular status,[57] and we can be sure that after 27 BC everyone knew at least one passage from Ennius, without necessarily knowing its context:[58]

---

53 Dio Cassius 57.18.4–5 (Xiphilinus): λόγιόν τέ τι ὡς καὶ Σιβύλλειον, ἄλλως μὲν οὐδὲν τῷ τῆς πόλεως χρόνῳ προσῆκον, πρὸς δὲ τὰ παρόντα ᾀδόμενον, οὐχ ἡσυχῇ σφας ἐκίνει· ἔλεγε γὰρ ὅτι· τρὶς δὲ τριηκοσίων περιτελλομένων ἐνιαυτῶν Ῥωμαίους ἔμφυλος ὀλεῖ στάσις . . . The Loeb translator loses the sense of ᾀδόμενον ('applied to the situation then existing'); cf. n. 46 above.

54 Dio Cassius 62.18.3 (Xiphilinus): καὶ μάλισθ' ὅτι αὐτοὺς ἡ μνήμη τοῦ λογίου τοῦ κατὰ τὸν Τιβέριόν ποτε ᾀσθέντος ἐθορύβει. Still unwilling to countenance chanting, the Loeb translator renders ᾀσθέντος as 'the oracle which . . . had been on everybody's lips'.

55 Dio Cassius 62.18.4 (Xiphilinus): μεταβαλόντες ἕτερον λογίον ὡς καὶ Σιβύλλειον ὄντως ὂν ᾖδον· ἔστι δὲ τοῦτο· ἔσχατος Αἰνεαδῶν μητροκτόνος ἡγεμονεύσει. For ᾖδον the Loeb translator has 'proceeded to repeat'.

56 *CIL* I².1, pp. 1–50; Degrassi 1947.1–87. Nineteen AUC dates survive on the *fasti consulares*, more than ninety on the *triumphales*.

57 See for instance Cicero *De republica* 5.1: '*moribus antiquis res stat Romana uirisque*' [Ennius *Annales* 156 Sk], *quem quidem ille uersum uel breuitate uel ueritate tamquam ex oraculo mihi quodam esse effatus uidetur*.

58 Ennius *Annales* 154–5 Sk, in Varro *De re rustica* 3.1.2: *nam in hoc nunc denique est ut dici possit, non cum Ennius scripsit: 'septingenti sunt paulo plus aut minus anni augusto augurio postquam inclita condita Roma est'*. Applied to Augustus: Suetonius *Diuus Augustus* 7.2.

> *septingenti sunt, paulo plus aut minus, anni*
> *augusto augurio postquam incluta condita Roma est.*
>
> Seven hundred years there are, a little more or less,
> since glorious Rome was founded with august augury.

If it had become known, two centuries after Ennius, that the Sibyl had allocated Rome just nine hundred years, it's not surprising that the citizens were panicky.

AD 19 was an ill-omened year from the very first day, when a mysterious trumpet-blast was heard at dawn.[59] When that happened in 88 BC, the *haruspices* announced that the eighth Etruscan *saeculum* had come to an end.[60] The conclusion of the ninth *saeculum* was marked by the comet of 44 BC—or so the *haruspex* Vulcatius declared to the Roman People in the Forum, and fell dead as he finished his speech.[61] The tenth *saeculum* was the last: when would it end, and what would happen when it did?

If the Roman People had read their Varro, they would have learned that each Etruscan *saeculum* lasted over a hundred years, and that the eighth was still in progress when Varro was writing in the late Republic.[62] However, most Roman citizens did not read books. They trusted what their prophets told them by direct inspiration from the gods, however terrifying the message might be.[63] And if that was true in the sophisticated Rome of the first century AD, it was true *a fortiori* in the time of Ennius.

V

Why did Ennius call his epic *Annales*? Diomedes, in the passage with which we began, says it was because it contained 'the events of practically each year, like the public annals composed by the priests and scribes'.[64] But that cannot be the whole story. Even if the chronicle of the *pontifices* did indeed go back to the fifth century BC, as Tim Cornell and Stephen Oakley believe,[65] it could have provided a year-by-year framework only from the fourth book of the *Annales* onwards. The narrative from Aeneas to Tarquin could not have been written in that way, and even for the early Republic there is no evidence that anyone

---

59 Dio Cassius 57.18.3, explained as the consul L. Norbanus practising.
60 Plutarch *Sulla* 7.3–5; *Suda* s.v. Σύλλας (attributing it to Livy and Diodorus). Cf. Servius on *Aeneid* 8.526: *Varro de saeculis auditum sonum tubae de caelo dicit.*
61 Augustus *De uita sua* fr. 5P (Servius *auctus* on *Ecl.* 9.46), specifying an *oratio in contione.*
62 Censorinus *De die natali* 17.5–6: *ut Varro testatur . . . octauum tum demum agi.*
63 Cf. Lucretius 1.102–3 (n. 36 above).
64 Above, n. 1.
65 Cornell 1995.13–15, Oakley 1997.24–27; see pp. 263–5 below for a sceptical view.

used the annalistic form, consular year by consular year, before L. Piso Frugi in the 120s BC.[66]

But that was not the only way of measuring years. The latest work on chronography in Ennius' time was by Eratosthenes of Cyrene, who was interested in the origins of Rome. He believed Romulus was the son of Ascanius, and since he put the fall of Troy in 1184/3 BC, that implies a date in the region of 1140–1120 for the foundation of the city.[67] Ennius too has Romulus as Aeneas' grandson; but he gained some chronological leeway by making him the son of Aeneas' younger daughter, who was born in Italy,[68] rather than of the son who fled with Aeneas from Troy. So if, as is likely, the famous lines about the seven hundred years belong in a speech of Camillus after the sack of Rome by the Gauls, he may have had a somewhat later foundation-date in mind.[69]

The date of the sack of Rome was known pretty accurately: Polybius' '387/6 BC' is probably from Timaeus, and the detailed chronology in his account of Rome's subsequent wars with the Gauls no doubt represents what Fabius Pictor knew.[70] So one might guess that Ennius' chronological era was constructed backwards from the triumph of M. Fulvius Nobilior in 187 BC. A thousand years before that was close enough to Eratosthenes' date for the fall of Troy; the foundation of Rome by the son of the daughter of Aeneas' old age could be put a hundred years later, in 1087,[71] and narrative landmarks could be put at century intervals thereafter; hence the seven hundred years in 387 BC.

Nobody knows how Ennius imagined the regal period, or when he thought the Republic began. But once the list of seven kings became canonical,[72] and the first consuls were firmly placed in the twenty-eighth year before Xerxes' invasion of Greece,[73] his system was no longer viable. By that point the foundation was agreed to be much later than Ennius had it—for instance in

---

66 For Piso as the innovative annalist, see Forsythe 1994.42; cf. Dionysius of Halicarnassus *Ant. Rom.* 4.7.5, 4.15.5, 12.9.3 (Πείσων δὲ ὁ τιμητικὸς ἐν ταῖς ἐνιαυσίοις ἀναγραφαῖς).

67 Eratosthenes *FGrH* 241 F1 (Troy date), F45 (Romulus): respectively Clement of Alexandria *Stromateis* 1.138.1–3 and Servius *auctus* on *Aeneid* 1.273.

68 Ennius *Annales* 36 Sk: Ilia's speech to her half-sister, '*Eurydica prognata, pater quam noster amauit*'. Cf. Pausanias 10.26.1 for Eurydice = Creusa.

69 Ennius *Annales* 154–5 Sk (n. 58 above). According to Skutsch (1968.12), 'without a doubt, both Eratosthenes and Ennius assumed that Rome was founded about 1100 BC'; but that ignores the difference between the two accounts.

70 Polybius 1.6.1–2, 2.18.6–19.7; Walbank 1957.46–8, 185–7.

71 Cf. Syme 1958.772–4, inferring a tradition that Rome was founded in 1084 BC, 1200 years before Trajan's death in AD 117.

72 The reign of Tullus Hostilius may have originated with the emergence of the senatorial Hostilii (praetors in 209 and 207 BC). For the eight bronze statues on the Capitol, supposedly the seven kings plus L. Brutus (Asconius 29C, Pliny *Nat. Hist.* 33.9, 33.24, Dio Cassius 43.45.3–4, Appian *Civil Wars* 1.16.70), see Coarelli 1999.

73 Polybius 3.22.2 (from Fabius?).

747 BC (Fabius Pictor), or 728 (Cincius Alimentus), or 751 (Cato)[74]—and a dynasty of Alban kings had been created to reach back to Aeneas.[75]

New patterns had to be found for the passing of time. In Virgil, Jupiter prophesies three years for Aeneas, thirty for Ascanius, three hundred for the Alban kings.[76] In Livy, Camillus dates the sack of Rome to *ab urbe condita* 365, the magical number representing a 'year of years'.[77]

It is tantalising not to know on what grounds the learned senator Manilius in 97 BC calculated the 'great year' marked by the life-cycle of the phoenix: evidently the current era had begun in 312 BC (Ap. Claudius' revolutionary censorship), and the previous one in 852 BC.[78] The latter date looks like a century before the foundation; is it completely a coincidence that Jerome, who had access to otherwise unknown traditions on early Rome, put the first 'centenary games' in 452 BC?[79] Whatever arcane systems were devised, the simple hundred-year *saeculum* always retained its power.

The annalist Piso Frugi marked the opening of Rome's seventh *saeculum* in 158 BC;[80] other historians noted significant events in *ab urbe condita* 400 (a patrician 'backlash') and 700 (a disastrous fire);[81] and Claudius Caesar held Secular Games, and displayed a fake phoenix, in the eight hundredth year of the city.[82] But as we have seen already, not everyone believed the chronology of historians and emperors. If the prophets were chanting that thrice three hundred years had come and gone, that was enough to cause panic among the People.[83]

A late-republican expert on prophecy told Varro that provided the historians' narrative about Romulus' augury was true, the gods had promised that

74 Dionysius of Halicarnassus 1.74.1–2.
75 Diodorus 7.5.6–12 (from the Armenian version of Eusebius' *Chronicle*), Livy 1.3.6–10, Dionysius of Halicarnassus *Ant. Rom.* 1.71, Ovid *Metamorphoses* 14.609–21, *Fasti* 4.39–54, *Origo gentis Romanae* 17.4–19.1. The new system was already in being in the third century BC: see Forsythe 1994.113–23.
76 Virgil *Aeneid* 1.265–74. Servius (on *Aeneid* 1.272) was puzzled: *quomodo trecentos annos dicit, cum eam* [i.e. *gentem Hectoream*] *quadringentis regnasse constet sub Albanis regibus?*
77 Livy 5.54.5; see Hubaux 1958.13–88. Magical: *Papyri Graecae magicae* XII.139; cf. (e.g.) Pliny *Nat. Hist.* 19.12, 34.33, Quintus Curtius 3.3.10, Heliodorus *Aethiopica* 9.226, Augustine *City of God* 18.53.
78 Pliny *Nat. Hist.* 10.4–5: the 215th year of a 540-year era (if the numerals in Pliny's text are reliable).
79 Jerome *Chron.* 112 Helm (*Romae ... agon centenarius primum actus*); cf. 88 Helm for the unique version of Remus' death (*a Fabio Romuli duce occisus*). On the rival sequences of *ludi saeculares*, see Wiseman 1998.165–7.
80 Piso fr. 46 Forsythe (Censorinus *De die natali* 17.13).
81 Livy 7.18.1 (perhaps from Licinius Macer); Orosius 6.14.5, 7.2.11 (from Livy).
82 Tacitus *Annals* 11.11.1; Pliny *Nat. Hist.* 10.5.
83 Above, nn. 53–4.

the Roman People would last 1200 years, one century for each vulture.[84] What is interesting is the reservation. Historians were notoriously capable of lying,[85] whereas prophets could claim that their knowledge came straight from the gods. Poets were liars too, and yet privileged to see the gods;[86] the Muses themselves taught Hesiod that they could tell both lies and truth alike.[87]

Ennius was inspired by the Muses of Olympus, who were also the Latin Camenae.[88] He used the metre of Homer rather than that of the Fauns and prophets, and no doubt his sweet-voiced Egeria sounded quite different from the terrifying threats of the Lucretian *uates*.[89] Nevertheless, the title of his great work suggests that he saw the world in much the same way that they did. It is appropriate that later readers could treat his lines as the oracles of a prophet.[90]

Of course Ennius is rightly celebrated as a pioneering innovator, the founder of a great tradition, a poet who deserves his place in Raphael's *Parnassus* next to Homer, Dante and Virgil. But he is no less interesting as a witness of his own time, when the conditions of pre-literary Rome were still familiar.

---

84 Varro *Antiquitates humanae* book 18 (fr. 4 Mirsch), cited in Censorinus *De die natali* 17.15: *ait fuisse Vettium Romae in augurio non ignobilem ingenio magno, cuius docto in disceptando parem; eum se audisse dicentem,* **si ita esset ut traderent historici** *de Romuli urbis condendae auguriis ac XII vulturis, quoniam CXX annos incolumis preterisset populus Romanus, ad mille et ducentos peruenturum.*
85 Evidence and discussion in Wiseman 1993a.
86 Ovid *Fasti* 6.23 ('*ius tibi fecisti numen caeleste uidendi*', says Juno), but also 6.253 (*non equidem uidi—ualeant mendacia uatum!*).
87 Hesiod *Theogony* 22–8.
88 Ennius *Annales* 1 and 487 Sk.; n. 34 above.
89 Ennius *Annales* 113 Sk: *olli respondit suauis sonus Egeriai.* Threats: n. 36 above.
90 Cicero *De republica* 5.1 (n. 57 above); cf. Cole 2006.532–3.

CHAPTER FOUR

The God of the Lupercal

I

On 15 February, two days after the Ides, there took place at Rome the mysterious ritual called *Lupercalia*, which began when the *Luperci* sacrificed a goat at the *Lupercal*. There was evidently a close conceptual and etymological connection between the name of the festival, the title of the celebrants, and the name of the sacred place: as our best-informed literary source on Roman religion, M. Terentius Varro, succinctly put it, 'the *Luperci* [are so called] because at the *Lupercalia* they sacrifice at the *Lupercal* . . . the *Lupercalia* are so called because [that is when] the *Luperci* sacrifice at the *Lupercal*'.[1]

What is missing in that elegantly circular definition is the name of the divinity to whom the sacrifice was made. Even the sex of the goat is unclear—Ovid and Plutarch refer to a she-goat, other sources make it male[2]—which might perhaps imply a similar ambiguity in the gender of the recipient.[3] Varro does indeed refer to a goddess Luperca, whom he identifies with the she-wolf of the foundation legend; he explains the name as *lupa pepercit*, 'the she-wolf spared them' (referring to the infant twins), so I think we can take this as an elaboration on the myth, and not much help for the ritual.[4]

Roman Society Presidential Address, November 1993. I am very grateful to those who commented on earlier versions of the argument, given at the British School at Rome, at Stanford (the T.B.L. Webster Lecture) and at Berkeley. But my greatest debt is to the marvellous collection of material in Dr Elisabeth Smits' Utrecht thesis *Faunus* (Smits 1946).

1 Varro *De lingua Latina* 5.85, 6.13: *Luperci, quod Lupercalibus in Lupercali sacra faciunt. . . Lupercalia dicta, quod in Lupercali Luperci sacra faciunt.*
2 Ovid *Fasti* 2.361, Plutarch *Romulus* 21.4 (αἶγες), Quintilian *Institutio* 1.5.66 (*luere per caprum*), Servius on Virgil *Aeneid* 8.343 (*de capro luebatur*). The *Luperci* skinned the sacrificial goat and used its hide for wearing and for striking those whom they met: Dionysius of Halicarnassus 1.80.1 (Tubero fr. 3P), Nicolaus of Damascus *FGrH* 90 F130.71, Festus (Paulus) 75–6L, Ovid *Fasti* 2.445–6, Plutarch *Romulus* 21.4–5, Valerius Maximus 2.2.9. They were called *crepi*, evidently a form of *capri*: Festus (Paulus) 49L, cf. 42L.
3 Arnobius *Aduersus gentes* 7.19: *dis feminis feminas, mares maribus hostias immolare.* (Female offerings to Faunus at Ovid *Fasti* 4.652 and Horace *Odes* 1.4.11–12 are regarded by the commentators as 'un-Roman'.)
4 Arnobius *Aduersus gentes* 4.3 = Varro *Antiquitates rerum diuinarum* fr. 221 Cardauns.

'*Lupercalia*' is just one of the festival days (*dies feriati*) that are named in large letters on the pre-Julian calendar. (Whether that list goes back to the early regal period, as Mommsen thought, or no further than the fifth century BC, as is argued by Agnes Kirsopp Michels in her book on the Roman calendar,[5] it is the earliest evidence we have for the *Lupercalia*.) There are forty-two such names, of which thirty end in *-alia*; and at least twenty of those thirty are formed from the name of the divinity concerned—*Liberalia, Floralia, Neptunalia, Saturnalia*, and so on. But there are others that are not (e.g. *Agonalia, Feralia, Vinalia*), and I think it likely that '*Lupercalia*' belongs in that category.[6]

Like the names of the 'large-letter' festivals, so too the names of the *flamines* (priests of individual divinities, of which thirteen out of fifteen are known) must reflect the pantheon of early Rome.[7] As one might expect, the two lists overlap substantially: corresponding to the *flamen Quirinalis* and six of the minor *flamines*—*Carmentalis, Cerialis, Furrinalis, Portunalis, Volcanalis* and *Volturnalis*—are the calendar items *Quirinalia, Carmentalia, Cerialia, Furrinalia, Portunalia, Volcanalia* and *Volturnalia*. But no name corresponds to the *Lupercalia*, and in fact we know that there cannot have been a specialist *flamen* to look after that cult; on 15 February the *flamen Dialis*, Jupiter's priest, was in charge.[8] That fact, together with Varro's circular explanation of *Lupercalia-Luperci-Lupercal*, seems to imply that for the Romans no one god (or goddess) was particularly associated with the ritual.

In modern accounts it is normally taken for granted that the divinity honoured at the *Lupercalia* was Faunus, and that is indeed what Ovid says.[9] Other authors, however, give other names, as we shall see; and for Faunus in particular there is a strong *prima facie* argument against. His festival was the Ides, 13 February, very close to the *Lupercalia* but not the same day. It was in fact the dedication day of Faunus' temple on the Tiber island, founded in 193 BC, which *ought* to imply that Faunus was thought of as closely associated with the *Lupercalia* cult, but not himself the recipient of it.[10]

---

5   Michels 1967.207–20 for a history of the controversy. Cf. North 1989.574: 'We do not know when this form of calendar was introduced, though it may well have been in the course of the republican period; its introduction might or might not have coincided with the fixing of the list of festivals in capitals.'

6   The list is in Degrassi 1963.364–5; I have omitted the Ides of each month from the totals. Degrassi gives 'Lupercalia Luperco sive Fauno', but that begs the question.

7   Varro *De lingua Latina* 5.84: *horum singuli cognomina habent ab eo deo cui sacra faciunt* (similarly 7.45, citing Ennius *Annales* 116–18 Sk); Vanggard 1988, esp. 24–8 [who however omits the *flamen Virbialis* (*ILS* 6457)].

8   Ovid *Fasti* 2.282. (Conversely, minor *flamines* without corresponding 'large-letter' festivals are *Falacer, Floralis, Palatualis, Pomonalis* [and *Virbialis*].)

9   Ovid *Fasti* 2.267–8, 303–4, 423–4; 5.99–102. Like Horace (*Odes* 1.17.1–4), Ovid assumes the identity of Faunus and Pan (*Fasti* 2.423–4, 2.84, 4.650–3); see now Parker 1993.

10 Faunus temple: Ovid *Fasti* 2.193–4, Degrassi 1963.4, 223, Livy 33.42.10, 34.53.4. But see n. 51 below.

The *Lupercalia* ritual and its associated myth, of the suckling of Remus and Romulus at the *Lupercal*,[11] have been a subject of inexhaustible fascination for scholars both ancient and modern. In recent years the prevailing mode of enquiry has been that of the comparativists, beginning in 1964 with Gerhard Binder's very influential monograph *Die Aussetzung des Königskindes*,[12] and continuing with Andreas Alföldi's formidably learned argument on 'the structure of the pre-Etruscan Roman state', almost entirely based on his comparative interpretation of the *Lupercalia* ritual and the myth of the twins.[13] Since then, we have had Christoph Ulf's book *Das römische Lupercalienfest*, arguing from the supposed parallel of African initiation rites, and Jan Bremmer's anthropological interpretation of the foundation story in the Bremmer and Horsfall collection *Roman Myth and Mythography*.[14] (One might expect the name of Georges Dumézil to appear in this doxology; but Dumézil's only extended treatment of the *Lupercalia* was in an early work, and in his later years he disowned it.[15])

The trouble with comparativist analysis is that it argues synchronically, and makes no adequate allowance for change over time.[16] Alföldi, for instance, claims to extrapolate, from the details given in our historical sources, the model of a ritual which had served a society thousands of years earlier and thousands of miles away (unimaginable to the Romans themselves) and which remained essentially unchanged into the historical period, effectively dictating to the Romans the performance of ritual acts that had little or no significance for their own thought-world. Surely that is absurd. No doubt religious behaviour is inherently conservative; perhaps Roman religion was more conservative than most. But any community's dealings with its gods must reflect, at some level, its own needs and preoccupations, and adjust, with whatever time-lag, as those needs and preoccupations change.

There have, of course, been some protests at some of the comparativists' excesses,[17] but perhaps the time has come for a new look at the *Lupercalia* from

---

11 Ovid *Fasti* 2.381–422, *Origo gentis Romanae* 22.1, Servius on *Aeneid* 8.343; cf. Plutarch *Romulus* 21.4, Dionysius of Halicarnassus 1.32.3–4, 1.79.7–8. Detailed analysis in Wiseman 1995.77–88.

12 Binder 1964, esp. 96–115 (ch. 10, 'Der Romulusmythos und das Lupercalienfest').

13 Alföldi 1974, esp. 69–180 (chs 3–6, 'Der Mythos von der Wölfin-Urahnin', 'Das Luperkalienfest', 'Hirtenkriegertum und Männerbund', 'Zweiteilung und Doppelmonarchie').

14 Ulf 1982; Bremmer 1987a. For earlier literature see Ulf's bibliography, and add Pötscher 1984.

15 Dumézil 1929.197–222; cf. Dumézil 1970.349 n. 33. The *Lupercalia* offered no support for Dumézil's 'tripartite' theory, on which see Momigliano 1984 = 1987.135–59, and Belier 1991.

16 Bremmer, however (1987a.38–43), does argue for a historically specific context.

17 E.g. Welwei 1967, responding to Binder 1964; Versnel 1976, reviewing Alföldi 1974. As an analogy, cf. Momigliano 1984 on Dumézil, and 1989.55: 'What Dumézil cannot do, because it is contradictory in terms, is to postulate an invariable Indo-European pattern as the explanation of the continuously changing relations between the social groups of Rome.'

an empirical historian's viewpoint, plotting the evidence over time and looking for the ways the ritual developed in a constantly changing world. It may help to keep the material under control if we focus in particular on that puzzling question: to whom did the *Luperci* sacrifice at the *Lupercal* on the morning of the *Lupercalia*?

II

Our earliest evidence for the god of the *Lupercal* dates back to the middle of the third century BC. It is a fragment of Eratosthenes, and I draw particular attention to it because for some unaccountable reason it is not included in Jacoby's *Fragmente der griechischen Historiker*.[18] It comes in the scholia to Plato's *Phaedrus*, at the point where Socrates mentions the Sibyl. The scholiast gives a list of Sibyls, including this item at no. 4:[19]

τετάρτη Ἰταλική. ἡ ἐν ἐρημίᾳ τῆς Ἰταλίας τὴν διατριβὴν λαχοῦσα, ἧς υἱός ἐγένετο Εὔανδρος, ὁ τὸ ἐν Ῥώμῃ τοῦ Πανὸς ἱερόν, τὸ καλούμενον Λούπερκον, κτίσας. περὶ ἧς ἔγραψεν Ἐρατοσθένης.

The fourth is the Italian [Sibyl]. It was her lot to spend her life in the wilderness of Italy; her son was Evander, who founded the cult-place of Pan in Rome, which is called Luperkon. Eratosthenes wrote about her.

Clement of Alexandria, who was very well read in the Greek philosophers, evidently had the same passage in mind when he wrote his *Stromateis* about AD 200. Arguing that the Sibyls, like Moses, pre-date Orpheus and the other sages of Greece, he discusses the Phrygian and Erythraean Sibyls, and then goes on:[20]

μέμνηται τούτων Ἡρακλείδης ὁ Ποντικὸς ἐν τῷ περὶ χρηστηρίων. ἐῶ δὲ τὴν Αἰγυπτίαν καὶ τὴν Ἰταλήν, ἢ τὸ ἐν Ῥώμῃ Κάρμαλον ᾤκησεν, ἧς υἱός Εὔανδρος ὁ τὸ ἐν Ῥώμῃ τοῦ Πανὸς ἱερὸν τὸ Λουπέρκιον καλούμενον κτίσας.

Heraclides Ponticus refers to them in his *On Oracles*. I say nothing of the Egyptian [Sibyl], or the Italian one who dwelt at the Karmalon in Rome; her son was Evander, who founded the cult-place of Pan in Rome, which is called Luperkion.

The last phrases, agreeing almost word for word with the Plato scholiast, show that Clement too knew of the Italian Sibyl, and the cult of Pan at the *Lupercal*, from Eratosthenes.[21]

---

18 The passage is referred to, but not quoted, at *FGrH* 241 F26; no comment in Jacoby 1962.713.
19 Schol. Plato *Phaedrus* 244b, Ruhnk p. 61. [Greene 1938 includes the passage only in the *apparatus criticus*; no explanation is offered.]
20 Clemens Alexandrinus *Stromateis* 1.108.3; cf. Heraclides Ponticus fr. 130 Wehrli.
21 Eratosthenes was clearly expanding Heraclides' list; see Parke 1988.23–36, who however does not refer to these two passages.

This fourth Sibyl must be the 'Cimmerian Sibyl in Italy' mentioned by Naevius and Piso.[22] She clearly owes her existence to the early identification of Lake Avernus as the scene of Odysseus' visit to the dead:[23]

> The vessel came to the bounds of eddying Ocean, where lie the land and city of the Cimmerians, covered with mist and cloud. Never does the resplendent sun look on this people with his beams, neither when he climbs towards the stars of heaven nor when once more he comes earthwards from the sky; dismal night overhangs these wretches always.

That doesn't sound much like the Bay of Naples. Nevertheless, Pliny and Festus are explicit that the city of the Cimmerians had been next to Avernus, between Baiae and Cumae; and though there is a textual corruption, the *Origo gentis Romanae* evidently made it the home of the Sibyl.[24] That idea probably goes back at least as far as the fifth century: Aeschylus' *Psychagogoi* seems to have been set at Lake Avernus, with a chorus descended from Hermes; and Hermes was the father of Evander.[25]

At some stage the story of Evander and his prophetic mother was moved to Rome. In Eratosthenes she is still a Sibyl, living at the Cermalus, the site of the *Lupercal*;[26] later, when the story of the Cumaean Sibyl had developed, with a canonical date in the time of King Tarquin, Evander's mother became Carmentis, 'a prophetess before the Sibyl came to Italy', as Livy puts it.[27] So Eratosthenes' item on the Italian Sibyl and the Roman cult of Pan belongs to a quite early stratum of Roman legend. But how early?

Evander was an Arcadian from Pallantion, from which was named Palatium, the Palatine hill.[28] Pallantion was mentioned in Stesichorus' *Geryoneis*, the sixth-century poem that told the story of Herakles' tenth labour, the cattle of Geryon. The Roman legend of Herakles and the cattle, which explained the Forum Bovarium and the Ara Maxima, was evidently current by

---

22 Lactantius *Div. inst.* 1.6.10 = Varro *Antiquitates rerum diuinarum* fr. 56a Cardauns. Parke 1988.33 wrongly assumes she was invented by Naevius.

23 Homer *Odyssey* 11.14–19 (trans. W. Shewring), Strabo 5.4.5 (244); cf. Sophocles *TrGF* 4 F748 for the *nekyomanteion* at 'Aornos' [but Ogden 2001.47–51 puts it at the Acheron in Thesprotia].

24 Pliny *Nat. Hist.* 3.61, Festus (Paulus) 37L; *Origo gentis Romanae* 10.1, *Sibylla in oppido quod uocatur* †*Cimbarionis*†—i.e. *Cimmerium*, as in Pliny?

25 Aeschylus *TrGF* 3 F273, 273a (Aristophanes *Frogs* 1266, Maximus of Tyre 8.2b); cf. n. 23 above (Sophocles). Hermes as father of Evander: Dionysius of Halicarnassus 1.31.1, 1.40.2 (by Themis = Carmenta), Virgil *Aeneid* 8.138, 336 (by Carmentis), Pausanias 8.43.2 (by the daughter of Ladon); *contra* Ovid *Fasti* 1.472 (not a god), Servius on *Aeneid* 8.130 (Echemos).

26 Varro *De lingua Latina* 5.54, Plutarch *Romulus* 3.5 = Fabius Pictor *FGrH* 809 F4.3).

27 Livy 1.7.8; cf. Strabo 5.3.3 (230), Dionysius of Halicarnassus 1.31.1, 1.40.2, Virgil *Aeneid* 8.336, etc; see also n. 35 below. Cumaean Sibyl: Lactantius *Div. inst.* 1.6.10–11 = Varro *Antiquitates rerum diuinarum* fr. 56a Cardauns; Parke 1988.76–9.

28 Varro *De lingua Latina* 5.53, Dionysius of Halicarnassus 1.31.4, Livy 1.5.1, etc.

about 530 BC, when the hero's deification was celebrated on a temple in the Forum Bovarium itself.[29] In our later literary sources Evander greets Herakles, and his mother prophesies the apotheosis; but whether that too goes back to the sixth century BC it is impossible to say.

Certainly the sixth century is too early for Pan. Even in Athens, the Arcadian god found a home only in the fifth century, after his help at the battle of Marathon.[30] In fact, the Athenian cult may well be helpful for our purposes. It was set up in thanks for victory, in a cave below the Acropolis, close to the point where the temple of Victory guarded the entrance to the citadel.[31] The Roman topography corresponds exactly.

The temple of Victory at the western corner of the Palatine was begun in or about 307 BC, but not finished till 294.[32] Archaeological evidence now reveals why it took so long. First, it was a very large and imposing building, even bigger than its later neighbour, the temple of Magna Mater. Second, the building programme evidently involved more than just the temple itself: the side of the Palatine overlooking the Forum Bovarium was built up with great terracing walls in *opus quadratum*, and it is probable that the programme included a new monumental approach, the *cliuus Victoriae*. The effect must have been like the entrance to an acropolis, with a Victory temple at the gate.[33]

We know from Dionysius that there was a clear conceptual and topographical relationship between the Victory temple and the *Lupercal*. Both cults were supposedly founded by Evander, and both came from Arcadia. The victory goddess, according to Arcadian legend, was the daughter of Pallas son of Lykaon, eponyms respectively of the Palatine (*Pallantion*) and the *Lupercal* (*Lykaion*). As Dionysius tells us, her temple was at the top of the hill, and the *Lupercal* cave at the bottom—just as in Athens.[34] In view of this close association of the two cults, it is not surprising to find that one of the names our sources give us for Evander's mother is Nikostrate, 'victorious army'.[35]

There is another parallel with the Pan cave in Athens, this time involving the foundation myth. In one version of the story of the twins, Mars ravishes

---

29 *PMGF* Stesichorus 85 (Pausanias 8.3.2); *Enea* 1981.121–2, Cristofani 1990.119–20 and tav. IX.

30 Herodotus 6.105; Borgeaud 1988.133–62, Garland 1992.47–63.

31 For the topography see Travlos 1971.70–1, 148–57, 417–21; the juxtaposition of Pan's cave and the Nike temple is illustrated in Garland 1992, pl. 11.

32 Livy 10.33.9: begun by L. Postumius Megellus as *aed. cur.*, dedicated by him as *cos. II*.

33 Pensabene [1998, esp. 26–34, 115–19]; Wiseman 1981 = 1987a.187–204.

34 Dionysius of Halicarnassus 1.32.3–33.1, with Wiseman 1981.35–6 = 1987a.187–8.

35 Strabo 5.3.3 (230), Servius on *Aeneid* 8.336. Otherwise Themis (Dionysius of Halicarnassus 1.31.1, 1.40.2) or Tiburs (Servius *auctus* on *Aeneid* 8.336), the latter implying an identification with the Tiburtine Sibyl. Cf. n. 27 above, and for the Tiburtine Sibyl (Albunea) see Lactantius *Div. inst.* 1.6.12 = Varro *Antiquitates rerum diuinarum* fr. 56a Cardauns, with Coarelli 1987.103–10.

their mother inside the *Lupercal* cave itself, just as Apollo rapes Creousa in Pan's cave in Athens, and fathers on her the founder-hero Ion.[36] Pan himself uses caves for raping nymphs, and a comic version of that idea is applied by Ovid to Faunus, his Roman Pan, in one of the aetiological stories for the *Lupercalia*.[37]

So the Eratosthenes fragment enables us to see Pan in Rome in two different areas of life: on the one hand, sex and conception; on the other, war and victory. We shall be pursuing both those aspects—the former in sections III and IV, the latter in section V—but first it is worth noting that the very idea of Pan in Rome is not as paradoxical as one might think. Herakles had his cult at the Ara Maxima by the sixth century BC; the Dioscuri had theirs in the Forum in 484, and Apollo his in the Flaminian fields in 431; Asklepios was brought from Epidauros to the Tiber island in 291.[38] Why should Pan not have been introduced at the *Lupercal* some time in (say) the late fifth or early fourth century?

<h1 style="text-align:center">III</h1>

An interesting contemporary sidelight on Eratosthenes' Roman Pan is provided by a series of engraved bronze mirrors from Praeneste. A third-century example [fig. 10] portrays a sprightly little ithyphallic goat-legged Pan, labelled *PAINSSCOS* for *Paniskos*, dancing with '*Marsuas*' the satyr;[39] Marsyas was a figure of some importance in Rome, the legendary ancestor of the *gens Marcia* and the symbol of *libertas*, with his statue in the Forum.[40]

A much more elaborate scene, dated to the third quarter of the fourth century [fig. 11], evidently shows the *Lupercal* myth itself, with a she-wolf in the centre suckling human twins.[41] To the left stands a male figure, naked but for boots and a goatskin loosely knotted round his neck by the forelegs;[42] he is wild and unkempt, and carries a *lagobolon*, the shepherd's throwing-stick. I think he is Pan. The contemporary iconography of Pan in his native Arcadia

---

36 Servius *auctus* on *Aeneid* 1.273: *repentino occursu lupi turbata refugit in speluncam, in qua a Marte compressa est*. Euripides *Ion* 491–506, 936–41; for Ion as a founder, ibid. 74, cf. 1571–94; I am grateful to Christina Kraus for pointing this out to me. Cf. Borgeaud 1988.151–2 for the cave as a 'wild spot in the heart of town'.

37 Euripides *Helen* 188–90; Ovid *Fasti* 2.315, 332 (Faunus and Omphale in a very well-appointed cave), cf. n. 9 above. A hint of rape from Silenus in his cave: Virgil *Eclogues* 6.13, 26 (cf. 6.27 for dancing *Fauni*).

38 Herakles: n. 29 above. Castor and Pollux: Livy 2.42.5. Apollo: Livy 4.29.7. Asklepios: Livy 10.47.7, *Epit.* 11.

39 Gerhard et al. 1897.54, Taf. 45; *ILLRP* 1201 for the inscription.

40 Torelli 1982.99–106; Coarelli 1985.91–119. For satyrs at Rome, see Wiseman 1988 = 1994.68–85, esp. 1988.4–5 = 1994.73–4 on Marsyas.

41 Adam and Briquel 1982; cf. *Lexicon Iconographicum Mythologiae Classicae* 4.1 (1988) 131. For an interpretation of the scene as a whole, see Wiseman 1993b, 1995.65–71.

42 As in Philostratus *Life of Apollonius* 6.27: a libidinous satyr on Lemnos.

Fig. 10 Praenestine mirror, third century BC (*ILLRP* 1201): Paniskos and Marsyas.

Fig. 11 Praenestine mirror, fourth century BC (Adam and Briquel 1982): on the left, Pan Lykaios?

shows him in human form, as a young man with a *lagobolon*, while Pan as a wild man is attested on the coins of the Black Sea colony of Panticapaeum, which was named after the god [fig. 12].[43] The only sign of bestiality is very unobtrusive horns, effectively undetectable in the dishevelled hair of the 'wild man' version, which is what I think we have here.

---

43 Arcadia: Head 1911.445, fig. 241; Hübinger 1992.208, 210. Panticapaeum: Kraay and Hirmer 1966.335, nos. 440–2. See in general Brommer 1949–50.

Fig. 12 Fourth-century BC coins of (left) the Arcadian federation and (right) Panticapaeum on the Black Sea: Pan in human form with *lagobolon*, and as a wild man.

The closest analogue to the figure on the mirror is a passage in Justin's abridgement of the first-century BC historian Pompeius Trogus, on the Arcadian Evander at Rome:[44]

> *in huius radicibus templum Lycaeo, quem Graeci Pana, Romani Lupercum appellant, constituit; ipsum dei simulacrum nudum caprina pelle amictum est, quo habitu nunc Romae Lupercalibus decurritur.*
>
> At the foot of this hill [the Palatine] he established a shrine to Lycaeus, whom the Greeks call Pan and the Romans Lupercus. The actual image of the god is naked with a goatskin cape, the costume in which the running is done nowadays at the *Lupercalia* in Rome.

We know that the Luperci of the first century BC wore their goatskins as loincloths, and brandished goatskin thongs, not throwing-sticks.[45] However, Trogus was evidently describing a statue which may have represented an earlier state of affairs, as illustrated on the mirror.

Trogus calls the god of the *Lupercal* 'Lycaeus'—that is, Pan Lykaios, named after the Arcadian Mount Lykaion.[46] The Roman name he offers is merely a

---

44 Justin 43.1.7.

45 Dionysius of Halicarnassus 1.80.1 (Tubero fr. 3P), Nicolaus of Damascus *FGrH* 90 F130.71; cf. Ovid *Fasti* 2.445–6 (thongs), 5.101 (*cinctuti*), Plutarch *Romulus* 21.4–5, *Quaestiones Romanae* 68 (*Moralia* 280b). Justin's *nunc* is inexplicable.

46 Livy 1.5.1–2, Virgil *Aeneid* 8.343–4 and Servius *ad loc.*, Dionysius of Halicarnassus 1.32.3, 1.80.1, Ovid *Fasti* 2.423–4, Plutarch *Romulus* 21.3, *Caesar* 61.1, *Antony* 12.1, *Quaestiones Romanae* 68 (*Moralia* 280c); see also Augustine *City of God* 18.16 = Varro *De gente populi Romani* fr. 29 Fraccaro. For the mysterious cults of Mt Lykaion, see Burkert 1983.84–93, Borgeaud 1988.34–42, Hübinger 1992.189–212.

calque—*lupus* for *lykos*—and a back-formation from the ritual itself, like 'the god Februarius' evidently named by Livy in his lost book 14.[47] Livy offers a more interesting name in book 1, where he reports the capture of Remus at the *Lupercalia*:[48]

> *iam tum in Palatio monte Lupercal hoc fuisse ludicrum ferunt, et a Pallanteo, urbe Arcadica, Pallantium, dein Palatium montem appellatum; ibi Euandrum, qui ex eo genere Arcadum multis ante tempestatibus tenuerit loca, sollemne allatum ex Arcadia instituisse ut nudi iuuenes Lycaeum Pana uenerantes per lusum atque lasciuiam currerent, quem Romani deinde uocarunt Inuum.*

> They say that even at that time there existed this *Lupercal* festival at the Palatine hill (called Pallantium, and then Palatine, after the Arcadian city of Pallantion), and that Evander, a man of Arcadian descent who held that region many generations earlier, had brought the rite from Arcadia and instituted it there: naked young men ran about in shameless sport in honour of Lycaean Pan, whom the Romans afterwards called Inuus.

Inuus was the god of sexual penetration (*inire*, to enter),[49] an appropriate identity for Pan, whose rampant sexuality was one of his defining features. Ovid on the other hand identifies Lycaean Pan with Faunus, a god of prophecy but also a dweller in the wild with strong sexual appetites.[50] The idea of Faunus as the god of the *Lupercal* goes back at least as far as the historian C. Acilius in the mid-second century BC.[51]

---

47 Livy fr. 63 Weissenborn = 'Gelasius' *Adu. Andromachum* 11–12 (*CSEL* 35.1, 456–7): *Dic mihi, cum saepenumero in Romanis historiis legatur Liuio oratore saepissime in hac urbe exorta pestilentia infinita hominum milia deperisse atque eo frequenter uentum ut uix esset unde illis bellicosis temporibus exercitus potuisset adscribi, illo tempore deo tuo Februario minime litabatur an etiam cultus hic omnino nil proderat? illo tempore Lupercalia non celebrabantur? nec enim dicturus es haec sacra illo tempore non coepisse, quae ante Romulum ab Euandro in Italiam perhibentur adlata. Lupercalia autem propter quid instituta sunt, quantum ad ipsius superstitionis commenta respectat, Liuius in secunda decade loquitur nec propter morbos inhibendos instituta commemorat sed propter sterilitatem, ut ei uidetur, mulierum quae tunc acciderat exigendam.* For *februare* as the purification ritual of the *Luperci*, see Varro *De lingua Latina* 6.13, 6.34, Ovid *Fasti* 2.19–36, Plutarch *Quaestiones Romanae* 68 (*Moralia* 280b), *Romulus* 21.3, *Numa* 19.5, Festus (Paulus) 75–6L, Censorinus 22.15.
48 Livy 1.5.1–2; cf. also Macrobius *Saturnalia* 1.22.2 (*Pan ipse quem uocant Inuum*).
49 Festus (Paulus) 98L: *init ponitur interdum pro concubitu*. E.g. Suetonius *Diuus Augustus* 69.2, Seneca *Epistles* 95.21. Usually of animals (Varro *De re rustica* 2.7.9, Livy 41.13.2, etc); see Arnobius *Aduersus gentes* 3.23 for Inuus as guardian of flocks.
50 Ovid *Fasti* 2.423–4. Faunus *a fando* (or from φωνή): Cicero *De natura deorum* 2.6 (with Pease's commentary), Varro *De lingua Latina* 7.36, *Origo gentis Romanae* 4.4, Servius *auctus* on Virgil *Georgics* 1.10–11, Servius on *Aeneid* 7.47, 7.81. Sexuality: Horace *Odes* 3.18.1 etc. Nonnus, no doubt from a Hellenistic source, makes Faunus the son of Circe, with clear reference to the Hesiodic 'wild man' Agrios, brother of Latinos: Hesiod *Theogony* 1011–16, Nonnus *Dionysiaca* 13.328–32, 37.56–60.
51 Plutarch *Romulus* 21.7 = Acilius *FGrH* 813 F2.

The three gods Pan, Faunus and Inuus are often identified,[52] and also a fourth, Silvanus, whose characteristics notoriously overlap with those of Faunus.[53] Silvanus is never mentioned in relation to the *Lupercalia*, but I think one of his cult-places in Rome may well be associated with the ritual.

The naked *Luperci* 'ran about' this way and that: *discurrere* and *diatheein* are the words most often used to describe them. According to Varro, they ran up and down the Sacra Via.[54] But Varro also calls their run a *lustratio* of the ancient Palatine settlement, which should mean an encircling route *round* the hill; and that is what Dionysius and Plutarch both imply.[55] There is no real contradiction, however. It was not a race, and the *Luperci* evidently spent much of the day running about performing their antics; on the other hand, they began from the *Lupercal* and they evidently ended in the Comitium, as is clear from the *Lupercalia* of 44 BC, when a large crowd in the Forum, and Caesar on the Rostra, were watching the climax of the show.[56] That makes a very credible *lustratio* of the Palatine [fig. 13], if we imagine a date for its institution when the Velabrum was still a marsh, or a backwater of the Tiber.[57]

The *Lupercal* and the Comitium were both, paradoxically, the site of the *ficus Ruminalis*, the fig-tree under which the she-wolf suckled the twins. The duplication was explained by a miraculous relocation of the tree from *Lupercal*

---

52 Servius on *Aeneid* 6.775, Probus on *Georgics* 1.10, ps.Acro on Horace *Odes* 1.17.1, Rutilius Namasianus *De reditu* 31–6 (*multa licet priscum nomen deleuerit aetas,* | *hoc Inui castrum fama fuisse putat,* | *seu Pan Tyrrhenis mutauit Maenala siluis* | *siue sinus patrios incola Faunus init;* | *dum renouat largo mortalia semina fetu,* | *fingitur in uenerem pronior esse deus*). Cf. Plutarch *Numa* 15.3 (*Fauni* like *Panes*).

53 *Origo gentis Romanae* 4.6. Silvanus as Faunus: Dionysius of Halicarnassus 5.16.3, Livy 2.7.2, Valerius Maximus 1.8.5 (the voice in the *silua Arsia*). Silvanus as dangerous rapist: Augustine *City of God* 6.9 (Varro *Antiquitates rerum diuinarum* fr. 111 Cardauns), 15.23. Dorcey 1992.33–40 vainly tries to argue away the similarities.

54 *Discurrere*: Festus (Paulus) 49L, *Origo gentis Romanae* 22.1; cf. Ovid *Fasti* 2.285 (of the god). *Diatheontes* etc: Plutarch *Quaestiones Romanae* 68 (*Moralia* 280b-c), *Romulus* 21.5, *Caesar* 61.2, *Antony* 12.1. *Lupercorum per sacram uiam ascensum atque descensum*: Augustine *City of God* 18.12 = Varro *De gente populi Romani* fr. 21 Fraccaro.

55 Varro *De lingua Latina* 6.34: *tum februatur populus* [n. 47 above]*, id est Lupercis nudis lustratur antiquum oppidum Palatium gregibus humanis cinctum*. *Lustrare* also at Ovid *Fasti* 2.32, 5.102, Festus (Paulus) 75L, Censorinus 22.15; cf. Dionysius of Halicarnassus 1.80.1 (*perielthein*), Plutarch *Romulus* 21.4 (*peridromē*), 21.8 (*peritheein*).

56 Cicero *Philippics* 2.85, Plutarch *Caesar* 61.3, *Antony* 12.1, Appian *Civil Wars* 2.109, Cassius Dio 44.11.2.

57 Varro *De lingua Latina* 5.43–4, 5.156. Cicero (*Pro Caelio* 26) was probably right to date the origin of the *Luperci* 'before civilisation and the rule of law'. [Deep-core analysis has now disproved the Varronian picture of the early Velabrum: it is clear that the valley between the Capitol and the Palatine had been neither a marsh nor a backwater, but an area of clay-beds that was flooded only when the Tiber overflowed its banks (Ammerman 1998 and 2006.305–7, pp. 12–13 above).]

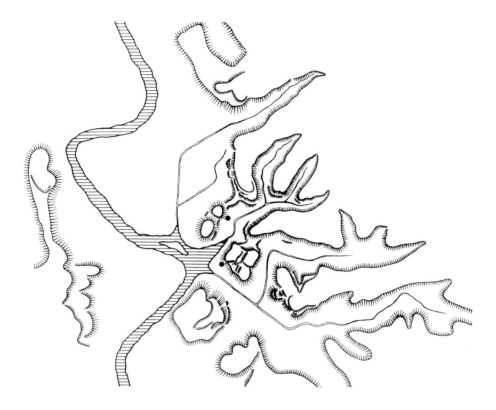

Fig. 13 Map of the site of Rome. The dots represent the suggested beginning and end of the course of the *Luperci*, each the site of a fig-tree: lower, the *Lupercal*; upper, 'in front of the temple of Saturn' (Pliny *Nat. Hist.* 15.77).

to Comitium effected by the wonder-working augur Attus Navius.[58] One is tempted to guess that there were necessarily two fig-trees, one at each end of the *Lupercalia* run. Fig trees were associated with fertility and with goats, both prominent aspects of the *Lupercalia*,[59] and late authors give 'Ficarius' as an epithet of Faunus.[60] In the passage where he describes Attus Navius' miracle,

58 *In comitio*: Tacitus *Annals* 13.58.1, Festus 168L; Conon *FGrH* 20 F48.8, Dionysius of Hali-carnassus 3.71.5; Torelli 1982.98–9. *In Cermalo* (i.e. *Lupercal*): Varro *De lingua Latina* 5.54, Livy 1.4.5, Ovid *Fasti* 2.411–12, Plutarch *Romulus* 4.1, *Origo gentis Romanae* 20.3. Both (miracle of Attus Navius): Pliny *Nat. Hist.* 15.77.

59 Isidorus *Origines* 17.7.17 (*ficus a fecunditate*); the wild fig-tree is *caprificus*. See n. 2 above for the *Luperci* as goats.

60 Jerome *Ad Isaiam* 13.21 (*PL* 24.159, n. 66 below), Isidorus *Origines* 8.11.104 (*quem autem uulgo Incubonem uocant, hunc Romani Faunum ficarium dicunt*). Cf. Pelagonius 31 (p. 41 Ihm) for *Fatuus ficarius*; Fatuus was another name for Faunus (e.g. Servius on *Aeneid* 6.775).

Pliny refers to a fig-tree, possibly the same one, that grew in front of the temple of Saturn but had to be removed, with a sacrifice by the Vestals, because it was undermining the statue of Silvanus.[61]

Silvanus and a fig-tree, in front of the temple of Saturn; and Propertius, in his poem on Tarpeia, offers a grove of Silvanus, complete with a cave and a spring, below the *arx* of the Capitol on the Forum side.[62] The imagined landscape is very like that of the *Lupercal*.[63] The area in front of the Saturn temple was supposed to be where the bones of Orestes were placed after he had brought the image and cult of Artemis Tauropolos to Aricia. In the more usual version of the myth, Orestes died in Arcadia.[64] The details escape us, but it looks as if the Comitium below the Capitol, like the *Lupercal* below the Palatine, was the site of an early cult imported from Arcadia, and that the two were linked by the course of the *Luperci*, from one fig-tree to the other.

IV

In dealing with Pan, Inuus, Faunus and Silvanus as gods of sexual energy and desire, we must not omit two minor characters who are frequently associated—or indeed identified—with them in this respect. They are Incubus, or Incubo, and Ephialtes: he who lies on you (in Latin) and he who jumps on you (in Greek).[65] They in turn are associated, or identified, with the *pilosi*, 'the hairy ones'.[66]

---

61 Pliny *Nat. Hist.* 15.77 (*fuit et ante Saturni aedem. . .*); he gave the date of its removal, but the numerals have been lost from the text.

62 Propertius 4.5.3–6, cf. 13–14 for a spring at the site of the *Curia*; the 'springs of Janus' (Varro *De lingua Latina* 5.156, Ovid *Fasti* 1.257–76, *Metamorphoses* 14.778–804) must have been thereabouts. For 'the wood below the Capitol' in what was later the Forum, see Dionysius of Halicarnassus 2.50.2; for the possibility that the Comitium was once a *lucus*, see Vaahtera 1993.103–7.

63 Dionysius of Halicarnassus 1.32.4, 1.79.8. 'Satyr country': Wiseman 1988.12–13 = 1994.84.

64 Servius on *Aeneid* 2.116; cf. Herodotus 1.67–8 (bones of Orestes in Tegea), Pausanias 8.5.5, Strabo 13.1.3 (582).

65 Servius on *Aeneid* 6.775, ps.Acro on Horace *Odes* 1.17.1, Augustine *City of God* 15.23, Artemidorus *Oneirocritica* 2.37 (ὁ δὲ Ἐφιάτης ὁ αὐτὸς εἶναι τῷ Πανὶ νενόμισται. . .), Caelius Aurelianus *De morbis chronicis* 1.54–5 (*Incubonem aliqui ab hominis forma uel similitudine nomen dicere dixerunt. . . item quidam ueteres Ephialten uocauerunt, alii Epophelen, quod utilis patientibus perhibeatur*), Jerome *Vita Paulli* 8 (*PL* 23.23: *unus ex accolis eremi quos uario delusa errore gentilitas Faunos satyrosque et Incubos uocans colit*), ps.Augustine *De spiritu et anima* 25 (*PL* 40.789). For the etymology of Ephialtes, cf. *Scholia Graeca in Homeri Iliadem* (ed. Dindorf) 3.248, Eustathius on the *Iliad* 560.10–11.

66 Jerome *Ad Isaiam* 13.21 (*PL* 24.159: *et pilosi saltabunt ibi, uel Incubones uel satyros uel siluestres quosdam homines, quos nonnulli Faunos ficarios uocant aut daemonum genera intellegunt*), *Mythographus Vaticanus* 2.24 Bode (*Fauni autem sunt qui uulgo Incubae uel pilosi appellati sunt, et a quibus, dum a paganis consulerentur, responsa uocibus dabantur*), Gregorius Magnus *Moralia* 7.36 (*PL* 75.786: *qui namque alii pilosi appellatione fingantur nisi hi quos Graeci Panas, Latini Incubos uocant?*), Isidorus *Origines* 8.11.103 (*Pilosi, qui Graece Panitae, Latine Incubi appellantur, siue Inui ab ineundo passim cum animalibus, unde et Incubi dicuntur ab incumbendo, hoc est stuprando*).

The *pilosi* happen to be attested first in the Vulgate, as the wild creatures who Isaiah predicts will dance in the wilderness that once was Babylon, but St Jerome took them from an earlier tradition in authors unknown to us.[67] Strabo has Ephialtes along with Lamia, Gorgo and Mormolyke as a bogey to frighten children;[68] Petronius has Incubo as a goblin sitting on treasure—snatch his cap off, and it's yours;[69] coins of Bithynian Nicaea in the second and third centuries AD show Ephialtes, goat-legged and wearing a cap, in his guise as Epopheles, 'the helpful one'.[70] But above all Ephialtes and Incubus (or Incubo) were the names of the god of nightmare, who sits on your chest while you're asleep and stops you breathing.[71] Peonies will keep him away; Pliny, who tells us this, calls the nightmare demons *Fauni*,[72] and since their nocturnal assaults were often sexual,[73] it is clear that we are dealing with the libidinous and many-faceted god of the *Lupercal*.

At this point we return to the Praenestine mirrors, and in particular to a pair, dated to the late fourth or early third century BC and clearly from the same workshop, which are engraved with related scenes.[74] The first, now in Baltimore [fig. 14], shows a Dionysiac scene surrounded by a vine with grapes. To the left, a flute-girl. To the right, with an amphora ready to hand, a young man, apparently naked, blows into a conch-shell(?); he is not garlanded, and two little horns appear from his hair. In the centre, a man with a garland on his head sprawls on the cushions, clearly dead drunk, while behind him, evidently trying to revive him by pouring wine from a *kylix*, is a garlanded and bearded figure with a thyrsus in the crook of his left arm. He seems at first to be hairy, but the left forearm and right wrist show that he is wearing a tight-fitting hairy

---

67 Vulgate *Isaias* 13.21, 34.13; Jerome *Ad Isaiam* 34.13 (*PL* 24.372: *onocentauri et pilosi et Lamia, quae gentilium fabulae et poetarum figmenta describunt*).

68 Strabo 1.2.8 (19), cf. Phrynichus *Ephialtes* (*PCG* 7.395–7), Aristophanes *Wasps* 1037–8 and scholia.

69 Petronius *Satyrica* 38.8, cf. Porphyrio on Horace *Satires* 2.6.12. *Incubare* was the *mot juste* for guarding treasure (references in Otto 1890.173), but it was more often dragons that did it: e.g. Phaedrus 4.21, Martial 12.53.3, Festus (Paulus) 59L. For the cap, cf. Hübinger 1992.198, 204: worn by dedicants (hunters and shepherds) at Pan's sanctuary on Mt Lykaion.

70 *Lexicon Iconographicum Mythologiae Classicae* 3.1 (1986) 802. Epopheles: Caelius Aurelianus *De morbis chronicis* 1.3.54 (n. 65 above), Hesychius s.vv. *Opheles* and *Epopheles*; cf. also Artemidorus *Oneirocritica* 2.37 (μεγάλας ὠφελείας προαγορεύει).

71 Caelius Aurelianus *De morbis chronicis* 1.3.54–7, Macrobius *Ad Somnium Scipionis* 1.3.7, Eustathius on the *Iliad* 561.8, on the *Odyssey* 1687.52; Aristophanes *Wasps* 1037–8, etc.

72 Pliny *Nat. Hist.* 25.29, 30.84, Dioscorides *Materia medica* 3.140; cf. Aetius Amidenus *Med.* 1.84 (*CMG* 8.1.50) on the peony as *ephialtia*.

73 Caelius Aurelianus *De morbis chronicis* 1.3.56, Paulus Aegineta 3.15 (*CMG* 9.1.158–9). *Incub(it)are* in sexual sense: Plautus *Persa* 284, Pomponius Mela 3.83.

74 Gerhard et al. 1897.51–3, Taf. 42–3.

Fig. 14 Praenestine mirror, late fourth or early third century BC: drinking scene.

costume.[75] He looks rather sad; and the young man and the flute-girl seem to have somewhat disapproving expressions.

---

75 Compare the 'curious papposilen, obviously wearing a costume' on a volute-crater of the Arpi painter, also of late fourth- or early third-century date: Trendall and Cambitoglou 1982.924, pl. 362, better illustration in Trendall 1989 fig. 266. See also the actor playing Silenos on the 'Pronomos vase' (Attic red-figure, c.400 BC): Seaford 1984.3–4, pl. III. Such hairy-costumed performers evidently pre-date the genre of satyr-play, and appear on black-figure vases from the first half of the sixth century onward: see Hedreen 1992.113–14, 125–6, 128, 163–4, pls 4, 31, 37, 44; also Hedreen 1994 pl. IV(a), where the hairy skin of the ithyphallic silen/satyr stops at the elbows, and is therefore presumably a costume.

Fig. 15 Praenestine mirror, late fourth or early third century BC: bedroom scene.

For the second scene [fig. 15] (the mirror is in the Villa Giulia at Rome), we have moved from the *triclinium* to the *cubiculum*. A lady, garlanded and with an elaborate coiffure, lies on the bed naked, holding back the mantle round her shoulders in a gesture of invitation. She is being pawed by what looks like the same bearded figure in the hairy costume (his thyrsus is propped up behind him), while to the right a colleague in the same gear leaps up high, with a torch in one hand and an amphora in the other. Between them the young man, his horns now much more prominent, gallops across the bed playing the *syrinx* with his left hand and pointing with his right at the lady's private parts. They still don't look very happy, and it is worth noticing that they are not ithyphallic.[75a]

Given that mirrors were often wedding presents, it is the marriage-torch that tells the story for us. The bride awaits; the bridegroom is incapably drunk; and the gods of sexual desire try to wake him up and show him what to do. The iconography even tells us who they are. The two figures in costume are 'hairy ones', *pilosi*. The one on the left is lying on the lady: *incumbere*, whence Incubus or Incubo. The one on the right is leaping up: *ephallesthai*, whence Ephialtes. The young man plays Pan's pipes, and has Pan's horns; but the direction of his pointing finger is a clear instruction to *inire*, whence Inuus.

Inuus is named by Livy as the god of the *Lupercal*. He had a cult-place, Castrum Inui, on the coast of Latium between Antium and Ardea;[76] it was either identical with, or very close to, the place called *Aphrodision* by Strabo, Pliny and Pomponius Mela. Cicero refers to a birth-goddess, Natio, whose shrine was one of a group in the territory of Ardea at which sacrifice was still regularly offered in the first century BC.[77] It looks as if Inuus was part of a complex of ancient cults concerned with human reproduction and fertility. Moreover, Antium and Ardea were the nearest ports to Praeneste, and linked to the inland city by the cult of Fortuna.[78] Fortuna, the guardian goddess of Servius Tullius, was a neighbour of the *Lupercal* at Rome.[79]

Before we leave the mirror scene, let us remember that the *pilosi* Incubus and Ephialtes are evidently in costume. Are we to think of them as supernatural beings, or human performers? If the latter, are they performing in a stage drama or a sacred ritual? Perhaps these categories are too schematic: are they human performers impersonating supernatural beings, in a drama which is in itself a ritual?[80] The questions cannot be answered, but are relevant equally to the *Lupercalia*. For according to Varro the *Luperci* were *ludii*, players or

---

75a [The argument is ignored by Gury 1998.1013–15, who believes that the woman on the bed is 'sans doute une Ménade', and that 'la mise en scène suggère l'idée d'une épiphanie panique nocturne' (reference only to Borgeaud 1988.76).]

76 Livy 1.5.2, Virgil *Aeneid* 6.775, Martial 4.60.1, Silius Italicus 8.359; Rutilius Namasianus *De reditu* 227–36 (n. 52 above) confuses it with Castrum Novum in Etruria. Cf. Tomasetti 1910.460–1 on a *villa Priapi in agro Ardeatino*, tenth century AD.

77 Strabo 5.3.5 (232), Pliny *Nat. Hist.* 3.57, Pomponius Mela 2.71; Cicero *De natura deorum* 3.47. For the archaic context, see Torelli 1993. Note that Horace (*Odes* 3.18.6) calls Faunus *Veneris sodalis*, and that the Rutuli of Castrum Inui are *Faunigenae* in Silius Italicus 8.356. Cf. also Vitruvius 8.3.2 for springs smelling of sulphur *in Ardeatino*—like Faunus' oracle at Albunea (Virgil *Aeneid* 7.84).

78 Coarelli 1987.74–9; cf. Torelli 1993.98: 'il rapporto tra Preneste e Anzio è strettissimo.'

79 Ovid *Fasti* 6.476–9, 569–80; Coarelli 1988.305–28.

80 Cf. Seaford 1994.266–9 for men dressed as satyrs as part of wedding ritual; ibid. 308 for weddings and Dionysiac mysteries, 270 n. 154 for the mysteries as a *spectacle*.

performers; the first stone theatre in Rome, begun in 154 BC but destroyed soon after, was to have overlooked the *Lupercal*;[81] and in Lactantius' time (though by then the circumstances were somewhat different) the *Luperci* even wore masks.[82]

V

I think it is clear from all this that the Roman Pan attested by Eratosthenes is perfectly explicable as the Hellenized form of an archaic Latin god of fertility. But there is another aspect of his personality to be explored.

The longer version of Servius' commentary on Virgil's phrase *gelida sub rupe Lupercal* adds this learned comment to the identification of Pan Lycaeus:[83]

> *sunt qui dicant hunc* Πᾶνα Ἐνυάλιον, *deum bellicosum; alii Liberum patrem, eo quod capro ei fit diuina res, qui est hostia Liberi propria.*
>
> There are those who say that this Pan is Enyalios, the warlike god; others call him Liber Pater, because a he-goat is sacrificed to him, which is the offering appropriate to Liber.

Liber Pater, otherwise identified as Dionysus, is intelligible enough; but why 'man-slaying Enyalios', 'the warrior with the flashing helmet'?[84] That doesn't sound like Pan. However, Virgil at one point calls the *Lupercal* the cave of Mars, and in one version of the foundation story Mars fathers the twins there.[85] There was also an aetiology of the running of the *Luperci* which derived it from the victory of Romulus and Remus over Amulius, and their triumphant run homewards waving their swords.[86]

That is appropriate to the cult supposedly founded below the temple of Victory by Evander the son of Nikostrate, a cult analogous to that of Pan the bringer of victory at Athens.[87] The military associations are made to extend also to the god's Latin analogues: Faunus is a son of Ares in Dionysius and Appian, and by a wonderful bilingual pun Inuus (Ἐνυοῦς) is made the son of

---

81 *Ludii*: Varro *Antiquitates rerum diuinarum* fr. 80 Cardauns (Tertullian *De spectaculis* 5.3); see Schmidt 1989, esp. 88–9. Theatre: Velleius Paterculus 1.15.3; for the circumstances, see North 1992.

82 Lactantius *Diu. Inst.* 1.21.45: *nudi, uncti, coronati, aut personati aut luto obliti currunt.* But see pp. 79–81 below.

83 Servius *auctus* on *Aeneid* 7.343.

84 Homer *Iliad* 2.651, 22.132.

85 Virgil *Aeneid* 8.630, with Servius *auctus*' commentary (Fabius *Annales Latini* fr. 4P); Servius *auctus* on *Aeneid* 1.273 (n. 36 above).

86 Plutarch *Romulus* 21.6, from Butas' elegiac *Aitia*.

87 See above, p. 57.

Enyo, the war-goddess whose Roman name was Bellona.[88] The obvious context for these versions is the Roman conquest of Italy; the real temple of Victory was dedicated in 294, and the temple of Bellona was vowed in 296 and dedicated a few years later.[89]

Now, an Inuus who is really *Enuous* is no longer derived from *inire*, and has presumably lost his penetrative function. The source that gives us this eccentric etymology carefully explains that Bellona's son was goat-footed, and very quick at running up and down hills. What defines him now is not sex but speed.[90] And the reason for that, I think, is that he has become the god of the *equites*.

The original Roman cavalry were the *celeres*, 'the swift ones'—supposedly the flying squad of three hundred horsemen who served as Romulus' body-guard.[91] Their real origin was probably the late fourth century, when the Romans, who had had no significant cavalry up to then, borrowed the idea from the Samnites.[92] The defining ritual of the *equester ordo*, the parade (*trans-uectio*) to the temple of Castor every 15 July, was introduced by Q. Fabius Rullianus in his censorship in 304 BC,[93] evidently an innovation in recognition of a new élite corps. The first commander of Romulus' *celeres* was called Fabius in one surviving version of the story.[94]

In view of the later reputation of the Fabii, based on the patient caution of the great *Cunctator*, it may seem paradoxical to associate them with *celeritas*, of all characteristics. But that is what their enemies evidently said of them. The two most notorious Fabian exploits in the tradition of the early Republic are, first, their offer to fight the Veientes on their own, which led to the disastrous defeat at the Cremera, and second, their rash engagement with the Gauls at Clusium, which led to the even more disastrous sack of Rome. Before the *Cunctator* redefined their image, the Fabii could be represented as men who

---

88 Dionysius of Halicarnassus 1.31.2, Appian *Basilike* fr. 1 (identifying Faunus and Latinus). Diomedes in *Grammatici Latini* 1.475 Keil: <. . . > *et Bellonae, id est* Ἐννοῦς, *filio, quem caprino pede Inuum poetae fingunt, quod summa montium et difficilia collium concitato cursu caprae more superaret, quotiens praedatoria uice grassaretur, citipedem hunc cursum sibi repperisse testificantur.*

89 Livy 10.33.9; Livy 10.19.17–21, Ovid *Fasti* 6.201–4.

90 Diomedes at n. 88 above. So too Faunus: Horace *Odes* 1.17.1–2 (*uelox*), Ovid *Fasti* 2.285–6.

91 Dionysius of Halicarnassus 2.13.2, Festus (Paulus) 48L, Pliny *Nat. Hist.* 33.35, Servius on *Aeneid* 11.603 (*a celeritate*). The *tribunus celerum* had the same relationship to the king as the *magister equitum* to the dictator (and the Praetorian Prefect to the emperor): Pomponius in *Digest* 1.2.2.15–19, Lydus *De magistratibus* 1.14, cf. 37.

92 *Ineditum Vaticanum*, *FGrH* 839 F1.3 (lines 19–22).

93 Valerius Maximus 2.2.9, *De uiris illustribus* 32.3.

94 Jerome *Chronica* on Olympiad 6.3 (Fotheringham p. 152): *Remus rutro pastorali a Fabio Romuli duce occisus.* The implement is significant, given the ancient etymology of *Fabius* from words meaning 'to dig': Festus (Paulus) 77L, Plutarch *Fabius Maximus* 1.2.

acted first and thought afterwards—gallantly courageous or dangerously head-strong, according to your prejudice.[95] The *celeres* themselves were similarly controversial: according to Plutarch's version, they were one of the symptoms of Romulus' increasingly tyrannical rule, and the first thing Numa did was to disband them.[96] Perhaps what was at issue, in the social and political context of the late fourth century, was the behaviour of young aristocrats liberated from the discipline of the phalanx by the innovation of swift and mobile cavalry. Was it flair, promptness and glamorous high spirits, or rashness, arrogance and mindless exhibitionism?

In his account of Roman military institutions, Polybius makes a very inter-esting observation about the Roman cavalry. Nowadays, he says, they are armed like Greek cavalry; but originally they used no body-armour and fought naked except for loincloths (*perizomata*), in order to maximise their *speed* in getting on and off their horses.[97] There is no reason to doubt the accuracy of Polybius' information, and it gives valuable confirmation of the military role of the *celeres* in the late fourth century. It also directs us back to the *Lupercalia*.

'Naked except for loincloths' is also a description of the *Luperci*, as we meet them in Dionysius and Plutarch. Ovid calls them *cinctuti*, a very rare word meaning not just 'girt' (that would be *cincti*), but 'wearing the *cinctus*'—that is, the minimal covering used by young men at exercise, sometimes called *campestre* after the Campus where the young men trained.[98] Pompeius Trogus, however (as excerpted by Justin), describes an ancient statue of the god of the *Lupercal* naked but for a goatskin used as a cape—exactly the costume of Pan on the Praenestine mirror in about 330 BC.[99] His assertion that that is also what the *Luperci* wore directly contradicts the descriptions in Dionysius, Ovid and Plutarch.

I suggest that the statue represented an archaic form of the *Lupercus* costume, which was then superseded, perhaps for reasons of modesty, by the goatskin loincloth. And since the 'reformed' *Luperci* were thus dressed (or undressed) like the *celeres*, it is an economical hypothesis to assume that the redefinition of Inuus as a quasi-*celer* dates from the same time. Faunus as the son of Mars, Inuus as the son of Bellona, Pan as Enyalios, the run of the *Luperci* as the triumphant waving of swords, Evander's *Lupercal* shrine associated with

---

95 The Fabian legends, favourable and hostile, are discussed by Montanari 1976.83–187, esp.114–15, 130–1 on Fabii as *celeres*. Cf. Ovid *Fasti* 2.205 (the Fabii reach the Cremera *celeri passu*), 2.223 (*latis discursibus*, cf. n. 54 above for *discurrere*).

96 Plutarch *Romulus* 26.2, *Numa* 7.4.

97 Polybius 6.25.3–4; Rawson 1971.20–1 = 1991.43–5, suggesting the heavy cavalry were introduced between 212 and 206 BC.

98 See n. 45 above. *Cinctus*, *campestre*: Varro *De lingua Latina* 5.114, ps.Acro on Horace *Epistles* 1.11.18, Augustine *City of God* 14.17, Isidorus *Etymologiae* 19.22.5, 19.33.1.

99 See pp. 58–61 above.

the temple of Victory above—all these things fit most comfortably into the years between the vowing and the dedication of the Victory temple (*c.* 307–294 BC). The key moment was no doubt the censorship of Q. Fabius Rullianus in 304.[100]

Valerius Maximus provides a confirmation of the hypothesis, in the second section of his chapter on traditional customs (*de institutis antiquis*).[101] The examples he offers are in hierarchical order, from the Senate and magistrates down to the *populus*, interpreted in military terms as the infantry. His one item on the *equester ordo*—of which the *celeres* were the original nucleus—refers to the two occasions each year on which the young cavalrymen were allowed to 'show themselves off' to the city: *equestris uero ordinis iuuentus omnibus annis bis urbem* **spectaculo sui** *sub magnis auctoribus celebrabant*. Those two occasions were the parade (*transuectio*) on 15 July, and the *Lupercalia* on 15 February.

The *magni auctores* to whom Valerius refers are respectively Fabius Rullianus, who instituted the equestrian parade as censor in 304, and Romulus and Remus, who were supposed to have instituted the *Lupercalia* after their grandfather Numitor, now restored as king of Alba, had given them permission to found a city at the place where they had been brought up. The foundation of the *Lupercal* by the twins is an aetiological explanation for the division of the *Luperci* into two groups, the *Fabiani* and the *Quinctiales*;[102] Valerius refers to this element of the ritual with the phrase *diuisa pastorali turba*.

Many items in Valerius' collection of anecdotes, including some in this chapter,[103] come from the family history of the Fabii Maximi. The fact that he associates the *Lupercalia* with the cavalry, and that one of the two groups of *Luperci* was named after the Fabii, makes one suspect that perhaps *both* the events he mentions were innovations by Fabius Rullianus in 304. The parade was a wholly novel institution, for which Fabius himself properly took the responsibility; but if he also introduced changes in the traditional ritual of the *Lupercalia*, they would need to be disguised as a return to ancient practice, with an appropriate aetiology from the distant past.

Ovid too tells the story of the origin of the *Lupercalia*, and his narrative includes a very revealing detail. While the meat was being prepared after the sacrifice of a goat to Faunus, the twins and their followers were exercising naked. It was reported that robbers were stealing their flocks. They ran off in pursuit in different directions; Remus and the Fabii caught the robbers, brought back the booty, and helped themselves to the meat, which was now

---

100 See pp. 57, 70–1 above.
101 Valerius Maximus 2.2.9.
102 Ovid *Fasti* 2.375–8, Festus (Paulus) 78L, Festus 308L; *CIL* 6.1933, 6.33421, 11.3205.
103 Valerius Maximus 2.2.1 and 4. Fabian items take up nearly a page in the index to Kempf's Teubner edition.

ready; Romulus and the Quincti(li)i returned empty-handed, and had to go hungry.[104] The story is very similar to that of the Pinarii at the Ara Maxima: they came late and had to go without.[105] In each case, there must have been a ritual reason why certain persons involved in the sacrifice were not allowed to share the feast.

We know that the cult of Hercules at the Ara Maxima was reorganised in 312. I suggest that the *Lupercalia* were reorganised in 304, that the two teams of *Luperci* were introduced at that time, and that this doubling of the number of the potential participants made necessary an aetiological explanation why only one of the two groups could share the sacrificial meat. If we are right to attribute the innovation to Fabius Rullianus in 304, it is no surprise that the Fabian group was privileged.

It was Mommsen who pointed out that the Fabii and the Quinctii, after whom the two groups of *Luperci* were named, were the only patrician *gentes* who ever used the *praenomen* Kaeso. The name, he suggested, was derived from *caedere*, to beat, with reference to the ritual at the *Lupercalia* in which the young men beat whomever they ran into.[106] Now, the best known Kaeso Quinctius was the young patrician who was supposedly put on trial in 461 BC for beating up plebeians. His combination of glamour and arrogance reflects, I think, the ambivalent image of the *celeres*.[107]

The Fabii who bore the name Kaeso are also significant. There were at least two of them, and possibly four. The two certain ones were K. Fabius Vibulanus, who as consular tribune in 479 led the ill-fated Fabian army to the Cremera, and K. Fabius Ambustus, who in 391 led the embassy to Clusium which provoked the Gauls to march on Rome.[108] That is, both the episodes in which Fabian haste and thoughtlessness led to disaster were attributed to Fabii called Kaeso. However, there also traces of a tradition which gave the name to Fabian heroes. In one version of the story of the priest who during the siege of the Capitol miraculously walked through the Gallic lines to perform sacrifice, his name is given as K. Fabius Dorsuo (otherwise Gaius).[109] And in one version

---

104 Ovid *Fasti* 2.359–80, esp. 374 '*haec certe non nisi victor edet*'.

105 Plutarch *Quaestiones Romanae* 60 (*Moralia* 278e-f), Servius on *Aeneid* 8.269, Servius *auctus* on *Aeneid* 8.270, *Origo gentis Romanae* 8.3, Lydus *De magistratibus* 1.23: Pinarii ἀπὸ τοῦ πεινᾶν, another bilingual etymology.

106 Mommsen 1864.17; also plebeian K. Duilii (*Xuir* 450, *cos.* 336) and K. Acilii (grandfather of *cos.* 150). Valerius Maximus 2.2.9 (*obuios*), Nicolaus of Damascus *FGrH* 90 F130.71, Plutarch *Romulus* 21.5, *Caesar* 61.2.

107 Livy 3.11.5–13.10, Dionysius of Halicarnassus 10.5-8.

108 Livy 2.48.5–50.11, Dionysius of Halicarnassus 9.14.1, 15.3, 16.3, 22.5. Of the 'three sons of M. Fabius Ambustus' sent to Clusium in 391 (Livy 5.35.5), the senior was evidently Kaeso, who had already held the consular tribunate three times (Livy 4.61.4, 5.10.1, 5.24.1).

109 Cassius Dio 7 fr. 25.5; Gaius in Livy 5.46.2 and 52.3, Valerius Maximus 1.1.11.

of the story of the exploration of the Ciminian forest during the war against the Etruscans in 310, the heroic spy is named as K. Fabius (otherwise Marcus), the brother of Fabius Rullianus himself.[110]

It looks as if the Kaesones, both Fabii and Quinctii, were exploited by both sides in the political controversies of the late fourth century, as patrician charisma strove with plebeian constitutionalism for ideological supremacy. That in turn implies that the *Luperci* were now controversial, one of the symbols of a patrician ideology which claimed credit for Rome's military success but was resisted by its opponents as arrogant and tyrannical.

VI

The half-century from the Caudine Forks to the defeat of Pyrrhus was a period of intense conflict, crisis, and innovation. It is unrealistic to try to separate out religious, political and military elements. Just as Appius Claudius' censorship in 312 revolutionised both the cult of Hercules and the political influence of the urban *plebs*, so that of his enemy Fabius Rullianus in 304 honoured the new military role of the young aristocrats and also, I suggest, radically reorganised the *Lupercalia*.

Two teams of *Luperci* were created, named after aristocratic *gentes* and consisting of young cavalrymen, dismounted but stripped for action. The loin-cloths that were the uniform of the *celeres* enabled them to show off their physique without the undignified nudity of the traditional *Luperci*. The explicitly sexual associations of the Pan cult were minimised, Inuus, Faunus and Pan himself being reinterpreted as divinities of war. The ritual run, if we may trust the aetiology preserved in Plutarch, now took place with the waving of swords. The *Lupercal* cave itself must have been involved in the ambitious restructuring of the hillside below the new temple of Victory, which was dedicated the year after Rullianus' great victory at Sentinum in 205.

Such innovations would not please everyone, and when the victory in 295 was followed by three years of continuous pestilence,[111] we can reasonably guess that Rullianus' enemies attributed it to the anger of the gods. This was the epidemic that caused the Romans to summon Asklepios (Aesculapius) from Epidauros in 292.[112] The word used of it is *lues*, plague, a contagion of the sort that lustration rituals like the *Lupercalia* were designed to prevent,[113] and it seems to have been sent by the god of the *Lupercal* himself.

---

110 Frontinus 1.2.2; cf. Livy 9.36.2, *M. Fabium, Caesonem alii . . . tradunt*.

111 Valerius Maximus 1.8.2 (*triennio* before 293), Zonaras 8.1 (prophesied in 297).

112 Ovid *Metamorphoses* 15.622–744, Valerius Maximus 1.8.2, Livy 10.47.6–7, Plutarch *Quaestiones Romanae* 94 (*Moralia* 286d), Lactantius *Inst. diu.* 2.7.13, *De uiris illustribus* 22.

113 *Lues*: Ovid *Metamorphoses* 15.626, Lactantius *Inst. diu.* 2.7.13. Purification: see above, nn. 47 and 55.

The first-century AD medical writer Soranus, discussing the choking symptoms of nightmare, insisted that Incubus/Ephialtes was not a god but a disease, of which the symptoms were pallor and emaciation.[114] He quotes a Greek authority 'Silimachus the Hippocratic' (possibly Callimachus, and if so third century BC), as saying that many people in Rome had died of this disease, incurring it through contagion as if in plague (*uelut lue*). The reference must surely be to the plague that caused the embassy to Epidauros, of which Ovid mentions *pallentia corpora* among the symptoms.[115] When Asklepios came to Rome, he stopped on the way at Antium, in Inuus' territory; he was finally installed on the Tiber island, where a century later a temple was also set up to Faunus. Not only that, but Ephialtes is named by the late medical writer Oribasius as 'the sacred interpreter and minister' of Asklepios.[116] It seems that the Romans, and Asklepios on their behalf, were going out of their way to mollify an offended god.

Fifteen years later, Rome was affected by another epidemic. This time the problem was miscarriages and still-births, both animal and human. The date, 276 BC, is given by Orosius, and a fragment of Livy reveals that this was the occasion when the *Lupercalia* flagellation ritual was introduced. According to Augustine, Asklepios was no help; he announced that gynaecology was not his speciality.[117]

What happened can be read in Ovid, in a narrative transposed to the time of Romulus. Juno, goddess of childbirth, was consulted; she announced, with a clear allusion to the name Inuus, that 'the sacred he-goat must enter the women of Rome'. Pan is the goat-god, and we know that the *Luperci*, ministers of Pan Lykaios, were called *crepi*, a corruption of *capri*, he-goats.[118] One obvious way to fulfil the command would be for the women of Rome to submit to sexual penetration by the *Luperci*. However, an alternative interpretation was found and adopted. When the *Luperci* made their goat-sacrifice on 15 February, the victim was to be skinned and the pelt cut up into thongs, with which the women of Rome must allow themselves to be whipped. In

114 Soranus *Causae*, quoted in Caelius Aurelianus *De morbis chronicis* 1.3.55–6.
115 Caelius Aurelianus *De morbis chronicis* 1.3.57, Ovid *Metamorphoses* 15.627. For Callimachus (Polybius 12.25d.4, Pliny *Nat. Hist.* 21.12, etc), see von Staden 1989.480–3. The alternative emendation is 'Lysimachus', date uncertain but pre-Neronian (von Staden 1989.564).
116 Antium: Ovid *Metamorphoses* 15.719–28, Valerius Maximus 1.2.8, *De uiris illustribus* 22.3. Faunus: n. 10 above. Ephialtes: Oribasius *Synopsis* 8.2 (οὔκ ἐστιν ὁ καλούμενος Ἐφιάλτης δαίμων κακός, ἀλλὰ ὁ μέν τις νόσος ἰσχυρά, ὁ δὲ ὑποφήτης ἱερὸς καὶ θεράπων Ἀσκληπιοῦ). The *celeres* were evidently portrayed in Asklepios' temple, but now renamed *ferentarii* (Varro *De lingua Latina* 7.57, unarmoured cavalry).
117 Orosius 4.2.2, Livy fr. 63 Weissenborn (n. 47 above), Augustine *City of God* 3.17. See Holleman 1974.20–1; innovation already emphasised by Otto 1913.183–5.
118 Ovid *Fasti* 2.425–52 (441 for '*sacer hircus inito*'). Crepi: n. 2 above.

that way, if the skin was broken, the he-goat would have 'entered' them.

According to Festus, the goatskin thongs were called *amiculum Iunonis*; no doubt 'wearing Juno's little cloak' was a euphemistic formula for offering yourself half-naked to the lash. Plutarch and Juvenal tell us that by the second century AD ladies used merely to hold out their hands to the *Luperci* 'like children in school'; but Ovid's phrase *terga percutienda dabant* suggests that originally it was more serious than that.[119]

All the literary evidence makes it clear that the *Lupercalia* ritual was an occasion for laughter and enjoyment: the words used are *paidia*, *gelōs*, *hilaritas*, *lusus* and *lasciuia*. Naked young men, their bodies oiled or smeared with mud, ran about striking anyone who got in their way. The fertility ritual introduced in 276 made the fun more brutal, and no doubt more exciting for the onlookers: the young women were no longer to run away, but to offer themselves to a flagellation that was a metaphor for sexual union. It was a female divinity who demanded a carnal remedy, and a male interpreter of the divine will who had it commuted to flagellation. No doubt the husbands of the women of Rome were not eager to have their wives literally impregnated by the *Luperci*.

It is important to remember the sheer sexiness of the *Lupercalia*. The young men themselves were objects of desire, which is why Augustus would not allow beardless boys to take part in the run. And from 276 onwards, the ritual encouraged young married women to bare their bodies in public.[120] One can see why it was such a popular spectacle.

But the reason for its introduction was specific to the third century BC. The secession of the plebeians in 287 shows that social and political tensions were still acute; a new and dangerous war with Pyrrhus began with costly defeats in 280 and 279. When pestilence returned, despite Asklepios, in 276, Juno evidently demanded a return to traditional ways. A compromise was reached, and once more the ritual of the *Lupercalia* was reformed. When the flagellation ritual was introduced, the necessary aetiological explanation was again attributed to Romulus, attached this time to the story of the Sabine women.[121] As in 304, innovation was disguised as a return to ancient custom.

This reconstruction is, of course, in the highest degree speculative. But enough evidence survives to make a reconstruction possible, to explain the phenomena in a coherent way, provided that we entertain the possibility of development, controversy and change, and reject the premise that ritual must

---

119 Festus (Paulus) 75–6L, Plutarch *Caesar* 61.2 ('shaggy thongs', as at *Antony* 12.1), Juvenal 2.142; Ovid *Fasti* 2.445–6. There may have been an Arcadian precedent: see Pausanias 8.23.1 for the flagellation of women at the Dionysos festival at Alea, on the instructions of Delphi.

120 Suetonius *Diuus Augustus* 31.4. *Matronae nudato corpore uapulabant*: 'Gelasius' *Aduersus Andromachum* 16 (CSEL 35.1.458).

121 Ovid *Fasti* 2.431–4.

remain essentially the same despite fundamental changes in the community
whose prosperity it is meant to guarantee. In times of very rapid change, like
the late fourth and early third centuries BC, far-reaching social and political
developments must have affected myth and ritual along with everything else.

VII

The next time Rome was convulsed by revolutionary change on that scale was
in the first century BC, and it is no surprise to find that the next development
in the ritual of the *Lupercalia* takes place precisely then.

Among the special honours granted to Caesar the dictator late in 45 BC was
the creation of a third group of *Luperci*, the *Iuliani*.[122] Their leader at the next
Lupercalia was the consul himself, M. Antonius, who used the occasion to
offer Caesar the crown. Cicero was disgusted. Running as naked *Luperci* was all
very well for young men, but quite incompatible with the dignity of a consul;
after the Ides of March, Cicero never tired of taunting Antony with the time
he had run into the Comitium *nudus, unctus, ebrius*, and mounted the Rostra in
an attempt to make Caesar king.[123]

The Senate in 43 withdrew Caesar's funding from the *Luperci*, and may
have abolished the *Iuliani*; but the historian Aelius Tubero, writing in the thir-
ties BC, clearly implies three groups in his account of the origin of the ritual,
and it is likely enough that the Triumvirs restored them.[124] Suetonius tells us
that the *Lupercalia* were one of the ancient ceremonies that Augustus restored
from oblivion, and Augustus himself in the *Res gestae* includes the *Lupercal*
among buildings he constructed. That probably implies a reorganisation analogous to the one in 304, though all we know for certain about it is his
prohibition of boys before the age of puberty from taking part in the run.[125]

The concern for sexual morality is very characteristic. In the late Republic
the college of *Luperci* had evidently had a somewhat equivocal reputation;
Cicero, for instance, did not approve of his nephew becoming a member.[126]
Augustus re-emphasised the connection with the *equester ordo*,[127] but seems to

---

122 Cassius Dio 44.6.2, 45.30.2, Suetonius *Diuus Iulius* 76.1.
123 Cicero *Philippics* 2.84–7, 3.12, 13.17, Cassius Dio 45.30.1–5.
124 Cicero *Philippics* 13.31 and fr. 19 (Nonius 418L); Dionysius of Halicarnassus 1.80.2 =
    Tubero fr. 3P.
125 Suetonius *Diuus Augustus* 31.4, Augustus *Res gestae* 19.1.
126 Cicero *Ad Atticum* 12.5.1. Late-republican *Luperci* included Geganius Clesippus (*ILLRP*
    696, Pliny *Nat. Hist.* 34.11), A. Castricius Myriotalentus (*CIL* 14.2105), (P.) Cornelius P.l.
    Surus (*AE* 1968.33, Panciera 1986); also M. Caelius Rufus and L. Herennius Balbus
    (Cicero *Pro Caelio* 26), though the latter claimed to be a strict moralist (ibid. 25–30).
127 *CIL* 6.31200.b.2.5–9: equestrian honours to Drusus at the *Lupercal* and on the day of the
    transuectio (15 July). *Luperci* as essentially equestrian: *CIL* 6.2160, 8.9405–6, 21063, *AE*
    1924.41 (second to third century AD).

have introduced attendants to minimise any danger to the young *equites'* moral well-being, and no longer required them either to wear goatskin or to brandish goatskin thongs.

The gravestone of Ti. Claudius Liberalis in the Vatican Museum shows us how a young *eques* who died at sixteen years of age was remembered in the early Empire: on one side, Liberalis riding in the *transuectio* parade, attended by a man with a flag; on the other, Liberalis as a *Lupercus*, wearing a substantial loincloth certainly not of goatskin, carrying a whip, not a goatskin thong, and escorted by two attendants.[128] The dignity and moral probity of the equestrian order are conspicuously on display, but what has happened to the *hilaritas* and *lasciuia* of the republican ritual? The evidence of Plutarch and Juvenal, that in the second century AD all the ladies had to do was to put out their hands to be struck by the *Luperci*, suggests that the ritual's traditional erotic charge had been deliberately neutralised.

The next great period of crisis and innovation in Roman history—one which involved the ultimate revolution in the Romans' religious outlook— was the late third and early fourth centuries AD, from (let us say) the building of Aurelian's wall to the founding of Constantinople. We have two images of the *Lupercalia* from this period, and very astonishing they are.

The first is on a mosaic floor from Thysdrus in North Africa; there is a scene for each month, and February is represented by the *Lupercalia*. Here the *Lupercus* is not running but standing; he is wearing a substantial apron, and raising a whip to bring down on the body of a woman who is being held in place by the two attendants. She looks back over her left shoulder at where her dress is raised to bare her body for the blow.[129] The same scene in greater detail appears on a late third-century sarcophagus from Rome [fig. 16].[130] Here the hieratic pose of the *Lupercus* and the humiliating exposure of the woman are even more explicit. The lady wears bracelets and an elegant coiffure, and the *Lupercus* carries out the rite with a very conscious dignity. His equestrian rank is symbolised by the man on the right carrying the *uexillum*. Behind him, shouldering the tree-branch which is his regular attribute, appears Silvanus, the god whose ancient grove by the temple of Saturn probably marked the ritual conclusion of the *Luperci*'s run.[131] The *Lupercalia* are still just recognisable, but fundamentally changed. This young equestrian is static and solemn, not naked

---

128 Illustrated and discussed by Veyne 1960, cf. Wiseman 1995.83, fig. 10. For the whip (appropriate to a horseman), cf. Daremberg and Saglio 1896.1153–4. [See now Tortorella 2000.249; Tortorella's article is the standard work on the iconography of the *Lupercalia*.]

129 Stern 1968, esp. 181–2 and pl. III, fig. 2; also in Holleman 1974.138 and Foucher 1976.278 [see now Tortorella 2000.252, cf. 245–6 for an analogous scene on a mirror in New York].

130 Schumacher 1968–9, Solin and Brandenburg 1980 [see now Tortorella 2000.253–4].

131 See p. 65 above; for the iconography of Silvanus, see Dorcey 1992.17–19, with illustrations 2, 3 and 6.

Fig. 16 Detail of sarcophagus from the S. Praetexta catacomb, Rome, third century AD (Schumacher 1968–9).

but wrapped up tightly as far as the chest. The high spirits have disappeared, replaced by a cold-blooded formality.

To us, this scene is repulsive. But it was evidently not offensive at the time; when the *Lupercus'* sarcophagus was re-used for the burial of a Christian lady about AD 340, his portrait and inscription were removed but the flagellation scene was not touched. Moreover, the *Luperci* in the late Empire seem to be rising in status, with even senators appearing among them from the late second century AD onwards.[132] One such was Crepereius Rogatus, who early in the fourth century created an elegant triple-naved *lararium*, its design very like a Christian basilica, on his property on the Viminal slope.[133] The apse was decorated with mosaics, showing the she-wolf and twins behind the altar, a male figure with a spear at the top of the arch, and on the pilaster at each side a *Lupercus* carrying a whip.[134]

If this was the headquarters of a *sodalitas* of *Luperci*, as Lanciani thought, then they met in formal and luxurious surroundings, and the god they worshipped was evidently Mars. Inuus, Faunus, Pan Lycaeus, Incubo and Ephialtes were well known to the learned (much of our evidence about them comes from this period), but perhaps rituals involving the elite demanded something more dignified. Faunus, however, was still respectable in distant Britain, where his name is prominently featured on the silverware of the Thetford treasure; and Macrobius shows how Pan and Inuus could be reinterpreted as allegory to satisfy the sensibilities of serious persons.[135]

The god of the *Lupercal* had to recede into the background, but the *Lupercalia* remained as an important element in the civic life of Rome. When a late fifth-century pope—probably Felix III rather than Gelasius—tried to abolish it, a senator called Andromachus complained that the city was being deprived of its protection against pestilence and famine.[136] The pope returned to the attack, in that spirit of hostility to the 'neutral ground' of secular observance which Robert Markus has recently documented.[137] The episcopal polemic reveals

---

132 E.g. *CIL* 6.1397, 6.1474, 6.31716, 11.2106 (a Fabius from Clusium!). If Lactantius was right that they sometimes wore masks (n. 82 above), that may have been to protect their dignity.

133 Lanciani 1891, and *Forma urbis Romae* (1893–1901) sheet 23: on the line of Via Cavour below S. Maria Maggiore; Dulière 1979.255–9 and fig. 128 [see now Tortorella 2000.254–5].

134 Vatican MSS Lat. 2733.IIf.285: 'in utroque ipsarum [i.e. parastatarum] latere dicto opere [i.e. musivo] duo nudi luperci efficti erant, gestantes ferulas intortas.'

135 Johns 1986; Macrobius *Saturnalia* 1.22.2–7.

136 'Gelasius', *Aduersus Andromachum* 3, 13, 23 (CSEL 35.1.454, 457, 460–1); Duval 1977, esp. 246–50 for the date (suggesting c.488). [See now Cameron 2004b.512–13: 'What Gelasius saw was not a genuine survival but a picturesque revival.']

137 Markus 1990.131–5, esp. 133: 'The attack on the Lupercalia is not so much an attack on "remnants of paganism" as on traditions of Roman urban living.'

that the flagellations still took place, but as a performance by 'vile and common persons of the lowest class', to the accompaniment of obscene songs.[138] The pope challenges the senator and his fellow traditionalists: if the ritual is so important, why don't you do it the old way and run around naked yourselves with your little whip?[139] It is likely that the rite was suppressed not long after that.

In Constantinople, on the other hand, the *Lupercalia* were still celebrated in the tenth century, in a curious performance at the circus-races, where the charioteers dismounted and ran on foot, using the reins on each other.[140] A springtime hymn was sung, which shows how the *Lupercalia* (15 February) had been assimilated to the date for the start of spring and the coming of the *genitabilis aura Fauoni* (7–8 February).[141] An even more harmless association was with the beginning of Lent; the Byzantine *Lupercalia* ritual was defined as *makellarikon*, to do with the eating of meat, no doubt to mark the last day (before Easter) when it was allowed.[142]

That sort of tolerantly creative reinterpretation contrasts strongly with the hostility of the Roman Church. One of the things that made the difference was clearly the flagellation of women, which was giving trouble again a thousand years later. In 1481 the Carmelite friar Baptista Spagnuoli of Mantua—'good old Mantuan' to Holofernes in *Love's Labour's Lost*—published his long poem *De sacris diebus*, which did for the Christian calendar what Ovid's *Fasti* had done for the pagan one. His fourth item under February (after St Agatha on the 5th) concerns 'the evil custom of Shrove Tuesday'[143]—nothing less than a revived *Lupercalia*, with youths running about the town in masks, taking advantage of their anonymity to manhandle the young married

---

138 *Aduersus Andromachum* 16, 19–20 (CSEL 35.1.458, 459): *uiles triuialesque personas, abiectos et infimos.* The *cantilenae* were evidently a charade, confessions of sexual misconduct to justify the whipping.

139 Ibid. 17 (CSEL 35.1.458): *ipsi celebrate more maiorum, ipsi cum resticulo nudi discurrite.* Resticulo (cf. n. 128 above) is Guether's emendation for the MSS *ridiculo*; for *discurrere*, see n. 54 above.

140 Constantinus Porphyrogenitus *De caerimoniis* 1.79 (70), 82 (73); Duval 1977.223–43. Does ἡνιοχοῦντες ἀλλήλους describe a 'fossilised' derivative of the thong-wielding *Luperci* of classical Rome (n. 2 above)?

141 Ibid. 1.82 (73); Ovid *Fasti* 2.148, Pliny *Nat. Hist.* 2.122, Columella 11.2.15; Duval 1976.264–7. *Favonius*: Lucretius 1.11, Horace *Odes* 1.4, etc; for the connection with Faunus and the *Lupercalia* even in Horace's time, see Barr 1962.

142 Duval 1977.226–7.

143 Mantuanus 1481, *de carnisprivii mala consuetudine: Nam iuvenes istis facit insanire diebus | Pan Deus Arcadiae quondam: totasque per urbes | currere et acceptis facies abscondere larvis. | Est pudor in facie: facies velata pudorem | ora tegit: Scelus est pavidum metuitque videri. | Cuncta sub ignotis petulantia vultibus audet | quae ablegat gravitas et quae proscribit honestas. | Per fora per vicos it personata libido: | et censore carens subit omnia tecta voluptas: | nec nuruum palmas sed membra recondita pulsat: | perque domos remanent foedi vestigia capri.*

women, bare their bodies and whip them. The same licensed sadism is attested in Saxony in the seventeenth century, again as part of the 'carnival' permissiveness of Shrove Tuesday.[144]

Northern Europe may also provide a somewhat more spectacular manifestation of the god of the *Lupercal*. Behrend Pick's derivation of Mephistopheles from *Opheles*, one of the names of Ephialtes,[145] may not be right—in the *Faustbuch* of 1587 the name is spelt 'Mephostophiles'[146]—but even so, the horns and goat's feet of Pan and his equivalents have made a contribution to the iconography of Christian Europe which is literally diabolical.[147]

---

144 Paul Heinrich Tilemann, *Commentatio historico-moralis et juridica de eo quod justum est circa nuditatem* (1692), as cited in Mannhardt 1904.225–6: 'Tempore quadragesimali im Fachtnacht mulieres sibi obviam factas inhonesto ioco interdum denudatis posterioribus virgis vel etiam herba aliqua pungente feriunt' (no mention of masks). Mannhardt (1904.252–6) offers many examples of striking on the hands (cf. n. 119 above).

145 Pick 1917 = 1931.105–12, citing the coins showing Ephialtes Epopheles at Nicaea and elsewhere (n. 70 above).

146 So too in Marlowe: Bevington and Rasmussen 1993.127, 211 (the *apparatus criticus* reports 'Mephostophiles' for both texts).

147 Bernheimer 1952.93–101; cf. Merivale 1969 [and now also Boardman 1997].

CHAPTER FIVE

Liber: Myth, Drama and Ideology in Republican Rome

I

By name and by nature, Liber is the god of freedom. His gift of wine frees men from cares, his mysteries free the soul from mortality, his power frees the seed in sexual union;[1] one of his many Greek names is *Lyaeus*, 'the releaser' (Λυαῖος from λύειν).[2] Though many explanations were offered by ancient sources to account for his name, the simplest and most obvious was an ideological one: *Liber a libertate*.[3] Political freedom, *libertas*, was the defining quality of the Roman Republic, achieved by the expulsion of Tarquin and under threat ever after.[4] It can hardly be accidental that Liber's festival (the *Liberalia*) was held on 17 March, just two days after the magistrates of the Republic entered office and twenty days after 'the flight of the king' (*Regifugium*).[5]

But the freedom of the Roman People was always potentially in conflict with the *dignitas* of the *principes uiri*.[6] Roman politics, like Athenian, could be conceived as a struggle between the many and the few,[7] and what the many called *libertas* the few redefined as *licentia*, anarchic and dangerously 'un-Roman'.[8]

---

1 Respectively: Seneca *De tranquillitate animi* 17.8, Servius on Virgil *Georgics* 1.166, Varro *Antiquitates rerum diuinarum* fr. 93 Cardauns; Maltby 1991.337.

2 *Etymologicum magnum* 571.18; Bruckmann 1893.87–8.

3 Servius on *Aeneid* 4.638, cf. 3.20 (*causa libertatis*), 4.57 (*Lyaeus . . . apte urbis libertatis est deus*).

4 Wirszubski 1950; Hellegouarc'h 1963.542–59.

5 *Regifugium*: Mastrocinque 1988.46–7. Consuls enter office on Ides of March: Livy 26.26.5, 31.5.2, 33.43.1, etc. The only festivals marked in the ancient calendar between *Regifugium* and *Liberalia* are the two *Equirria* horse-races in honour of Mars on 27 February and 14 March; in the foundation-story of the Republic, the expulsion of Tarquin was followed by the confiscation of his property and its dedication to Mars (the Campus Martius).

6 *Contentio libertatis dignitatisque*: Livy 4.6.11, cf. 7.33.3. *Res olim dissociabiles . . . principatum ac libertatem*: Tacitus *Agricola* 3.1.

7 Sallust *Bellum Iugurthinum* 8.2. *Multi, plurimi*: Cicero *De republica* 2.39, 6.1. *Pauci*: Sallust *Bellum Catilinae* 20.7, 39.1, *Bellum Iugurthinum* 31.2, 31.9, 31.20, 41.7, *Histories* 1.55.12, 1.55.23, 3.48.28.

8 E.g. Cicero *Pro Flacco* 16, *De republica* 1.68, 3.23; Livy 3.37.8, 3.53.6, 3.59.4, 23.2.1; Phaedrus 1.2.2–3; Tacitus *Dialogus* 40.2. Cf. Cicero *De domo* 110–11 and *De legibus* 2.42 on Clodius' shrine of Libertas (*templum Licentiae*).

Not surprisingly, therefore, it was when the Senate's authority was strong, in the early second century BC, that the 'licentious' aspects of Liber—the so-called *Bacchanalia*—were stamped out throughout Italy in a ruthless police action.[9]

The fluctuations of ideological attitude, of which the '*Bacchanalia* affair' was a particularly violent example, make it pointless to attempt a synchronic account of Liber in the Roman Republic. Our literary sources almost all post-date 186 BC, and naturally reflect the Senate's hostile view. A tiny glimpse of earlier attitudes is provided by a line of Naevius quoted in Festus' dictionary:[10]

> *Liberalia Liberi festa, quae apud Graecos dicuntur* Διονύσια. *Naeuius: Libera lingua loquimur ludis Liberalibus.*
>
> *Liberalia*: the festival of Liber, called *Dionysia* by the Greeks. See Naevius: 'At the *Liberalia* games we enjoy free speech.'

We know from Ovid that the *Liberalia* had once been *ludi*.[11] Naevius' reference may suggest that they were theatre games (*ludi scaenici*), but a line of Plautus implies that the women celebrating the festival were also a part of the performance, and from Livy's hostile description, which may well go back to a second-century BC source, we may infer that ritual and stage spectacle overlapped.[12]

Before Naevius, there is no contemporary literary evidence—but that does not mean that there is no contemporary evidence at all. A crucially important, and much neglected, source of information is the corpus of engraved bronze *cistae* and mirrors dating from the late fourth and early third centuries BC. These artefacts are usually called 'Praenestine', because of the accident that Praeneste's cemeteries have been more thoroughly explored than those of any other Latin city; but since one of the finest of the *cistae* was certainly made in Rome, this material should be understood as illustrating the story-world of Latium in general, just as contemporary vase-painting illustrates that of Etruria, Campania and southern Italy.[13]

---

9   Livy 39.8–19 (*licentia* at 39.13.10), *ILLRP* 511; Cicero *De legibus* 2.37, Valerius Maximus 6.3.7 (exercise of *seueritas*); Pailler 1988.

10 Festus (Paulus) 103L = Naevius fr. 113R; Wiseman 1998.35–43. [According to Csapo and Slater 1994.209, 'it is notable that there are no games [at Rome] for Dionysus or his Latin equivalent.']

11 Ovid *Fasti* 3.784–6 (later transferred to the *Cerialia* on 19 April).

12 Plautus *Casina* 980 (*nunc Baccae nullae ludunt*); Livy 39.10.7, 39.13.12–13, cf. 39.15.7 (*concessum ludum ac lasciuiam*); Cazanove 1983, esp. 103–13. Livy's source: Wiseman 1998.47–8.

13 Battaglia and Emiliozzi 1979 and 1990: no. 68, the 'Ficoroni *cista*' carries Novios Plautios' 'made in Rome' inscription (*ILLRP* 1197). Vase-painting: Beazley 1947; Martelli 1987; Trendall 1967 and 1987; Trendall and Cambitoglou 1982. A detailed comparative study of the iconography of the Latin engravers and the Etruscan, Campanian and South-Italian vase-painters is urgently needed.

As on the vases, so on the engraved bronzes Dionysiac imagery is ubiquitous. It is clear that all over Italy, Latium included, the iconography of the
thiasos was perfectly familiar in the fourth and third centuries BC, as it had been
in the sixth and fifth.[14] When the consul in Livy's narrative of 186 BC warns the
Roman People against outlandish foreign rituals, we should not take his words
as reliable evidence. If something like that really was said at the time, it can
only have been a disingenuous pretext for interference with a cult that had
become politically undesirable.[15] Liber and *libertas* had to be controlled.

II

A *cista* in Berlin, no. 5 in the corpus [fig. 17], names *LEIBER* in a group of
gods witnessing what seems to be the initiation of the young Mars at the *Liberalia*.[16] The combination of the familiar iconography of the gods and the
mysterious scene of young Mars kneeling on an amphora under the sign of
Cerberus may serve as a reminder of how little we know; we need not expect
everything portrayed on these artefacts to correspond to what our literary
sources tell us about two or three centuries later. (It would be good to know,
for instance, what Liber's right-hand gesture means. Is he warning Apollo off,
or is just the artist's way of filling the space?) Another Berlin *cista*, no. 4 [fig.
18], portrays Liber in a younger guise, with Venus and Adonis(?), one of the
Dioscuri, Jupiter and Diana.[17]

A *cista* in Karlsruhe [fig. 19, p. 89] shows Liber and the satyrs with a female
figure. Since she and Liber balance each other in a very symmetrical composition, it is tempting to identify her as Libera.[18] Or she may be Semele, mother
of Dionysus, brought back from the Underworld by her son to become the
goddess Thyone, whose Latin equivalent is Stimula; the *lucus Stimulae*, centre

---

14 Early fifth-century antefixes etc: Cazenove 1986, esp. 185–90 for bibliography and discussion. Note that the satyrs' female partners were more often nymphs than maenads: Hedreen
    1994. The Phase IIB vase with the graffito *euoin* from tomb 482 at Osteria dell'Osa (Gabii)
    attests Latin familiarity with Dionysiac ritual as early as the eighth century BC: see Peruzzi
    1998.81–90 [however, the reading may be *eulin*: Ridgway 1996].
15 Livy 39.15.1–3, 39.16.8–9; Beard, North and Price 1998.1.93–6.
16 Suggested by Pairault Massa 1992.163–4; other suggestions in Battaglia and Emiliozzi
    1979.52–4 and 61 ('nota aggiunta').
17 Battaglia and Emiliozzi 1979.49.
18 Cf. Pliny *Nat. Hist.* 36.29 (a statue group of satyrs with Liber and Libera). Libera was sometimes identified with Persephone (Cicero *De natura deorum* 2.62, *Verrines* 5.187, Dionysius of
    Halicarnassus 6.17.2, 6.94.3, Arnobius 5.21), sometimes with Ariadne (Ovid *Fasti* 3.459–
    516, Hyginus *Fabulae* 224.2), sometimes with Venus (Varro *Antiquitates rerum diuinarum* fr.
    93 Cardauns, *CIL* 8.15578). See now Jurgeit 1999.524, who identifies the scene as the
    preparation of a bride by her girl friends, with Dionysus bringing his own bride Ariadne.
    (But why are the satyrs so surprised? And which of the five young women is the bride?)

Fig. 17 *Cista* no. 5, in the Staatliche Museen, Berlin (Battaglia and Emiliozzi 1979.50–54): the gods witness Minerva's anointing of the young Mars (third figure from the right, beneath Cerberus in the upper border).

Fig. 18 *Cista* no. 4, in the Staatliche Museen, Berlin (Battaglia and Emiliozzi 1979.48–50): the young Liber (second figure from the right).

Fig. 19 *Cista* no. 22, in the Badisches Landesmuseum, Karlsruhe (Battaglia and Emiliozzi 1979.95–7), with nineteenth-century additions omitted (Jurgeit 1992): Liber and Libera(?) escorted by satyrs.

of the Bacchic rites in Rome, was also known as 'Semele's Grove'.[19]

This *cista* is also notable as the most elaborate example of a frequently recurring iconographic motif, women naked at the washing-basin.[20] Mauro Menichetti, in his important book on the *cistae*, sees this as an allusion to the 'feminine *paideia*' of an aristocratic society, celebrating the beauty and seductiveness that lead to marriage,[21] and it is certainly true that this scene seems to have something in common with the women's festival on 1 April, as described by Ovid.[22] We shall return to this motif; for the moment, however, I want to concentrate on Liber and his followers, particularly the satyrs.

Cista no. 72, in the Villa Giulia [fig. 20], shows a wide range of satyr-types.[23] Note in particular the old fat satyr with the long beard, riding on a goat; he reminds us of old Silenus in the Augustan poets, the father of the satyrs, on his hollow-backed donkey.[24] In the centre is a sober, mature satyr, respectably clothed, playing a pipe; he too may remind us of Silenus in the literary texts, this time as the source of wisdom and sage advice.[25]

But neither characterisation of Silenus is necessarily applicable in the fourth century BC. It is true that Silenus as father of the satyrs is already a familiar figure in Athenian satiric drama, but Herodotus continues to use σιληνός in its original generic sense and not as a proper name.[26] Alcibiades in Plato's

19 Semele: Diodorus Siculus 4.25.4, Apollodorus 3.5.3, Hyginus *Fabulae* 251.1; Carpenter 1997.62–4. Thyone παρὰ τὸ θύειν, ὅ ἐστιν ὁρμᾶν: Scholiast on Pindar *Pythians* 3.177, Suda s.v. *Thyone*. Stimula from *stimulare*: Varro *Antiquitates rerum diuinarum* fr. 130 Cardauns. *Lucus*: Livy 39.12.4, Ovid *Fasti* 6.503, *CIL* 6.9897; Cazenove 1986.56–66.

20 See also *cistae* nos. 24 (Leningrad), 67 (Providence RI, authenticity disputed), 74 and 75 (both Villa Giulia). See below, pp. 111 and 115 on nos. 50–51 (and n. 33 on no. 100).

21 Menichetti 1995.57: 'Tutte queste raffigurazioni che pongono in primo piano la toletta della donna alludono in un linguaggio greccizante alla *paideia* femminile della cura del corpo tramite cui si acquisisce quel potere di seduzione dell'uomo mediante il quale si accede alla sfera di matrimonio.' Ibid. 19: 'La donna visibile sui grandi fregi incise non corrisponde ad una banalizzante prospettiva dell'*oikos*, ma è invece investita da una valorizzazione tipica di una società aristocratica che individua nella donna un veicolo privilegiato di trasmissione di lignagge e fortune...'

22 Ovid *Fasti* 4.133–62 (*Latiae matres nurusque*); Menichetti 1995.62–3 [and see now pp. 140–54 below].

23 Also an ithyphallic herm (Priapus?) on the altar; the young Pan, in human form with tiny horns in his hair, identified by the throwing-stick (*pedum*); and a goose with an upright neck, as on the base of one of the phallic pillars of the *choregos*' monument at Delos (also late fourth century). For the Dionysiac context of the Delos monument, see Cole 1993, esp. 30–3. [For a goose as *deliciae Priapi*, see Petronius *Satyricon* 137.1.]

24 The *locus classicus* is Ovid *Ars amatoria* 1.541–8; also *Fasti* 1.399, 3.749, 6.339.

25 Cicero *Tusculanae* 1.114, Virgil *Eclogues* 6.13–30; also Theopompus *FGrH* 115 F75, though it is not clear whether he used *Silenos* as a proper name or a description (cf. Herodotus 8.138.3 ὁ σιληνός, Xenophon *Anabasis* 1.2.13 τὸν σάτυρον). A serious, clothed, elderly satyr appears on *cista* no. 96 (Villa Giulia), among respectable women in the *gynaeceum*; see also the lyre-playing Silenus and the Silenus with the mirror in the Villa of the Mysteries frieze at Pompeii.

26 Aeschylus *Diktyoulkoi* 805, Euripides *Cyclops* 82–4, 272, 431 etc; Herodotus 7.26.3, ὁ τοῦ Μαρσύεω ἀσκός. Seaford 1984.6–7.

Fig. 20 *Cista* no. 72, in the Villa Giulia Museum, Rome (Battaglia and Emiliozzi 1990.239–44): various satyrs.

Symposion likens Socrates to 'those *silenoi* in the sculptors' workshops which the craftsmen portray as holding pan-pipes or *auloi*, and when you take them apart you see they have statues of gods inside'; but since he then goes on to say that Socrates is like 'the satyr Marsyas' even though he doesn't play the *aulos*, it is clear enough that he means not statues of Silenus but statues of *silenoi* in general, of whom Marsyas was one.[27] As for fat Silenus' donkey, in Ptolemy's great Dionysiac procession in 270 BC there were five troops of donkeys ridden by *satyroi* and *silenoi* alike.[28]

So it would be rash to identify either the old fat satyr or the sober one as Silenus. On the contrary, the young dancing satyr at the far left of fig. 20, and the one at the far right with the short beard, carrying a wineskin, may have a better claim to the name. On *cista* no. 66, at Vassar College [fig. 21], a fragmentary scene showing Jupiter or Dis Pater, Diana, the Dioscuri and Victoria includes at the far right a short-bearded satyr carrying a wineskin; he is named as *SILANOS*.[29] And on a *cista* in New York, no. 45 [fig. 22], the name *SILANVS* is attached to the young satyr dancing at the far left with a naked young woman, and playing *kottabos* at the same time.

On the lid of no. 45 a grossly fat old satyr, whom first-century BC Romans might have identified as Silenus, is given the appropriate name *EBRIOS* [fig. 23, p. 95]. He wears a crown of a very distinctive type, which appears again on a mirror in the British Museum [fig. 24, p. 96], showing a mythological scene involving Telis (Thetis?), Ajax and Alcumena.[30] At the right, the little fat satyr wearing the crown, and making good use of a drinking-bowl, may be Ebrios again.

The same sort of crown is worn by a different sort of 'satyr'-figure at a drinking-party on a mirror in Baltimore [fig. 14, p. 67 above]. He has a straggly triangular beard and is evidently playing *kottabos*—or perhaps dropping wine on the drunken figure sprawled in front of him. His companions are a young woman, naked to the waist, playing the pipes, and a naked young man (perhaps Pan, to judge by the horns in his hair), blowing on a conch-shell. Unlike them, he is wearing a tight-fitting hairy suit, the sleeve visible at the left

27 Plato *Symposion* 215a, 216d, 221d (*silenoi*); 215b–e, 216c (Marsyas); cf. Herodotus 7.26.3 (previous note).

28 Athenaeus 5.200e = Callixenus of Rhodes *FGrH* 627 F2 (p. 173.7–8); ibid. 197e, 197f–198a, 199b (pp. 168.10–11, 168.21–5, 170.17–18) for generic *satyroi* and *silenoi*, 199a (p. 170.12) for a singular Silenus.

29 For the inscriptions, including [?*DIES*]*PATER* and [*P*]*ORLOU*[*CES*], see Battaglia and Emiliozzi 1990.202–4. They draw attention to the fact that the 'thunderbolt' in 'Jupiter's' hand is 'stilizzato in maniera insolito'. I suggest that it is not a thunderbolt at all but the edge of the god's cloak, that his hand is resting on the arm of his throne, and that the inscription could more naturally be restored as [*DIS*] *PATER*.

30 Pairault Massa 1992.168–70, Menichetti 1995.120: Ajax in the Isles of the Blessed, receiving the arms of Achilles?

Fig. 21 *Cista* no. 66, in Vassar College, New York (Battaglia and Emiliozzi 1990.200–6): far right, a satyr called Silanos.

Fig. 22 *Cista* no. 45, in the Pierpont Morgan Library, New York (Battaglia and Emiliozzi 1979.146–50): second figure from the left, a satyr called Silanus.

Fig. 23 Lid of *cista* no. 45 (fig. 22): a satyr called Ebrios.

forearm, which must mean that he is an actor or performer of some sort.[31]

On a *cista* also in Baltimore, no. 1 [fig. 25, p. 97], the hairy-suited figure appears again, in the company now of two girl musicians and a young satyr with an amphora. What is striking about this scene is the way the Dionysiac *thiasos* merges into the mythological scene of the death of Medusa, the birth of Pegasus, and the pursuit of Perseus by one of the Gorgons.[32]

---

31 For an interpretation of this mirror and its companion-piece (in the Villa Giulia), see pp. 66–9 above.

32 Battaglia and Emiliozzi 1979.42: 'Si tratta di due scene ben distinte: 1) nascita di Pegaso dal corpo di Medusa; 2) thiasos.' But the scenes are not distinct: the upright thyrsus divides the composition into two unequal halves, but the *thiasos* extends beyond it (veiled woman dancing). Perseus with the head of Medusa appears also on *cista* no. 76 (Villa Giulia), along with Peleus and Thetis.

Fig. 24 Mirror in the British Museum: 'Telis', Aiax, Alcumena and satyr.

Before trying to pull together some of these data, let us complete our typology of Latin satyrs. On *cista* no. 14, in Chicago [fig. 26, p. 98], we have a *thiasos* including at the left the young Liber with a thyrsus, and at the right a short, plump, short-bearded satyr with a cup. He reappears in a mysterious scene on a mirror of doubtful provenance in the Villa Giulia [fig. 27, p. 100], carrying a caduceus and offering a garland to a tall young woman who seems to be feeling inside her dress with her left hand. He appears again on a rectangular *cista* in the Villa Giulia, no. 100 [fig. 28, p. 101], sitting beneath a basin and

Fig. 25 *Cista* no. 1, in the Walters Art Gallery, Baltimore (Battaglia and Emiliozzi 1979.41–3): Bacchic procession with Medusa and Perseus.

Fig. 26 *Cista* no. 14, in the Field Museum, Chicago (Battaglia and Emiliozzi 1979.76–7): Bacchic scene with plump satyr at far right.

feeling the sexual parts of a winged naked female.[33] What stories these scenes refer to, we do not know.

A satyr with the same physique, short and plump, but with a fuller beard and moustache, appears in an early-third century context of some importance for the ideology of the Roman Republic. This is Marsyas, as portrayed in the forum of the Latin colony of Paestum, founded in 273 BC [fig. 29, p. 102].[34] Since part of a similar statue has turned up at Alba Fucens, founded in 303 BC,[35] it is a natural inference that both colonies had put up replicas of the Marsyas statue that stood in the Comitium at Rome, and that the Rome statue, for which our earliest direct evidence is in Horace, therefore dated from the fourth century BC.[36]

The Paestum Marsyas has shackles on his feet. Filippo Coarelli brilliantly suggested the abolition of slavery for debt (*nexum*), in 326 or 313 BC, as the likely context for the erection of the Marsyas statue in Rome.[37] In mythological terms, however, the reference must surely be to Marsyas' musical contest with Apollo, illustrated on *cista* no. 70 in the Villa Giulia [fig. 30, p. 103]. According to what Herodotus calls 'the Phrygian story', victorious Apollo had the presumptuous satyr hung up and flayed alive, but some mythologists were evidently uneasy about this gruesome tale; Diodorus, for instance, says that Apollo did it but later regretted it.[38] Silius Italicus and the elder Pliny attest what we may call the Italian story, that Marsyas escaped and fled to Italy, where he became the ancestor of the Marsi.[39]

How did he escape? Surely he must have been freed by his patron Liber, whom no chains could resist.[40] And that, as Servius explains in his commentary on the *Aeneid*, is the meaning of those statues in the *fora* of Italian cities:[41]

33 Cf. Menichetti 1995.62, who ignores the wings and takes this as another example of the *sfera femminile* and seduction leading to marriage. Pairault Massa 1992.165–6 more plausibly describes the winged figures as 'due "geni" femminili', and rightly insists on their uniqueness.

34 See Coarelli 1985.98–9, figs. 13–17.

35 See Liberatore 1995.

36 Colonial copies: Charax of Pergamum *FGrH* 103 F31. Rome: Horace *Satires* 1.6.115–17 with Porphyrio and ps.Acro *ad loc*.: illustrated on *denarii* of L. Marcius Censorinus in 82 BC (Crawford 1974.377–8, no. 363) and on the *anaglypha Traiani* (Torelli 1982.99–106, Coarelli 1985.91–119).

37 Coarelli 1985.97–100 and 102–11. The Twelve Tables specified shackles (*compedes*) for debtors (Aulus Gellius 20.1.45). Date of abolition: Livy 8.28 (326 BC), Varro *De lingua Latina* 7.105 (313 BC); Oakley 1998.688–91.

38 Herodotus 7.26.3, Diodorus Siculus 3.59.2–5, 5.75.3.

39 Silius Italicus 8.502–4, Pliny *Nat. Hist.* 3.108; Weis 1992.367, 377.

40 Euripides *Bacchae* 613–21, Ovid *Metamorphoses* 3.696–700; in a different sense, cf. Tibullus 1.7.41–2 (*Bacchus et adflictis requiem mortalibus adfert,* | *crura licet dura compede pulsa sonent*).

41 Servius on *Aeneid* 3.20, 4.58; Veyne 1961.

in liberis ciuitatibus simulacrum Marsyae erat, qui in tutela Liberi patris est. ...
'Patrique Lyaeo', qui, ut supra diximus, apte urbibus libertatis est deus; unde etiam
Marsyas, eius minister, est in ciuitatibus in foro positus libertatis indicium, qui erecta
manu testatur nihil urbi deesse.

In free cities there was a statue of Marsyas, who is under the protection of Liber
Pater. .... 'To Father Lyaeus', who as we said above is appropriately the god of
freedom for cities; whence Marsyas too, his servant, is placed in the forum in
cities as a symbol of freedom, with his hand raised to show the city lacks
nothing.

Fig. 27 Mirror in the Villa Giulia Museum, Rome: woman and satyr.

Fig. 28 One side of *cista* no. 100, in the Villa Giulia Museum, Rome (Battaglia and Emiliozzi 1990.312–6): satyr and winged girls.

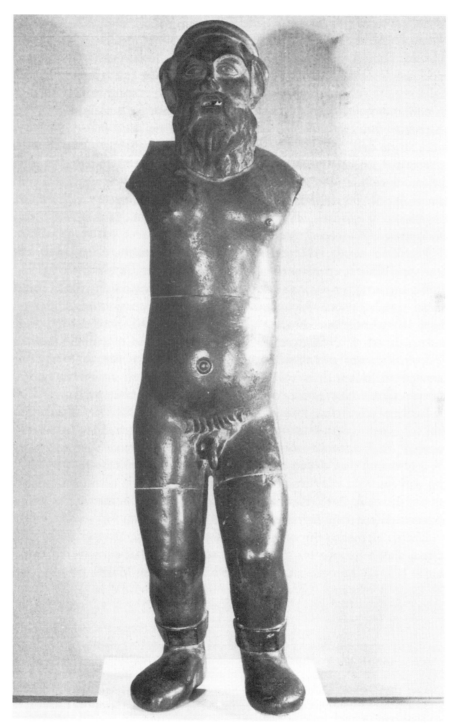

Fig. 29 Marsyas statue at Paestum (Coarelli 1985.98, fig. 13).

Fig. 30 *Cista* no. 70, in the Villa Giulia Museum, Rome (Battaglia and Emiliozzi 1990.232–6): Apollo and Marsyas.

III

On a mirror in the Villa Giulia, signed by the artist Vibis (=Vibius) Pilipus, Marsyas is portrayed dancing cheerfully with an ithyphallic goatlegged Paniskos [fig. 10, p. 59 above]. Little Pan is clearly imitating him, as the fat old satyr on the Ficoroni *cista* in the Villa Giulia, no. 68 [fig. 31], imitates the Argonaut working out at the punch-bag. Marsyas 'stamps his foot and waves the tail of an ass': thus Anne Weis in the *Lexicon Iconographicum*, but the stamping is clearly a dance, as illustrated on a near-contemporary Lucanian *oinochoe* [fig. 32].[42] The hand-gesture too is evidently part of the satyrs' dance-repertoire, as is clear from many scenes on Athenian and Italian vases,[43] and it brings us back to young Silanus on the New York *cista* [fig. 22, p. 94 above].

Fig. 31 Detail of the 'Ficoroni *cista*' (no. 68) in the Villa Giulia Museum, Rome (Battaglia and Emiliozzi 1990.211–25): Argonauts and old satyr.

According to the description of that scene in *Le ciste prenestine*, the young woman 'solleva ambedue le mani in un gesto che sembra di protesta'.[44] But that is a misreading: the young satyr is not assaulting her, and her hand-movements correspond to his. Iconographically, what we have here is a scene familiar from the Satricum antefixes of the early fifth century BC [fig. 33], the

---

42 Weis 1992.368; Trendall 1967.141, no. 784 (plate 66.6). Is Marsyas on the mirror waving his own tail? If so, we must think of him as a performer.

43 Athenian evidence conveniently collected in Brommer 1944: see figs 2, 4, 9, 10, 38, 40–3, 67. An early Italian example, c. 470–460 BC, is a cup from Vulci in the Rodin Museum in Paris (Beazley 1947.25–7, Plate IV.1, Martelli 1987 fig. 160); it carries the name of Aules Vipinas.

44 Battaglia and Emiliozzi 1979.147.

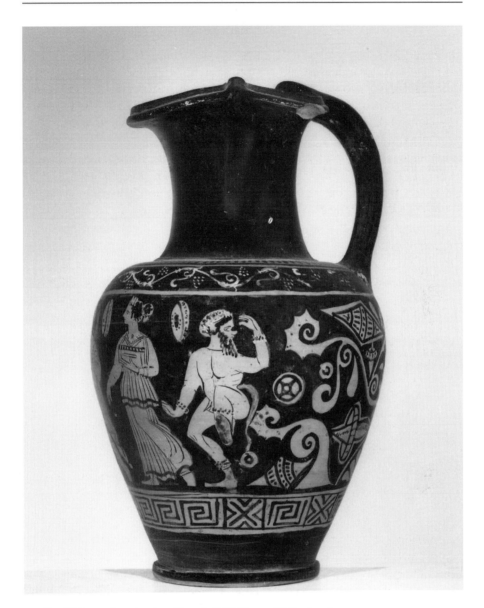

Fig. 32 Lucanian *oinochoe* (Trendall 1967, no. 784): dancing satyr.

Fig. 33 Antefix from Satricum in the Villa Giulia Museum, Rome (Giglioli 1935, tav. cclxxxv.2): satyr and nymph dancing.

Fig. 34 Faliscan cup in the Villa Giulia Museum, Rome (Giglioli 1935, tav. cclxxii.2): satyr-performer and dancing girl.

dance of a satyr with a nymph.[45] But the 'nymph' on the New York *cista* is no creature of the wild; she wears very elaborate jewellery. I think she is a dancing girl playing the part of a nymph, analogous perhaps to the hairy-suited performer on the Baltimore mirror [fig. 14, p. 67 above]. Indeed, we see the two together on a fourth-century Faliscan cup in the Villa Giulia [fig. 34]. A closer parallel for Silanus and his partner is a scene on an Apulian dish in the British Museum [fig. 35], showing a young satyr with the *kottabos*-cup on his finger and a dancing girl using the turned-up hand gesture.[46] The context

45 Not a maenad, as wrongly stated in Wiseman 1994.71 and 77; see Hedreen 1994. Also mistaken is the description of the satyr's gesture in Giglioli 1935.35: 'con la mano destra fa un gesto come di riluttanza'.

46 At Trendall and Cambitoglou 1982.281, the satyr is wrongly described as 'a nude youth'.

Fig. 35 Apulian dish in the British Museum (F 133): young satyr and dancing girl.

seems to be a symposion, but it is worth noticing that the rest of the scene shows two bacchantes attacking the disguised Pentheus.

A mid-fourth-century comment from an Athenian who knew southern Italy may help us to see what is going on. In the seventh book of the *Laws*, Plato discusses acceptable and unacceptable types of dance:[47]

ὅση μὲν βακχεία τ' ἐστὶν καὶ τῶν ταύταις ἑπομένων, ἃς Νύμφας τε καὶ Πᾶνας καὶ Σειληνοὺς καὶ Σατύρους ἐπονομάζοντες, ὥς φασιν, μιμοῦνται κατῳνωμένους, περὶ καθαρμούς τε καὶ τελετάς τινας ἀποτελούντων, σύμπαν τοῦτο τῆς ὀρχήσεως τὸ γένος οὔθ' ὡς εἰρηνικὸν οὔθ' ὡς πολεμικὸν οὔθ' ὅτι ποτὲ βούλεται ῥᾴδιον ἀφορίσασθαι.

Any [dancing] that is Bacchic in nature, or that resembles those in which, while celebrating certain ceremonies of purification and initiation, the dancers 'imitate', as the phrase is, drunken persons, calling them nymphs, Pans, Sileni and satyrs—this kind of dancing is, as a whole, neither peaceful nor warlike, and it is hard to determine what its purpose is.

---

47 Plato *Laws* 7.815c. For text and meaning, see England 1921.302–3 and Morrow 1960.362–3 and n. 221; I have borrowed part of Morrow's translation.

As a modern commentator observes, 'despite the questionable character of these dances, Plato hesitates to legislate against them; and this hesitation may be due to a reluctance to lay hands upon long-established religious practices.'[48] The Senate showed no such reluctance in 186 BC; presumably ceremonies of purification and initiation were what the 'ignoble' Greco-Etruscan *sacrificulus et uates* had been offering.[49]

One detail of the Plato passage is particularly important for our purposes; ὥς φασιν introduces the technical term μιμοῦνται, which means 'represent in the form of a μῖμος'.[50] We have already noticed examples of visually-represented imitation: Marsyas and Paniskos, the Argonaut and the old fat satyr. The hairy body-suit, worn on the Baltimore mirror by someone at a symposion,[51] was also one of the regular costumes for actors in satyr-play.[52] The common ground of drinking parties, Dionysiac ritual and dramatic *mimesis*, clearly implied by Plato but not easy for moderns to visualise, has been explored from various angles in recent years,[53] and it seems to me that interpretation of the iconography of the Latin bronzes must also take account of it.

The ubiquity of the satyrs makes it natural to think first of satyric drama and quasi-drama. The hairy-suited *papposilenos* is a very familiar character in south-Italian, and particularly Paestan, vase-painting, frequently portrayed in boots, which make it clear that he is a performer even though the scenes are not obviously dramatic.[54] An Apulian bell-crater in Cleveland [fig. 36] shows him in a mask, but a mask quite different from that of Attic satyr-play, and his companion in the scene is a slave from comedy.[55] Mime too is relevant here, for even in Athens satyr-play was beginning to be associated with mime by the fourth century BC.[56] In Italy the dramatic genres were even less watertight, as is shown by Apulian and Paestan vases showing naked girl acrobats performing with comic actors.

---

48 Morrow 1960.365.
49 Livy 39.8.3; cf. 39.16.6–11 for the consul's attempt to reassure the *populus* that ancient rites were not being violated.
50 England 1921.302.
51 Evidently associated with a wedding ceremony (p. 69 above); cf. Seaford 1994.308 for the analogies between marriage and Dionysiac initiation. Hairy-suited satyrs on Delos, perhaps to be associated with the *phallephoria* procession: Cole 1993.32–3.
52 See the 'Pronomos Vase' (late fifth century), with the actor in the hairy suit at upper right: conveniently illustrated in Seaford 1984 plate III, and in Green 1994.44, fig. 2.19.
53 E.g. Seaford 1984.5–10, Seaford 1994.266–9, Green 1994.38–46 and 89–93. See in general Green 1995.
54 E.g. Trendall 1987, plates 28e, 71c, 92, 93b, 99c, 101e, 105a-b, 105e, 107a, 107c, 120b, 162a, 162c, 241a, 241c; Green 1995.92–3, figs 4.3–4.
55 Green 1995.102–3 and plate 8; contrast the 'pronomos Vase' (n. 52 above).
56 See Luce 1930.339, Simon 1982.19–20 and plate 8: Dionysus entertained by, respectively, a *mima* playing a satyr, and a satyr called Mimos.

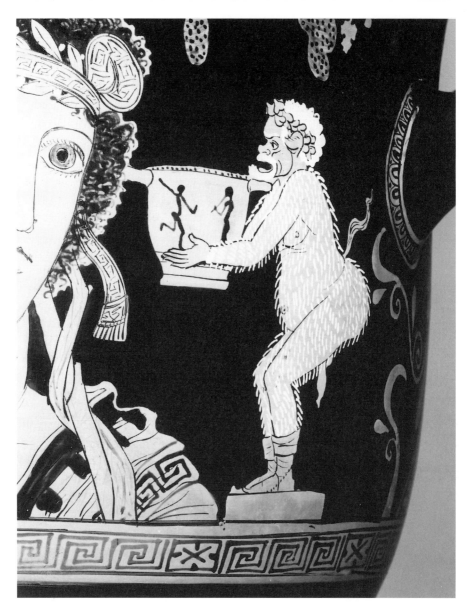

Fig. 36 Bell crater with Dionysiac scene in the Cleveland Museum of Art: South Italy, Apulia, early fourth century BC, c. 400–390 BC. Earthenware with slip decoration, 37.8 x 40.3 cm.

As C.W. Dearden puts it (though I think the evidence justifies a less tentative formulation),[57]

> the argument to be made is that the tight lines drawn around the individual dramatic genre in fifth-century Athens may not have been so watertight in Magna Graecia in the fourth century and later. . . The evidence is by no means conclusive but it could be taken to suggest that vase painters in Southern Italy and, more importantly, their customers, saw drama of whatever genre in a comprehensive light.

So—to return to the New York *cista* [fig. 22, p. 94 above]—a young woman, naked but adorned with jewellery, dancing with a satyr, might be seen either as a nymph, or as a Bacchic worshipper imitating a nymph, or as a *mima* playing a nymph on stage.

Another recurring motif may help us. A fourth-century Etruscan cup in the Vatican [fig. 37] shows a dancing satyr, his left hand in the now-familiar turned-up position, with two naked and bejewelled young women, who are not dancing but using a mirror and a perfume jar; their clothes hang on a tree behind. Another cup from the same 'Clusium' group [fig. 38] shows three such young women, adorned in just the same way, playing the roles of Leda and her maidservants—and the eagle shows that the scene is taken from Euripides' *Helen*.[58]

On *cista* no. 82 in the Villa Giulia [fig. 39, p. 114], at the right hand side of the composition a young dancing satyr (same gesture of the hand) looks across at a naked young woman wearing jewellery and using a mirror. Between them, playing the *auloi*, sits an old fat satyr wearing the same type of crown as Ebrios [fig. 23, p. 95 above]. The piping satyr reappears on two *cistae* at Palestrina, nos. 50 and 51 [fig. 40, p. 115], both illustrating the same scene; but this time he sits and plays beneath a basin at which two naked and bejewelled young women are washing.

For Menichetti, these are examples of the feminine *paideia* that leads to marriage,[59] but a different and more specific explanation is available if we keep *mimesis* in mind. In the iconographic conventions of Athenian vase-painting, the presence of a piper (*auletes*) indicates that the scene is not 'real life' but a performance.[60] Let us suppose for the sake of argument that the same convention applies to the piping satyr in *cistae* nos. 50–51 and 82.

---

57 Dearden 1995 plate 1 (quotations from 85 and 86). See also Hughes 1997, identifying a naked female comic dancer ('Konnakis') on a fourth-century Tarentine *krater*.

58 Euripides *Helen* 17–21; Martelli 1987.331, fig. 180.

59 See above, p. 90.

60 Green 1994.24 ('a conventional symbol whose function is to indicate that what we have here is a performance in the theatre'); Carpenter 1997.78 ('a signal that the context for the scene is a performance').

Fig. 37 Etruscan cup (Clusium group) in the Vatican, Museo Gregoriano (inv. 14962): showgirls and dancing satyr.

The first of the two scenes [fig. 40, p. 115] is described in *Le ciste prenestine* as 'scena di toletta ed immagini di repertorio . . . sei personaggi aggruppati due a due, senza il minimo legame narrative o, comunque, logico'.[61] It is true that this is not a story that we can recognise, but it doesn't follow that it is not a story at all.[62] The naked, kneeling captive is not just a stock figure; he looks up at the tall man with the staff, and the lady wrapped up in a cloak clearly belongs in the same scene, as does the young man to the right (not shown on no. 50).

---

61 Battaglia and Emiliozzi 1979.158–9 and 160.
62 There are plenty of unfamiliar stories on the *cistae*: e.g. the man, the dwarf and the girl with the knife (handle of no. 47), the chariot-race of Venus and Aucena (lid of no. 9), the attack on the palace (no. 54), the Dioscuri and the *pater poimilionum* (no. 27), etc. For Aucena see Peruzzi 1998.161–4.

Fig. 38 Etruscan cup (Clusium group) in the Musée d'art et d'histoire, Geneva: showgirls playing Leda and the swan.

It is not clear whether the bearded warrior with the horse, and the tall lady accompanied by a winged *daimon* carrying a parasol, are part of the same story, or another. But they are surely in a story of some sort.

With no. 82 [fig. 39] we are on firmer ground. The identification of the warrior to the left, with horse and dog, is uncertain, as is that of the naked young man with spear and sword just to the left of the dancing satyr. But the figures between them are recognisable: grieving Achilles, Iphigeneia, Clytemnestra (or Diana?) at the window, Agamemnon.[63] It is a scene familiar

---

63 Battaglia and Emiliozzi 1990.274–6; Menichetti 1995.66. [See Graham 1998 for 'the woman at the window' as normally a prostitute or an adulteress; the latter would be appropriate for Clytemnestra.]

Fig. 39 *Cista* no. 82, in the Villa Giulia Museum, Rome (Battaglia and Emiliozzi 1990.273–7): sacrifice of Iphigeneia, with piping satyr.

Fig. 40 *Cista* no. 51, in the Museo Archeologico, Palestrina (Battaglia and Emiliozzi 1979.160–2): unidentified scene, with piping satyr.

from tragedy, and Bordenache Battaglia and Emiliozzi are right to point out its 'indubbi riflessi di una rappresentazione teatrale', including the window: 'la finestrella cioè, potrebbe indicare, in modo compendiario, lo sfondo architettonico della scena stessa.'[64]

So our hypothesis about the piping satyr may be justified: one of the two scenes is certainly theatrical, and the other could be. In one case the satyr is accompanied by two women at the basin, in the other by a woman with a mirror and a young satyr dancing—stock figures, according to the editors of the corpus, but it is hardly possible to believe that they have their place in the composition just because the artist had some space to fill.[65] If we are right that the piping satyr represents theatricality, then so, in some sense, must the other figures.

Let us look again at Iphigeneia [fig. 39]:[66]

> La fanciulla è rappresentata nell'atto di denudarsi, sollevando con ambedue le mani un ampio mantello per lasciarlo ricadere dietro le spalle, quasi a sottolineare, in maniera un po' teatrale, l'inumana condanna a metter fine alla sua splendida giovinezza.

What sort of theatre would expose her 'splendida giovinezza' in this way? Why should a tragic heroine have nothing on under her cloak? Perhaps we may approach an answer if we notice that what little she is wearing is the same jewellery as the girl with the mirror: necklace, bracelets, earrings. So too on the New York *cista*, no. 45 [fig. 22, p. 94 above], the young woman dancing with Silanus wears practically the same jewellery as the woman called *DOXA* in the main scene. There is no piping satyr there, but otherwise the juxtaposition of the dancing satyr and a young woman next to a narrative scene is very close to what we have in no. 82.[67]

Apart from young Silanus and his partner, what is happening on the New York *cista*? The scene is flanked by two female figures named as *DOXA* and *LAVIS* (i.e. *laus*?). Between them, from left to right: *LADVMEDA* with a stag, in front of a bearded herm; *AIAX ILIOS*, holding the reins of two horses; a column with a notice attached (*LECES*, i.e. *leges*?); a naked young man with a sword and two spears, named as *SORESIOS*; *ACMEMONO*, i.e. Agamemnon, in a pose similar to that on no. 82; two horses looking out of a double window; and a young man in a short cloak, named as *ISTOR*. It is a

---

64 Battaglia and Emiliozzi 1990.275. Windows often appear in theatrical scenes on Paestan vase-painting: see Green 1995.109–10 and plate 10.

65 Battaglia and Emiliozzi 1990.276: 'l'incisore colma lo spazio rimasto libero, senza soluzione di continuità, con tre figure di repertorio. . .'

66 Battaglia and Emiliozzi 1990.274–5 (cf. 1979.148).

67 For the similarities between the two scenes, see Battaglia and Emiliozzi 1979.148–9.

very symmetrical scene, and one which implies a contest: 'Glory' and 'Praise' at the sides, 'the rules' in the centre, two sets of two horses, and a man whose name means 'judge' (ἴστωρ). How Laodamia, Ajax and Agamemnon fit in we do not know, but their presence makes it clear that this is not just the celebration of a chariot-race victory (by Soresios?). The contest or race must belong in the age of heroes, or in the afterlife. Here too, as in nos. 50–51, we have an unknown story, but one which could have been a stage performance.

My suggestion is that the young woman dancing with Silanus on no. 45, the young woman with the mirror on no. 82, and the two young women at the basin on nos. 50 and 51, are performers whom we might best describe as *mimae*, portrayed next to but outside the dramas in which they appeared. The matching jewellery suggests that Silanus' partner could have played Doxa, and the girl on no. 82 could have played Iphigeneia; but what about the girls on nos. 50–51? Here, very tentatively, I should like to make a further suggestion.

The editors of the corpus rightly note the 'ampio mantello' of which Iphigeneia is divesting herself on no. 82 [fig. 39 above]. Is it possible that before she took it off, she was wrapped up in it like the woman behind the kneeling captive on nos. 50 and 51 [fig. 40 above]? Young women wrapped up like that are seen dancing in the Bacchic *thiasos* on no. 72 [fig. 20, p. 91 above] and no. 1 [fig. 25, p. 97 above], and also on a *cista* we have not considered yet, no. 31 in the British Museum [fig. 41]. The scene on no. 72 is not obviously dramatic, but it does include a piping satyr. Nos. 1 and 31 show 'composite' scenes, with the *thiasos* merging into a particular story.[68] On no. 31, Dis Pater and Proserpina receive a messenger announcing the death of a youth, who dismounts from his horse just as winged Victoria holds out a diadem to him;[69] the *thiasos* consists of Liber, bowed and supported by a young boy, a grimacing satyr holding a torch reversed, the wrapped-up young woman dancing, another satyr, and a bearded male figure turning to observe the scene in the Underworld.

I suggest that these 'composite' scenes are similar in intention to the piping-satyr motif observed above—that is, they play on the viewer's understanding that Liber is among other things a god of drama,[70] and thus indicate that his followers are not only singing and dancing but also imitating (Plato's word) the legendary story. If that is so, then the young women so conspicuously wrapped up may indeed be part of the performance.

---

68 See n. 32 above for the 'merging' of the *thiasos* and the Perseus and Medusa story on no. 1; on no. 31 the scenes are linked by the turned head of the man on the right.

69 Battaglia and Emiliozzi 1979.117; cf. n. 29 above for Dis Pater.

70 In Athens, the god of drama was Dionysos *Eleuthereus*: for the identification with Liber see Alexander 'Polyhistor' *FGrH* 273 F109 (Plutarch *Moralia* 289a = *Quaestiones Romanae* 104).

Fig. 41 *Cista* no. 31, in the British Museum (Battaglia and Emiliozzi 1979.116–18): scene in Hades, with satyrs.

IV

To sum up the argument so far, I think these *cista* scenes may imply a kind of Dionysiac dramatic performance, perhaps not separable from Dionysiac ritual, in which one feature was the participation of *mimae*. Their role may have evolved from the imitation of nymphs dancing with satyrs, which would at least help to explain its startlingly erotic quality; for what we seem to infer is a dramatic convention by which young women performed wrapped up completely in voluminous cloaks, and then removed them ('in maniera un po' teatrale') to appear spectacularly naked. Not only that, but the stories in which they did so were sometimes plots from the repertoire of Attic tragedy like *Iphigeneia at Aulis*.

Two further *cistae* may illuminate the phenomenon. No. 9, in Berlin [fig. 42], shows *CRISIDA* (Chryseis?) and Ajax between two mounted Amazons called *CASENTER* (Cassandra?) and *OINVMAMA*, watched by a young man in *petasos* and *chlamys* called *ALSES*. Behind Alses, *ALIXENTR* is carrying out a version of the Judgement of Paris in which the contestants are *ATELETA* (Atalanta?), *ALSIR* and *HELENA*. All three of the contestants are naked except for jewellery (the disgruntled Helen is either dropping her cloak or about to put it on again), and Crisida's dress has fallen open at the front. On no. 83, in the Villa Giulia [fig. 43], *CREISITA* and *ELENA* are at the washing-basin by a fountain, both naked and bejewelled, with Helen holding her cloak out behind her in a pose identical to that of Iphigeneia on no. 82. To the left stand *TONDRVS* (Tyndareus?), a figure whose name has been lost, and a warrior called *SECI.LVCVS* holding a horse; to the right are *ACILES* with a horse, a slave called *SIMOS*, and *ORESTE[s]*.

These scenes could be burlesque mythology, with characters and stories deliberately mixed up. If they are from drama, it is probably paratragic. It may not be accidental that Ajax and Atalanta, who feature on *cista* no. 9, both had satyr-plays named after them.[71] But the scenes on the *cistae* may be closer to a less formal dramatic genre, the *paignion*, recently discussed in an important article by James Davidson.[72] Mimic, erotic, with plots from tragedy, *paignia* could be appropriate entertainment for a symposion.[73] The form dates back at least to the fifth century at Athens, with the work of a certain Gnesippus, mentioned by Cratinus as a tragic poet, whom Athenaeus describes as 'a *paignion*-author of the cheerful muse'.[74]

---

71 Aristias' *Atalante* (Pollux 8.31), Polemaeus of Ephesus' *Aias* (*SIG* 3³.1079): Steffen 1952.117, 257.

72 See Davidson 2000.

73 Plutarch *Moralia* 712e-f (*Quaest. conv.* 8); Athenaeus 14.638d–639a. παίζειν and *mimus*: Suetonius *Diuus Augustus* 99.1; cf. Plutarch *Caesar* 10.2 for παίζειν at the Bona Dea rites, on which see Wiseman 1974.130–4. Laevius' *Erotopaignia*: Courtney 1993.118–43.

74 *TGF* 27 T1 = Athenaeus 14.638d (παιγνιαγράφου τῆς ἱλαρᾶς μούσης); Cratinus fr. 256.

Fig. 42 *Cista* no. 9, in the Staatliche Museen, Berlin (Battaglia and Emiliozzi 1979.64–5): Crisida and Ajax.

Fig. 43 *Cista* no. 83, in the Villa Giulia Museum, Rome (Battaglia and Emiliozzi 1990.277–80): Creisita and Elena.

That description is reminiscent of the 'cheerful tragedy' pioneered by Rhinthon of Tarentum in the third century BC.[75] Rhinthon's work has often been associated with the scenes of comedy and mythological burlesque on south-Italian vase-painting (the so-called 'phlyax vases'), but they belong a generation or more earlier.[76] The natural inference is that the vases illustrate various forms of fourth-century dramatic performance in various parts of southern Italy, from sophisticated Tarentum to Oscan-speaking Campania, influenced in varying degrees by the Athenian theatre (and we may add the Syracusan too) but not bound by its generic rules.[77] The scenes on the *cistae* extend that range into Latium, and the spelling of the names implies a culture in which the names of the characters of Greek mythology were known orally, and not (or not primarily) by texts. So if in Latium we seem to find the un-Attic phenomenon of *mimae* displaying themselves naked in roles otherwise appropriate to tragedy, there is no *a priori* reason to doubt the validity of the inference.

A late fourth-century jug in Naples [fig. 44] offers a close iconographic parallel to Iphigeneia and Helen on *cistae* nos. 82 and 83 [figs 39 and 43, pp. 114 and 121 above]: the jewellery, the cloak and the raised arms are the same, but here the young woman's arms and cloak are separately attached to two uprights which look like oars. She is Andromeda, heroine of Euripides' most popular play, 'an openly romantic tale, complete with magic, monsters, and a happy ending'.[78] In all earlier representations of Andromeda's exposure to the monster, she is richly dressed as a barbarian princess. The first time she is represented naked, as was the norm in later Roman art, is precisely here, in Campania in the late fourth century, close in both time and space to the world of the Latin *cistae*.[79] Andromeda was above all a subject for the stage—not only Euripidean tragedy but probably satyr-play too, and later in Latin plays by

---

75 Suda s.v. *Rhinthon*: Ῥίνθων, Ταραντῖνος κωμικός, ἀρχηγὸς τῆς καλουμένης ἱλαροτραγῳδίας, ὃ ἔστι φλυακογραφία. Stephanus of Byzantium s.v. *Taras*: Ῥίνθων, Ταραντῖνος φλύαξ, τὰ τραγικὰ μεταρρυθμίζων ἐς τὸ γελοῖον. Most of his titles are Euripidean (*Herakles, Iphigeneia in Aulis, Iphigeneia in Tauris, Medea, Orestes, Telephus*).

76 Trendall 1959.9; Taplin 1993.48–54.

77 See above, pp. 109–11. See Taplin 1993.89–99 on the 'transplantation of Attic comedy' to Magna Graecia; ibid. 40–1 (plate 16.15) and 94 on Oscan-speaking Campania. Syracusan theatre: comedies by Epicharmus, Phormis and Deinolochus, mimes by Sophron and Xenarchus (Kaibel 1899.87–182); Epicharmus wrote an *Amykos*, a favourite subject on the Latin bronzes (e.g. *cistae* nos. 8, 38, 49, 68), and an *Atalantai* (cf. *cista* no. 9) was attributed to both Epicharmus (frr. 14–18 Kaibel) and to Phormis (Athenaeus 14.652a).

78 Euripides frr. 114–56 Nauck; for its popularity, Aristophanes *Frogs* 52–4 (and the parody at *Thesmophoriazusae* 1009–1134), Athenaeus 12.537d, Lucian *De historia conscribenda* 1; quotation from Michelini 1987.77 [and see now Wright 2005].

79 Phillips 1968.9; Schauenberg 1981.788. Indeed, there is a precise parallel if (as Phillips thinks, 1968.13) the Andromeda scene on *cista* no. ⋆60, in the Louvre, is genuine—but alas, it seems unlikely to be so: see R. Leprévots Trogan, in Battaglia and Emiliozzi 1990.187–8.

Livius Andronicus, Ennius and Accius.[80] The comparable iconography makes it likely, I think, that Helen and Iphigeneia on the *cistae* are on stage too.

The complex iconographic evidence presented here indicates, I think, a common fourth-century culture of mimetic representation extending far beyond the Greek cities of southern Italy into Latium and Etruria. In Apulia [fig. 35, p. 108 above], we see a *kottabos*-playing satyr, a piper, a naked dancing-girl, and a scene from Euripides' *Bacchae*. At Etruscan Clusium [figs 37 and 38, pp. 112–13 above], we have a dancing satyr and a scene described in the prologue of Euripides' *Helen*, with the *mimae* losing their cloaks and displaying themselves naked as they protect the delusive swan from the eagle. In Naples [fig. 44], a naked *mima* plays Euripides' *Andromeda*. In Latium [fig.

Fig. 44 Campanian jug (Trendall 1967, Campanian 2/138): Andromeda.

---

80 Satyr-play: a plot involving Perseus is inferred from vase-painting (Brommer 1944.25–9, figs 21–3). Livius fr. 18R (Nonius 86L), Ennius frr. 97–106R (=112–19 Jocelyn), Accius frr. 100–118R (=380–97 Dangel).

39, p. 114 above], the *cista* scene shows satyrs piping and dancing, and a naked *mima* dropping her cloak as Euripides' *Iphigeneia at Aulis*. There is no reason to suppose that Rome was in any way immune to this culture of Dionysiac *mimesis*, or that it had been somehow lost before literary drama was introduced there by Livius Andronicus three or four generations later.

V

Livius Andronicus came from Tarentum.[81] If the Varronian chronology is correct, and he produced his first play in Rome in 240 BC,[82] he was a near-contemporary of Rhinthon and must have been very familiar with the 'cheerful tragedy' mode; perhaps his *Andromeda* was an example of it.[83]

Just at the time of his Roman debut, at a date variously transmitted as 241 and 238 BC, the plebeian aediles, who had their headquarters at the temple of Liber, struck a blow for the Roman People by prosecuting wealthy landowners who were grazing their beasts on public land.[84] They used the fines to build a new temple to Flora, immediately next door to the Liber temple, and set up games in honour of the goddess. According to Ovid (who reports Flora's own account), the Senate refused to fund the games on an annual basis until forced to do so by the goddess' anger in 173 BC.[85] The reason was presumably the Senate's disapproval of the licentious nature of the games, which in later times at least involved *mimae* undressing on stage.[86]

Three and a half centuries of ill-attested cultural change lie between the engraving of the *cistae* and our literary evidence for the *ludi Florales*. Inevitably, the argument connecting them is a tenuous one. But inadequate though the evidence is, I think there is enough of it to justify the tentative hypothesis that the scenes on the *cistae* reflect one type at least of mimetic performance in fourth-century Latium. If Greeks called it *paignia*, Latins might translate that as *ludi*.[87]

---

81 Accius fr. 18 Funaioli (Cicero *Brutus* 72).

82 Varro *De poetis* fr. 55 Funaioli (Aulus Gellius 17.21.42); Cicero *Brutus* 72, *De senectute* 50; cf. Cassiodorus *Chronica* on 239 BC. For the chronological problem (Accius put it much later), see most recently Oakley 1998.61–3.

83 *Rhinthonica* known at Rome: Cicero *Ad Atticum* 1.20.3, Donatus *De comoedia* 6.1, Evanthius *De comoedia* 4.1, Lydus *De magistratibus* 1.40.

84 Ovid *Fasti* 5.279–90; Velleius Paterculus 1.14.8 (241 BC), Pliny *Nat. Hist.* 18.286 (238 BC). Cf. Wiseman 1979.93–4 and n. 124, arguing for 240 BC (the consulship of C. Claudius Cento) as a possible date for the origin of the *Floralia*; note that *cento* means 'patchwork', and that at Flora's games it was the custom to wear multi-coloured clothes (Ovid *Fasti* 5.356, *cultu uersicolore*).

85 Ovid *Fasti* 5.291–330, Tacitus *Annals* 2.49.1; cf. Varro *De lingua Latina* 5.158, Festus 276L.

86 Valerius Maximus 2.10.8 (*priscus mos iocorum*), Seneca *Epistles* 97.8; cf. Ovid *Fasti* 4.946 and 5.331–56, Martial 1 pref. and 1.35.8–9, Tertullian *De spectaculis* 17, Arnobius 3.23 and 7.33, Lactantius *Institutiones diuinae* 1.20.6–10, Augustine *City of God* 2.27, Historia Augusta *Heliogabalus* 6.5, Ausonius 7.24.25–6. [See pp. 175–86 below for the games of Flora.]

87 For *ludere* and παίζειν, see above, nn. 12 and 73.

This suggestion is of course hardly compatible with the late-republican history of the origin and development of Roman drama, as reconstructed by Varro and transmitted to us by Livy, Horace and Valerius Maximus.[88] Varro's view depended on the assumption that drama derived from rustic festivals, and that in the early Republic the Romans were peasants innocent of Greek literary culture. As Horace puts it in a too-famous passage,[89]

> *agricolae prisci fortes paruoque beati,*
> *condita post frumenta leuantes tempore festo*
> *corpus et ipsum animum spe finis dura ferentem,*
> *cum sociis operum pueris et coniuge fida*
> *Tellurem porco, Siluanum lacte piabant,*
> *floribus et uino Genium memorem breuis aeui . . .*
> *Graecia capta ferum uictorem cepit et artes*
> *intulit agresti Latio. sic horridus ille*
> *defluxit numerus Saturnius et graue uirus*
> *munditiae pepulere; sed in longum tamen aeuum*
> *manserunt hodieque manent uestigia ruris.*
> *serus enim Graecis admouit acumina chartis,*
> *et post Punica bella quietus quaerere coepit*
> *quid Sophocles et Thespis et Aeschylus utile ferrent.*

The men of old were tough farmers content with little. After the harvest was brought in, they relaxed body and mind at holiday time, for the mind endures hard work by the prospect of an end to it. With the boys and faithful wives who shared their labours, they appeased Tellus with a pig, Silvanus with milk, and Genius, who knows how short life is, with flowers and wine...

When Greece was captured, it took the fierce victor captive and brought the arts into rustic Latium. That's how the crude Saturnian metre drained away, and elegance drove out the offensive smell; but traces of the farmyard remained for a long time, and still remain today. For it was only late that [the Roman] applied his intelligence to Greek pages, and in the peace after the Punic Wars began to ask what use Sophocles and Thespis and Aeschylus could be.

This passage represents just one of the paradigms of early Rome in the antiquarian tradition; precisely the opposite picture is offered by Cicero in *De republica*, who argues that since Romulus post-dated Homer, the Romans at the time of the foundation lived in an age when literary culture was long familiar and primitive conditions had long been dispelled.[90] Both notions are

---

88 Livy 7.2, Horace *Epistles* 2.1.139–76, Valerius Maximus 2.4.4; cf. also Virgil *Georgics* 2.380–96; Schmidt 1989, Oakley 1998.40–58.

89 Horace *Epistles* 2.1.139–44, 156–63; detailed commentary in Brink 1982.175–215.

90 Cicero *De republica* 2.18–19: *iam inueteratis litteris atque doctrinis omnique illo antiquo ex inculta hominum uita errore sublato.*

learned reconstructions deployed as part of an argument, and neither has any historical validity. How could Horace or Cicero have known what early Rome was like?

Unfortunately, however, Horace's epigram about *Graecia capta* has predisposed some modern scholars to reject the possibility of significant Greek influence on Roman culture before the second century BC. So for instance Richard Beacham, in an otherwise valuable book on Roman stagecraft, can follow his account of the theatre in Magna Graecia with this assertion:[91]

> It is most unlikely that Rome of the mid-fourth century was in any position either geographically or culturally to benefit directly from such a sophisticated theatrical culture. Roman visitors may possibly have been bemused observers from time to time of performances in Greek theatres, but they would have brought back only travellers' tales of practices, entertaining perhaps to recount to their families and friends, but aesthetically too advanced to be understood or to influence the growth of whatever crude drama was germinating at Rome.

The influence of Horace's patronising paradigm is clearly detectable here; but the iconography of the *cistae*, and the artistic sophistication they represent, are enough to refute it completely.

Varro's 'theoretical construction' of the prehistory of the Roman theatre is much indebted to Eratosthenes' researches into Attic drama.[92] That is a familiar technique: in the absence of good evidence, analogy can provide the material.[93] But Varro also had an ideological reason to attribute a native and rustic origin to Roman drama. He had strong views about the theatre in his own time, particularly its portrayal of the gods,[94] and it is very likely that he blamed its deplorable aspects on Greek influence corrupting an honest native tradition. So those tough old farmers are imagined as sacrificing not to Ceres (Demeter) or Liber (Dionysus), but to Latin gods untainted by Greek myth—Tellus, Silvanus and Genius.

As the power of fertility both human and agricultural,[95] Genius receives flowers and wine, offerings that Horace's readers would associate with Flora

---

91 Beacham 1991.7–8.
92 See Horsfall 1994, esp.66–70; quotation from Rawson 1985.274.
93 For examples in historiography, see Soltau 1909.73–91. There evidently was some archival evidence for the Roman theatre (the *commentarii* cited at Cicero *Brutus* 60 and 72), but it is not likely to have gone back to the fourth century BC.
94 Varro *Antiquitates rerum diuinarum* frr. 7 and 10 Cardauns (cf. Wiseman 1998.17–24); note that one of the 'tales unworthy of the gods' to which he objects is the birth of Pegasus (fr. 7, *ex guttis sanguinis natus*), as illustrated on *cista* no. 1.
95 Varro *Antiquitates rerum diuinarum* fr. 248 Cardauns: *uim habet omnium rerum gignendarum*. He was thought of as the father of Tages, who was born from a ploughed field (Festus 492L, Cicero *De diuinatione* 2.50); and he was identified as the *Lar familiaris* (Censorinus 3.2), who manifested himself as the phallus in the hearth to beget Servius Tullius (Pliny *Nat. Hist.* 36.204).

Mater and Liber Pater; and it is Genius who is mindful of the shortness of human life, which according to Ovid was Flora's justification for the licentiousness of her games.[96] Liber and Flora were the gods of fertility honoured in Roman public ritual, and their conspicuous omission here must be by deliberate choice.[97] So the Varronian model for the origin of Roman drama is indeed of great historical importance—but not as evidence for the real conditions of the fourth century BC. Rather it is an example of the ongoing ideological sensitivity of Liber and Flora.

Liber had his ancient cult and temple, shared with Ceres and Libera, at the foot of the Aventine; it was the headquarters of the plebeian aediles, and their use of it as an archive for senatorial decrees was represented as an important aspect of the *libertas* restored after the tyranny of the Decemvirs.[98] The *cistae* reveal total familiarity with Dionysiac imagery and ritual in the fourth century BC, and seem also to attest a type of drama, or mimetic performance, which combined mythic narrative with erotic burlesque. About 240 BC the People's representatives built a temple to Flora next to that of Liber, Ceres and Libera, and introduced games of which the Senate refused to approve. At the end of the third century BC we find Naevius, a politically controversial playwright, referring to the *ludi* of the *Liberalia* as a forum for freedom of speech. In 186 BC the specifically Dionysiac aspects of the cult of Liber were brutally suppressed. Flora's games, however, were recognised at last in 173 BC, perhaps as a necessary concession to popular feeling.[99]

In the light of all that, it is not surprising that a culturally conservative antiquarian like Varro would create a prehistory of Roman drama which left out Liber completely. His reconstruction, as transmitted by Livy, Horace and Valerius Maximus, cannot stand against the visual evidence of the *cistae*. The scenes they show are hard to interpret, but they are at least a contemporary source.

---

96 Horace *Epistles* 2.1.144, Ovid *Fasti* 5.353–4. Flora Mater: e.g. Cicero *Verrines* 5.36, Lucretius 5.739. Liber Pater: e.g. Varro *De re rustica* 1.2.19, Horace *Epistles* 2.1.5. Association of sex, flowers and wine: Ovid *Fasti* 5.331–54 on Flora and Bacchus.

97 Liber as phallic god of fertility: Varro *Antiquitates rerum diuinarum* fr. 262 Cardauns (Augustine *City of God* 7.21). Flora presides over all fertility, including human: Ovid *Fasti* 5.261–74.

98 Temple: Dionysius of Halicarnassus 6.17.2–4, 6.94.3 ('vowed in 496 BC, dedicated in 493'), with Wiseman 1998.35–6. Aediles: Livy 3.55.7 and 13 (3.55.1–56.1 on *libertas* restored in 449), 10.23.13, 26.6.19, 26.36.9, 33.25.2–3.

99 See above, pp. 84–5, 124. I have suggested elsewhere that Ampelius' reference to Liber the son of Flora (9.11) may reflect the post–186 situation, when Semele as Liber's mother was too closely associated with the Bacchanals: Wiseman 1998.41–2.

VI

The cult of Ceres, Liber and Libera and the cult of Flora both involved games which were set up as a result of famine, after consultation of the Sibylline books;[100] the goddess of agriculture, the god of viticulture and the goddess of the flowering spring had to be placated or the Roman People would starve. But both sets of *ludi* were politically controversial: as we have seen, the Senate refused for sixty-five years to make Flora's games annual, and at some point in the second century BC Liber's games were taken away from the *Liberalia* and merged with those of Ceres in April.[101]

Marsyas too, the servant of Liber,[102] may have featured in these ill-attested ideological tensions. His old enemy Apollo was honoured with *ludi* in 212 BC, and it is clear from Livy's account that the innovation was the Senate's reaction to the demands of agitators at a time of popular dissatisfaction. But Apollo failed to bring about the end of the war, which had been the purpose of the exercise; that was done by the Phrygian Magna Mater, who was brought to Rome in 204 and granted her own temple and *ludi*.[103] Marsyas was part of the Magna Mater's story:[104]

> συναναστρέφεσθαι δ' αὐτῇ καὶ φιλίαν ἔχειν ἐπὶ πλέον φασὶ Μαρσύαν
> τὸν Φρύγα, θαυμαζόμενον ἐπὶ συνέσει καὶ σωφροσύνῃ· καὶ τῆς μὲν
> συνέσεως τεκμήριον λαμβάνουσι τὸ μιμήσασθαι τοὺς φθόγγους τῆς
> πολυκαλάμου σύριγγος καὶ μετενεγκεῖν ἐπὶ τοὺς αὐλοὺς τὴν ὅλην
> ἁρμονίαν, τῆς δὲ σωφροσύνης σημεῖον εἶναι φασι τὸ μέχρι τῆς
> τελευτῆς ἀπείρατον γενέσθαι τῶν ἀφροδισίων.
>
> The man who associated with her and loved her more than anyone else, they
> say, was Marsyas the Phrygian, who was admired for his intelligence and
> chastity. A proof of his intelligence they find in the fact that he imitated the
> sounds made by the pipe of many reeds and carried all its notes over into the
> flute, and as an indication of his chastity they cite his abstinence from sexual
> pleasures until the day of his death.

Here is a very different Marsyas from the presumptuous satyr who was taught his place by Apollo. That surprising quality of sexual abstinence may have been emphasised at the time when the rites of his master Liber—the *Bacchanalia* held

---

100 Ceres, Liber, Libera: Dionysius of Halicarnassus 6.17.2–4, [Cyprian] *De spectaculis* 4.1. Flora: Pliny *Nat. Hist.* 18.286, Degrassi 1963.132–3 (*Fasti Praenestini* on 28 April); cf. Ovid *Fasti* 5.311–30 on the games made annual in 173.

101 Ovid *Fasti* 5.311–30 (Flora), 3.785–6 (Liber).

102 See above, pp. 99–100.

103 Livy 25.1.6–12, 25.12.2–15 (*ludi Apollinares*); 29.14.14, 34.54.3, 36.3.4 (*ludi Megalenses*).

104 Diodorus Siculus 3.58.3. Cf. Solinus 1.8–9 (Cn. Gellius fr. 7P) on the Phrygian Megales, ambassador of king Marsyas, who taught the Sabines the art of augury; his name evidently alludes to the Magna Mater.

at Stimula's grove close to the temple of Ceres, Liber and Libera—were alleged to be orgies of sexual abuse.[105]

It is tempting to see the suppression of the *Bacchanalia* in 186 BC as the Senate's reimposition of Apolline authority. Perhaps something of the sort may be inferred from the censors' arrangements in 179 and 174:[106]

> *theatrum et proscaenium ad Apollinis ... locauit ... scaenam aedilibus praetoribus praebendam ... curauerunt.*
>
> [M. Lepidus the censor] contracted for a theatre and proscaenium at the temple of Apollo ... [The censors] saw to it that a stage be placed at the disposal of the aediles and praetors.

Does this mean that the temple of Apollo *in circo Flaminio* was being organised as the centre for *ludi* in general? (Only the *ludi Apollinares* were under the praetor's control; the aediles looked after the other games.) We don't know when Liber lost his *ludi* at the *Liberalia*,[107] but this would certainly be an appropriate time. However, Ovid is explicit that a famine in 173 forced the Senate to make Flora's games annual; since Flora could be thought of as the mother of Liber, it seems that the ideological issue was not quite settled after all.[108]

Forty years later, in the political crisis after the murder of Tiberius Gracchus, the Sibylline books ordered the Romans to placate *Ceres antiquissima*; that was interpreted to mean the Demeter of Enna in Sicily, whose daughter Persephone was now identified as Libera. Cicero notes that the *decemuiri sacris faciundis* deliberately did not involve the goddess at the Roman temple of Ceres, Liber and Libera.[109] Yet again, though the details escape us, there seems to be an ideological question at stake. Though it was clear who would be offended at the death of the People's champion, the senatorial interpreters of the will of the gods were evidently eager to move the confrontation out of Rome.

At Philippi in 41 BC, 'the last struggle of the Free State',[110] Brutus' password was *Libertas*, and that of the Caesarians was *Apollo*. Part of the mythology of the defeat was that Brutus had applied to himself the words of the dying Patroclus: 'deadly fate and the son of Leto have killed me.'[111]

---

105 Livy 39.8–19; for the location of the *lucus Stimulae* (Livy 39.12.5, Ovid *Fasti* 6.503, *CIL* 6.9897) see Cazanove 1986.56–66.

106 Livy 40.51.3, 41.27.5.

107 The *terminus post quem* is Naevius fr. 113R (p. 85 above).

108 Ovid *Fasti* 5.311–30; Ampelius 9.11 (n. 99 above).

109 Cicero *Verrines* 4.108, cf. 106, 109 and 5.187 for Libera.

110 Syme 1939.205.

111 Dio Cassius 47.43.1, Valerius Maximus 1.5.7, quoting *Iliad* 16.849. Plutarch's version (*Brutus* 24.7), that 'Apollo' was Brutus' own password, is probably an error; it is preferred by Gurval 1995.98–100, who however ignores the Dio reference.

The young Caesar claimed to be Apollo's son, or Apollo himself,[112] but when he masqueraded as the god at a time of famine (probably in 40 or 39), popular reaction was very hostile:[113]

> *cena quoque eius secretior in fabulis fuit, quae uulgo* δωδεκάθεος *uocabatur; in qua deorum dearumque habitu discubuisse conuiuas et ipsum pro Apolline ornatum non Antoni modo epistulae singulorum nomina amarissime enumerantis exprobrant sed et sine auctore notissimi uersus:*
>
>> *cum primum istorum conduxit mensa choregum*
>>> *sexque deos uidit Mallia sexque deas,*
>> *impia dum Phoebi Caesar mendacia ludit,*
>>> *dum noua diuorum cenat adulteria,*
>> *omnia se a terris tunc numina declinarunt*
>>> *fugit et auratos Iuppiter ipse thronos.*
>
> *auxit cenae rumorem summa tunc in ciuitate penuria ac fames, adclamatumque est postridie omne frumentum deos comedisse et Caesarem esse plane Apollinem sed Tortorem, quo cognomina is deus quadam in parte urbis colebatur.*

There was besides a private dinner of his, commonly called that of the 'twelve gods', which was the subject of gossip. At this the guests appeared in the guise of gods and goddesses, while he himself was made up to represent Apollo, as was charged not merely in letters of Antony, who spitefully gives the names of all the guests, but also in these anonymous lines, which everyone knows: 'As soon as that table of rascals had secured a choragus and Mallia saw six gods and six goddesses, while Caesar impiously played the false role of Apollo and feasted amid novel debaucheries of the gods, then all the deities turned their faces from the earth and Jupiter himself fled from his golden throne.' The scandal of this banquet was the greater because of dearth and famine in the land at that time, and on the following day there was an outcry that the gods had eaten all the grain and that Caesar was in truth Apollo, but Apollo the Tormentor, a surname under which the god was worshipped in one part of the city.

There is an interesting parallel between this passage and the description of Antony in Asia after the Philippi campaign:[114]

εἰς γοῦν Ἔφεσον εἰσιόντος αὐτοῦ, γυναῖκες μὲν εἰς Βάκχας, ἄνδρες δὲ καὶ παῖδες εἰς σατύρους καὶ Πᾶνας ἡγοῦντο διεσκευασμένοι, κιττοῦ δὲ

---

112 Domitius Marsus fr. 8 (Courtney 1993.304–5), Dio Cassius 45.1.2, Suetonius *Diuus Augustus* 94.4 (= Asclepiades of Mendes *FGrH* 617 F2). See now Gurval 1995.87–136, who puts Octavian's association with Apollo very late.

113 Suetonius *Diuus Augustus* 70.1–2 (trans. J.C. Rolfe, Loeb Classical Library 1913). Famine: Appian *Civil Wars* 5.67–8, Dio Cassius 48.31.1.

114 Plutarch *Antony* 24.3–4 (trans. Ian Scott-Kilvert, Penguin Classics 1965); cf. 26.3 on Antony in Cilicia.

καὶ θύρσων καὶ ψαλτηρίων καὶ συρίγγων καὶ αὐλῶν ἡ πόλις ἦν πλέα,
Διόνυσον αὐτὸν ἀνακαλουμένων Ψαριδότην καὶ Μειλίχιον. ἦν γὰρ
ἀμέλει τοιοῦτος ἐνίοις, τοῖς δὲ πολλοῖς Ὠμηστὴς καὶ Ἀγριώνιος.
ἀφῄρειτο γὰρ εὐγενεῖς ἀνθρώπους τὰ ὄντα, μαστιγίαις καὶ κόλαξι
χαριζόμενος.

At any rate, when Antony made his entry into Ephesus, women arrayed like
Bacchantes and men and boys like satyrs and Pans led the way before him, and
the city was full of ivy and thyrsus-wands and harps and pipes and flutes, the
people hailing him as Dionysus Giver of Joy and Beneficent. For he was so,
undoubtedly, to some; but to the greater part he was Dionysus Carnivorous
and Savage. For he took their property from well-born men and bestowed it on
flatterers and scoundrels.

In each case the divine identification has to be accepted. Opponents may insist
on the harmful aspects of the respective gods, but Octavian *is* Apollo, Antony
is Dionysus (i.e. Liber).

Moreover, it seems that this mythology reflects the same ideological
polarity that can be detected in the third and second centuries BC. For 'Apollo
the torturer' must surely be an allusion to the Marsyas myth, where the god's
victory consists of Marsyas hanging from the tree, flayed alive. But Marsyas is
the servant of Liber, his statue is the guarantee of the People's freedom, his
gesture announces that the city lacks nothing.[115] If he is tortured, of course
there's a famine!

VII

It was not until the corn supply was under control again, after the defeat of
Sextus Pompeius, that Octavian vowed his temple to Apollo and began
creating the great complex on the Palatine that would eventually be dedicated
on 9 October 28 BC.[116] The site was on the brow of the hill, overlooking the
Forum Bovarium and the lower part of the Circus Maximus valley. Directly
opposite was the temple of Ceres, Liber and Libera, on the lower slope of the
Aventine 'just above the starting-gates of the Circus'; described by Cicero as
pulcherrimum et magnificentissimum,[117] it was a splendid monument to Antony's
patron god—and therefore, perhaps, offensive to Apollo and Octavian. In 31
BC, however, with the Apollo temple still under construction and Octavian

---

115 See above, pp. 99–100. The connection is made by Feeney 1991.220–1.
116 Vow: Velleius Paterculus 2.81.3, Dio Cassius 49.15.5. Dedication: Dio Cassius 53.1.3,
    Degrassi 1963.209 (*Fasti Antiates* on 9 October).
117 Dionysius of Halicarnassus 6.94.3 (site), Cicero *Verrines* 4.108. Had the old fifth-century
    temple been rebuilt? If so, it is not known when or by whom.

away fighting the Actium campaign, the eyesore was suddenly and fortuitously removed:[118]

> καὶ πῦρ ἄλλα τε οὐκ ὀλίγα καὶ αὐτοῦ τοῦ ἱπποδρόμου πολὺ τό τε Δημήτριον καὶ ἕτερον ναὸν Ἐλπίδος ἔφθειρεν. ἔδοξαν μὲν γὰρ οἱ ἐξελεύθεροι αὐτὸ πεποιηκέναι· πᾶσι γὰρ τοῖς ἔν τε τῇ Ἰταλίᾳ αὐτῶν οὖσι καὶ πέντε μυριάδων οὐσίαν ἢ καὶ πλείω κεκτημένοις τὸ ὄγδοον αὐτῆς συντελέσαι ἐκελεύσθη, κἀκ τούτου καὶ ταραχαὶ καὶ φόνοι καὶ ἐμπρήσεις ὑπ' αὐτῶν πολλαὶ ἐγένοντο, καὶ οὐ πρότερόν γε κατέστησαν πρὶν ἢ τοῖς ὅπλοις καταδαμασθῆναι.

Fire also consumed a considerable portion of the Circus itself, along with the temple of Ceres, another shrine dedicated to Spes, and a large number of other structures. The freedmen were thought to have caused this; for all of them who were in Italy and possessed property worth two hundred thousand sesterces or more had been ordered to contribute an eighth of it. This resulted in numerous riots, murders, and the burning of many buildings on their part, and they were not brought to order until they were subdued by armed force.

Flora's temple too must have been destroyed—and it is a remarkable fact that in the *Georgics*, published the following year, the goddess of bloom and growth is not so much as mentioned.[119]

In 28 BC, the year of the dedication of the Apollo temple, Octavian on the Senate's instructions rebuilt 82 temples, 'omitting none which deserved to be rebuilt at that time'.[120] What exactly does *quod eo tempore refici debebat* mean? It is clear that neither the Ceres-Liber-Libera temple nor the temple of Flora qualified for inclusion, since the date of their rededication is given by Tacitus as AD 17, forty-seven years after the fire that destroyed them.[121] Evidently Augustus was content to do without those two temples for the greater part of his principate. For the citizens in the bustling Circus Maximus quarter there was to be no rival centre of loyalty. They had only to look up, and there against the blue sky was the great marble pediment of Apollo's temple, with his bronze *quadriga* flashing in the sun. It was from above (*desuper*) that Apollo exerted his authority.[122]

---

118 Dio Cassius 50.10.3–4 (included in a list of portents, 50.10.6).

119 See Fantham 1992, esp. 49–52; contrast Lucretius 5.739, Cicero *Verrines* 5.36, Varro *De re rustica* 1.1.5–6.

120 Augustus *Res gestae* 20.4, cf. Livy 4.20.7 (*templorum omnium conditorem aut restitutorem*), Suetonius *Diuus Augustus* 30.2, Dio Cassius 53.2.4–5.

121 Tacitus *Annals* 2.49.1: *isdem temporibus deum aedis uetustate aut igni abolitas coeptasque ab Augusto dedicauit, Libero Liberaeque et Cereri iuxta circum maximum, quam A. Postumius dictator uouerat, eodemque in loco Florae ab Lucio et Marco Publiciis aedilibus constitutam...*

122 Propertius 2.31.9–11; Virgil *Aeneid* 8.705, 9.639.

It is a measure of Augustus' effective power that he could do such a thing. In 23 BC, when his life was threatened by serious illness, the *Odes* of Horace were published, including one which must have touched some anxieties in Rome:[123]

> *delicta maiorum inmeritus lues,*
> *Romane, donec templa refeceris*
>   *aedesque labentis deorum et*
>   *foeda nigro simulacra fumo.*
> *dis te minorem quod geris, imperas:*
> *hinc omne principium, huc refer exitum.*
>   *di multa neglecti dederunt*
>   *Hesperiae mala luctuosae.*

Roman, though innocent you will pay for your ancestors' misdeeds until you have restored the gods' temples and falling shrines and statues foul with black smoke. You only rule because you recognise the gods' superiority: put down every beginning and end to that. Neglected gods have inflicted many evils on sorrowing Hesperia.

The following year there was famine. Surely Ceres, Liber and Flora must be propitiated, as they had been in the past? But no: Augustus took the *cura annonae* on himself, and the crisis passed.[124]

Meanwhile, the talismanic statue of Marsyas still stood in the Forum, crowned with flowers by the citizens he protected. The elder Pliny reports a curious story:[125]

> *P. Munatius cum demptam Marsuae coronam e floribus capiti suo inposuisset atque ob id*
> *duci cum in uincula triumuiri iussissent, appellauit tribunis plebis, nec intercessere illi.*
> Publius Munatius took a chaplet of flowers from the statue of Marsyas and put it on his own head. Ordered by the *triumuiri* [*capitales*] to be put in chains for his offence, he appealed to the tribunes of the *plebs*, who refused to intervene.

But Pliny goes on to quote a letter of Augustus complaining about his daughter Julia for doing just the opposite—not taking a garland from Marsyas but

---

123 Horace *Odes* 3.6.1–8 (the last of the 'Roman Odes'); Dio Cassius 53.30.1–4 for Augustus' illness.

124 Dio Cassius 54.1.1–4, Augustus *Res gestae* 5.1–2. It was to Terra Mater, not Ceres, that sacrifice was made at the Secular Games in 17 BC (*CIL* 6.32323.136, but Ceres in Horace *Carmen saeculare* 30); and it may have been an Augustan innovation to have the *lectisternium* to Ceres on the festival day of Tellus, at her temple on the Carinae (Arnobius 7.32; Degrassi 1963.136–7, *Fasti Praenestini* on 13 December).

125 Pliny *Nat. Hist.* 21.8 (on the *licentia* of wearing garlands during the day).

putting one on him. The natural inference is that her gesture was a statement of *libertas*, which he interpreted as *licentia* and *luxuria*.[126]

The letter was no doubt his justification to the Senate for the banishment of Julia in 2 BC. Seneca's description of that event also implies the significance of Marsyas as a symbol of *licentia*:[127]

> *Diuus Augustus filiam ultra impudicitiae maledictum impudicam relegauit et flagitia principalis domus in publicum emisit: admissos gregatim adulteros, pererratam nocturnis comissationibus ciuitatem, forum ipsum ac rostra, ex quibus pater legem de adulteriis tulerat, filiae in stupra placuisse, cotidianum ad Marsyam concursum, cum ex adultera in quaestuariam uersa ius omnis licentiae sub ignoto adultero peteret.*

The deified Augustus banished his daughter, whose immorality went beyond her bad reputation for it, and he brought the scandals of the imperial house into the open—the adulterers admitted in droves, the nocturnal parties roaming round the city, the Forum itself (and the Rostra from which her father had proposed the law against adultery) as the favourite place for her sexual debauchery, the daily gathering at the statue of Marsyas, where from being an adulteress she became a paid harlot, and claimed the right to every licence under a lover she didn't even know.

Marsyas was the servant of Antony's patron god; the most conspicuous of Julia's lovers, now duly executed for treason, was Antony's son.[128]

VIII

Apolline authority was still being exercised, but progressively from now on matters slipped out of Augustus' control. By AD 4 *atrox fortuna* had robbed him of his sons Gaius and Lucius; by AD 7 Agrippa Postumus had been disinherited and Pannonia was in revolt; what was worse, throughout that three-year period there was disastrous famine in Rome.[129]

This was probably the time when Ovid was writing his *Fasti*. In that poem Augustus' Apollo is hardly mentioned;[130] Ceres, Liber and Flora, on the other hand, are given extensive treatment, as is required by their respective festivals. For the *Liberalia* in book 3, Ovid elaborately declines to narrate the birth and *res gestae* of the god, preferring to concentrate on the honey-cakes (*liba* from Liber) provided at his festival:[131]

---

126 Pliny *Nat. Hist.* 21.9: *apud nos exemplum licentiae huius non est aliud quam filia diui Augusti, cuius luxuria noctibus coronatum Marsuam litterae illius dei gemunt.*

127 Seneca *De beneficiis* 6.32.1; cf. Velleius Paterculus 2.100.3 on Julia's *licentia* (*quidquid liberet pro licito uindicans*).

128 Velleius Paterculus 2.100.4, Tacitus *Annals* 4.44.3, Dio Cassius 55.10.15.

129 Dio Cassius 55.22.3, 55.26.1–3, 55.27.1, 55.31.3–4, 55.33.4.

130 Only at 4.951 and 6.91.

131 Ovid *Fasti* 3.715, 724–6.

nec referam Semelen . . .

. . . non est carminis huius opus;

carminis huius opus causas exponere quare

uitisator populos ad sua liba uocet.

I shall not tell of Semele [or the birth from Jupiter's thigh, or the conquest of Thrace, Scythia and India, or Pentheus or Lycurgus or the Tyrrhenian pirates]; that is not the business of this song. The business of this song is to explain the reasons why the Vine-planter invites the people to eat his honey-cakes.

Feeding the People is what matters. For the *Cerialia* in book 4, Ovid tells the old story of Demeter and Persephone, ending with the goddess' restoration of the grain harvest:[132]

tum demum uoltumque Ceres animumque recepit

imposuitque suae spicea serta comae;

largaque prouenit cessatis messis in aruis,

et uix congestas area cepit opes.

Then at last Ceres recovered her looks and her spirit and put wreaths of corn-ears in her hair; a generous harvest came forth in the fallow fields, and the threshing-floor could hardly hold the heaped-up riches.

And for the *Floralia* in book 5, Ovid has the goddess herself tell how she punished the Senate's neglect of her:[133]

'nos quoque tangit honor; festis gaudemus et aris,

turbaque caelestes ambitiosa sumus. . .

at si neglegimur magnis iniuria poenis

soluitur et iustum praeterit ira modum. . .

longa referre mora est correcta obliuia damnis.

me quoque Romani praeteriere patres.'

'We too are touched by honour; enjoying festivals and sacrifices, we dwellers in heaven are an ambitious lot. . . But if we are neglected the crime is paid for with heavy punishments, and our anger goes beyond the just limit. . . It would take a long time to list examples of forgetfulness corrected by disasters. Even I was once overlooked by the Roman Senate.'

And the punishment she inflicted, in 173 BC, was famine. We should remember that it was the Senate who had authorised the programme of temple restoration in 28 BC, and thus left Ceres, Liber and Flora for all this time without their temples in the Circus Maximus. Not even the subtlest of poets

---

132 Ovid *Fasti* 4.615–18; for the famine, see *Metamporphoses* 5.474–86 (from *Homeric Hymn to Ceres* 305–13).

133 Ovid *Fasti* 5.297–8, 303–4, 311–12.

could blame the *princeps*; but whoever was thought to be responsible, it is hard to believe that in a time of famine Ovid's readers failed to notice the topicality of these passages.

This time, it seems, Augustus gave in. The temples were rebuilt, and rededicated in due course by Tiberius. But it would be wrong to see that as a victory in the long ideological struggle. Palatine Apollo at the house of Augustus retained his supremacy, and *libertas* was now defended by the Praetorian Guard.[134] Marsyas in the Forum still presided over the welfare of the city, but now it took the form of imperial munificence, celebrated in grand marble reliefs for the citizens to admire.[135] The mythology of Liber and Marsyas had been a republican phenomenon, an example of what Tacitus called *plebis et optimatium certamina*. It still had real life in it for the first generation or two of the Augustan principate, but gradually the reality of power turned all such phenomena into mere *simulacra libertatis* (another Tacitean phrase).[136]

IX

Inevitably, given the nature of the evidence, this story of Liber, *ludi* and *libertas* has been uneven and incomplete. And only now, at the end of it, are we in a position to ask how it began.

According to Dionysius of Halicarnassus, the temple and games of Ceres, Liber and Libera were vowed in 496 BC by the dictator A. Postumius Albus, victor of the battle of Lake Regillus, and inaugurated three years later. That tradition, unknown to Livy, can be traced to the history of A. Postumius Albinus in the mid-second century BC; but since the historian was a cousin of the consul Sp. Postumius Albinus who in 186 BC was responsible for the suppression of the *Bacchanalia*, his testimony on the origin of the cult is not to be accepted without question.[137] There is no contemporary evidence, but events in Athens may suggest another possibility.

According to the *Athenaion Politeia*, the Pisistratids were expelled from Athens in the archonship of Harpaktides, i.e. 511/10 BC.[138] The dramatic contests at the 'City Dionysia', which took place towards the end of March at the precinct of Dionysus Eleuthereus on the slope of the Acropolis, probably began in 502/1 BC.[139] The chronological sequence strongly suggests an ideo-

---

134 Josephus *Antiquities* 19.42 (a claim denied by an old-fashioned lover of liberty, Cassius Chaerea).
135 *Anaglypha Traiani*: Torelli 1982.89–109, with figs IV.1–16 (Marsyas at IV 8–9, 14).
136 Tacitus *Annals* 4.32.1, 1.77.3.
137 Dionysius of Halicarnassus 6.10.1, 6.17.2–4, 6.94.3; Wiseman 1998.35–6.
138 [Aristotle] *Athenaion politeia* 19.6; Rhodes 1981.191–9.
139 *IG* 2².2318; Pickard-Cambridge 1968.101–7. Alleged earlier dates for victories by Thespis and Choerilus are not reliable: West 1989.

logical connection between Eleuthereus and the freedom of Athens from the tyranny of Hippias.[140]

Compare Rome. According to Polybius, the Tarquins were expelled twenty-eight years before Xerxes' invasion of Greece, i.e. 508/7 BC.[141] The *Liberalia* took place on 17 March at the temple of Ceres, Liber and Libera on the slope of the Aventine overlooking the open space of the Circus Maximus. At least by the first century BC, Liber could be identified as Dionysus Eleuthereus.[142] It is tempting to infer that the association of Liber and *libertas* had the same origin as that of Eleuthereus and ἐλευθερία, celebrating the expulsion of Tarquin three years after the Athenians expelled Hippias.

Unfortunately, such synchronisms are suspiciously common in early Roman history. The expulsion of the tyrant Tarquin/Hippias is paralleled by the ambush and heroic death of the three hundred Fabii/Spartans, or the exile by an ungrateful people of Coriolanus/Themistocles.[143] The details of particular episodes are frequently reminiscent of Greek history—the war provoked by the kidnap of prostitutes, the speech given at the congress of the enemy alliance, the invaders who spare the defending commander's estates, and so on.[144] The Tarquin story itself contains two classic examples, with Sextus at Gabii playing first Zopyrus at Babylon and then Periander consulting Thrasybulus.[145]

In particular, as Attilio Mastrocinque has pointed out, the events immediately following the expulsion seem to be largely borrowed from Herodotus.[146] Porsena comes to bring back Tarquin, but abandons the siege because he is impressed by the Romans' courage and love of freedom; so Cleomenes came to bring back Hippias, but abandoned the invasion because he was impressed by the evils of tyranny.[147] The Veientes attack Rome to bring back Tarquin, there is a closely-fought battle, and Silvanus (or Faunus) speaks in favour of the Romans; so the Persians attacked Athens to bring back Hippias, there was a closely-fought battle, and Pan announced that he would fight on the Athe-

---

140 See Connor 1989, Seaford 1994.243–4.
141 Polybius 3.22.1; Walbank 1957.665–9. The date probably comes from Eratosthenes, who used the διάβασις of Xerxes as one of the fixed points of his chronology (*FGrH* 241 F1(a) = Clemens Alexandrinus *Stromateis* 1.138.1–3) and evidently included material on Rome (F45 = Servius *auctus* on *Aeneid* 1.273); cf. Dionysius of Halicarnassus 1.74.2 for the importance of Eratosthenes for synchronising Roman and Greek chronology.
142 Alexander Polyhistor *FGrH* 273 F109 (Plutarch *Moralia* 289a = *Quaestiones Romanae* 104).
143 See respectively Pliny *Nat. Hist.* 34.17, Aulus Gellius 17.21.13, Cicero *Brutus* 41–3. On the Fabii parallel see Soltau 1909.88–90, Ogilvie 1965.359–60.
144 See respectively Livy 2.18.2 (Aristophanes *Acharnians* 523–9), Dionysius of Halicarnassus 5.50.3 (Thucydides 1.72.2), Livy 2.39.5–6 (Thucydides 2.13.1).
145 Dionysius of Halicarnassus 4.55–6 (Herodotus 3.154, 5.92–3).
146 Mastrocinque 1988.33–4.
147 Herodotus 5.90–3 (including the story of Thrasybulus and the poppies, n. 145 above).

nians' side.[148] Tarquinius of Collatia is consul in the first year of the Republic, but because his relationship with the exiled tyrant arouses suspicion, he goes into voluntary exile; so Hipparchus of Collutos was archon in Cleisthenic Athens, but because his relationship with the exiled Hippias aroused suspicion, he was the first to go into ten-year exile under the new system of ostracism.[149]

As the last example shows, the template was not Herodotus alone; Hipparchus' ostracism probably comes from Androtion or one of the other Atthidographers.[150] It was evidently the events themselves, not just one narrative of them, which provided the inspiration. Who did it? Possibly Fabius Pictor, possibly Timaeus or some other Greek historian who dealt with Rome; the involvement of the exiled Tarquins with Aristodemus of Cumae makes it likely that the outline of their story was remembered – and elaborated?—in Greek historiography.[151]

What these examples show is not just a means of creating plausible history out of little or nothing (though it *is* that), but also a predisposition to think of the Roman experience in Athenian terms. Rather than some Greek historian, it may have been the Romans themselves who constructed their freedom narrative on the lines of Athenian democracy. Late in the fourth century, at the time of the Samnite wars, they set up a statue of Alcibiades at the Comitium. A few years later, they placed the new temple of Victory on the Palatine above the cave of Pan (the *Lupercal*), and incorporated into the complex a newly-fortified access to the hill (the *cliuus Victoriae*), thus reproducing the topography of the Nike temple in the Propylaea of the Athenian acropolis. Nike, Pan and Alcibiades had made the Athenians victorious; perhaps they would do the same for Rome.[152]

By that time at least, we may reasonably imagine that Liber, *libertas* and the *Liberalia* were firmly associated in the Romans' minds with Dionysus Eleuthereus, ἐλευθερία and the City Dionysia. But did the association go back to the actual events—whatever they were—of the end of the tyranny at Rome?

Given the Cumae connection, which brought the story into Greek historiography, Polybius' date for the expulsion of the Tarquins may be roughly

---

148 Herodotus 6.105.2–3, Pausanias 1.28.4 on Pan; cf. Livy 2.7.2 (Silvanus), Dionysius of Halicarnassus 5.16.2–3 (Faunus).
149 [Aristotle] *Athenaion politeia* 22.4, cf. Livy 2.2.3–10; the version in Dionysius and Plutarch makes Collatinus deserve his exile (Wiseman 1998.81–2 [and pp. 299–301 below]). The particular parallel of Tarquinius Collatinus and Ἵππαρχος Κολλυτεύς was pointed out by Griffiths 1998.
150 For the sources of the *Athenaion politeia*, see Rhodes 1981.15–30.
151 Mastrocinque 1988.34–5. Detailed Cumaean history (possibly Hyperochus, *FGrH* 576) inferred from Dionysius of Halicarnassus 7.3–11 on Aristodemus; Alföldi 1965.56–72.
152 Alcibiades: Pliny *Nat. Hist.* 34.26, Plutarch *Numa* 8.10. Victory temple complex: pp. 57–8 above. Pan and Marathon: n. 148 above.

right. As for Liber, his temple was decorated by the famous artists Damophilus and Gorgasus, whose work was attested by a Greek inscription; no remains survive, but a likely parallel is provided by the early fifth-century temple of Mater Matuta at Satricum, evidently the work of itinerant Greek master-craftsmen.[153] So the expulsion and the temple may indeed have been roughly contemporary, and Liber could have signified *libertas* even as early as about 500 BC.

Because of the absence of good contemporary evidence, and the consequent impossibility of deciding the historical value, if any, of the foundation-legends of the Republic,[154] we cannot be sure that the ideological significance of Liber and his *ludi* goes back to the very beginning of the Republic. But it is certainly possible.

---

153 Pliny *Nat. Hist.* 35.154; Lulof 1996.204–8. Mater Matuta was identified as Ino, the sister of Semele, and was therefore part of Liber's story (Ovid *Fasti* 6.484, *si domus illa tua est*).

154 I wish I could accept Mastrocinque's estimate of the historicity of the literary tradition (1988.235), but I think it is not enough to 'rassegnarsi, *faute de mieux*, ad accettare senza entusiasmo i dati della tradizione' (182) just because modern reconstructions are no more plausible than the ancient ones (213). Nor can I follow him in using Macrobius *Saturnalia* 1.7.34–5, on Brutus' supposed reform of the supposedly Dionysiac Lares Compitales ritual, as evidence for a historical connection between Liber and the new Republic (Mastrocinque 1988.37–41, 145–50; appendix on Liber at 245–75).

CHAPTER SIX

The Kalends of April

I

The Kalends of April were one of the three days in the year when a man was expected to give a woman a present (the other two were her birthday and the *Sigillaria*). As Ovid points out in his *Ars amatoria*, the economical seducer should avoid those dates:[1]

> *siue dies suberit natalis siue Kalendae*
> > *quas Venerem Marti continuasse iuuat,*
> *siue erit ornatus non, ut fuit ante, sigillis,*
> > *sed regum positas Circus habebit opes,*
> *differ opus. . .*

If her birthday is coming, or the Kalends whose pleasure it is to have joined Venus to Mars, or if the Circus, not as of old adorned with statuettes, is going to have royal treasures on display—postpone your campaign.

Note the phrase Ovid uses to describe the 'joining' of March and April (the months of Mars and Venus respectively). Appropriately for the context, it is a sexual allusion; the first day of April is, as it were, the moment when Mars enters Venus. The same expression is used in the *Fasti*, where the poet introduces the 1 April ritual:[2]

> *et formosa Venus formoso tempore digna est,*
> > *utque solet, Marti continuata suo est.*
> *uere monet curuas materna per aequora puppes*
> > *ire nec hibernas iam timuisse minas.*

Lovely Venus both deserves the lovely season and is joined, as usual, to her own Mars. In spring she tells the curved ships to sail through the seas that bore her, and no longer to fear the threats of winter.

---

1 Ovid *Ars amatoria* 1.405–9. For the *Sigillaria* (20 December, part of the Saturnalia), see Macrobius *Saturnalia* 1.11.46–50, Suetonius *Diuus Claudius* 5, SHA *Hadrian* 17.3, *Caracalla* 1.8.
2 Ovid *Fasti* 4.129–32.

What follows in *Fasti* 4, the description of the ritual of Venus Verticordia and Fortuna Virilis, is notoriously controversial. Many important contributions have been made in the last twenty years, since Jacqueline Champeaux' seminal work on Fortuna in 1982,[3] but I think there is more to be said. This chapter begins as a close reading of the Ovid passage, but then develops into a hypothetical reconstruction of one aspect of the culture of archaic Italy. I offer it in memory of Martin Frederiksen as an example of what literary scholarship and archaeology can do for each other.[4]

II

Ovid *Fasti* 4.133–62:

> *rite deam colitis Latiae matresque nurusque*
> > *et uos, quis uittae longaque uestis abest.*
>
> 135 *aurea marmoreo redimicula demite collo,*
> > *demite diuitias: tota lauanda dea est.*
>
> *aurea siccato redimicula reddite collo:*
> > *nunc alii flores, nunc noua danda rosa est.*
>
> *uos quoque sub uiridi myrto iubet ipsa lauari,*
> 140 > *causaque cur iubeat (discite) certa subest.*
>
> *litore siccabat rorantes nuda capillos;*
> > *uiderunt satyri, turba proterua, deam.*
>
> *sensit et opposita texit sua corpora [tempora] myrto;*
> > *tuta fuit facto uosque referre iubet.*
>
> 145 *discite nunc quare Fortunae tura Virili*
> > *detis eo calida [gelida] qui locus umet aqua.*
>
> *accipit ille locus posito uelamine cunctas*
> > *et uitium nudi corporis omne uidet;*
>
> *ut tegat hoc celetque uiros, Fortuna Virilis*
> 150 > *praestat et hoc paruo ture rogata facit.*
>
> *nec pigeat tritum niueo cum lacte papauer*
> > *sumere et expressis mella liquata fauis.*
>
> *cum primum cupido Venus est deducta marito,*
> > *hoc bibit; ex illo tempore nupta fuit.*

---

3   Champeaux 1982.375–409. See also Torelli 1984.77–89; Greco 1985; Porte 1985.388–93, 458–60, 469; Coarelli 1988.293–301; Boëls-Janssen 1993.321–35; Barchiesi 1994.207–16 = 1997.219–28; Menichetti 1995.61–3; Fantham 1998.115–23; Torelli 1999.65–8, 74–8, 177–8. [See now Schultz 2006.148, 202–3.]

4   Martin supervised my Oxford doctoral thesis on *noui homines* (1961–7). When I first met him, I was a traditional text-based English classicist. I still am; but what little I know about the archaeology of ancient Italy I owe to him, and to the British School at Rome, where I was Rome Scholar in Classical Studies in 1962–3.

155   *supplicibus uerbis illam placate: sub illa*
               et forma et mores et bona fama manet.
          Roma pudicitia proauorum tempore lapsa est;
               Cumaeam, ueteres, consuluistis anum.
          templa iubet fieri Veneri, quibus ordine factis
160   *inde Venus uerso nomina corde tenet.*
          semper ad Aeneadas placido, pulcherrima, uoltu
               respice totque tuas, diua, tuere nurus.

You pay the goddess proper respect, matrons and young wives of Latium, and you who don't wear ribbons and long dresses.

Take off from her marble neck the golden necklaces, take off her wealth; the goddess must be washed all over. Put back on her new-dried neck the golden necklaces; fresh flowers, new roses, must be given her now.

Wash yourselves too, under green myrtle. She gives the order herself, and there is a sure reason for it. Listen! She was naked, drying her dripping hair on the shore, when a lecherous gang of satyrs caught sight of the goddess. She realised, and put myrtle in the way to screen her body [*or* brow]. That made her safe, and she bids you remember it.

Now learn why you give incense to Fortuna Virilis in the place which is wet with warm [*or* cold] water. That place receives all women without their clothes, and sees each blemish of the naked body. Fortuna Virilis guarantees to conceal it and hide it from men, and she does so when asked with a little incense.

And don't be reluctant to take ground poppy, in white milk and liquid honey squeezed from the honeycomb. When Venus was first brought to her eager bridegroom, this is what she drank, and from that moment she was a wife.

Appease her with words of supplication; in her control beauty and character and good reputation stay fixed. Rome slipped from chastity in our ancestors' time, and the men of old consulted the old woman of Cumae. She ordered a temple to be built for Venus, and it was duly done; since then Venus has a name from the turning of the heart.

Goddess most fair, look always with a kindly face on the descendants of Aeneas, and protect all your young wives.

The conspicuous 'ring-composition' of lines 133 (*deam, nurusque*) and 162 (*diua, nurus*) defines the passage as a single coherent unit. It is organised around a sequence of imperatives (lines 135, 136, 137, 140, 145, 155), as the poet takes on the role of 'master of ceremonies'.[5] But it is also divided into seven recognisable paragraphs:

---

5   A favourite technique: see also *Fasti* 1.663–96, 2.532–64, 2.623–38, 4.407–16, 4.731–82, 6.775–80.

1 [133–4]	definition of worshippers
2 [135–8]	washing of Venus statue
3 [139–44]	worshippers bathe, myrtle crown *aition*
4 [145–50]	incense to Fortuna Virilis
5 [151–4]	poppy drink, Venus as bride
6 [155–60]	Venus Verticordia *aition*
7 [161–22]	closing prayer to Venus

The first and last of these are a single couplet each; the second is a conspicuously antithetical pair of couplets; the third is marked out by an internal 'ring', with *uos* (*quo*)*que* and *iubet* at 139 and 144, *myrto* at 139 and 143; so too is the fourth, with *tura/ture* at 145 and 150 and the goddess's name at 145 and 149. The fourth paragraph is thus the central '*omphalos*' of a symmetrical structure.

The construction of this complex passage makes it clear that the offering to Fortuna Virilis is an integral part of the Venus ritual, and also that the same group of women—Roman citizens, rich and poor—is being addressed throughout. Ovid's careful and deliberate presentation rules out any reconstruction that presupposes a distinction between the women who worship Venus and those who worship Fortuna.[6] It was a single ritual with two goddesses involved, no doubt the result of an ancient Fortuna cult being combined with Venus Verticordia in the third or second century BC.[7]

The distinction that Ovid does make, in the first couplet, is sometimes taken as being between respectable women and prostitutes.[8] But that too is surely wrong. Those who don't wear the *stola* are just women definable as *humiliores*, with no connotations of immorality; if Ovid had wanted to specify prostitutes, he could have referred to women who wore the *toga*.[9] As the

---

6   According to Fantham (1998.116–18), 'these rituals honouring more than one deity may well have been observed in different places'; it 'seems unlikely that the same group is addressed throughout'; 'elite wives in the main ritual' are to be distinguished from 'the working women's offering to Fortuna Virilis'. *Contra* Barchiesi 1994.209–10 = 1997.222, surely rightly. Mommsen's supplement to the *Fasti Praenestini* (wrongly attributed to Degrassi by Fantham 1998.116) would distinguish *honestiores* worshipping Venus Verticordia from *humiliores* worshipping Fortuna Virilis; but it is gratuitous, and has been rightly rejected by all scholars since Champeaux (1982.379–80). [However, Schultz (n. 3 above) tacitly accepts it: 'the poet then conflates the two rituals'.]

7   Thus Champeaux 1982.383 and 390–4, Torelli 1984.78–81, Coarelli 1988.293.

8   E.g. Champeaux 1982.382 (Champeaux' argument slides tacitly from '*humiliores*' to '*humiliores et courtisanes*': 1982.384, 387, 390, 392, 393, 394, 404, 405, 407); Boëls-Janssen 1993.328; Barchiesi 1994.209–10 = 1997.222; Pasco-Pranger 2006.149–52. 'Patrician and plebeian' (Torelli 1984.83, 1999.67) is closer to Ovid's formulation.

9   Cicero *Philippics* 2.44, Horace *Satires* 1.2.63 and scholiasts, Sulpicia [Tibullus] 3.16.3, Martial 2.39.2, 10.52, Juvenal 2.68–70. For 'those who don't wear the *stola*', cf. Ovid *Ars amatoria* 1.31–2, 2.600; presumably the poet did not want to characterise all his female readers as prostitutes.

descendants of Aeneas are the Romans, so the 'daughters-in-law of Venus' (162) are the women of Rome, and the poet addresses all of them.[10]

The context of the third paragraph is the myth of Venus *anadyomene*, already alluded to in the introductory passage (*materna per aequora*, 131). For Ovid, as for Horace,[11] April's goddess is *Venus marina*. There were myrtles growing where she emerged naked from the sea, and according to Servius she hid herself behind the bush.[12] That seems to be what Ovid asks us to imagine (143–4); but such a banal scenario does not fit the *aition* at all well, since the women who imitate her do so by wearing only myrtle garlands. Moreover, the eleventh-century Vatican manuscript has *tempora*, not *corpora*, at 143. If that is the true reading, and *corpora* a rationalising 'correction', then the protection was not physical but magical.[13] Crowned with myrtle, Venus was safe even though the satyrs were watching.

Whatever the correct solution of the textual crux, that idea of magical protection must be valid for the ritual, where it is certain that the women's only protection was myrtle round the head. The parallel with the myth must mean that there are men watching, like the satyrs.[13a] Under normal circumstances, of course, the women would cover their bodies, but on the Kalends of April it seems that wearing Venus' myrtle garland makes it all right.

Certainly the watching males are a necessary feature of the fourth paragraph: the whole purpose of the offering to Fortuna Virilis is to make the less beautiful women's bodies attractive to the men (*uiros*, 149). This privileged exhibition—a startling idea, but one clearly implied by Ovid's text—may account for the goddess's name, if 'Fortuna Virilis' expresses the men's good fortune. Where it took place depends on the solution of another textual uncertainty. If *calida* is the correct reading at 146, it was in the public baths; if *gelida*, it was outside, no doubt at the *piscina publica*. In any case, the *piscina publica* must have been the site of the ritual from the late fourth century, when it was built to exploit the water of the Aqua Appia,[14] until the introduction of public baths (and warm water) in the second century BC.[15]

---

10 Cf. *cunctas* at 147, the middle point of the whole passage.

11 Horace *Odes* 4.11.15–16, cf. 3.26.5.

12 Servius on *Eclogues* 7.62: *myrtum ideo dicatum Veneri uolunt quia cum a mari exisset latuit in myrto ne nuda conspiceretur.*

13 Torelli 1984.83. I think Porte (1985.469) and Boëls-Janssen (1993.327) are right to prefer *tempora*, though Porte wrongly supposes that the story is an Ovidian invention.

13a [*Pace* Pasco-Pranger 2006.154, who assumes without argument that men were excluded.]

14 Since the Paestum colony had its own *piscina publica* (Greco 1985), 273 BC is a firm *terminus ante quem*.

15 So Greco 1985.229–31, Coarelli 1988.299–300, Torelli 1999.65–7. Boëls-Janssen 1993.329 less convincingly suggests the Tiber.

A Praenestine *cista*, now in the Badisches Landesmuseum at Karlsruhe [fig. 19, p. 89 above], seems to offer a mythologised illustration of the ritual as it may have existed in the fourth century BC.[16] The columns mark off the bath-house or nymphaeum where the women are washing themselves at the fountain; they are observed by two satyrs, one followed by Liber Pater, the other by an unidentified goddess. The symmetrical composition makes one think of Libera,[17] but Fortuna Virilis is also a possibility.

Are we to think of men dressed as satyrs? That was certainly a familiar phenomenon in Dionysiac cult;[18] and we have visual evidence for it in two contemporary bronze mirrors from Latium, one in the Villa Giulia in Rome [fig. 10, p. 59 above], the other in Baltimore [fig. 14, p. 67 above].[19] Marsyas in fig. 10 is waving his tail, which must therefore be detachable, and the central figure in fig. 14 is wearing the outfit of an actor playing a hairy satyr (visible at the left forearm). It is not inconceivable that in the fourth century BC the Kalends of April ritual involved a similar type of masquerade.

Since satyrs symbolise male sexual desire, the purpose of the ritual is clear enough, and confirmed by Ovid's fifth paragraph. The mythic *aition* (153–4) is of Venus on her wedding night, taking a sedative before submitting to the enthusiastic embrace of Vulcan.[20] So the women of Rome must allow the men to have their way. The nearest parallel is the Spartan custom, allegedly introduced by Lycurgus, of having citizen girls dance naked at certain festivals with the young men looking on, as an incentive to marriage by seizure (ἁρπαγή).[21]

The community must encourage sex, but also control it. Marriage, however defined, is the seed-bed of the Republic, producing warriors who will defend its territory.[22] It is surely not accidental that the two festivals of

---

16 Jurgeit 1999.528–33, no. 885. It is no. 22 in the standard catalogue (Battaglia and Emiliozzi 1979.95–7, tav. cxiii-cxvii), but the illustrations there include some nineteenth-century additions; see Jurgeit 1992.85–94. See Menichetti 1995.61–2 for the relevance of Fortuna Virilis.

17 See p. 86 above.

18 See Plato *Laws* 7.815c (nearly contemporary with the *cista*): p. 108 above.

19 *Etruskische Spiegel* 5 (1883) Taf. 43 and 45.

20 Sedative: Champeaux 1982.381 and 387–8, Porte 1985.459, Boëls-Janssen 1993.326, Barchiesi 1994.213 = 1997.225; Torelli 1984.83 assumes it is an aphrodisiac. The 'eager husband' cannot be Mars, as assumed without argument by Bömer 1958.218, tentatively followed by Fantham 1998.121.

21 Plutarch *Lycurgus* 14.2 (εἴθισε … τὰς κόρας γυμνάς τε πομπεύειν καὶ πρὸς ἱεροῖς τισιν ὀρχεῖσθαι καὶ ᾄδειν τῶν νέων παρόντων καὶ θεωμένων); cf. 15.3 for ἁρπαγή. The Spartan custom clearly influenced Plato (*Laws* 771e–772a).

22 Cicero *De officiis* 1.54: *nam cum sit hoc natura commune animantium, ut habeant lubidinem procreandi, prima societas in ipso coniugio est, proxima in liberis, deinde una domus, communia omnia; id autem est principium urbis et quasi seminarium rei publicae.* Cf. Catullus 61.71–5, on Hymenaeus: *quae tuis careat sacris | non queat dare praesides | terra finibus.* For the marriage formula *liberorum quaerendorum causa*, see Festus 312L, Valerius Maximus 7.7.4, Suetonius *Diuus Iulius* 52.3, Aulus Gellius 4.3.2.

Carmentis the goddess of childbirth (11 and 15 January) come just over nine months after the Kalends of April.[23] Various stories of Roman history or pseudo-history betray anxieties about the birth-rate;[24] no less conspicuous are anxieties about unregulated sexual activity, as in the Dionysiac rites banned in 186 BC.[25] The combined festival of Fortuna Virilis, who gives men what they want, and Venus Verticordia, who turns women's hearts to chastity (Ovid's sixth paragraph),[26] may be seen as an expression of those conflicting priorities.

III

So far, I have deliberately restricted the discussion to the Ovid passage and what can be inferred from it. But other authors also refer to the Kalends of April, if only briefly:

1. Verrius Flaccus Fasti Praenestini (Inscriptiones Italiae 13.1.126–7):

> frequenter mulieres supplicant Fortunae Virili, humiliores etiam in balineis, quod in iis ea parte corpor[is] utique uiri nudantur qua feminarum gratia desideratur.

The women en masse pray to Fortuna Virilis, those of lower rank even in the baths, because there men reveal that particular part of the body by which the favour of women is sought [or the beauty of women is desired].

2. Macrobius Saturnalia 1.12.15:

> non tamen negat Verrius Flaccus hoc die postea constitutum ut matronae Veneri sacrum facerent, cuius rei causam, quia huic loco non conuenit, praetereundum est.

However, Verrius Flaccus agrees that on this day it was later laid down that the married women should sacrifice to Venus. I must pass over the reason for it, because in this place it is not appropriate.

3. Plutarch Numa 19.2:

> ...δεύτερον δὲ τὸν Ἀπρίλλιον, ἐπώνυμον ὄντα τῆς Ἀφροδίτης, ἐν ᾧ θύουσί τε τῇ θεῷ καὶ ταῖς καλάνδαις αἱ γυναῖκες ἐστεφανωμέναι μυρσίνῃ λούονται.

---

23 Carmentis and childbirth: Ovid Fasti 1.627–8, Plutarch Romulus 21.2 and Moralia 278b-c (Quaestiones Romanae 56), Augustine City of God 4.11.

24 E.g. Ovid Fasti 2.429–48 (Romulus); Festus 478L (Tarquinius Superbus); Orosius 4.2.2, Augustine City of God 3.18 (276 BC); Ovid Fasti 1.619–28 (195 BC).

25 Livy 39.8.6–7 (stupra promiscua); cf. 13.10, 13.12, 15.9, 15.12, 18.5–6.

26 Valerius Maximus 8.15.12: quo facilius uirginum mulierumque mens a libidine ad pudicitiam conuerteretur. Ovid may be referring to the temple built in 119 BC (Obsequens 37); but since the consultation of the Sibylline books in that year is recorded only in the context of human sacrifice (Plutarch Moralia 284a-b = Quaestiones Romanae 83), it may be better to take it as a reference to the earlier dedication of a statue (Valerius Maximus loc. cit., Pliny Nat. Hist. 7.128). The date of the latter is evidently before 204 BC, since Pliny puts it before the story of Q. Claudia; however, Torelli (1984.79–81) argues for 178 BC.

[Romulus named] the second month April after Aphrodite. In that month they sacrifice to the goddess and on the Kalends the women bathe garlanded with myrtle.

4. John Lydus *De mensibus* 4.65:

ταῖς τοίνυν καλάνδαις Ἀπριλίαις αἱ σεμναὶ γυναικῶν ὑπὲρ ὁμονοίας καὶ βίου σώφρονος ἐτίμων τὴν Ἀφροδίτην· αἱ δὲ τοῦ πλήθους γυναῖκες ἐν τοῖς τῶν ἀνδρῶν βαλανείοις ἐλούοντο πρὸς θεραπείαν αὐτῆς μυρσίνῃ ἐστεμμέναι.

On the Kalends of April the women of rank used to honour Aphrodite for the sake of harmony and a respectable character; but the women of the people used to bathe in the men's baths, garlanded with myrtle in honour of the goddess.

All four passages clearly derive from the antiquarian tradition. Only Verrius Flaccus (item 1) refers to Fortuna Virilis; for the others, it is solely a festival of Venus, and since the day is named as 'Veneralia' in the Calendar of Furius Filocalus, it is normally (and plausibly) assumed that after the Augustan age Fortuna's share in it was gradually forgotten.[27] Lydus in item 4 was probably using the Verrius Flaccus tradition (item 1), but assuming that the goddess concerned was Venus. Since Verrius Flaccus and Plutarch use the present tense, Macrobius and Lydus the past, the whole ritual was probably obsolete by the fourth century AD.

What we can infer from these passages is the way sophisticated Augustan Rome handled a ritual that had become embarrassing. Its erotic nature is admitted in Verrius Flaccus' prim little note in the Fasti Praenestini (item 1),[28] and implied by Macrobius' reluctance to discuss the subject (item 2). How did a lady of the Roman elite carry out her ritual obligations on the Kalends of April? If she took the necessary bath at home, the proper place for the next stage would surely be the *lectus genialis* in the *atrium*.[29] Named after Genius, the god of human reproduction, it was the *matrona*'s particular place in the house.[30] That may seem public enough, but of course the doors could be kept closed and witnesses excluded. For the *humiliores* who had neither an *atrium* nor their own water supply, there was no alternative to the traditional public display, now held in the baths.

---

27 So Champeaux 1982.391–2, Boëls-Janssen 1993.323–4; Fantham 1998.115 assumes it was already the Veneralia in Ovid's time.

28 It 'seems absurd' (Fantham 1998.120), but that is all the more reason to take it seriously as evidence.

29 Horace *Epistles* 1.1.87 (*lectus genialis in aula est*), Cicero *Pro Cluentio* 14, Lucan 2.356–7—all in the context of marriage.

30 Genius: Festus (Paulus) 83L; cf. Varro in Augustine *City of God* 7.13, Festus (Paulus) 84L, Censorinus 3.1. *Matrona*'s place: Laberius fr. 30R (Aulus Gellius 16.9.4), Propertius 4.11.85–6, Asconius 43C.

There may be an analogy in the flagellation ritual of the *Lupercalia* on 15 February. In the time of Plutarch and Juvenal, the women just held out their hands to be struck, 'like children in school'.[31] If that was already the custom in the Rome of Augustus, Ovid's aetiology ignores the fact; he refers only to women 'offering their backs'.[32] So too on the Kalends of April, he gives the respectable ladies no option of avoiding the public exposure of their bodies. Alessandro Barchiesi is surely right to see that as mischievous.[33]

IV

The temple of Venus Verticordia, referred to by Ovid in his sixth paragraph, was situated in the valley of the Circus Maximus (*uallis Murcia*), presumably close to the *piscina publica*. The evidence is in a passage of Servius, commenting on Virgil's reference to the rape of the Sabine women:[34]

> *uallis autem ipsa ubi circenses editi sunt ideo Murcia dicta est, quia quidam uicinum montem Murcum appellatum uolunt; alii quod fanum Veneris Verticordiae ibi fuerit, circa quod nemus e murtetis fuissent, inmutata littera Murciam appellatam; alii Murciam a Murcido, quod est marcidum, dictam uolunt; pars a dea Murcia, quae cum Bacchanalia essent furorem sacri ipsius murcidum faceret.*

The valley itself where the circus games were held is called Murcia for this reason, because some think the nearby hill is called Mons Murcus; others say that because this is where the temple of Venus Verticordia was, around which there had been a myrtle grove, [the valley] was called Murcia by the change of a letter; others think it is called Murcia from Murcidus, i.e. *marcidus* [rotten]; some think it is from the goddess Murcia, who, when the Bacchanalia were taking place here, made slow the madness of the god's ritual.

The myrtle grove is located by Varro at the temple of Venus Murtea, which must therefore be another name for the same goddess.[35] It can hardly be an accident that this was where the story of Rome's primeval 'marriage by seizure' was set.

If our inference from the Ovid passage is valid, the Fortuna Virilis cult must

31 Plutarch *Caesar* 61.2, Juvenal 2.142; contrast Gelasius *Adu. Andr.* 16 (CSEL 35.1.458), *matronae nudato corpore publice uapulabant*. See now Stefano Tortorella in Carandini and Cappelli 2000.244–55, especially the illustrations at 246, 252 and 253.
32 Ovid *Fasti* 2.445–6, *iussae sua terga puellae | pellibus exsectis percutienda dabant*.
33 Barchiesi 1994.209–10 = 1997.222; cf. 1994.212 for his *malizia* (1997.224, 'mischief').
34 Servius *auctus* on *Aeneid* 8.636; Coarelli 1988.95–7.
35 Varro *De lingua Latina* 5.154 on *ad Murciae*: *alii dicunt a murteto declinatum, quod ibi id fuerit; cuius uestigium manet, quod ibi est sacellum etiam nunc Murteae Veneris*. Cf. Pliny *Nat. Hist.* 15.121 (in the context of myrtles and the Sabine women story, 119–20): *quin et ara uetus fuit Veneri Murteae quam nunc Murciam uocant*.

have been in the same place. Plutarch mentions it in his list of the Roman aspects of the goddess in *De fortuna Romanorum*:[36]

ἔστι δὲ καὶ παρὰ τὸν τῆς Ἀφροδίτης ἐπιταλαρίου βωμὸν ἄρρενος Τύχης ἔδος. [ἐπιταλασίου Bernadakis]

... and by the altar of Aphrodite Epitalarios there is a shrine of male Tyche [Fortuna Virilis].

That evidently gives us yet another name for the goddess of the myrtle grove; but why should Venus be associated with a basket (τάλαρος)? Mario Torelli sees an allusion to the Bacchic *cista mystica* containing the phallus, and given the cult's Dionysiac associations (the watching satyrs, and Servius' reference to the Bacchanalia), that is certainly a possibility. Filippo Coarelli, however, suggests a better solution, one that brings in the site's association with the story of the rape of the Sabines.[37]

The shout of good wishes at Roman weddings was '*Talas(s)io*'—or '*Thalas(s)io*', as it was sometimes spelt.[38] (All the spellings presumably render an archaic *Talasio* from a time when Latin did not aspirate or duplicate consonants.) Many authors explain it as the dative form of the name of an influential Roman whose agents seized the most beautiful of the Sabine girls and carried her off; challenged by rival suitors, they shouted that she was 'for T(h)alassius'.[39] It seems an improbable name for a Roman, even one of Romulus' time, and it is not surprising that the antiquarian tradition offered a different explanation:

1. Festus 478–80L:

> [*talas*]*sionem in nuptiis Varro ait* [*signum esse lani*]*fici*, τάλαρον, *id est quassillum; i*[*nde enim so*]*litum appellari talassionem.* [*Sed . . .*] *historiarum scriptor Talassium* [*ait. . .*]
>
> Varro says that '*talassio*' at weddings is *talaros*, the sign of wool-working, i.e. a basket; that is the reason for the custom of calling '*talassio*'. But . . . the historian says ['girl for Talassius' story follows].

2. Plutarch *Moralia* 271f (*Quaestiones Romanae* 31):

> διὰ τί ὁ πολυθρύλητος ᾄδεται Ταλάσιος ἐν τοῖς γάμοις; πότερον ἀπὸ τῆς τααςίας; καὶ γὰρ τὸν τάλαρον τάλασον ὀνομάζουσι· καὶ τὴν

---

36 Plutarch *Moralia* 323a (*De fortuna Romanorum* 10).
37 Torelli 1984.78; Coarelli 1988.298–9.
38 Unaspirated: Catullus 61.127, Festus 478–80L, Sidonius Apollinaris *Epistles* 1.5; Plutarch *Quaestiones Romanae* 31, *Romulus* 15.1–4, *Pompey* 4.3. Aspirated: Livy 1.9.12, Festus 492L, Servius on *Aeneid* 1.651; Martial 1.35.6–7, 3.93.25, 12.42.4, 12.95.5. MSS vary: [Virg.] *Catalepton* 12.9, 13.6.
39 Livy 1.9.12, etc; Servius on *Aeneid* 1.651 makes *Thalassio* the nominative form of the name.

νύμφην εἰσάγοντες νάκος ὑποστρωννύασιν·᾿ αὐτὴ δ' εἰσφέρει μὲν
ἠλακάτην καὶ τὴν ἄτρακτον, ἐρίῳ δὲ τὴν θύραν περιστέφει τοῦ
ἀνδρός. ἢ τὸ λεγόμενον ὑπὸ τῶν ἱστορικῶν ἀληθές, ὅτι...

Why is the famous 'talasios' sung at weddings? Is it from spinning? For they call
the wool-basket *talasos*. And when they bring the bride in, they spread a fleece
beneath her; she herself brings a distaff and the spindle, and she uses wool to
garland the bridegroom's door. Or is what the historians say true ['girl for
Talassius' story follows]?

3. Plutarch *Romulus* 15.2–4:

Σέξτιος δὲ Σύλλας ὁ Καρχηδόνιος, οὔτε μουσῶν οὔτε χαρίτων ἐπιδεὴς
ἀνήρ, ἔλεγεν ἡμῖν ὅτι τῆς ἁρπαγῆς σύνθημα τὴν φωνὴν ἔδωκε ταύτην ὁ
Ῥωμύλος. ἅπαντες οὖν τὸν Ταλάσιον ἐβόων οἱ τὰς παρθένους
κομίζοντες· καὶ διὰ τοῦτο τοῖς γάμοις παραμένει τὸ ἔθος. οἱ δὲ
πλεῖστοι νομίζουσιν, ὧν καὶ Ἰόβας ἐστί, παράκλησιν εἶναι καὶ
παρακέλευσιν εἰς φιλεργίαν καὶ ταλασίαν, οὔπω τότε τοῖς Ἑλληνικοῖς
ὀνόμασι τῶν Ἰταλικῶν ἐπικεχυμένων. εἰ δὲ τοῦτο μὴ λέγεται κακῶς,
ἀλλ' ἐχρῶντο Ῥωμαῖοι τότε τῷ ὀνόματι τῆς ταλασίας, καθάπερ ἡμεῖς,
ἑτέραν ἄν τις αἰτίαν εἰκάσειε πιθανωτέραν. ἐπεὶ γὰρ οἱ Σαβῖνοι πρὸς
τοὺς Ῥωμαίους πολεμήσαντες διηλλάγησαν, ἐγένοντο συνθῆκαι περὶ
τῶν γυναικῶν, ὅπως μηδὲν ἄλλο ἔργον τοῖς ἀνδράσιν ἢ τὰ περὶ τὴν
ταλασίαν ὑπουργῶσι.

['Girl for Talassius' story.] But Sextius Sulla the Carthaginian, no stranger to
either the Muses or the Graces, told me that Romulus gave this word as the
signal for the abduction; so those who were carrying off the girls kept shouting
'*talasios*', and that is why the custom survives at weddings. Most authorities,
including Juba, think that it is an exhortation and encouragement to diligence
and spinning, since Greek words had not yet been submerged by Latin ones.
And if this is not mistaken, and the Romans did at that time use the word *talasia*
as we do, then one might conjecture a different and more plausible explanation:
when the Sabines made peace after their war with the Romans, there were arti-
cles in the treaty about the women, to the effect that they should do no work
for their husbands except for tasks involved with spinning.

It is possible, as Coarelli suggests, that Plutarch's 'Aphrodite Epitalarios'
belongs in this aetiological context. In that case Venus the Turner of Hearts
(Verticordia), Venus of the Myrtle Grove (Murtea), would be also Venus of
the Spinning-Basket.

However, item 3 above incorporates a third explanation, otherwise unattested. The learned Sextius Sulla thought the cry was Romulus' signal for the
'marriage by seizure'. Unfortunately Plutarch doesn't explain why the word
would have been appropriate in that context, but I think a reason can be

found. Let us suppose that baskets have nothing to do with it, that the rhotacism of items 1 and 2 (τάλαρος = τάλασος) is an unnecessary expedient, and that *Talasio* originally meant *Thalassio*—that is, Θαλασσίῳ, 'for Poseidon'.[40]

The games to which Romulus had invited the Sabines and their daughters were in honour of Poseidon Hippios, Latinised as Neptunus Equester.[41] The god was identified with Consus, whose underground altar was in the valley of the Circus Maximus at the point where the chariots turned. The turning-post was called *metae Murciae*, just opposite the myrtle grove of Murcia who was also Venus Murtea.[42]

The reason for Poseidon Hippios was brilliantly revealed by Fausto Zevi in an article demonstrating the historicity of Rome's 'Corinthian kings', the Tarquinii.[43] If the first *ludi circenses* were set up by the son of Demaratus, as the tradition insists,[44] then naturally they would be on the model of the Isthmian Games, and in honour of the same god. The valley flooded every winter, when you needed a boat to reach the Aventine,[45] so the idea that it was somehow Poseidon's realm was not as strange as it seems today. It may explain why the *scalae Caci*, down from the Palatine to the Circus Maximus, were called 'the steps of the Fair Shore'.[46] At the bottom of those steps, at or near the Lupercal, was a building decorated with sea-shells (perhaps a *nymphaeum*), which its sixteenth-century discoverers naturally identified as a temple of Neptune.[47]

If Consus was Poseidon, and his altar was next to the myrtle grove, and the goddess of the myrtle grove was not only Venus Murtea but also Aphrodite Epitalarios, then perhaps we can explain that mysterious epithet as another unnecessary rhotacism. Was she originally Epitalasios, an early Latin transliter-

---

40 For Θαλάσσιος as Poseidon, see Aristophanes *Wasps* 1519 (= *trag. adesp.* fr. 69 Nauck), *Plutus* 396.

41 Dionysius of Halicarnassus 1.33.2, Livy 1.9.6, Plutarch *Romulus* 14.3, *Moralia* 276C (*Quaestiones Romanae* 48), Servius *auctus* on *Aeneid* 8.635, Servius on *Aeneid* 8.636, Lydus *De magistratibus* 1.30.

42 Dionysius of Halicarnassus 2.31.2, Plutarch *Romulus* 14.3, Tertullian *De spectaculis* 5.7, 8.6 (*apud metas Murcias*, cf. Apuleius *Golden Ass* 6.8.2); Humphrey 1986.60–2, 95–7, 258–9, 290–1. For the place-name *ad Murciae*, see Varro *De lingua Latina* 5.154, Livy 1.33.5, *Inscriptiones Italiae* 13.3.60 and 78 (*elogium* of M'. Valerius Maximus).

43 Zevi 1995.307–8. [See below, p. 233 n. 18.]

44 Cicero *De republica* 2.36, Livy 1.35.7–9, Dionysius of Halicarnassus 3.68.1, *De uiris illustribus* 6.8.

45 Cicero *Ad Quintum fratrem* 3.5.8 (54 BC: *magna uis aquae usque ad piscinam publicam*), Varro *De lingua Latina* 5.43; cf. Varro *De lingua Latina* 5.44, 5.156, Propertius 4.9.5–6, Tibullus 2.5.33–4, Ovid *Fasti* 6.405–8, Plutarch *Romulus* 5.5 (Velabrum).

46 Plutarch *Romulus* 20.4: παρὰ τοὺς λεγομένους βαθμοὺς καλῆς ἀκτῆς.

47 Lanciani 1990.230: discovered by Ulisse Aldovrandi in 1549 between S. Teodoro and S. Anastasia. [It was rediscovered in 2007, and identified—prematurely, I think—as the Lupercal itself.]

ation of ἐπιθαλάσσιος? That would at least account for the myrtles: if the
flooded valley was thought of as the sea, then this is where 'marine Venus'
emerged naked before the satyrs' lustful eyes. And here, as Plutarch says, was
the shrine of Fortuna Virilis.

V

According to the earliest surviving version of the myth, Aphrodite came ashore
on the coast of Cyprus.[48] The goddess was honoured there by a ritual of 'sacred
prostitution', as we know from a passage in Justin:[49]

> *mos erat Cypriis uirgines ante nuptias statutis diebus dotalem pecuniam quaesituras in*
> *quaestum ad litus maris mittere, pro reliqua pudicitia libamenta Veneri soluturas. harum*
> *igitur ex numero LXXX admodum uirgines raptas nauibus inponi Elissa iubet, ut et*
> *iuuentus matrimonia et urbs subolem habere posset.*
>
> It was the custom among the Cypriots to send their virgins before marriage to
> the sea-shore on fixed days, for employment to earn money for their dowries,
> and to pay a first-fruit offering to Venus in return for chastity thereafter. So
> Elissa ordered as many as eighty of these girls to be taken and put on the ships,
> so that her young men could have marriages and her city could have posterity.

Elissa is Dido, in flight from Tyre. Her motive in seizing the Cypriot girls was
the same as that of Romulus with the Sabines, to provide women for a new
city. The story may well come from Timaeus, just at the time when the legend
of the Sabines was probably taking shape.[50]

Parallels to the Cypriot custom are reported from Lydia, Syria, Armenia
and Babylonia,[51] but also, more relevantly, at the Greek city of Locri
Epizephyrii in south Italy. Hard pressed in a war with their neighbours of
Rhegium in 477/6 BC, the Locrians vowed to Aphrodite that if she gave them
the victory their daughters would serve the goddess as prostitutes each year on
her festal day; she did, and the vow was carried out. Later it lapsed, during a
difficult war with the Lucanians, but Dionysius II of Sicily demanded that it be
reinstated, this time with the service lasting a month.[52]

---

48 Hesiod *Theogony* 193, *Homeric Hymns* 6.1–5; cf. Homer *Odyssey* 8.363, *Homeric Hymns* 5.58,
    Herodotus 1.105.3 (Paphos).
49 Justin 18.5.4–5, presumably from Pompeius Trogus in the first century BC; MacLachlan
    1992.152–7.
50 Timaeus *FGrH* 566 F82, cf. 60. That the Sabines story originated with the incorporation of
    the historical Sabines into the Roman state in 290 (*ciues sine suffragio*) and 266 (*ciues optimo*
    iure) is strongly suggested by the tradition that T. Tatius' Sabines were given *ciuitas sine*
    suffragio (Servius on *Aeneid* 7.709); see Wiseman 1995.127.
51 Clearchus fr. 43a Wehrli (Athenaeus 12.516), Herodotus 1.199.2, Strabo 11.14.6, Lucian *De*
    dea Syria 6; cf. also Valerius Maximus 2.6.15 (past tense) on Sicca in north Africa.
52 Justin 21.3.1–4: *uouerant, si uictores forent, ut die festo Veneris uirgines suas prostituerent.*

At Locri and in Cyprus, the duty imposed by the goddess was carried out by citizen women at specific times, as a kind of public contribution. Elsewhere, at wealthy cult centres that could afford to feed and clothe them, the goddess's precinct might have a permanent staff of slave girls (*hierodouloi*). The best known examples of the latter custom are Eryx, at the western tip of Sicily, and Corinth.[53]

When Strabo discusses 'wealthy Corinth', and tries to account for that ancient epithet (no longer valid in his own time, of course), the sequence of his material is as follows:[54] first the city's geographical situation, enabling it to exact tolls both from north-south traffic by land and from east-west traffic by sea; then the Isthmian Games, bringing in spectators from all over Greece; then the city's Bacchiad rulers, enriched by exploiting the market but later expelled in Cypselus' coup; then Demaratus, the wealthy Bacchiad who took refuge in Etruria and whose son moved to Rome to become king Tarquinius 'Priscus'; and finally the famous cult of Aphrodite, with more than a thousand *hierodouloi* attracting the custom of sea-captains from all over the world. It gave rise to the proverb 'Not for every man is the voyage to Corinth', implying 'only for the fortunate'.[55]

Strabo's train of thought entitles us, I think, to extend Zevi's inference about Demaratus' son and the Isthmian Games: if he brought one of Corinth's profitable cults to his new city, why not the other one as well? If Poseidon Hippios (Neptunus Equester) could be superimposed on Consus, couldn't Aphrodite (Venus) be superimposed on Fortuna?

I suggest, therefore, that at some time in the seventh or early sixth century BC, two Corinthian cults, each designed to bring in visitors from far afield, were established in the valley between the Palatine and Aventine hills. In August there were horse-races in honour of Poseidon/Consus; and all the year round there were *hierodouloi* serving the needs of men who could afford an offering to Aphrodite/Fortuna. The latter, at least, could only be maintained by the munificence of a wealthy ruler; but wealth, as Zevi rightly insists,[56] was the recurring theme of the Tarquins' story from first to last.

What would happen to such a 'tyrannical' cult when the tyrant was expelled and the funding cut off? The goddess must still be honoured. I suggest

---

53 Strabo 6.2.6, Diodorus Siculus 4.83 (Eryx); Pindar fr. 122 Snell, Strabo 8.6.20, 12.3.36 (Corinth); MacLachlan 1992.157–60.

54 Strabo 8.6.20; for Corinth after the destruction of 146 BC, see Cicero *Ad familiares* 4.5.4 (Ser. Sulpicius on *oppida quodam tempore florentissima* . . . *nunc prostrata et diruta*). By Strabo's time there was a Roman colony.

55 οὐ παντὸς ἀνδρὸς ἐς Κόρινθον ἔσθ' ὁ πλοῦς, Latinised by Horace (*Epistles* 1.17.36) as *non cuiuis homini contingit adire Corinthum*.

56 Zevi 1995.294–8.

that the community adopted the Cypriot system, as the Locrians did a generation later: citizen women would serve, but only on the goddess's festal day. Just
as August was the driest month of the year at Rome, and therefore the most
suitable for horse-races in the valley, so in April the river was at its height,
swollen with melted Apennine snow, and the valley was flooded like the sea.[57]

The connection with Liber, attested on the Karlsruhe *cista* and by Servius'
definition of Murcia,[58] may well belong to this stage. Certainly the proximity
of the two festivals in the calendar—the Liberalia on 17 March and Fortuna
Virilis on 1 April—is consistent with a conceptual link, while Liber's role as
the guarantor of public freedom makes his cult necessarily *post reges exactos*,
whether or not the date of 493 BC for his temple is accurate.[59]

The next stage, I suggest, was a long-drawn out ideological dispute, probably in the fourth and third centuries BC, between orgiastic traditionalists and
puritanical modernisers.[60] The cult of Venus Obsequens, introduced in 295,
may have been an attempt to control the goddess ('Venus who complies'); if
so, the effect was surely cancelled out by the introduction of Venus Erycina in
215.[61] The cult of Venus Verticordia, whenever it began, was evidently
designed to shift the emphasis of Fortuna Virilis. It celebrated chastity and
marital concord,[62] and offered the ladies of Rome a respectable reason ('in
imitation of the goddess') to do what they traditionally had to do on that day
of the year.

All of that, I think, is necessary to make sense of the Ovid passage in *Fasti* 4.
To return to the very beginning, I take it as confirmation of the hypothesis
offered here that on the Kalends of April a man was expected to give a woman
a present. It was the last vestige of the long-forgotten origin of the ritual in
sacred prostitution.

---

57 For the modern statistics, see the table in Le Gall 1953.12.
58 See above, at pp. 145, 148.
59 Liber and *libertas*: Servius on *Aeneid* 3.20, 4.57 and 4.638. See pp. 84–6 above.
60 Such a conflict can be inferred about the Lupercalia, roughly between 304 and 276 BC: pp.
    70–8 above.
61 For Erycina and prostitutes, see Ovid *Fasti* 4.865–76. I cannot follow Torelli (1999.93) on
    Venus Obsequens: *aliquot matronas ad populum stupri damnatas pecunia multauit* (Livy 10.31.9)
    can hardly mean that the adulterous women were 'obliged to prostitute themselves near the
    new sanctuary'.
62 Valerius Maximus 8.15.12, Pliny *Nat. Hist.* 7.120, Lydus *De mensibus* 4.65

CHAPTER SEVEN

Summoning Jupiter:
Magic in the Roman Republic

I

There is a long passage in Varro's *De lingua Latina* where the great antiquarian seeks to explain the archaic word *inlicium*. In the course of his argument he cites early attestations not only of the noun itself but also of the verb *inlicere* ('to entice, bring in'), and its cognates *pellicere* and *elicere*.[1] All but one of the citations are from early texts; the exception is his example of *elicere* ('to elicit, bring out'), which is not a text but the name of a Roman cult site:[2]

> *sic Elicii Iouis ara in Auentino, ab eliciendo.*
> Thus the altar of Jupiter 'Elicius' on the Aventine, from 'eliciting'.

The name of the altar was explained by a famous story of Numa 'eliciting' Jupiter from heaven, bringing him down to the Aventine to bargain about what sacrifice he would accept to expiate thunderbolts.[3]

Livy has a much less sensational explanation of the name, in keeping with his policy of distancing himself from miracle stories and divine epiphanies.[4] In his account of Numa's institution of the *pontifices*, he reports that their duties included teaching the citizens what portents sent by lightning or other visible means should be recognised and properly expiated:[5]

> *ad ea elicienda ex mentibus diuinis Ioui Elicio aram in Auentino dicauit deumque consuluit auguriis quae suscipienda essent.*

---

1 *De lingua Latina* 6.86–95, citing *censoriae tabulae* (86), *commentarii consulares* (87), the *commentarius* of a quaestor's indictment (90), *Chorus Proserpinae* (a play?) and Pacuvius' *Hermiona* (94), and the *Commentarii* of Marcus Iunius (95); Iunius is probably the early jurist M. Iunius Brutus, praetor *c.* 140 BC (Cicero *Brutus* 175, Pomponius in *Digest* 1.2.2.39).
2 Varro *De lingua Latina* 6.94 (R.G. Kent's Loeb text; the MSS read *iobis uisa ara*).
3 Valerius Antias fr. 6P (Arnobius *Aduersus nationes* 5.1): . . . *quibus ad terras modis Iuppiter posset et sacrificiis elici*. Ovid *Fasti* 3.327–8: *eliciunt caelo te, Iuppiter, unde minores | nunc quoque te celebrant Eliciumque uocant.* Cf. Plutarch *Numa* 15.3–6, who naturally does not have the Latin etymology.
4 Levene 1993.16–30 on Livy's attitude to the supernatural; see also pp. 245–6 below.
5 Livy 1.20.7.

To elicit that information from the divine mind, Numa consecrated an altar to
Jupiter Elicius on the Aventine, and enquired of the god by auguries which
phenomena should be formally recognised.

Since augury was a traditionally acceptable means of ascertaining the will of the
gods, this version preserved the dignity of sober history; Livy will not tell the
story of Numa bargaining with Jupiter in person, though we can be sure he
knew it.

There is a sequel to this episode, reported by Livy a few paragraphs later in
his account of Numa's warlike successor Tullus Hostilius. Rome was struck by
a plague, and the citizens were anxious to regain the goodwill of the gods, as in
Numa's time:[6]

> ipsum regem tradunt uoluentem commentarios Numae, cum ibi quaedam occulta
> sollemnia sacrificia Ioui Elicio facta inuenisset, operatum his sacris se abdidisse; sed non
> rite initum aut curatum id sacrum esse, nec solum nullam ei oblatam caelestium speciem
> sed ira Iouis sollicitati praua religione fulmine ictum cum domo conflagrasse.
>
> They say that the king himself was turning over the commentaries of Numa,
> and when he found certain secret and solemn sacrifices that had been made to
> Jupiter Elicius, he hid himself away in order to carry out these rites. But the
> ritual was not properly entered on or carried out. Not only was no divine
> appearance manifested to him, but Jupiter was angry at being solicited by
> perverted religion. Struck by a thunderbolt, the king and his palace were
> destroyed by fire.

If Tullus was expecting a 'divine appearance' (caelestium species), what he found
in Numa's commentaries must have been instructions for more than just
augury.

We happen to know what it was from one of Livy's sources, whose account
he chose not to reproduce:[7]

> L. Piso primo annalium auctor est Tullum Hostilium regem ex Numae libris eodem quo
> illum sacrificio Iouem caelo deuocare conatum. . .
>
> According to Lucius Piso in the first book of his Annals, king Tullus Hostilius
> used the same sacrificial ritual as Numa, from Numa's books, to try to call
> Jupiter down from heaven.

But even what Livy does tell us about the death of Tullus is enough to disprove
the sanitised version of Numa and Jupiter Elicius that he has just offered; it

---

6   Livy 1.31.8. Cf. Dionysius of Halicarnassus 3.35.1–2 (with a rationalised version at 35.3–4),
    Plutarch Numa 22.7.
7   Pliny Nat. Hist. 28.14 (Piso fr. 17 Forsythe); cf. Nat. Hist. 2.140 (fr. 20 Forsythe). Piso too
    had the ritual performed parum rite.

presupposes the story which at that point he declined to tell, of a face-to-face encounter between the king and the god.

Why did Tullus fail where Numa had evidently succeeded? 'Incorrect ritual' is an odd explanation: what could count as the proper ritual for such an act? It must have been self-evident to Livy's readers that someone who tried to compel a god to appear before him was asking for a thunderbolt. However, they did know that there were people who claimed to be able to do that, and *elicere* was the verb used for what they did; it was the imposition of a binding spell by what we would call magic, and what Livy here calls 'perverted religion' (*praua religio*).[8]

In 56 BC, for instance, Cicero was attacking the credibility of a hostile witness in a court case:[9]

> *quae te tanta prauitas mentis tenuerit, qui tantus furor, ut cum inaudita ac nefaria sacra susceperis, cum inferorum animas **elicere**, cum puerorum extis deos manes mactare soleas, . . .*

What great perversion of mind, what great madness possessed you, that although you have undertaken unheard-of and impious rites, although it is your habit to bring out the spirits of the underworld and sacrifice the entrails of children to the gods of the dead, [yet you ignore the auspices of traditional religion].

The witness, Publius Vatinius, was a Pythagorean, and that philosophical sect had always been associated with magical practices.[10] Of course we need not believe forensic invective, but the allegation must have been at least an intelligible one to the senators and *equites* on the jury. In the early years of Tiberius, a young aristocrat with an interest in 'the rites of magicians' who could 'bring out the shades of the underworld by incantations' ended up facing a charge of treason, and took his own life.[11]

These examples from the world of public life provide a context for the more lurid descriptions of magic in the poets—Horace on the witches Canidia and Sagana in the graveyard,[12] Tibullus on the witch who will help adulterous

---

8 Attested already in Plato: *Republic* 364c (ἀγύρται δὲ καὶ μάντεις . . . ἐπαγωγαῖς τισιν καὶ καταδέσμοις τοὺς θεούς, ὥς φασιν, πείθοντές σφισι ὑπηρετεῖν); *Laws* 909b.
9 Cicero *In Vatinium* 14; Ogden 2001.149–50.
10 Sources in Guthrie 1962.253–4; cf. also MacMullen 1966.95–127, Ogden 2001.116–23. Vatinius was an associate of the learned P. Nigidius Figulus (*Scholia Bobiensia* 146St), who was described as *Pythagoricus et magus* (Jerome *Chron.* on 45–44 BC); for Pythagoreanism in late-republican Rome see Griffin 1994.707–10.
11 Tacitus *Annals* 2.27.2 (*magorum sacra*), 2.28.2 (*temptatus ut infernas umbras carminibus* **eliceret**).
12 Horace *Satires* 1.8.23–50, esp. 28–9: *cruor in fossam confusus, ut inde | manis* **elicerent**, *animas responsa daturas.* In *Epode* 5, Canidia is about to sacrifice a child, as Cicero claimed Vatinius did. See Ogden 2001.199–200.

lovers,[13] and above all Lucan on the terrifying Erictho, who can summon not only spirits of the dead but the Furies themselves.[14] Lucan states explicitly that Thessalian witches like Erictho had power to compel even the gods by their incantations.[15] What he describes as foul and barbaric sorcery seems to be exactly what Tullus Hostilius was punished for trying to do; yet Tullus was following the instructions of good king Numa, and Numa himself—as Livy was reluctant to reveal—had evidently been able to compel Jupiter, and call him down from heaven.

We do not know when the story about Numa 'eliciting' Jupiter was first created; but it is very clear that by the time Livy was writing attitudes to such activities had shifted fundamentally. That is not surprising. 'In archaic times magic was "embedded", that is, an integrated part of everyday practice. Nobody thought about it as "magic".'[16] Circe's powers are taken for granted in the *Odyssey*, including her instructions for calling up the shades of the dead.[17] But the disciplines of the city-state defined more rigorously what was acceptable in the community's relationship with the gods, and what was not. The creation of magic as a category came about when certain practices were identified as both objectionable and alien—the malign inventions of the Persian *magoi*.[18] When did that happen in Rome?

The tradition of Numa as a pupil of Pythagoras probably goes back at least to the fourth century BC.[19] At that time it was accepted doctrine that Pythagoras had travelled to Persia to learn the wisdom of 'Zaratas the Chaldaean'—i.e. Zoroaster.[20] Three centuries later both Cicero and Livy rejected the whole idea of Numa's connection with Pythagoras, partly on chronological grounds but also because Rome's wise king could surely not have derived his wisdom from foreign sources.[21] Their attitude was the result of a major shift

---

13 Tibullus 1.2.43–54, esp. 47–8: *haec cantu finditque solum manesque sepulcris | **elicit***.
14 Lucan 6.507–830, esp. 732–3: '*iam uos* [the Furies] *ego nomine uero* | **eliciam** . . .' Cf. Pliny *Nat. Hist.* 30.14 for Nero's wish to use magic 'to command the gods' (*imperare dis concupiuit*); Ogden 2001.152–3 .
15 Lucan 6.440–51, 492–9, 527–8 (esp. 443–4, 497–8, 528 for the *carmina*); cf. Statius *Thebaid* 3.144–5 (*plurima . . . imperet ad superos*), Apuleius *Metamorphoses* 1.8.4 (*deos infimare*), 3.15.7 (*coguntur numina*), 3.18.3 (*numinum coactorum uiolentia*).
16 Ankarloo and Clark 1999.xv. Cf. Ogden 1999.85: 'there is no easy way to separate binding spells from what can uncontroversially be termed "religion" in an ancient context.'
17 As noted by Pliny *Nat. Hist.* 30.6; Homer *Odyssey* 10.504–40, carried out at 11.23–50.
18 See Gordon 1999, esp. 162–5, 229–31, 244–52.
19 Numa and Pythagoras: Diodorus Siculus 8.14, Cicero *De republica* 2.28 (*falsum*), Livy 1.18.2 (*falso*), Dionysius of Halicarnassus 2.59.1, Ovid *Metamorphoses* 15.1–484, Plutarch *Numa* 1.2–4, 8.4–10, 22.4; Storchi Marino 1999, esp. 82–3 on the date of the tradition.
20 Aristoxenus fr. 13 Wehrli.
21 Cicero *De republica* 2.28–9 (*non esse nos transmarinis nec inportatis artibus eruditos, sed genuinis domesticisque uirtutibus*), Livy 1.18.2–4 (*non tam peregrinis artibus quam disciplina tetrica ac tristi ueterum Sabinorum*).

in Roman attitudes in the late third and second centuries BC, marked by the Senate's successive purges of 'alien' religious experts—'prophets and sacrificers' in 212, Bacchanals in 186, Chaldaean astrologers in 139.[22]

It was in 181 BC that the tomb of Numa was 'discovered' on the Janiculum, containing no body but several volumes of pontifical law and Pythagorean philosophy. When the content of the books became known, the urban praetor demanded to read them, declared that they were dangerous to religion, and with the backing of the Senate had them publicly burned in the *comitium*.[23] We may, I think, interpret this mysterious episode as someone's attempt to validate the traditional belief in a Pythagorean Numa by providing 'authentic' evidence. If so, the authorities defeated it; but the book-burning did not stamp out the belief itself, which was still being defended by Plutarch three centuries later.[24]

It is against that background that we can now consider the story that Livy wouldn't tell, but which Varro alluded to in the passage with which we began. We have three authorities for it: the historian Valerius Antias, writing probably in the mid-first century AD,[25] the poet Ovid, writing at the very beginning of the first century AD,[26] and the biographer and philosopher Plutarch, writing early in the second century AD.[27]

II

Numa was worried about thunderbolts. They were portents, signs of the gods' anger; but what was the proper sacrifice of expiation?[28] He consulted his divine consort Egeria for advice.[29]

Egeria was the nymph of a spring near the ancient grove of Diana at

---

22 213 BC: Livy 25.1.8–12 (*alieno errore . . . externo ritu*). 186 BC: Livy 39.8–19, esp. 15.2–3 for the consul's speech on *prauae et externae religiones*. 139 BC: Valerius Maximus 1.3.3, Livy *Oxyrhynchus epitome* 54.

23 Livy 40.29 (*cum animum aduertisset pleraque dissoluendarum religionum esse*, 29.11), Valerius Maximus 1.1.12, Pliny *Nat. Hist.* 13.84–7, Plutarch *Numa* 22.2–5; detailed analysis of the discrepant sources in Forsythe 1994.207–15. Pythagorean content: Cassius Hemina fr. 37P (Pliny *Nat. Hist.* 13.86), Piso fr. 19 Forsythe (Pliny *Nat. Hist.* 13.87), Valerius Antias fr. 9P (Livy 40.29.8).

24 See Gruen 1990.158–70, esp. 167–8.

25 Valerius Antias fr. 6P (Arnobius *Aduersus nationes* 5.1). For the date of Antias, see Wiseman 1979.113–35 and 1998.75–89, Forsythe 2002.99–103.

26 Ovid *Fasti* 3.259–392.

27 Plutarch *Numa* 15.

28 Valerius Antias fr. 6P (*cum procurandi fulminis scientiam non haberet essetque illi cupido noscendi*); Ovid *Fasti* 3.285–8.

29 Valerius Antias fr. 6P (*Egeriae monitu*), Ovid *Fasti* 3.289–90, Plutarch *Numa* 15.5 (cf. 13.1). Both Ovid (*Fasti* 3.261–76) and Plutarch (*Numa* 15.2) introduce the story with a 'preface' on Egeria.

Aricia.[30] But she was also a goddess at Rome, one of the *Camenae*, whose sacred grove and spring were just outside the Porta Capena.[31] She was Numa's wife (or lover), and his adviser on relations with the gods.[32] (Sceptical historians preserved the story by reporting it as what Numa himself told the Roman People, an invention to confirm his authority.[33]) She was thought of as having magical powers, for instance in miraculously furnishing Numa's frugal table with costly food and drink—a feat otherwise attributed in ancient authors to sorcerers and witches.[34]

Thanks to St Augustine's interest in the subject, we know that Varro dealt at length with Numa in his dialogue *De cultu deorum*.[35] The long peace of Numa's reign was due to the benevolence of the gods, which was achieved, according to Varro, by Numa's practice of hydromancy.[36] This technique, which originated in Persia and was later employed also by Pythagoras (thus Varro avoided the chronological impossibility of Numa as a Pythagorean disciple), involved seeing the gods' reflections in water; Numa was thus able to consult them on what form of ritual they required him to use.[37] Because he 'brought out' (*egerere*) water for this purpose (no doubt from the spring of the Camenae), the story arose that Numa had a divine counsellor called 'Egeria'. By this means Varro was able to avoid attributing to the pious king a sexual relationship which would have been unworthy of the dignity of the gods.[38]

Varro did, however, attribute to Numa the desire to keep secret his method of communicating with the immortals. He had the books that explained the

---

30 Virgil *Aeneid* 7.762–4; Ovid *Fasti* 3.263–75, *Metamorphoses* 15.487–92; Statius *Siluae* 5.3.290–1, Martial 6.47.3.
31 *Camenae*: Livy 1.21.3; Dionysius of Halicarnassus 2.60.5 ('Muses'); Ovid *Fasti* 3.275, *Metamorphoses* 15.482; Martial 6.47.3–4, Juvenal 3.16; Plutarch *Numa* 8.6, 13.2 ('Muses'). Porta Capena: Juvenal 3.10–20, cf. Martial 2.6.15–16.
32 Cicero *De legibus* 1.4 (*fabula*), Dionysius of Halicarnassus 2.60.4–5 (μυθολογοῦσιν); Ovid *Fasti* 3.262, 276, *Metamorphoses* 15.482–4; Martial 10.35.13–14; Plutarch *Numa* 4.1–2 (λόγος), *Moralia* 321c (μυθωδέστερον).
33 Livy 1.19.5; Plutarch *Numa* 4.8, 8.6, 15.1.
34 Dionysius of Halicarnassus 2.60.5–7, Plutarch *Numa* 15.2; cf. Origen *Contra Celsum* 1.68 (τὰ ἔργα τῶν γοήτων), Philostratus *Vita Apollonii* 3.27 (Indian sage), 4.25 (*empousa* at Corinth).
35 Augustine *City of God* 3.9, 7.34–5 (Varro *Logistorici* frr. 42–4 Chappuis).
36 Varro *Logistorici* fr. 42 Chappuis: *quid ille* [Numa] *molitus sit et quibus artibus deos tales sibi uel illi ciuitati consociare potuerit, Varro prodit.* For compulsion of gods by hydromancy (also called lecanomancy), see *Papyri magici Graeci* IV.222–60 (Ogden 2002.205–6), with discussion in Ogden 2001.192–3.
37 Varro *Logistorici* fr. 44 Chappuis: *ut in aqua uideret imagines deorum* [*uel potius ludificationes daemonum*, comments Augustine], *a quibus audiret quid in sacris constituere atque obseruare debet.* Cf. also Strabo 16.2.39 (C762) on Persian ὑδρομάντεις.
38 Augustine *City of God* 7.35: *quod ergo aquam egesserit . . . ideo nympham Egeriam coniugem dicitur habuisse, quemadmodum in supra scripto libro Varronis exponitur.* Cf. Augustine *City of God* 18.10: *Marcus Varro non uult fabulosis aduersus deos fidem adhibere figmentis, ne de maiestate eorum dignitate indignum aliquid sentiat.*

technique buried with him, and when in 181 BC they accidentally came to light, 'the senators agreed with the dead king' and told the praetor to burn them.[39] Varro had no problem with the use of hydromancy as such—he had witnessed hydromantic divination at Tralles during the Mithridatic war[40]—but he understood why Numa and the senators of 181 BC did not want the technique divulged. He took the view that the understanding of the wise was not something to be shared with the population at large.[41]

His interpretation of Numa's piety precisely exemplifies the tripartite scheme he set out at the beginning of the *Divine Antiquities*:[42] 'mythical theology', with its tales unworthy of the divine majesty, offers the story of Numa and Egeria as lovers; 'physical [i.e. natural] theology', which philosophers understand, provides what Varro regards as the true explanation, that Numa used hydromancy to consult the gods; 'civic theology' is represented by the cult of Jupiter Elicius, and the very particular offerings made at the altar on the Aventine.

How do these Varronian categories relate to each other? Varro himself took it for granted that 'mythical theology' was necessarily secondary to 'natural theology'; the truth was turned into myth by the poets.[43] Augustine accepted that, though naturally without endorsing the truth of the philosophers' theology. Modern scholars are more likely to take the opposite view, assuming a primeval myth subsequently rationalised by etymology. But not all myths are 'primeval' (whatever that unhelpful term signifies), and since the poets Varro had in mind were clearly inventing their stories for the stage,[44] the origin of 'mythical theology' is bound up with the question of the origin of the Roman *ludi scaenici*.

Where Augustine disagreed with Varro was about the separation of the first and third categories. Since the theatre games were an integral part of pagan religion, 'civic theology' too depended on myths unworthy of the gods.[45] Over a century earlier, Arnobius had argued that this very narrative of Numa and Jupiter was both grossly offensive to divine dignity and at the same time

39 Augustus *City of God* 7.34, citing Varro's own words (*Logistorici* fr. 43 Chappuis): *ubi cum primores quasdam causas legissent, cur quidque in sacris fuerit institutum, Numae mortuo senatus adsensus est, eosque libros tamquam religiosi patres conscripti praetor ut comburet censuerunt.*
40 Apuleius *Apologia* 42.
41 Varro *Antiquitates diuinae* fr. 8 Cardauns (Augustine *City of God* 6.5): *sic alia, quae facilius intra parietes in schola quam extra in foro ferre possunt aures.*
42 Varro *Antiquitates diuinae* frr. 6–10 Cardauns (Augustine *City of God* 6.5, 6.12).
43 Augustine *City of God* 7.35: *ita enim solent res gestae aspersione mendaciorum in fabulas uerti.* See pp. 246–9 below for the same assumption in Varro's *De gente populi Romani* (Augustine *City of God* 18.10–13).
44 Augustine *City of God* 6.6 (*di poetici theatrici ludicri scaenici*), 6.7 (*theologia fabulosa theatrica scaenica*); Wiseman 1998.17–24.
45 Augustine *City of God* 6.6–7 *passim*.

essential to the Romans' traditional civic cult.[46] On that point, at least, the critics had a good case. The whole comic tale of Egeria's advice was indeed embedded in the cult practice of the Roman Republic.

III

Our sources call Egeria a nymph or a goddess interchangeably. But I think it is clear that when her story was first created she was only a nymph—a *semidea*, one of the humblest members of the immortal world.[47] She did not know the answer to Numa's problem, so she advised him to consult powers one step up in the divine hierarchy, the deities of the woods and hills of Rome, Picus and Faunus.[48] Ovid describes them as horned and hoofed; elsewhere, he identifies Faunus with Pan. According to Plutarch, 'one might liken them to satyrs and Pans'—but with an added characteristic to which we shall come in a moment.[49]

Below the Aventine was a holm-oak grove, with a cave and a spring where Picus and Faunus used to come to drink.[50] Numa left bowls of wine there, and hid in the cave with a picked group of twelve young men. Picus and Faunus came, drank deeply, and fell asleep; the twelve leapt out and bound them fast, only releasing them when they promised to tell Numa what he needed to know.[51] The obvious analogue for this story is Midas' capture of Silenus, to learn from him the workings of the universe;[52] but there are also echoes of the consultation of Proteus, since Plutarch refers to Picus and Faunus shape-shifting in their attempt to avoid capture.[53]

Picus and Faunus are known from other sources as oracular deities, and in the Euhemerised version of their myth—where they feature as kings of ancient

---

46 Arnobius *Aduersus nationes* 5.1–4 (exploiting Valerius Antias fr. 6P).

47 *Semideae*: e.g. Ovid *Heroides* 4.49, *Metamorphoses* 1.192.

48 Ovid *Fasti* 3.292 (*Romani numen utrumque soli*), 3.303 (*siluestria numina*), 3.315–16 (*'di sumus agrestes et qui dominemur in altis | montibus'*).

49 Ovid *Fasti* 3.312, cf. 2.361, 4.663, 5.99–101 (horns and hoofs); 2.423–4, 3.84, 4.650–3 (Faunus as Pan); Plutarch *Numa* 15.3.

50 Ovid *Fasti* 3.295–9, cf. 302 and 305 for the *antrum*; Calpurnius Siculus 1.8–12 describes a generic grove-cave-spring habitat for Faunus.

51 Only Antias (fr. 6P) mentions the twelve *casti iuuenes*, in what was probably an aetiology of the leaping Salii (Wiseman 1998.21–2).

52 Herodotus 8.138.2–3, Xenophon *Anabasis* 1.2.13, Theopompus *FGrH* 115 F75; Gantz 1993.138 for the iconographic evidence. Virgil (*Eclogues* 6.13–30) has Silenus captured by two boys and a nymph.

53 Plutarch *Numa* 15.4; cf. Homer *Odyssey* 4.454–61 (Proteus and Menelaus), Virgil *Georgics* 4.437–47 (Proteus and Aristaeus). Proteus could be thought of as a magician: Petronius *Satyricon* 134.12, Pliny *Nat. Hist.* 30.6.

Latium—they are described as skilled prophets or augurs.[54] But Plutarch knew another and more sensational interpretation of their powers:[55]

δυνάμει δὲ φαρμάκων καὶ δεινότητι τῆς περὶ τὰ θεῖα γοητείας λέγονται ταῦτα τοῖς ὑφ' Ἑλλήνων προσαγορευθεῖσιν Ἰδαίοις Δακτύλοις σοφιζόμενοι περιιέναι τὴν Ἰταλίαν.

It is said that they go around Italy practising the same craft, by the power of their potions and the skill of their sorcery regarding divine matters, as those called by the Greeks the Idaean Daktyloi.

According to Ephorus the Idaean Daktyloi were wizards, who moved from their native Phrygia to the island of Samothrace and astonished the people there by their skill in 'incantations, initiations and mystery rituals'.[56] The Samothracian mystery cult was well known to the Romans; Varro claimed that Aeneas had brought the Penates from there, that Tarquinius Priscus had been an initiate, and that some Roman religious terminology was derived from Samothrace.[57]

The main purpose of the Numa story was to explain why the offerings made at the altar of Jupiter Elicius consisted of fish, hair and onions: the wise king had discovered that the god wanted live human heads, but would be satisfied with live fish, human hair and onion-heads.[58] Our sources report three different versions of how Numa discovered this.

The first is the simplest: Picus and Faunus told him.[59] But how did they know? As Faunus points out in Ovid's version, rustic divinities are hardly experts on thunderbolts:[60]

'magna petis nec quae monitu tibi discere nostro
   fas sit: habent finis numina nostra suos.
di sumus agrestes et qui dominemur in altis
   montibus: arbitrium est in sua tela Ioui.'

---

54 Oracles: Plutarch *Moralia* 268f (Picus); Virgil *Aeneid* 7.81–103, Ovid *Fasti* 4.649–68 (Faunus). Prophet-kings: Augustine *City of God* 18.15 (Picus); Plutarch *Moralia* 268d, *Origo gentis Romanae* 4.4 (Faunus). See Ogden 2001.91–2 on Virgil's story of Latinus consulting the oracle of his father Faunus, 'an amalgamation of a *nekuomanteion* and a hero-oracle'; Ovid, however, thinks of the oracular Faunus as a hoofed divinity (n. 49 above).

55 Plutarch *Numa* 15.3.

56 Ephorus *FGrH* 70 F104 (Diodorus 5.64.4): ὑπάρξαντας δὲ γόητας ἐπιτηδεῦσαι τάς τε ἐπῳδὰς καὶ τελετὰς καὶ μυστήρια.

57 Varro *Antiquitates humanae* fr. 2.8 Mirsch (Aeneas), *Antiquitates diuinae* fr. 205 Cardauns (Tarquinius); *De lingua Latina* 5.58 (a phrase in the *augurum libri*), 7.34 (*camillus*); for Varro on Samothrace, see also *Antiquitates diuinae* fr. 206 Cardauns (Augustine *City of God* 7.28), *Logistorici* fr. 40 Chappuis.

58 Arnobius *Aduersus nationes* 5.1 (Antias fr. 6P), Ovid *Fasti* 3.337–44, Plutarch *Numa* 15.5.

59 Plutarch *Numa* 15.4: τούτους φασὶ ... τὸν ἐπὶ τοῖς κεραυνοῖς ἐκδιδάξαι καθαρμόν, ὃς ποιεῖται μέχρι νῦν διὰ κρομμύων καὶ τριχῶν καὶ μαινίδων.

60 Ovid *Fasti* 3.313–16.

'You're asking a lot, and for something you are forbidden to know by our instruction. Our powers have their limits. We are gods of the countryside, masters of the high hills; Jupiter's weapons are under *his* control.'

Somehow, Numa had to talk to Jupiter himself. Hence the second and third versions of the story, which differ slightly but significantly.

According to Valerius Antias, Picus and Faunus told Numa 'by what means and by what sacrifices' Jupiter could be brought out of heaven.[61] That cautious formulation allows the assumption that the pious king did nothing unlawful, and that Jupiter came of his own free will. 'It is rational enough,' observed Plutarch,[62] 'to suppose that the deity would not place his affection upon horses or birds, but rather upon human beings eminently distinguished by virtue, and that he neither dislikes nor disdains to hold conversation with a man of wisdom and piety.'

The third version, however, stated without concealment that Picus and Faunus brought Jupiter out by the arts of magic, and that Jupiter was angry.[63] Ovid is explicit that he was *compelled* to come:[64]

> 'deme tamen nobis uincula,' Picus ait:
> 'Iuppiter huc ueniet, ualida perductus ab arte.
>   nubila promissi Styx mihi testis erit.'
> emissi laqueis quid agant, quae carmina dicant,
>   quaque trahant superis sedibus arte Iouem,
> scire nefas homini: nobis concessa canentur
>   quaeque pio dici uatis ab ore licet.

'Just take the shackles off us,' said Picus, 'and Jupiter will come here, drawn by powerful art. Cloudy Styx will be the witness of my promise.' What they did when they were set free, what incantations they said, by what art they dragged Jupiter from his high seat, it is forbidden for man to know. I shall sing what I'm allowed, what may be spoken from the mouth of a pious bard.

Although the story has a happy ending—Jupiter is amused by Numa's ingenuity and goes back to heaven in a good mood[65]—the fact remains that he has been forced to obey a magic spell, just as if wicked Erictho had been practising her *polluta ars.*[66]

---

61 Arnobius *Aduersus nationes* 5.1 (Antias fr. 6P): *illos statim perdocuisse regem quibus ad terras modis Iuppiter posset et sacrificiis elici.*
62 Plutarch *Numa* 4.3, trans. John and William Langhorne (1770).
63 Plutarch *Numa* 15.5: ἔνιοι δὲ οὐ τοὺς δαίμονας φασιν ὑποθέσθαι τὸν καθαρμόν, ἀλλ᾽ ἐκείνους μὲν καταγαγεῖν τὸν Δία μαγεύσαντας, τὸν δὲ θεὸν ὀργιζόμενον . . .
64 Ovid *Fasti* 3.320–6.
65 Plutarch *Numa* 15.6 (τὸν μὲν θεὸν ἀπελθεῖν ἵλεω γενόμενον); Ovid *Fasti* 3.343 (*risit*).
66 Lucan 6.509; see above, p. 158.

I think it is inconceivable that this story is a late invention. Why should anyone want to impute the use of forbidden magic to the pious king, if the tradition did not exist already? Besides, the problematic element in the story seems to be inherent in the cult itself—not only the god's title (from *elicere*) but also the nature of the offerings, since hair and fish were much used in magical rituals.[67] Some scholars resort to the concept of 'folktale',[68] which does at least imply antiquity, but is otherwise an unhelpful description of the aetiological explanation of a public cult.

Certainly the story as we have it is a comedy, perhaps first created for the stage.[69] I think it is likely that 'tales unworthy of the gods' were characteristic of the plays put on at the Roman dramatic festivals, and that such plays were intended to be educational as well as entertaining.[70] At any rate, what we seem to have here is an old story designed to encourage the Roman People to believe that their wise king could call on magical powers—and that the eventual outcome was the shield that fell from heaven, a divine talisman to guarantee Rome's prosperity.[71]

IV

Modern work on magic in the ancient world tends to move straight from Hellenistic Greece to late-Republican Rome.[72] The Roman Republic's knowledge of magic is assumed to be part of its assimilation of Greek culture, supposedly in the early second century BC.[73] The tacit premise, that Rome was free of outside cultural influences until 'after the Punic Wars' (as Horace put it),[74] is demonstrably false: the Greek language was known in Latium by about 800 BC, and Greek mythology is attested at Rome as soon as recognisable iconography becomes available in the sixth century.[75] Given the evident early interest in Pythagoras, and the prohibition of casting spells in the *Twelve*

---

67 Hair: e.g. Euripides *Hippolytus* 513, Apuleius *Metamorphoses* 3.16; Ogden 1999.14–15. Fish: e.g. Ovid *Fasti* 2.577–8, Apuleius *Apologia* 27.

68 Rose 1928.318; Grant 1971.145–6.

69 Valerius Antias fr. 6P (Arobius *Aduersus nationes* 5.1, *excogitata et comparata derisui*), Plutarch *Numa* 15.6 (μυθώδη καὶ γελοῖα); see above, n. 44.

70 Augustine *City of God* 4.26–7; Varro *De lingua Latina* 6.18 (a play that *docuit populum*). For a possible example, see Wiseman 2004a.116–17 (on Ovid *Fasti* 2.583–616).

71 Ovid *Fasti* 3.259–62, 349–92; implicit also at Plutarch *Numa* 13.1. See Wiseman 1998.21–2 for the suggestion that the 'twelve chaste youths' of Antias fr. 6P were an aetiology for the Salii.

72 E.g. Luck 1999.120: Theocritus followed by Nigidius Figulus.

73 E.g. Dickie 2001.124–8, esp. 126 on 'new ways of thinking and new forms of behaviour' in the time of the elder Cato.

74 Horace *Epistles* 2.1.156–63, a disastrously influential passage.

75 See briefly Wiseman 1994.6–8, 26–8; on the Gabii graffito, see Ridgway 1996, Peruzzi 1998.19–22, Wiseman 2004a.13–16.

Tables,[76] we can be confident that the Romans of the fifth and fourth centuries BC were well aware of the magic arts.

They evidently disapproved of the malicious use of such arts against individuals, but we have no reason to suppose that the arts themselves were regarded as un-Roman. On the contrary, the implication of the Numa and Jupiter story is that in the archaic period (whenever it was that the Elicius cult was set up) they were taken for granted as an acceptable way for a wise and pious king to make contact with the gods. The trouble came in the second century BC, when the Senate arrogated to itself the duty of deciding which traditional practices were acceptable, and which not. The burning of the Pythagorean 'books of Numa' in 181 BC was an early manifestation of Roman authoritarianism, later so familiar under the emperors.[77] But it seems that the story of Numa and Jupiter was firmly fixed in the popular mind, no doubt through the medium of stage performances, and so it survived to be preserved in literature.

As a poet, Ovid could tell the story straight, so long as he virtuously dissociated himself from any knowledge of magic; so too could a frivolous historian like Valerius Antias, much to the indignation of Arnobius.[78] But a philosophical antiquarian could allow only a rationalised reference to hydromancy, while serious historians, protecting Numa's reputation, referred to magic and the compulsion of deities only as sacrilegious rites, as in the exemplary case of Tullus Hostilius, blasted by the angry god.[79] Plutarch, the Greek philosopher who wanted to insist on Numa's Pythagoreanism despite the chronological impossibility,[80] narrated the story only as a *mythos*—not what really happened, but a Platonic 'noble lie' told to the unruly Romans by Numa the philosopher-king.[81]

For our purpose, the value of the story is as an example of how something that belonged exclusively to the archaic world of pre-literary Rome can nevertheless become visible to us, even through the medium of literature itself.

---

76 *Tabulae* VIII.1 and 4: texts and discussion at Crawford 1996.677–9, 682–4.
77 See Dio 52.36.1–3 (Maecenas' advice to Augustus), and Paulus *Sententiae* 5.23.17–19 (Ogden 2002.279) on the punishment of magicians, including the public burning of their books.
78 Arnobius *Aduersus nationes* 5.1: *quid? illa quae historiae continent graues seriae curiosae ... poetarum sunt excogitata lasciuia?*
79 See above, pp. 160–1 (Varro), 155–7 (Livy and Piso).
80 Plutarch *Numa* 1.2–3, 8.3–10, 14.2–3, 22.3–4.
81 Plutarch *Numa* 15.1, cf. 4.8 ('not ignoble' story about Egeria), 8.1–3 (Plato).

CHAPTER EIGHT

Origines ludorum

I

si Latinis ciuitatem dederitis, credo, existimatis uos ita ut constitistis in contione habituros locum aut ludis et festis interfuturos. nonne illos omnia occupaturos putatis?
'I suppose you imagine that if you give the Latins citizenship, you'll have space at public meetings and take part in games and festivals in just the same way as now. Don't you think they'll take over everything?'

C. Fannius (*cos.* 122 BC)[1]

The consul's argument tells us what mattered most about being a Roman citizen: participation in politics, and in the games and festivals of the gods. The audience at the games was the Roman People, and their reactions could be taken as those of the citizen body as a whole.[2] When Polybius comments on the importance of religious belief in holding the Roman state together, he explains it by the use of 'tragedy' to influence the People;[3] presumably that refers to plays performed at the *ludi scaenici*, which often featured the Furies punishing evildoers and the gods announcing to the audience the benefits they had conferred on them.[4]

So the origins and development of the 'public games', as the Romans called them, are a significant part of the political history of the Republic, and the appearance of a learned and detailed monograph on the subject is a reason for gratitude and congratulation.[5] Deservedly, Frank Bernstein's book will be for the foreseeable future the standard work on the history of the *ludi*, and for that

---

1   *Oratio de sociis et nomine Latino contra Gracchum* fr. 3 Malcovati (Julius Victor 6.4 = *Rhetores Latini* 402 Halm).
2   Cicero *Pro Sestio* 106, 116–18, *De haruspicum responso* 22–5, *In Pisonem* 65, *Ad Atticum* 2.19.3, 14.3.2, *Philippics* 1.36.
3   Polybius 6.56.8 and 11: ἐπὶ τοσοῦτον γὰρ ἐκτετραγῴδηται καὶ παρεισῆκται τοῦτο τὸ μέρος [sc. δεισιδαιμονία] παρ' αὐτοῖς εἴς τε τοὺς κατ' ἰδίαν βίους καὶ τὰ κοινὰ τῆς πόλεως ὥστε μὴ καταλιπεῖν ὑπερβολήν. [. . .] λείπεται τοῖς ἀδήλοις φόβοις καὶ τῇ τοιαύτῃ τραγῳδίᾳ τὰ πλήθη συνέχειν. See Mazzarino 1966.61–2, Zorzetti 1980.64–5.
4   Cicero *Pro Roscio Amerino* 67, *In Pisonem* 46, *De haruspicum responso* 39, *De legibus* 1.40, *Academica* 2.89 (Furies); Plautus *Amphitruo* 41–5 (gods).
5   Bernstein 1998.

very reason it is important to draw attention to any arguments in it which may seem to be less than compelling.

II

A convenient summary of the dates of origin of the different *ludi* is offered in Bernstein's Appendix 2:[6]

ludi maximi/Romani	about 509 or 507
ludi plebeii	probably 220
ludi Ceriales	probably 220 or 219
ludi Apollinares	208
ludi Megalenses	191
ludi Florales	173
ludi Victoriae (Sullanae)	81
Ludi Victoriae Caesaris	45

In fact, only the last two of these dates are secure. Cicero and Livy are explicit that the *ludi Romani* were instituted by Tarquinius Priscus;[7] Livy gives 212 for the origin of the *ludi Apollinares*,[8] and 204 and 194 (as well as 191) for that of the *Megalenses*;[9] the *ludi Florales* dated from 241 or 238, according to Velleius Paterculus and Pliny respectively.[10]

In the case of the *Apollinares*, which were the responsibility of the urban praetor, we know that at first they were vowed by the praetor each year and held on a day of his choosing, and then in 208 they were made annual with a fixed date.[11] The *Florales* similarly were not at first a regular part of the calendar, and we do not know how often (or even whether) the plebeian aediles of each year held them before the consuls of 173, acting on a *senatus*

---

6   Bernstein 1998.358.
7   Cicero *De republica* 2.36 (*eundem primum ludos maximos, qui Romani dicti sunt, fecisse accepimus*), Livy 1.35.9 (*sollemnes deinde annui mansere ludi, Romani magnique uarie appellati*); Eutropius 1.6.1 and *De uiris illustribus* 6.8 are probably dependent on Livy. Cf. also ps.Asconius 217 Stangl: *Romani ludi sub regibus instituti sunt magnique appellati, quod magnis impensis dati.*
8   Livy 25.12.1–15 (concluding *haec est origo ludorum Apollinarium*), 27.23.5.
9   Livy 29.10.4–11.8 and 14.5–14 (concluding *ludi fuere, Megalesia appellati*, 204); 34.54.3 (*Megalesia ludos scaenicos A. Atilius Serranus L. Scribonius aediles curules primi fecerunt*, 194); 36.36.4 (*ludique ob dedicationem eius facti, quos primos scaenicos fuisse Antias Valerius est auctor, Megalesia appellatos*, 191).
10   Velleius Paterculus 1.14.8 on colonial foundations (...*proximoque anno Torquato Sempronioque consulibus Brundisium et post triennium Spoletium, quo anno Floralium ludorum factum est initium*); Pliny *Nat. Hist.* 18.236 (*itaque iidem Floralia IV kal. easdem instituerunt urbis anno DXVI ex oraculis Sibyllae, ut omnia bene deflorescerent*). Cf. Ovid *Fasti* 5.277–94 on the Publicii, plebeian aediles no doubt in one or other of those years; also the Flora coins of C. Clodius Vestalis in 41 BC (Crawford 1974.521, no. 512), which may have been for the two-hundredth anniversary.
11   Livy 27.23.5–7, by a law of the urban praetor P. Licinius Varus.

consultum, made them annual.[12] But it is worth noticing that Livy doesn't mention the reform of 173;[13] evidently it was a less important stage than the founding of the games 65 or 68 years earlier.

Bernstein argues that the *Megalenses* only became annual with the dedication of the temple of Magna Mater in 191, and applies the same logic to the *ludi Romani*: in honour of Jupiter Optimus Maximus, they can only have been regular after the Capitoline temple was dedicated.[14] That is of course a possible solution (in both cases), but it is certainly not a necessary one. No doubt Rome already had a cult of Jupiter before the Capitoline temple was built, and the famously wealthy Tarquins could certainly afford to put on games every year.[15]

There is a particular problem with the *ludi Romani*, arising from what ought to be the best of evidence, a statement by an aedile-elect concerning the games for which he was going to be responsible:[16]

> *habeo rationem quid a populo Romano acceperim; mihi ludos sanctissimos maxima cum cura et caerimonia Cereri Libero Liberaeque faciundos, mihi Florem matrem populo plebique Romanae ludorum celebritate placandam, mihi ludos antiquissimos, qui primi Romani appellati sunt, cum dignitate maxima et religione Ioui Iunoni Mineruaeque esse faciundos.*
>
> 'I think carefully about the task the Roman People has laid upon me. I shall have to put on, with all possible care and ceremony, the most sacred games of Ceres, Liber and Libera; I shall have to secure the goodwill of Mother Flora for the people and *plebs* of Rome by the popularity of her games; and for Jupiter, Juno and Minerva, with the utmost dignity and religious piety, I shall have to put on the most ancient games, the first that were called "Roman".'

This puzzling passage was brilliantly explained by Lily Ross Taylor long ago.[17] The *ludi Ceriales* and *Florales* were certainly the plebeian aediles' responsibility, as the *Romani* and *Megalenses* were that of the curule aediles;[18] it is therefore inevitable that Cicero was a plebeian aedile, and that the third games he refers to were the *ludi plebeii*.

According to one strand of the historiographical tradition, the Plebeian Games went right back to the beginning of the Republic.[19] What Cicero

---

12 Ovid *Fasti* 5.295–330; the famine that caused the Senate to act may have been the result of the plague of 175–4 (Obsequens 10, Livy 41.21.5–8, 42.2.7).

13 There was an opportunity at 42.2.3–7, on *prodigia* and the *pax deorum*; cf. also 42.10.7–8 on the locust cloud in Apulia.

14 Bernstein 1998.193–5 on Magna Mater, 50–1 on Iuppiter Optimus Maximus.

15 For the historicity of the tradition about the Tarquins' wealth, see Zevi 1995.

16 Cicero *Verrines* 5.36; cf. *Pro Murena* 40 (*ego qui trinos ludos aedilis feceram*).

17 Taylor 1939, esp. 194–7 on the games.

18 Dio Cassius 37.8.1 (curule), 47.40.6 and Ovid *Fasti* 5.287–92 (plebeian).

19 Valerius Maximus 1.7.4 (491 BC); ps.Asconius 217 Stangl (*plebeii ludi, quos exactis regibus pro libertate plebis fecerunt, an pro reconciliatione plebis post secessionem in Auentinum*).

implies is that they were originally the only 'Roman Games', and that only after 367, when the curule aediles took over, did the *ludi plebeii* and *Romani* become two separate events.[20] I suspect that this narrative was the creation of Licinius Macer, himself an ex-tribune of the *plebs*, whose history was probably coming out at just the time Cicero was speaking.[21]

III

Bernstein, however, rejects Taylor's argument outright, and thinks the Cicero passage must be emended. That is a desperate expedient, and not a convincing one—for what would be the point of calling them 'the ancient games which were first called Plebeian'? It is clear that Bernstein is driven to it by the ill-founded belief that the *ludi plebeii* were a creation of the late third century, and that the Circus Flaminius was created in 220 BC to provide a site for them.[22] That idea comes with the authority of Mommsen,[23] but even so it must be wrong.

In both title and structure, the *ludi plebeii* are analogous to the *Romani*. Neither games are named after a god; both are centred on Jupiter's day,[24] in the only two months of the Roman calendar which feature no 'large-letter' festivals except the Kalends, Nones and Ides. That in itself suggests that the *ludi plebeii* and *Romani* coexisted at the time the calendar was put together (no later than the fourth century BC), and in any case the very existence of a specifically plebeian festival suggests a fifth- or fourth-century origin.

By contrast, the *ludi* that were introduced in the third century all have very specific foundation stories arising out of the particular issues of the day. The *Florales* resulted from the plebeian aediles fining landowners who encroached on the public land, the *Apollinares* from the praetor's alleged discovery of the prophecies of Cn. Marcius after a crack-down on 'seers and sacrificers', the *Megalenses* from the Sibylline Books' advice on how to drive the foreign enemy out of Italy.[25] The only foundation story that survives for the *ludi plebeii*,

---

20 Livy 6.42.12–14 (*recusantibus id munus aedilibus plebis*, 367). Cf. Dionysius of Halicarnassus 5.57.5 for 'the games named after the city' in 500 BC (probably from Aelius Tubero: Wiseman 1994.54–5); it is not clear who was thought to be organising them.

21 See Wiseman 1995.107–8 and 135–6. Macer was tribune in 73; he died in 66, when his history had reached at least as far as 299 BC (Livy 10.9.10, fr. 19P).

22 Bernstein 1998.79–80 and 158–63: 'problematisch ist aber, dass die Angabe des Relativsatz über die *Romani* als *ludi antiquissimi* zu *plebeii* emendiert werden muss' (79).

23 Mommsen 1887.519–20: 'Wann diese Spiele eingerichtet worden sind, ist zweifelhaft, wahrscheinlich erst im J. d. St. 534.' The doubt has disappeared in Mommsen 1893.335: 'Ludi plebeii post Romanos magnos antiquissimi et honoratissimi instituti sunt a.u.c 534.'

24 Ides sacred to Jupiter: Ovid *Fasti* 1.56, Macrobius *Saturnalia* 1.15.14–15, Lydus *De mensibus* 3.10. The idea that the calendar must pre-date the dedication of the Capitoline temple, because 'of the feast-days which it marks with large letters none is connected with that cult' (Rose and Price 1996.274), is simply invalid.

25 See notes 8–10 above.

that they celebrated the liberty of the *plebs* after the expulsion of the kings or the secession to the Aventine, is in a late Ciceronian scholiast. Too late to be reliable, according to Bernstein; but if there had been a genuine historical origin for the games in 220 BC, one might have expected a scholiast to know it.[26]

Finally, the building of the Circus Flaminius is certainly irrelevant to the question. It is true that Valerius Maximus anachronistically puts the *ludi plebeii* in the Circus Flaminius in 491 BC;[27] but there is no other evidence that C. Flaminius' creation was ever used for major *ludi*, and ample evidence that it was a piazza surrounded by very substantial public buildings, quite unsuitable for chariot racing.[28] It is also true that theatrical performances were held in the piazza at the *ludi Apollinares*;[29] but that was only because the temple of Apollo was there, and no connection with the *ludi plebeii* in honour of Jupiter. Mommsen's theory has nothing to recommend it.

IV

In Bernstein's list, the *ludi plebeii* and *Ceriales* belong together. Since the first reliable evidence for them comes in Livy, respectively in 216 and 202 BC, he assumes that they were introduced soon before that time.[30] The reason for the assumption is his belief in the 'hellenizing' of the Roman religious experience in the third century BC.[31] But it is an illusion to suppose that Greek ideas influ-

---

26 See n. 19 above; Bernstein 1998.79–80.

27 Valerius Maximus 1.7.4; he may have been imagining the open space of the *prata flaminia*, the site enclosed by C. Flaminius in 220 (Livy 3.54.15). For the gloss *in circo* [*maximo et Flaminio*] *spectaculi locus* at Valerius Maximus 4.4.8, see Wiseman 1976.45.

28 See Humphrey 1986.540–5, Viscogliosi 1993. The only *ludi* Varro knew about in the Circus Flaminius were the horse-races of the obscure *ludi Taurei* (*De lingua Latina* 5.154).

29 Plutarch *Cicero* 13 (the temples of Bellona and Apollo were adjacent); cf. Livy 3.63.7 (*in prata flaminia, ubi nunc aedes Apollinis est*), 40.51.3 (censor of 179 lets contracts for *theatrum et proscaenium ad Apollinis*).

30 Bernstein 1998.157–8; Livy 23.30.17 (*plebei ludi aedilium M. Aurelii Cottae et M. Claudii Marcelli ter instaurati*), 30.39.8 (*Cerialia ludos dictator et magister equitum ex senatus consulto fecerunt*). [So too Csapo and Slater 1994.208: *ludi plebeii* 'instituted in 220 BC', *Ceriales* 'celebrated from 202 BC' (no evidence or argument offered).]

31 Bernstein 1998.227: 'Veränderungen und Neuerungen wurden in der Regel auf ein gewandeltes Religionsverständnis zurückgeführt. Neue, vor allem griechisch-hellenistische Gottesvorstellungen führten zur Erweiterung des Ritus und veranlassten die Einführung neuer *ludi publici*. Diese Ausweitung des öffentlichen Spielbetriebs in Rom vollzog sich allerdings auf mehreren Ebenen. Nur vereinzelt konnte aufgrund der Überlieferungssituation beobachtet werden, wann es zu einer Vermehrung der Spieltage kam. Gleichwol dürfte von einer sukzessiven Zunahme ausgehen sein. Andererseits wurden in einem ziemlich kurzen Zeitraum fünf weitere statarische *ludi publici*, die *ludi plebeii*, *Ceriales*, *Apollinares*, *Megalenses* und *Florales*, eingerichtet. Diese Tatsache ist um so bemerkenswerter, als es von spätarchaischer Zeit bis in das späte 3. Jahrhundert nur die *ludi maximi* bzw. *Romani* für Iuppiter Optimus Maximus gegeben hat.' I think there is a circular argument hiding in that final sentence.

enced the Romans only then; the iconographic evidence illustrates the phenomenon at least as far back as the sixth century.[32] So there is no *a priori* reason to
attribute the origin of the undatable games to the latest period possible.

In fact, each of the Livy passages offers no more than a *terminus ante quem*.
Since they refer to exceptional circumstances which happened to occur in
those years, the games concerned may have been regularly held for many
generations before then, and in the case of the *ludi plebeii* we have seen that
they probably were. I think the same applies to the *Ceriales*.

If the games of Ceres had really been introduced in 220 or 219 BC, one
would expect some account of their introduction to have survived, as it has for
the games of Flora, Apollo and the Great Mother. Certainly one would not
expect a foundation story attributing it to the battle of Lake Regillus in the
early fifth century BC; but that is what we have, not in a late scholiast but in the
narrative of Dionysius of Halicarnassus, very probably taken from a second-
century BC source.[33] We needn't suppose that the account is necessarily
historical. The point is rather that if the Romans of the second and first
centuries BC believed that Ceres' games were introduced in the early
Republic, the existence of that tradition puts the onus of proof on those who
claim, like Bernstein, that they were really introduced nearly three centuries
later, in circumstances that happen not to have been recorded.

The moneyer C. Memmius claimed on his coins in 56 BC that one of his
ancestors was the first to hold the *ludi Ceriales*: MEMMIVS AED. CERIALIA
PREIMVS FECIT.[34] At first glance, that seems a good argument for a late
foundation date; the first securely dated Memmius was praetor in 172 BC, so an
aedile a generation or two earlier would bring us to the period suggested by
Bernstein. Indeed, all the standard works confidently place the moneyer's
ancestor as 'aedile ?211' and father of the praetor.[35] But despite the question
mark, the date 211 is not uncertain; it is worthless. It should be only 'before
210', when Livy started recording the names of plebeian aediles.[36] Here too,
we have no more than a *terminus ante quem*.

It is important to remember that the late-republican Memmii claimed to be
a very ancient family indeed, descended from Assaracus and the kings of Troy.[37]

---

32 For a brief statement, see North 2000a.15–16.
33 Dionysius of Halicarnassus 6.10.1, 6.17.2–4, 6.94.3. Probably from the history of A. Postu-
    mius Albinus, consul in 151 and descendant of the victor of Lake Regillus: see Wiseman
    1998.35–6 and 86–7.
34 Crawford 1974. 451–2, no. 427.
35 Münzer 1932; Broughton 1951.276; Sumner 1973.87.
36 See Münzer 1932.303, Broughton 1951.277 n. 4.
37 Virgil *Aeneid* 12.127 (*genus Assaraci Mnestheus*), 5.117 (*mox Italus Mnestheus, genus a quo
    nomine Memmi*); the name is a calque on μεμνῆσθαι = *meminisse*. Mnestheus was evidently
    named on the late-republican monument of C. Memmius C.f. at Ephesus: see Torelli
    1997.152–74, esp. 164–7.

What were they supposed to have been doing between the arrival of Aeneas in Italy and the praetorship of 172 BC? Compare the Sicinii, who claimed descent from the aristocracy of Alba Longa; they too are first securely attested in the early second century BC.[38] But someone in the historiographical tradition gave the Sicinii a heroic role in the early history of the plebs, from 493 to 387 BC; it was almost certainly Licinius Macer, honouring a fellow-*popularis* of the post-Sullan years.[39] The Memmii too had *popularis* credentials (the radical tribune of 111 BC was the moneyer's grandfather),[40] and since the cult of Ceres, Liber and Libera was the centre of the early plebeian movement, it is quite possible that Macer—and the Memmii themselves—attributed the origin of Ceres' games to a plebeian aedile of the early fifth century BC.

The following fifth-century plebeian aediles are named in the historical tradition: L. Iunius Brutus and L. Sicinius, 492; T. Iunius Brutus and C. Visellius(?) Ruga, 491; L. Alienus, 454.[41] The Iunii Bruti clearly owe their existence to the story of the Liberator, though in a version which evidently denied the execution of his sons.[42] The Sicinii we have considered already; Visellii and Al(l)ieni are otherwise known only as late-republican tribunes of the *plebs*.[43] Memmius the aedile would fit as easily into that pseudo-historical context as into the real history of the late third century.

So the coin legend does not disprove the presumption that the *ludi Ceriales*, like the *plebeii*, are more probably an early fifth-century than a late third-century phenomenon. As noted above, that doesn't mean that the account of their origin in Dionysius, as the result of a vow for victory at the battle of Lake Regillus, is necessarily historical. On the contrary, one can see that it incorporates an allusion to a quite different version, that the games were vowed at a time of famine.[44] As with the *plebeii*,[45] different accounts of their origin were

---

38 Dionysius of Halicarnassus 3.13.4 (Alban); Cn. Sicinius, praetor in 183 and 172 BC. One of the supposed consuls of 487 BC is variously named as 'T. Sicinius' (Livy 2.40.14, Festus 180L), 'T. Siccius' (Dionysius of Halicarnassus 8.64.1), and 'Sabinus' (*Fasti Hydatiani*, Chronicle of 354, *Chronicon Paschale*).

39 Sallust *Histories* 3.48.8 (speech of Macer) on L. Sicinius *tr. pl.* 76. For Macer and the alleged early Sicinii, see Ogilvie 1965.337, 382 (on Livy 2.40.14 and 58.2), and Briscoe 1971.10; Ogilvie's brief comments are justified in detail by Hodgkinson 1997.

40 Sallust *Jugurtha* 27.2, 30.3–34.1; for the stemma, see Sumner 1973.85–90.

41 Dionysius of Halicarnassus 7.14.2, cf. 6.89.1 for the full names (492 BC); 7.26.3, cf. 6.89.1 for 'Visellius', name corrupted in the MSS (491); Livy 3.11.5, cf. Dionysius of Halicarnassus 10.48.3 (454). There is also M'. Marcius (440 BC), named by Pliny *Nat. Hist.* 18.15.

42 For the dispute, see Plutarch *Brutus* 1.4–5 (Posidonius *FGrH* 87 F 40).

43 *CIL* I² 744 (*lex Visellia*), cf. Cicero *Brutus* 264 on C. Visellius Varro; Campbell 2000.216, 321–2 (*lex . . . Alliena*); cf. Crawford 1974.471, no. 457, on A. Allienus.

44 Dionysius of Halicarnassus 6.17.3–4; ps.Cyprian *De spectaculis* 4.1 (*cum urbem fames occupasset, ad auocationem populi adquisiti sunt ludi scaenici et Cereri et Libero dicati postmodum*). For the *ludi* of Liber, see Festus (Paulus) 103L, Ovid *Fasti* 3.784–6.

45 Ps.Asconius 217 Stangl (n. 19 above).

evidently circulating as the historiographical tradition took shape. Which, if any, was the right one is now beyond our knowledge.

V

The main importance of the Memmius coin-legend is that it reveals how significant the games were in late-republican society. It mattered to be able to claim credit for having introduced them. A moneyer of the previous year, C. Servilius C.f., had made what may be a similar boast about the *Florales* (FLORAL. PRIMVS),[46] and traces of similar '*primus*' claims are easily detectable in the historical sources on the origins of the various *ludi*.[47]

There was a very lively literature on the subject: not only Varro's *De scaenicis originibus*, *De quaestionibus scaenicis*, and the ninth and tenth books of his *Antiquitates diuinae* (on *ludi circenses* and *scaenici* respectively), but also Sinnius Capito's *Spectacula*, and whatever other late-republican sources Suetonius had for his two books of *Historia ludicra*.[48] Like the *De familiis Troianis* of Varro and Hyginus, these works no doubt incorporated the competitive historical claims of ambitious Romans engaged in the *contentio nobilitatis* of late-republican politics.[49]

As it turns out, Bernstein's innocent list of the origins of the Roman games conceals a ferment of aetiology, pseudo-history and self-promoting publicity. And that is just what we should expect. How the games began could be a subject for plays put on at the games themselves,[50] and for most people what they saw on the stage was a large part of what they knew about the past, an uncheckable amalgam of fact and legend.[51] For us, what matters most is what the consul pointed out to the populace in 122 BC: the games were part of the definition of Roman citizenship.

---

46 Crawford 1974.447, no. 423, interpreting the legend as [*flamen*] *Floral*[*is*] *primus*; the traditional interpretation *Floral*[*ia*] *primus* [*fecit*] is defended by Badian 1984.56–8.

47 E.g. Livy 27.23.5 and 7, 34.54.3, 36.36.3 (Valerius Antias fr. 40P); Censorinus *De die natali* 17.10 (probably also from Antias).

48 Varro: frr. 70–7 and 307–18 Funaioli; Augustine *City of God* 6.3 on the *Antiquitates*. Sinnius Capito: Lactantius *Diuinae institutiones* 6.20.35; cf. Festus 186L, 438L, 500L. Suetonius: Aulus Gellius 9.7.3, *Suda* s.v. 'Trankullos'; cf. Tertullian *De spectaculis* 5 (he found his material *apud Suetonium Tranquillum uel a quibus Tranquillus accepit*).

49 Lucretius 2.11 (*certare ingenio, contendere nobilitate*), Horace *Odes* 3.1.10–13 (*hic generosior . . . contendat*).

50 *Megalensia* was the title of comedies (*togatae*) by Afranius and Atta; Ovid *Fasti* 4.326 for a play about the arrival of the Great Mother. Afranius and the mime-writer Laberius also wrote plays called *Compitalia* (for the *ludi compitalicii* see Cicero *In Pisonem* 8 and Asconius 7C); some idea of the content may be inferred from Pliny *Nat. Hist.* 36.204 and Macrobius *Saturnalia* 1.7.34–5.

51 Cicero *De legibus* 1.47 (*scaena* as source of *opiniones*), Pausanias 1.3.3 (learning from 'choruses and tragedies'); cf. nn. 3–4 above, and Wiseman 1994.16–20.

CHAPTER NINE

The Games of Flora

I

Spectacle can take many forms, but in the Roman Republic it came to have a particular significance, in the festivals or 'games' (*ludi*) that were put on by the aediles at public expense, at regular dates throughout the year, in honour of the gods of Rome. Each of these festivals consisted of two different types of entertainment: 'stage games' (*ludi scaenici*), dramatic performances in temporary theatres erected for the occasion, and 'circus games' (*ludi circenses*), chariot races and wild-beast hunts in the Circus Maximus.

These were the occasions when the Roman community met *en masse* to honour its gods and celebrate its identity. They were a powerful force for social cohesion, and the right to 'view' them (*spectaculum* means 'a viewing') was one of the chief privileges of citizenship. By the mid-first century BC, which is the period much of our evidence comes from, there were seven such festivals: the *ludi Megalenses*, for the Great Mother of the Gods (4–9 April); the *ludi Ceriales*, for Ceres (12–18 April); the *ludi Florales*, for Flora (28 April—2 May); the *ludi Apollinares*, for Apollo (6–12 July); the *ludi Romani*, for Jupiter (4–12 September); the *ludi Victoriae*, for Victory (26–31 October); and the *ludi plebeii*, for Jupiter again (4–12 November). The dates refer to the 'stage games' only; the 'circus games' came afterwards in each case.

That makes forty-nine days of public stage performance every year. What went on? We have texts only for one type of comedy (Plautus and Terence), played by an all-male cast in masks. It is obvious that this cannot have been the only dramatic genre in republican Rome. Entertaining the Roman People and its gods for five, six, seven or nine consecutive days necessarily required plenty of variety, but we are very ill informed about the different types of performance that must have been offered. What follows is an investigation of one particular dramatic festival, the *ludi Florales* in April and May.

II

Flora was a goddess of flowers and blossoms, and a deity of some significance in Rome. Fabius Pictor gave her name (in Greek) to a character in the foundation story; according to Varro, her cult was introduced by Titus Tatius and his Sabines in the reign of Romulus; John Lydus, from what source we do not know, even reports that 'Flora' was the sacred name of Rome itself.[1]

The original site of her cult was just at the point where the ancient Via Salaria, coming over the high ground from Antemnae, descended into the floodplain of the Tiber before entering the city at the foot of the Capitol; her grove and altar, and later her temple, evidently sheltered below the north-west slope of the Quirinal, facing west across the meadows of the Campus Martius [fig. 45].[2] She was one of the select divinities that had their own designated priests, the *flamines* allegedly created by Numa.[3] She appears on coin-types minted in 57 and 41 BC; the former, by C. Servilius C.f., carries the legend FLORAL. PRIMVS, interpreted by Michael Crawford as *Floralis primus*, referring to an ancestor of the moneyer who was the goddess' first *flamen*.[4] If that is right, no doubt the ancestor was a legendary one, like Marcius the first *pontifex*.[5]

The other coin-type, by C. Clodius Vestalis in 41 BC, probably refers to the moment in the third century BC when Flora received a new temple and the *ludi Florales* were introduced.[6] In or about the year 240 BC, two plebeian

---

1   Fabius Pictor *FGrH* 809 F 4a (Plutarch *Romulus* 3.3), on Antho the daughter of Amulius, who saves the life of her cousin, the mother of the twins; Varro *De lingua Latina* 5.74 (citing *annales*); Lydus *De mensibus* 4.73: ἱερατικὸν δὲ Φλῶρα οἱονεὶ ἄνθουσα (compare 4.75: Ῥώμη Φλῶρα).

2   Varro *De lingua Latina* 5.158, Vitruvius 7.9.4, Martial 5.22.3–4, 6.27.1. Coarelli 1995.254: 'sulle pendici del colle che scendono verso Via della Panetteria,' just below the Quirinal Palace. (The descent of the Via Salaria is represented by Via di Porta Pinciana and Via Francesco Crispi.)

3   Varro *De lingua Latina* 7.45, quoting Ennius *Annales* fr. 116–18 Skutsch; cf. Vanggaard 1988.

4   Crawford 1974.447, no. 423, pl. LI. The traditional interpretation 'FLORAL[ia] PRIMVS [fecit]', referring to an aedile of 173 BC (cf. Ovid *Fasti* 5.329–30), is restated by Badian 1984.56–8. But Badian's appeal (1984.56) to the legend MEMMIVS AED. CERIALIA PREIMVS FECIT on C. Memmius' *denarii* (Crawford 1974.451–2, no. 427 [see p. 172 above]) as 'inspired by that of the "first Floralia" in the previous year' is unconvincing. As Badian himself observes (1984.57), Memmius' legend 'could not be more explicit—perhaps by contrast with Servilius' obscure conciseness'; surely the only reason for the explicitness would be to distinguish it from a *different* message?

5   Livy 1.20.5; cf. also Plutarch *Moralia* 264c-d (Juba *FGrH* 275 F 91) on the *pontifex* Cornelius; Plutarch *Numa* 10.1 on the Vestal Verania. Badian (1984.57–8) argues that since the Servilii were among the Alban families brought to Rome by Tullus Hostilius, there could not have been a *flamen* Servilius under Numa. But that is to impute too much consistency to 'accepted belief'. Numa was supposed to have created the priesthood of the Vestal Virgins, but its previous existence in Alba is a necessary premise of the foundation story (indeed, in one version the Vestal mother of the twins was called Servilia: *Anthologia Palatina* 3.19.pref.). Perhaps the flaminate, mentioned by Livy 1.20.2–3 in just this context, was also thought of in Servilian tradition as an Alban institution.

6   Crawford 1974.521, no. 512, pl. LXII. See also Wiseman 1979.92–4 and n. 124, arguing that Vestalis was a descendant of C. Claudius Cento *cos.* 240 and that he attributed the *Floralia* to Cento's consulship. Pliny *Nat. Hist.* 18.286 dates the games to 238 BC, Velleius Paterculus 1.14.8 to 241. Note that *Cento* means 'patchwork', and that at Flora's games it was the custom to wear multicoloured clothes (Ovid *Fasti* 5.356, *cultu uersicolore*).

Fig. 45 Republican Rome in its geographical context.

aediles with the appropriate name of Publicius punished rich landowners who were illegally occupying public land; they brought the culprits to trial before the People, fined them heavily, and with the proceeds built the Clivus Publicius up from the Circus Maximus to the Aventine.[7] At the bottom of the Clivus, next to the ancient temple of Ceres and Liber, they built a new temple of Flora and instituted her games.[8] The Senate, evidently resenting this manifestation of popular sovereignty, refused to honour Flora, but she made them change their minds (as she explained in person to the poet Ovid), and the games were duly established as regular and annual in 173 BC.[9]

According to Pliny, Flora's games were set up at the behest of the Sibylline books. So too was the cult of Venus of Eryx, with her tradition of ritual prostitution.[10] This same period saw the introduction of the erotically charged flagellation spectacle at the *Lupercalia*, and of the *Saturnalia* with its carnivalesque role-reversals.[11] Members of the senatorial elite may have disapproved, but licensed popular revelry seems to have been not only permitted but even prescribed as a means of honouring the gods in the Rome of the third century BC.

Whatever the reason, Flora's games were notoriously licentious.[12] Her day was 28 April, and by the Augustan period at least, the *ludi scaenici* extended till 2 May—five days of theatrical performances, followed by one day of *ludi circenses* in the Circus Maximus. In fact, the whole festival probably took place in the Circus, immediately in front of the new temple, where there was plenty of room for the erection of *ad hoc* stages and auditoria.[13] The Circus was famous for showgirls and prostitutes,[14] and it was precisely showgirls and pros-

---

7   Ovid *Fasti* 5.279–94, Varro *De lingua Latina* 5.158. Festus (276L) has a variant attributing the Clivus to the curule aediles L. and M. Publicii Malleoli.

8   Tacitus *Annals* 2.49.1; according to Ampelius 9.11, Liber was the son of Flora. Games: Ovid *Fasti* 5.277, 291–2, Velleius Paterculus 1.14.8, Pliny *Nat. Hist.* 18.286.

9   Ovid *Fasti* 5.295–330. The ideological dispute evidently gave rise to rival myths. Flora tells Ovid (*Fasti* 5.195–228) that she was the nymph Chloris—from χλωρός, the fresh green of spring growth—and that Zephyrus abducted and married her, and made her the goddess of flowers. A much less flattering version, alluded to by Ovid (*Fasti* 5.191, *hominum sententia fallax*), made her out to be a wealthy prostitute who made the Roman People her heir, and left them a fund to pay for games in her honour (Lactantius *Diuinae institutiones* 1.20.5–10, Minucius Felix *Octavius* 25.8, Cyprian *De uanitate idolum* 4).

10 Pliny *Nat. Hist.* 18.286, Livy 22.9.8–10 (215 BC). For the Sibyl's innovations in the third century BC, see North 1989.616–18.

11 Lupercalia: Livy fr. 63 Weissenborn; cf. Orosius 4.2.2 (for the date 276 BC), Ovid *Fasti* 2.425–52 (by order of Juno); for the context see pp. 75–8 above. Saturnalia: Livy 22.1.19–20 (217 BC), Accius *Annales* fr. 4 Courtney (Macrobius *Saturnalia* 1.7.36), Pliny *Letters* 2.17.24, Ausonius 7.24.15; Macrobius *Saturnalia* 1.24.23.

12 Ovid *Fasti* 4.946, 5.331–56, Martial 1.pref., Historia Augusta *Elagabalus* 6.5, Ausonius 7.24.25, Arnobius 3.23, Augustine *City of God* 2.27.

13 Hanson 1959.16–17; see also ps.-Acro on Horace *Satires* 2.3.182.

14 *Priapea* 27 (*deliciae populi, magno notissima Circo,* | *Quinctia, uibratas docta mouere nates*), Suetonius *Nero* 27.2, Juvenal 3.65.

titutes who performed at the *ludi Florales*.[15] At least by the late Republic, it was a traditional part of the entertainment that they should undress at the audience's demand. On a famous occasion in 55 BC, the presence of Marcus Cato in the audience inhibited the usual calls for the striptease; when he realized, he left the theatre and the show went on.[16]

Naturally, Christian polemicists seized on this indecency as typical of paganism.[17] Cicero, as plebeian aedile-elect, had included the *ludi Florales* among the solemn responsibilities of his office:[18]

> *habeo rationem quid a populo Romano acceperim; . . . mihi Floram matrem populo plebique Romanae ludorum celebritate placandam.*
>
> I think carefully about the task the Roman People has laid upon me; . . . I shall have to secure the goodwill of Mother Flora for the People and *plebs* of Rome by the celebration of games.

St Augustine was appalled: Cicero was a serious man, and claimed to be a philosopher![19] 'Secure the goodwill', indeed! This *placatio* of the goddess was *petulantissima, impudentissima, nequissima, immundissima. . .* However over the top Augustine's rhetoric may have been, one can see his point. How could a striptease show be a traditional part of the public religion of Rome, formally entrusted to the dignified magistrates of the Republic? Why didn't Cato stay where he was, and let the force of his moral authority prevent the disgraceful exhibition?

I think an answer to the puzzle may be found if we ask another question: what were the plays in which Flora's girls performed? They were not, of course, anything like the formal genres of comedy and tragedy, with their male actors and masks. These were 'mimes', traditionally sexy and farcical,[20] but not *restricted* to sex and farce. A whole collection of ethically improving one-liners was put together from the mimes of Publilius Syrus.[21] The epitaph of a mime-actress of the late Republic emphasizes her skill in dance, and in all the Muses' arts.[22] Mimes had plots and dialogue; there was more involved than just 'bumps and grinds'. But what sort of plots offered parts to numerous young women and required them to undress?

---

15 Lactantius *Diuinae institutiones* 1.20.10: *meretrices, quae tum mimarum fungantur officio. Mimae:* Valerius Maximus 2.10.8. *Meretrices:* Ovid *Fasti* 5.349, Seneca *Epistulae* 97.8, Martial 1.35.8–9, Tertullian *De spectaculis* 17.3, Arnobius 7.33.
16 Valerius Maximus 2.10.8, Seneca *Epistulae* 97.8, Martial 1.pref.
17 Lactantius *Diuinae institutiones* 1.20.6–10, Tertullian *De spectaculis* 17.3–4, Arnobius 7.33.
18 Cicero *Verrines* 5.36 (70 BC).
19 Augustine *City of God* 2.27 (*uir grauis et philosophaster Tullius*); see also n. 58 below.
20 Ovid *Tristia* 2.497–520; see Rawson 1993.
21 Collected in Duff and Duff 1934.14–111; see Giancotti 1967.275–462.
22 *ILLRP* 803 = *CIL* I² 1214 = *ILS* 5213, Eucharis Liciniae l.; see Wiseman 1985.30–5.

I have argued elsewhere that much of what went on at the Roman dramatic festivals represented the Romans' own mythology and history—aetiological stories to explain gods and rituals, exemplary stories to celebrate the deeds of men.[23] I believe that there were performances of this sort at Rome long before Livius Andronicus introduced the formal genres of Greek drama. If that hypothesis is valid, then we may be able to trace some possible scenarios for Flora's games in the mythological and historical narratives offered by our literary sources.

III

In the second or third year of the Republic,[24] Rome was besieged by Lars Porsena of Clusium, in alliance with the exiled Tarquins. The literary tradition narrates the siege as a succession of heroic exploits by 'the three prodigies and wonders of the Roman name': Horatius Cocles, Gaius Mucius, and Cloelia.[25] All three stories were probably aetiological in origin: to explain a statue, supposedly of Horatius, at the Volcanal,[26] the 'Mucian Meadows' across the Tiber,[27] and another statue, of a girl on a horse, at the top of the Sacra Via.[28] All three stories were told in various forms,[29] and among the variants of one, the Cloelia narrative, we find our first example.

Cloelia was one of a group of boys and young women sent by the Romans as hostages to Porsena's camp across the Tiber. What is common to all the versions of the story is that she escaped back to Rome, the Romans honourably gave her up, and Porsena equally honourably freed her in admira-

---

23 Wiseman 1994.10–19; Wiseman 1995.133–8.

24 Second: Livy 2.8.9–9.1, Plutarch *Publicola* 16.1–2. Third: Dionysius of Halicarnassus 5.21.1.

25 Florus 1.10.3 (*illa tria Romani nominis prodigia atque miracula, Horatius, Mucius, Cloelia*); thus e.g. Livy 2.10–13, Plutarch *Publicola* 16–19, *De uiris illustribus* 11–13. Georges Dumézil interpreted Horatius and Mucius as reflections of the Indo-European 'one-eyed god' and 'one-handed god' (Dumézil 1988.139–59, Dumézil 1973.274–6); for the context in Dumézil's theory, see Belier 1991.146–56. The concept was extended to Cloelia by Luciano Arcella (Arcella 1985.30–1 on 'i tre eroi-mostri'). Quite apart from the general problems raised by Dumézil's theories, on which see Belier 1991, there are good reasons for considering at least two of the stories to be comparatively late inventions: Horatius' exploit at the bridge seems to presuppose a wall circuit that included the Janiculum and can therefore hardly predate the third century BC (Gjerstad 1969, Wiseman 1979.44), while Mucius' sacrifice of his right hand explained the use of the *cognomen* Scaevola by the Mucii (Livy 2.13.1, Plutarch *Publicola* 17.3), which is first attested in a praetor of 215 BC (Livy 25.3.6).

26 Aulus Gellius 4.5.1–4, Plutarch *Publicola* 16.7, *De uiris illustribus* 11.2; cf. Livy 2.10.12 (*in comitio*), Dionysius of Halicarnassus 5.25.2 (in the Forum). See Coarelli 1983.161–2, 168–9.

27 Festus 131L, Livy 2.13.5, Dionysius of Halicarnassus 5.35.1, *De uiris illustribus* 12.6.

28 Livy 2.13.11, Dionysius of Halicarnassus 5.35.2, Seneca *Consolatio ad Marciam* 16.2, Plutarch *Publicola* 19.5, Annius Fetialis in Pliny *Nat. Hist.* 34.29 [see pp. 289–90 below]; cf. *De uiris illustribus* 13.4 (*in foro*).

29 Horatius: in Polybius 6.55.3, unlike the later writers, he sacrifices his life. Mucius: εἴρηται μὲν ὑπὸ πολλῶν καὶ διαφορῶς (Plutarch *Publicola* 17.1).

tion of her bravery. But how did she cross the river? (The bridge, of course, had been broken at the time of Horatius' exploit.) According to one version, she got hold of a horse and rode it across.[30] Since the statue that gave rise to the story was of a girl on a horse,[31] this version is likely to be the original one. But it did not go unchallenged: some said she swam across, and explained the statue by having Porsena honour her with the gift of a war-horse, to show that she had the courage of a man.[32] It is a variant of the 'swimming' version that concerns us here.

Dionysius of Halicarnassus relates that the girl hostages asked their guards for permission to bathe in the river. Permission was granted. The girls then asked the men to withdraw a little from the bank until they had bathed and dressed again, so as not to see them naked. The guards behaved like gentlemen, and the girls, now unsupervised, followed Cloelia's suggestion and swam across *en masse*. Plutarch has the same version, but he does not just follow Dionysius; it is clear that the two authors were independently using the same source.[33]

Also found only in Dionysius and Plutarch is the episode of an ambush by the Tarquins as the girls are being returned to Porsena. The heroine of this story is Valeria, daughter of Publius Valerius Publicola; the author from whom Dionysius and Plutarch took it was probably Valerius Antias.[34]

The mass escape offers no starring role for Cloelia. She is no longer the uniquely courageous heroine, but at the most *prima inter pares*, with no particular claim to an honorific statue. The story's aetiological significance is lost, but what has been gained—carefully signaled by the request for the guards to withdraw—is the scene where the girls get undressed. It is, however, a scene which the non-visual medium of historiography is ill equipped to convey, and I imagine it was originally conceived for the stage: the guards withdraw, but we the audience are privileged to watch.

There is nothing paradoxical in this hypothesis. The historians of Rome

---

30 Valerius Maximus 3.2.2, Plutarch *Publicola* 19.4, Florus 1.10.7, *De uiris illustribus* 13.1.

31 See n. 28 above. As a curiosity, cf. Arcella 1985.39: 'statua equestre come enfatizzazione e cristallizzazione del rifiuto di un'unione esogamica.'

32 Swimming: Livy 2.13.6, Virgil *Aeneid* 8.651, Dionysius of Halicarnassus 5.33.1, Plutarch *Publicola* 19.1, Polyaenus 8.31. Gift from Porsena: Dionysius of Halicarnassus 5.34.3, Plutarch *Publicola* 19.4, Cassius Dio 4.14. Gift from Romans at Porsena's suggestion: Servius on *Aeneid* 8.646.

33 Dionysius of Halicarnassus 5.33.1, Plutarch *Publicola* 19.1; also Polyaenus 8.31, who adds the detail that they wrapped their dresses round their heads as turbans, presumably to have something to wear on the other side.

34 Dionysius of Halicarnassus 5.33.2–4, Plutarch *Publicola* 19.2–3. Plutarch *Publicola* 19.5 reports a variant that attributed the 'girl on a horse' statue to Valeria. I think it can be shown (see Wiseman 1998.75–89) that Antias systematically retold the famous stories of the early Republic with a 'Valerian dimension' in each case.

were well aware that 'historical' episodes were presented on the stage, and that some of the material in their own sources might be suspected of having originated there.[35] Most historical drama was serious, and literary historians equated the genre of *fabula praetexta* with Greek tragedy.[36] But the *praetexta* was not the only dramatic form that exploited the history of Rome. What sort of play was it that starred the glamorous Quinta Claudia in the story of the Great Mother's arrival in 204 BC?[37] The *ludi scaenici* of the Roman Republic no doubt presented performances in many more various forms than later antiquarians were ever able to categorise;[38] for some of them, no doubt (to borrow modern phraseology), the contribution of the producer and director will have been more important than that of the scriptwriter. The mimes at the *Floralia* could be an example.

I suggest, therefore, that the version of the Cloelia story reported by Dionysius and Plutarch started life as a lightheartedly patriotic showpiece for the girls at the games of Flora, and that it was then incorporated, probably by Valerius Antias,[39] into a historical narrative from which our two surviving authors took it in good faith. If we accept that as a working hypothesis (and the nature of the evidence means that it can hardly be anything more), we may look for analogous examples in some other unexpected places.

IV

The *ludi Florales* ran from 28 April to 2 May.[40] The first day of May, which fell in the middle of the games, was the festival of Bona Dea, the women's goddess, at her shrine below the so-called 'little Aventine'.[41]

---

35 Livy 5.21.9 (fall of Veii), Dionysius of Halicarnassus 3.18.1 (triplets' fight in war with Alba), 9.22.1–3 (Fabii at the Cremera), Plutarch *Romulus* 8.7 (foundation legend).

36 Diomedes in *Grammatici Latini* 1.489K: *in quibus imperatorum negotia agebantur et publica et reges Romani uel duces inducuntur, personarum dignitate et [personarum] sublimitate tragoediis similes.* *Praetexta* fragments in Manuwald 2001.131–248; see Zorzetti 1980, Flower 1993 [and pp. 194–9 below].

37 Ovid *Fasti* 4.291–348: *mira, sed et scaena testificata, loquar* (326). Cf. also Varro *De lingua Latina* 6.18, on the Nonae Caprotinae.

38 See Zorzetti 1980.83: 'La pretesta arcaica . . . non è che la punta di un *iceberg*, la parte cioè emergente nel campo del teatro letterario di un ben più nutrito gruppo di manifestazioni culturali, in cui il popolo romano era sollecitato ad esprimere, per mantenerla o adattarla, la coscienza della propria tradizione.'

39 See n. 34 above. Antias was interested in the stage: frr. 18P, 22P, 55P (Censorinus 17.8–11) on the *ludi saeculares*, fr. 37P (Asconius 69C) on the *ludi Romani*, fr. 40P (Livy 36.36.4) on the *ludi Megalenses*, fr. 46P (Livy 39.22.9) on votive *ludi*. Two items in his history have been thought to derive from dramatic sources: see Wiseman 1998.21–3 on fr. 6P, Mazzarino 1966.451 and 542 on fr. 48P.

40 Ovid *Fasti* 4.943–8, 5.183–6; Degrassi 1963.449–51.

41 Ovid *Fasti* 5.148–58, cf. Cicero *De domo* 136 (*sub Saxo*); Degrassi 1963.453.

That is the scene of Propertius 4.9, one of the legendary narratives in a book of Callimachean aetiology. What has to be explained is the Forum Bovarium, and its cult of Hercules at the Ara Maxima. In twenty lines, Propertius tells the story made famous in the eighth book of the *Aeneid*, how Hercules overcame the monstrous cattle-thief Cacus. And then:[42]

> ... *sicco torquet sitis ora palato,*
> *terraque non ullas feta ministrat aquas.*
> *sed procul inclusas audit ridere puellas,*
> *lucus ubi umbroso fecerat orbe nemus,*
> *femineae loca clausa deae fontesque piandos,*
> *impune et nullis sacra retecta uiris.*

His palate is dry, thirst tortures his mouth, and the earth, teeming with water, offers him none. But far off he hears the laughter of girls, enclosed where the wood had made a grove with a circle of shade—the secret place of the women's goddess, and her sacred waters, and rituals never with impunity revealed to men.

The parched hero hurries to the precinct and begs for admission: 'O you who sport [or dance] in the grotto of the grove...'[43] But the priestess refuses him ('May the gods give you other springs; this water flows for girls'),[44] at which Hercules forces his way in and drinks the stream dry.[45]

What girls, what sport, what dance? The grotto (*antrum*) mentioned by Propertius features also in Juvenal's wonderfully overheated description of the rites of Bona Dea, where the women of Rome, in a drunken frenzy, challenge the brothel-keepers' slave girls to a contest of erotic dancing.[46] It is far from clear whether Juvenal was thinking about the Kalends of May festival or about the Bona Dea ritual in December at the house of a senior magistrate (the occasion notoriously desecrated by Publius Clodius in 62 BC).[47] However, since the May festival took place at the time of the *ludi Florales*, when we know the mimes were performed by *meretrices*, Juvenal's reference to the girls from the brothels may allude to them.

Propertius' poem has been much studied of late,[48] but none of its recent

---

42 Propertius 4.9.21–6 (the translation of line 22 is adapted from G.P. Goold's Loeb Classical Library version).

43 4.9.33: '*o luci quae luditis antro*'. For *ludere* as 'dance' (*Thesaurus linguae Latinae* 7.1772.45–74, 1789.48–63), see Cairns 1992.74.

44 4.9.59–60: '*di tibi dent alios fontes; haec lympha puellis ... fluit*'.

45 4.9.65, *exhausto iam flumine*.

46 Juvenal 6.314–34 (328 for the *antrum*); cf. Wiseman 1974.130–4.

47 Cicero *Ad Atticum* 1.12.3, 1.13.3, Plutarch *Cicero* 28, *Caesar* 9–10, Scholia Bobiensia 85–91 Stangl; Juvenal refers to the Clodius scandal at 6.335–45.

48 Cairns 1992, Anderson 1992, Fox 1996.169–75. See also Hardie 1996.222–3, 225: the girls 'are celebrating the festival of the Bona Dea with their dance' (223).

interpreters has picked up J.C. McKeown's suggestion that in this poem, as in others, Propertius may have been 'mythologising mime'.[49] Although it is not quite what McKeown meant (he sees Hercules as a mimic komast), I take this poem as another scenario for Flora's girls, but conceptually reversed. Propertius focuses on Hercules; for the stage, the scene would be *inside* the precinct, with the audience again in the role of voyeurs.

Bona Dea shared the first day of May with the guardian gods of Rome, the Lares Praestites. They were the twin sons of Mercury by a nymph called Lara, whose story is told by Ovid as an aetiology of 'the silent goddess'.[50] Jupiter is pursuing the nymph Juturna, but she persistently eludes him. Frustrated beyond endurance, he summons all the nymphs of Latium and issues a stern warning: next time Juturna runs away, stop her before she gets in the water! The nymphs agree, but Lara can't hold her tongue. Not only does she warn Juturna, she even goes to Juno and tells her what Jupiter is up to, sympathizing with married women.[51] Furious, Jupiter tears out her tongue and banishes her to the underworld, giving Mercury, as *psychopompos*, the job of escorting her there. On the way, in a grove (no doubt the grove of his mother Maia, whom some identified as Bona Dea),[52] Mercury takes advantage of her condition and fathers on her the twin Lares.

Since the action is almost wholly articulated in speeches—Jupiter to the nymphs, Lara to Juturna, Lara to Juno, Jupiter to Mercury—I infer that this too is probably the elegiac reworking of a dramatic original. If so, the assembled nymphs, like the girls in Propertius' precinct,[53] may suggest what sort of performance was involved. In the spring, as Horace tells us, the nymphs dance naked in the warm west wind; the bride of the west wind, a nymph who became a goddess, is Flora herself.[54]

As we have noted already, these two scenarios in Propertius and Ovid both involve divinities whose festival day fell in the middle of Flora's games. But they have something else in common, which is particularly relevant to our enquiry. Here is Hercules, dying for a drink, pleading at the gate in 'words unworthy of a god [*uerba minora deo*]'; here is Jupiter, dying for something else, his treatment by the elusive Juturna 'unworthy of so great a god [*tanto non patienda deo*]'. Both phrases echo, no doubt deliberately, the polemical intro-

---

49. McKeown 1979.77–8.
50 Ovid *Fasti* 2.583–616, on the *Feralia* (21 February) and *dea Muta*.
51 Ovid *Fasti* 2.605, *miserataque nuptas*.
52 Maia as Bona Dea: Macrobius *Saturnalia* 1.12.20–1, citing Cornelius Labeo. Maia as the goddess of the month of May: Ovid *Fasti* 5.79–106. The Bona Dea precinct was close to Mercury's temple: see Wiseman 1995.113, 139, 204, and also 67–71, on the myth of the silent goddess.
53 Cf. Hardie 1996.223–5, on the analogy of water-nymphs and human girl dancers.
54 Horace *Odes* 4.7.5–12, Ovid *Fasti* 5.195–220.

duction to Varro's *Antiquitates rerum diuinarum*, in which the great antiquarian attacked traditional mythology as 'contrary to the dignity and nature of the immortal gods'.[55] And what Varro says about this deplorable type of theology is that it belongs in the *theatre*.[56]

Much of our knowledge of Varro's work comes indirectly from Christian writers, who exploited it for their own polemical purposes. Their arguments confirm that the disgraceful stories, unworthy of the gods, to which Varro objected (but which they seized on as characteristic of paganism), were performed on the stage at the public games.[57] Not only that, but Arnobius and Augustine, in passages clearly dependent on Varro, associate them in particular with the games of Flora.[58]

V

So I think we have found three stories that have some claim to be the sort of thing the *mimae* performed at the *ludi Florales*—one preserved in historical narrative, the other two in aetiological elegy. And perhaps we can even see how such performances may have been structured—for we need not imagine any great complexity of plot. (No doubt choreography was more important.)

First, on come the girls, with enough dialogue to establish who they are and what they are doing: Porsena's hostages; worshippers of Bona Dea; nymphs of the streams of Latium. They dance, and in due course take off their dresses as required by the plot; it is striking that all three scenarios involve water and streams or rivers.[59] When the audience has duly enjoyed the spectacle, enter the heavies: the Tarquins, attacking the girls on their way back to the chivalrous Porsena; Hercules, causing a rumpus at a place where men are forbidden; Jupiter (with Mercury in attendance), haranguing the nymphs, tearing out Lara's tongue.

---

55 Propertius 4.9.32, Ovid *Fasti* 2.586; Varro *Antiquitates diuinae* fr. 7 Cardauns (Augustine *City of God* 6.5): *multa contra dignitatem et naturam immortalium ficta.*

56 Varro *Antiquitates diuinae* fr. 10 Cardauns (Augustine *City of God* 6.5): *prima theologia maxime accommodata est ad theatrum.* This was the theology *quo maxime utuntur poetae* (fr. 7), and by 'poets' Varro primarily meant dramatists: cf. Augustine *City of God* 6.6 (using Varro) on *di poetici theatrici ludicri scaenici.*

57 E.g. Tertullian *Apologeticus* 15.1–3, Arnobius 4.35, Augustine *City of God* 6.6–8.

58 Arnobius 7.33: *existimatue tractari se honorifice Flora, si suis in ludis flagitiosa conspexerit res agi et migratum ab lupanaribus in theatra? itane istud non est **deorum imminuere dignitatem**, dicare et consecrare turpissimas res eis, quas censor animus respuat. . . ?* Augustine *City of God* 2.27 (having just quoted Cicero *Verrines* 5.36 on the *Floralia*): *hanc, inquam, pudendam ueraeque religioni auersandam et detestandam talium numinum placationem, fabulas in deos inlecebrosas atque criminosas, haec **ignominiosa deorum** uel sceleritate turpiterque facta uel sceleratius turpiusque conficta oculis et auribus publicis ciuitas tota discebat.* Varro is cited by name at Arnobius 7.1 and Augustine *City of God* 3.4 (respectively frr. 22 and 20 Cardauns).

59 Cf. Griffin 1985.88–111 (on 'the pleasures of water and nakedness'), and Traversari 1960. Could the temporary theatres of the late Republic have been flooded? It is hard to imagine it.

One imagines these scenes performed in very broad burlesque; the tongue-tearing scene would be intolerable in any other mode. Cato, of course, is not in the audience, and if his fellow philosopher Marcus Varro is there, he will not approve of this treatment of the gods. But it is all done for the best of motives. Heroic Valeria escapes from the ambush and brings help; Porsena banishes the Tarquins and the Romans are saved.[60] Hercules breaks in and drinks his fill—and that, citizens, is why women may not worship at the Ara Maxima. Exit Mercury, ogling the helpless Lara; she will conceive, and bear the guardian gods of Rome. And at each satisfactory ending, no doubt, the girls dance again before they make their bow.

To moralists like Cato and religious purists like Varro, it was all very disgraceful. But to the Roman People, and the ambitious aediles whose job it was to entertain them at the games, it was surely a proper way to honour the goddess at her holiday time. For all their raunchy style, Flora's games were like the other dramatic festivals in providing an opportunity for the creation and re-creation of the Romans' concepts of their gods, their city, and their past.

---

60 Dionysius of Halicarnassus 5.34, Plutarch *Publicola* 19.5–6.

CHAPTER TEN

The Games of Hercules

I

In 78 BC, the year of Sulla's death, a moneyer called M. Volteius issued the following series of *denarii* [fig. 46]:

1. *Obv.*: Laureate head of Jupiter r. *Rev.*: Capitoline temple; below, M.VOLTEI.M.F.
2. *Obv.*: Head of Hercules r. *Rev.*: Erymanthian boar r.; in exergue, M.VOLTEI.M.F.
3. *Obv.*: Head of Liber r., wearing ivy-wreath. *Rev.*: Ceres in *biga* of snakes r., holding torch in each hand; behind, control-symbol; in exergue, M.VOLTEI.M.F.
4. *Obv.*: Helmeted bust r., draped (helmet bound with laurel-wreath); behind, control-symbol. *Rev.*: Cybele, wearing turreted crown and veil, in *biga* of

Fig. 46 The coins of M. Volteius, 78 BC.

lions r., holding reins in l. hand and *patera* in r. hand; above, control-numeral; in exergue, M.VOLTEI.M.F.

5. *Obv.*: Laureate head of Apollo r. *Rev.*: Tripod with snakes coiled round front leg and rearing head above; on l., S.C.; on r., D.T.; in exergue, M.VOLTEI.M.F.

What these images have in common was recognised by Mommsen in 1860: they represent, he thought, the *ludi Romani* (in honour of Jupiter), the *ludi plebeii*, the *ludi Ceriales*, the *ludi Megalenses* and the *ludi Apollinares*.[1]

There are some problems, however. First, can the tetrastyle temple on the reverse of no. 1 really be that of Jupiter Optimus Maximus on the Capitol? Perhaps it can: as Michael Crawford points out, 'since the temple had been destroyed and not yet rebuilt at the time of this issue, the representation is not necessarily accurate'. Next, whose is the bust on the obverse of no. 4? Duncan Fishwick suggests 'the Cappadocian Goddess', whose cult was similar to that of 'the Phrygian Goddess' Cybele. In the civil war of 88 BC she encouraged Sulla in a dream to smite his enemies; Plutarch's account, which probably comes from Sulla's memoirs, identifies the goddess as 'Selene, Athena, or Enyo', and the garlanded helmet is indeed sometimes found in the iconography of Athena.[2]

What surely confirms Mommsen's hypothesis is the combination of images on no. 3. In the late third century BC (the evidence comes from Naevius), Liber had his own *ludi* at the Liberalia; by Ovid's time, he had lost them and now shared the games of Ceres.[3] Evidently the same was true in 78 BC, since he shares the coin issue with her as well. So four of the five issues represent major annual *ludi*, identified by the divinities in whose honour they were held. But what about Hercules?

Mommsen assumed that Hercules must represent the *ludi plebeii*, otherwise absent from the list. But the *ludi* of Flora and of Victoria are absent too, so that in itself is not a sufficient argument. More important is the fact that the *ludi plebeii*, like the *Romani*, were centred on a 'feast of Jupiter' (*epulum Iouis*) and were therefore presumably thought of as offered to that god.[4] Certainly there is nothing in our surviving sources to connect the Plebeian Games with Hercules. The logic of the Volteius coin issue seems to require that in 78 BC

1   Crawford 1974.399–402 (no. 385.1–5), whose descriptions I repeat (except 'border of dots' for each type). *Ludi*: Mommsen 1860.620–1 n. 451, followed by Crawford 1974.402.

2   Crawford 1974.400; Fishwick 1967.152–4; Plutarch *Sulla* 9.4; *Lexicon Iconographicum Mythologiae Classicae* s.v. Athena nos. 302, 305 (Thurii coins), Athena-Minerva no. 2 (Pompeii).

3   Naevius fr. 113R (Festus [Paulus] 103L), cf. Ausonius 7.24.29–30, Ovid *Fasti* 3.785–6. See now Wiseman 1998.35–51 [and ch. 5 above].

4   Degrassi 1963.449–52, 525–6 (*ludi Florales* 28 April–3 May, *ludi Victoriae Sullanae* 26 Oct.–1 Nov.). *Epula Iouis*: Degrassi 1963.509, 530 (*ludi Romani* 13 Sept., *ludi plebeii* 13 Nov.).

there were games of Hercules comparable with those of Ceres, Apollo and the Great Mother.

Certainly there were games of Hercules at Rome in the first century BC. Two late-republican inscriptions attest them. The first was found on the Via Appia between the sixth and seventh milestones:

>]R.MAG.LVDOS
> her]COLEI.MAGNO
>]NEO.FECIT

The first letter is thought to be the remains of a *cognomen*. In the third line Mommsen read [*in theatro lig*]*neo*; Whatmough in 1921 suggested [*in circo Flami*]*neo*, which may be preferable in that the temple of Hercules Magnus Custos stood in the Circus Flaminius. The god's cult day was 4 June, on which date the late-imperial calendars report '*ludi*' (*fasti Siluii*) or '*ludi in Minicia*' (*fasti Filocali*). The Severan marble plan identifies as *MINI[CIA]* the rectangular portico north of the theatre of Balbus, not far from the probable site of the Hercules Custos temple (modern Via Arenula); Filippo Coarelli plausibly suggests that that by the late empire the Porticus Minucia *frumentaria* provided a better site for the games than the Circus Flaminius piazza.[5]

The second inscription comes from the Caelian, near Quattro Coronati:

> MAG.HE[rc
> SVFFRAGIO.PAG.PRIM[i creati
> LVDOS.FECERV[nt

Here too we have games given by *magistri*, and it seems that the men in charge are not only *magistri He*[*rculani*] but also *magistri pagi*, their responsibility defined both topographically and by reference to the god. The nearest parallel may be the *ludi Tarpeii* or *Capitolini*, set up in honour of Jupiter Feretrius on the Capitol and organised by a *collegium* of 'those who lived on the Capitol and the *arx*'.[6]

Games held in a portico, or in a piazza like the Circus Flaminius (which despite its name was not a race-track), were clearly not *ludi circenses* with chariot-racing.[7] Theatrical performances would be possible, and perhaps a small-scale *uenatio* (Augustus once flooded the Circus Flaminius to show crocodiles), but these local games were clearly on a less ambitious scale than the

---

5   *CIL* 6.335 = 1².985 = *ILLRP* 703. Degrassi 1963.284–9 (*fasti Filocali*), 269 (*fasti Siluii*); Coarelli 1997.296–345 (Porticus Minucia), 498–503 (Hercules Custos temple); cf. Zevi 1993 (esp. 679–92), whose siting of the Porticus Minucia *frumentaria* inside the Circus Flaminius itself is refuted by Coarelli 1997.304–10.

6   *CIL* 6.30888 = 1².984 = *ILS* 6081 = *ILLRP* 701. Piso fr. 7P (Tertullian *De spectaculis* 5), Livy 5.50.4 (*collegium . . . ex iis qui in Capitolio atque arce habitarent*).

7   *Pace* Coarelli 1997.499, who restores the first inscription '. . . *ludos* [*circenses*]'.

series of great annual *ludi* entrusted to the aediles. If the *ludi Tarpeii* are indeed analogous, they may have consisted of amateur athletics and boxing.[8]

The *magistri* in the second inscription were the first to be elected by their *pagus*. Mommsen thought that this might mean they were the first elected after Clodius restored the *collegia* in 58 BC. However, the ban in 64 BC had exempted religious associations, and we know that even before Clodius' law was passed Sex. Cloelius, as *magister collegii*, was holding *ludi compitalicii* in honour of the Lares.[9] But whether or not that was the occasion, the wording of the inscription makes it clear that some sort of change had taken place in the selection of those responsible for the games of Hercules.

That may offer a solution to the dilemma presented by our two near-contemporary sources of information: the coins of Volteius imply games like the *ludi Romani* and the other annual festivals put on by the aediles; the inscriptions attest games put on by *magistri*, evidently on a much smaller scale. Is it possible that the games of Hercules were at first what the coins imply, but were then reorganised as merely local and entrusted to *magistri* elected by their fellow-*pagani*?

The hypothesis is in two parts: first, that major *ludi* of Hercules had been instituted before 78 BC, and second, that they were soon afterwards 'demoted' to local games of a particular *pagus*. Neither event is attested, but it seems to me that both are perfectly possible.[9a]

II

Sulla took the gods seriously. In the dedication passage of his *Memoirs* he advised Lucullus to regard dreams as reliable divine messages, and the *Memoirs* themselves were full of prophecies, portents and communications from the gods. Fortuna, Venus, Apollo and Bellona feature particularly, but they were not the only deities he honoured. In 79 he consecrated a tithe of his whole

---

8 Circus Flaminius piazza: Humphrey 1986.540–5. Crocodiles: Cassius Dio 55.10.8 (2 BC). *Ludi Tarpeii*: Ennius *Annales* 1 fr. li Sk (Scholia Bernensia on Virgil *Georgics* 2.384), *sic ludos edidit ut caestibus dimicarent et cursu contenderent*.

9 Cicero *In Pisonem* 8, Asconius 7C (cf. 75C for exemptions); Pliny *Nat. Hist.* 36.204 (Lares); Lintott 1968.77–83.

9a [See Keaveney 2005 for a determinedly sceptical reaction to the second part of the hypothesis. However, his own preferred solution, that the inscriptions are pre-Sullan and that 'games that were lowly fell into the hands of Sulla, the great devotee of Hercules, and it was he who gave them their enhanced standing' (Keaveney 2005.223), takes no account of *prim*[*i creati*] in the Caelian inscription, and fails to explain the absence of the 'enhanced' games of Hercules from the calendar *fasti* and from Ovid *Fasti* 6.209–12.]

property to Hercules, with huge banquets for the populace, and it is possible to conjecture why the hero-god was important to him.[10]

The campaigns in the War of the Allies which made Sulla's reputation as a general, and won him the consulship in 88 and the command against Mithridates, were concentrated in Campania; also in Campania, at Mount Tifata, he defeated the armies of Norbanus and the young Marius in 83; and it was to Campanian Cumae that he retired, after laying down his power, to spend his last years writing his memoirs.[11] Campania, and the Bay of Naples in particular, was a part of Italy particularly associated with Hercules. It was at the Campi Phlegraei that the hero met and defeated the rebellious Giants, at Bauli that he penned up the cattle of Geryon, at Pompeii that he held his triumphal procession; he built the causeway across the Lucrine bay, and he founded the town called Herakleion, the Roman Herculaneum.[12]

Sulla derived his *cognomen* from 'Sibylla'. The Sibyl's home at Cumae, which was Sulla's home too in his retirement, was a part of this Herculean neighbourhood. A pair of huge tusks was preserved there in the ancient temple of Apollo, and identified as those of the Erymanthian boar.[13] Since the boar was what M. Volteius chose to use on the reverse of his issue no. 2, it must somehow have symbolised the games of Hercules at Rome.

Ovid is explicit that it was on the instructions of the Sibyl that Sulla set up the temple of Hercules Magnus Custos in the Circus Flaminius:

> *altera pars circi Custode sub Hercule tuta est,*
> > *quod deus Euboico carmine munus habet.*
> *muneris est tempus, qui Nonas Lucifer ante est:*
> > *si titulum quaeris, Sulla probauit opus.*

> The other part of the Circus is under the protection of Guardian Hercules; the god holds office through the Euboean oracle. The time of his taking office is the day before the Nones; if you are enquiring about the inscription, it was Sulla who approved the work.

Since the inscription from the Via Appia specifies Hercules Magnus as the recipient of the games, it is reasonable to infer that the games were set up at the

10 *To theion, to daimonion*, etc: Plutarch *Sulla* 6.5–7 (Sulla fr. 8P), 7.2–6, 9.3–4, 14.7, 17.1–2, 27.3–4. Ibid. 6.5 (Fortuna); 7.6, 9.4, 27.6, 30.2 (Bellona); 12.4–5, 19.6, 29.6 (Apollo); 19.5, 34.2 (Venus); 35.1 (tithe to Hercules). Cf. Velleius Paterculus 2.25.4: Sulla thanks Diana for his victory at Mt Tifata.

11 89 BC: Sulla frr. 9–10P, Appian *Civil Wars* 1.50–1, Orosius 5.18.22, Velleius Paterculus 2.16.2. 83 BC: Appian *Civil Wars* 1.84–6, Plutarch *Sulla* 27.4–5, Velleius Paterculus 2.25, Cicero *Philippics* 2.27. Cumae villa: Appian *Civil Wars* 1.104, cf. Valerius Maximus 9.3.8, *De uiris illustribus* 75.12 (Puteoli).

12 Diodorus Siculus 4.21.5–22.2, cf. Strabo 5.4.4 (Giants); Servius on Virgil *Aeneid* 7.662 (Bauli, Pompeii), Dionysius of Halicarnassus 1.44.1 (Herculaneum).

13 Macrobius *Saturnalia* 1.17.27, Charisius *Ars grammatica* 140B (Sibylla); Pausanias 8.24.5.

same time as the temple, as had happened a century earlier with the Magna Mater and the *ludi Megalenses*. No doubt 'Hercules the Great Guardian', like his neighbour Bellona, played some part in Sulla's personal myth.[14] What part it was we do not know, but the events of 89 and 83 BC offered plenty of opportunity for the protective hero to earn his temple and his games.

But what happened afterwards? Why should the games have been reduced to the humbler sphere of the local *magistri*?

Here we must remember the ideological sensitivity of *ludi*. The *ludi plebeii*, for instance, represented plebeian freedom—either from the Tarquins or from the patricians, according to the alternative origin stories offered by a Ciceronian scholiast. The *ludi Romani* were the subject of a dispute between the plebeians and the patricians at a turning point in the 'struggle of the orders', the election of the first plebeian consul; the story cannot be made sense of in Livy's abbreviated account, but the games were evidently thought to be an important issue. The *ludi Florales* were founded by plebeian aediles, and paid for with fines exacted from landowners encroaching on public land; for over sixty years the Senate refused to recognise the games, and only yielded when a famine was attributed to the goddess's anger.[15]

A similarly contentious background may be inferred for the *ludi Apollinares*. In 213 BC the urban praetor carried out a police action, on the Senate's instructions, against 'prophets and sacrificers' in the Roman Forum. These people were evidently considered a threat to the authority of the Senate and magistrates, and their prophetic books and sacrificial manuals were duly confiscated. The following year, however, it was announced that two important prophecies of Cn. Marcius had been discovered among this material. The Senate ordered a consultation of the Sibylline Books; the Sibyl evidently agreed with Marcius, and the games of Apollo were set up as a result.[16] It is natural to infer that the Senate was alarmed by the prophets' influence, and made sure that any innovations that had to be conceded would be carried out under senatorial control. That is, the *ludi Apollinares* were set up in order to forestall something more dangerous.[16a]

The vicissitudes of the 'games of Liber' may give us some idea of what that 'something more dangerous' was. As we noted in the context of Volteius' coin issue no. 3, the Liberalia had been *ludi* in the time of Naevius, but the games

---

14 Ovid *Fasti* 6.209–12 (4 June), cf. 199–208 for Bellona; Livy 36.36.3–4 (Magna Mater, temple and games).

15 Ps.Asconius 217St (on Cicero *Verrines* act. pr. 31); Livy 6.42.12–14; Ovid *Fasti* 5.279–330.

16 Livy 25.1.6–12, 12.2–15. An ancestor of Sulla was involved in the consultation of the Sibyl (Macrobius *Saturnalia* 1.17.27).

16a [See now North 2000b.100–102. Keaveney, however (2005.222 n. 45), finds this whole argument 'pointless and irrelevant'.]

were later merged with the *ludi Ceriales*. The Naevius fragment—'*libera lingua loquimur ludis Liberalibus*'—suggests that the games exploited the ideological implication of the god's name, and therefore that their suppression may have had a political dimension. The most likely context for it is surely the consuls' crack-down on the 'Bacchanals' in 186 BC, a particularly brutal example of senatorial authority being exerted over what could be perceived as a rival focus of loyalty. The leader of the Bacchic cult was a 'prophet and sacrificer', just like those supposedly subversive characters in the Forum in 213 BC.[17]

If that could happen in the second century BC, perhaps it could also happen in the first, but in the opposite ideological direction. What we have inferred from the combination of Volteius' coins and the *magistri* inscriptions is a 'demotion' of Sullan games. The likely context for that is the reform movement of 70–67 BC, when the Sullan oligarchy was tainted with gross corruption and abuse of power, and Sulla's more contentious legislation was reversed.[18] There would have to be a good reason to take the god's games out of the hands of the aediles, but what the reason was we can only guess. Since Sulla's *ludi Victoriae* continued as a regular part of the aediles' annual programme, mere association with the dictator was clearly not enough to justify it.

The Victoria games celebrated the battle of the Colline Gate, which could quite reasonably be presented as a victory over an external enemy.[19] If the Hercules games were associated with specifically civil war campaigns, or with victories over allies who accepted the Roman citizenship in 89 (and were now at last enrolled by the censors of 70–69), one can imagine hostile tribunes not wanting the spilling of citizen blood to be publicly commemorated. No offence to the god, who would still be honoured on 4 June, but his games would now be a local affair rather than a celebration by the people as a whole.

We cannot know whether it happened like that; but some such hypothesis seems to be required to make sense of the conflicting evidence we have. Perhaps the games of Hercules may count as another example of the inextricable interrelation of 'religion' and 'politics' in the Roman republic.

---

17 See n. 3 above; exhaustive treatment of the events of 186 in Pailler 1988. *Sacrificulus et uates*: Livy 39.8.3, cf. 25.1.8.

18 Crook, Lintott and Rawson 1994.210–15, 223–8 (Seager); 327–8 (Wiseman).

19 Velleius Paterculus 2.27.1–2 on Pontius Telesinus as a quasi-Hannibal [disputed by Keaveney 2005.221–2].

CHAPTER ELEVEN

Praetextae, Togatae *and Other*
Unhelpful Categories

> ... *uel qui praetextas uel qui docuere togatas.*
> ...whether those who have staged *praetextae* or those who have staged *togatae*.
>
> Horace Ars poetica 288

> *cur hoc, togata praetexta data †eis† Apollinaribus ludis docuit populum.*
> The *togata praetexta* given at the Games of Apollo taught the People why this
> was so.
>
> Varro De lingua Latina 6.18

Horace clearly implies that *praetextae* and *togatae* were not the same thing;
equally clearly, Varro refers to a play that is both. That is because Varro had his
own categorisation of dramatic forms (reported for us by the fourth-century
grammarian Diomedes), which did not coincide with what Horace took for
granted.[1] In exploring the reasons for that, I want to take further Patrick
Kragelund's excellent discussion about the nature of the sources.[2]

It was characteristic of Varro to organise whatever subject he was addressing
into categories and sub-categories,[3] and the two main *genera* into which he
divided drama were defined according to national costume. Greek plays were
palliatae, Roman *togatae*. Each *genus* was subdivided into four *species*: respectively tragedy, comedy, satyr-play, mime, and their equivalents *praetexta*,
tabernaria, *Atellana*, *planipes*.[4] Diomedes takes all this as gospel, and describes
Horace's view as a *communis error*, but there is no need to accept his verdict. In
my view it is much more likely that Varro's schema is an attempt to define the
indefinable, to impose artificial order on essentially disorderly data, and that
Horace more accurately represents the reality of his time.

It does not follow, however, that Horace was distinguishing between tragic

---

1 Varro fr. 306 Funaioli (Diomedes in *Grammatici Latini* 1.489 Keil).
2 Kragelund *et al.* 2002.11–17.
3 E.g. Varro *De lingua Latina* 5.10–13, *De re rustica* 1.9.1–6, 2.1.11–12, *De philosophia* ap.
  Augustine *City of God* 19.1; see Rawson 1991.327–9.
4 Diomedes in *Grammatici Latini* 1.489–90 Keil; see Kragelund *et al.* 2002.14 and n. 28.

and comic Roman plays.[5] The natural sense of the two terms he uses ought to be that *praetextae* dealt with the doings of senators and magistrates, and *togatae* with those of ordinary citizens. The example Varro refers to (not, in fact, a good argument for his own categories) shows that stories of Roman history might be wholly un-tragic; the *Nonae Caprotinae* play not only has a happy ending, for the Romans at least, but is clearly erotic in nature.[6] Could the scene where the girls are handed over to the lecherous Latins have been performed by male actors in masks? It seems unlikely—but what place was there for *mimae* in a *praetexta*?

Perhaps our own categories are too rigid. Any attempt to define a 'dramatic genre' is bound to be artificial. Performance takes place in an infinite number of ways, and its forms are constantly changing. Whatever the moral, political or religious constraints in particular places at particular times, the only rule performers consistently observe is the necessity of pleasing their audience.

Even the apparently fundamental distinction between tragedy and comedy is too crude to be helpful. At least as far back as the fifth century BC, comedy exploited tragedy, not only mocking it but seeking to borrow its authority,[7] and in Periclean Athens there was recognisable common ground between tragedy and the 'cheerful muse' of erotic mime.[8] Plays entitled *Komoidotragoidia* are known from fourth-century Athens, and probably also from early fifth-century Syracuse.[9]

Evidence for drama in the west is provided by the red-figure vases of South Italy and Sicily from the late fifth century to the end of the fourth; particularly important are the mid-fourth-century theatrical scenes on the pottery of Lucanian Paestum, which show a flourishing tradition of 'tragic' mythological themes played as broad farce.[10] At much the same time—the second half of the fourth century—engraved bronze *cistae* from Latium appear to illustrate a type of Dionysiac performance in which heroic myth is combined with erotic spectacle by female performers whom one can only describe as *mimae*.[11] At Tarentum in the early third century, Rhinthon specialised in a form called

5   As is normally assumed, e.g. by Kragelund (Kragelund *et al.* 2002.16, Niall Rudd's translation); judicious discussion in Brink 1971.319–21.
6   Wiseman 1998.8–11, 68.
7   See now Silk 2000, esp. 42–98, 415–17. For tragic parody in Old Comedy, see Bowie 2000.322–4.
8   On Gnesippus, described by Cratinus (fr. 256 K-A) as a tragic poet, see Athenaeus 14.638d (παιγνιαγράφου τῆς ἱλαρᾶς μούσης); Davidson 2000, esp. 48–9 on the Cratinus passage.
9   Alcaeus and Anaxandrides (Kassel-Austin *PCG* 2.9–10 and 249–50); Dinolochus (cf. *Suda* s.v. for his date), cited by the *Antiatticista Bekkeri* 112.29 (Kaibel *CGF* 149).
10 Trendall 1989, esp. 12, 262–4; ibid. 196–232 for Paestum; Trendall 1987.433, index of 'vases with theatrical subjects'. [See now Pontrandolfo 2000.]
11 Battaglia and Emiliozzi 1979 and 1990: nos. 9 (judgement of Paris), 22, 45, 50, 51, 82 (Iphigeneia at Aulis), 83; see pp. 109–27 above.

'cheerful tragedy'.[12] One of his plays was *Amphitryon*, and Plautus' play of that name a century later is described in Mercury's prologue speech as a *tragicomoedia*.[13]

Half way between Rhinthon and Plautus, at just the time when the Tarentine Andronicus produced his first play at Rome,[14] erotic mime performances were featured at the plebeian *ludi Florales*.[15] I think there is good reason to believe that the repertoire of the *mimae* included scenarios that claimed to be historical.[16] It is certain that 'mime' was a polymorphous mode, ranging from the outrageously licentious to the morally exemplary;[17] we know that it could deal with contemporary events and characters in a satirical way,[18] and there is no reason to suppose that it would regard any subject as beyond its scope.

The type of drama that was normally called *fabula togata* (in Horace's definition, not Varro's) flourished in the second and first centuries BC: its classic authors were Titinius, Quinctius Atta and Afranius. Like mime, it could be obscene;[19] like mime, it could be ethically improving.[20] Known titles common to both forms are *Aquae caldae* (Atta and Laberius), *Augur* (Afranius and Pomponius), *Compitalia* (Afranius and Laberius), *Fullones* (Titinius and three different mime authors), *Satura* (Atta and Pomponius), and *Virgo* (Afranius and Laberius). *Satura* is interesting, given the Dionysiac context of the perform-

---

12 *Suda* s.v. (ἀρχηγὸς τῆς καλουμένης ἱλαροτραγῳδίας); Stephanus of Byzantium s.v. *Taras* (Ῥίνθων ... τὰ τραγικὰ μεταρρυθμίζων ἐς τὸ γελοῖον).

13 Rhinthon fr. 1 Kaibel (Athenaeus 3.111c), Plautus *Amphitruo* 50–63; Christenson 2000.7–12, 47–50.

14 240 BC: Varro *De poetis* fr. 55 Funaioli (Aulus Gellius 17.21.42), Cicero *Brutus* 72, *De senectute* 50; Oakley 1998.61–3. Livius Andronicus from Tarentum: Accius fr. 18 Funaioli (Cicero *Brutus* 72).

15 241 BC: Velleius 1.14.8. 238 BC: Pliny *Nat. Hist.* 18.286. Made annual in 173 BC: Ovid *Fasti* 5.295–330. Mimae, erotic: Valerius Maximus 2.10.8 (*priscum morem iocorum*); cf. Ovid *Fasti* 4.946 (*ioci morem liberioris*), 5.331–54, Seneca *Epistles* 97.8, Martial 1 pref. and 1.35.8–9. Plebeian: Ovid *Fasti* 5.279–94, cf. 352.

16 See pp. 175–86 above, esp. 180–5 on Dionysius of Halicarnassus 5.33.1 and Plutarch *Publicola* 19.1 (Cloelia and the Tarquins), Propertius 4.9.21–70 (Hercules and Bona Dea), Ovid *Fasti* 2.583–616 (conception of the Lares). Cf. also Wiseman 1998.64–74, esp. 72–4 on Ovid *Fasti* 3.661–96 (Anna Perenna and the secession of the *plebs*).

17 Mime and *ethologia*: Diogenes Laertius 3.18 (Sophron and Plato), Cicero *De oratore* 2.242–4. On Publilius' moral maxims (cf. Seneca *De tranquillitate animi* 11.8), see Giancotti 1967.275–462; Rawson 1991.570–1.

18 E.g. Cicero *Ad familiares* 7.2.3 (53 BC), *Ad Atticum* 14.3.2 (44 BC); Suetonius *Domitian* 10.4 (AD 93), where *exodium* probably refers to mime. For Laberius' treatment of contemporary issues, see Wiseman 1985.187–8.

19 Quintilian 10.1.100, Ausonius *Epigrams* 67.2–4 (both on Afranius). Priapus was appropriate to both modes: Macrobius *Saturnalia* 6.5.6 (Afranius), Augustine *City of God* 6.7 (mime).

20 Seneca *Epistles* 8.8: *non attingam tragicos nec togatas nostras. habent enim hae quoque aliquid seueritatis et sunt inter comoedias et tragoedias mediae.* Afranius compared with Menander: Cicero *De finibus* 1.7, Horace *Epistles* 2.1.57, Macrobius *Saturnalia* 6.1.4.

ances illustrated on the fourth-century *cistae*, and the evidence of Vitruvius and Horace for satyr-play in Rome.[21] *Compitalia* is interesting too: if it was an aetiology for the *ludi compitales*, it may have had a 'historical' plot about Servius Tullius or Lucius Brutus.[22]

Two *togata* authors, Atta and Afranius, wrote plays called *Megalensia*, for which the coming of the Great Mother in 204 BC is clearly a possible subject. As Patrick Kragelund rightly points out,[23] the play about Quinta Claudia to which Ovid refers is analogous to the *Nonae Caprotinae* play mentioned by Varro. He assumes they were *praetextae*, which may be right in one sense, since Roman magistrates must have featured in both. But neither can have been remotely like a tragedy; the main action of both was essentially comic.[24] Wherever we look, the Varronian categories seem to dissolve.

An added complication came in Varro's own time, with the introduction by Bathyllus and Pylades of the solo ballet sometimes called *pantomimus*. The plot might be a tragedy, a comedy, an *Atellana*, a *togata*, or a theme from a poet like Virgil or Ovid.[25] Since Lucian includes Polycrates of Samos and Seleucus and Stratonice among the themes appropriate to tragic dance,[26] there was evidently no prohibition on historical subjects; nor on contemporary ones, since fulsome flattery of the reigning emperor was always a safe and popular theme.[27]

I am not wholly convinced by Patrick Kragelund's idea of a 'transition from the republican system focused on the *ludi* to the more diversified imperial literary scene', in which 'the *ludi* no longer were a viable setting for aristocratic self-promotion'.[28] A precious but neglected description of *ludi* in Augustan Rome reveals an aristocrat in charge (*erat facturus ludos quidam nobilis*),[29] and just the same creative mixture of performance genres as we have detected in the

---

21 *Cistae*: n. 11 above. Satyr-play: Vitruvius 5.6.9 (cf. 7.5.2), Horace *Ars poetica* 220–50; Wiseman 1994.68–85.

22 Pliny *Nat. Hist.* 36.204 (Ser. Tullius), Macrobius *Saturnalia* 1.7.34–5 (Brutus). Performances at *compita*: Propertius 2.22a.3–8.

23 Kragelund *et al.* 2002.18–20.

24 Ovid *Fasti* 4.293–326, with Fantham 1998.154: 'these lines sketch a kind of comedy.' See in general pp. 210–11 below.

25 E.g. [Seneca *Controuersiae* 3.pref.10 (Pylades for comedy, Bathyllus for tragedy);] Juvenal 7.86–92 (tragedy plots), Plutarch *Quaestiones conuiuiales* 7.8 (comedy), Tertullian *De spectaculis* 17.2 (*Atellana*), Pliny *Nat. Hist.* 7.159 (*togatae*), Suetonius *Nero* 54 (Virgil's Turnus), Ovid *Tristia* 2.519 and 2.7.25 (*mea poemata* and *carmina nostra*). [Possibly also satyr play? See Persius 5.123 on Bathyllus' *Satyr*.]

26 Lucian *Saltatio* 54, 58; cf. 72 on dance as a source of knowledge about the past (διδάσκουσα δὲ πολλὰ τῶν πάλαι).

27 E.g. Domitian: Pliny *Panegyric* 54.1, clearly referring to *pantomimi* (cf. 46.4); for the *commissiones*, cf. Suetonius *Diuus Augustus* 89.3 (Augustus discouraging flattery).

28 Kragelund *et al.* 2002.34–5.

29 Phaedrus 5.7.16 (cf. 5.5.4–10, *diues et nobilis*).

republican evidence. Phaedrus is telling the story of a *tibicen* called Princeps, Bathyllus' regular accompanist, who had fallen and broken his leg while 'flying' on the stage-crane in the course of his performance. Now convalescing, he makes a guest appearance at the noble's games:[30]

> *aulaeo misso, deuolutis tonitribus,*
> *di sunt locuti more translaticio.*
> *tunc chorus ignotum modo reducto canticum*
> *insonuit, cuius haec fuit sententia:*
> *'laetare incolumis Roma saluo principe.'*

The curtain was removed, thunders were rolled, and the gods spoke in the traditional way. Then the chorus started singing a song unknown to the man just returned, which went like this: 'Rome, rejoice, you are safe while the *princeps* is safe.'

The thunder rolls; the gods speak 'in the traditional way', perhaps in a prologue (in Plautus' time gods speaking from the stage were a feature of *tragoedia*);[31] the chorus sings a patriotic song about the safety of the emperor. It could be the start of a *praetexta* about the safe return of Augustus in 24 or 19 or 13 BC—or it could be a mime, a *togata*, or any mixture of the available forms. So multifarious is the theatrical world implied by the sources that to say 'it must have been' (or 'it cannot have been') this form or that would be merely to announce one's own prejudice. The evidence does not allow us to make that sort of judgement.

The same applies to the *Octavia*, about which Patrick Kragelund's discussion seems to me exemplary.[32] The text presents itself as a play for performance; what sort of evidence or argument would be needed to show that it cannot be what it purports to be? The text makes repeated reference to the traditional liberties of the Roman People;[33] what sort of evidence or argument would be needed to show that it was written not for a popular audience at the *ludi scaenici*, but for a literary coterie at a private *recitatio*?

One feature seems to me decisive, the absence from the text of the day of the royal wedding. The ghost of Agrippina refers to it in advance (lines 593–7), and Poppaea's nurse describes it in retrospect (693–709); in the intervening scene, the chorus of citizens tells us it has already happened (671–3, 683–5). So more than twenty-four hours have passed, without explanation, between Agrippina's exit at 645 and the entrance of Octavia and the chorus at 646. At a

---

30 Phaedrus 5.7.23–7; Henderson 2001.95–118, cf. 220 n. 42, where Henderson is surprisingly uncurious about what sort of show it was.
31 Plautus *Amphitruo* 41–4.
32 Kragelund *et al.* 2002.7–11, 41–50.
33 Kragelund 1982.

recitatio, where the text has to do all the work, that would be an artistic failure. In a stage performance, music and action can carry the plot forward without words; and as we have seen, the Roman theatrical tradition offered many different styles in which the haughty harlot's wedding-orgy could be played.[34]

Was there a play about the fall of Messallina in AD 48? Tacitus' description of her marriage to Silius reads like a satyr-play scenario.[35] What Tacitus' later text owes to the *Octavia* no doubt comes indirectly (perhaps through Cluvius Rufus, a historian much involved with Neronian theatre),[36] but is nevertheless important evidence for the way such plays might affect historical narrative. We can see that clearly enough in Livy's stories of Tullia and Verginia, and may suspect it also in Plutarch's treatment of Gaius Gracchus.[37]

So when Octavia attributes Messallina's downfall to the anger of Venus,[38] and the chorus dwells on the crime of Tullia and the deaths of Verginia, the Gracchi and Messallina herself,[39] I think we are entitled to infer (at least provisionally) an on-going tradition of historical drama from which, much more than from historians, the Roman People derived its knowledge of the significant past. Whether the literary elite called such plays *praetextae*, *togatae*, or anything else, seems to me of peripheral importance. For understanding the history of Roman drama, the Varronian categories are more of a hindrance than a help.

---

34 I have sketched one possibility in Wiseman 2004a.265–72. *Superba paelex*: *Octavia* 125.

35 Tacitus *Annals* 11.31.2, *strepente circum procaci choro*; the doomed Silius wears tragic *cothurni*.

36 Tacitus *Annals* 14.60.5 (*Octavia* 896–8), 63.2 (*Octavia* 933–46). Cluvius: Suetonius *Nero* 21.2, Dio Cassius 63.14.3; Wiseman 1991.111–18.

37 Tullia: Livy 1.46.3 (*tragicum scelus*), 59.13 (Furies). Verginia: Livy 3.58.10–11 (ghost). Gracchus: see now Beness and Hillard 2001.

38 *Octavia* 257–9; Messallina had caused the deaths of two of Venus' descendants, Julia Livilla and Livia Julia (Seneca *Apolocyntosis* 10.4, Dio Cassius 60.18.4).

39 *Octavia* 304–8 (Tullia), 295–303 (Lucretia and Verginia), 882–6 (Gracchi), 947–51 (Messallina). Lucretia was the tragic heroine of plays by Accius and Cassius: Kragelund *et al.* 2002.21 and nn. 46–7.

CHAPTER TWELVE

Octavia *and the Phantom Genre*

Octavia: A Play Attributed to Seneca, edited with introduction and commentary by Rolando Ferri (Cambridge Classical Texts and Commentaries 41), Cambridge U.P., 2003. pp. x + 471.

I

In one sense, as an example of what traditional classical scholarship can do with a Latin text, Rolando Ferri's commentary on the pseudo-Senecan *Octavia* is superb. On manuscript readings and textual questions, on Latin idiom and semantics, on prosody and metrical technicalities, his detailed notes provide a treasure-house of erudition and judicious comment, with particularly thorough citation of parallels in the Senecan corpus and other 'Silver Latin' authors. A worthy addition to the 'orange cover' Cambridge series, it will be an indispensable aid to the study of this important and surprisingly neglected text. In another sense, however, those who are interested in the history and society of Rome as well as her language and literature may find it less than completely helpful.

Ferri begins his Introduction with a short section on the genre of *Octavia*, announcing somewhat dogmatically that reference to the play as *Octavia praetexta* is 'a practice which should be abandoned'. He sees it as influenced much more by Greek tragedy than by the republican *fabulae praetextae*, and concludes with this firm statement (pp. 2–3):

> Political caution, a propensity for themes increasingly irrelevant to popular audiences at large, and a long-term process of 'gentrification' of literature at Rome made *praetextae* more suitable for recitation in the auditoria of a few aristocratic patrons than for onstage performance before large theatre audiences.

The only evidence offered for this far-reaching generalisation is a reference forward to section 5 of the Introduction ('Structure and Dramatic Technique in *Octavia*'), where the same view is taken as already established (pp. 54–5):

> The cultural setting in which *Octavia* must be placed is that of the flourishing production of dramas for recitation in Roman literary circles. Abundant evidence for the popularity of tragedy in these circles comes from Pliny,

Juvenal and Martial. Whether any of these dramas were in fact composed for regular theatre performance is doubtful, and a multiplicity of factors have been thought to account for this: the lack of state patronage, the corruption of popular taste, a snobbish reluctance, on the part of the elite, to produce elaborate dramas in the style of fifth-century Athenian tragedy and expose them to the whimsical reaction of the uneducated.

Note 'must' in the first sentence, insisting on the relevance of one genre alone, 'the Senecan *Rezitationsdrama*' (p. 56). Note too the confident assumption of 'lack of state patronage', which an author as well read as Ferri must know to be untrue: Tiberius didn't put on shows, but all the other emperors did, and of course the praetors continued to present the regular *ludi scaenici* every year; one of the playwrights we happen to know about (because the theatre audience barracked him) was P. Pomponius Secundus, consul in AD 44 and author of tragedies, including a *praetexta* entitled *Aeneas*.[1]

It is important to understand that there is *no* ancient evidence for dramatic texts written solely for recitation. Otto Zwierlein coined the phrase *Rezitationsdrama* to describe what he believed Seneca's tragedies to be;[2] but of course there is a lively and still unresolved debate on whether (or how) Seneca's tragedies were staged, and it is by no means clear that Zwierlein's assumption is correct.[3] The scene of Tacitus' *Dialogus* is set the day after Maternus' tragedy *Cato* had been presented at a *recitatio*, and the interlocutors refer repeatedly to that type of presentation; but when Marcus Aper says to him 'I summon you from the lecture-room *and the theatre* to the law court' it is clear that Maternus is not thought of as writing for *recitatio* alone.[4] The whole point is that his plays were dangerously controversial; there would be no chance of having them staged under the present circumstances, but that does not mean that Maternus never wanted them staged at all.

What there *is* evidence for is the playwright presenting his drama to a small audience of friends before risking it in front of the *populus Romanus* in the theatre;[5] but that is something very different. As Pliny observed, if you write tragedy you need actors and a stage.[6] It is surely counter-intuitive to imagine

---

1 Tacitus *Annals* 11.13.1: *At Claudius . . . theatralem populi lasciuiam seueris edictis increpuit, quod in Publium Pomponium consularem (is carmina scaenae dabat) . . . probra iecerat.* Tragedies: Quintilian 10.1.98, Pliny *Letters* 7.17.11. *Aeneas*: Charisius in *Grammatici Latini* 1.132 Keil; Manuwald 2001.243–8.

2 Zwierlein.1966, esp. 156–65.

3 See for instance Kragelund 1999, Harrison 2000.

4 Tacitus *Dialogus* 10.5: *nunc te ab auditoriis **et theatris** in forum et ad causas et ad uera proelia uoco.* Cf. 2.1, 3.3, 9.4, 10.2, 11.2 (*recitatio*); 9.3, 10.7 (*auditoria*).

5 Horace *Ars poetica* 386–9, 438–52 on honest criticism (cf. 419–37 on flatterers), 474 for the *recitator*. Contrast 125, 179–92 (*scaena*); 113, 153–5, 248–50 (theatre audience).

6 Pliny *Letters* 7.17.3: *. . . cur tragoediam, quae non auditorium sed scaenam et actores, cur lyrica, quae non lectorem sed chorum et lyram poscunt.*

an author choosing a dramatic genre with no expectation at all of dramatic performance. When Ferri supposes that 'a reciter could have supplemented his words with expressive gesture or even prefaced his recitation with a short description of what was to happen' (p. 55 n. 137), the reader may wonder about the value of a hypothesis that needs such special pleading to make it plausible.

It is very striking that Ferri has Octavia 'come out of the palace' at the start of the text, 'withdraw into her apartments' at line 33, and 'return on stage' at line 57 (pp. 120, 122). We also have the Nurse's 'appearance on stage' at line 34 (p. 134); Poppaea 'appears on stage' at line 690 (p. 321), and the chorus 'comes on stage' at line 762 (p. 342). Ferri does sometimes use scare-quotes (e.g. p. 308, 'as she leaves the "stage"...'), but it seems clear enough that normally as he reads the text he imagines a dramatic scenario and not a recitation. No doubt he would say that he is imagining an *imaginary* dramatic scenario (p. 226: 'conventionally portrayed as "outside" the royal palace, Seneca nervously paces up and down...'), but I think most readers will find that an unnecessary complication.

Why should the text *not* be written for performance on the stage? Ferri seems unaware that the burden of proof is on him: the default position must be that a text in dramatic form is a text for performance, unless it can be shown that that is impossible. Ferri does look for non-dramatic characteristics at pp. 59–63, but the results are unimpressive, falling far short of the absolute cogency his position requires. The fact is that he assumes the '*Rezitationsdrama* hypothesis' *a priori*, and thus feels no obligation to prove it.

II

In the same way, he assumes a late date of composition. 'Consideration of the play's structure strongly suggests that it was composed by someone who worked from written sources' (p. 9)—i.e. after the appearance of what Ferri calls 'the historical *vulgata*', the histories of Cluvius Rufus, Fabius Rusticus and the elder Pliny. His principal reason for this seems to me quite extraordinary. 'We may imagine that in 68–69 much of what happened in the household of the *princeps* was still shrouded in obscurity' (p. 10); 'unless the *auctor Octaviae* was one of the political protagonists of the Neronian court, he would have found it impossible to have first-hand, independent knowledge of the inside story of imperial intrigues' (p. 16); 'this dwelling on the details and personalia of Julio-Claudian Rome presupposes an "audience" well acquainted with the stories of court intrigue of the period, as perhaps made popular by Flavian historians' (p. 398).

I doubt if many readers will share Ferri's belief that nobody in Rome knew what happened in Nero's court until the Flavian historians told them. This very text refers to the glamour of the court (*fulgor*, line 34) and the constant operation of *fama* (line 67), and as the note on the latter passage rightly observes, 'the role of *fama* in creating public opinion at Rome, and often bringing about important events, is constantly stressed in Tacitus' historical works' (p. 314). Besides, Ferri himself points out that the character of Nero in *Octavia* is not the same as in Tacitus, Suetonius and Dio. He explains it by 'reasons of literary decorum' leading the playwright 'to sketch a figure more suited to tragedy' (p. 248)—but one might prefer to suppose that the playwright simply wrote before the 'historical *vulgata*' had been created.

That seems particularly clear in the case of one key element in the plot, the explicit linking of the popular rising in support of Octavia and the fire of Rome two years later. We know from Tacitus that his sources were divided over whether Nero was responsible for the fire;[7] but those who said he was (reflected in Suetonius and Dio) evidently did not attribute to him the motive of vengeance on the *populus Romanus* which is so striking a feature of the play. No 'historical *vulgata*' here, then (tacitly admitted at p. 363); and the emphasis on the people's hunger at line 833, evidently referring to the brief food shortage after the fire (p. 365), might suggest that the playwright was a contemporary, reflecting the immediate impact of events. But no: at p. 15 Ferri interprets the invention of the vengeance motive

> as a clear sign that the author was composing from written sources, and collecting in his portrayal of Nero everything that was best known and, as it were, *typical* about Nero: Nero had to be *recognizable* as the legendary emperor that everybody had read about.

To describe that as a *non sequitur* would be putting it mildly.

Over twenty years ago, simultaneously but independently, Patrick Kragelund and T.D. Barnes made the case for the reign of Galba (June 68 to January 69) as the date of *Octavia*.[8] Ferri discusses their arguments at pp. 5–9, and is unconvinced. In particular, he dismisses Kragelund's inferences from the 'populism' of the play (p. 7):

> [T]he lines in which the chorus summons itself to rebel against the *princeps* display little Republicanism: the rebels only want to restore the Claudian princess to her legitimate share in the government . . . The *praetexta* is remarkably vague and non-committal on all constitutional issues regarding the position of the *princeps*. No traces of the so-called Senatorial opposition under Vespasian can be detected. The language in which political issues are discussed applies to situations which range through the whole of the first century.

---

7   Tacitus *Annals* 15.38.1: *forte an dolo principis incertum (nam utrumque auctores prodidere)*.
8   Kragelund 1982, esp. 38–54; Barnes 1982.

Ferri prefers to see the author's motive as exploiting the Flavians' supposed sympathy for the memory of Claudius (pp. 16–17). In that case it is surprising that there is nothing in the text that even hints at the coming dynasty, but that is an argument Ferri legitimately makes about Galba too. Much more important is the reference to the 'Senatorial opposition', and his later judgement that 'the authority of the "Roman people" . . . need mean no more than the Roman Senate' (p. 315). But the Roman Senate did not regard the Gracchi as heroes (lines 882–6, no comment in Ferri's notes); far from being language common throughout the first century, that passage explicitly contradicts the views of Velleius Paterculus, Valerius Maximus, and Lucan.[9]

I think the problem here is the basic premise of Ferri's political analysis, as made clear at p. 316:

> It is risky to draw any conclusions about the author's political stance from the confidence that the people may be won over by a just cause . . . Rousing the people to an insurrection has no parallels in extant Roman imperial history . . . This nostalgic celebration of Republican Rome does not lead to an open condemnation of the Principate as such.

Of course there is no sign in the text that the *populus Romanus* wanted to overthrow the principate. In 49 BC, the first Caesar crossed the Rubicon 'in order to free the Roman People from its oppression by an oligarchic faction', a motive repeated almost word for word by his adopted son when he marched on Rome five years later;[10] in AD 41, when the consuls restored the Republic after the death of Caligula, the People were delighted at the prospect of Claudius being imposed as emperor, because they disliked senatorial authority and needed the protection of a *princeps* 'to keep the Senate's rapacity in check'.[11] The Caesars were the People's tribunes (*tribunicia potestas* meant what it said),[12] and the last thing the *populus Romanus* wanted was to go back to an oligarchic Republic. In *Octavia* the people dislike Nero not because he is a *princeps* but because he is an overbearing tyrant. They love the daughter of their old emperor, just as they had loved the daughter of Augustus, and now, as then,[13] they react with violence when their favourite is wronged.

An emperor could lose the People's allegiance by abandoning his responsibility to protect them. Nero realised that in 64, when he decided not to go to

---

9   Velleius Paterculus 2.3.2, 2.6.2; Valerius Maximus 4.7.1, 7.2.6b, 9.4.1; Lucan 6.796.
10 Caesar *Civil War* 1.22.5 (his own speech at Corfinium): *ut se et populum Romanum factione paucorum oppressum in libertatem uindicaret*. Augustus *Res gestae* 1.1: *rem publicam a dominatione factionis oppressam in libertatem uindicaui*.
11 Josephus *Antiquities* 19.228; cf.115, 158 (and 189, 272 for a different view, probably from a different source); Suetonius *Claudius* 10.4, Dio 59.30.3.
12 Tacitus *Annals* 1.2.2 on Augustus: . . . *ad tuendam plebem tribunicio iure contentum*.
13 Dio 55.13.1 (demonstrations in AD 3).

Greece;[14] but the effect of the fire more than cancelled out the popularity he earned by staying in Rome, and at the end of 66 he went to Greece anyway. Popular reaction to his death was mixed, but it is clear that some, at least, of the populace were delighted at the news.[15] The circumstances of summer 68 were unprecedented—the last of the Caesars dead, having failed the People— and nobody knew at the time what was going to happen next. The attitudes presupposed in *Octavia* may be easier to understand in that context than under the safely established successor dynasty of the Flavians.

Ferri, however, has convinced himself that the author of *Octavia* was writing (for recitation) under Domitian. And he places him very specifically (p. 26):

> The author of *Octavia* may have been an old pupil of Seneca, a survivor left with little to rejoice at by the advent of the Flavian dynasty, who had found a haven in the house of the last surviving grand ladies of that circle [e.g. Lucan's widow Polla Argentaria], and set about composing *Octavia* hoping to ingratiate himself with them.

That would be surprising, given the anti-Senecan reaction of the Domitianic period (pp. 26–7); nor is it clear how many of Seneca's pupils were 'on the margins of the literary field', with 'a mind full of remembered verse, but . . . ill at ease with the tools of those who had made them', as the anonymous author is described later (pp. 31, 39). However, Ferri himself describes this idea as a fantasy (p. 72), and it is hard to disagree.

III

If the hypotheses put forward about the nature and date of *Octavia* by a Latinist of Ferri's quality are not acceptable, the critic has an obligation to offer something better. I think that can be done, but only if we rid ourselves of preconceptions about 'the corruption of popular taste' or 'the gentrification of literature'.

It is very easy, especially for classicists, to forget that drama is performance first and literature only second (if that). The aediles of the Republic had about fifty days of *ludi scaenici* per year to fill with spectacle for the Roman People— and that only counts the regular festivals, not the extra *ludi* for triumphs, funerals, temple dedications and so on. For the praetors under the principate (they were given the responsibility in 23 BC), the total was substantially more. How much of what they put on had written texts that would be preserved afterwards? The texts of Plautus, Terence and Seneca predispose us to think that comedy and tragedy on the Greek model were the norm, and that seems

---

14 Tacitus *Annals* 15.36.3–4.
15 Suetonius *Nero* 57.1, Dio 63.29.1; cf. Tacitus *Histories* 1.4.

to be confirmed, at least as far as tragedy is concerned, by the surviving fragments of lost plays. The index of Otto Ribbeck's *Tragicorum Romanorum
fragmenta* lists the titles of 141 tragedies on Greek mythological themes, but of
only sixteen *fabulae praetextae* on Roman subjects. However, there are good
reasons for supposing that those statistics may be misleading.

In the first place, *fabulae praetextae* were sometimes on topical subjects. The
classic examples are Naevius' *Clastidium* (on M. Marcellus' victory in 222 BC),
Ennius' *Ambracia* (on M. Nobilior's victory in 189 BC) and Pacuvius' *Paullus*
(probably on L. Paullus' victory in 168 BC). But the very fact that they *are*
classic examples—plays so famous that their texts were preserved—may make
them untypical. More valuable for our purposes is the evidence in Pollio's
letter to Cicero in June 43 BC, reporting the games organised by L. Balbus in
Spain: one of the plays put on was a *praetexta* about Balbus' own part in the
civil war five years earlier. There is no reason to suppose that the text of that
was ever preserved, and we would never have known about it if Pollio's letter
had not been incorporated into Cicero's collected correspondence. There may
have been many such plays on topical subjects, significant at the time but soon
forgotten, which never found their way into libraries and were therefore never
quoted by scholars and grammarians. 'C'étaient des pièces de circonstance,'
wrote Gaston Boissier in 1893,[16] 'et le plupart n'ont pas dû survivre aux
circonstances mêmes pour lesquelles on les avaient faites.' In which case the
Ribbeck statistics tell us nothing about the theatrical reality of the time.

Secondly, the evidence of authors who happen to mention theatrical matters
seems to imply that Roman themes were important. Plautus, for instance, in the
prologue to *Amphitruo*, refers to the way gods like Neptune, Virtus, Victoria,
Mars and Bellona appear in tragedies to tell the audience what benefits they
have conferred on Rome. Two hundred years later, Phaedrus reports a
performance that began with a roll of thunder and 'the gods speaking in the
traditional way', followed by a choral song of thanks for the safety of the *princeps*.[17] It is very likely that topical themes under the principate involved much
loyal flattery; Augustus had to tell the praetors to keep it to a minimum, and
Trajan too did his best to discourage it after gross excesses under Domitian.[18]

Themes from Roman history are of course attested in the fragments
(Ennius' *Sabinae*, Accius' *Brutus*, and so on), and historical writers not infre-
quently comment that stories they have found in their sources seem
appropriate to plays. Livy calls the death of Servius Tullius 'a crime from
tragedy', and remarks that the transfer of Juno Regina from Veii to her new

---

16 Boissier 1893.107.
17 Plautus *Amphitruo* 41–4; Phaedrus 5.7.16–27.
18 Suetonius *Diuus Augustus* 89.3 (cf. 43.5 and Cicero *Ad Atticum* 16.5.1 for *commissio* referring
    to *ludi scaenici*); Pliny *Panegyricus* 54.1–2.

home on the Aventine involved miracle stories 'more appropriate to the stage'.[19] Plutarch makes a similar comment about the foundation story, and Dionysius about the battle of the triplets and the Fabii at the Cremera.[20] The strong inference, that there were indeed influential plays on these subjects, is confirmed in the case of the foundation story by Naevius' known play (or plays) on Romulus;[21] but all we need to insist on is a weaker inference, that these were the sort of historical stories that plays *might* be written about.

Livy's treatment of the Juno Regina story suggests that drama could provide aetiologies for particular Roman cults. When Ovid tells of the coming of the Magna Mater to Rome and the miraculous vindication of Quinta Claudia, he comments that the story is 'amazing, but attested by the stage'.[22] And then there is Varro's account of the Nonae Caprotinae ritual on 7 July, explained by a pseudo-historical story set in the immediate aftermath of the sack of Rome by the Gauls: 'the People learned the reason for this from the *togata praetexta* given at the Games of Apollo.'[23]

It may be significant that Varro does not attribute that play to an author. Does it date back to a time before the magistrates responsible for the games dealt with authors at all? (We might imagine them hiring the actors to do a performance, and telling them what was required.) If that is the case, then the fact that Varro knows the play may imply that it was repeated every year as a traditional item on the programme, part of the educational function of the games. The same may be true of plays about historic Roman victories. When Horace complains of the modern taste for mere spectacle in the theatre, his example, featuring a four-hour triumphal procession, is of a play on the taking of Corinth in 146 BC.[24] That was hardly a topical subject at the time he was writing; but it may be evidence for the way the citizens of Rome acquired their knowledge of their own history.

Of course such conjectures cannot be proved. All I want to insist on is the importance of Roman themes in the normal business of the Roman stage. Two final witnesses may be enough to prove the point. Here is Horace again, this time in the *Ars poetica*:[25]

> *nil intemptatum nostri liquere poetae,*
> *nec minimum meruere decus uestigia Graeca*

---

19 Livy 1.46.3 (*sceleris tragici exemplum*), 5.20.9 (*ad ostentationem scaenae gaudentis miraculis aptiora*).
20 Plutarch *Romulus* 8.7; Dionysius of Halicarnassus *Ant. Rom.* 3.18.1, 9.22.3.
21 Varro *De lingua Latina* 7.107, Festus 334L, Donatus on Terence *Adelphoe* 537; Manuwald 2001.141–61.
22 Ovid *Fasti* 4.326: *mira sed et scaena testificata loquar.*
23 Varro *De lingua Latina* 6.18: *cur hoc, togata praetexta data eis Apollinaribus ludis docuit populum*; Manuwald 2001.66–71.
24 Horace *Epistles* 2.1.187–93; Manuwald 2001.71–5.
25 Horace *Ars poetica* 285–8; for the sense of the fourth line see above, pp. 194–5.

> *ausi deserere et celebrare domestica facta,*
> *uel qui praetextas uel qui docuere togatas.*

Our poets have left nothing unattempted, earning not the least glory when they have dared to leave the Greek tracks and celebrate our own deeds, whether producing *praetextae* or *togatae*.

A generation later, Manilius tells us that one born under the constellation Cepheus may be a talented actor, playing either Romans or Greek heroes: *scaenisque togatos | aut magnos heroas aget*.[26] There is no evidence here for 'the progressive disappearance of *praetextae* from the stage' (Ferri p. 2).

IV

Having suggested above that 'the Senecan *Rezitationsdrama*' is a phantom genre, created out of preconceptions about Seneca and a misunderstanding of the *recitationes* of Maternus in Tacitus' *Dialogus*, I need to offer something in its place. Here too there is evidence, if one is prepared to look for it, which shows authors continuing to write for stage performance throughout the early principate.

Ovid counters Augustus' charge of obscenity against his *Ars amatoria* by pointing at the plots of erotic mimes, where successful adultery always wins the prize. Then he goes on:[27]

> *quoque minus prodest, scaena est lucrosa poetae,*
> *tantaque non paruo crimina praetor emit.*
> *inspice ludorum sumptus, Auguste, tuorum:*
> *empta tibi magno talia multa leges.*

The stage is profitable for poets, the less edifying it is. The praetor pays high prices buying such crimes. Take a look at the accounts of your own games, Augustus: you'll see that many such plots were expensively bought for you.

Writing for money isn't the most glorious way of achieving literary fame, as the elder Seneca pointed out about Abronius Silo, who wrote scripts for the *pantomimi* ('he didn't abandon his gift, he polluted it').[28] But that is not the point at issue here. Lucan himself left fourteen volumes of *salticae fabulae*; Statius sold his *Agaue* to Paris, the star actor-dancer of his day.[29] Martial did not think it at all demeaning; he lists the literary specialities of his friend Varro—Sophoclean tragedy, Horatian lyric, mime and elegy—without any sense that the third genre was less respectable than the others.[30]

---

26 Manilius *Astronomica* 5.282 (I follow G.P. Goold's ordering of the text in the Loeb edition).
27 Ovid *Tristia* 2.507–10.
28 Seneca *Suasoriae* 2.19 (*pantomimis fabulas scripsit*). Cf. *Anthologia Palatina* 9.543 (Crinagoras 39 Gow-Page): Philonides writing for Bathyllus.
29 *Vita Lucani*; Juvenal 7.86–7.
30 Martial 5.30.1–4 (*facundi scaena Catulli* at line 3).

Authors had to live, and there was a market to supply. The biggest demand was for the *pantomimi*, who drew huge crowds of enthusiastic and sometimes violent fans. The subject matter of their art was totally eclectic, including Roman themes as well as Greek. Pliny tells us that Stephanio, who had the distinction of performing in the Secular Games of both 17 BC and AD 47, was the first to dance as a *togatus*; Nero himself tried to recover his popularity in 68 by offering to dance Virgil's Turnus.[31] Like modern dramatists writing for television, Roman authors evidently adapted traditional genres to the new medium, and since Lucian includes 'teaching historical events' among the lofty aims of the actor-dancer,[32] the *praetexta* must have been given the same treatment. Even those who wrote in the traditional form were no doubt affected by the new theatrical conditions. Ferri briefly notes the possible influence of mime on the *Octavia* (pp. 294, 309, after D.F. Sutton); I think it can be assumed, and exploited as a solution to the main problem in the text as we have it, the way the marriage of Nero and Poppaea seems to have been 'spliced out of the sequence of events'.[33]

Lucian defined the possible range of the actor-dancer's material as everything 'from the emergence of the world out of Chaos to the days of Cleopatra of Egypt'.[34] But that was for Greek readers, ending where Greek history ended. Romans could still find new historical themes in the turbulent history of the principate. As we noted above, under normal circumstances the contemporary concerns of the *ludi scaenici* were no doubt confined to loyal praise of the *princeps* and his family. But when there was a dynastic crisis, the house of Caesar could provide plots as dramatic as the house of Atreus. It is easy to imagine a changed atmosphere in the theatre after the disgrace of Julia in 2 BC, the death of Germanicus in AD 19, the destruction of Sejanus in AD 31, the death of Tiberius in AD 37, the assassination of Gaius in AD 41, the fall of Messallina in AD 48, the execution of Agrippina in AD 59, and so on. All the playwright needed was a stage villain safely dead or disgraced, and the full melodrama of the imperial court could be staged with impunity.

That, I think, is the background we need if we are to understand the *Octavia*. We can, if we want, interpret it merely as a literary text, to be explained by its relation to other literary texts; but it seems to me more fruitful to read it as a document of the Roman stage, composed for performance at one of the most dramatic moments of Roman history.

---

31 Pliny *Nat. Hist.* 7.159; Suetonius *Nero* 54.
32 Lucian *Saltatio* 72; see above, p. 197.
33 Problem: Smith 2003.403–4 (quotation from 404). Hypothetical reconstruction: Wiseman 2004a.265–72.
34 Lucian *Saltatio* 37.

CHAPTER THIRTEEN

Ovid and the Stage

scaena sonat ludique uocant: spectate, Quirites.

Ovid *Fasti* 4.187

I

The fourth book of the *Fasti* contains Ovid's account of the *ludi Megalenses*, the games of the Great Mother. The din of her procession is deafening, but he has lots of questions to ask. The Mother deputes to the Muses the job of explanation, and Erato tells him what he needs to know. There are ten questions and ten answers, of which much the longest (102 lines out of the total 194) is the story of how the Phrygian goddess came to Rome. A major part of that story (*Fasti* 4.297–328) concerns her reception at Ostia and the miracle of the grounded ship.[1]

The tale of Claudia Quinta's undeserved reputation, and her vindication by the goddess as she pulled the ship from the sandbank single-handed, was known to Propertius and probably to Livy (though he didn't use it), but evidently not to Cicero or Diodorus.[2] Erato reveals that it was the plot of a play: *mira, sed et scaena testificata loquar* (326). What sort of play was it? The standard catalogues of Ribbeck and Klotz include it among the *fabulae praetextae*;[3] on the other hand, since it must have been particularly relevant to the *ludi Megalenses*, it is worth noting that the title 'Megalensia' was used by two of the known authors of *fabulae togatae*.[4]

According to the grammarians of late antiquity, *praetextae* were tragedies— or at least, serious plays—and *togatae* were comedies.[5] However, Seneca

1   On which see Wiseman 1979.94–9 and Bremmer 1987.105–11.
2   Propertius 4.11.51–2, Livy 29.14.12; Cicero *De haruspicum responso* 27, *Pro Caelio* 34, Diodorus Siculus 34.33.2.
3   Ribbeck 1897.335; Klotz 1953.371.
4   Nonius 829L (Afranius), Servius on *Eclogues* 7.33 (Atta).
5   Donatus *De comoedia* 6.1, Diomedes in *Grammatici Latini* 1.482 and 489 Keil, Lydus *De magistratibus* 1.40.

describes *togatae* as 'between comedy and tragedy',[6] and Varro seems to refer to a play on a somewhat similar historical theme (an *aition* for the Nonae Caprotinae festival) as a *togata praetexta*.[7] Certainly the attractive young noble-woman of Ovid's scenario, with her 'ready tongue for the strict old men',[8] sounds like a character in a comedy, however pious and patriotic its outcome; and a crowd of men hauling on a rope has comic potential too, as in Aristophanes' *Peace* and Aeschylus' satyr-play *Diktyoulkoi*.[9]

A detailed discussion of 'Ovid at the *ludi Megalenses*' came to this conclusion about the Claudia passage:[10]

> It would seem that dramatic entertainment at Roman festivals provided, as did the medieval mystery plays, a representation of the cult story appropriate to the festal day. [. . .] At all events we may conclude that Ovid deliberately accentuated the flavour of his descriptions of Roman holidays if not by the inclusion of appropriate material from the festal stage at any rate by dramatic colour and stage effects.

For this passage, at least, the conditional in the last sentence is unnecessarily cautious: Ovid evidently *is* including 'material from the festal stage'. To make sense of it, however, requires a hard look at two inter-related questions. First, what evidence is there for the sort of performances the Romans watched at the *ludi scaenici* in the first century BC? And second, what can we infer from Ovid's texts about the kind of drama he used as a source for his stories?

II

For most aspects of the social and cultural history of the late Republic, the works of Cicero offer an unparalleled wealth of information. But not for the stage, and there may be a reason for that. The audience at the games was the *populus Romanus*;[11] Cicero's relationship with the Roman People was fundamentally changed by the execution of the conspirators on 5 December 63 BC;

---

6 Seneca *Epistles* 8.8: *quam multi poetae dicunt quae philosophis aut dicta sunt aut dicenda! non adtingam tragicos, nec togatas nostras: habent enim hae quoque aliquid seueritatis et sunt inter comoedias ac tragoedias mediae.* Cf. Diomedes in *Grammatici Latini* 1.489–90 Keil, classing *praetextatae* as a type of *togatae*. See Brink 1971.319–20.

7 Varro *De lingua latina* 6.18, on which see Drossart 1974 and Wiseman 1998.8–11.

8 *Fasti* 4.309–10: *cultus et ornatis uarie prodisse capillis | obfuit, ad rigidos promptaque lingua senes.*

9 *Fasti* 4.297–304, with Fantham 1998.154: 'these lines sketch a kind of comedy.' Emphasis on *funis*: 4.297, 325, 331, 333 (also Propertius 4.11.51); cf. Aristophanes *Peace* 458–519, Aeschylus fr. 46a.16–21 Radt.

10 Littlewood 1981.387.

11 Cicero *Pro Sestio* 106, 116–18, *De haruspicum responso* 22–5, *In Pisonem* 65, *Ad Atticum* 2.19.3, 14.3.2, *Philippics* 1.36.

and the greater part of his *oeuvre*, including almost all the surviving correspondence, was written after that date.

As a young outsider challenging the entrenched *nobilitas*, Cicero could speak on the People's behalf—as in the prosecution of Verres, the debate on Pompey's eastern command and the defence of the *popularis* tribune C. Cornelius.[12] He was still able to exploit that popular goodwill in the first weeks of his consulship, when he presented himself as a *consul popularis* in order to defeat Rullus' land bill.[13] Up to that point, we may be sure that Cicero was greeted with warm applause whenever he took his seat in the theatre at the *ludi scaenici*. But the execution of citizens without trial must have changed all that. Cicero himself evidently presented it as a conscious act of *aristokratia*,[14] and from then on it seems he was regularly hissed at the games, except when he could shelter behind the popularity of Pompey.[15] Not surprisingly, though he still went to the games when politics required it, Cicero in his late years was not an enthusiastic theatre-goer. With that in mind, let us see what the Ciceronian evidence has to offer on the subject of the Roman stage.

In 80 BC (he was twenty-six) Cicero defended Sex. Roscius on a charge of parricide. In the course of a long purple passage on the heinousness of the crime, he appealed to what the jury had often seen on the stage, Orestes or Alcmaeon pursued by Furies for the murder of his mother:[16]

> *nolite enim putare, quem ad modum in fabulis saepenumero uidetis, eos qui aliquid impie scelerateque commiserint agitari et perterreri Furiarum taedis ardentibus. sua quemque fraus et suus terror maxime uexat. . .*

> Do not imagine that those who have committed some impious or criminal act are driven in terror by the blazing torches of the Furies, as you often see in plays. What hounds them is above all their own crime and their own terror.

The phrase *taedis ardentibus* is used by Cicero on two other occasions where he is making the same point, and otherwise only in a quotation from tragedy.[17]

---

12 E.g. Cicero *Verrines I* 34–7, *Verrines II* 5.174–6; *Pro lege Manilia* 63–4, 69–71; Asconius 71–79C. The *pro Cornelio* speeches are reconstructed by Kumaniecki 1970.

13 Cicero *De lege agraria* 2.6–10.

14 Plutarch *Cicero* 22.1, cf. Cicero *Ad Atticum* 2.3.4 (ἀριστοκρατικῶς). Plutarch's source at this point was probably Cicero's περὶ ὑπατείας, the Greek monograph on his consulship: Pelling 1985.315.

15 Cicero *Ad Atticum* 1.16.11, q.v. for Cicero's view of the Roman People at this time (also *Ad Atticum* 2.1.8, 2.16.1).

16 Cicero *Pro Roscio Amerino* 67, cf. 66 (*uidetisne quos nobis poetae tradiderunt. . .*) and 46 for *fabula* as 'play' (a comedy by Caecilius).

17 Cicero *In Pisonem* 46 (*ut in scaena uidetis*), *De legibus* 1.40 (*sicut in fabulis*), *Academica* 2.89 (tragedy); cf. *De haruspicum responso* 39 (*in tragoediis*) on the Furies and madness. The *topos* dates back at least as far as Aeschines (*In Timarchum* 190): μὴ γὰρ οἴεσθε . . . τοὺς ἠσεβηκότας, καθάπερ ἐν ταῖς τραγῳδίαις, Ποινὰς ἐλαύνειν καὶ κολάζειν δᾳσὶν ἡμμέναις.

Ennius wrote an *Alcmeo* and a *Eumenides*, and Pacuvius evidently had the Furies on stage lying in wait for Orestes at Delphi.[18] Such plays were no doubt what Polybius had in mind when he drew attention to the Romans' use of tragedy for controlling the populace;[19] fear of punishment by the gods was always a powerful deterrent from wrongdoing, and one medium of exemplary moral education was evidently the tragic stage.[20] Cicero's rationalisation of it is merely the recognition that educated people will not take the imagery literally.

It was probably some time in the late seventies that Cicero defended the great comic actor Q. Roscius in a private suit brought by a business partner. How absurd to imagine that a man of Roscius' stature would stoop to fraud for a mere fifty thousand sesterces![21]

> *pro deum hominumque fidem! qui HS CCCIƆƆƆ CCCIƆƆƆ CCCIƆƆƆ quaestus facere noluit (nam certe HS CCCIƆƆƆ CCCIƆƆƆ CCCIƆƆƆ merere et potuit et debuit, si potest Dionysia HS CCIƆƆ CCIƆƆ merere), is per summam fraudem et malitiam et perfidiam HS IƆ appetiit?*
>
> I ask you! A man who declined to make a profit of 300,000 sesterces used utter deceit, wickedness and treachery to make 50,000? For he certainly could and should have earned 300,000 if Dionysia can earn 200,000.

Who was Dionysia? The jury evidently knew without being told; they must have seen her often on the stage. Aulus Gellius, quoting a *bon mot* of Q. Hortensius, calls her a *saltatricula*, which must mean a mime actress; and a fragment of Varro's *Menippean Satires*, probably dateable to just about the time of the Roscius case, reveals the sort of performance she may have starred in:[22]

---

18 Ennius frr. 16–31, 144–8 Jocelyn (= 19–32, 132–6 R³), cf. Accius *Alcmeo*, frr. 608–20 Dangel (= 58–70 R³). Pacuvius: Servius on *Aeneid* 4.473 (fr. LIII R³)

19 Pol. 6.56.8: ἐπὶ τοσοῦτον γὰρ ἐκτετραγῴδηται καὶ παρεισῆκται τοῦτο τὸ μέρος [sc. δεισιδαιμονία] παρ' αὐτοῖς εἴς τε τοὺς κατ' ἰδίαν βίους καὶ τὰ κοινὰ τῆς πόλεως ὥστε μὴ καταλιπεῖν ὑπερβολήν. Failing a community of philosophers, the people have to be controlled (56.11): λείπεται τοῖς ἀδήλοις φόβοις καὶ τῇ τοιαύτῃ τραγῳδίᾳ τὰ πλήθη συνέχειν. See Mazzarino 1966.2.61–2 and Zorzetti 1980.64–5.

20 Aristotle *Metaphysics* 12.8.20 (1074b4–5), Diodorus Siculus 1.2.2 (on ἡ τῶν ἐν ᾅδου μυθολογία), Cicero *In Catilinam* 4.7–8, *De legibus* 2.15–16; cf. Cicero *De legibus* 1.47 on the stage as a source of *opiniones*. See Liebeschuetz 1979.39–54 for the ethical demands of Roman religion, and Rawson 1991.570–81 for theatrical moralising ('the theatre … provided much of the mental furniture of the poor', 581).

21 Cicero *Pro Roscio comoedo* 23 (Roscius was a rich man, and did not accept a fee for his performances).

22 Varro *Menippean Satires* 513 Astbury (Nonius 563L); cf. Lucian *Saltatio* 41 for Actaeon as a subject for tragic mime. [Atalanta was evidently another mythological mime subject: see *CIL* 6.37965.21 (the second- or third-century AD epitaph for Allia Potestas): *quid crura? Atalantes status illi comicus ipse*, translated by Horsfall 1985.256 as 'What about her legs? She had quite the pose of Atalanta on the comic stage'. The reference at that date is probably to mime, and we know that already in Ovid's time (*Amores* 3.2.29–30, *Ars amatoria* 3.775) Atalanta's legs were famous for more than just running (Horsfall 1985.263).] Hortensius: Aulus Gellius 1.5.3 (against L. Torquatus in 62 BC).

crede mihi, plures dominos serui comederunt quam canes. quod si Actaeon occupasset et
ipse prius suos canes comedisset, non nugas saltatoribus in theatro fieret.

I tell you, more masters have been gobbled up by their slaves than by their
dogs. But if Actaeon had got in first and eaten his dogs himself, he wouldn't be
rubbish for dancers in the theatre.

Presumably the *saltatores* (masculine) played the dogs who tore Actaeon to
pieces; naked Diana and her nymphs would be roles for *saltatriculae*.

In his defence of Q. Gallius in 64 BC,[23] Cicero reminded the jury of what
he and they were seeing at the games—the huge success enjoyed by one
'dominant' playwright with his 'Banquets of Poets and Philosophers',
presenting Euripides arguing with Menander, Epicurus with Socrates.[24] It is
not at all clear what dramatic genre was involved. On the one hand, the
subject matter might suit the more ethically-improving end of the mime-
writers' repertoire, known to us mainly from the collection of *sententiae*
attributed to Publilius Syrus.[25] On the other hand, the banquets of philosophers had been satirised in Lycophron's third-century satyr-play *Menedemos*,
and both Vitruvius and Horace clearly imply that satyr-play was a familiar part
of the Roman theatrical experience in the first century BC; indeed, Q. Cicero
evidently produced Sophocles' satyr-play 'The Banqueters' to amuse Caesar's
officers in Gaul.[26]

Coming now to Cicero's career after the consulship, we find him reporting
political allusions at the *ludi Apollinares* of 59 and 58 BC (the latter at second
hand, since he was in exile at the time); the plays concerned are tragedies, a
praetexta, and a comic *togata*.[27] In the *pro Caelio* of April 56, delivered at the
very time of the *ludi Megalenses*, he quotes from tragedy and comedy, and
alludes to tragedy, *praetexta* and mime.[28] At Pompey's lavish games in 55, he

---

23 For the date, see Ramsey 1980.
24 Fr. 4 Puccioni = Jerome *Ad Nepotianum* 52.8: *unus quidam poeta dominatur, homo perlitteratus,*
    cuius sunt illa conuiuia poetarum ac philosopharum. . . . See Giancotti 1967.119–28 and Wiseman
    1994.80, both of whom wrongly date the speech to 66 BC.
25 Conveniently available in the Loeb *Minor Latin Poets* (ed. J.W. Duff and A.M. Duff, 1934)
    3–111; cf. Rawson 1991.579f. Giancotti (see previous note) assumes that the play Cicero
    refers to was a mime, and tentatively suggests D. Laberius as the author.
26 Athenaeus 2.55d, 10.419e–420c (Lycophron); Vitruvius 5.6.9, 7.5.2, Horace *Ars poetica*
    220–50; Cicero *ad Q. fratrem* 2.16.3 (July 54 BC), Συνδείπνους Σοφοκλέους, *quamquam a*
    te actam fabellam uideo esse festiue, nullo modo probaui (for the vulgar content of the play, cf.
    Athenaeus 1.17d). See Wiseman 1994.68–85.
27 Cicero *Ad Atticum* 2.19.3 (unknown tragedy); *Pro Sestio* 118 (Afranius' *Simulans*), 120–2
    (Accius' *Eurysaces*), 123 (Accius' *Brutus*).
28 Cicero *Pro Caelio* 1 (*diebus festis ludisque publicis*), 18 (Ennius' *Medea exsul*), 36 (unknown
    comedy), 37 (comedy by Caecilius), 38 (Terence's *Adelphi*), 64–5 (*fabulae*, mime), 67 (tragic
    Equus Troianus?): see Hollis 1998. The *prosopopoeia* of Ap. Claudius Caecus at *Pro Caelio* 34
    is presented as a stage scenario (*ita grauem personam induxi*, 35), necessarily a *praetexta*.

found the mimes soporific and the tragedies disappointing; also on the programme, though he gives no details, were 'Greek and Oscan shows'.[29]

In 54 BC, at a time when his political *volte-face* may have brought him temporarily back into popular favour, he was at Apollo's games again, evidently in support of the praetor responsible for them:[30]

> *redii Romam Fontei causa a.d. vii Id. Quint. ueni spectatum, primum magno et aequa-*
> *bili plausu—sed hoc ne curaris, ego ineptus qui scripserim. deinde Antiphonti operam. is*
> *erat ante manu missus quam productus. ne diutius pendeas, palmam tulit. sed nihil tam*
> *pusillum, nihil tam sine uoce, nihil tam. . . uerum haec tu tecum habeto. in Andromacha*
> *tamen maior fuit quam Astyanax, in ceteris parem habuit neminem. quaeris nunc de*
> *Arbuscula. ualde placuit. ludi magnifici et grati; uenatio in aliud tempus dilata.*

I returned to Rome for Fonteius' benefit on 9 July, and went to the theatre. To begin with, the applause was loud and steady as I entered—but never mind that, I am a fool to mention it. To proceed, I saw Antipho, who had been given his freedom before they put him on the stage. Not to keep you too long in suspense, he won the prize; but never have I seen such a weedy little object, not a scrap of voice, not a—but don't say I said so! As Andromache at any rate he stood head and shoulders above Astyanax. In the other roles he didn't have his equal. Now you'll want to know about Arbuscula. First-rate. The games were fine and much appreciated. The hunt was put off to another time.

Antipho was evidently a tragic actor. Arbuscula must have been a *mima*, presumably also a novice and an ex-slave. Twenty years later Horace refers to her as saying 'It's enough if the knights applaud me' when the rest of the audience booed her off the stage; in 54 she may have been like the young freedwoman Epicharis, starring in 'the games of the nobles' at fourteen.[31]

A letter to Trebatius the following year reveals another aspect of the mimic stage—topical satire, of which Trebatius may be a victim if he stays in Gaul too long without getting rich.[32] The mimes used to come first at the games, in the morning programme; a letter to Paetus in 46 implies that a mime now follows a tragedy, in the slot previously occupied by a *fabula Atellana*.[33] Whenever they came, Cicero found them as tedious at Caesar's games that autumn as he had

29 Cicero *Ad familiares* 7.2.1–3; for Greek shows, cf. *Ad Atticum* 16.5.1, Plutarch *Marius* 2.1 and *ILLRP* 803.13 = *CIL* 1².1214.13.
30 Cicero *Ad Atticum* 4.15.6 (Shackleton Bailey's translation); cf. 4.5.1 and *Ad familiares* 1.9.4– 18 on the 'palinode'.
31 Horace *Satires* 1.10.76–7; *ILLRP* 803 = *CIL* 1².1214, with Wiseman 1985.30–35.
32 Cicero *Ad familiares* 7.11.2: *si diutius frustra afueris, non modo Laberium sed etiam sodalem nostrum Valerium pertimesco; mira enim persona induci potest Britannici iuris consulti.* For Valerius Catullus the mimographer, see n. 41 below.
33 Cicero *Ad familiares* 9.16.7 (contrast 7.2.1).

done at Pompey's nine years earlier.[34] What excited him were the serious genres of tragedy and *praetexta* that could be taken as commenting on the high issues of contemporary politics, as at the *ludi Apollinares* in July 44 BC.[35] However, even the mimes' ad-libbing had been worth hearing at that year's *ludi Megalenses*, immediately following the Ides of March.[36]

The ubiquity of mime, in its many forms, is the main thing that emerges from the Ciceronian evidence. Small wonder that in Lucretius the man who has been watching the games all day sees dancers in his dreams, and not the masks of comedy or tragedy.[37] Despite recent doubts on the subject, it is more likely than not that this popular and versatile dramatic form influenced, and even overlapped with, the literary genres of 'high culture'.[38]

The star *mima* of the forties BC, mistress of Antony and Cornelius Gallus,[39] sang (and danced?) in a performance of Virgil's sixth *Eclogue*. So at least Servius tells us; Donatus too believed that the *Eclogues* were performed on the stage, and it is not easy to see why these late sources should have invented the idea.[40] It has been argued that Catullus the poet, Catullus the mime-writer and Catullus the theorist of mime were one and the same person—a startling notion, but not at all inconsistent with what we can infer about the literary culture of the mid-first century BC.[41] The same applies to the Augustan age, and particularly to the elegiac poets, since 'contemporary mime is precisely the sort of literary production which we should expect to find exploited in elegy'.[42] With that in mind, we may turn to Ovid, whose own works, he tells us, were often 'danced' on the stage.[43]

---

34 Cicero *Ad familiares* 12.18.2 on *Laberi et Publilii poemata* (cf. 7.2.1); *Pro Rabirio Postumo* 35 for a dismissive comment about mimes in 54 BC.

35 Cicero *Philippics* 1.36, *Ad Atticum* 16.2.3 (Accius' *Tereus*); cf. *Ad Atticum* 16.5.1 (Brutus had expected Accius' *Brutus*).

36 Cicero *Ad Atticum* 14.3.2 (9 April 44): *tu si quid* πραγματικὸν *habes rescribe; sin minus, populi* ἐπισημασίαν *et mimorum dicta perscribito*.

37 Lucretius 4.973–83, cf. 788–93; the mask is exploited in a different context (4.296–9).

38 See McKeown 1979 and Fantham 1989; the latter calls mime 'the missing link in Roman literary history'. Contra Rawson 1993, who insists on 'the vulgarity of the Roman mime', but with so many proper reservations that the essentials of the McKeown-Fantham view remain valid. Evidently mime could be both vulgar *and* sophisticated, morally sententious *and* obscene.

39 Volumnia Cytheris: Cicero *Ad familiares* 9.26.2; *Ad Atticum* 10.10.5, 10.16.5, *Philippics* 2.20, 2.58, 2.62, 2.69, 2.77, Plutarch *Antony* 9.4–5, Pliny *Nat. Hist.* 8.55 (Antony); Servius on *Eclogues* 10.1, *De uiris illustribus* 82.2 (Gallus).

40 Servius on *Eclogues* 6.11, Donatus *Vita Vergilii* 26 OCT; see Van Sickle 1986.17–23.

41 Wiseman 1985.183–98, 258–9, and 1994.92–4. For the theorist, see Scholia Bernensia on Lucan 1.544: *in libro Catulli qui inscribitur* περὶ μιμολογιῶν (Müller's reading for *quis cribitur permimologiarum*).

42 McKeown 1979.71; among the mime-influenced passages he goes on to discuss are Horace *Satires* 1.2.127–34, Propertius 2.29, 4.7, 4.8 and 4.9.

43 *Tristia* 2.519–20: *et mea sunt populo saltata poemata saepe.*

III

For the following fifteen episodes in the *Metamorphoses* and *Fasti*, various scholars in the past thirty years or so have suggested direct influence from the Roman theatre:

1. Pentheus and Acoites (*Met.* 3.562–83, 692–700): from Pacuvius' tragedy *Pentheus*?[44]

2. The Calydonian boar-hunt (*Met.* 8.273–413): from a mime by Laberius?[45]

3. Circe, Picus and Canens (*Met.* 14.320–434): from a satyr-play?[46]

4. Pomona and Vertumnus (*Met.* 14.622–94, 765–71): from a satyr-play?[47]

5. Priapus and Lotis (*Fasti* 1.391–440): from a mime?[48]

6. Faunus, Hercules and Omphale (*Fasti* 2.303–56): from a satyr-play?[49]

7. Jupiter, Lara and Mercury (*Fasti* 2.583–616): from a mime?[50]

8. Ariadne and Liber (*Fasti* 3.459–516): from a mime?[51]

9. Anna, Aeneas and Lavinia (*Fasti* 3.543–656): from a mime?[52]

10. Anna Perenna and Mars (*Fasti* 3.675–96): from a mime by Laberius?[53]

11. Silenus and the bees (*Fasti* 3.738–60): from 'burlesque drama'?[54]

12. Priapus and Vesta (*Fasti* 6.319–48): from a mime or satyr-play?[55]

13. Ino, Hercules and Carmentis (*Fasti* 6.501–50): from a mime or satyr-play?[56]

14. Fortuna and Servius (*Fasti* 6.573–80): from a mime?[57]

15. Servius, Tarquin and Tullia (*Fasti* 6.585–624): from a *praetexta*?[58]

---

44 Otis 1966.371–2: Pacuvius ap. Servius on *Aeneid* 4.469.

45 Horsfall 1979b: Laberius fr. 176 Bonaria = 148 R³.

46 Wiseman 1994.83: cf. Steffen 1952.134 on Aeschylus' satyr-play *Circe* (frr. 113a–115 Radt). See further p. 220 below.

47 Brief reference at Wiseman 1994.82, 84.

48 McKeown 1979.76; cf. also Littlewood 1980.317 and Wiseman 1998.23–4.

49 Satyr-play: Littlewood 1975.1063–7: Steffen 1952.230–4, 241–2 on *Omphale* satyr-plays by Ion and Achaios. 'Popular drama': Fantham 1983.196–8, 200–1.

50 Wiseman 1998.24.

51 Barchiesi 1994.230 = 1997.243: 'una scena di teatro leggero'. The putative drama must post-date Catullus 64.

52 Giancotti 1967.63–5; cf. also McKeown 1979.75–6 and Barchiesi 1994.232 = 1997.245. The putative drama must post-date Virgil *Aeneid* 4.

53 Giancotti 1967.61–3: Laberius fr. 10 Bonaria = 2 R³; cf. also McKeown 1979.76, Littlewood 1980.316–17, Wiseman 1998.72–4.

54 Brief reference at Littlewood 1980.317. See further pp. 223–4 below.

55 Mime: McKeown 1979.76; cf. Littlewood 1980.317. Satyr-play: Wiseman 1994.82.

56 Wiseman 1998.48–51.

57 Barchiesi 1994.217 = 1997.229; Wiseman 1998.27–30.

58 Wiseman 1998.30–4: *Fasti* 6.612, *mira quidem, sed tamen acta*.

There is more to be said about one or two of these, and further examples may be added to the list. But first, it may be helpful to expose certain prejudices that have hampered enquiry hitherto.

First, the idea that 'mythological burlesque ... seems not to have been a common feature in mime'.[59] That goes against the explicit evidence of Varro, who refers to mimes about Liber and the Nymphs, and of Augustine on Priapus, the protagonist of nos. 5 and 12 in the list above:[60]

> *numquid Priapo mimi, non etiam sacerdotes enormia pudenda fecerunt? an aliter stat*
> *adorandus in locis sacris, quam procedit ridiculus in theatris?*
> It is not only the mimes who give Priapus an enormous phallus; the priests do
> the same. He stands there in his sacred places to claim men's adoration in just
> the same guise as he comes on the stage to provoke laughter.

The context is Augustine's challenge to Varro's distinction between the gods of the poets and the gods of the city, *theologia fabularis* and *theologia ciuilis*.[61] Since the whole lengthy passage is devoted to Varro's argument, it is likely that Priapus too featured in the mimes of Varro's time, and not just Augustine's.[62]

Second, it is said that 'satyr play [was] a genre which despite Horace's encouragement had probably lapsed for good in Augustan Rome'.[63] Why should we suppose so? Horace, like Vitruvius, provides the evidence that in one form or another it was still a living genre, as it probably had been since at least the fourth century BC.[64]

Coupled with this is a third unfounded prejudice, that 'the theory of decorum' prevented any common ground existing between the world of the satyrs and that of contemporary Rome: 'no common language or socially acceptable container can exist for a mixture of themes and styles which amounts to a breakdown of the conventional hierarchies.'[65] But if that were the case one would hardly expect dignified senatorial families to claim descent (as they did) from Pan, Silenus and Marsyas,[66] or Suetonius to include in his

---

59 McKeown 1979.75; *contra* Horsfall 1979b.331, 'both mimes and Atellan farces on mytho-
    logical themes are attested'. [See n. 22 above.]
60 Varro *Antiquitates diuinae* fr. 3 Cardauns; Augustine *City of God* 6.7 (CSEL 40.284), trans. H.
    Bettenson (Penguin Classics 1967).
61 Augustine *City of God* 6.5 = Varro *Antiquitates diuinae* frr. 7–10 Cardauns.
62 *City of God* 6.2–10 *passim* (Varro *Antiquitates diuinae* frr. 2a–12, 47, 62 Cardauns). Agahd (fr.
    39d) included Priapus in his Varro fragment; Cardauns (fr. 35) is more cautious.
63 Fantham 1983.187; cf. Barchiesi 1994.231–2 = 1997.244, 'un genere letterario di cui
    sappiamo poco, o, soprattutto, non possiamo richiamare con certezza la presenza a Roma: il
    dramma satiresco'. (The phrase 'genere letterario' begs a big question.)
64 Horace and Vitruvius: n. 26 above. Fourth century BC: for satyrs and the Bacchic *thiasos* on
    bronze *cistae*, sometimes apparently in the context of performance, see above, pp. 86–124.
65 Barchiesi 1994.234 = 1997.247.
66 See the coin-types of the Vibii Pansae (90 and 48 BC), the Iunii Silani (91 BC) and the Marcii
    (82 BC): Crawford 1974.336–7, 346, 377, 464–5, 467.

narrative of Caesar's crossing of the Rubicon (as he does) a supernatural figure piping to shepherds like Pan.[67]

What we do not know is the extent to which satyr-play and mime could be combined on the Roman stage. Mutual influence of the two genres can be detected as early as the fourth century BC in Athens,[68] and is likely to have increased in the innovative world of Hellenistic theatre. At Rome, the jesters in the processions at funerals, triumphs and festivals could be described as either mimes or *satyristai*; the satyr-dance called *sikinnis* was one of the elements of mime as performed by Bathyllus and Pylades; and Horace's purist polemic in the *Ars poetica* clearly implies that in his time the ancient rustic form of satyr-play had given way to a more sophisticated urban type, with obscene dialogue like that attributed to mime.[69] The interdependence of the genres is illustrated two generations after Ovid by Petronius' *Satyrica*, a novel full of references and allusions to mime, with a plot that depends on the anger of Priapus.[70]

Satyr-play naturally had a chorus of satyrs; mime, or one type of it at least, had a chorus of dancing girls[71]—and once we are free of the notion that *mimae* never played mythological burlesque, we can cast them as nymphs.[72] Nymphs and satyrs had danced and made love together since the beginning of Greek iconography, and their interplay of sexual desire was still celebrated in the art of Rome.[73] It would be very surprising if they were kept strictly separate in Roman popular drama. In the Ovidian episodes listed above (nos. 3, 4, 5 and 12), we find them both symmetrically separate—naiads and dryads in love with Picus: satyrs, Pans, Silenus and Priapus in love with Pomona—and also together, pursued and pursuing in the two stories of the 'feast of the gods'.[74] The natural inference is that the same *corps de ballet* of male and female dancers could put on different scenarios in different styles, as the producers of each set of games required.

---

67 Suetonius *Diuus Iulius* 32; Wiseman 1998.60–2.

68 See Simon 1982.19–20 and Plate 8, and Beazley 1963.1519 no. 13: Dionysus being entertained by, respectively, a satyr called Mimos and a *mima* dressed as a satyr.

69 Dionysius of Halicarnassus 7.72.10–12, Suetonius *Diuus Vespasianus* 19.2; Aristonicus of Alexandria ap. Athenaeus 1.20e; Horace *Ars poetica* 234–50, esp. 247 *immunda crepent ignominiosaque dicta* (cf. Ovid *Tristia* 2.497 on *mimos obscaena iocantes*).

70 Full details and bibliography in Panayotakis 1995.

71 Cf. Ovid *Fasti* 5.349–52 on the *mimae* at the *ludi Florales*. See Wiseman 1998.70–1.

72 See pp. 213–14 above on the Actaeon scenario attested by Varro.

73 See Hedreen 1994 on the sixth century BC, and Dierichs 1997.41–55 (who wrongly calls all the female partners 'maenads'). [See above, pp. 106–8.]

74 Ovid *Metamorphoses* 14.326–32, 637–41, *Fasti* 1.405–14, 6.323–4, 333–5. Just nymphs at *Fasti* 2.589–98, just satyrs at 3.737–58 (nos. 7 and 11). Cf. also *Fasti* 2.307 (no. 6, Faunus' farewell to the mountain nymphs), 3.467 (no. 8, Bacchus' girl captives) and 6.499–500 (no. 13, sea-nymphs bringing Ino and Melicertes): the dancers perform first, then leave the stage as the play proper begins?

IV

It is clear enough from the late-Republican evidence that performers like Dionysia, Arbuscula and Cytheris were not just chorus girls but stars in their own right,[75] no doubt with enough pulling power to have shows created specifically as vehicles for their particular talents. If that was the case, we may have an example in Ovid's treatment of Circe in *Metamorphoses* 14 (no. 3 above). The nymphs and Nereids are there, but in a subordinate capacity as Circe's maids;[76] no one is allowed to upstage the 'elemental sexuality' of the sorceress.[77]

Her first scene is with Glaucus, himself the subject of an Aeschylean satyr-play.[78] He wants Scylla, a girl who plays with the Nereids,[79] but Circe wants him. Spurned, she poisons Scylla's bathing pool.[80] Now here comes handsome Picus, king of Latium, galloping after wild boar. All the nymphs pined for him, but he loved just one, and married her—Canens, the singer, whose song perhaps the audience have already heard.[81] Circe lures him with her magic and begs for his love. Spurned again, she turns him into a woodpecker. Enter his companions, who threaten her with their spears; more sorcery, and they are turned into monstrous beasts.[82] 'This magic and its results,' writes a modern critic,[83] 'project the disordered, irrational state of Circe's whole being and convey her passion's blind, willful megalomania.' What a part for an actress! No doubt she watches from above in triumphant malice as the dancers mime the search for their missing king, and the scene ends with the singing nymph's despairing lament.[84]

One of the reasons for inferring a dramatic origin for this Ovidian story is the lavish use of dialogue.[85] The same applies to the Lara, Ino and Tullia episodes in the *Fasti* (nos. 7, 13 and 15 above), whereas the lecherous pursuits

---

75 See above, nn. 22, 31, 39.

76 *Metamorphoses* 14.264–7, cf. 311 (exploited by Ovid to make the Picus episode a story within a story).

77 Segal 1968.442; *Metamorphoses* 14.25–7, cf. Virgil *Aeneid* 7.189 *capta cupidine*. For sorcery as a mime subject, see Theocritus 2 (taken from a Sophron mime, according to the scholiast), and Page 1941.328–31.

78 Steffen 1952.119–23: Aeschylus frr. 25c–35 Radt.

79 *Metamorphoses* 13.735–7, 898–903.

80 *Metamorphoses* 14.8–74. Scylla's pool is like Thetis' (p. 221 below): 14.51–4, 11.229–37.

81 *Metamorphoses* 14.341, *feminea modulatur carmina uoce*.

82 *Metamorphoses* 14.320–415. For variants of the Picus-Circe story, see Moorton 1988.

83 Segal 1968.438; *Metamorphoses* 14.320–415.

84 *Metamorphoses* 14.416–34. For a search in the final scene, but with a happier outcome, cf. *Fasti* 3.649–56 (no. 9 in the list above).

85 *Metamorphoses* 14.12–39, 335–7, 372–85, 397–402. Another reason is Shakespeare's borrowing of the name Titania (14.438) and the transformation of man into beast ('Bottom, thou art translated!').

of Priapus and Faunus (nos. 5, 6 and 12) are performed without words,[86] in a tiptoeing silence before the sudden uproar of the dénouement. A combination of both styles is suggested by an episode that I think has not yet been considered in this context, that of Peleus and Thetis.[87] Here too we have an erotic quest, but with a very different outcome.

First, a dialogue between the Nereid Thetis and the prophetic seagod Proteus, another figure from Aeschylean satyr-play.[88] He tells her to conceive: her son will be mightier than his father, which is why Jupiter has stopped pursuing her and granted permission to do so to the hero Peleus. The next scene is the sea-cave where the naked nymph comes to sleep. Peleus finds her, pleads with her to accept his love, and seizes her when she refuses. But Thetis is a shape-shifter, and when she turns herself into a tigress even Peleus is discouraged (like Circe's transformations, this scene is a choreographer's challenge and opportunity). Dialogue again, as Proteus tells Peleus to bring bondage equipment next time. And so he does:[89]

> *pronus erat Titan inclinatoque tenebat*
> *Hesperium temone fretum, cum pulchra relicto*
> *Nereis ingreditur consueta cubilia ponto.*
> *uix bene uirgineos Peleus inuaserat artus;*
> *illa nouat formas, donec sua membra teneri*
> *sensit et in partes diuersas bracchia tendi.*
> *tum demum ingemuit 'neque' ait 'sine numine uincis'*
> *exhibita estque Thetis. confessam amplectitur heros*
> *et potitur uotis ingentique implet Achille.*

The sun was sinking, touching the western strait in his descending chariot, when the beautiful Nereid left the sea and mounted her accustomed couch. Unfairly, Peleus had taken control of her virgin limbs; she changed her shape, until she realised that her legs were being held and her arms stretched out on either side. Then at last she cried 'You only win with divine help'—and Thetis was displayed. She admitted defeat; the hero embraced her, took possession of what he had prayed for, and filled her with huge Achilles.

Two details may allude to stage performance. First, the grotto itself, Thetis' private bedroom: 'hard to tell whether nature or art had made it—but no, it was artificial.'[90] And then the dénouement, with the nymph on display to the

---

86 Priapus woos Lotis with 'nods and signs', and she rejects him with a glance (*Fasti* 1.417–20).
87 *Metamorphoses* 11.221–65.
88 Steffen 1952.137–9: Aeschylus frr. 210–15 Radt.
89 *Metamorphoses* 11.257–65. For dancers performing metamorphosis, see Lucian *Saltatio* 19, 57.
90 *Metamorphoses* 11.235–6, *natura factus an arte | ambiguum, magis arte tamen.*

audience as well as to Peleus, in the position of total exposure used to portray Andromeda and Hesione.[91] She gives in, so Peleus can release her (as Perseus and Hercules do in the other stories), no doubt for a closing *pas de deux*.[92]

As early as the fourth century BC, to judge by the visual evidence, mythological performances in which *mimae* appeared naked were familiar in Latium; the literary sources on the *ludi Florales* attest similar spectacles from the third century BC to the first.[93] The discovery of Ariadne could be an example. L. Pomponius wrote a satyr-play *Ariadne*,[94] and Catullus' dramatically 'disobedient *ekphrasis*' in poem 64 has the distraught heroine lose her clothes before delivering her great aria of passion and despair; meanwhile the god and his satyrs are looking for her, and he is burning with desire.[95]

Ovid's sequel to Catullus' Ariadne (no. 8 above) is much more decorous, ending with a confirmation of conjugal love. It is an *aition* not only for the constellation of Ariadne's crown but also for Ariadne as Libera, the mysterious third occupant of the Roman temple of Ceres, Liber and Libera, allegedly founded after the battle of Lake Regillus.[96] Annual games were part of the cult, the Liberalia on 17 March and the Cerealia on 19 April. Ovid's *aition* for the Liberalia (no. 11 above) is also—like the Ariadne narrative—surprisingly uncharacteristic of the licentious wine-god and his satyrs.

It begins with a long and deliberately anticlimactic priamel:[97]

> *tertia post Idus lux est celeberrima Baccho;*
> *Bacche, faue uati, dum tua festa cano.*
> *nec referam Semelen, ad quam nisi fulmina secum*

---

91 Not, I think, 'spreadeagled on the ground', as suggested by Griffin 1997.140. Andromeda [fig. 44, p. 123 above]: Schauenberg 1981.787–90; for illustrations see particularly 628 no. 20 (Campanian vase, fourth century BC), 640 no. 146a (temple relief at Falerii, second century BC), 641 no. 152 (grave relief of performance at Roman games, second century AD). Hesione: Oakley 1997.628–9, illustrations at 386–9 nos. 18–41.

92 Hardly an imitation of the sex act itself, though in some contexts that may have been acceptable on the mimic stage: Ovid *Tristia* 2.515, *imitantes turpia mimos*; Valerius Maximus 2.6.7, *quorum argumenta maiore ex parte stuprorum continent actus*.

93 See above, pp. 109–24. Floralia: Valerius Maximus 2.10.8 (*priscus mos iocorum*), Seneca *Epistles* 97.8; cf. Ovid *Fasti* 4.946 and 5.331–56, Martial 1 pref. and 1.35.8–9, Tertullian *De spectaculis* 17, Arnobius *Aduersus nationes*. 3.23 and 7.33, Lactantius *Institutiones*. 1.20.6–10, Augustine *City of God* 2.27, Historia Augusta *Elagabalus* 6.5, Ausonius 7.24.25f.

94 Porphyrio on Horace *Ars poetica* 221; Wiseman 1994.70.

95 Catullus 64.60–70, 251–3 (*te quaerens, Ariadna, tuoque incensus amore*, 253); note the music-and-dance scene at 64.254–65. See Laird 1993, esp. 20 ('sound, movement and temporality') and 29 ('succession of time, movement, sound, and especially speech') on the qualities that make the *ekphrasis* 'disobedient': he relates them to rhetoric, but they seem even more relevant to dramatic performance.

96 Ovid *Fasti* 3.459–516, esp. 469 (*coniunx*), 498 (*coniugis*), 512 (*Libera*). Temple: Dionysius of Halicarnassus 6.10.1, 6.17.2–4, 6.94.3, on which see Wiseman 1998.35–6.

97 3.713–26: *partus* for *paruus* at 716 is Heinsius' emendation. For *uitisator* at 726 some MSS and editors read *uilis anus* (cf. 765), an unnecessary simplification.

> *Iuppiter adferret, partus inermis eras;*
> *nec, puer ut posses maturo tempore nasci,*
> * expletum patrio corpore matris opus;*
> *Sithonas et Scythicos longum narrare triumphos*
> * et domitos gentes, turifer Inde, tuas;*
> *tu quoque Thebanae mala praeda tacebere matris,*
> * inque tuum furiis acte, Lycurge, genus;*
> *ecce libet subitos pisces Tyrrhenaque monstra*
> * dicere, sed non est carminis huius opus.*
> *carminis huius opus causas exponere quare*
> * uitisator populos ad sua liba uocet.*

The third dawn after the Ides is famed for Bacchus: Bacchus, favour a poet while I sing of your festival. But I shall not tell of Semele, to whom Jupiter came—if he had left his thunderbolts behind you would have been born unarmed. Nor shall I tell how a mother's function was fulfilled in your father's body, so that you could be born a boy at the proper time. It would take too long to narrate your Sithonian and Scythian triumphs and the conquest of the peoples of incense-bearing India. You too [Pentheus], wrongful prey of your Theban mother, will not be spoken of, nor you, Lycurgus, driven by the Furies against your own kin. See, I would like to tell of sudden fish and Tyrrhenian miracles, but that is not the purpose of this song. The purpose of this song is to explain why the Vine-planter calls the peoples to his own honey-cakes.

The Vine-planter is Liber, his own cakes are *liba*—and the song is of what happened when the god discovered honey.

The stories Ovid is not going to tell here—though he tells them in the *Metamorphoses*—were about the god's miraculous origin and miraculous powers, well known in Rome as subjects for tragedy. (Pacuvius wrote a *Pentheus*, Naevius a *Lycurgus*, Accius a *Tropaeum Liberi* which presumably dealt with the god's triumphant progress.) The story he does tell here could hardly be further from tragedy, and it isn't really satyr-play either, though the satyrs feature in it:[98]

> *ibat harenoso satyris comitatus ab Hebro*
> * (non habet ingratos fabula nostra iocos),*
> *iamque erat ad Rhodopen Pangaeaque florida uentum...*

He was on his way from sandy Hebrus, attended by the satyrs (my story contains no unwelcome frolics), and already they had come to Rhodope and flowery Pangaeus...

These are satyrs for a children's party. They enjoy their honey, and they laugh

---

98 3.737–9.

when old Silenus gets stung on his bald head, but their usual phallic antics—
hinted at in *iocos*[99]—are explicitly ruled out. Ovid at the Liberalia leaves out
sex, plays down the god's awesome power, and draws attention to the fact that
he is doing so.

A reason why may be hinted at a few lines further on, in one of the explanations for the granting of the *toga uirilis* at the Liberalia. In the old times when
the Romans were horny-handed farmers, when senators worked their fathers'
fields and the consul took up the *fasces* straight from the plough, the population
lived in the country and only came to town for the games; so perhaps that was
why the day was chosen for the ceremony, to get a crowd together to congrat-
ulate the new adult.[100] A parenthesis interrupts the argument:[101]

> *sed dis, non studiis ille dabatur honor;*
> *luce sua ludos uuae commentor habebat,*
>   *quos cum taedifera nunc habet ille dea.*

But that honour [games] used to be given to the gods, not to popular enthusiasm; the discoverer of the grape used to have games on his own day, but now
he shares them with the torch-carrying goddess [Ceres].

The games of the Liberalia are attested for the time of Naevius, and it is likely
that their cancellation had something to do with the Roman government's
violent suppression of the 'Bacchanalia' in 186 BC.[102] That event was long
remembered; it is cited in Cicero's treatise on the laws as a salutary example of
traditional moral standards.[103] Augustus is unlikely to have disagreed, especially
in the light of Antony's masquerade as Liber-Dionysus.[104]

The ancient temple of Ceres, Liber and Libera was burned down in 31 BC;
astonishingly, it was not included in the temple-restoration programme of 28,
but rededicated only in AD 17. Augustus evidently did without it for most of
his principate. That must surely have been a deliberate gesture to demote
Liber: since Ceres had also a joint cult with Tellus at the Carinae, the goddess
of the harvest could now be honoured without any unfortunate association

---

99 Barchiesi 1997.133, 240: 'Ovid uses the word *ioci* and its cognates to refer to a whole comic
    and sexual sphere in the *Fasti*. . . The use of terms like *ioci, iocosus, obscenus,* and also *fabula*
    seems to be reserved for burlesque tales, almost always of a sexual nature.'
100 *Fasti* 3.779–88.
101 3.784–6. For *studia* used of actors' rowdy fans, cf. Tacitus *Annals* 1.16.3, *Dialogus* 29.3; for
    the phenomenon in general, see Valeius Maximus 2.4.1, Tacitus *Annals* 1.77, 4.14.3,
    11.13.1, 13.24.1, Suetonius *Tiberius* 37.2, *Nero* 20.3, Pliny *Epistles* 7.24.7.
102 Naevius fr. 113 R³; Wiseman 1998.35–43.
103 Cicero *De legibus* 2.37, *seueritas maiorum* in defence of *mulierum fama*; cf. Varro *Antiquitates*
    diuinae fr. 45 Cardauns. Livy's great set-piece narrative at 39.8–19 must have been very
    familiar to Ovid and his readers.
104 Seneca *Suasoriae* 1.6, Dio Cassius 48.39.2, Plutarch *Antony* 24.2–3, 26.3, 60.3, 75.3–4; see
    above, pp. 130–1.

with Antony's patron god.[105] In that context, it seems permissible to wonder whether Ovid's account of the Liberalia reflects the god's reduced prestige.

Since the derivation of Liber from *liberi* is found already in Cicero,[106] it may not be absurd to suggest that the Liberalia festival was actually reorganised as a show suitable for children. Whatever the explanation, Ovid seems to be illustrating a deliberately emasculated version of the Roman games in honour of the god. The phallic comedies he does bring on (nos. 5, 6 and 12 above) are all safely set in a Greek landscape.[107]

V

Discussion of Liber has brought us back to our starting point, Ovid's use of stage material about the gods and goddesses who were honoured at the *ludi scaenici* themselves.[108] My last example concerns the goddess Flora, whose *ludi Florales* (28 April–2 May) were famous for just the sort of erotic entertainment that Ovid's narratives have allowed us to infer.[109]

Flora was closely associated with Liber (his mother, in one story), and her temple was next to his at the Circus Maximus; it must have been burned down at the same time, and like his was only rededicated in AD 17.[110] Her games had been controversial from the start, so here too we may guess that Augustus chose to distance himself from so uninhibited a festival.[111] Ovid, however, gives himself a long and affectionate interview with Flora, enjoying her physical presence and emphasising the Liber-like liberty of her games.[112]

He begins by asking her to tell him in person who she is, 'for the opinion of men is fallacious'. That may refer to the story known from Christian sources, that Flora was a successful prostitute who bequeathed her riches to the

---

105 Dio Cassius 50.10.3–4 (31 BC), Augutus *Res gestae* 20.4 (28 BC), Tacitus *Annals* 2.49.1 (AD 17); perhaps Augustus' hand was eventually forced by the great famine of AD 4–7 (Dio Cassius 55.22.3, 26.1–3, 27.1, 31.3–4, 33.4). Ceres and Tellus: Arnobius *Aduersus nationes*. 7.32, *Fasti Praenestini* on 13 December (*Inscriptiones Italiae* 13.2.537f), Horace *Carmen saeculare* 29–30; see Palombi 1997.154–8 on frr. 577 and 672 of the Severan Forma Urbis, showing twin temples *in Tellure*. The goddess of plenty on the Ara Pacis is indistinguishably Ceres or Tellus: see most recently Spaeth 1996.125–51, esp. 133–5.

106 Cicero *De natura deorum* 2.62, *quod ex nobis natos liberos appellamus*.

107 *Fasti* 1.393 (*Graecia*), 2.313 (Lydia), 6.327 (Ida).

108 *Fasti* 4.326, with Littlewood 1981.387.

109 See pp. 175–86 above.

110 Tacitus *Annals* 2.49.1, *eodem in loco* (n. 105 above); Ampelius 9.11, *secundus Liber ex Merone et Flora*; Ovid *Fasti* 5.335–46 for Flora and Bacchus, in the context of her games.

111 Games not recognised by the Senate till 173 BC (Ovid *Fasti* 5.295–330); Augustus' Palatine Vesta installed on the *Floralia* (ibid. 4.943–54), on which see Barchiesi 1994.122 = 1997.133.

112 *Fasti* 4.946 (*scaena ioci morem liberioris habet*), 5.331–2 (*quare lasciuia maior | his foret in ludis liberiorque iocus*); 5.195, 199, 275, 376 (physical presence). Note that the narrator, uniquely in the *Fasti*, is named as Naso the poet (5.377).

Roman People, out of which games were set up in her honour.[113] But she knows better:[114]

> sic ego. sic nostris respondit diua rogatis
>   (dum loquitur uernas efflat ab ore rosas):
> 'Chloris eram quae Flora uocor: corrupta Latino
>   nominis est nostri littera Graeca sono.
> Chloris eram, nymphe campi felicis, ubi audis
>   rem fortunatis ante fuisse uiris.
> quae fuerit mihi forma graue est narrare modestae. . . '

That was what I asked. This is what the goddess replied to my question (and while she spoke, she breathed spring roses): 'I who am called Flora used to be Chloris; a Greek letter in my name has been corrupted in Latin speech. I used to be Chloris, a nymph of the happy field where once upon a time, as you have heard, fortunate men had business. It's hard to tell you modestly what my figure was like. . .'

The nature of the 'business' is one of Flora's tactful reticences. But who were the fortunate men who enjoyed it?

In Homer, the Elysian Field is a country club with a tight membership policy; Menelaus only gets in as a son-in-law of Zeus. In Hesiod, you qualify if you fought in the epic wars at Thebes or Troy. By Pindar's time the criterion is a moral one: 'whoever have thrice dared to keep their soul utterly free from deeds of wrong.'[115] Just as evil-doers are threatened with the punishments of Tartarus, so this is the reward for a life of virtue.

Tartarus was a real threat for pious Romans; it is presupposed by Lucretius' great poem, and references to it are found even in senatorial speeches.[116] As we saw with reference to the Ciceronian evidence about drama, tragedy put the threat on the stage in the form of the Furies, to enforce moral behaviour in the way Polybius had described.[117] One might infer as a corollary that the rewards of virtue could be advertised on the comic stage.

The paradise of Hesiod and Pindar was the Isles of the Blessed, but the facilities there were the same as in Elysium—the river of Oceanus at the ends of the earth, and the mild breath of Zephyrus, god of the west wind. Pindar

---

113 *Fasti* 5.191 (*ipsa doce, quae sis: hominum sententia fallax*); Lactantius *Institutiones* 1.20.5–10, Minucius Felix *Octavius* 25.8, Cyprian *De uanitate idolum* 4. For a well-known prostitute called Flora in the first century BC, see Plutarch *Pompeius* 2.2–4, Varro *Menippean Satires* fr. 136 Astbury, Philodemus 12 Gow-Page (*Anthologia Palatina* 5.132).

114 *Fasti* 5.193–9; for *rem* at 198, see Adams 1982.203.

115 Homer *Odyssey* 4.561–9, Hesiod *Works and Days* 166–73, Pindar *Olympians* 2.68–77.

116 Lucretius 1.62–110, 3.37–56 etc; Cicero *In Catilinam* 4.7–8, Sallust *Catiline* 54.20, *Histories* 2.47.3M.

117 See above, pp. 212–13.

adds flowers and garlands; in Hesiod it is 'sweet-smelling fruit'.[118] In the
Aeneid, the abode of the blessed is a combination of grassy turf and shady
woods, including a grove scented with laurel.[119] All these items appear in
Flora's story. Chloris the nymph was ravished by Zephyrus, who gave her a
garden and made her the goddess of flowers; she was visited by Juno, on her
way to Oceanus to complain about Jupiter, and she gave her a herb to make
her pregnant. Outside Ovid, Martial refers to Flora fleeing into her laurel-
grove to escape the attentions of Priapus.[120]

At some time after Hesiod (whose text was interpolated to make it fit),
Kronos came to be thought of as the king of the blessed ones.[121] The Latins
called Kronos Saturnus, and attributed to him the naming of their own land;
for it was there that he hid (*latebat*) when banished by Jupiter. He was
welcomed by primeval Janus, and his reign was the golden age.[122] The *Saturnia
regna* were either here but impossibly long ago or now but impossibly far away,
ideas symbolised respectively by 'the castle of Saturnus' at the foot of the
Capitol, supposed origin of the treasury of the Roman People, and by 'the
tower of Kronos', a feature of Pindar's Isles of the Blessed.[123] Here *and* now
was only possible at the god's own festival, the Saturnalia.

The Roman cults of Saturnus and Flora had much in common. Both were
ancient,[124] both were extended with new features in the third century BC, and
in both cases the innovation involved popular *licentia*, freedom from the
normal constraints of society. In 241 or 238 the plebeian aediles built 'rustic
Flora' a new temple next to Liber's, with luxurious Corinthian columns, and
honoured her with permissive games which the Senate refused to make annual
until forced to do so by the goddess's anger.[125] In 217, with Hannibal already
in Italy and social cohesion an urgent necessity, the Senate not only allowed

---

118 Oceanus: Homer *Odyssey* 4.568, Hesiod *Works and Days* 170, Pindar *Olympians* 2.71.
      πείρατα γαίης: Homer *Odyssey* 4.563, Hesiod *Works and Days* 168. Zephyrus: Homer
      Odyssey 4.567, cf. Pindar *Olympians* 2.72 αὖραι περιπνέοισι. Flowers and fruit: Hesiod
      Works and Days 171, Pindar *Olympians* 2.72, 74.
119 Virgil *Aeneid* 6.638, 642, 656, 674 (grass); 639, 658, 673 (groves).
120 Ovid *Fasti* 5.200–12, 229–60 (for Flora and Zephyrus, cf. also Lucretius 5.738–40); Martial
      10.92.10. [See Bremer 1975.268–74 for the erotic implication of flowery meadows, from
      Archilochus to Petronius.]
121 West 1978.195, on Hesiod *Works and Days* 173a.
122 Virgil *Aeneid* 8.314–27, Festus 430L, Justin 43.1.3–5. Janus: Ovid *Fasti* 1.232–53, *Origo
      gentis Romanae* 3.1–7, Macrobius *Saturnalia* 1.7.19–24. See Versnel 1993.89–135 ('Kronos
      and the Kronia'), 136–227 ('Saturnus and the Saturnalia').
123 *Saturni castrum*: Festus 430L, Varro *De lingua Latina* 5.42, *Origo gentis Romanae* 3.6 (*aerarium*).
      Κρόνου τύρσις: Pindar *Olympians* 2.70.
124 Flora had her own *flamen* (Ennius *Annales* 2.117 Sk, *ILS* 5007); the Saturnalia were part of
      the archaic calendar (*Fasti Antiates*, 17 Dec.).
125 Velleius 1.14.8, Pliny *Nat. Hist.* 18.286 (date); Tacitus *Annals* 2.49.1 (site), Vitruvius 1.2.5
      (columns); Ovid *Fasti* 5.279–94 (aediles), 297–330 (Senate). *Rustica Flora*: Martial 5.22.4
      (her old temple at the foot of the Quirinal).

but instructed the populace to celebrate Saturnus' festival every year with drunken revelry and gambling, wearing symbolic caps of liberty (*pillei*).[126]

Ovid tactfully refrains from asking Flora herself about her games:[127]

> *quaerere conabar quare lasciuia maior*
> *his foret in ludis liberiorque iocus,*
> *sed mihi succurrit numen non esse seuerum*
> *aptaque deliciis munera ferre deam.*
> *tempora sutilibus cinguntur pota coronis*
> *et latet iniecta splendida mensa rosa. . .*
> *scaena leuis decet hanc: non est, mihi credite, non est*
> *illa coturnatas inter habenda deas.*
> *turba quidem cur hos celebret meretricia ludos*
> *non ex difficili causa petita subest:*
> *non est de tetricis, non est de magna professis,*
> *uolt sua plebeio sacra patere choro,*
> *et monet aetatis specie dum floreat uti;*
> *contemni spinam cum cecidere rosae.*

I was trying to inquire why these games have more sexiness and freer fun; but it occurred to me that the goddess's nature is not strict, and the gifts she brings are appropriate to pleasure. Drunken brows are wreathed with stitched garlands, and thrown roses cover the polished table. [*There follow ten lines on what Flora and Liber have in common, including a cross-reference to Ariadne's crown.*] A lightweight stage is proper for her; she isn't, believe me she isn't, to be counted among the goddesses in tragic boots. As for why a troupe of prostitutes performs these games, the reason isn't hard to find. She is not one of the frowners, not one of those who make big claims. She wants her festival open to a plebeian chorus, and she warns us to use the beauty of youth while it's in flower: the thorn is despised once the roses have fallen.

Note the *deae coturnatae* at line 348. Since goddesses wearing *coturni* are goddesses on the tragic stage, we may infer that Flora is on the stage too, but in the 'barefoot' genre of mime.[128] Ovid's emphatic 'believe me. . .', with his earlier admission that he couldn't keep his eyes off her,[129] has a particular impact if we imagine the theatre. The goddesses of tragedy are static, masked,

---

126 Livy 22.1.19–20; Seneca *Epistles* 18.3–4, Martial 11.6, 14.1; full details in Versnel 1993.146–50.

127 Ovid *Fasti* 5.331–6, 347–54. This part of the argument first appeared in *JACT Review* 24 (Autumn 1998) 6–8.

128 Mimes were *excalceati* (Seneca *Epistles* 8.8) or *planipedes* (Juvenal 8.191, Diomedes in *Grammatici Latini* 1.490 Keil, etc).

129 Ovid *Fasti* 5.275–6: *talia dicentem tacitus mirabar; at illa* | *'ius tibi discendi, si qua requiris' ait.*

and played by male actors; the goddesses of mime are showgirls who sing and dance.[130]

So I suggest that here too Ovid was alluding to a stage scenario familiar to his readers. It was a performance for the torchlit nights of the *ludi Florales*; the scene was the Elysian Field, and the girls played the nymphs whose availability was one of the rewards of the righteous; after the show, they would be available in real life.[131] Chloris was the leading lady's role (*partes tuae*, as Ovid says to Flora at 5.184), in what was probably an episodic plot like that suggested above for Circe.[132] Enter Priapus, whose attentions she avoids; enter Juno, whose pregnancy problem she solves (hoping Jupiter doesn't find out); enter Zephyrus, who successfully pursues her; and the play ends, as it should, with an *aition* for the cult of the goddess in whose honour the games are held.[133]

Ovid calls Flora's girls a *chorus plebeius*, and in telling the story of how the plebeian aediles set up her games he emphasises their significant name by pointedly repeating the words *populus*, *publicus* and *Publicius*.[134] Flora was a goddess of the People; it was the *populus* who in 55 BC were inhibited by Cato's presence from enjoying the 'ancient custom' of her games.[135] That the popular idea of Elysium was a garden of fleshly delights may be illustrated from Ovid's own text, in the passage on the Anna Perenna festival: those who have spent the day drinking and making love in her riverside meadow and grove are hailed on their return as 'the blessed ones'.[136] The purpose of such festivals was to make the mythical real, for a day.

But there was no escape from the social hierarchy. Even the gods were subject to it, as Ovid explains in his item on the birth of Maiestas; so too in the *Metamorphoses*, Jupiter's neighbourhood is carefully defined as 'the Palatium of the sky', away from the dwellings of the plebeian gods.[137] Nymphs, who dwell on earth, are among the humblest of the immortals, but by pleasing the greater

---

130 Tragedy: Plautus *Amphitruo* 41–3 (Virtus, Victoria, Bellona). Mime: Augustus *City of God* 7.26 = CSEL 40.340, Arnobius 4.35 (Venus, Cybele); and cf. nn. 60–2 and 74 above.

131 Ovid *Fasti* 5.361–8 (*deliciis nocturna licentia nostris* | *conuenit*, 367f), cf. Dio Cassius 58.19.1–2; for *mimae* as *meretrices* (*Fasti* 5.349), cf. Seneca *Epistles* 97.8, Lactantius *Institutiones* 1.20.10, Arnobius 7.33; for 'after the show', cf. Plautus *Casina* 1016–18, *Truculentus* 965–6, and Cicero *De finibus* 2.23 (*ludos et quae sequuntur*) with Wiseman 1985.44–5.

132 See p. 220 above.

133 Martial 10.92.10 (Priapus), Ovid *Fasti* 5.229–60 (Juno, 230 for Jupiter), 201–11 (Zephyrus).

134 *Fasti* 5.352, 283–94. At the time, the aediles probably spelled their name *Populicius* (cf. *ILLRP* 35 = *CIL* 1².28).

135 Seneca *Epistles* 97.8, Valerius Maximus 2.10.8 (*quem [Catonem] abeuntem ingenti plausu populus prosecutus priscum morem iocorum in scaenam reuocauit*), cf. Martial 1 pref.

136 Ovid *Fasti* 3.523–40; Wiseman 1998.64–74. [See also Tibullus 1.3.57–64, and Mace 1996.239–40 on the erotic afterlife.]

137 *Fasti* 5.19–32, *Metamorphoses* 1.173–4. For *illa turba quasi plebeiorum deorum*, see Augustine *City of God* 4.11, 6.1, 7.1, 7.2 (CSEL 40.178, 270, 302, 305), certainly from Varro.

gods in their amorous moods they may earn promotion to goddess status—as a slave-girl may become a *libertina*.[138] Flora was just like the *mima* who played her. And the grand and humbler gods were just like the audience in the theatre, from the senators in the orchestra to the ordinary citizens in the *cauea*, chewing their roasted nuts.[139] The illusion of the theatre merged the two worlds.

Ovid, I suggest, exploited that illusion in the *Fasti*. He could take advantage of what all his readers had vividly in their minds, the doings of gods and men made visible on the stage in the festivals of the Roman People.

VI

'Peleus and Thetis' and 'Flora (The Musical)' are offered as further items for the list on p. 217. Naturally, all these suggestions about Ovid's 'sources' (or 'influences', or 'intertexts') are hypothetical, and hypotheses are judged by how well or badly they explain the phenomena.

What needs explanation is not Ovid but the stage. The history of Roman drama cannot be understood just from the texts of Plautus, Terence and Seneca. The dramatic festivals were so central a part of the community life of Rome that allusions to what went on at them can be found throughout the vast range of our literary sources; but such allusions are rarely explicit, since the authors had no need to explain what their readers knew already. Our problem is to imagine what they took for granted.

One such passage is Erato's declaration at *Fasti* 4.326: 'I shall tell you marvels, but marvels attested also by the stage.' That at least is direct evidence for Ovid's use of theatrical material, and it encourages inference from other Ovidian episodes as possible testimony for the history of Roman show business.

---

138 On earth: Ovid *Metamorphoses* 1.192–5 (under the protection of Jupiter–Augustus). Promotion: e.g. Juturna (Virgil *Aeneid* 12.138–41), Pomona (Ovid *Metamorphoses* 14.635–42, 765–71), Carna (Ovid *Fasti* 6.101–28).
139 Lucretius 4.78–9, Horace *Ars poetica* 249.

CHAPTER FOURTEEN

The Prehistory of Roman Historiography

I

The Greeks come before the Romans, in this book as in all accounts of the ancient world. That priority is not a historical datum—on the contrary, the city-states of Athens and Rome came into being at much the same time—but in the discussion of ancient literature it is inevitable. Uniquely, and astonishingly, in the sixth century BC Greeks used the medium of alphabetic writing not just for lists or laws or epitaphs, but also to preserve the songs of epic bards and lyric poets; and so they created a literature. Neither Latins nor (so far as we know) Etruscans did that until three centuries later.

It is not that the Latins and Etruscans were backward, or peripheral. Horace's famous lines on the rude farmers of the Roman Republic, wholly innocent of Greek culture until 'the peace that followed the Punic Wars',[1] are demonstrable nonsense. Of course classicists want to believe what a classic author tells them; but a few archaeological glimpses of the archaic world of Latium and south Etruria may help us to overcome that mindset.

The earliest alphabetic Greek inscription known from anywhere was scratched on a pot about 800 BC in an Iron-Age community in Latium, just 20 km east of Rome;[2] Euboean potters can be detected working at Veii in the eighth century BC;[3] in the mid-seventh century, Kleiklos, 'famed for fame', is attested on a Corinthian vase in the Esquiline cemetery at Rome,[4] and Aristonothos, 'bastard noble', painted the blinding of Polyphemos on a mixing bowl made for an Etruscan magnate at Caere;[5] other Greeks known as living and working in Etruria at that time include Larth Telikles and Rutile Hipukrates;[6] in the sixth century, Ionians and Samians were frequenting the trading post of Gravisca,[7] at about the same time as a bronze plaque attests the

---

1   Horace *Epistles* 2.1.156–63.
2   Ridgway 1996.
3   Ridgway 1992.131–7.
4   *SEG* 31.875.
5   Schweitzer 1955.
6   Ridgway 1988.664–5.
7   *SEG* 27.671, 32.940–1017.

cult of the Dioskouroi at Lavinium,[8] while at Rome an Attic black-figure krater showing Hephaistos appears at the Volcanal,[9] and a terracotta statue group portrays the apotheosis of Herakles in the Forum Bovarium.[10]

These are just the most striking examples of an archaeological record which led its most authoritative interpreter to the following conclusion:[11] 'The effect of the refined Ionian civilisation on the cities of Tyrrhenian Italy is widespread and deeply felt in the second half of the sixth century BC. We could even say that there comes into being a genuine cultural and artistic *koine* consisting equally of the Greek colonies and the Campanian, Latin and Etruscan centres.'

So it should be no surprise that Hesiod—or a sixth-century pseudo-Hesiod—makes Latinos, eponym of the Latins and ruler of 'the famed Etruscans', a son of Kirke and Odysseus.[12] Kirke's island was just off the coast of Latium, directly across the water from the north coast of Sicily, where in the early sixth century lived the greatest poet of the Greek West, Stesichoros of Himera. Though he wrote in lyric metres, Stesichoros' grandeur and ambitious heroic narratives put him in almost the same category as Homer himself.[13] A late source, not necessarily untrustworthy, says that Stesichoros related Aeneas' voyage to the West, and recent discoveries have revealed much of his *Geryoneis*, the narrative of Herakles' tenth labour which ultimately lies behind the Roman story of Hercules' meeting with Evander.[14]

Pallantion, Evander's Arkadian home, was mentioned in the *Geryoneis*, and one of the versions of the poet's own life says that he was born in Pallantion but went into exile—just like Evander.[15] If that reflects the characteristic biographical method of borrowing episodes from an author's works as if they were evidence for his life,[16] perhaps we might even infer that the Roman story goes back to Stesichoros himself. Of course we do not know enough to *assert* that, but it is not inconceivable. Rome and early Greek poetry did not exist in separate worlds.

The same is true of early Greek prose. Those Ionian dedications at Gravisca were set up by people not unlike the pioneer *logopoios* Hekataios of Miletos, whose 'circuit of the earth' naturally included western Italy—not only the predictable islands (Elba, Capri etc) but also inland centres like Nola and Capua in Campania, the latter of which he derived from 'Capys the Trojan'.[17]

---

8   *ILLRP* 1271a.
9   Coarelli 1983.176–7.
10 Cristofani 1990.115–18.
11 Pallottino 1981.44 (my translation).
12 Hesiod *Theogony* 1011–16; West 1966.435–6.
13 Quintilian 10.1.62.
14 Horsfall 1979a; Page 1973.
15 *Suda* s.v. 'Stesichoros'.
16 Harvey 2004.298–300.
17 Hekataios *FGrH* 1 F 59–63.

Rome would not have been beyond his scope. The early fifth century may be when Promathion of Samos wrote his *Italika*, which contained the earliest version of the Romulus legend; and the unknown author of the 'Kymaian chronicle', which probably dealt with the descendants of Demaratos of Korinth who ruled in Rome, may also belong to that period.[18] Towards the end of the fifth century Hellanikos of Lesbos reported a view of Rome's origin—founded by Aeneas 'with Odysseus'—which looks like a combination of two separate traditions existing already. Hellanikos also seems to have known some Latin, since his account of Herakles' return with the cattle of Geryon includes a derivation of 'Italia' from *uitulus*.[19]

He may have regarded Latin as a Greek dialect.[20] Certainly in the fourth century BC Herakleides of Pontos called Rome 'a Hellenic *polis*', and Aristotle believed it had been founded by Achaians blown off course by storms in the return from Troy.[21] Theophrastos knew the Roman colony at Kirkaion, where the inhabitants pointed out the tomb of Elpenor, and his circumstantial report of a Roman attempt to found a city in Corsica shows that he was well informed.[22] At this point we have visual evidence again, with the engraved bronze mirrors and *cistae* which attest the thorough familiarity of Latin and Roman craftsmen with Greek artistic traditions; the inscribed names on some of the scenes depicted provide vivid evidence of their creative exploitation of the stories of Greek mythology.[23]

In the third century BC, Eratosthenes of Kyrene found it natural to include Romulus, son of Ascanius and grandson of Aeneas, in his chronological researches, and it is not at all paradoxical that his contemporary Kallimachos used the story of 'Gaius the Roman' to illustrate the virtues of *Panhellas*.[24]

II

It is clear, then, that as far back as our information extends—more than half a millennium before Horace imagined the dawn of Hellenic consciousness in his Roman peasants—Rome and her Latin and Etruscan neighbours were an inte-

---

18 Wiseman 1995.57–61 (Promathion); Alföldi 1965.56–72 (chronicle); Zevi 1995 (Demaratos). [Gallia 2007 attacks the Alföldi/Zevi hypothesis on *a priori* grounds; his argument depends on the very questionable assumptions that an early fifth-century Greek source interested in the Tarquins is an impossibility ('no such record could have existed', p. 64), and that the story of Tarquin's association with Aristodemus and death at his court was the invention of a Roman annalist.]

19 Hellanikos *FGrH* 4 F 84, 111.

20 Gabba 2000.159–65.

21 Herakleides of Pontos fr. 102 Wehrli; Aristotle fr. 609 Rose.

22 Theophrastos *History of Plants* 5.8.1–3.

23 Wiseman 2004a.87–118. [See above, pp. 86–124.]

24 Eratosthenes *FGrH* 241 F 45; Kallimachos *Aitia* 4.106.

gral part of the Greek world. What effect did that have on the Romans' perception of themselves?

Whether or not the expulsion of the Tarquins was inspired by that of the Peisistratids, the Romans must have been aware of the parallel. The early-republican cult of Liber may well have been influenced by the Athenian Dionysos Eleuthereus; much more certain is the influence of the 'Solonian' law-code on the Twelve Tables, visible even in the fragments that survive.[25] Moreover, there are structural elements in the 'history' of the early Republic, as we have it in Livy and Dionysios, which strongly suggest the influence of Athenian events: the attack of Porsenna to restore Tarquin parallels that of the Spartans to restore Hippias, the exile of Collatinus parallels the ostracism of Hipparchos, the exile of Coriolanus parallels the ostracism of Themistokles, and so on.[26] The cults of the Spartan Dioskouroi in the Forum and of Arkadian Pan at the Lupercal, and the 'chapels of the Argives' listed in a liturgical document quoted by Varro,[27] show that Athens was not the only influence, but by the end of the fourth century her imperial democracy may well have seemed a particularly appropriate paradigm for the Roman republic's domination of central Italy. It was at the time of the Samnite wars that the statue of Alkibiades, 'the bravest of the Greeks', was erected in the Comitium.[28]

That choice implies familiarity with recent historiography—Thucydides, Xenophon, Ephoros of Kyme. And there is reason to suppose that some Romans also read the 'Atthidographers', whose narratives of the long history of their city's political development conspicuously prefigured the later historiography of Rome. A particularly revealing parallel is the description in Kleidemos of Theseus' battle with the Amazons in what was in historical times the middle of Athens:[29] the topographical details are used as 'evidence' in just the same way as the Lacus Curtius and the Iuppiter Stator temple in the story of Romulus' battle with the Sabines in what was in historical times the middle of Rome.

Kleidemos was probably an *exegetes*,[30] using his cultic expertise to create the material for his history. In Rome the *annales* of the *pontifices*, considered by Cicero to be fundamental for the development of Roman historiography, may have begun in 300 BC with the creation of the reformed college of *pontifices*, now with plebeian parity of membership.[31] It is usually thought that the *annales* began much earlier than that; but the main evidence for that position has been

25 Crawford 1996.560–1.
26 Mastrocinque 1988.32–5.
27 Varro *De lingua Latina* 5.45–54.
28 Pliny *Nat. Hist.* 34.26.
29 Kleidemos *FGrH* 323 F 18.
30 Kleidemos *FGrH* 323 F 14.
31 Livy 10.9.2; cf. Cicero *De oratore* 2.51–3.

shown to be textually unreliable,[32] and in any case it may be thought unlikely that the unreformed patrician college had been interested in making its knowledge public.

A similar point may be made about another potential source of historical information, the list of annual magistrates. Such lists certainly existed after the power-sharing compromise of 367 BC, which required the election of one plebeian and one patrician consul each year; however, magistrate lists reaching right back to the expulsion of the Tarquins were available to the historians of the first century BC, and to whoever created the sequence of consuls and triumphs inscribed on Augustus' triumphal arch, and it is usually thought that they are broadly reliable.[33] But if the reform of 367 marked the final achievement of a *polis* constitution which required formal record-keeping, it may well be doubted whether the patrician magistrates of the previous 140 years felt the need for such an archive. We know that some later historians, faced with an absence of authentic record for the years before the Gallic sack of the city in 387, were driven to the conclusion that the Gauls had burned the city, and all the records had perished in the fire.[34] In fact, as the archaeological evidence shows, there was no fire. The suspicion must be that what passed for the 'early-republican' magistrate list in Livy's time was the result of antiquarian scholarship of the same kind as that of the Atthidographers who reconstructed the earliest Athenian archon-list.

It happens to be recorded that in 304 BC the aedile Cn. Flavius set up a shrine of Concordia to mark the reconciliation of the 'orders', and that in the inscription he dated it to 204 years after the dedication of the Capitoline temple.[35] That may imply that the only way of counting the years before 367 BC was by the nails that were annually driven into the wall of the temple of Iuppiter Optimus Maximus on the Capitol.[36] That great monument to the power and ambition of the archaic tyranny, conceived on the lines of the cult of Zeus at Olympia, still dominated the Romans' memory of their own past.[37] Kleidemos was writing in the mid-fourth century BC. Whether or not his work in particular was influential in Rome, it now seems clear that it was in the generation after that—the pivotal period at the turn of the fourth and third centuries—that the main outlines of 'Roman history' were formed.[38]

32 Humm 2000.106–9, on Cicero *De republica* 1.25; *contra* Cornell 1995.13–15.
33 Cornell 1995.218–21.
34 *FGrH* 840 F 3. [See above, pp. 13–14.]
35 Pliny *Nat. Hist.* 33.119–20.
36 Livy 7.3.5.
37. Purcell 2003.26–33.
38 Gabba 2000.16–19.

III

How that came about is a question fraught with methodological difficulty. What can we know about the communal memory of a pre-literary society, when our evidence comes from much later literary texts whose authors (remember Horace!) had little or no understanding of it? Any hypothesis can only be tentative—but even so, there are hints in our literary sources that may help us to imagine some aspects of the Rome of 300 BC.

The most famous such item, first exploited by the Dutch scholar Perizonius in 1685, is Cicero's reference to a passage in the elder Cato's *Origines* about a custom—obsolete in Cato's own time—of guests at banquets singing songs to the music of the pipe 'in praise of famous men'.[39] Modern scholarship is divided on the value of this evidence, which on the one hand is certainly consistent with what we know of the archaic *symposion*, but on the other might be just Cato's exploitation of Greek antiquarian scholarship about the archaic past.[40] My own view is that it may well have been a genuine memory from the pre-literary world, offering an insight into how the past was remembered in one stratum of Roman society. One might imagine that banquets where the friends and relatives of an Appius Claudius or a Quintus Fabius were gathered were not unlike those implied by the poetry of the early Greek elegists, with the values of an aristocratic elite being rehearsed and reinforced by the example of admired ancestors.[41]

Aristocrats also had more public ways of making sure the deeds of their ancestors were remembered. Cicero refers to the survival of early funeral orations, Livy to the inscriptions attached to ancestral portraits, and the earliest Scipionic epitaphs give us an idea of the sort of information that might be transmitted.[42] The fact that both Cicero and Livy thought it was unreliable need not concern us: what matters is the creation of communal memory through the pride of noble families.

Was that all there was? One influential modern view holds that the creation of the Roman historical tradition was solely the work of the elite, as if the Roman ruling class were identical with the Republic.[43] But since the Latin for 'Roman history' is *res* (*gestae*) *populi Romani*,[44] that can hardly be true. The deeds of noble leaders do indeed feature prominently in the later historical tradition, but they do not monopolise it. Where should we look for the communal memory of the People as a whole?

39 Cato fr. 118P; cf. Momigliano 1957.
40 Horsfall 1994.70–3; *contra* Zorzetti 1990.
41 Wiseman 1994.30–2.
42 Cicero *Brutus* 62; Livy 8.40.2; *ILLRP* 309–10 [pp. 6–7 above].
43 Timpe 1988.283–5.
44 Sallust *Cat.* 4.2, Livy pref. 1.

It may be helpful to apply to the citizens of Rome something that Pausanias wrote in the second century AD about the Athenians, who believed that their democracy was set up by Theseus. As Pausanias rather snobbishly comments, 'there are many false beliefs current among the mass of mankind, since they are ignorant of historical science and consider trustworthy whatever they have heard from childhood in choruses and tragedies.'[45] The 'choruses' he refers to were part of everyday experience, hymns in honour of the gods at the sacrifices and rituals that were familiar to every adult and child in the *polis*; and since Plato says much the same thing about 'stories repeated in prayers at sacrifices',[46] I think we are entitled to use Pausanias here as evidence for more than just his own time and place.

There are three passages in Dionysios of Halikarnassos' history of early Rome where the author alludes to hymns still sung in Rome in his own time. At 1.31.2 he refers to Faunus, king of the Aborigines, 'a man of prudence as well as energy, whom the Romans in their sacrifices and songs honour as one of the gods of their country'; at 1.79.11 he comments that the young Romulus and Remus were looked on as offspring of the gods, 'and as such they are still celebrated by the Romans in the hymns of their country'; and at 8.62.3 he says of Marcius Coriolanus 'though nearly five hundred years have already elapsed since his death down to the present time, his memory has not become extinct, but he is still sung and hymned by all as a pious and just man'. A possible context for the first of these may be the sacrifice to Faunus at the Tiber Island on 13 February; for the second, either the Lupercalia two days later, scene of the suckling of the twins, or the Parilia, anniversary of the foundation of the city, on 21 April; and for the third, the sacrifice to Fortuna Muliebris at the fourth milestone of the Via Latina on 6 July.[47] It is not necessary to suppose that the hymns Dionysios knew in the late first century BC were themselves archaic compositions; the mere fact that such hymns were sung at Roman sacrifices is enough to attest one more traditional source of communal memory.

Tragedies, according to Pausanias, were the other main source of the ordinary Athenian's historical knowledge. Here too there is a Roman analogy, in Plautus' casual remark that gods in tragedies regularly reminded the audience of the good things they have done for Rome. That suggests plays on Roman historical themes, no doubt the *fabulae praetextae* discussed by historians of Roman drama from Varro onwards.[48] Since the earliest *praetexta* our sources refer to is Naevius' *Clastidium*, on the single combat of the consul Marcellus

---

45 Pausanias 1.3.3.
46 Plato *Laws* 887d; cf. Buxton 1994.21–6.
47 Dionysios 8.55.3–5 gives the date and the reason.
48 Plautus *Amphitruo* 41–4; cf. Kragelund et al. 2002.

with a Gallic king in 222 BC, modern scholars have usually inferred that the genre was an invention of Naevius himself—and no doubt that is true as far as *literary* drama is concerned. The question is, was there drama before there was literature?

One revealing piece of evidence is Varro's citation of a play on a quasi-historical subject not by the author's name, or even the title, but by the context of its performance: 'the People were taught the reason for this by the *togata praetexta* presented at the Games of Apollo.'[49] What matters here is the assumption that performances at the theatre games 'teach the People'. The particular play Varro refers to can hardly predate 212 BC, when the *ludi Apol-linares* were inaugurated, but the principle may well date back to before our imagined 300 BC horizon, since the *ludi Romani* certainly, and the *ludi plebeii*, *Ceriales* and *Liberales* probably, were already in existence at that time (see above, pp. 168–74). Moreover, it is clear from the iconography of the bronze mirrors and *cistae* mentioned above that Latins and Romans in the fourth century BC were familiar with dramatic performance, in a Dionysiac context which might even involve the plots of Euripidean tragedies (see above, pp. 109–24).

So it may well be that when the citizens of Rome gathered at the 'games' in honour of their gods—Iuppiter Optimus Maximus at the *ludi Romani* and *plebeii*, Ceres, Liber and Libera at the others—they were taught what they needed to know about the gods, about their rights and duties, and about the history of their city, by exemplary narratives presented in dramatic form. As always, our inference can only be a provisional hypothesis. But it is at least consistent with the little we know about plays presented in the later Rome of our literary sources, which dealt with divine punishment of wrongdoers,[50] the power of the gods as revealed on earth,[51] the miraculous ways in which the Romans of the past overcame their enemies,[52] and the rewards of victory as manifested in the triumphal celebration.[53] It is, I think, reasonable to assume that much of Rome's communal memory consisted of what the citizen body saw regularly performed before its eyes.

The very fact that later historians might suspect material in their sources of having been invented for the stage is enough to confirm that dramatic performance was one of the ways in which historical knowledge could be created and perpetuated. There were of course other ways, which hardly need argument: the instruction of the young by parents and teachers, for example,

---

49 Varro *De lingua Latina* 6.18.
50 Cicero *In Pisonem* 46.
51 Ovid *Fasti* 4.326.
52 Livy 5.21.9.
53 Horace *Epistles* 2.1.187–93.

or the commercial activity of professional story-tellers.[54] But the contexts suggested above, preserving the remembered past of the leading families or of the citizen body as a whole, may be more important for our purposes, as possible conduits for the historical tradition of the Roman People.

IV

In his preface to the *Lays of Ancient Rome*, Macaulay notes with regret that the Romans—unlike Sir Walter Scott—never sought out and recorded examples of oral poetry in order to prevent them from being forgotten. But Macaulay was wrong: it seems that at least one such collection was indeed made, 'a book of very ancient *carmina*, which was said to have been put together before anything written in Latin'.[55] Only scraps from it survive, preserved in learned authors from Varro to Macrobius, but some of them may be of interest for our subject.

Here for instance is a quasi-Homeric moment quoted by Festus from the *uetera carmina*: 'But now Aurora, withdrawing from the sky, reveals her father.'[56] That must be from a narrative poem, as perhaps was this line, quoted by Varro in his *De uita populi Romani*: 'There the shepherds hold the Consualia games with hides.'[57] The reference is evidently to Consus' altar in the valley north of the Aventine; that was where the Sabine women were abducted at the Consualia on 21 August in the first year of Rome, so the 'shepherds' may well be Romulus' men. Two other *carmina* were certainly narrative, entitled 'Priam' and 'Neleus'.[58] Priam's sceptre was one of the divine talismans of Rome,[59] and Neleus was one of a pair of divinely begotten twins who were exposed, rescued, and brought up in secret before freeing their mother from servitude; the parallel with Romulus and Remus extends even to the cradle (*skaphê*) which featured in the recognition scene.[60]

The most important feature of these tantalisingly enigmatic fragments is their anonymity, which suggests that they did indeed originate in a world before authors. The transition to literature proper is marked by the *carmen belli Punici*, which is always attributed in our sources to its author Cn. Naevius. This was a poem of which the written text was preserved—but even so, it was not designed primarily for reading. Before C. Octavius Lampadio divided it into seven books, it existed as 'a continuous script',[61] which I think means that

---

54 Pliny *Epistles* 2.20.1, Dio Chrysostom 20.10.
55 Macrobius *Saturnalia* 5.20.18.
56 Festus 214L.
57 Nonius 31L.
58 Varro *De lingua Latina* 7.28 (an invocation to the *Casmenae*); Festus 418L, 482L.
59 Servius *auctus* on *Aeneid* 7.188.
60 Aristotle *Poetics* 1454B, Dionysius of Halicarnassus 1.82–3.
61 Suetonius *De gramm.* 2.2.

Naevius wrote it for recitation in the traditional way: the script was his personal property, not copied until after his death.

Naevius' *carmen* is an important milestone in the development of Roman historical consciousness. No doubt bigger, better and more comprehensive than any of its predecessors, it must have taken five or six hours to deliver. Its audience of Roman citizens—at the *ludi Romani*, perhaps—will have learned about Aeneas' flight from Troy, Jupiter's prophecy of Roman greatness, the origins of Carthage and its enmity with Rome, the foundation of Rome by Aeneas' grandson Romulus, and the course of the great Punic war in which the poet himself had fought. Ennius was right about Naevius' Saturnian metre, 'in which of old the Fauns and prophets sang'.[62] It was indeed a traditional form—but it was used at a high level of literary sophistication,[63] and Naevius' poem deserves to be thought of as the first true history of Rome.

There was another form of literary sophistication, however, which despised the historical epic and its mass audience.[64] Those who knew the Greek historians knew Thucydides' pointed contrast between the performances of poets and *logographoi*, competing for a particular audience's favour, and his own historical research, entrusted to a written text which would be a possession for ever.[65] The Hannibalic War was a time when men might well remember Thucydides, and his insistence that the war he narrated was the greatest and most terrible in history: no doubt that had been true two centuries earlier, but the Romans knew it was true no longer. Even so, the first *historiai* of Rome were not (or not only) Thucydidean war narratives.

Fabius Pictor and Cincius Alimentus—and Postumius Albinus too, in the next generation—were Roman senators who wrote their histories in Greek. Despite authoritative opinion to the contrary,[66] that must mean that at least they hoped for a Greek readership. Since 1974 we have known that Fabius Pictor's history began with 'the coming of Herakles into Italy';[67] Plutarch tells us that Fabius' detailed and theatrical narrative of the overthrow of Amulius by Romulus and Remus was taken from a Greek author, Diokles of Peparethos;[68] Postumius Albinus is likely to be responsible for casting the victory of his ancestor Aulus Postumius at Lake Regillus into the 'purely Homeric' narrative followed by Livy and Dionysios.[69] That looks like *prima facie* evidence that these authors were writing for an international Greek-speaking audience.

62 Ennius *Annales* fr. 207 Sk.
63 Goldberg 1995.73–82.
64 Kallimachos *Anth. Pal.* 12.43.1–4.
65 Thucydides 1.21.1, 22.4.
66 Gruen 1992.231.
67 *SEG* 26.1123.3a.
68 Plutarch *Romulus* 3.1, 8.7.
69 Wiseman 1998.86–7.

Part of their motive was no doubt to present Rome in a sympathetic light. Fabius will have presented Herakles as the ancestor not only of himself but of the great commander who defied Hannibal.[70] One of the few surviving items of Cincius' history reassuringly presents the Roman ruling class as a strong oligarchy trusted by the People: the Senate decrees the execution of Sp. Maelius without trial, and entrusts the deed to Servilius Ahala, who takes a sword and cuts Maelius down in the Forum; the citizens are indignant, but when he shouts that he has killed a tyrant by order of the Senate, they accept the sentence without demur.[71]

One can hardly imagine Naevius, that scourge of the nobility,[72] telling the story to the Roman People in quite those terms. And of course there were other differences too between the Saturnian bard and the Hellenizing historians. 'Naevius . . ., by choosing to write a poem rather than a history, did not submit the Roman past to the process of rational elucidation in the interest of truth which is characteristic of Greek historiography.'[73] But there is no need to privilege one style over the other. It was a combination of their methods (and their prejudices) that defined the past of a city which in their day had already seen a century and a half of military struggle and success, three centuries of creative tension between the respective interests of the many and the few, and more than half a millennium (*pace* Horace) of varied cultural evolution. It is not surprising that the resulting tradition of Roman historiography was so rich and complex.

Recommended reading

First, six chapters from three separate volumes of the second edition of *The Cambridge Ancient History*: David Ridgway, 'The Etruscans', vol. 4 (1988), 634–75; R.M. Ogilvie and A. Drummond, 'The sources for early Roman history', vol. 7.2 (1989), 1–29; M. Torelli, 'Archaic Rome between Latium and Etruria', ibid. 30–51; A. Momigliano, 'The origins of Rome', ibid. 52–112; A. Drummond, 'Rome in the fifth century', ibid. 113–71 and 172–242; Elizabeth Rawson, 'Roman tradition and the Greek world', vol. 8 (1989), 422–76.

Tim Cornell's chapters in *CAH²* 7.2 are subsumed into his magisterial synthesis *The Beginnings of Rome* (London, 1995), an essential work; much of interest will also be found also in Stephen Oakley's chapter 'The Annalistic Tradition', in his *Commentary on Livy Books VI–X*, vol. 1 (Oxford, 1997), 21–109, and in the essays in Erich Gruen's two collections, *Studies in Greek Culture and Roman Policy* (Leiden, 1990) and *Culture and Identity in Republican Rome* (Ithaca NY, 1992). Two valuable studies on Roman religion are relevant to the theme: the chapter 'Early Rome' in Mary Beard, John

---

70 Plutarch *Fabius* 1.1.
71 Cincius Alimentus *FGrH* 810 F 4.
72 Aulus Gellius 3.3.15.
73 Momigliano 1990.91.

North and Simon Price, *Religions of Rome* (Cambridge, 1998), vol. 1, 1–72, and Denis Feeney's short but stimulating *Literature and Religion at Rome* (Cambridge, 1998).

All those are predominantly background reading. For the central problem of how to understand non-literary culture, three recent items may be recommended, not least as examples of contrasting scholarly approaches: Nicholas Horsfall, *The Culture of the Roman Plebs* (London, 2003); Nicholas Purcell, 'Becoming Historical: the Roman Case', in David Braund and Christopher Gill (eds), *Myth, History and Culture in Republican Rome* (Exeter, 2003), 12–40; and chapters 2–7 of T.P. Wiseman, *The Myths of Rome* (Exeter, 2004).

CHAPTER FIFTEEN

History, Poetry, and Annales

I   Livy and Varro

Livy begins his preface with a conspicuous half-hexameter and an allusion to Ennius, and ends it with the wish that he could exploit the prefatory conventions of epic poetry.[1] In the central passage, however, he emphasises the differences between what he does and what the poets do:[2]

> *quae ante conditam condendamue urbem poeticis magis decora fabulis quam incorruptis rerum gestarum monumentis tradita, ea nec adfirmare nec refellere in animo est.*
>
> I intend neither to endorse nor to refute those traditions of events before the city was founded or planned which are more appropriate to the stories of poets than to the uncorrupted records of history.

More appropriate in what way? Livy is evidently expressing a generic distinction between poetry and history,[3] but on what criterion?

The temporal phrase *ante conditam condendamue urbem* implies that chronology is what marks off poetic from historical material, and that is perhaps what we should expect. Just a few years earlier, in 43 BC, Varro had published his major work on history and chronology, the four books *De gente populi Romani*,[4] in which he had carefully distinguished three periods of the past (*discrimina temporum*).[5] The first, the ἄδηλον or obscure, ran from the creation of mankind to the first flood (that of Ogyges, not Deucalion), and could not be calculated in years. The second, about 1600 years from the flood to the first Olympiad, he called μυθικόν, because many of the supposed events of that period were *fabulosa*—and it is clear from the fragments that he attrib-

---

1   Livy pref. 1, 13. On §1, cf. Quintilian 9.4.74 (*T. Liuius hexametri exordio coepit*) and Ennius *Annals*. fr. 494 Skutsch; Moles 1993.141–2. On §13, see Moles 1993.156–8.
2   Livy pref. 6: this passage and pref. 13 are the only places in the whole of Livy's extant text where the noun *poeta* or the adjective *poeticus* occurs.
3   Moles 1993.148: '*decora* is used of what is generically appropriate.'
4   Fragments in Peter 1906.10–24 and Fraccaro 1907.255–86; for the date, see Fraccaro 1907.77–8, and Horsfall 1972.124–5.
5   Fr. 3P (Censorinus 21.1–5); cf. Fraccaro 1907.255–7.

uted the *fabulae* to poets.[6] Only the third period, from the first Olympiad onwards, could be called ἱστορικόν, because the events that took place in it were recorded in 'true histories'.

Varro's choice of 776 BC as the dividing-line between the realms of poetic fiction and historical truth corresponds quite closely with Livy's dating, since it just allows the beginning of the foundation story (*condenda urbs*) to fall within the historical period. The dispute over the Alban kingship which resulted in Amulius' overthrow of Numitor and murder of his son, and the consecration of Numitor's daughter as a Vestal Virgin, took place three years before the conception of Romulus and Remus, and thus, on Varro's chronology, in 775 BC.[7]

However, it is not as simple as that. As Livy's next sentence makes clear, the particular poetic legend he has in mind is the conception story itself:[8]

> *datur haec uenia antiquitati ut miscendo humana diuinis primordia urbium augustiora faciat; et si cui populo licere oportet consecrare origines suas et ad deos referre auctores, ea belli gloria est populo Romano ut cum suum conditorisque parentem Martem potissimum ferat, tam et hoc gentes humanae patiantur aequo animo quam imperium patiuntur.*

> Antiquity is granted this licence, to make the origins of cities more august by mingling the human with the divine; and if any people ought to be allowed to sanctify its origins and claim gods as founders, such is the martial glory of the Roman people that when it declares Mars in particular as its parent and the father of its founder, the nations of the world may put up with that too, as readily as they put up with our imperial rule.

So now it seems that what marks off the poet's territory from the historian's is the participation of gods in human affairs, the 'mingling of human and divine'. And if the poets say that Mars really appeared on earth to father the twins on Rhea Silvia, they must mean that he did so in 772 BC, four years into Varro's historical period.[9]

Of course it is absurd to be so pedantic. Both Varro and Livy were serious authors dealing with a serious issue, and neither of them was content with a merely mechanical solution.

---

6 Fr. 6P (Augustine *City of God* 18.8), on the birth of Minerva from the head of Jupiter: *poetis et fabulis, non historiae rebusque gestis est adplicandum* (the antithesis accepted as Varronian by Fraccaro 1907.42). Fr. 13P = 23F (Augustine *City of God* 18.12), on Jupiter and Europa: *quod de Ioue poetae cantant*, as opposed to *historica ueritas*. Fr. 17P = 29F (Augustine *City of God* 18.16), on the metamorphosis of Diomedes' companions, which Varro thought was not fictitious: *non fabuloso poeticoque mendacio sed historica adtestatione confirmant.*
7 Conception on 24 June 772 (Varro in Plutarch *Romulus* 12.3–6), τετάρτῳ ἔτει after Ilia's consecration (Dionysius of Halicarnassus 1.77.1).
8 Livy pref. 7.
9 Above, n. 7: Plutarch citing the calculations of Varro's friend Tarutius.

The way Livy dealt with the problem has been well explored by David Levene.[10] There were plenty of allegedly supernatural events in Roman history, and Livy's consistent technique in dealing with them is to distance himself with an exculpatory formula (*dicitur, ut ferunt, traditur memoriae,* etc), sometimes offering an alternative explanation on the merely human level;[11] but he will often report, as a fact, that contemporaries accepted the event as supernatural, and by narrating the favourable outcome he allows his reader to infer that they were right to do so.[12] Sometimes he leaves out a famous divine-intervention story altogether, but leaves a hint to remind his readers of it, as when he refers to the *caelestia arma* of the Salii, or the dictator's vow to the Dioscuri at the battle of Lake Regillus, or the *insigne nomen* of Claudia Quinta at the reception of the Magna Mater in 204.[13]

One particularly revealing instance of his technique is the narrative of the disappearance of Romulus.[14] After the sudden storm that left the king's throne mysteriously empty, the Romans were prepared to believe the *patres* who had been standing close to him when they said he had been snatched up by a whirlwind. On the initiative of just a few people (presumably the *patres* themselves), the Romans now hailed Romulus as a god and the son of a god. But then Livy goes on (1.16.4):

> *fuisse credo tum quoque aliquos qui discerptum regem patrum manibus taciti arguerent; manauit enim haec quoque sed perobscura fama; illam alteram admiratio uiri et pauor praesens nobilitauit.*
>
> I believe that even then there were some who claimed in secret that the king had been torn to pieces at the hands of the *patres*; for this tale too has spread, very obscure though it is. Admiration of Romulus and the fear felt at the time has made the former version famous [or noble].

What made the Romans believe in Romulus the god was the prudent judgement (*consilium*) of one man, Julius Proculus, who reported to the people's

---

10 Levene 1993, esp. 16–30. See also Feldherr 1998.64–78 and Forsythe 1999.87–98.

11 E.g. 1.4.7 (Acca Larentia as *lupa*), 1.31.4 (either divine voice or response of *haruspices*), 5.22.5 (either divine inspiration or young man's joke). Note also the use of *certe* (e.g. 1.36.6, 2.7.2, 5.22.6) to mark the transition to what Livy is prepared to endorse.

12 E.g. the warning voice at 5.32.6–7: Livy commits himself only to the fact that M. Caedicius reported to the tribunes that he had heard it, but acceptance of its genuineness is part of the *religio* which enables Rome to survive the disaster (5.50.5, 5.52.11).

13 1.20.4, 2.20.12 (*nihil nec diuinae nec humanae opis dictator praetermittens*), 29.14.12; cf. respectively Ovid *Fasti* 3.259–392, Dionysius of Halicarnasus 6.13 and Ovid *Fasti* 4.291–344. Cicero uses the same technique at *De republica* 2.13 (*orantibus*), 2.37.4 (*scintilla ingenii*), 2.45.3 (*caede maculatus*): see Zetzel 1995.170, 192, 201. Otherwise unattested divine-intervention stories may be inferred from Livy 1.12.7 on Romulus and Jupiter Stator (*tamquam caelesti uoce iussi*) and 10.19.17 on Ap. Claudius and Bellona (*uelut instigante dea*).

14 Livy 1.16.2–8; Levene 1993.132–3.

assembly that Romulus had descended from heaven and told him to tell the Romans of his deification.

Livy reports as fact Proculus' report, and the belief it created,[15] but his use of the word *consilium* clearly implies that it was a piece of deliberate policy to keep the people happy—a 'noble lie' (γενναῖον ψεῦδος), as in Plato's *Republic*. His use of the ambiguous word *nobilitauit* may be an allusion to that famous passage; so too Plutarch describes as 'not ignoble' (οὐ φαῦλον) the tradition that Numa invented the story of his divine mistress and adviser Egeria, for the same reason.[16] Livy may not have been as much of a philosopher as Plutarch, but he was interested in the subject, and wrote philosophical dialogues.[17] So an allusion to Plato is not out of the question.

As for Varro, who certainly was a philosopher (among many other things), his complex argument in *De gente populi Romani* about myth, history and divine intervention can be reconstructed from book 18 of Augustine's *De ciuitate Dei*, which is largely based on it.[18] Varro ended book 2 of *De gente* with the Trojan War, which divided his 'mythical' period—from Ogyges' flood to the first Olympiad—into two unequal parts, of which the latter was closer to the 'historical' category.[19] But even in the earlier period, as Augustine remarks in a passage which is agreed to be Varronian,[20] there were true histories which were turned into myth by the poets.

Augustine has just given a long list of *fabulae fictae*, all of which involved physical impossibilities: Triptolemus and his winged serpents; the Minotaur; the Centaurs; three-headed Cerberus; Phrixus and Helle on the flying ram; the Gorgon's gaze; Bellerophon on Pegasus; Amphion and his miraculous lyre; Daedalus and Icarus; Oedipus and the Sphinx; Antaeus the son of Earth. Then he comments:[21]

> *hae fabulae bellum ad usque Troianum, ubi secundum librum Marcus Varro de populi Romani gente finiuit, ex occasione historiarum, quae res ueraciter gestas continent, ita sunt ingeniis hominum fictae ut non sunt opprobriis numinum adfixae.*
>
> Down to the time of the Trojan War, which is where Marcus Varro ended the second book of *De gente populi Romani*, these mythical stories were made up by the ingenuity of men, taking the opportunity offered by histories which contain things that truthfully happened, in such a way as not to link them with slanders on the divine powers.

---

15 Livy 1.16.5 (*consilium, fides*), 1.16.8 (*fides*, twice).
16 Livy 1.16.4; Plato *Republic* 3.414B–415D; Plutarch *Numa* 4.8 (also Lycurgus and his lawcode 'from Apollo').
17 Seneca *Epistles* 100.9.
18 See Fraccaro 1907.23–67 for an analysis of Augustine's sources in book 18.
19 Fr. 3P (n. 5 above), fr. 14P = 28F (Augustine *City of God* 18.13).
20 Fr. 14P = 28F (Augustine *City of God* 18.13).
21 Augustine *City of God* 18.13.

That last phrase alludes to a Varronian obsession, the 'tales unworthy of the gods' which made up the *theologia fabularis* of poets and playwrights,[22] and Augustine goes on to some examples of such stories, such as Jupiter's alleged abduction of Ganymede (not true, it was king Tantalus who did it, just as it was the Cretan king Xanthus who abducted Europa).[23]

But whether slanderous or not, these myths were made up by poets out of true historical records. That is how Varro and Augustine saw it; we of course see it the other way round, as the creation of 'history' by the rationalising of myth. So Erichthonius was not conceived by the earth from Vulcan's ejaculation as he tried to rape Minerva: that was an *opinio fabulosa* arising from the 'fact' that the infant was found in the temple of those two gods.[24] And the dispute between Minerva and Neptune over the city of Athens was settled not by a vulgar display of miracle-working, as the myth has it, but by a ballot of the Athenians themselves in which the women defeated the men by one vote; as Augustine observes, for Varro this was *non fabulosa sed historica ratio.*[25]

So the chronological criterion for poetic myth or factual history was by no means hard and fast. Nor, more surprisingly, was that of supernatural intervention in human life.

It may well be that Varro had a strictly natural 'historical' version of all those miraculous stories listed by Augustine. But he certainly did not rule out the supernatural *a priori*. In book 3 of *De gente* he reported as historical fact the metamorphosis of the companions of Diomedes into birds, citing as support the transformation of Ulysses' men by Circe, and the werewolves of the Arcadian Lycaeus cult.[26] Augustine insists on Varro's judgement—*historica adtestatio*, not *fabulosum poeticumque mendacium*—and it leads him into a long digression on the powers of *daemones.*[27]

That was a matter of some importance to Augustine, and he returns to it more than once in *De ciuitate Dei*. In book 10, discussing the 'miracles of the gods of the gentiles', which resulted from the power of demons, he cites as examples the migration of the Penates from Alba to Lavinium, Attus Navius'

---

22 Varro *Antiquitates diuinae* frr. 7 and 10 Cardauns (Augustine *City of God* 6.5); see Wiseman 1998.17–24. Varro *De gente populi Romani* fr. 8P = 18F (Augustine *City of God* 18.10): *Marcus Varro non uult fabulosis aduersus deos fidem adhibere figmentis, ne de maiestatis eorum dignitate indignum aliquid sentiat.*

23 Augustine *City of God* 18.12 (Europa), 18.13 (Ganymede)—both passages with explicit reference to the stage. Xanthus' abduction of Europa counted as *historica ueritas* (cf. n. 6 above).

24 Fr. 13P = 24F (Augustine *City of God* 18.12).

25 Fr. 7P = 17–18F (Augustine *City of God* 18.9–10).

26 Fr. 17P = 29F (Augustine *City of God* 18.16–17). Contrast Pliny *Nat. Hist.* 10.127 (on the *fabula* of Diomedes' companions), 8.81–2 (on the Arcadian story as *Graeca credulitas*).

27 Augustine *City of God* 18.18: he leaves open the possibility that Apuleius' *Golden Ass* was a factual narrative. On *daemones*, see Brenk 1986.

cutting of the whetstone, the voyage of Aesculapius' snake from Epidaurus to Rome, Claudia Quinta pulling the ship from the mudbank, and the Vestal who proved her innocence by carrying water in a sieve. When Tertullian had dealt with the same question, he too cited Claudia Quinta and the Vestal with the sieve, but also the epiphany of Castor and Pollux and the reddening of Domitius' beard.[28] Both writers knew Varro's works well and used them extensively, and I think it is likely that all these examples come from him.

One of them certainly did, as is proved by a neglected passage in *De ciuitate Dei* book 22:[29]

> *nam si ad eorum miracula ueniamus, quae facta a dis suis obponunt martyribus nostris, nonne etiam ipsa pro nobis facere et nobis reperientur omnino proficere? nam inter magna miracula deorum suorum profecto magnum illud est quod Varro commemorat, Vestalem uirginem, cum periclitaretur falsa suspicione de stupro, cribrum implesse aqua de Tiberi et ad suos iudices nulla eius parte stillante portasse. quis aquae pondus supra cribrum tenuit? quis tot cauernis patentibus nihil inde in terram cadere permisit? responsuri sunt: 'aliquis deus aut aliquis daemon.'*

And now if we turn to examine the miracles of paganism, the achievements of their gods which they oppose to those of our martyrs, we shall find that those achievements support our side, and supply us with invaluable assistance. In fact, among their greater miracles is the one recorded by Varro concerning a Vestal Virgin who had come under suspicion of unchastity and was in danger of her life. The story goes that she filled a sieve with water from the Tiber and carried it to her judges without spilling a drop. Now who was it that kept that weight of water in the sieve? Who was it who prevented the water from pouring out on to the ground from all those gaping holes? The reply will be, 'Some god, or some demon.'

The Vestal's name was Tuccia, and her trial before the *pontifices* took place about 230 BC.[30] The way Varro dealt with her story is not beyond detection.

At the beginning of the twenty-eighth book of the *Natural History*, for which Varro was one of his named sources, the elder Pliny discusses the power of words, in particular prayers and incantations. One of his prime examples is

---

28 Augustine *City of God* 10.16 (*illa ... miracula deorum gentilium, quae commendat historia*); Tertullian *Apologeticus* 22.12. For Domitius, see Suetonius *Nero* 1.1 and Plutarch *Aemilius Paullus* 25.3–4.

29 Augustine *City of God* 22.11, trans. H. Bettenson (Penguin Classics). The passage escaped the notice of Cichorius 1922.20–1, Münzer 1939 (see also n. 31 below), and Broughton 1951.227.

30 Livy *Epitome* 20, mentioned after the subjection of Sardinia and Corsica in 231. The MSS of Pliny *Nat. Hist.* 28.12 give *anno urbis DCVIIII* (145 BC), to be emended to *DXXIIII* (230 BC): Münzer 1897.177 n. 1 and 1937.206.

the *deprecatio* which enabled Tuccia to carry the water in the sieve.[31] When Valerius Maximus tells the Tuccia story, he quotes her rash prayer to Vesta as the cause of the miracle.[32] Dionysius of Halicarnassus, in a part of his *Roman Antiquities* for which he certainly used Varro, inserts into his account of the foundation of the Vesta cult a digression on the manifestations of the goddess: two Vestals, Aemilia and Tuccia, are cited as having prayed to Vesta and been empowered to perform miracles.[33] Aemilia's prayer is quoted verbatim; Tuccia's is only referred to, but is clearly an important part of the story.[34]

From this triangulation of the extant sources, the outline at least is visible of the Varronian treatment of Tuccia's story as evidence of the power of Vesta's *numen*. Perhaps it was one of a series of examples of divine manifestation in Roman history, as in Tertullian and Augustine.[35] It was certainly a question as important to Varro's theology as it was to theirs.

Livy had quite different priorities, either omitting miracle stories altogether or distancing himself from them by the use of *oratio obliqua*.[36] He wanted his readers to draw appropriate moral conclusions from his narrative whether or not they believed in supernatural manifestations. It was a controversial question—and though he may have relegated such stories to the 'appropriate to poetic legends' category, there is no reason to suppose that all Romans would agree with him.

II   Cicero

The *locus classicus* for the respective modes of poetry and history is the conversation that opens Cicero's *De legibus*. It takes place by the river Liris, in the grounds of the Cicero house at Arpinum. This ancient oak, says Atticus—it

---

31 Pliny *Nat. Hist.* 28.12, *qua usa aquam in cribro tulit*; cf. 28.10, *polleantne aliquid uerba et incantamenta carminum*. See Münzer 1897.177–8 for Varro as the source, and 1937.205: 'Es liegt ohne Zweifel hier überall eine mehr antiquarisch als annalistische Überlieferung zugrunde.' See n. 29 above: Münzer was evidently unaware of the Augustine passage which confirmed his conjecture.

32 Valerius Maximus 8.1.abs.5 [see now Mueller 2002.50–2]. For Valerius' use of Varro, see Bloomer 1992.113–26.

33 Dionysius of Halicarnassus 2.68–9 (ἐπιφάνεια at 68.1 and 69.3); Varro cited at 2.21.2, 2.47.4 and 2.48.4. For Aemilia (also Valerius Maximus 1.1.7, Prop. 4.11.53–4), see Münzer 1920.173–7 and 1937.199–203 [and Mueller 2002.47–8]: the legendary version of a real event in 178 BC (Livy *Epitome* 41, Obsequens 8).

34 Dionysius of Halicarnassus 2.68.4 (Aemilia), 2.69.2 (Tuccia, τὴν θεὸν ἐπικαλωσαμένην ἡγεμόνα τῆς ὁδοῦ γενέσθαι).

35 See n. 28 above. The subject may have been treated in the last book of Varro's *Antiquitates diuinae* (on the *di selecti*, including Vesta: frr. 229 and 281–3 Cardauns), or in *Curio de cultu deorum* (cf. Augustine *City of God* 7.34–5), or just possibly in *Gallus de admirandis* (cf. Macrobius *Saturnalia* 3.15.8).

36 See p. 245 above. He evidently reported Tuccia's condemnation (Livy *Epitome* 20); if he mentioned the miracle as an alternative tradition (as suggested by Münzer 1937.207), it will have been to reject it.

must be the very one where Marius saw the eagle in Marcus' epic poem. If you like, says Quintus; but Marius' oak was planted by a poet, and that's the sort of tree that never dies.[37] So Atticus consults the author himself: was it his own verses that planted the tree, or did Cicero have a factual source for what he wrote?[38]

Marcus replies by asking Atticus two questions of his own. Did Romulus really appear to Julius Proculus (on the Quirinal, close to Atticus' house in Rome), and did the north wind really carry off Oreithyia (at the Ilissus, close to Atticus' old house in Athens)?[39] 'Why do you ask?', says Atticus.[40]

> nihil sane, nisi ne nimis diligenter inquiras in ea quae isto modo memoriae sint prodita.
> 'No reason – except this, that you shouldn't inquire too carefully into events that are recorded in that manner.'

At first sight, it looks straightforward enough: if *isto modo* means 'like a poet', then *modus* should mean something like 'generic convention'. But this *modus* is a means of *memoriae prodere*, which is the historian's job.[41]

In any case, Atticus is still not satisfied:

> atqui multa quaeruntur in Mario fictane an uera sint, et a nonnullis, quod et in recenti memoria et in Arpinati homine uersere, ueritas a te postulatur.
> 'But people ask about many things in the *Marius*, whether they are true or invented; and since you're dealing with recent events and a man of Arpinum, some people are demanding the truth from you.'

Evidently not everyone thought it was enough just to say 'this is poetry, not history'. But Marcus insists that it is:

> et mehercule ego me cupio non mendacem putari; sed tamen nonnulli isti, Tite noster, faciunt imperite qui in isto periculo non ut a poeta sed ut a teste ueritatem exigant; nec dubito quin idem et cum Egeria conlocutum Numam et ab aquila Tarquinio apicem inpositum putent.
> 'Well, I certainly don't want to be thought a liar! But my dear Titus, those "some people" of yours are naive in demanding the truth in such a case, not as from a poet, but as from a witness. I've no doubt they think Numa really talked with Egeria, and the eagle really put the cap on Tarquin's head!'

---

37 Cicero *De legibus* 1.1–2 (1.14 for the Liris bank). Cicero's *Marius*: Courtney 1993.174–8.
38 Cicero *De legibus* 1.3: *tuine uersus hanc quercum seuerint, an ita factum de Mario, ut scribis, acceperis.*
39 Ibid.: *certen ... uerumne sit ... sic enim est traditum.* (Plato *Phaedrus* 229B for the Ilissus, surely a deliberate allusion by Cicero.)
40 Cicero *De legibus* 1.4 (the following three quotations).
41 *TLL* 8.677.70–8: e.g. Cicero *De diuinatione* 1.55 (*omnes historici*), Nepos *Themistocles* 10.5 (Thucydides). The phrase occurs sixteen times in Livy (*memoriae tradere* seven times, *memoriae mandare* twice).

So, says Quintus, you think that different laws are to be observed in a history and in a poem? Of course, replies Marcus, for in a history what matters is truth, in a poem it's mostly enjoyment.[42]

That 'mostly' (*pleraque*) is important, as is the concession Marcus immediately makes, that there are countless *fabulae* in Herodotus and Theopompus.[43] He knows that his schematic distinction between poetry and history is not universally valid, and that people like Atticus, naive or not, are entitled to ask whether a poem on a historical subject is to be believed. So if, as Denis Feeney puts it, the question at issue in this conversation is 'what you can narrate in a particular genre', 'the appropriate treatment of the data of received tradition',[44] it is clear that more than one type of answer could legitimately be given.

That is spectacularly demonstrated in another dialogue of which Cicero and his brother were the interlocutors (this time without Atticus), namely *De diuinatione*. Do the gods really communicate their will to men?[45] In book 1 Quintus argues that they do: although its workings are mysterious, genuine divination can and does exist, as is proved by the overwhelming testimony of past authorities.[46] In book 2 Marcus speaks for the sceptics: since divination is inherently improbable and cannot be explained, the supposed evidence for it must be either invented or explicable by other means.[47]

Although the negative argument comes second, Cicero as author is careful to keep both possibilities open. The Academic philosopher's purpose is 'to compare arguments, to set out what can be said for any proposition, and without asserting his own authority to leave the audience's judgement free and unimpaired'.[48] Who knows how many of the audience agreed with Quintus?

The distinction between history and *fabula* is central to the whole discussion. Quintus insists on the authority of written records, which may be either poetry or prose.[49] One of his prime exhibits is the whetstone cut in half by Attus Navius:[50]

---

42 Cicero *De legibus* 1.5: *Quippe, cum in illa [historia] omnia ad ueritatem, Quinte, referatur, in hoc [poemate] ad delectationem pleraque.*

43 Ibid.; cf. Strabo 1.2.35 (C43). For myths in history see Marincola 1997.117–27.

44 Feeney 1991.259, 260; the whole chapter on 'epic of history' (250–312) is fundamental.

45 Cicero *De diuinatione* 1.1: *magnifica quaedam res et salutaris, si modo est ulla, quaque proxime ad deorum uim natura mortalis possit accedere.*

46 E.g. 1.12: *nihil est autem quod non longinquitas temporum excipiente memoria prodendisque monumentis efficere atque assequi possit.*

47 E.g. 2.27: *hoc ego philosophi non esse arbitror, testibus uti qui aut casu ueri aut malitia falsi fictiue esse possunt.*

48 2.150: . . . *conferre causas et quid in quamque sententiam dici possit expromere, nulla adhibita sua auctoritate iudicium audientium relinquere integrum ac liberum.* See Beard 1986, Schofield 1986.

49 *Scriptores*: 1.31. *Scribere*, with named author: poetry 1.22, 87; prose 1.33, 36, 46, 48, 50, 53, 56, 121, 130. *Scriptum est* etc., anonymous: 1.31, 39, 52, 89, 101, 121. *Historia*: 1.37, 38, 49, 50, 55, 121. *Annales*: 1.43, 51, 100. *Monumenta*: 1.12, 33, 72, 87.

50 1.33; cf. Livy 1.36.4–5, who narrates it with *ut ferunt. . . ferunt. . . memorant. . . .*

negemus omnia, comburamus annales, ficta haec dicamus, quiduis denique potius quam deos res humanas curare fateamur.

'Let's deny it all, let's burn the annals, let's say it's an invention—anything at all rather than admit that the gods care about human affairs!'

Which is precisely the answer Marcus gives in book 2: philosophy shouldn't accept invented stories.[51] Again, such stories may be in poetry or prose. After all, says Marcus, why should I believe Herodotus any more than Ennius?[52] Literary genre seems not to be the main issue here.

However, there is a passage in book 1 which does address the status of poetic stories. Quintus has been citing examples from Greek historians, including Philistus' report of what the mother of Dionysius of Syracuse dreamed when she was pregnant.[53] That reminds him of the dreams of Ilia and Priam in Ennius, which he admits are invented *fabulae*; but he quotes them all the same, because they are no different from historical examples like the dream of Aeneas in Fabius Pictor.[54]

All three of those dreams (since Ennius' Ilia was the daughter of Aeneas) were far back in what Varro called the mythical period. But now Quintus takes a historical example:[55]

sed propiora uideamus. cuiusnam modi est Superbi Tarquinii somnium, de quo in Bruto Acci loquitur ipse?

'But let's look at something more recent. Of what sort is Tarquinius Superbus' dream, which he talks about himself in Accius' *Brutus*?'

What exactly is Quintus asking here? *Cuiusnam modi est?* can hardly mean 'What genre is it?', because the genre is obvious: it's a play, a *fabula praetexta*. At this point his concern is not primarily with poetry or prose,[56] but with fact or fiction in any genre. Accius' play was on a historical subject, so the question 'Did Tarquin really have that dream?' is a perfectly reasonable one, even though Marcus in book 2 doesn't bother to answer it.[57]

---

51 2.80: *contemne cotem Atti Nauii; nihil debet esse in philosophia commenticiis fabellis loci.*

52 2.115: *Herodotum cur ueraciorem ducam Ennio? num minus ille potuit de Croeso quam de Pyrrho fingere Ennius? Fingere* also at 2.27, 58, 136; *fabula* and/or *commenticius* at 2.27, 80, 113.

53 1.37: *age, barbari uani atque fallaces; num etiam Graiorum historia mentita est?* Chrysippus on the Delphic oracle (1.37–8), Chrysippus and Philistus on dreams (1.39); the theme resumes after the digression with Heraclides Ponticus, Dinon, and one of the Alexander-historians (1.46–7).

54 1.40–3 (*fabulae* at 40 and 43, *ficta* and *commenticium* at 42): Ennius *Annales* 1.34–50 Skutsch and *Scaenica* 50–61 Jocelyn; Fabius Pictor *FGrH* 809 F1.

55 1.43: Accius *Brutus* 651–72 Dangel (= 17–38R).

56 He ends the digression at 1.46 with *age nunc ad externa redeamus*: Greek v. Latin is as important as prose v. poetry.

57 Cf. *De diuinatione* 2.136 on *multa ... a te ex historiis prolata somnia*, not citing the examples from Ennius or Accius and dismissing those from the Greek historians (*quis enim auctor istorum?*).

What Marcus' answer would have been, we can guess from the contemptuous reference in *De legibus* to 'events recorded *isto modo*'. For him, as no doubt for Cicero the author, the only *modus* that counted as valid history was one where the author guaranteed his report with evidence and argument; mere narrative had no authority in itself.[58] But not everyone took that view. Cicero is careful to let us see both sides of the argument, and to give them spokesmen of equal status. Quintus speaks not only for the naive majority, the *imperiti*, but also for thinking people, readers of philosophical dialogues, who chose not to be bound by the scepticism of the Academy.

III   Dionysius and Plutarch

Twenty years or so after Livy made his prefatory comment about stories more suitable to poetry, Dionysius of Halicarnassus faced the problem of narrating the conception of Romulus.

He reported as fact the rape of Ilia in the grove sacred to Mars. Someone did it[59]—but who? Some say it was one of the girl's suitors (a version hardly consistent with Ilia being a Vestal); others that it was Amulius himself, dressed in armour to terrify her (a version evidently designed to rationalise the story that Mars was responsible).[60] But those are the exceptions:

οἱ δὲ πλεῖστοι μυθολογοῦσι τοῦ δαίμονος εἴδωλον, οὗ τὸ χωρίον ἦν, πολλὰ καὶ ἄλλα τῷ πάθει δαιμόνια ἔργα προσάπτοντες ἡλίου τε ἀφανισμὸν αἰφνίδιον καὶ ζόφον ἐν οὐρανῷ κατασχόντα.

Most authors relate the legend that it was an apparition of the divine power to whom the place was sacred, adding to the incident many supernatural occurrences, including a sudden disappearance of the sun and darkness spread over the sky.

The apparition was bigger and more beautiful than a man; they say that it comforted the girl afterwards ('by which it became clear that it was a god'), and then disappeared up to the sky wrapped in a cloud.[61]

Dionysius is aware that more is involved here than just a disagreement among authorities. He suggests two possible approaches. One is to reject such stories outright because they attribute to the gods the frailties of humanity; on

---

58 Cicero *De legibus* 1.4. For the rival modes of *historia* and *aphegesis* (inquiry and story-telling), see Wiseman 1993a.135–8.

59 Dionysius of Halicarnassus 1.77.1, with βιάζεταί τις ἐν τῷ τεμένει delayed for emphasis to the end of the sentence.

60 Ibid.: τινες μὲν ἀποφαίνουσι ... οἱ δὲ ... (cf. Plutarch *Romulus* 4.2 for the second version).

61 Dionysius of Halicarnassus 1.77.2; *Origo gentis Romanae* 20.1 (from Fabius Pictor book 1).

this view (which is that of Varro), sexual desire is 'unworthy of the incorrupt-
ible and blessed nature' of the gods. The other approach is to suppose that the
substance of the universe is mixed, and that between human and divine a third
category exists, a race of *daimones* who couple sometimes with mortals, sometimes with gods. It is not for a historian to decide:[62]

ὅπως μὲν οὖν χρὴ περὶ τῶν τοιῶνδε δόξης ἔχειν, . . . οὔτε καιρὸς ἐν τῷ
παρόντι διασκοπεῖν ἀρκεῖ τε ὅσα φιλοσόφοις περὶ αὐτῶν ἐλέχθη.

What view should we take of such matters? This is not the appropriate place to
consider it; what the philosophers have said on the subject is sufficient.

The only safe thing to say is 'The Romans believe that the twins were the sons
of Mars'.[63]

The next miracle story in the narrative is the suckling of the twins by the
she-wolf. Dionysius reports it from Fabius Pictor as an apparently supernatural
event,[64] but then offers the rationalised version in which the *lupa* was really
Acca Larentia.[65] He attributes the latter to 'those who think that mythical
material does not belong in historical writing', but he himself does not privilege that version. Like Livy, no doubt he wanted to satisfy readers of both
persuasions.[66]

So too on the disappearance of Romulus, Dionysius juxtaposes the 'more
legendary' story, that he was swept up to heaven by his father Mars, and the
'more credible' version, that he was killed by the senators.[67] But this time he
adds a comment of his own:

ἔοικε δ' οὐ μικρὰν ἀφορμὴν παρέχειν τοῖς θεοποιοῦσι τὰ θνητὰ καὶ εἰς
οὐρανὸν ἀναβιβάζουσι τὰς ψυχὰς τῶν ἐπιφανῶν τὰ συμβάντα ἐκ τοῦ
θεοῦ περὶ τὴν σύγκρισιν τοῦ ἀνδρὸς καὶ τὴν διάκρισιν.

But the things that happened by divine agency concerning both the formation
and the dissolution of that man seem to provide no little material for those who
make mortality divine and take the souls of famous men up to heaven.

---

62 1.77.3 (cf. n. 22 above for Varro); *pace* Gabba 1991.124–5, Dionysius does not endorse the
first (or either) of these alternatives. [For the *daimones*, see Plato *Symposium* 203A.]
63 2.2.3 (Dionysius' summary of book 1).
64 1.79.7, δαιμόνιόν τι χρῆμα. 1.83.3 for Fabius *FGrH* 809 F4(b).
65 1.84.4; cf. Livy 1.4.7 (*inde locum fabulae ac miraculo datum*), Plutarch *Romulus* 4.3 (ἐπὶ τὸ
μυθῶδες ἐκτροπὴν τῇ φήμῃ παρασχεῖν), *Origo gentis Romanae* 21.1 (from Valerius
Antias).
66 1.84.1. Cf. 1.8.3 for the various categories of his readership, including those who like their
enjoyment undistracted (ἀόχλητος).
67 2.56.2–4; for the μυθωδέστερα/πιθανώτερα contrast, cf. 1.39.1 and 41.1 on Hercules (τὰ
μὲν μυθικώτερα τὰ δ' ἀληθέστερα).

He refers to the two mysterious eclipses of the sun that took place at the conception and the death of Romulus, even though the former had been part of his 'mythical' narrative of that event.[68]

The impression that Dionysius' sympathy did not lie with the sceptics is strengthened by his treatment of Numa. He knows, of course, the standard explanation of the Egeria story, that it was Numa's 'noble lie' to impress the people; but he attributes it to 'those who remove all legends from history', and conspicuously fails to endorse it himself, saying that such matters relating to the gods would require too long a discussion.[69]

When he comes to Numa's establishment of the Vesta cult, his digression on the historical evidence for the goddess's miracle-working powers is introduced with a very explicit declaration:[70]

ὅσοι μὲν οὖν τὰς ἀθέους ἀσκοῦσι φιλοσοφίας, εἰ δὴ καὶ φιλοσοφίας αὐτὰς δεῖ καλεῖν, ἁπάσας διασύροντες τὰς ἐπιφανείας τῶν θεῶν τὰς παρ' Ἕλλησιν ἢ βαρβάροις γενομένας καὶ ταύτας εἰς γέλωτα πολὺν ἄξουσι τὰς ἱστορίας ἀλαζονείαις ἀνθρωπίναις αὐτὰς ἀνατιθέντες, ὡς οὐδενὶ θεῶν μέλον ἀνθρώπων οὐδενός. ὅσοι δ' οὐκ ἀπολύουσι τῆς ἀνθρωπίνης ἐπιμελείας τοὺς θεούς, ἀλλὰ καὶ τοῖς ἀγαθοῖς εὐμενεῖς εἶναι νομίζουσι καὶ τοῖς κακοῖς δυσμενεῖς διὰ πολλῆς ἐληλυθότες ἱστορίας, οὐδὲ ταύτας ὑπολήψονται τὰς ἐπιφανείας εἶναι ἀπίστους.

Those who practise the atheist philosophies (if they deserve to be called philosophies at all), who ridicule all the manifestations of the gods which have taken place among either Greeks or foreigners, will reduce these reports as well to mocking laughter and attribute them to human trickery, on the grounds that none of the gods is concerned with anything human. But those who do not absolve the gods from the care of humanity, but after going deeply into history conclude that they are favourable to the good and hostile to the wicked, will not suppose that even these manifestations are incredible.

'Going deeply into history' is just what Dionysius claimed to be doing, and this sort of subject matter was well worth recording.[71] Indeed, it was an essential part of the usefulness of history for statesmen and politicians, as Dionysius points out when narrating the part played by *daimones* in revealing a conspiracy in the ninth year of the Republic.[72]

---

68 2.56.6, cf. 1.77.2.

69 2.60.5–61.3 (quotation from 61.1); see above, n. 16.

70 2.68.1–2 (see above, nn. 33–4), citing the reports of οἱ συγγραφεῖς. [Cf. Livy 10.40.10 on *doctrina deos spernens*.]

71 1.5.4, 3.18.1, 7.66.1–3, 11.1.4–5 (*akribeia*); 2.68.1 (πάνυ δ' ἄξιον ... ἱστορῆσαι).

72 5.56.1, cf. 5.54.1–3; not in Livy. (Probably from Tubero: see Wiseman 1994.54–7.) Dionysius writing for *politikoi*: 1.8.3, 5.75.1, 11.1.1.

That could hardly be further away from our Polybian preconceptions about what is appropriate to history.[73] But perhaps it would not have surprised Varro, or the Q. Cicero of *De diuinatione*. I think Emilio Gabba was mistaken in saying that Dionysius 'sought, as far as it lay within his power, to leave aside any myth involving divine intervention in human affairs'.[74] On the contrary, he not only related such myths but even drew his readers' attention to the philosophical issues involved in them.

The clearest statement of Dionysius' position comes in book 8. Coriolanus has yielded to his mother and withdrawn his army; the Senate has honoured the women of Rome by the dedication of a temple to Fortuna Muliebris. There follows an episode which Livy omits, but which Dionysius expressly describes as 'appropriate to the form of history'.[75] The *matronae* had had a statue of the goddess made at their own expense; on the day of the dedication, this statue spoke, not once but twice (so there could be no mistake), confirming the propriety of the women's act.[76] The event was recorded in the chronicle of the *pontifices*, and Dionysius reports it for two very specific reasons:[77]

> ... ἐπανορθώσεως ἕνεκα τῶν οἰομένων μήτ' ἐπὶ ταῖς τιμαῖς ταῖς παρ' ἀνθρώπων χαίρειν τοὺς θεοὺς μήτ' ἐπὶ ταῖς ἀνοσίοις καὶ ἀδίκοις πράξεσιν ἀγανακτεῖν ... ἵνα τοῖς μὲν εὐλαβεστέροις περὶ τὸ συνέχειν ἃς παρὰ τῶν προγόνων δόξας ὑπὲρ τοῦ δαιμονίου παρέλαβον ἀμεταμέλητος ἡ τοιαύτη προαίρεσις καὶ βεβαία διαμένῃ, τοῖς δ' ὑπερορῶσι τῶν πατρίων ἐθισμῶν καὶ μηθενὸς ποιοῦσι τὸ δαιμόνιον τῶν ἀνθρωπίνων λογισμῶν κύριον μάλιστα μὲν ἀναθέσθαι ταύτην τὴν δόξαν, εἰ δ' ἀνιάτως ἔχουσιν, ἔτι μᾶλλον αὐτοῖς ἀπεχθάνεσθαι καὶ κακοδαιμονεστέροις εἶναι.

> To correct those who think that the gods are neither pleased by honours received from mortals nor offended at unholy and unjust acts... [and] that those who are more scrupulous in preserving the beliefs about the divine power which they have inherited from their forefathers may keep their conviction firm and unwavering, while those who despise ancestral custom and claim that the divine power has no control over human reason may either abandon that view or, if they are incorrigible, become even more hateful and god-forsaken.

---

73 Cf. Polybius 3.47.6–9 on the participation of gods and heroes in real events as πάσης ἱστορίας ἀλλοτριώτατον.

74 Gabba 1991.118; but cf. Dionysius of Halicarnassus 1.40.5 (epiphany of Hercules in 312 BC, story promised), 2.68.3 (much more to say on Vesta's epiphanies), 6.13 (Castor and Pollux at Lake Regillus), etc. What Dionysius rejected at 2.18.3–19.1 was not myth as such (Gabba 1991.119–20) but 'tales unworthy of the gods' (n. 22 above).

75 8.56.1 (ἱστορεῖται at 56.2, ἱστορίαν at 56.4). For the ἱστορίας σχῆμα, cf. 1.41.1, with Fox 1993.44–5.

76 8.56.2–4; cf. Valerius Maximus 1.8.4 and Plutarch *Coriolanus* 37.3.

77 8.56.1 (ὡς αἱ τῶν ἱεροφαντῶν περιέχουσι γραφαί) = *Annales pontificum* fr. 20 Chassignet; cf. Frier 1979.118.

Yet again we find that the question asked was not so much 'What is appropriate to the genre?' as 'What ought we to believe?'.

That order of priorities is even more evident in Plutarch, whose biographical format allowed him more space than Dionysius had for philosophical reflection. On the disappearance of Romulus: can we really believe that the body of a great man, and not just his soul, might be borne up to heaven? On Numa and Egeria: although the gods must love virtuous mortals, and may instruct wise rulers, surely they cannot take sexual pleasure in a mortal body? On the appearance of Castor and Pollux in the Forum at the time of the battle of Lake Regillus: why should it not be credible, when even in modern times the divine power can bring instant news of battles far away?[78] These are important questions, and Plutarch is not dogmatic about them. 'If anyone says otherwise, "Broad is the way", as Bacchylides has it.'[79]

As for the speaking statue, of course it was impossible (statues have no vocal cords), and if the historical evidence forces us to believe it, then we must assume that some dream-like power of the imagination caused people to believe they heard it speak.[80] But as Plutarch knows, there is also quite another way of looking at it:

οὐ μὴν ἀλλὰ τοῖς ὑπ᾽ εὐνοίας καὶ φιλίας πρὸς τὸν θεὸν ἄγαν ἐμπαθῶς ἔχουσι, καὶ μηδὲν ἀθετεῖν μηδ᾽ ἀναίνεσθαι τῶν τοιούτων δυναμένοις, μέγα πρὸς πίστιν ἐστὶ τὸ θαυμάσιον καὶ μὴ καθ᾽ ἡμᾶς τῆς τοῦ θεοῦ δυνάμεως.

Nevertheless, for those who are passionate in their devotion and love for the divine, and incapable of rejecting or denying anything of this kind, the main argument for belief is the wonderful and transcendant nature of the divine power.

On this view, miracles are impossible only in human terms: divine power is beyond our understanding. Plutarch himself urges a cautious middle way, between empty superstition and arrogant contempt for the gods.[81]

It seems therefore that what we are disposed to think of as a matter of literary decorum was in reality a profound philosophical and theological question. Those who argued that myths had no place in history were not just defining a genre; they were putting into practice a controversial belief about

78 Plutarch *Romulus* 28, *Numa* 4, *Aemilius Paullus* 25; [Nock 1972.535–6,] Wardman 1974.163–6.
79 Plutarch *Numa* 4.8. Other gnomic quotations in the same context: *Romulus* 28.6 (Pindar), *Coriolanus* 38.4 (Heraclitus), *Camillus* 6.4 (Delphi motto).
80 Plutarch *Coriolanus* 38.3, ὅπου δ᾽ ἡμᾶς ἡ ἱστορία πολλοῖς ἀποβιάζεται καὶ πιθανοῖς μάρτυσιν. . . For Romans who believed in animate statues, cf. Lucilius 484–9M = 524–9W (on *terriculas Lamias, Fauni quas Pompiliique instituere Numae*).
81 Plutarch *Coriolanus* 38.3–4; *Camillus* 6.4 for another talking statue (Juno's, at Veii).

the nature of the gods. Dionysius and Plutarch were both familiar with that
school of thought,[82] but neither endorsed it himself, and there is no reason to
suppose that they were unusual in that.[83]

IV   Valerius Maximus and Livy

My final witness is an author whose evidential value has been long neglected
because of a misconception about the purpose of his work. It is a widely held
view—but one based on no evidence that I know of—that Valerius Maximus'
collection of historical *exempla* was written as a handbook 'for students and
practitioners of declamation'.[84] The author's own statement of his aim is set
out clearly enough in the preface, which deserves quoting in full:[85]

> (1) *urbis Romae exterarumque gentium facta simul ac dicta memoratu digna, quae apud
> alios latius diffusa sunt quam ut breuiter cognosci possint, ab inlustribus electa auctoribus
> digerere constitui, ut documenta sumere uolentibus longae inquisitionis labor absit. (2) nec
> mihi cuncta complectendi cupido incessit: quis enim omnis aeui gesta modico uoluminum
> numero comprehenderit, aut quis compos mentis domesticae peregrinaeque historiae seriem
> felici superiorum stilo conditam uel attentiore cura uel praestantiore facundia traditurum se
> sperauerit? (3) te igitur huic coepto, penes quem hominum deorumque consensus maris ac
> terrae regimen esse uoluit, certissima salus patriae, Caesar, inuoco, cuius caelesti
> prouidentia uirtutes, de quibus dicturus sum, benignissime fouentur, uitia seuerissime
> uindicantur: (4) nam si prisci oratores ab Ioue Optimo Maximo bene orsi sunt, si excel-
> lentissimi uates a numine aliquo principia traxerunt, mea paruitas eo iustius ad fauorem
> tuum decucurrerit, quo cetera diuinitas opinione colligitur, tua praesenti fide paterno
> auitoque sideri par uidetur, quorum eximio fulgore multum caerimoniis nostris inclutae
> claritatis accessit: reliquos enim deos accepimus, Caesares dedimus. (5) et quoniam
> initium a cultu deorum petere in animo est, de condicione eius summatim disseram.*

---

82   No myths in history: Dionysius of Halicarnassus 1.84.1, 2.61.1. No divine involvement in
     human affairs: Dionysius of Halicarnassus 1.77.3, 2.56.6, 2.68.2, 8.56.1; Plutarch *Coriolanus*
     38.3, *Camillus* 6.2–4.

83   Cf. Dio Cassius 55.1.4 on a miraculous apparition in 9 BC: θαυμαστόν μὲν οὖν . . . οὐ
     μέντοι καὶ ἀπιστεῖν ἔχω. Dio became a historian when τὸ δαιμόνιον appeared in his
     sleep and encouraged him. See n. 159 below, and Millar 1964.179–81: 'an unquestioning
     adherent of traditional pagan belief and observance' (179).

84   Bloomer 1992.1, cf. Fantham 1996.133: 'a reference work for orators, or more likely
     declaimers, needing precedents for the subjects of their speeches.' *Contra* Skidmore
     1996.xvi–xvii, 53–4. Wardle 1998.12–15 hedges his bets: 'I would argue that the serious
     moral purpose envisaged by Skidmore should be combined with a primary audience of those
     involved in declamation...' (The reference to *declamantes* in the preface to Iulius Paris'
     epitome is evidence only for the fourth or fifth century AD.)

85   Text as in J. Briscoe's 1998 Teubner edition and D.R. Shackleton Bailey's Loeb (2000); R.
     Combàs' Budé (1995) reads *alacritatis* (with the best MSS), not *claritatis*, at §4. I have added
     the section numbers. [See now Mueller 2002.17–19 for a good defence of *alacritatis*.]

(1) I have decided to set in order a selection, from distinguished authors, of the memorable deeds and sayings of Rome and of foreign nations, which are too widely scattered in other writers for knowledge of them to be acquired in a short time, in order to save those who wish to receive the lessons the labour of long research.

(2) I have not been seized by the desire to include everything. For who could embrace the events of all time in a small number of volumes? Who in his right mind could hope to hand on the whole sequence of Roman and foreign history, recorded in the happy style of previous writers, either with more careful accuracy or with more outstanding eloquence?

(3) You therefore, Caesar, the surest salvation of our country, I invoke for this enterprise – you whom the consensus of men and gods has wished to be the ruler of land and sea, you whose heavenly providence most generously favours the virtues, and most strictly punishes the vices, of which I am about to speak.

(4) For if the orators of old rightly began with Jupiter Best and Greatest, if the most excellent bards took their beginnings from some divine power, all the more properly will my humble self have had recourse to your favour, in that the rest of divinity is inferred from mere opinion, whereas yours is seen by immediate faith as equal to the star of your father and grandfather, whose exceptional brightness added much splendid brilliance to our ceremonies; for the other gods we have received [from the past], the Caesars we have given [to the future].

(5) And since it is my intention to seek my starting point in the worship of the gods, I shall deal briefly with its nature.

Valerius uses the idiom of historiography—not just *omnis aeui gesta* and *historiae series* (§2), but the title phrase itself, *facta ac dicta memoratu digna* (§1), which is reminiscent of Cicero's definition of the subject-matter of history in *De oratore*.[86] His opening phrase, and *cupido incessit* in §2, seem to be borrowed from Sallust.[87] But the most striking feature of this passage is its repeated inter-textual reference to a famous preface of about sixty years earlier, that of Livy himself.

---

86 Cicero *De oratore* 2.63: *uult enim, quoniam in rebus magnis **memoriaque dignis** consilia primum, deinde acta, postea euentus exspectentur, et de consiliis significari quid scriptor probet et in rebus bestis declarari non solum quid **actum aut dictum** sit, sed etiam quo modo. . .* [Cf. Tacitus *Annals* 3.65.1 on exemplary *dicta factaque* as the subject matter of *annales*.]

    For *memoratu dignum*, and the more frequent *memoria dignum*, see Oakley 1998.138–9; the idea goes back at least to Herodotus (1.16.2, 1.117 ἀξιαπηγητότατα). Servius *auctus* on *Aeneid* 1.373 (*digna memoratu*) and Isidore *Etymologiae* 1.44.3 (*digna memoria*) preserve Verrius Flaccus' account of the *annales maximi*: Frier 1979.27–37, 40–1.

87 Sallust *Catiline* 6.1 (*urbem Romam*, imitated by Tacitus *Annals* 1.1.1), 7.3 (*cupido incesserat*); cf. Guerrini 1981.29–60, 'Valerio Massimo e Sallustio'. Tony Woodman reminds me that *omne aeuum* (§2) may be an allusion to Catullus 1.6, and thus to Nepos' *Chronica*.

The first allusion defines Valerius' purpose (§1). Livy had carefully regis-
tered the ethical value of history:[88]

> *hoc illud est praecipue in cognitione rerum salubre ac frugiferum, omnis te exempli docu-*
> *menta in inlustri posita monumento intueri; inde tibi tuaeque rei publicae quod imitere*
> *capias, inde foedum inceptu foedum exitu quod uites.*
>
> It is this in particular which is salutary and beneficial in the knowledge of
> history, that you behold lessons of every sort of example set forth in a conspic-
> uous monument. From there you may take, for yourself and your republic,
> what to imitate and what, corrupt in origin and corrupt in outcome, to avoid.

Valerius repeats the key word *documenta* and applies to it the verb *sumere*, corresponding to Livy's *capias*. Failure to recognise this has resulted in some strange
translations of *documenta sumere uolentibus*,[89] but the allusion and the meaning
are both clear enough: *documenta* is from *docere*, and history teaches.

Livy's conspicuous second-person address to the reader is transferred by
Valerius to the emperor (§3)—no longer the citizen of a republic choosing
what to imitate or avoid, but a god-like arbiter meting out reward and punishment. Even so, Valerius' *uirtutes* and *uitia* are recognisably the *quod imitere* and
quod uites of Livy's preface. Similarly Livian are the passages where Valerius
identifies accuracy and style as the possible ways to surpass one's predecessors
(§2),[90] and appeals to the poets' habit of beginning with the gods (§4).[91] Finally,
where Livy had referred to the *magnitudo* of his rivals, Valerius speaks of *mea
paruitas* (§4).[92]

In view of all this, and of the brute fact that in his time Livy's huge narrative was the classic statement of *domestica historia*, one might expect Valerius to
share Livy's attitude to stories of miracles and divine intervention. But no: in
his first book alone, he presents gods and goddesses acting as protagonists in
one story after another,[93] and his moral lesson on the ubiquity of divine

---

88 Livy pref. 10; Moles 1993.152–5.
89 E.g. 'those who want concrete evidence' (Bloomer 1992.14); 'those who wish to embrace
    the examples' (Wardle 1998.29); 'chi volesse compulsare tali fonti' (Faranda 1971.65). The
    key explanatory text is Varro *De lingua Latina* 6.62, defining *documenta* as *exempla docendi
    causa*.
90 Livy pref. 2, *noui semper scriptores aut in rebus certius aliquid allaturos se aut scribendi arte rudem
    uetustatem superaturos credunt.* Parallel noted by Herkommer 1968.79 n. 1.
91 Livy pref. 13, *precationibus deorum dearumque, si ut poetis nobis quoque mos esset...*; cf. n. 1
    above.
92 Livy pref. 3, *nobilitate ac magnitudine eorum qui nomini officient meo consoler.* Valerius perhaps
    alludes to his own cognomen Maximus, itself evidently a badge of *nobilitas* (Skidmore
    1996.113–17); but if so, the allusion is modest, not 'ludic' (Wardle 1998.70).
93 1.1.18 (Apollo), 1.1.19 (Aesculapius), 1.1.ext.1 (Juno), 1.6.12 (Jupiter). [Add 3.2.1 (*di
    immortales* keep Cocles safe), 3.4.4 and 4.5.3 (acts of Fortuna), 8.15.5 (gods send crow for
    Valerius).]

concern for mortals, and divine punishment of wickedness, is spelt out again and again.[94]

The fire burns on Servius Tullius' head;[95] the voice of Silvanus is heard in the wood;[96] Castor and Pollux fight for the Romans at Lake Regillus;[97] T. Latinius reports his vision to the Senate, and is cured;[98] the statue of Fortuna addresses the matrons;[99] queen Juno of Veii says she wants to go to Rome;[100] a divine vision warns Decius Mus and his colleague in a dream;[101] the angry Hercules blinds Appius Claudius and wipes out the Potitii.[102] Miracle stories which Livy either omits altogether or keeps in careful *oratio obliqua* are narrated by Valerius in a confident indicative mode which leaves no room for doubt.[103]

Particularly revealing is what he does with the material he takes from Cicero. In book 2 of Cicero's *De natura deorum*, the Stoic spokesman Lucilius Balbus uses divine epiphanies as part of his argument for the existence of the gods; for instance, on the day of the battle of Pydna in 168 BC, P. Vatienus of Reate was met by two young men on white horses who told him that king Perses had just been captured. In book 3, however, C. Cotta pours scorn on all such stories as mere unsubstantiated rumour. Valerius ignores the sceptic's point, and reports the epiphany story as simple fact,[104] just as he does with two dream stories adduced by Quintus Cicero in book 1 of *De diuinatione* and refuted by Marcus in book 2.[105]

Valerius was writing moral protreptic, not philosophical argument. He sets out his position with admirable clarity:[106]

---

94 1.1.ext.3, *lento enim gradu ad uindictam sui diuina procedit ira*; 1.6.1, *sic humana consilia casti-gantur ubi se caelestibus praeferunt*; 1.6.12, *quibus apparet caelestium numen . . . uoluisse*; 1.7.1, *quid ergo aliud putamus quam diuino numine effectum . . . ?*; 1.8.2, *numen ipsius dei . . . compro-bauit*.

95 1.6.1 (Livy 1.39.1, *ferunt*). Also L. Marcius in 211 BC: 1.6.2 (Livy 25.39.16, *miracula addunt*).

96 1.8.5 (Livy 2.7.2, *adiciunt miracula*).

97 1.8.1 (not in Livy: see n. 13 above).

98 1.7.4 (Livy 2.36.8, *traditum memoriae est*).

99 1.8.4 (not in Livy); see above, pp. 256–7.

100 1.8.3 (Livy 5.22.6, *fabulae adiectum est*).

101 1.7.3 (Livy 8.6.9, *dicitur*).

102 1.1.17 (Livy 9.29.10, *traditur*).

103 Not only in book 1: see also 5.6.2 on M. Curtius and the chasm (Livy 7.6.1, *dicitur, ferunt*), 5.6.3 on Genucius Cipus (not in Livy: see n. 112 below), 8.1.abs.5 on Tuccia (Livy *Epitome* 20, cf. pp. 248–9 above). [See also Mueller 2002.39 on Valerius Maximus 1.1.20 (contrast Livy 42.28.12) on the anger of Juno Lacinia, and 2002.40–1 on Valerius' miracles in general.]

104 Cicero *De natura deorum* 2.6 (3.11–13); Valerius Maximus 1.8.1, with close verbal parallels. For the name (not Vatinius) see Taylor 1960.262–3.

105 Cicero *De diuinatione* 1.56 and 59 (2.136–41); Valerius Maximus 1.7.5–6, verbal parallels again.

106 Val. Max. 1.8.7. Wardle 1998.59 unfortunately translates Kempf's 1888 Teubner text, which made nonsense of the passage by printing Novák's conjecture *uera* for *uana* in the final phrase.

nec me praeterit de motu et uoce deorum immortalium humanis oculis auribusque percepto
quam in ancipiti opinione aestimatio uersetur, sed quia non noua dicuntur sed tradita
repetuntur, fidem auctores uindicent: nostrum sit inclutis litterarum monumentis conse-
crata perinde ac uana non refugisse.

I am not unaware how controversial is the question of the perception by
human sight and hearing of the movement and voices of the immortal gods.
But since what is said is not new, but a repetition of what has been handed
down, my authorities may defend their own credibility. Let it be my part not to
have avoided, as if they were false, events that have been consecrated in famous
literary monuments.

The particular event that gave rise to this declaration was the miraculous
double migration of the Penates from Alba Longa back to their home in
Lavinium. We know some of the famous literary monuments in which that
story was consecrated: the fourth book of the pontiffs' *Annales maximi*,[107] the
second book of L. Cincius Alimentus' history,[108] the second book of L. Iulius
Caesar's *Pontificalia*,[109] the first book of Q. Aelius Tubero's *Historiae*,[110] and the
first book of Dionysius of Halicarnassus' *Roman Antiquities*.[111] Not one of them
was the work of a poet.

V   Poetry and *Annales*

So Varro, Cicero, Dionysius, Plutarch and Valerius Maximus have brought us
to an unexpected conclusion. Livy's comment on what is appropriate to poets'
stories, far from being a truism, turns out to be a partisan statement of philosophical scepticism. Other historians took the opposite view, and did accept
miracle stories and divine epiphanies as a proper part of their subject matter.
The issue was one not of literary convention but of theological belief.

The common ground of prose and poetry is well illustrated by an item in
Valerius Maximus' chapter on patriotism. The praetor Genucius Cipus, leaving
the city on campaign, finds that he has grown horns; the soothsayers tell him
that it signifies he will be king if he returns; he goes into voluntary exile. The

---

107 *Origo gentis Romanae* 17.3 = *Annales pontificum* fr. 3 Chassignet; Frier 1979.50–2.
108 *Origo gentis Romanae* 17.3 = *FGrH* 810 F9 (unnecessarily categorised as doubtful); Richard
     1983.165–6. [See now Cameron 2004.329–34 on *OGR*'s source citations, esp. 330 on this
     passage.]
109 *Origo gentis Romanae* 17.3, cf. 9.6, 15.5; Richard 1983.139.
110 *Origo gentis Romanae* 17.3, not in Peter's *HRR* fragments. Preliminary material on Tubero
     in Wiseman 1979.135–9.
111 Dionysius of Halicarnassus 1.67.2 (θαῦμα μέγιστον λέγεται γενέσθαι). Possibly from
     Timaeus (cf. *FGrH* 566 F59); but Dionysius used authors who used the pontifical chronicle
     (1.73.1, 1.74.3, 4.2.1, 7.1.6, 8.56.1), and Tubero was one of his Roman patrons (Dionysius
     of Halicarnassus *Thucydides* 1).

same story is told in Ovid's *Metamorphoses*.[112] Valerius' account of the Penates' migration offers a similar parallel. He introduces it as something 'recognised in its own time [which] has come down to later generations'—just what Virgil puts more succinctly when he has a miracle to report: *prisca fides facto, sed fama perennis*.[113]

It was a way of thinking very familiar to the Romans. To believe in miracles and divine intervention is to believe that the gods are concerned with the world of humans, that they take note of moral excellence and its opposite, and reward or punish it accordingly. Cicero, in his guise as legislator, made it the programme of his law-code to secure that belief in the minds of the citizens, and we have seen both Dionysius and Valerius Maximus deliberately selecting their material to do the same.[114]

So it should not be a surprise to find that the *pontifices*—whose duty it was to instruct the people,[115] and whose chronicle was consulted as a repertory of precedent and example[116]—included in that chronicle such exemplary paradigms of divine power as the migrating Penates and the speaking statue of Fortuna Muliebris.[117] They also included one of the weirdest of all such manifestations, the phantom phallus that appeared in the royal hearth and fathered a miraculous child on queen Tanaquil's maidservant. Dionysius, Pliny and Plutarch all have that story, and so does Ovid, in a poem about 'sacred matters drawn from the old *annales*'.[118] We may as well burn the *annales*, says Quintus Cicero, if we're not going to believe in the gods' concern for mortals. He was talking about the story of Attus Navius and the whetstone, which no doubt also featured in the pontiffs' chronicle.[119]

Modern historians treasure the idea of the *annales pontificum* as an ancient archive, guaranteeing at least the framework of early Roman history.[120] In my

---

112 Valerius Maximus 5.6.3, *noui atque inauditi generis prodigium*; Ovid *Metamorphoses* 15.565–621. Pliny (*Nat. Hist.* 11.123) calls Cipus *fabulosus*, like Actaeon.

113 Valerius Maximus 1.8.7, *quod suo saeculo cognitum manauit ad posteros* (trans. Wardle 1998.59); Virgil *Aeneid* 9.79. Cf. Ovid *Metamorphoses* 1.400 (*quis hoc credat, nisi sit pro teste uetustas?*), *Fasti* 4.203–4 (*pro magno teste uetustas | creditur: acceptam parce mouere fidem*).

114 Cicero *De legibus* 2.15–16; see above, nn. 70, 77 (Dionysius), 94 (Valerius).

115 Livy 1.20.6–7, on Numa's appointment of the first *pontifex*: . . . *ut esset quo consultum plebes ueniret . . . ut idem pontifex edoceret . . .* Cicero *De oratore* 2.52, on the notice-board put up in the house of the *pontifex maximus*: *potestas ut esset populo cognoscendi*.

116 Livy 8.18.11–12, 27.8.8–9; Frier 1979.98–100.

117 See above, nn. 77, 107.

118 Dionysius of Halicarnassus 4.2.1–3 = *Annales pontificum* fr. 13 Chassignet; Pliny *Nat. Hist.* 36.204, Plutarch *Moralia* 323b–c (*De fortuna Romanorum* 10); Ovid *Fasti* 6.625–36; also Arnobius *Aduersus nationes* 5.18. *Sacra. . . annalibus eruta priscis*: Ovid *Fasti* 1.7, cf. 4.11.

119 Cicero *De diuinatione* 1.33 (p. 252 above); cf. Frier 1979.222.

120 See most recently Cornell 1995.13–15 and Oakley 1997.24–7. Servius *auctus* (on *Aeneid* 1.373) says the *pontifex maximus* recorded *digna memoratu . . . domi militiaeque terra marique gesta*; but that evidently reflects the eighty-book edition described by Verrius Flaccus (Frier 1979.27–37).

view that is a somewhat sanguine idea. It was certainly an archive, but what the pontiffs chose to record for the good of the citizens was not necessarily what the historian of *res gestae* would like to know. It is ironic that the very item which is supposed to show how far the chronicle went back—the report in the *annales maximi* of an eclipse on 21 June 'about 350 years after the foundation of the city'—is cited by Cicero not from a historian but from Ennius' epic poem.[121] Indeed, Ennius evidently took the title, and perhaps the concept, of his *Annales* from the pontiffs' chronicle, long before any prose writer ever used that title for a historical work.[122]

The word *annales* occurs in the first book of the *Aeneid*, where the shipwrecked hero introduces himself to his disguised mother:[123]

> 'o dea, si prima repetens ab origine pergam
> et uacet annalis nostrorum audire laborum,
> ante diem clauso componet Vesper Olympo.
> nos Troia antiqua, si uestras forte per auris
> Troiae nomen iit, diuersa per aequora uectos
> forte sua Libycis tempestas appulit oris.
> sum pius Aeneas, raptos qui ex hoste penatis
> classe ueho mecum, fama super aethera notus;
> Italiam quaero patriam, et genus ab Ioue summo.'

'O goddess, if I were to start at the beginning and retrace our whole story, and if you had the time to listen to the annals of our suffering, before I finish the doors of Olympus would close and the Evening Star would lay the day to rest. We come from the ancient city of Troy, if the name of Troy has ever reached your ears. We have sailed many seas and by the chance of the winds we have been driven ashore here in Libya. I am Aeneas, known for my devotion. I carry with me on my ships the gods of my house, the Penates, wrested from my enemies, and my fame has reached beyond the skies. I am searching for my fatherland in Italy. My descent is from highest Jupiter.'

By *annales* in line 373 Aeneas refers to the long story he will eventually tell in books 2–3, a narrative full of miracles and divine interventions. But the ancient commentators took the word to be a specific allusion to the pontiffs' chronicle; indeed, it is from their commentary on that line that much of our information

---

121 Cicero *De republica* 1.25 = *Annales pontificum* fr. 8 Chassignet = Ennius *Annales* 153 Sk (*ex hoc die quem apud Ennium et in annalibus maximis consignatum uidemus*); Skutsch 1985.311–13. The year date is very uncertain: see most recently Humm 2000.106–9.

122 Skutsch 1985.6–7; Frier 1979.216–19. The first certain use of *Annales* as the title of a prose history was evidently by L. Piso *censorius* after 120 BC: Wiseman 1979.12–16, Forsythe 1994.42 ('Piso's work is the earliest Roman history for which a strictly annalistic treatment of the early and middle republic is attested').

123 Virgil *Aeneid* 1.372–80, trans. D. West (Penguin Classics).

about the chronicle derives.[124] They inferred that Aeneas is to be thought of as a *pontifex*, which seems reasonable enough given his self-definition as *pius Aeneas* and the carrier of the Penates.

The *Aeneid* was being composed at the time of Augustus' restoration of the 82 temples, when the people wanted him to be *pontifex maximus*.[125] Horace in the last of his 'Roman Odes' was repeating the traditional lesson that the gods control everything, and success depends on their goodwill.[126] Aeneas the pious *pontifex*, ancestor of Augustus, fits well into that context.

On 6 March 12 BC, Augustus finally did become *pontifex maximus*, to the huge enthusiasm of the Roman people;[127] and at some point not far distant from that date (between Cicero and Verrius Flaccus), a vast new eighty-book edition of the *annales pontificum* was produced.[128] It seems to have been a characteristically Augustan project. Just like the great lists of consuls and *triumphatores* that decorated his triumphal arch, or the annotated statues of the heroes of the Roman past that thronged his new Forum, so too the accumulated (and no doubt expanded) documentation of all past *pontifices maximi* would encompass the whole of Roman history in a teleological sequence culminating in Augustus himself.[129]

If we are right to see miracle stories and reports of divine intervention as part of the pontiffs' traditional material—and two of the four certain fragments of the eighty-book edition are clear examples of that[130]—it is worth remembering that Augustus' own memoirs were full of such stories,[131] and according

---

124 Macrobius *Saturnalia* 3.2.17; Servius *auctus* on *Aeneid* 1.373.

125 Augustus *Res gestae* 10.2 (*populo id sacerdotium deferente mihi*), 20.4 (temples, begun in 28 BC).

126 Horace *Odes* 3.6, esp. 5–6: *dis te minorem quod geris, imperas: hinc omne principium, huc refer exitum*. Compare Cicero *De legibus* 2.15: *sit igitur hoc iam a principio persuasum ciuibus, dominos esse omnium ac moderatores deos, eaque quae gerantur eorum geri iudicio ac numine.*

127 Augustus *Res gestae* 10.2, cf. Ovid *Fasti* 3.415–28. For the importance of the pontificate in Augustus' self-presentation, see Bowersock 1990.

128 Frier 1979.193–200; Chassignet 1996.xxxvi–xl refuses to accept Frier's conclusion, but nowhere engages with his arguments.

129 For learning and scholarship as tools of Augustan authority, cf. Wallace-Hadrill 1997.11–22; the eighty books were 'a great collection of aetiological explanations of Roman rites and institutions' (Rawson 1991.15).

130 *Annales pontificum* frr. 3 and 5 Chassignet (*Origo gentis Romanae* 17.3, 18.3); the others are frr. 4 and 7 (ibid. 17.5 and Aulus Gellius 4.5.1–6).

131 Augustus *De uita sua* frr. 4, 6, 7, 12 Malcovati (Tertullian *De anima* 46; Pliny *Nat. Hist.* 2.93; Servius *auctus* on *Eclogues* 9.46; Plutarch *Brutus* 41.5): prophetic visions seen by Cicero and M. Artorius, the comet signifying *Caesaris animam inter deorum immortalium numina receptam*, and the instant punishment of a *haruspex* who revealed the secrets of the gods. For the autobiography and its context, see Ando 2000.139–43: 'to remind people of the reasons for their gratitude and their loyalty' (141).

Sulla's memoirs were similarly full of divine interventions (frr. 6, 8, 9, 15, 16, 18, 21 Peter); and a later imperial author, Marcus Aurelius in his *Meditations* (2.11, 9.27, 12.28), was quite sure that the gods exist, care about human affairs, and communicate their will through dreams and oracles.

to Suetonius one of his favourite entertainments was listening to *aretalogi*, story-tellers who specialised in tales of the deeds and power of the gods.[132] Yet that was the type of story that Livy in his preface saw as appropriate to poetry.

Perhaps this is the place to bring in something Livy says in book 5, where the phraseology, clearly reminiscent of the passage in the preface, may cast some light on what sort of poetry he had in mind:[133]

> *sed in rebus tam antiquis si quae similia ueris sint pro ueris accipiantur, satis habeam;*
> *haec ad ostentationem scenae gaudentis miraculis aptiora quam ad fidem neque adfirmare*
> *neque refellere est operae pretium.*
>
> But in matters so ancient let me be content if some things like the truth are accepted as true. It is not worth the trouble either to endorse or to refute these things: they are more appropriate to the ostentation of the stage, which delights in miracles, than to credibility.

This refers to an episode which Livy carefully introduces as a *fabula*, the next act of which was the speech of Juno Regina, signifying her willingness to go to Rome.[134] Since *fabula* can also mean the plot of a play, perhaps, as in Varro,[135] the *poetae* Livy was thinking of were dramatists.

The stage that delighted in miracles was among other things a vehicle for the moral and political education of the Roman people,[136] and that included instruction about the gods—how they helped Rome,[137] how they championed virtue,[138] how they punished sinners.[139] That is something not often mentioned in histories of Roman drama, but the evidence for it is clear enough. Nor is it often mentioned in accounts of the pontiffs' chronicle that those responsible for the eighty-book edition saw fit to include (at book 11) a learned explanation for an iambic senarius line, *malum consilium consultori pessimum est*, allegedly sung by children round the city when the wicked machinations of Etruscan *haruspices* were foiled.[140] Perhaps it was a catch-phrase from a popular play on

---

132 Suetonius *Diuus Augustus* 74. Examples of aretalogy are listed, with bibliography, in Engelmann 1975.37, 55–6.

133 Livy 5.21.9. The echo of pref. 6 is noted by (e.g.) Moles 1993.148–9, Kraus 1994.283–4, Forsythe 1999.43.

134 Livy 5.21.8 (*inseritur huic loco fabula*), 5.22.6 (*inde fabulae adiectum est uocem quoque dicentis uelle auditam*). *Fabula praetexta* inferred by Ribbeck 1881.

135 Augustine *City of God* 6.5 (= Varro *Antiquitates diuinae* frr. 7–10 Cardauns), cf. 6.6 (on *di poetici theatrici ludicri scaenici*).

136 Moral: full documentation and discussion in Rawson 1991.570–81. Political: Polybius 6.56.8 and 11, with Zorzetti 1980.64–5; Cicero *Pro Rabirio Postumo* 29, with Leigh 1996.186–8.

137 Plautus *Amphitruo* 41–5 (gods in tragedies reporting their benefactions).

138 Ovid *Fasti* 4.326 (the miracle of Magna Mater and Q. Claudia).

139 Cicero *Pro Roscio Amerino* 66–7, *In Pisonem* 46, *De legibus* 1.40, *Academica* 2.89, *De haruspicum responso* 39 (the Furies and their blazing torches as a commonplace of tragedy).

140 *Annales pontificum* fr. 8 Chassignet (Aulus Gellius 4.5.5). Cf. Pliny *Nat. Hist.* 28.15 (citing *annales*) for a similar story.

the subject; at any rate, it suggests common ground in the preoccupations of the pontiffs and the stage.

What I think may have happened is this.

First, it was an ancient custom (though we don't know how ancient) for the *pontifex maximus* to put up in the public part of his house a notice-board listing events for the information of the Roman People. According to Cato, crop failures and eclipses were characteristic items; no doubt the main purpose was to make known items that might reveal the gods' attitude towards Rome, and thus to encourage the citizens in pious and god-fearing behaviour.[141]

This material was also accumulated into a chronicle, variously known as *annales publici*,[142] *annales populi Romani*,[143] *annales pontificum*,[144] or *annales maximi*.[145] Presumably the chronicle consisted of a series of volumes,[146] added to by successive *pontifices maximi*, and kept in a place where they could be consulted by the learned and literate.[147]

I imagine the ordinary people had little use for the chronicle. A bulletin board was one thing (Roman citizens were used to reading notices, or having notices read to them[148]), but they needed no consolidated archive to discover how the immortal gods had manifested their power and majesty in times past. They had prophets (*uates*) to tell them that, and to keep the fear of divine punishment firmly before their eyes.[149] And those who were too sophisticated to 'listen to a prophet' (one of the signs of superstition, according to Cicero) would get the same message from the performances at the *ludi scaenici*.[150]

---

141 Cicero *De oratore* 2.52, Servius *auctus* on *Aeneid* 1.373, Dionysius of Halicarnassus 1.74.3; Cato *Origines* fr. 77P = *Annales pontificum* fr. 2 Chassignet (Aulus Gellius 2.28.6). Cf. Livy 1.20.6 on the *pontifices'* responsibility for *omnia publica priuataque sacra*.
142 Cicero *De republica* 2.28; Seneca *Consolatio ad Polybium* 14.2; Diomedes in *Grammatici Latini* 1.484K.
143 Cicero *De domo* 86.
144 Cicero *De legibus* 1.2.6; *Origo gentis Romanae* preface, 17.3, 17.5, 18.3.
145 Cicero *De oratore* 2.52, *De republica* 1.25; Aulus Gellius 4.5.6; Festus (Paulus) 113L; Macrobius *Saturnalia* 3.2.17; Servius *auctus* on *Aeneid* 1.373.
146 Cf. Horace *Epistles* 2.1.26 (*pontificum libros*), which could be a reference to the chronicle. Its original form may be inferred by comparison with the evidence for Etruscan 'linen books' in the fourth century BC: see most recently Torelli 1996.13–22, esp. 19–20, figs 2–3.
147 E.g. by Ennius, and probably by L. Cincius Alimentus about 200 BC: see above, nn. 121 and 108.
148 Public notices: e.g. Cicero *De lege agraria* 2.13 (text of law), *Ad Atticum* 2.20.4, 4.3.3 (edicts, speeches); cf. Millar 1998.45, 103. Private notices (lost property, debts, etc): e.g. Plautus *Rudens* 1294; Cicero *Pro Quinctio* 50, *Ad Atticum* 1.18.8; Propertius 3.23.23; Seneca *De beneficiis* 4.12.2.
149 Lucretius 1.102–9 and Dionysius of Halicarnassus 5.54.3, with Wiseman 1994.49–67. Cf. Livy 25.1.7–10 (*uates* in the Forum, 213 BC); Isidore *Origines* 6.8.12 (*praecepta* of the *uates* Marcius).
150 See above, p. 266. Cicero *De diuinatio* 2.149 on *superstitio*: *instat enim et urget et quo te cumque uerteris persequitur, siue tu uatem siue tu omen audieris . . .*

Part of the prophets' task was taken over by the poets of early Roman literature (which is why in post-Varronian Latin *uates* can also mean a poet). In the preface to book 7 of his *Annales*, a famous passage, Ennius carefully distanced himself from the Saturnian metre of 'the Fauns and the *uates*', but his subject-matter, especially in the early books, must have substantially overlapped with theirs.[151] About seventy years later, L. Piso the ex-censor published a dry historical chronicle in prose—a very different author and a very different work, but he evidently called it *Annales*, and what it had in common with Ennius' epic poem may be seen from how they dealt with the Trojan pre-history of their subject. Ennius' Anchises foretells the future, Venus having given her lover the power of prophecy; Piso's Aeneas passes through the victorious Greek forces at Troy by a miracle, thanks to his piety.[152] Either of those items could have come from the pontiffs' chronicle, which indeed both authors evidently used.[153]

It is difficult for moderns to imagine a world in which prophecy, poetry, history and moral exhortation were not always thought of as separate conceptual categories. The best evidence is provided not by the great thinkers but by the commonplace minds of antiquity. Here is Diodorus Siculus in the preface to his *Universal History*:[154]

εἰ γὰρ ἡ τῶν ἐν ᾅδου μυθολογία τὴν ὑπόθεσιν πεπλασμένην ἔξουσα πολλὰ συμβάλλεται τοῖς ἀνθρώποις πρὸς εὐσέβειαν καὶ δικαιοσύνην, πόσῳ μᾶλλον ὑποληπτέον τὴν προφῆτιν τῆς ἀληθείας ἱστορίαν, τῆς ὅλη φιλοσοφίας οἱονεὶ μητρόπολιν οὖσαν, ἐπισκευάσθαι τὰ ἤθη μᾶλλον πρὸς καλοκαγαθίαν;

If the [poets'] mythology of Hades, fictitious though its subject-matter is, makes a great contribution to piety and justice among men, how much more must we assume that the prophetess of truth, history, which is as it were the mother-city of philosophy in general, is even more able to equip men's characters for a noble way of life?

---

151 Ennius *Annales* fr. 206–7 Skutsch (quoted by Varro *De lingua latina* 7.36; Cicero *Brutus* 71, 75–6, *Orator* 157, 171, *De diuinatione* 1.114; Quintilian 9.4.115; *Origo gentis Romanae* 4.5); cf. frr. 54–5 and 110–11Sk (Romulus' deification), 113Sk (Egeria), 139Sk (Lucumo and the eagle), etc.

152 Ennius *Annales* fr. 15–16 Skutsch; Piso fr. 3 Forsythe (= 2P). Forsythe 1994.96–7 wrongly translates *miraculo* as 'by way of inspiring awe and amazement': awe and amazement are the result, not the cause, of the *miraculum*, as is clear from Livy (5.46.3) on the similar story of Fabius Dorsuo.

153 Ennius: n. 121 above. Piso fr. 33 Forsythe = *Annales pontificum* fr. 5 Chassignet (*Origo gentis Romanae* 18.3), a story of divine punishment.

154 Diodorus Siculus 1.2.2, cf. Polybius 6.56.12; Polybius, not a commonplace mind, treats it as a means of social control.

Narrative set in the underworld was reserved to the poets. So too was narrative set in heaven, as Servius remarks about the *Aeneid*:[155]

> ... *constat ex diuinis humanisque personis, continens uera cum fictis; nam Aeneam ad Italiam uenisse manifestum est, Venerem uero locutam cum Ioue missumue Mercurium constat esse compositum.*
>
> It is made up of divine and human characters, and contains both truth and fiction; for Aeneas' journey to Italy is plain fact, whereas Venus' conversation with Jupiter and the mission of Mercury are agreed to be invented.

Virgil himself marks the transition from the underworld back to the historical mode by the passage of Aeneas through the ivory gate.[156] Everything that happens on earth, including divine manifestations and even Jupiter brought down to earth to bargain with Numa, could appear equally in a historian, and for the same hortatory purpose.[157]

P. Mucius Scaevola, who was *pontifex maximus* from 130 to about 115 BC, ended the practice of putting up the notice-board in his house. Presumably, though we cannot be sure, that means that under the next seven *pontifices maximi* there were no further additions to the pontiffs' chronicle.[158] But during those hundred years there was plenty of material to be recorded, as the disasters of the dying Republic offered evidence of the gods' anger. We see the late Republic through the rational eyes of Cicero, but other sources can give us a different angle: Dio, for instance, reveals the anxiety of the people in 55–54 BC when Gabinius restored the king of Egypt against the express instructions of the Sibyl.[159]

The prophets were busy throughout that time.[160] So too were the historians, the poets and the playwrights, recording and dramatising the

---

155 Servius on *Aeneid* 1 pref. The clearest statement is by an anonymous poet of the first century AD (*Aetna* 74–91), inveighing against the stage (*plurima pars scaenae rerum est fallacia*, 75) and the *mentiti uates* (79): his examples of their *mendosae uulgata licentia famae* (74, cf. *libertas* at 91) are the sinners and lawgivers in the underworld, the wars of the gods, and Jupiter's adulterous disguises.

156 Virgil *Aeneid* 6.893–9. Cf. Donatus *uita Vergilii* 38 and ps.Probus *uita Vergilii* ad fin., quoting a poem on Augustus' refusal to allow the *Aeneid* to be burned: *tu, maxime Caesar, | non sinis et Latiae consulis historiae.* According to Servius (on *Aeneid* 1.382), Lucan's epic was a *historia*, not a *poema*; it is noteworthy that the underworld narrative is not in the poet's voice but at third hand, as the revived corpse tells what he says the ghosts told him (Lucan 6.776–9).

157 Valerius Antias fr. 6P (Arnobius *Aduersus nationes* 5.1); cf. Wiseman 1998.21–3.

158 L. Metellus Delmaticus, ?115–103 BC; Cn. Domitius Ahenobarbus, 103–?89; Q. Mucius Scaevola, ?89–82; Q. Metellus Pius, 82–63; C. Iulius Caesar, 63–44; M. Aemilius Lepidus, 44–12.

159 Dio Cassius 39.15.1–4, 55.3, 56.4, 59.3, 60.4–61.4 (esp. 61.1 on the Tiber flood, 61.3 on the anger of τὸ δαιμόνιον); cf. n. 83 above.

160 E.g. Cicero *De diuinatione* 1.4 and Plutarch *Marius* 42.4 (87 BC); Sallust *Histories* 1.67.3M (78 BC); Cicero *De consulatu suo* quoted in *De diuinatione* 1.18 (63 BC).

catastrophes.[161] When the crisis was eventually over, the charismatic son of Divus Iulius would find no shortage of pious examples and moral paradigms to present to the grateful people, whether in his own memoirs or in a great new edition of the pontiffs' chronicle.[162] What I think we have to infer is a complex process of mutual borrowing and mutual influence among the poets, the prose-writers and the *pontifices*, lasting from at least the third century BC to the time of Augustus. The eighty books of the new pontiffs' chronicle will have contained a vast amount of stuff taken from literary sources, but those sources themselves may well have been influenced by the chronicle in its earlier manifestations. And the whole enterprise would have been meaningless without the fundamental motivation that we have found in one ancient source after another—the need to understand the true relationship between gods and men.

If this is a credible reconstruction, then Livy's position becomes a little clearer. I take it that when he wrote his preface, at a time when guilt and anxiety were still prevalent, the old pontiffs' chronicle was largely forgotten and the new one not yet created. What we see in him is not so much Augustan piety as a tolerant and patriotic form of Ciceronian scepticism.

For Livy, divine intervention was not appropriate to 'uncorrupted' history—but we know that other historians thought it was. For Cicero, different rules applied when history was written in prose or in verse—but Quintus had had to ask him whether that was his view, which shows that not everybody thought so.[163] The very fact that purists tried to insist on rational criteria entitles us to infer that the general attitude was different from theirs. Even in the sophisticated Rome of the first century BC, for many readers the distinction between the proper pursuits of poets and historians was far from clear-cut, and certainly not a simple matter of literary genre.

---

161 Playwrights: no fragments or titles known, but lost plays—on the death of C. Gracchus, the crossing of the Rubicon, the Ides of March—are inferred by Wiseman 1998.52–63 and Weinstock 1971.353–4. [See Keaveney 2003 for a sceptical view.]
162 See above, p. 265.
163 Livy pref. 6; Cicero *De legibus* 1.5.

CHAPTER SIXTEEN

The House of Tarquin

I

The archaeological evidence for archaic Rome has been spectacularly increased in the last twenty years by Andrea Carandini's ongoing excavations on the north slope of the Palatine, between the Arch of Titus and the temple of Vesta [fig. 47]. His first campaign, begun in 1985, revealed the remains of four substantial houses, dateable to about 530 BC and evidently occupied continuously for the next three centuries.[1] Destroyed in the third century (serious fires are recorded at Rome in 241, 213 and 210 BC),[2] they were rebuilt and survived in their new form until 'Nero's fire' in AD 64.

Enough survives of one of the sixth-century houses ('domus 3') to show that it was designed round an *atrium* [figs 48–9, pp. 274–5].[3] The remains of the other three are much more fragmentary (indeed, hardly anything at all survives of 'domus 1' and 'domus 2'), but they are confidently reconstructed by Carandini on the assumption that they too were *atrium* houses.[4] That is not what a cautious archaeologist would do, but Andrea Carandini is not a cautious archaeologist. He takes the generous view that reconstruction is the highest aim of excavation, 'the one moral justification for our work'. He believes that archaeologists have an obligation to make explicit, and visible, for the lay public what they as experts can infer from the remains they have uncovered. He has nothing but contempt for those of his colleagues who are too 'academically *comme il faut*' to take risks. 'In life and in research, you get nowhere without risk and error.'[5]

---

1 First published in Carandini 1990, whence Holloway 1994.67 (plan of 'domus 3'), Smith 1996.252 (general plan). Detailed excavation report in Carandini and Carafa 1995.215–59; historical summary and reconstruction drawings in Carandini 1995.50–67.
2 Orosius 4.11.8–9, Augustine *City of God* 3.18 (241 BC); Livy 24.47.15–16 (213 BC), 26.27.1–5 (210 BC).
3 Plan in Carandini 1990.98 (= Holloway 1994.67) superseded in Carandini 1995.60–1, tav. 57–8.
4 Carandini 1995.52 and 54, tav. 49 and 51, for the surviving remains of 'domus 1 and 2'; contrast 53 and 55–9, tav. 50 and 52–6, for the reconstructions.
5 His position is stated with candour and eloquence in Carandini 2000.148–55; the phrases quoted in the text are from pp. 149 and 155.

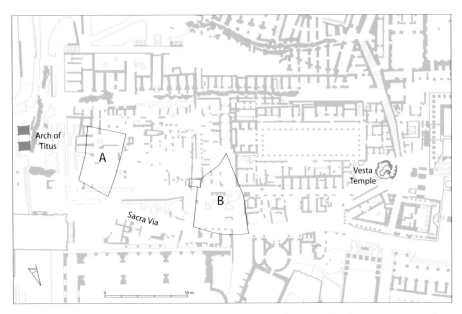

Fig. 47 The 'Sacra Via' from the arch of Titus to the temple of Vesta. A: site of 'domus 3' (figs 48–9). B: site of 'house of Tarquin' and 'Porta Mugonia' (figs 52–4).

Error is indeed always possible, as Carandini knows perfectly well: 'Reconstructions, by their nature, are nothing but combinations of hypotheses . . . Any scientific hypothesis may lead us into error, especially in the absence of a critical sense, and thus be taken as proved fact.'[6] That is the risk Carandini is proud to take. The trouble is that the more plausible the reconstruction looks, the less motivation there will be to apply one's critical sense and ask whether the data justify the hypotheses.

It is important to understand the motive for Carandini's method. As he says himself, what drives him is 'the magic of discovering the materials to construct something . . . the pleasure of giving shape to the shapeless'.[7] He cites with approval Italo Calvino's idea of a 'mental cinema' for ever projecting images inside our heads:[8]

6   Carandini 2000.153 ('Le ricostruzioni sono per loro natura nient'altro che combinazioni di ipotesi'), 154 ('Qualsiasi ipotesi scientifica può indurre in errore, specie in assenza di senso critico, ed essere quindi assunta come verità provata').
7   Carandini 2000.73.
8   Carandini 2000.155 (citing Calvino 1988.83): 'Ciò accade quando pensiamo, quando conversiamo, quando leggiamo . . . e sopratutto quando sogniamo e in un secondo riusciamo ad ammobiliare un intero castello e a vestire tutti i cortigiani. Cosí anche l'archeologo, partendo da indizi e frammenti, non può impedirsi di autoproiettare nella propria mente il "cinema mentale" di quelle cose e di quell'edificio finalmente capiti. Se è onesto, lavora su questa imagine, la perfeziona e la trasforma in una figura che sia visibile anche ad altri, grazie a un disegno di cui è responsabile.'

That's what happens when we think, when we talk, when we read ... above all when we dream, and in one second succeed in furnishing an entire castle and putting all the courtiers in costume. So too the archaeologist, starting from indications and fragments, cannot stop himself projecting in his mind the 'mental cinema' of those objects and that building finally understood. If he is honest, he works on the image, perfects it, and transforms it into a shape visible to others as well, by means of an illustration for which he takes the responsibility.

Note the phrase 'cannot stop himself'. Carandini is not just recommending good professional practice; he is describing a psychological disposition.

So it is no surprise to find the same phrase at the climax of his presentation of the sixth-century houses:[9]

We cannot stop ourselves imagining the following scenes: Ocrisia in the kitchen, possessed by the phallus of the Lar emerging from the hearth to beget Servius Tullius, as was believed to have happened in the palace of Tarquinius Priscus in the grove of Vesta; the mistress of the house weaving in her chamber; the store-house under lock and key, full of furnishings and foodstuffs; the throne, the marriage bed, the boxes of writing-tablets in the *tablinum*; the banquet-songs sung in the dining-room; the servants on the upper floor; the clients in the *atrium* (about five hundred of them could get in for the *salutatio*); and the family on the terrace, nearly twice as wide as the Sacra Via, following the course of the Luperci, the triumphal procession or other rituals in the narrow street below, and three metres away the terrace of the family opposite.

Naturally, the hypothetical rooms in Carandini's reconstruction drawings are all labelled, as he sees them in his mental cinema.

None of this is meant as criticism. How else can hypotheses be created, if not by the exercise of an informed imagination?[10] The purpose of this introductory section has been merely to make clear Carandini's method, before considering his hypothesis about the house of Tarquin.

9 Carandini 1995.51: 'Non possiamo impedirci di immaginare le seguenti scene...'
10 As one of Carandini's distinguished predecessors protested when criticised—'quasi che l'intuizione non fosse la somma di dati positivi, che sfuggono all'occhio delle moltitudini' (Giacomo Boni, letter of June 1899 quoted in Wiseman 1987b.132).

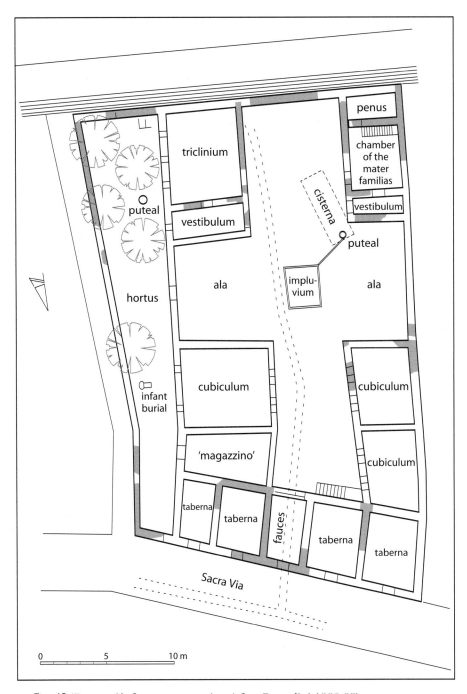

Fig. 48 'Domus 3', first reconstruction (after Carandini 1990.98).

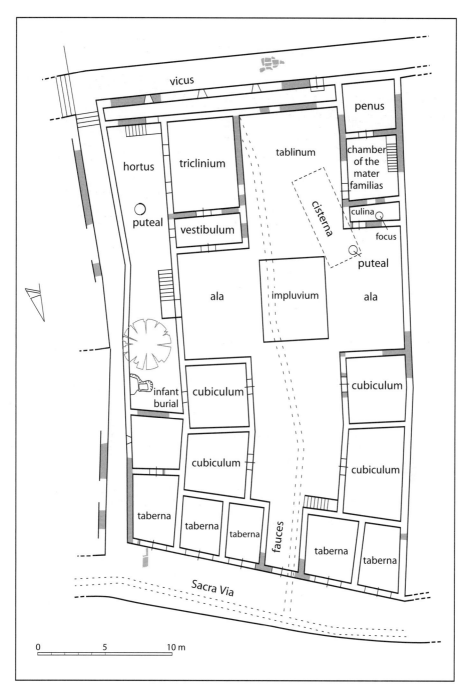

Fig. 49 'Domus 3', second reconstruction (after Carandini 1995.60, fig. 57).

II

I think it is no accident that at the end of the first stage of his excavation programme Andrea Carandini had in his mind a story set 'in the palace of Tarquinius Priscus in the grove of Vesta'.[11] There are only two ancient sources for the site of the house of Tarquinius Priscus. Solinus, probably using Varro, says that it was 'by the Porta Mugonia, above [or beyond] the top of the Nova Via',[12] while according to Livy one of its windows looked out on the Nova Via, 'for the king lived by the temple of Jupiter Stator'.[13] In 1990 Carandini thought he knew where the Nova Via and the Porta Mugonia were, and that they adjoined the grove of Vesta [fig. 50].[14] All that area would be explored in the second stage of his programme.

How the second stage altered Carandini's conception of the archaic topography can be seen in the sketch-plan he published in 2004 [fig. 51]. The Nova Via and the Porta Mugonia have now been moved, the grove of Vesta is much reduced from its former size, and a large area is newly marked off as 'the house of the Tarquins and of Servius Tullius'. Carandini's paradoxical description in 1995 of the house of Tarquinius Priscus as 'in the grove of Vesta' (why should there be a palace in a sacred grove?) marked a transitional phase in his reinterpretation, after the remains of an early house were discovered at the eastern end of the area marked on the 1990 plan as Vesta's grove.[15]

The full report of the new excavations is still to come,[16] but Carandini has now provided some preliminary information about 'the house of the Tarquins'. Three construction periods are identified: 'second half/last quarter of the seventh century' (construction in *scaglie di tufo rosso e cappellaccio*); 'second quarter of the sixth century' (construction in *scheggioni di tufo rosso*); 'last quarter of the sixth century or first half of the fifth' (construction in *opera quadrata di cappellaccio*).[17] The first two of these phases are interpreted as the house of Tarquinius Priscus and the 'official' house of Servius Tullius, respectively.[18] Rebuilt with a grandiose cryptoporticus after the fire of 210 BC, the house survived to the time of Augustus, when it was destroyed and replaced with a warehouse (*horreum*).[19]

---

11 Carandini 1995.51: 'come si credeva fosse avvenuto nella *regia* di Tarquinio Prisco nel *lucus Vestae*.'
12 Solinus 1.24 : *ad Mugoniam portam supra summam nouam uiam*. Cf. Varro *De uita populi Romani* fr. 7 Riposati = 290 Salvadore (Nonius 852L) for the list of the kings' houses.
13 Livy 1.41.4: *per fenestras in nouam uiam uersas, habitabat enim rex ad Iouis Statoris.*
14 Carandini 1990.97, fig. 4.2; contrast Carandini 2004.89, fig. 5.
15 Carandini and Carafa 1995.264: 'sulla base della scoperta in quest'area durante indagini ancora in corso di strutture in cappellaccio. . .'
16 Carandini, Carafa and Filippi, forthcoming.
17 Carandini 2004.46, cf. 68. 73.
18 The concept of a king's 'official' residence, though evidently important to Carandini ('precisione necessaria', Carandini 2004.53, cf. 56, 63 etc), is never explained, and seems to be an anachronism. Where did the king actually live?
19 Carandini 2004.46, cf. 59, 63–4.

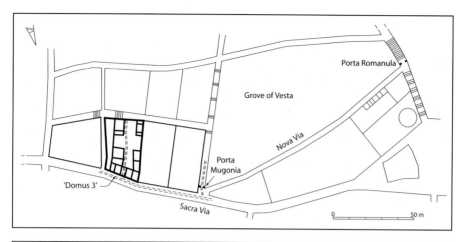

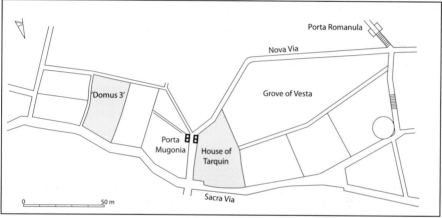

Fig. 50 Grove of Vesta and Porta Mugonia, first reconstruction (after Carandini 1990.97).

Fig. 51 Grove of Vesta and Porta Mugonia, second reconstruction (after Carandini 2004.89, fig. 5).

Carandini's plan of the house very helpfully distinguishes preserved remains, probable structures and hypothetical structures,[20] though naturally the degree of probability (and the criteria employed to establish it) will not become clear until the full excavation report is published. When the three categories are presented separately [figs 52–4], the extent of Carandini's hypothetical reconstruction becomes clear.

---

20 Carandini 2004.93, fig. 9c.

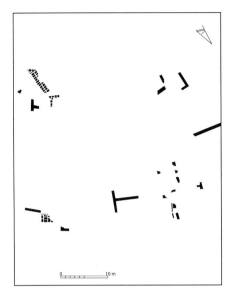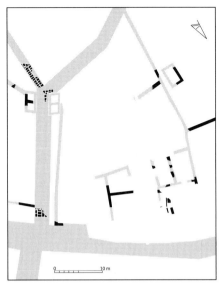

Fig. 52 'House of the Tarquins', surviving remains (after Carandini 2004.93, fig. 9c).

Fig. 53 'House of the Tarquins', surviving remains and 'probable structures' (after Carandini 2004.93, fig. 9c).

It is based, once again, on the reasonably well attested layout of 'domus 3' [figs 48–9 above]. Carandini at first believed that the two houses were contemporary, and he attributed the newly-discovered one to Tarquinius Superbus in the late sixth century.[21] Now that its origin has been taken back a century earlier and attributed to the first Tarquinius, 'domus 3' is a much less obvious paradigm for its layout; so Carandini now suggests, without argument, that the *atrium* houses of his first excavations deliberately imitated the pre-existing house of the Tarquins.[22]

We must assume that they imitated it down to the last detail, for Carandini reproduces the layout of 'domus 3' very precisely [fig. 54], even to the mysterious corridor across the back of the house. (The corridor did not appear in his first reconstruction of 'domus 3',[23] and it is far from clear what purpose it served.) However, the rooms on either side of the *tablinum* are reversed in comparison with 'domus 3', the kitchen, the chamber of the *mater familias* (*gineceo*) and the storehouse exchanging places with the *triclinium* and its associ-

---

21 Carandini 1995.42; Carandini 1997.ill.xx.
22 Carandini 2004.63 ('verosimilmente'), 69 ('è dunque possibile'), 72 ('verosimilmente').
23 Carandini 1990.98, whence Holloway 1994.67.

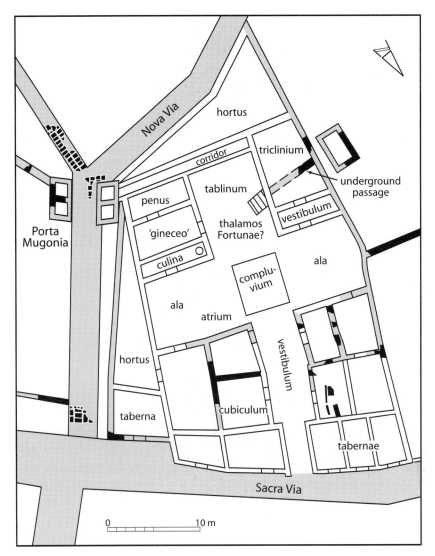

Fig. 54 'House of the Tarquins', hypothetical reconstruction (after Carandini 2004.93, fig. 9c).

ated anteroom.[24] There must be a good reason for these choices, but it cannot be archaeological; that part of the site is empty of 'preserved remains'.[25] Note too the identification of the front part of the *tablinum* as '*thalamos Fortunae*'. Since a *thalamos* should be a closed chamber, there must be a compelling reason to identify it as a space in a huge open *atrium* that could hold five hundred people.[26]

Of course there *are* reasons, and Carandini makes them very clear. They are to be found in Livy, Dionysius, Ovid and Plutarch—in the stories which stimulate his imagination and direct his mental cinema.

III

There are seven episodes of the 'myth-history' of sixth-century BC Rome which are set in different parts of the palace of the Tarquins. They are

(1) the conception of Servius Tullius,
(2) the fire portent,
(3) the assassination plot,
(4) Tanaquil at the window,
(5) the goddess and the king,
(6) the eagle and snake portents,
(7) the girl on a horse.

1. The conception of Servius Tullius.

ἀπὸ τῆς ἑστίας τῶν βασιλείων, ἐφ' ἧς ἄλλας τε Ῥωμαῖοι συντελοῦσιν ἱερουργίας καὶ τὰς ἀπὸ τῶν δείπνων ἀπαρχὰς ἁγίζουσιν, ὑπὲρ τοῦ πυρὸς ἀνασχεῖν λέγουσιν αἰδοῖον ἀνδρός. τοῦτο δὲ θεάσασθαι τὴν Ὀκρισίαν πρώτην φέρουσαν τοὺς εἰωθότας πελάνους ἐπὶ τὸ πῦρ...

They say that from the hearth [*hestia*] in the palace, on which the Romans offer various other sacrifices and also consecrate the first portions of their meals, there rose above the fire a man's privy member, and that Ocrisia was the first to see it as she was carrying the customary cakes to the fire...[27]

---

24 Bafflingly labelled '*vestibulum*' (Carandini 1995.51, 'il vestibolo del grande *triclinium*'); see pp. 283–4 below for the meaning of the Latin word.

25 Carandini 2004.69: 'Abbiamo alcune tracce archeologiche [*sic*], ma non sufficienti per proporre una ricostruzione archeologica vera e propria. Possiamo però—sempre a fine di spasso—riempire quello spazio...'

26 Plutarch *Moralia* 273B (ὁ καλούμενος Τύχης θάλαμος); for the *atrium* as a public space (*ad communem omnium usum*) see Varro *De lingua Latina* 5.161.

27 Dionysius of Halicarnassus 4.2.1 (Loeb translation).

...παρθένον τὴν Ὀκρησίαν ἀπάργματα καὶ λοιβὴν ἑκάστοτε
λαμβάνουσαν ἀπὸ τῆς βασιλικῆς τραπέζης ἐπὶ τὴν ἑστίαν κομίζειν· καί
ποτε τυχεῖν μὲν αὐτήν, ὥσπερ εἰώθει, τῷ πυρὶ τὰς ἀπαρχὰς
ἐπιβάλλουσαν, αἰφνίδιον δὲ τῆς φλογὸς μαρανθείσης μόριον ἀνδρὸς
ἀνατεῖναι γόνιμον ἐκ τῆς ἑστίας...

Ocrisia was a maiden who took the first-fruits and the libations on all occasions
from the royal table and brought them to the hearth [*hestia*]; and once on a
time, when she chanced, as usual, to be casting the offerings on the fire,
suddenly, as the flames died down, the member of a man rose up out of the
hearth...[28]

Ovid's version is only slightly different:

> hanc secum Tanaquil sacris de more peractis
>   iussit in ornatum fundere uina focum;
> hic inter cineres obscaeni forma uirilis
>   aut fuit aut uisa est...

After performing with her the sacred rites in due form, Tanaquil
ordered Ocrisia to pour wine on the hearth [*focus*], which had been
adorned. There among the ashes there was, or seemed to be, the shape
of the male organ...[29]

Carandini imagines this as taking place in the kitchen (*culina*),[30] but the sources'
emphasis on formal sacrifice, particularly Ovid's 'adorned hearth'
(*ornatum...focum*), seems to rule that out.

Where *was* the hearth in a palace in the sixth century BC—or rather, where
was it assumed to be when this story was first created? One possible analogy
might be the 'central hearth' in Agamemnon's palace (as imagined by
Aeschylus), where the sheep stood ready for sacrifice to greet the king's return;
or we might think of the hearth in the palace of Admetus, king of the Molos-
sians, where Themistocles took refuge in about 470 BC.[31] One could imagine
either scene in the central courtyard of the sixth-century Etruscan palace at
Murlo.[32]

---

28 Plutarch *Moralia* 323b (Loeb translation).
29 Ovid *Fasti* 6.629–32 (Loeb translation).
30 Carandini 1995.51; Carandini 2004.63.
31 Aechylus *Agamemnon* 1056 (ἑστίας μεσομφάλου), Thucydides 1.136.3.
32 Holloway 1994.56–9, fig. 4.7.

2. The fire portent.

> *eo tempore in regia prodigium uisu euentuque mirabile fuit. puero dormienti, cui Seruio*
> *Tullio fuit nomen, caput arsisse ferunt multorum in conspectu; plurimo igitur clamore*
> *inde ad tantae rei miraculum orto excitos reges...*
>
> At this time there happened in the house of the king a portent which was
> remarkable alike in its manifestation and in its outcome. The story is that while
> a child named Servius Tullius lay sleeping, his head burst into flames in the sight
> of many. The general outcry which so great a miracle called forth brought the
> king and queen to the place...[33]

Where were those numerous witnesses? Dionysius' version is more specific:

> καθημένου γάρ ποτ' αὐτοῦ μεσούσης μάλισθ' ἡμέρας ἐν τῇ παστάδι
> τῶν βασιλείων καὶ κατενεχθέντος ἐφ' ὕπνον, πῦρ ἀπέλαμψεν ἀπὸ τῆς
> κεφαλῆς αὐτοῦ, ἥ τε μήτηρ αὐτοῦ καὶ ἡ τοῦ βασιλέως γυνὴ
> πορευόμεναι διὰ τῆς παστάδος ἐθεάσαντο καὶ πάντες ὅσοι σὺν ταῖς
> γυναιξὶν ἐτύγχανον τότε παρόντες.
>
> When he had fallen asleep one day while sitting in the portico [*pastas*] of the
> palace about noon, a fire shone forth from his head. This was seen by his
> mother and by the king's wife, as they were walking through the portico, as
> well as by all who happened to be present with them at that time.[34]

Where would 'the portico of the palace' be in an *atrium* house? The scene
seems to be imagined in a colonnaded courtyard or peristyle, but there is no
room for that in Carandini's reconstruction.

3. The assassination plot.

The sons of Ancus Marcius plan to kill Tarquinius Priscus:

> *ex pastoribus duo ferocissimi delecti ad facinus, quibus consueti erant uterque agrestibus*
> *ferramentis <armati,> in uestibulo regiae quam potuere tumultuosissime specie rixae in*
> *se omnes apparitores regios conuertunt; inde, cum ambo regem appellarent clamorque*
> *eorum penitus in regiam peruenisset, uocati ad regem pergunt.*
>
> Two very desperate shepherds were selected to do the deed. Armed with the
> rustic implements to which they were both accustomed, they feigned a brawl in
> the entrance-court [*uestibulum*] of the palace and, making as much noise as
> possible, attracted the attention of all the royal attendants; then they appealed to

---

33 Livy 1.39.1 (Loeb translation). Cf. Valerius Maximus 1.6.1 (*domesticorum oculi adnotauerunt*).
34 Dionysius of Halicarnassus 4.2.4 (Loeb translation). For παστάς as the Greek for *porticus*, see
    Plutarch *Galba* 25.5.

the king, until their shouts were heard inside the palace and they were sent for and came before him.[35]

The forecourt and the king's attendants are not mentioned in Dionysius' version of the episode (he just says the brawl took place 'near the palace'), but he too makes it clear that the assassins were outside, and called in by the king to have their case heard.[36]

There is no forecourt in front of Carandini's *atrium* houses, just a row of shops with the terrace above from which the family could look out across the narrow street to their neighbours opposite. He puts the *uestibulum* inside the house, identifying it as the first part of the *atrium* itself. On this matter I think, with respect, that he is demonstrably wrong.

For the meaning of the term *uestibulum* we have something rather rare in our sources, an explicit definition from an expert authority. It is provided by Aulus Gellius, in his discussion of common errors:[37]

> *animaduerti enim quosdam hautquaquam indoctos uiros opinari uestibulum esse partem domus priorem, quam uulgus atrium uocat. C. Aelius Gallus in libro de significatione uerborum quae ad ius ciuile pertinent uestibulum esse dicit non in ipsis aedibus neque partem aedium, sed locum ante ianuam domus uacuum, per quem a uia aditus accessusque ad aedis est, cum dextra sinistraque ianuam tecta saepiunt uiae iuncta atque ipsa ianua procul a uia est, area uacanti intersita.*

For I have observed that some men who are by no means without learning think that the vestibule is the front part of house, which is commonly known as the *atrium*. Gaius Aelius Gallus, in the second book of his work *On the Meaning of Words Relating to the Civil Law*, says that the vestibule is not in the house itself, nor is it part of the house, but is an open space before the door of the house, through which there is an approach and access [*aditus accessusque*] to the house from the street, while on the right and left the door is hemmed in by buildings extended to the street and the door itself is at a distance from the street, separated from it by this vacant space.

Aelius Gallus' definition is confirmed by the consistent usage of ancient authors from Plautus onwards. The *uestibulum* was in front of the house,[38] and one

---

35 Livy 1.40.5 (Loeb translation).

36 Dionysius of Halicarnassus 3.72.2 (πλησίον τῶν βασιλείων), 72.3 (εἰσκαλέσας αὐτοὺς ὁ βασιλεὺς).

37 Aulus Gallius 16.5.2–3 (Loeb translation) = Aelius Gallus fr. 7 Funaioli; repeated almost verbatim in Macrobius *Saturnalia* 6.8.15–16.

38 E.g. Plautus *Mostellaria* 817 (*ante aedis*), Varro *de lingua Latina* 7.81 (*ante domum*), Varro *De re rustica* 3.9.7 (metaphor for yard in front of henhouse), Vitruvius 6.7.5 (*ante ianuas* = Greek προθύρα), Aulus Gellius 16.5.8 (*ante ianuam*), Servius on *Aeneid* 4.507 (*ne quis introeat*).

went *out* of the house to reach it;[39] it provided an approach to the door,[40] and might even be shared between two neighbouring houses.[41]

The *uestibulum* was where the clients congregated in the early morning, waiting for the moment when they would be admitted to pay their respects.[42] There was plenty of opportunity there for quarrels and fights,[43] as in the story of the brawling shepherds. The king's attendants (*apparitores*) were probably another authentic touch in the story, if, as seems likely, the lictors of a magistrate waited in his *uestibulum*.[44]

The more important the house, the bigger the *uestibulum*. There might be a colonnade, portrait statues of the ancestors, spoils of battle hung on the walls.[45] Pompey the Great's *uestibulum* even featured the rams of captured warships, while that of Nero's Golden House was designed to contain a colossal statue of the emperor 120 feet high.[46] When Catullus imagines the palace of king Peleus, he has the *uestibulum* lined with tall trees—beeches, laurels, poplars, cypresses.[47] The forecourt of the king of Rome's palace was no doubt thought of as similarly grand.

How is it that Carandini's reconstructed houses leave no room for so conspicuous a feature? The answer, I think, is that having once decided that the remains imply an *atrium* plan, he was over-influenced by the best-known form of that layout, in the town-houses of Pompeii and Herculaneum.[48] But there was no need for grand forecourts in the small towns of Campania.[49] For the capital, that paradigm is fundamentally misleading.

---

39 Varro *De lingua Latina* 7.81 (on Ballio at Plautus *Pseudolus* 953–5, *qui exit in uestibulum*); Statius *Siluae* 4.4.41–2 (*uestibulo . . . rogant exire clientes*).
40 *Aditus*: Cicero *Pro Caecina* 35, *Pro Milone* 75, *Orator* 50; Vitruvius 1.2.6, Paulus in *Digest* 10.3.19.1.
41 Paulus in *Digest* 10.3.19.1; cf. Cicero *Pro Milone* 75 (Clodius building a wall across his sister's *uestibulum*).
42 E.g. Cicero *Ad Atticum* 4.3.5, *De oratore* 1.200, Vitruvius 6.5.1–2, Seneca *Epistles* 84.12, *Consolatio ad Marciam* 10.1 (*exclusorum clientium turba referta uestibula*), Statius *Siluae* 4.4.41–2, Suetonius *Gaius* 22.2, Aulus Gellius 16.5.8–10 (*priusquam admitterentur*), Nonius 75L (*dum introeundi daretur copia*).
43 Seneca *Epistles* 84.12: *illa tumultuosa rixa salutantium limina*.
44 *De uiris illustribus* 20.1: *fasces lictorios foribus appositos*.
45 Plautus *Mostellaria* 817 (*ambulacrum*), Pliny *Nat. Hist.* 35.7 (*foris et circa limina . . . imagines*), Virgil *Aeneid* 7.177–86 (statues and *spolia*). The Ionic colonnade behind the shrine of Vesta on the 'Sorrento base' may represent the *uestibulum* of Augustus' house (Wiseman 1991.107–9).
46 Cicero *Philippics* 2.68; Suetonius *Nero* 31.1 (the Hadrianic temple of Venus and Rome probably represents the area of Nero's planned *uestibulum*).
47 Catullus 64.285–93 (wedding presents from a river god).
48 Marquadt 1886.213–50; McKay 1975.32–63.
49 Cf. Vitruvius 6.5.1 on those who don't need *uestibula*. For the few Pompeian exceptions, see Leach 1993.

4. Tanaquil at the window.

After the attack on Tarquinius, Tanaquil closes the palace doors to conceal the king's death and contrive the succession of Servius Tullius. The crowd outside is noisy and anxious:

> cum clamor impetusque multitudinis uix sustineri posset, ex superiore parte aedium per fenestras in nouam uiam uersas—habitabat enim rex ad Iouis Statoris—populum Tanaquil adloquitur.

> When the shouting and pushing of the crowd could hardly be withstood, Tanaquil went up into the upper storey of the house, and through a window looking out upon the Nova Via—for the king lived near the temple of Jupiter Stator—addressed the populace.[50]

The topographical reference was no doubt self-explanatory to Livy's readers, but for us the position of the Jupiter Stator temple and the course of the Nova Via are very controversial questions.[51]

In 1990 Carandini's line for the Nova Via was that argued by Filippo Coarelli in 1983 [fig. 50, p. 277]; it corresponds to the orientation of the archaic *atrium Vestae*, behind which Giacomo Boni had found traces of early paving.[52] There are difficulties with Coarelli's hypothesis (as there are with all attempts to reconstruct this most elusive of ancient Roman streets), but it does have the merit of fitting coherently into a comprehensive interpretation of all the relevant literary and archaeological evidence. In Carandini's 2004 version, however [fig. 51, p. 277], all coherence has been abandoned.[53]

The paving found by Boni is now an 'internal street' inside the Vesta sanctuary, leading nowhere and apparently closed at both ends.[54] Four different pre-imperial Novae Viae are now identified: the first two, for which there is no archaeological evidence, are hypothesised as running outside the respective eighth- and seventh-century BC archaic walls;[55] the third, on a totally different line and dated to the mid-sixth century, is inferred from paving and the

---

50 Livy 1.41.4 (Loeb translation).
51 See Coarelli 1983.26–33, 227–55; *contra* Ziolkowski 1989.231–6. For a new examination of the ancient evidence, see Wiseman 2004b on the Nova Via and Ziolkowski 2004 (esp. 8–19, 32–8, 46–50, 58–64) on the Jupiter Stator temple. I remain unconvinced by Ziolkowski's argument that the temple was close to the Arch of Titus, for three reasons: according to Appian (*Civil Wars* 2.11) it was close to the Forum; according to pseudo-Cicero (*Antequam in exsilium iret* 24) it was at the foot of the Palatine; and according to Plutarch (*Cicero* 16.3) it was 'at the beginning of the Sacra Via as you go up to the Palatine'.
52 Carandini 1990.97, fig. 4.2; Carandini and Carafa 1995.262–3; Coarelli 1983.227–30 (*contra* Ziolkowski 2004.43–6).
53 Carandini 2004.38–41, 87–92 (figs 3–9).
54 Carandini 2004.39, 'percorso di servizio e chiuso'.
55 Carandini 2004.39 ('Del percorso alto-arcaico della *Nova Via* non vi è traccia'), 88 (fig. 4); cf. Carandini 1997.ill.xvii–xix and xxx.

remains of a gate found in the second phase of the excavations;[56] the fourth, evidently late-republican and on a different line again (coming out above the Arch of Titus) is that identified by R. Santangeli Valenzani and R. Volpe in 1986.[57] It is the third of these, misleadingly described as only a slight adjustment of the Coarelli hypothesis,[58] which concerns us here.

Coarelli's Nova Via is outside the archaic city gate, as its name (*uia*, not *uicus*) clearly requires; and it is below the grove of Vesta, as Cicero explicitly states.[59] Carandini's Nova Via is *inside* the gate and *above* the grove.[60] The house of Tarquinius Priscus was 'above [or beyond] the top of the Nova Via',[61] but Carandini has the 'top of the Nova Via' sloping *down* towards it.[62] These difficulties are not mentioned, and it is clear that for Carandini they simply don't count in comparison with the scenario his mental cinema projects. For that, we must take the Tanaquil scene in conjunction with another story about the window.

5. *The goddess and the king.*

In the thirty-sixth of his *Roman Questions*, Plutarch asks: 'Why do they call one of the gates the Window ... and why is the so-called Chamber of Fortune beside it?' He gives two possible answers:[63]

πότερον ὅτι Σέρβιος ὁ βασιλεὺς εὐτυχέστατος γενόμενος δόξαν ἔσχε τῇ Τύχῃ συνεῖναι φοιτώσῃ διὰ θυπίδος πρὸς αὐτόν; ἢ τοῦτο μὲν μῦθός ἐστιν, ἐπεὶ δὲ Ταρκυνίου Πρίσκου τοῦ βασιλέως ἀποθανόντος ἡ γυνὴ Τανακυλλὶς ἔμφρων οὖσα καὶ βασιλικὴ διὰ θυρίδος προκύψασα τοῖς πολίταις ἐνέτυχε καὶ συνέπεισεν ἀποδεῖξαι βασιλέα τὸν Σέρβιον, ἔσχε ταύτην ὁ τόπος τὴν ἐπωνυμίαν;

Is it because King Servius, the luckiest of mortals, was reputed to have intercourse with Fortuna, who visited him through a window? Or is this but a fable, and is the true reason that when King Tarquinius Priscus died, his wife Tanaquil, a sensible and a queenly woman, put her head out of a window and, addressing the citizens, persuaded them to appoint Servius king, and thus the place came to have this name?

---

56 Carandini 2004.46–7, 92–3 (fig. 8 and 9c); cf. Carandini 1997.ill.xx–xxi and xxxii.

57 Carandini 2004.92, fig. 8; Santangeli Valenziani and Volpe 1996.348.

58 Carandini 2004.24, 38, 46 ('la ricostruzione di Coarelli e nostra'); Coarelli's Nova Via 'va ricostruita invece leggermente più a monte' (38).

59 Cicero *De diuinatione* 1.101: *. . . a luco Vestae, qui a Palati radice in nouam uiam deuexus est.*

60 Carandini 2004.36 ('retrostante il lucus Vestae'), 89 (fig. 5).

61 Solinus 1.24: *supra summam nouam uiam.* Though *supra* can sometimes mean 'beyond' (Wiseman 2004b.170), it would be hard to understand it as 'beyond and *below*'.

62 *Summa noua via* at Carandini 1997.ill.xx and xxxii; Carandini 2004.89 (fig. 5), 93 (fig. 9c).

63 Plutarch *Moralia* 273b–c; I have slightly adapted the Loeb translation, which renders συνεῖναι as 'have converse with'. Plutarch uses the same verb elsewhere of Servius and Fortuna (see next note).

Ovid and Plutarch (in another passage) tell us that the gate was called Porta Fenestella, 'Littlewindow Gate', after the goddess' amorous visits.[64]

Since we know from Solinus that Tarquinius Priscus lived by the Porta Mugonia, it is an easy conjecture that that gate was also known as Porta Fenestella because it was next to a little window in the upper floor of an adjoining house.[65] Now, the second phase of Carandini's excavations has revealed the remains of a sixth-century gate in *opus quadratum*, which can be reconstructed as abutting on to the very house he identifies as that of Tarquinius Priscus [figs 52–3, p. 278 above].[66]

The resulting scenario requires extended quotation (the translation and the footnotes are mine):[67]

> The piers of the archaic Porta Mugonia consist of two chambers (in one of which were found sacrificial remains of the fifth century); that implies the possibility of access to these rooms, of ascent to the attic of the arch, and of its illumination by windows.[68] In particular, the western pier abutted on to the perimeter wall of the *domus Regia*, which probably predated it. In this abutment an opening could have been arranged into the fabric of the house, through which the upper storey of the gate, equipped with one or more windows (over the passage or at the sides?), could have been put in direct communication with the upper floor of the royal residence. We could then imagine Fortuna entering at night by the *fenestella* of the gate, getting into the house of Servius by an opening and a passage or corridor, and 'coming down' to the ground floor.[69] By taking an identical route in the opposite direction, Tanaquil could have appeared at that same window of the house-gate,[70] to calm the crowd that filled the Nova Via[71] and put before the people Servius Tullius' succession to the throne of Tarquinius (who was dead, but supposedly only wounded).

---

64 Ovid *Fasti* 6.577–8 (*nocte domum parua solita est intrare fenestra;* | *unde Fenestellae nomina porta tenet*); Plutarch *Moralia* 322f (ὥστε καὶ συνεῖναι δοκεῖν αὐτῷ τὴν Τύχην διά τινος θυρίδος καταβαίνουσαν εἰς τὸ δωμάτιον, ἣν νῦν Φενέστελλαν πύλην καλοῦσιν).

65 Solinus 1.24 (n. 12 above); Wiseman 1998.28–9.

66 Carandini 2004.68 (attributed to Servius Tullius), 93 (fig. 9c). Argument must of course remain provisional until the full excavation report is published.

67 Carandini 2004.68–9.

68 Carandini cites Trajan's Column (see for instance Lepper and Frere 1988 plates vi, xxxv, lxxiii) for 'numerosissime porte urbiche con finestrella o finestrelle soprastanti'. But if the window of a guardroom above was so regular a feature of city gates, why should it have given its name to just this one?

69 See Plutarch *Moralia* 322f (n. 64 above) for Fortuna 'coming down' (from heaven) into the house—not, of course, coming downstairs once she was inside.

70 An evasive phrase. Contrast Carandini 2004.60 on Tanaquil at the window of the *house*, which is what Livy says.

71 Cf. Carandini 2004.60 and 61, insisting that the windows at the *back* of the house ('le finestre del retro') opened on to the Nova Via. Why was the crowd there, and not at the front door?

If Fortuna's window of entry is the same as that at which Tanaquil appeared, she must have been on the second floor, as Livy states. She is said to 'come down'—we may imagine to the ground floor, where the royal bed was in the *tablinum* (so it is not a question of a simple bedroom on the second floor).[72] The king dies in his own bed; a new sovereign takes power, is proclaimed king from the *Regia/Porta Mugonia/Fenestella*,[73] and is thus legitimated as sovereign by a 'divine marriage' which takes place in that same bed: as it were, a death followed by fertilisation and resurrection—on the model of the dying god.[74]

Now it becomes clear why Carandini's hypothetical plan of the house of the Tarquins was based so closely on that of the later 'domus 3', even down to the mysterious corridor, and why the only change in the layout was to put the chamber of the *mater familias* (what he calls the *gineceo*) on the other side.[75] But it doesn't work: in the reconstruction of 'domus 3', the corridor is on the ground floor only.[76]

Let's remind ourselves of what the sources actually say. Tanaquil spoke to the crowd from a window of the house, not from a gate; and far from announcing a new king (for Servius' succession was by no means guaranteed), she was at pains to conceal the death of the old one.[77] Fortuna came through a window into the house, not a gate; and far from celebrating a sacred marriage in the public part of the house, she was pursuing a shameful affair in a private chamber.[78]

6. The eagle and snake portents.

Servius' successor (and murderer) Tarquinius Superbus was warned by various portents that his reign was in danger. Dionysius reports that a pair of eagles built their nest in a tall palm tree that stood in 'the garden next to the palace', but were driven out by a flock of vultures.[79] Livy tells us that a huge snake

---

72 See n. 69 above. But Carandini insists (2004.67 n. 265): 'Il *cubiculum* non doveva trovarsi dietro la finestrella al secondo piano della casa', visto che la Fortuna vi deve "scendere".'
73 See n. 70 above: *Regia/porta* ('palace-gate') is another evasive phrase.
74 Cf. Carandini 2004.66–7 on the Athenian ἱερὸς γάμος between Dionysus and the wife of the *archon basileus*: 'Non vi è dunque impedimento a mettere in scena il mito erotico e intronizzante di Fortuna a di Servio nel talamo di una dimora regale...'
75 See above, pp. 278–80.
76 Carandini 1995.60 and 62, fig. 57 and 60; so too in the 'house of the Tarquins' (Carandini 2004.93, fig. 9b).
77 Livy 1.41.4 (p. 285 above), 41.5 (*iubet bono animo esse ... regem ... iam ad se redisse*, etc.).
78 Ovid *Fasti* 6.573 (*furtiuos amores*), 579 (*nunc pudet*); Plutarch *Moralia* 273b (θάλαμος), 322f (εἰς τὸ δωμάτιον).
79 Dionysius of Halicarnassus 4.63.1 (τὸν παρακείμενον τοῖς βασιλείοις κῆπον); see below, p. 295.

appeared out of a wooden column and drove those present 'into the palace' in terror.[80] A combination of the two accounts would imply a garden with a portico, perhaps the same portico that featured in Dionysius' version of the miraculous fire round young Servius' head. As we noted on item 2 above, there seems to be no room for that in Carandini's reconstruction.

7. The girl on a horse.

The elder Pliny begins his account of Roman equestrian statues with that of Cloelia, the girl who led the escape of the Roman hostages from Porsenna's camp in the second year of the Republic.[81] According to Livy, the statue of Cloelia on a horse was 'at the top of the Sacra Via'.[82] Pliny's account continues as follows:

> *hanc primam cum Coclitis publice dicatam crediderim . . . nisi Cloeliae quoque Piso traderet ab iis positam qui una opsides fuissent, redditis a Porsenna in honorem eius. e diuerso Annius Fetialis equestrem quae fuerit contra Iouis Statoris aedem in uestibulo Superbi domus Valeriae fuisse Publicolae consulis filiae.*

> I should have held the view that her statue and that of [Horatius] Cocles were the first erected at public expense . . . were it not for the statement of Piso that the statue of Cloelia also was erected by the persons who had been hostages with her, when they were given back by Porsenna, as a mark of honour to her; whereas on the other hand Annius Fetialis states that the equestrian [statue] which stood opposite the temple of Jupiter Stator in the forecourt [*uestibulum*] was of Valeria, daughter of Publicola the consul.[83]

Since Plutarch reports that some said the statue on the Sacra Via was not Cloelia but Valeria, it is clear that Annius Fetialis was not referring to a different statue;[84] there was only one 'girl on a horse', and authors differed over who she was.

What matters for our purposes is that Annius Fetialis said the statue was in the *uestibulum* of the house of the Tarquins. For Carandini, that means it was

---

80 Livy 1.56.4: *anguis ex columna lignea elapsus cum terrorem fugamque in regiam fecisset.*

81 Pliny *Nat. Hist.* 34.28; see above, pp. 180–1, on the Cloelia story.

82 Livy 2.13.11 (*in summa sacra uia fuit posita uirgo insidens equo*); cf. Dionysius of Halicarnassus 5.35.2 (ἐπὶ τῆς ἱερᾶς ὁδοῦ), Seneca *Consolatio ad Marciam* 16.2 (*in sacra uia celeberrimo loco*), Plutarch *Publicola* 19.5 (ἀνάκειται δὲ τὴν ἱερὰν ὁδὸν πορευομένοις εἰς Παλάτιον), Plutarch *Moralia* 250F (ἐπὶ τῆς ὁδοῦ τῆς ἱερᾶς λεγομένης), Servius on *Aeneid* 8.646 (*in sacra uia*).

83 Pliny *Nat. Hist.* 34.29. I have slightly adapted the Loeb translation, which renders *equestrem quae fuerit contra. . .* as 'an equestrian figure which once stood opposite. . .' (there is no 'once' in the Latin).

84 Plutarch *Publicola* 19.5, *Moralia* 250f. Ziolkowski 2004.11–12 argues for two different statues; rightly rejected by Carandini 2004.61 ('quasi che di statue equestri femminili potesse pullulare la città agli esordi della Repubblica').

inside the house[85]—but in that case how could Annius identify it as 'opposite the temple of Jupiter Stator'? Ignoring that, Carandini makes it part of the royal family's domestic cult. He thinks it was really the statue of a goddess; at first she is identified as Venus Equestris (mentioned very briefly by Servius), and then, without argument, she becomes Fortuna Equestris, a wholly unattested figure supposedly associated with the Fortuna who 'ensnared' Servius Tullius.[86] Naturally her statue stood in one part of the *atrium*, facing the 'shrine-room' of Fortuna in the other.[87]

All of that might be possible if the *uestibulum* were a room inside the house; but as we saw on item 3 above, it is not. An alternative hypothesis is worth considering, that the statue of the girl on a horse stood in a forecourt open to the Sacra Via—which is what our evidence tells us.[88]

IV

Methodologically, it is important to distinguish three separate questions:

1. What was a sixth-century Roman king's house really like?
2. What was it believed to be like when these stories were first created?
3. What was it believed to be like when our surviving sources were writing?

Carandini normally assumes the identity of the first two questions—and it is indeed possible (though not of course the only possibility) that the stories themselves dated back to the sixth century BC. And although he is always prepared, where his argument requires it, to posit errors or misunderstandings in our literary evidence, more usually he assumes the essential identity of the second and third questions too.

His basic premise was made clear in *La nascita di Roma*: 'Oral tradition, gathered and handed down in the texts, is often the only living memory that reaches us from within that distant past.'[89] As with the first two questions, it is indeed *possible* for later written texts to transmit authentic information about a much earlier world (this book could hardly have been written otherwise); but

---

85 Carandini 2004.61 ('nella stessa dimora regia'), 93 (fig. 9c).

86 Carandini 2004.22 ('Afrodite Ippia'), 60 ('una *Potnia Hippon* o *Venus Equestris*'), 61 ('una *Fortuna/Venus Equestris*'), 65 and 75 ('*Fortuna Equestris*'). 'Ensnared' is Carandini's interpretation of the cult of Fortuna Viscata on the Palatine (Plutarch *Moralia* 281E and 322F, Carandini 2004.63).

87 Carandini 2004.65; cf. 69 ('*tablinum/sacrarium*'), 75 ('sacrario/talamo').

88 Open to the street: pp. 283–4 above. Sacra Via: n. 82 above.

89 Carandini 1997.37 (in the context of 'residui delle più antiche memorie … quando sono stati fissati per iscritto'): 'La tradizione orale, raccolta e tramandata nei testi, è spesso l'unica vivente memoria che ci giunge dell'interno di quell lontano passato.'

it is very far from automatic. In particular, when we are dealing not with antiquarian scholarship but with poets' and historians' narratives, there is little likelihood of details being transmitted which were inconsistent with what their readers took for granted. When Livy says that Tanaquil spoke to the crowd in the Nova Via, 'for the king lived next to the Jupiter Stator temple', he is not handing down a living memory, but appealing to his readers' knowledge of the city in their own time.

Of course neither Livy nor Dionysius nor Ovid nor Pliny nor Plutarch had any idea of what 'the house of the Tarquins' was like in its sixth- or even fifth-century form. And it is not likely that their sources knew, either.[90] According to Carandini, the house was destroyed in the fire of 210 BC, and splendidly rebuilt some time after that.[91] The new building in turn was evidently destroyed under Augustus, but it may have helped to form the image of the king's palace in the minds of the authors on whom our literary tradition depended.

The palace that they imagined had a colonnade (item 2 above), which perhaps surrounded a garden (item 6); it had at least one window that opened on to the Nova Via (item 4), evidently next to the ancient Palatine gate (item 5); and it had a substantial forecourt (item 3), which opened on to the Sacra Via (item 7).

How many of those features belonged to the house as it was in the second and first centuries BC? One obvious possibility is the forecourt (*uestibulum*), so conspicuous a feature of the great houses of the late Republic.[92] The king's forecourt was opposite the temple of Jupiter Stator,[93] and in the story of the assassins it was where his attendants were waiting;[94] so it may be significant that in the second century AD the college of lictors had its own cult of Jupiter Stator, attested by dedication inscriptions evidently found near this very site.[95]

However, we must be careful not to assume too easy a continuity. There were several major fires in this area under Augustus, one of which destroyed the statue of Cloelia 'and the houses nearby'.[96] Such fires may have resulted in substantial changes to the urban landscape (Ovid, for instance, mentions a new

---

90 There may be one exception, if Dionysius of Halicarnassus 4.63.1 (on the eagles in Tarquin's garden) came from an early Greek source: see below, pp. 295–6.

91 Carandini 2004.46 (cf. 59, 69, 73, 'late-republican'): 'splendidamente riedificata in opera cementizia un certo tempo dopo l'incendio del 210 a.C., dotata questa volta di un cripto-portico (segno evidente di un edificio pubblico) sottostante un grande atrio con mosaico a tessere nere.'

92 See p. 284 above.

93 Pliny *Nat. Hist.* 34.29: *contra Iouis Statoris aedem.*

94 Livy 1.39.5 (*omnes apparitores regios*), cf. 39.6 and 41.1 (lictors); see n. 44 above.

95 *CIL* 6.435, 31295a; Coarelli 1983.32–3.

96 Fires: Dio Cassius 54.24.2 (14 BC), 55.8.5–6 (7 BC), 55.26.4 (AD 6); Augustus *Res gestae* 20.3 (undated). Statue: Dionysius of Halicarnassus 5.35.2 (ἐλέγετο δ' ἐμπρήσεως περὶ τὰς πλησίον οἰκίας γενομένης ἠφασίσθαι).

way through from the Nova Via to the Forum), and that no doubt accounts for Carandini's discovery of a warehouse of Augustan date on the site of the house of the Tarquins.[97] But we know that Cloelia's statue was replaced: Seneca mentions it as shaming the effeminate young men of his time, in about AD 40.[98] Then came the great fire of AD 64, which destroyed the temple of Jupiter Stator, along with most of the centre of the city. The replacement statue must have been lost as well, since Pliny in the 70s AD refers to it in the past tense.[99]

After Nero's fire the urban landscape was altered even more drastically, with the Sacra Via straightened into a formal approach to the *uestibulum* of the Golden House with its colossal statue of Nero.[100] It's hard to imagine any rival *uestibulum* being allowed to remain. The temple of Jupiter Stator was rebuilt,[101] but the lictors' dedications to the god can no longer have been in the historically significant context of the king's forecourt opposite the temple. And if the 'girl on a horse' statue was replaced again, as it probably was,[102] its new setting on the Sacra Via can hardly have suggested any connection with the house of the Tarquins.

Andrea Carandini believes that the continuous reconstruction of archaic features of the urban landscape represents a continuity of memory that could last for seven centuries or more.[103] In my opinion that is just wishful thinking. Of course the statue meant that the Roman People still remembered Cloelia (or was it Valeria?), but it was not 'the living memory of oral tradition'. When Annaeus Florus in the second century AD told the story of Porsenna's siege of Rome, he referred to Horatius, Mucius and Cloelia as 'those three prodigies and marvels of the Roman name . . . who today would seem mythical if they were not in the history books.'[104]

The unique importance of excavation as the source of new evidence for early Rome puts a particular responsibility on archaeologists. When the full excavation report on 'the house of the Tarquins' is published in due course, it will be interesting to see what the mute stones can be made to tell us.

---

97 Ovid *Fasti* 6.396: *qua noua Romano nunc uia iuncta foro est*. Warehouse: n. 19 above.
98 Seneca *Consolatio ad Marciam* 16.2 (for the date see Griffin 1976.396–7).
99 Pliny *Nat. Hist.* 34.29 (*quae fuerit*). Temple destroyed: Tacitus *Annals* 15.41.1.
100 Coarelli 1999.227 ('aspetto rettilineo e monumentale'). Colossus: Martial 1.70.5–9, *De spectaculis* 2.1–4; Suetonius *Nero* 31.1 (*uestibulum*), Dio Cassius 66.15.1 (ἐν τῇ ἱερᾷ ὁδῷ).
101 It is listed in the fourth-century 'Regionary catalogues' (Coarelli 1983.28).
102 Servius on *Aeneid* 8.646: *statua equestris quam in sacra uia hodieque conspicimus* (or was Servius just reproducing what his source said?).
103 Carandini 1997.519, 633 and 2000.89, on the 'Romulean' Palatine walls.
104 Florus 1.10.3: *qui nisi in annalibus forent hodie fabulae uiderentur*.

CHAPTER SEVENTEEN

The Legend of Lucius Brutus

I   Introduction

In the construction of Roman identity, the legend of L. Iunius Brutus has a significance rivalled only by that of Romulus himself. After the foundation of the city, what could be more important in the collective memory than the means by which freedom and constitutional government were attained? The legends of Brutus and Romulus are similar in this respect also, that the narratives of them in the sources that survive to our time are patently an amalgam of many different versions, dating from many different chronological contexts.[1] This chapter is an attempt to work out a possible 'stratigraphy' of the various versions of the Brutus legend.

I begin from the assumption, justified by a splendid recent article by Fausto Zevi,[2] that the story of L. Tarquinius 'Superbus'—his wealth, his Corinthian ancestry, his rule in Rome, his expulsion from the city, his alliance in exile with Aristodemus of Cumae, and his bequest to Aristodemus of the wealth which the Romans had confiscated—is guaranteed as essentially historical by the existence of an early and well-informed Greek historical source on the career of Aristodemus,[3] which will have narrated that material long before the Roman historiographical tradition began.

However, there is no reason to suppose that the unknown Greek historian took any interest in the internal history of Rome.[4] For him, it would be enough just to say that 'the Romans overthrew Tarquinius'; no doubt he identified the context as Tarquinius' absence at the siege of Ardea, but we cannot assume that he cared about the particular motives of the man or men who led the revolution. The stories about Brutus, Lucretia, Collatinus, Publius Valerius and the rest come from the Roman tradition, the modalities of which, before

---

1   I have tried to sort out some of the different strata in the Romulus story in Wiseman 1983 and 1995.
2   Zevi 1995.
3   For the 'Cronaca Cumana', source of Dionysius of Halicarnassus' narrative at 7.3–11, the best treatment is still that of Alföldi 1965.56–72.
4   On this fundamental point I differ from Mastrocinque 1988.35, 105, 235.

the beginning of Roman historiography about 200 BC, are notoriously obscure and controversial.[5]

A very recent treatment of Lucius Brutus calls him simply 'a fictitious revolutionary hero'.[6] Essentially, I think, that judgement is undeniable: by the time the Roman historiographical tradition took shape, the record of the real events of the expulsion of the Tarquinii must have been distorted and romanticised beyond recognition. If there was indeed a real Lucius Brutus in 507 BC (as we know there was a real Poplios Valesios), the relationship between what he really did and what Fabius Pictor attributed to him, after ten generations of oral recycling and elaboration, is analogous to the relationship between the 'real' Agamemnon of the Bronze Age, or the 'real' King Arthur of the fifth century AD, and the characters who bear those names in Homer and Geoffrey of Monmouth.

But that is not to say that the traditions that have come down to us are worthless. On the contrary, they are of very great interest, and it may even be possible to extract some historical inferences from them. And the first thing to notice is the ubiquity of portents, prophecies and oracles.

II   Warnings for the King

The earliest surviving version of the story comes in a passage from Accius' play *Brutus*, quoted in Cicero's *De diuinatione*.[7] Tarquinius dreams of a wonderful flock of sheep; two brother rams are selected for him, and he sacrifices the more splendid of the two. Then the other one attacks him, and he falls down 'gravely wounded'. As he lies on the ground, he sees the sun travelling in a new course towards the right (*dextrorsum*).

The flock must be the Roman people; since rams are the leaders of the flock,[8] the sacrifice must represent Tarquinius' policy of getting rid of dangerously prominent citizens; the attack by the surviving brother of course refers to Brutus.[9] This is how the king's prophets interpret the dream in Accius' play:

> *proin uide ne quem tu esse hebetem deputes aeque ac pecus,*
> *is sapientia munitum pectus egregie gerat*
> *teque regno expellat; nam id quod de sole ostentum est tibi,*

---

5   See for instance Cornell 1986; Ungern-Sternberg 1986; Ungern-Sternberg 1988; Timpe 1988; Wiseman 1994.1–22; Gabba 2000.11–23; Poucet 2000.27–75.

6   Welwei 2000.48–57.

7   Cicero *De diuinatione* 1.44–5 (Accius *Brutus* 651–72 Dangel = 17–38R). For detailed analysis see Mastrocinque 1983.

8   So Artemidorus *Oneirocritica* 2.12, with a play on κριός and κρείων.

9   For the murder of Brutus' elder brother (and his father), see Dionysius of Halicarnassus 4.68.1–2, Zonaras 7.11 (both of whom also report the murder of his father), Livy 1.56.7, *De uir. ill.* 10.1.

populo commutationem rerum portendit fore
perpropinquam. haec bene uerruncent populo! nam quod ad dexteram
cepit cursum ab laeua signum praepotens, pulcherrume
auguratum est rem Romanam publicam summam fore.

'Be careful, in case the man you think stupid like a sheep should have a heart well fortified with wisdom, and drive you from your kingdom. For your portent of the sun means that the people's affairs will be changed, and very soon. May these signs turn out well for the people! For because the mighty star took its course to the right, the fairest augury has been given, that the Roman state will be supreme.'

A warning for Tarquinius may be good news for Rome. And the details work exactly, as they should: the ram makes Tarquinius fall (from power); he is not killed, but badly hurt (exiled and impoverished).

In the historical tradition, the king receives different warnings. One of them is reported by Dionysius:[10]

... προθεσπίσαντος αὐτῷ τοῦ δαιμονίου τὴν μέλλουσαν γενήσεσθαι περὶ τὸν οἶκον συμφορὰν πολλοῖς μὲν καὶ ἄλλοις οἰωνοῖς, τελευταίῳ δὲ τῷδε. αἰετοὶ συνιόντες εἰς τὸν παρακείμενον τοῖς βασιλείοις κῆπον ἔαρος ὥρᾳ νεοττιὰν ἔπλαττον ἐπὶ κορυφῇ φοίνικος ὑψηλοῦ. τούτων δὲ τῶν αἰετῶν ἀπτῆνας ἔτι τοὺς νεοττοὺς ἐχόντων γῦπες ἀθρόοι προσπετασθέντες τήν τε νεοττιὰν διεφόρησαν καὶ τοὺς νεοττοὺς ἀπέκτειναν καὶ τοὺς αἰετοὺς προσιόντας ἀπὸ τῆς νομῆς ἀμύττοντές τε καὶ παίοντες τοῖς ταρσοῖς ἀπὸ τοῦ φοίνικος ἀπήλασαν.

The divine power had forewarned him of the future disaster to his house by many signs, and particularly this final one. A pair of eagles came in the spring to the garden by the palace and built their nest at the top of a tall palm tree. While the young of these eagles were still unfledged, a flock of vultures flew to the nest and destroyed it, killing the young birds. When the eagles returned from hunting, the vultures drove them from the palm tree, tearing them and beating them with their wings.

If we assume, as I think we must, that here too the details of the prophecy accurately foretell what is to come, then the conclusion is inevitable that this omen story was created for a narrative quite different from the one all our surviving sources take for granted. The eagles must be the king and his queen; the vultures must be the Romans. But in this story the eagles' young are still helpless chicks, and the vultures kill them.

---

10 Dionysius of Halicarnassus 4.63.1–2; also in Zonaras 7.11.

That is quite inconsistent with the developed story of the Tarquin clan, in which Sextus, Arruns and Titus are adult warriors who share their father's exile and live to fight again.[11] It must be a remnant from an older and simpler tradition, in which the tyrant was a comparatively young man, with young children who were killed in the uprising. It may even come from the putative early Greek source; certainly the total absence of any allusion to Brutus or to the Romans' reasons for expelling the king, coupled with the uncomplimentary symbolism of the vultures (scavengers and carrion-eaters),[12] strongly suggests a non-Roman origin for the story.

Livy reports another *portentum terribile*: a snake appeared out of a wooden column and caused terror and panic. Zonaras adds that the king was dining with friends, and the huge snake 'drove him and his guests out'.[13] Since Livy refers to *fuga in regiam*, I think we must imagine the scene as the same 'garden by the palace' referred to by Dionysius in the story about the eagles, and the wooden column as part of a peristyle. Out of the apparently lifeless wood there suddenly appears a fierce and threatening force that drives the king out of his garden. The allusion to Brutus is clear enough; but why is it the king and his friends who are driven out, rather than the king and his family? Is this omen too a remnant from an early version of the story, predating the Roman theme of *reges exacti*?

Two further portents are alluded to by the elder Pliny, as the final item in his discussion of dogs:[14]

> *Canem locutum in prodigiis, quod equidem adnotauerim, accepimus et serpentem latrasse cum pulsus est regno Tarquinius.*
>
> So far as I have noted, a dog speaking and a snake barking have been reported [only] among the prodigies when Tarquinius was expelled from his kingdom.

Evidently Pliny knew a narrative of the events which was independent of those in our surviving sources. The snake he refers to must be the same one as in Livy and Zonaras—but why did it bark like a dog? To find an answer, we must move on to the next stage in the story: perturbed by these warning signs, Tarquinius sends to Delphi to find out what the future holds.[15]

---

11 Arruns dies killing Brutus in the king's first attempt to regain power by force (Livy 2.6.6–9, Dionysius of Halicarnassus 5.15.1–2, Valerius Maximus 5.6.1, Plutarch *Publicola* 9.1–2); Sextus and Titus fall at the battle of Lake Regillus (Dionysius of Halicarnessus 6.11.1–2, 12.5), though Livy has Sextus killed by his old subjects at Gabii (1.60.2).

12 Note that Plutarch (*Romulus* 9.6–7) feels it necessary to apologise for the vultures that inaugurated the foundation of Rome; cf. Jocelyn 1971.54–7.

13 Livy 1.56.4 (*anguis ex columna lignea elapsus cum terrorem fugamque in regiam fecisset*. . .), Zonaras 7.11 (ὄφις μέγας ἐπιφανεὶς αὐτόν τε καὶ τοὺς συσσίτους ἐξέβαλε).

14 Pliny *Nat. Hist.* 8.153.

15 According to Dionysius of Halicarnassus (4.69.2), his reason for the consultation was a plague afflicting children and pregnant women; Apollo gave instructions *ut pro capitibus capitibus supplicaretur*, which Tarquinius interpreted as human sacrifice, commuted by Brutus as consul (Macrobius *Saturnalia* 1.7.34–5, on which see Mastrocinque 1988.37–41).

III   The Oracles

In Zonaras' narrative (but not in those of Livy or Dionysius), we come across the talking dog:[16]

δіά τοι ταῦτα ἐς Δελφοὺς Τίτον τε καὶ Ἀρροῦντα τοὺς υἱοὺς ἔπεμψε. τοῦ δὲ Ἀπόλλωνος χρήσαντος τότε τῆς ἀρχῆς ἐκπεσεῖσθαι αὐτὸν ὅτε κύων ἀνθρωπίνῃ φωνῇ χρήσαιτο, ἀγαθαῖς ἐλπίσιν ἠώρητο, μὴ οἰηθεὶς ποτε γενέσθαι τὸ μάντευμα.

Because of these portents he sent his sons Titus and Arruns to Delphi; but when Apollo declared that he would be driven from his realm only when a dog used human speech, he was borne up with confidence, believing that the oracle could never be fulfilled.

The explanation is clear enough. Brutus is pretending to be an idiot, unable to speak.[17] The king's sons have taken him with them to Delphi as a source of mockery and amusement; in short, they treat him like a dog.[18] When this dog speaks, Tarquinius' reign will be over.

That, I assume, is why the snake in Pliny barks: it represents Brutus himself. It lurked within the wood of the column, just as the rod of gold was hidden within the wooden staff that Brutus offered to Apollo.[19] As for the talking dog, either Pliny misinterpreted his source in making it a real portent (one of the warning signs), rather than the unsuspected fulfilment of the oracle, or else the theme was dealt with differently by different authors. For it is clear that there were many versions of the story of how the supposed idiot overthrew the king, and that the narratives in our surviving texts are a palimpsest of various elements.

Naturally, all our sources focus on the famous story of the king's sons' question about the succession, and how Apollo's answer is made to apply to Brutus himself. But what exactly was Apollo's answer? There is a revealing difference between the Latin and the Greek authorities. In Livy, the god says that whoever shall first kiss his mother will have *imperium summum* at Rome; in Valerius Maximus and in pseudo-Aurelius Victor, it is *summam potestatem*.[20] Those, of course, are phrases carefully chosen to be applicable also to the shared authority of a consul. Servius is less careful: he makes Apollo simply

---

16 Zonaras 7.11; cf. Livy 1.56.10 (*perfectis patris mandatis*), Dionysius of Halicarnassus 4.69.3 (ὡς δὲ παρεγενήθησαν ἐπὶ τὸ μαντεῖον οἱ νεανίσκοι καὶ τοὺς χρησμοὺς ἔλαβον ὑπὲρ ὧν ἐπέμφθησαν).

17 The adjective *brutus* is often used of dumb creatures: e.g. Pacuvius 176R (Nonius 109L: *et obnoxium esse aut brutum aut elinguem putes*), Seneca *Epistles* 121.24 (*tacitis quoque et brutis*).

18 Livy 1.56.9 (*ludibrium*), Dionysius of Halicarnassus 4.69.1 (ἵνα γέλωτα παρέχῃ); Dio 2.11.10, Zonaras 7.11 (ὥσπερ τι ἄθυρμα).

19 Livy 1.56.9, Dionysius of Halicarnassus 4.69.3, Valerius Maximus 7.3.2, *De uir. ill.* 10.2.

20 Livy 1.56.10, Valerius Maximus 7.3.2, *De uir. ill.* 10.3.

promise power (*imperium*), and comments that Brutus did indeed 'obtain the power', as if he were truly succeeding the king.[21] That is what the Greek sources say too (Apollo promises τὴν Ῥωμαίων ἀρχήν or τὸ κράτος),[22] and since the oracle would have been in Greek it is not unreasonable to privilege their version.

'The rule' and 'the power' are not the same as 'the kingship', which is how the oracle can apply to Brutus. But equally they do not imply a shared authority. Apollo tells Brutus that he can be the ruler, not the co-ruler, of Rome. It seems to me that this crucial element in the story must predate the institution of the consulship.

When supreme authority is shared between two men, one might expect a foundation myth to reflect that duality. I have argued elsewhere that that is the probable origin of the story of Remus and Romulus, and that what made the myth necessary was the introduction of the consulship as a power-sharing device in 367 BC.[23] Not everyone accepts that suggestion for the origin of the twins story, just as not everyone believes that the consulship was a fourth-century innovation.[24] But the normal assumption that the consulship dates right back to the origins of the Republic, and that Brutus was always imagined as sharing power with Collatinus, simply creates more trouble than it's worth.

The canonical story of the first year of the Republic, as it appears in Livy, Dionysius and Plutarch, is patently an artificial combination of rival claims to have inaugurated the Republic, and can only be made to fit the assumption of an original consulship by the most implausible succession of events—an exile, two deaths in office, and three elections of suffect consuls.[25] The identity of the 'first two consuls' as Brutus and Collatinus depends on the forced amalgamation of two originally separate stories, those of Brutus the idiot and the rape of Lucretia—for why should Brutus be present at Lucretia's suicide? In any case, some authorities claimed that the first consuls were Brutus and M. Horatius, or Brutus and P. Valerius.[26] Three hundred years of oral story-telling, followed by two hundred years of creative historiography, have produced a chaotically overcrowded narrative.

---

21 Servius on *Aeneid* 3.96: *nam Brutus et filii Tarquinii cum oraculum Delphici Apollinis peterent, responsum est eius imperium fore qui primus matrem reuersus oscularetur. quod solus Brutus agnoscens de naui egressus simulans casum osculatus est terram; unde et potitus imperio est.*

22 Respectively Dionysius of Halicarnassus 4.69.3 and Dio 2.11.12 (= Zonaras 7.11); in both narratives the king's sons assume the question is about βασιλεία.

23 Wiseman 1995.103–10.

24 I am glad to see that the latter view is shared by Welwei 2000.49–50.

25 I have tried briefly to account for the absurdities in 'Roman Republic, Year One' (pp. 306–12 below).

26 Polybius 3.22.1 (M. Horatius), Pliny *Nat. Hist.* 36.112 (P. Valerius); the first chapter of Plutarch's *Publicola* (1.3–4) seems to presuppose a rejected tradition of Valerius as the first consul.

Much of the chaos can be cleared up by the simple expedient of forgetting the consulship. Despite constant repetition to the contrary, there is no good reason to believe in an authentic consular list going back even to the fifth century, much less the sixth.[27] On the contrary, Livy gives us good evidence—which he himself was unable to exploit—that in the early Republic the chief magistrate was called *praetor maximus*, a title which surely rules out any notion of equally shared power.[28] If that office, or something like it, was what Apollo promised to Brutus, the wording of the oracle would at least make sense.

So let us assume, for the sake of argument, that the earliest form of the Romans' story of their liberation presupposed a single supreme magistracy, to which Brutus was elected—thus succeeding the king, as the oracle story requires. Let us further assume that by the second half of the fourth century BC, when the power-sharing consulship was taken for granted as the essential and inevitable magistracy of the Republic, the story was elaborated to take account of the new conditions, and a colleague was found to share office with the Liberator. No doubt various names were proposed, but we know which one eventually became canonical—that of tragic Lucretia's husband, L. Tarquinius Collatinus. I think the context of his incorporation into the story can be dated quite securely.

IV   The Man from Collatia

The rape of a virtuous lady by the king's son is a perfectly intelligible motive for the overthrow of the monarchy. But why must her husband be a Tarquinius himself? It complicates the story, and makes necessary the invention of an entire branch of the royal family which had remained miraculously untouched by both wealth and arrogance.[29] The reason is, of course, that Collatinus' name is needed to justify getting rid of him:[30]

> *consulis enim alterius, cum aliud nihil offenderet, nomen inuisum ciuitati fuit. nimium*
> *Tarquinios regno adsuesse; initium a Prisco factum; regnasse dein Ser. Tullium; ne*

---

27 See for instance Wiseman 1996.313–15, in a review of Cornell 1995. The absence of fifth-century records is attested by 'Clodius' (Claudius Quadrigarius?) in Plutarch *Numa* 1.1; he gave the wrong explanation, but the fact that he had to explain it shows that the phenomenon itself was real enough.

28 Livy 7.3.5: *Lex uetusta est, priscis litteris uerbisque scripta, ut qui praetor maximus sit idibus Septembribus clauum pangat; fixa fuit dextro lateri aedis Iouis optimi maximi, ex qua parte Mineruae templum est.* At 7.3.7 he cites *diligens talium monumentorum auctor Cincius*.

29 For Demaratus' supposed younger son 'Egerius' (from *egens*), see Livy 1.34.2–3, 1.57.6, Dionysius of Halicarnassus 3.50.3, 4.64.2–3. The Latin name (cf. Festus 128L for Manius Egerius of Aricia) is enough to show that he is a secondary element in the story.

30 Livy 2.2.3; cf. also Cicero *De oratore* 3.40 (*cum autem consilium hoc principes cepissent, cognationem Superbi nomenque Tarquiniorum et memoriam regni esse tollendam...*).

interuallo quidem facto oblitum tamquam alieni regni, Superbum Tarquinium uelut
hereditatem gentis scelere ac ui repetisse; pulso Superbo penes Collatinum imperium esse.
nescire Tarquinios priuatos uiuere; non placere nomen, periculosum libertati esse.

The citizens disliked the name of one of the consuls, even though he had done
nothing else wrong. 'The Tarquinii have got too used to royal power! Priscus
started it; then Servius Tullius reigned, but even in that interval of extraneous
rule it wasn't forgotten, and Tarquinius Superbus claimed it by crime and
violence as if it was a family inheritance. Superbus has been expelled, but now
Collatinus has power! The Tarquinii don't know how to live as private citizens.
The name is hateful, a danger to liberty.'

So Brutus' consular colleague goes into voluntary exile, to make way for P.
Valerius. The parallel with Athenian ostracism has often been noted, and
Attilio Mastrocinque has convincingly included it as one of a whole sequence
of alleged events in the Romans' story of their liberation which are evidently
based on equivalent motifs in Athenian history.[31]

One particular detail, recently pointed out by Alan Griffiths,[32] reveals that
the parallel in this case is taken not from Herodotus but from a fourth-century
Atthidographer, possibly Androtion, used by the author of the Aristotelian
Constitution of Athens:[33]

καὶ πρῶτος ὠστρακίσθη τῶν ἐκείνου συγγενῶν Ἵππαρχος Χάρμου
Κολλυτεύς, δι' ὃν καὶ μάλιστα τὸν νόμον ἔθηκεν ὁ Κλεισθένης,
ἐξελάσαι βουλόμενος αὐτόν. οἱ γὰρ Ἀθηναῖοι τοὺς τῶν τυράννων
φίλους, ὅσοι μὴ συνεξαμαρτάνοιεν ἐν ταῖς ταραχαῖς, εἴων οἰκεῖν τὴν
πόλιν, χρώμενοι τῇ εἰωθυίᾳ τοῦ δήμου πρᾳότητι· ὧν ἡγεμὼν καὶ
προστάτης ἦν Ἵππαρχος.

The first of [the tyrant's] relatives to be ostracized was Hipparchos son of
Charmos, of the Collutos deme. It was because of him in particular that Cleis-
thenes passed the law, wanting to drive him out of the city. For the Athenians,
showing the people's customary forebearance, allowed the tyrant's friends to
live in the city, with the exception of those who had been involved in his
crimes during the disturbances; of these the leader and champion was Hipparchos.

Late in the fourth century BC, at the time of the Samnite wars, the Romans
put up a statue of Alcibiades in the Comitium.[34] For the ambitious and ener-
getic city-state that dominated Latium and was now extending its control over

---

31 Mastrocinque 1988.32–5; p. 34 for Collatinus.
32 Griffiths 1998.
33 *Athenaion politeia* 22.4.
34 Pliny *Nat. Hist.* 34.26, Plutarch *Numa* 8.10: Pythian Apollo had told them to honour 'the
    bravest and the wisest of the Greeks' (they chose Pythagoras as the wisest).

all of central Italy, the history of fifth-century Athens must have been an example and an inspiration. I think Emilio Gabba was right to identify this particular period as the time when Rome's traditions about her own past were being somehow organised into the more or less coherent story that was later transmitted by Fabius Pictor and his successors;[35] and if that is the case, then the phenomenon identified by Mastrocinque, of episodes evidently constructed or elaborated on the model of Athenian history, is easily explicable.

For the particular case of the foundation-myth of the Republic, I suggest that the old story of heroic Brutus succeeding the king was reshaped to fit the now unquestioned republican model of two equal ruling magistrates. Lucretia's husband would make a fitting colleague for Brutus, but since he had no traditional role to play in the liberation story, he would have to be got rid of again (like Remus or T. Tatius). The Athenian model offered a solution. Make Lucretia's husband a relative of the tyrant; put their married home in Collatia (at whatever cost to the coherence of her story);[36] and the calque of Collutos and Collatia provides an honourable exit for Brutus' necessary but inconvenient consular colleague.

V   Iunius and the Herons

During the last quarter of the fourth century BC, one of the most prominent Roman commanders was C. Iunius Bubulcus. He is so named seven times in Livy:

9.20.7–9	Consul 317, campaigns in Apulia
9.28.2	Consul II 313
9.29.3	Dictator 312
9.30.1	Consul III 311, campaigns in Samnium (9.31)
9.38.15	Magister equitum 310, campaigns in Samnium (9.40.8–9)
9.43.25	Censor 307
10.1.8	Dictator II 302

Diodorus names him three times just as C. Iunius; but Valerius Maximus, referring to his censorship, calls him 'C. Iunius Brutus Bubulcus', and in the Capitoline consular and triumphal *fasti* he is consistently 'C. Iunius C.f.C.n. Bubulcus Brutus'.[37] Similarly, his elder relative Iunius Scaeva—so named in

---

35 Gabba 2000.20–2; cf. Wiseman 1994.14–16, suggesting dramatic performance as one of the means.

36 The morning after the rape, Lucretia must either travel to Rome herself (Dionysius of Halicarnassus 4.66.1), or else summon her menfolk from Rome and Ardea (Livy 1.58.5), thus awkwardly putting the dramatic exposure of her body and the resulting popular indignation at Collatia rather than Rome (Livy 1.59.3–5).

37 Diodorus Siculus 19.17.1, 19.77.1, 20.3.1; Valerius Maximus 2.9.2; *Fasti consulares* for 317, 313, 312, 311, 309, 307 BC (also his son at 277 BC, cf. Livy 27.6.8 'C. Iunius Bubulcus'); *Fasti triumphales* for 311 BC.

Festus as one of the *tresuiri* responsible for the colony at Saticula—appears in Livy as 'Iunius Brutus' or 'Iunius Brutus Scaeva'.[38]

The natural inference is that these distinguished plebeians, the first of their family to achieve the consulship, were originally nicknamed as 'clumsy' (*scaeuus*) and 'yokel' (*bubulcus*), insults which they or their descendants adapted to their honour by adding the name of the hero who pretended to be stupid. And if, as seems likely, the old story of Brutus the liberator was being elaborated at just this time, it may be that a *nomen gentilicium* was only now for the first time attributed to him.

L. Iunius Brutus, as we may now call him, took over the army at Ardea as soon as Tarquinius had left.[39] The end of the siege, and the subsequent truce between Ardea and Rome, are presumably real historical events. The importance of Ardea in the sixth and fifth centuries BC, and her status as an equal of Rome, can be inferred from the tradition reported by the Greek historian Xenagoras, that Rhomos, Anteias and Ardeias were brothers, the sons of Odysseus and Circe.[40] It may also account for a puzzling quotation in Festus from the fourth-century Sicilian historian Alcimus:[41]

> *Alcimus ait, Tyrrhenia Aeneae natum filium Romulum fuisse, atque eo ortam Albam Aeneae neptem, cuius filius Rhodius condiderit urbem Romam.*
>
> Alcimus says that Romulus was the son of Aeneas' wife Tyrrhenia, and from Romulus was born Aeneas' granddaughter Alba, whose son, called Rhodius, founded Rome.

Editors sometimes emend 'Rhodius' to 'Rhomus', but the principle of the *difficilior lectio* counts against that easy solution. An alternative explanation is available if we remember that *ardea* means 'heron', ἐρῳδιός or ῥῳδιός in Greek.[42] So Rhodius can be the eponym of Ardea, which evidently claimed at one time to be the mother-city of Rome.

In the tradition exploited by Virgil, Ardea is the city of Turnus' father Daunus.[43] Daunus is more familiar as the eponymous king of Daunia in northern Apulia, whose son-in-law Diomedes founded Arpi (Argyrippa) in that territory.[44]

---

38 Festus 458L; Livy 8.12.13 (*mag. eq.* 339), 8.29.2 (*cos.* 325).
39 Livy 1.60.1–2, Dionysius of Halicarnassus 5.1.2.
40 Xenagoras *FGrH* 240 F29 (Dionysius of Halicarnassus 1.72.5).
41 Alcimus *FGrH* 560 F4 (Festus 326–8L).
42 The three-syllable spelling is attested by the grammarian Herodian (2.924 Lentz), who cites an example from Hipponax (fr. 16 West). For *ardea*, see Servius on *Aeneid* 7.412: *nam Ardea quasi ardua dicta est, id est magna et nobilis, licet Hyginus in Italicis urbibus* [fr. 11P] *ab augurio auis dictum uelit. illud namque Ouidii in Metamorphoseos* [14.573–80] *fabulosum est, incensam ab Hannibale Ardeam in hanc auem esse conuersam.* (Servius misinterprets Ovid, whose *barbarus* is Aeneas, not Hannibal.)
43 Virgil *Aeneid* 10.688, 12.22; cf. 8.146, 10.616, 12.90 etc.
44 Daunos and Diomedes: Ovid *Fasti* 4.76, Antoninus Liberalis *Metamorphoses* 37. Arpi: Lycophron *Alexandra* 592, Strabo 6.3.9, Justin 22.2.10, Solinus 2.10, Servius on *Aeneid* 8.9.

But the idea of Daunii in Latium goes back at least as far as Lycophron;[45] moreover, there were traditions which brought Diomedes himself to Latium, and even made him instrumental in the foundation of Rome.[46]

A Homeric scholiast's report on the death of Diomedes includes a version which must belong somehow in this context:[47]

...ὅθεν αὐτὸν φυγόντα φασὶν ἥκειν εἰς Ἰβηρίαν κἀκεῖ, ὡς μέν τινες, δολοφονηθῆναι ὑπὸ Δαύνου τοῦ βασιλέως, ὡς δὲ ἔνιοι, ἀπολέσθαι ὑπὸ Ἰουνίου τοῦ Δαύνου παιδὸς ἐν κυνηγεσίοις· ὅθεν αὐτὸν μὲν ἀπεθέωσεν Ἀθηνᾶ, τοὺς δὲ ἑταίρους εἰς ἐρῳδιοὺς μετέβαλεν.

They say he fled from there [i.e. from Argos, where his wife and her lover had plotted to kill him] and came to Iberia, where according to some authorities he was treacherously murdered by king Daunus, and according to others he was killed by Daunus' son Iunius while out hunting. As a result Athena deified him and turned his companions into herons.

'Iberia' is clearly a mistake: this story must be about Apulian Daunia.[48] The first version of Diomedes' death, which may go back as far as Mimnermus,[49] makes Daunus a treacherous enemy. The second, however, seems to presuppose the friendly Daunus who gave Diomedes his daughter. The death in the hunt was presumably accidental, a tragedy requiring Athena's intervention. It was also a conveniently blameless way of removing Diomedes and allowing his brother-in-law Iunius to be Daunus' heir—thus justifying Roman control over Daunia, as expressed in the foundation of the colony at Luceria in 314 BC.[50] C. Iunius Bubulcus campaigned in Apulia as consul in 317, and held his second consulship in 313; he could well have been one of the *tresuiri coloniae deducendae*. In any case, his involvement in the subjection of Daunia must surely be the origin of the story of Iunius son of Daunus.

The herons, however, may be relevant to 'Daunian' Ardea. The name of the new colony reflects that of Lucerus, a legendary king of Ardea who assisted Romulus in his war against T. Tatius' Sabines; the Romulean tribe of 'Luceres'

---

45 Lycophron *Alexandra* 1253–5, on Aeneas: κτίσει δὲ χώραν ἐν τόποις Βορειγόνων | ὑπὲρ Λατίνους Δαυνίους τ' ᾠκισμένην. Cf. Polybius 3.91.5 for Daunii in Campania, and in general Briquel 1974. 8–19.

46 Diomedes in Latium: Solinus 2.14 (giving the Palladion to Aeneas), Appian *Civil Wars* 2.20 (founding Lanuvium). Diomedes sends Rhomos son of Emathion to found Rome: Plutarch *Romulus* 2.1.

47 Schol. *Iliad* 5.412 (b), Erbse 2.64–5; I owe my knowledge of this important passage to Curti 1993. For the stories of Diomedes in Italy, see Malkin 1998.234–57.

48 The hunt may be an allusion to the etymology of Canusium, another of Diomedes' foundations (Servius on *Aeneid* 11.246, cf. Horace *Satires* 1.5.91–2).

49 Cited by the scholiast on Lycophron *Alexandra* 610, though it is not clear how much of the story was in Mimnermus.

50 Livy 9.26.1–5, Diodorus Siculus 19.72.8–9. Ancient dedications in the temple of Athena at Luceria were taken as evidence for the dominion of Diomedes (Strabo 6.3.9, 284).

was supposedly named after him.[51] A likely explanation is that Ardea was involved in some way in the Roman colonisation of Daunia, and that her Daunian mythology was invented to reflect that.[52]

If so, then the presence at Ardea of Iunius Bubulcus' alleged ancestor Brutus is likely to be another feature of the elaboration of the legend in the late fourth century BC. Unlike Collatinus, however, it was an element which lost its significance in later times. Not all the levels of the palimpsest remained equally important.

VI   Conclusion

Our sources on the revolution that brought freedom to Rome date from the late second century BC (Accius) to the twelfth century AD (Zonaras), between four and seventeen centuries after the event. Close analysis of the narratives they offer enables us to identify (hypothetically, of course) some of the elements out of which they were composed, and thus some of the stages by which the story was built up over the centuries.

First, we can infer an early account (probably in a Greek historian) where the tyrant's young children were killed in the revolt. The author's sympathies were evidently with Tarquinius, the eagle driven out by vultures, and naturally there is no sign of any heroic liberator.

Second, there may have been a version where the champion of freedom did indeed appear, as a monstrous snake, but where only the king's companions shared his exile. That looks like the earliest trace of the patriotic Roman story.

The version in which the snake barked like a dog perhaps belongs to a later stage, featuring the embassy to Delphi, the king's sons and their 'idiot' companion, and Apollo's oracle about the dog that speaks. Grown-up sons imply a whole royal family to be driven from power, as implied by the later Roman date-formula *post reges exactos* (not *regem exactum*).

Whether that stage also included the sons' enquiry about the succession is not clear. But Apollo's reply on that subject clearly implies a post-expulsion regime in which Brutus alone would have power, and it therefore pre-dates what I believe to be the introduction of the consulship in 367 BC.

The creation of the consulship evidently made necessary the adjustment of the liberation story to accommodate the idea of shared power. That seems to have happened at a time when the Romans were elaborating their own history on the model of that of Athens, and the tale of Tarquinius Collatinus as Brutus' temporary colleague is best explained as a calque on the ostracism of

---

51 Festus (Paulus) 106L. Note also 'Leukaria', daughter of Latinus and mother of Rhomus (Diony-
    sius of Halicarnassus 1.72.6, cf. Plutarch *Romulus* 2.1), though she may be a calque on 'Alba'.
52 So Curti 1993: perhaps the colonists of Luceria were from Ardea?

Hipparchus of Collutos. This must be the point at which the story of the rape of Lucretia—by a third son of Tarquin evidently not involved in the question of the succession[53]—is linked to the Brutus story by the expedient of having the supposed idiot present at her suicide.

The consulship was a power-sharing device, with one patrician and one plebeian in office each year. Since Tarquinius Collatinus must have been thought of as a patrician, the expedient of retrojecting the new system to the origins of the Republic required the Liberator himself to have been in some sense a plebeian. It is clear from the nomenclature of the first consular Iunii, Scaeva and Bubulcus, that their plebeian family claimed him in the second half of the fourth century, and that ever afterwards Brutus was thought of as the ancestor of the plebeian *gens Iunia*.

Iunius Bubulcus' involvement in the conquest and settlement of Daunia evidently gave them an even earlier ancestor, Iunius the brother-in-law of Diomedes; it may also have given rise to an element in the liberation story, as Brutus takes over the Roman army at Ardea and makes peace with the tyrant's victims.

If the argument presented here is valid, it implies a fertile and creative narrative tradition existing long before the introduction of literary historiography at Rome. And I think that is what we should expect, in a pre-literary culture making sense of changing conditions over a period of two centuries. 'Oral tradition' does not 'hand down the memory of events'; it elaborates, recycles, omits, invents, creates a succession of stories for a succession of audiences with ever-changing priorities.

Moreover, the process goes on even after the introduction of written history. Historians always liked to differ from their predecessors, either with new material or by presenting a different slant on traditional narratives.[54] In the case of the Brutus story, the assassination of Caesar caused a serious reappraisal on the part of some writers. Either Marcus Brutus the tyrannicide was no true descendant of the Liberator,[55] or the reputation of Lucius Brutus himself must be rethought in more critical terms (as in Virgil's *Aeneid*, where the arrogance of Tarquinius himself is attributed to him).[56] Like the story of Remus,[57] so the story of Brutus took on a new aspect in the Rome of Augustus.

Identity, the construction of a people's idea of itself, is always changing; and myth, the memory by which that identity is established, is always changing too.

---

53 Note that in Dionysius of Halicarnassus Sextus is the eldest son, and offers to make Lucretia queen (4.55.1, 4.65.2); contrast Livy 1.53.5.
54 See for instance Wiseman 1998.75–89.
55 See Plutarch *Brutus* 1.2–3.
56 Virgil *Aeneid* 6.817–23 (*animamque superbam*, 817); cf. Dionysius of Halicarnassus 5.8.1, Plutarch *Publicola* 6.4 (ambivalent judgements of Brutus' character).
57 Cf. Wiseman 1995.144–50.

CHAPTER EIGHTEEN

Roman Republic, Year One

I

The Romans knew that they had once been ruled by kings, and they believed, perhaps rightly, that the fall of the monarchy had taken place at what we would call the end of the sixth century BC. The texts that tell us this—Livy, Dionysius, Plutarch, etc—all depend on a historical tradition that can be traced back as far as the second half of the third century BC, when the Roman literary genres of historical drama, historical epic, and prose historiography began. Before that, we do not know how the Romans conceived or recorded the memory of their own past.

There is some exiguous contemporary evidence. The word 'king' (*rex*) appears on two inscriptions found at deep levels in Giacomo Boni's excavation of the Forum in 1899–1903; both may well be of sixth-century date.[1] Another inscription—which does not survive, but was seen and copied by a Roman antiquarian in the first century BC—evidently referred to the 'chief magistrate' (*praetor maximus*) of the post-monarchic regime.[2]

Early evidence of a different kind is provided by the Roman ritual calendar, which probably dates back at least to the fifth century BC.[2a] It marks 24 February as 'Flight of the King' (*Regifugium*), the last item before the beginning of the new year on 1 March.[3] In the third century BC, and perhaps before, the newly-elected consuls entered office on 15 March. Does the sequence commemorate a real event, the flight of the king followed by the election of republican magistrates and their entry into office after a nineteen-day vacuum of power? Or was the 'event' a story to explain the sequence?

Of one thing we can be reasonably sure. Whenever, and however, the power of the king was ended, there will have been stories to account for it, foundation legends for the infant Republic.

---

1 A fragment of a bucchero bowl from the Regia, illustrated in Momigliano 1989.76, fig. 25; and the 'Lapis Niger' stele at the Volcanal (*CIL* 1² 1 = *ILLRP* 3).

2 L. Cincius, quoted in Livy 7.3.5–7 [see pp. 10–11 above].

2a [So I believed in 1998; I now think the fourth century BC is no less likely.]

3 See Ovid *Fasti* 2.685, 851; Festus (Paulus) 347L; Plutarch *Quaestiones Romanae* 63 (= *Moralia* 279d); Ausonius 7.24.13; Polemius Silvius in *CIL* 1² p. 259 = Degrassi 1963.265.

1. The Story of Lucius Junius

Lucius Junius was the youngest son of a worthy citizen foully murdered by the king's agents in the days of Tarquin the Proud. The other sons were killed too,[3a] but Lucius pretended to be an idiot, and was contemptuously spared by the assassins. He had to keep up the pretence as he grew up, and became known to all as Stupid Lucius. The king's sons, who were as arrogant as their father, used Stupid Lucius as a butt for their cruel mockery.

One day, an ominous portent was reported at the palace. The king decided to consult the oracle at Delphi, and sent his sons on the mission. They took Stupid Lucius with them for amusement on the long journey. They brought rich gifts for the god, and sneered at the simple staff of cornel-wood which was Stupid Lucius' offering—but Apollo could see, as they could not, that within the hollow wood was a rod of pure gold.

After the Pythian priestess had given them the instructions they had come for, the royal princes asked the question that was *really* on their minds. Which of them would succeed their father as king? And this was the god's reply: 'Whichever of you shall first kiss his mother, he shall have supreme authority in Rome.' They didn't notice that Stupid Lucius was in the temple too.

As the king's sons came out, each of them scheming how to get home first, Stupid Lucius tripped and fell flat on his face. As usual, they mocked his clumsiness. They didn't see that he had kissed Mother Earth.

When they returned to Rome, they found the citizens furious with indignation at Tarquin's cruelty and injustice. All that was needed was a leader. Confident of the gods' support, Lucius Junius at last threw off his disguise and led the Roman People in righteous revolt against their tyrant. Tarquin and his sons were banished from Rome for ever, and the free citizens resolved to elect a chief magistrate of their own. The choice fell naturally on Stupid Lucius Junius, as he was ever afterwards known. For the nickname that had been an insult was now a badge of pride, and his descendants use it still.

2. The Story of Lucretia

Lucretia was a beautiful and virtuous lady, daughter of Spurius Lucretius and devoted wife of Lucius Collatinus, in the days of Tarquin the Proud. Her husband was an excellent citizen; it is true he was related to the Tarquins, but he had none of their power, none of their wealth, and none of their vices. He and Lucretia loved each other and were faithful to each other; and when Collatinus had to go away to the wars, Lucretia stayed at home and prayed for his safe return.

3a [My mistake: the sources give Lucius only one brother. So he is the younger son, not the youngest.]

But Lucretia was beautiful, and Sextus, the king's son, lusted after her. Late one evening he came to his kinsman's house. Lucretia was puzzled (did he not know her husband was away?), but she received him politely and offered him the hospitality of the house, as she was in duty bound to do. That night he came to her bedroom. He offered his love, but she rejected it with horror. He demanded her obedience, but she proudly refused. He threatened her with his sword, but she was not intimidated.

'Very well,' said Sextus. 'I will take you by force and kill you afterwards. Then I will kill a slave and put his body in your bed, and I shall tell your husband and your father that I slew the adulteress and her paramour.' Then, and only then, Lucretia yielded.

Next morning Sextus rode away triumphant, and Lucretia sent urgently for Collatinus and her father. When they heard what had happened, of course they told her she was not to blame, but Lucretia would not be consoled. 'I cannot live with this shame,' she said. 'But give me vengeance!' With that, she drew a dagger from her dress, and drove it into her heart.

Horrified, Collatinus and Lucretius watched her die. In grief and anguish, remembering her last words, they laid the bloodstained body on a bier and took it in procession to the market-place. A crowd gathered, and the two men told the tragic tale. It was enough. The citizens had long been indignant at Tarquin's cruelty and injustice. Now, stirred to righteous fury at Sextus' villainy, they rose against the tyrants. Tarquin and his sons were banished from Rome for ever, and the free citizens resolved to elect a chief magistrate of their own. Who better than the husband, or the father, of brave Lucretia?

3. The Story of Publius Valerius

Publius Valerius was the best of men. He was brave and handsome and generous, and though he was rich, he used his wealth to benefit his fellow-citizens. When bad king Tarquin was banished from Rome, and the free citizens resolved to elect a chief magistrate of their own, the choice naturally fell on him.

Valerius had a fine house on the Velia, overlooking the market-place, conveniently close for consultation. But alas, there is malice even in a free republic, and his enemies whispered that it was a tyrant's castle, dominating the citizens. Valerius never listened to gossip, but his close friends warned him of the slander. One morning, as the citizens came to the market-place, they looked up to the Velia and saw the house was gone. Valerius and his friends had demolished it overnight, stone by stone and timber by timber.

When the chief magistrate, now homeless, came into the market-place that day, he ordered his lictors to lower their *fasces* in the presence of the citizen body. The Roman People was sovereign, not he. And so, in honour of his modesty, Publius Valerius was called 'The People's Friend'.

4. The Story of Marcus Horatius

Marcus Horatius was a Roman of the old school, stern, unbending and devoted to the public good. When bad king Tarquin was banished from Rome, and the free citizens resolved to elect a chief magistrate of their own, the choice naturally fell on him. And that is why you can see his name on the architrave of Jupiter's temple on the Capitol.

Everyone knows how the Capitol got its name. When they were digging the foundations of the great temple, the workmen found a human head, miraculously preserved. Even the Etruscan soothsayers had to admit that the place had been marked out by the gods to be the head of things, the centre of power. That was in the days of the first Tarquin, the father of the tyrant.

The temple was huge and magnificent, and took many years to build. The first Tarquin died, and his wicked son inherited the project. But naturally Jupiter did not want his temple dedicated by a king so hateful to gods and men alike. So he saw to it that Tarquin was banished when the temple was almost finished, and the duty of dedicating it fell to Marcus Horatius.

Now, the dedicant of a temple must be free of all connection with grief or mourning. Horatius had a son, a fine young man who was at that time on military service. Just as the dedication was under way, a tearful messenger interrupted the ceremony. 'Bad news, Marcus Horatius! There is sickness in the camp, and your son is dead.' The people groaned in horror, but Horatius thought only of his duty. 'That is nothing to me,' he said. 'Cast out the body; I will not grieve or mourn.' And so the temple was dedicated with no ill omen.

It was Horatius' nephew, another devoted patriot, who saved Rome the following year by holding the bridge against the Etruscan host of Lars Porsenna and his ally, the banished Tarquin.

II

Told like that, the stories are clearly independent, and mutually inconsistent. That is what one expects in an oral tradition, when every telling of a story is a particular occasion, to a particular audience, for a particular purpose. One imagines that part, at least, of the purpose was to honour the noble family whose ancestor was commemorated in each of these exemplary tales.

But the stories are *not* told like that in our surviving literary sources. Livy and Dionysius were dependent on a tradition of written history going back nearly two hundred years; in the case of Plutarch, it was three hundred.[4] Add

---

4   The main narrative sources for the first year of the Republic are Livy 2.1.7–8.9, Dionysius of Halicarnassus 5.1.2–19.5, and Plutarch *Publicola* 1.4–14.5. Up-to-date modern discussion in Cornell 1995, ch. 9; cf. also Drummond 1989.172–90. For a fascinating exploration of all the aspects of the Brutus legend, assuming (wrongly, in my view) its essential historicity, see Mastrocinque 1988.

to that another three centuries—more than half the entire history of the Republic—back from the origins of Roman historiography to the time of the events themselves (whatever they were), and we have to take account of half a millennium of creative story-telling.

One of the things that evidently happened during that time was that the *praetor maximus* was forgotten. The tradition takes it totally for granted that the king was replaced by consuls, two magistrates of equal authority, holding office for a year. The earliest contemporary evidence for the consulship is the sarcophagus inscription of Gnaeus Scipio Barbatus (about 260 BC);[5] but it is universally accepted that the institution dates back at least a century before that. Many modern historians even believe that the tradition is right, and that the consulship was introduced with the Republic; but they need pretty fancy footwork to explain away the evidence for the *praetor maximus*.

Once you accept the consulship as the original republican magistracy, two of the stories can at once be amalgamated: L. Brutus ('Stupid') and L. Collatinus (Lucretia's husband) can be the first two consuls. All you have to do is find a reason for Brutus to be present at Lucretia's suicide. As for Valerius, Horatius, and Lucretia's father, they can be brought in as 'suffects', replacing consuls who died in office or abdicated. And so, by the time our sources were writing, it was accepted doctrine that there had been five consuls in the first year of the Republic.

St Augustine, taking that in good faith as genuine history, naturally inferred that the Republic had begun with a chapter of disasters:[6]

> Indeed, the consuls did not complete their year of office. For Junius Brutus deposed his colleague Lucius Tarquinius Collatinus from office and expelled him from Rome; and soon afterwards Brutus himself fell in battle, after inflicting wound for wound upon his enemy [one of Tarquin's sons]. . . . Besides this, Lucretius, the substitute for Brutus in the consulship, was carried off by illness before the end of the year. And so Publius Valerius, successor to Collatinus, and Marcus Horatius, brought in to fill the place of the departed Lucretius, completed that year of mourning and misery, the year which saw five consuls, and the year in which the new Roman commonwealth solemnly inaugurated the consulship, the new office of authority.

The Roman historians, who were nothing if not patriotic, can hardly have intended that reading. That it was possible at all is eloquent testimony to a forced and factitious narrative.

What really happened cannot be known—though the evidence for burned buildings, at an archaeological level that may well correspond to the later sixth

---

5   *ILLRP* 309 [p. 6 above]; Wachter 1987.301–42.
6   Augustine *City of God* 3.16 (Penguin translation).

century BC, suggests that 'the flight of the king' was a violent episode. Archaeology has also revealed Publius Valerius as a historical character: at about the right date, 'the companions of Poplios Valesios' made a dedication to Mars at Satricum, a Latin town some forty miles south of Rome.[7] But that local warlord seems to have little in common with the democratic constitutionalist of the Roman story.

The trouble with archaeological discoveries is that they encourage the Schliemann fallacy: find the site of Troy, and you've proved the *Iliad* is true. Even the best modern historians sometimes succumb to this temptation.

The study of early Rome has been put on a wholly new footing by Tim Cornell's brilliant synthesis *The Beginnings of Rome* (1995). Cornell has no illusions about the tradition on the birth of the Republic: 'it has the appearance of a historical romance, and forms a self-contained saga of connected stories.' But, he goes on,

> there is no reason in principle why the tradition should not be a romanticized version of events that really happened. It is arbitrary to dismiss the rape of Lucretia (for instance) as fiction, when we have no way of knowing whether it is fiction or not.[8]

That is, it purports to be true; it could be true; why should it not be true? Further,

> we might be tempted to argue that the overthrow of Tarquin was followed by a confused period of turmoil in which various members of his family and other leading figures struggled for power, replacing each other in rapid succession...

—and the note makes it explicit that

> they would include his relatives Brutus and Collatinus, but perhaps also Valerius Publicola ['The People's Friend'], who held the consulship three years in succession, and in the traditional story was suspected of aiming at kingship.[9]

So perhaps there really were five 'consuls' in Year One.

How do we know Valerius held the consulship three years running? Cornell takes it as a fact because he believes that

> the practice of recording the names of the men who held the chief magistracy *must* go back to the very early years of the Republic, and it is *certain* that continuous lists were kept in written form.[10]

---

7   Illustrated in Momigliano 1989.97, fig. 33; see Stibbe et al. 1980.
8   Cornell 1995.217.
9   Cornell 1995.217–18, 439.
10 Cornell 1995.13 (my emphasis).

If that were so, then documentary evidence would guarantee the five names as authentic. But it is, to put it mildly, an adventurous hypothesis.[11] It's also inconsistent with Cornell's own suggested model for Year One: why should the victor in that putative power struggle carefully record his rivals' names as equal to his own?

So forget any idea of archival evidence. What we have is the tradition, and what matters is how we handle it. 'In each case,' says Cornell,

> one must ask, first, whether there are grounds for regarding a story as ancient, or as a relatively late invention; and second, whether there are reasons for thinking that it might be based on fact.

Well and good, as far as it goes. But then: 'The burden of proof lies as heavily on those who wish to deny as on those who wish to affirm.'[12] And that, with the greatest respect, just will not do.

The burden of proof is on whoever challenges the *prima facie* presumption. And what is the *prima facie* presumption here? Not, I think, that authors writing five hundred years later, in a tradition of written history no more than two hundred years old, are likely to have reported the events accurately, or even recognisably. In such circumstances, to treat 'Why *shouldn't* it be true?' as a no less valid question than 'Why *should* it?' comes pretty close to abdicating the historian's responsibility.[13]

Better, in any case, to ask a different type of question. What sort of stories *are* they, and how may they have come about?

Afterword (2008)

That is the sort of question the various studies in this book have tried to address. The expulsion of the Tarquins and the establishment of the Republic were a formative moment in Rome's history, and of course a subject that

---

11 See Wiseman 1996.313–15 for arguments against. Stephen Oakley, in the introduction to his magnificent new commentary on Livy 6–10, defends a position close to Cornell's: 'it is very hard to see whence Pictor and later annalists drew the basic framework of their narrative, if there were no state records which were in some sense official'; the Romans' belief that the *annales maximi* went back to the beginning of the Republic 'does not amount to proof that the chronicle was already in existence in the fifth century or before, but it would be surprising in a partly hellenized and partly literate society if the state did not keep records of some kind' (Oakley 1997.24, 25). I think that begs a big question about the nature of 'the state'; and Oakley's general treatment of archival evidence seems to me more relevant to the fourth century (the period covered by Books 6–10) than the fifth or late sixth. [See now Oakley 2005.479–84 for further discussion of the problem.]

12 Cornell 1995.11.

13 Cf. Oakley 1997.102: 'accepting annalistic information unless it is proved to be wrong [is] an absurd procedure given the inadequacies of our sources.'

mattered deeply to the Romans themselves. By the time Livy was writing his history, a satisfactorily coherent narrative had been evolved from the princes' trip to Delphi to the peace treaty with Porsenna.[14] Some of the elements out of which it was created can be identified without too much difficulty, but it is not so easy to see which of them, if any, date back to the shadowy world of unwritten Rome.

The story of Brutus and the story of Lucretia were both subjects for the literary drama of the second and first centuries BC,[15] and no doubt also for the pre-literary dramatic performances we have hypothesized in previous chapters. Such an origin seems likely for the story Livy and Ovid tell about how Sextus Tarquinius came to lust after Lucretia:[16] as the siege of Ardea was dragging on, the young royals amused themselves with drinking sessions; at one such, they decided to ride off home that very night to see what their respective wives were up to; in Rome, the 'royal daughters-in-law' were enjoying themselves at a party; at Collatia, chaste Lucretia was spinning wool with her maids.[17] Since the wives who failed the test are conspicuously anonymous, one suspects that their party was originally a dance-interlude performed by *mimae*, light relief of the kind we have inferred for other stories from drama.[18] It is possible too that the expulsion of the tyrants was presented on the stage by the Furies pursuing Tarquin's murderous queen.[19]

To the stories of the consuls of Year One we may add the three tales of Roman heroism in Year Two which supposedly persuaded Porsenna to lift the siege of Rome and abandon his alliance with the exiled Tarquins.[20] These were the exploits of Horatius Cocles, Mucius and Cloelia, 'those three prodigies and marvels of the Roman name, who if they were not in the history-books would seem mythical today'.[21] The seven stories celebrate heroes or heroines of six different aristocratic families, the Iunii, Lucretii, Valerii, Horatii, Mucii and Cloelii. We may guess at the date of their respective origins from the periods when each family was most prominent in Rome,

---

14 Livy 1.56.4–2.15.7, cf. Plutarch *Publicola* 2.3–19.6.
15 Brutus: Accius *Brutus* (fragments and discussion in Manuwald 2001.220–37). Lucretia: Varro *De lingua Latina* 6.7 and 7.72, citing a tragedian called Cassius (Manuwald 2001.237–43).
16 Livy 1.57.4–11, Ovid *Fasti* 2.723–80; also Dio Cassius 2.11.13–15, *De uiris illustribus* 9.1–2. Contrast Dionysius of Halicarnassus 4.64.2–4, where Sextus comes to Collatia from Gabii, not Ardea, having desired Lucretia for a long time.
17 *Regii iuuenes*: Livy 1.57.4, *De uiris illustribus* 9.1. *Regiae nurus*: Livy 1.57.9, Ovid *Fasti* 2.739, *De uiris illustribus* 9.1. Cf. Ogilvie 1965.219, 222 ('pure New Comedy').
18 See pp. 180–1 above on Porsenna's hostages, 198–9 (with Wiseman 2004a.269–70) on Poppaea's wedding.
19 Livy 1.59.13, with Michels 1951.19–20; for Furies on stage, see pp. 212–13 above.
20 Livy 2.13.8 (*in admirationem uersus*), Plutarch *Publicola* 17.5 (ἀγασθεὶς καὶ θαυμάσας τὸ φρόνημα καὶ τὴν ἀρετὴν τῶν Ῥωμαίων). Dionysius of Halicarnassus (5.21.1) puts the events in Year Three.
21 Florus 1.10.4. For Cloelia see above, pp. 180–1, 289.

as indicated by the consulships (or other chief magistracies) attributed to them in the later Roman tradition.[22]

The plebeian Iunii took effective advantage of the end of the 'struggle of the orders', with six consulships and two dictatorships in the thirty-five years from 325 to 291 BC; and they continued to be a distinguished family, with ten more consulships (and another dictatorship) at regular intervals down to 62 BC.[23] The plebeian Mucii have a similar record, though starting a century later, with six consulships between 220 and 95 BC.[24]

No inference can be made from the patrician Valerii, who were hugely influential throughout the republican period, and beyond.[25] The other three patrician families are more interesting, and important as a contrast with the Iunii and Mucii. Counting consulships and 'consular tribunates' together, the Lucretii have nine chief magistracies between 508 and 381, the Horatii seven between 507 and 378, and the Cloelii three between 498 and 378. No one knows how reliable those records are, but the early high status of the Horatii, at least, is confirmed by the use of their name for one of the original rural tribes.

It is natural to conclude that the stories of Lucretia and her father the consul, of M. Horatius the consul and Horatius Cocles, and of the heroine Cloelia, all date from the fifth century or early fourth, while those of Brutus and Mucius were created in the late fourth and late third centuries respectively. We must be cautious, however. The old families may have continued: Lucretii of senatorial rank are known from at least the late third century BC, Cloelii from at least the early second, and even Horatii from at least the mid-first.[26]

In this context it is worth considering also the names of the seven kings. That of Romulus is certainly ancient, known already to a fourth-century Sicilian historian (as the son of Aeneas and Tyrrhenia), and no doubt associated with the fifth-century Romulii, or Romilii, who gave their name to another of the original rural tribes.[27] Nor is there any reason to doubt the antiquity of

---

22 Magistrates after 366 BC probably come from authentic lists, and may be taken as historical; those before that date are presumably the work of Roman antiquarians (p. 235 above), and their status as historical data is very doubtful.

23 Consulships: 325, 317, 313, 311, 292, 291, 277, 266, 249, 230, 178, 167, 138, 109, 77, 62 BC. Dictatorships: 312, 302, 216 BC.

24 220, 175, 174, 133, 117, 95 BC—all with the *cognomen* Scaevola, explained by their legendary ancestor's exploit (Plutarch *Publicola* 17.3).

25 On my count, 43 consulships between 505 and 31 BC; five dictatorships between 501 and 302 BC; 18 military tribunates with consular authority between 414 and 367 BC. For the creation of Valerian pseudo-history in the late Republic, see Wiseman 1998.75–89.

26 Lucretii (now plebeian): e.g. praetors in 205, 172 and 171 BC. Cloelii: e.g. a *rex sacrorum* in 180 (Livy 40.42.11) and a senator in 39 BC (Sherk 1969.158, line 8). Horatii: a *legatus* in 43 BC (Cicero *Ad familiares* 12.30.7).

27 Alcimus *FGrH* 560 F 4; Festus (Paulus) 331L for *Romulia tribus*; T. Romilius Rocus Vaticanus was supposedly consul in 455 BC and subsequently one of the Decemvirs (Degrassi 1947.24–5, Diodorus Siculus 12.5.1, Livy 3.33.3 etc).

the Tarquinii, a family known to Vel Saties of Vulci in the fourth century (one of the scenes painted in his tomb was of Gnaeus Tarquinius of Rome being killed by Marcus Camillus) and probably already to a Greek historian of Cumae a century before that.[28] Numa's family name, Pompilius, is totally mysterious and practically unparalleled in the Republic.[29]

That leaves Ancus Marcius, Tullus Hostilius and Servius Tullius, all of whom bear the names of families attested in later times. A Tullius was supposedly consul in 500 BC; the much later Tullii, including three first-century consuls, evidently did not claim any connection.[30] The Marcii, on the other hand, had eight consulships and a dictatorship in the 76 years from 357 to 281 BC (and then twelve consulships between 186 and 38 BC), a profile very like that of the Iunii;[31] and the Hostilii, like the Mucii, first appear in the late third century and continue at a high rank in the second.[32] If it makes sense to think of Horatius Cocles as a creation of the fifth century, Iunius Brutus of the late fourth, and Mucius of the late third, the same inference may reasonably be made about Servius Tullius (fifth century), Ancus Marcius (late fourth) and Tullus Hostilius (late third).

So far as we can tell from Naevius and Ennius, both of whom knew Romulus as the grandson of Aeneas,[33] unwritten Rome did not have a continuous narrative of the regal period, but a series of independent stories about good king Numa, wicked king Tarquin, and so on. The idea of precisely seven reigns, of which the years could be counted, was the achievement of literary historiography, and it depended on the chronologies of Timaeus and Eratosthenes, who provided dates for the foundation of the city and the expulsion of the kings.[34] It is quite possible to imagine Fabius Pictor or Cincius Alimentus exploiting the family pride of the Marcii and Hostilii (the latter their own contemporaries) to link up the traditional stories into seamless 'real history'.

Of course one cannot say for certain that that is what happened. But the possibility (to put it no more strongly than that) should be borne in mind as an

---

28 François Tomb: e.g. Cornell 1995.135–9, Wiseman 2004a.41–3. Historian of Cumae: Zevi 1995; p. 293 above.

29 Ogilvie 1965.601: 'No Pompilius is known between Numa and Catiline's friend (Q. Cicero, *Comm. Pet.* 10).' Claims of descent from Numa were already challenged by Roman authors (Plutarch *Numa* 21.1, cf. 1.1).

30 Crawford 1974.297 for a moneyer in 120 BC; the consulships were in 81, 63 and 30 BC. No connection: Cicero *Brutus* 62.

31 Consulships: 357, 352, 344, 342, 310, 306, 288, 281, 186, 169, 162, 156, 149, 118, 91, 68, 64, 56, 39, 38 BC. Dictatorship: 356 BC. Compare n. 23 above. Descent from king: Suetonius *Diuus Iulius* 6.1 (Marcii Reges).

32 Three praetorships in 209 and 207, then consulships in 170, 145 and 137 BC. Descent from king implied by Tullus Hostilius, tribune designate in 43 (Cicero *Philippics* 13.26).

33 Servius *auctus* on Virgil *Aeneid* 1.273. See pp. 49–50 above on Ennius' chronology.

34 Eratosthenes *FGrH* 241 F1 and F45 (see p. 49 above); Polybius 3.22.1–2 (from Timaeus, or Fabius following Timaeus?).

antidote to the opposite assumption, as recently expressed by a very distinguished historian:[35]

> As is well known, there is an ancient and uncontested tradition that makes the
> reign of Ancus Marcius, fourth king of Rome (traditional dating 646–616 BC),
> the moment when Roman dominion expanded as far as the Tyrrhenian coast
> (*usque ad mare imperium prolatum*, Livy 1.33.9)...

As Fausto Zevi rightly points out, 'the story of Ancus Marcius had been grafted
on to a stock of Greek historiography'—but he assumes it was done very early,
with an authentic Ancus mentioned in the fifth-century Greek source that
evidently reported the alliance of Aristodemus of Cumae with the exiled
Tarquin.[36] With the greatest respect, I find it hard to believe that the putative
Greek historian would have concerned himself with any details about Rome
before the son of Corinthian Demaratus arrived there. The grafting was much
more probably done centuries later, by a Roman historian and for a Roman
reason, to create a continuous narrative of the kings.

As we saw in the first chapter, real evidence for early Rome was rare and
hard to interpret. One potential source of information was provided by
honorific statues that had been set up in the past. There was a group of eight
on the Capitol, one with a drawn sword, which by the late Republic at least
were identified as the seven kings plus Lucius Brutus.[37] But they were not the
canonical seven, since Titus Tatius was included,[38] and in any case they were
probably no older than the fourth century BC;[39] what they represented when
they were first made is anybody's guess. The same may be said of the old
statues identified as Porsenna,[40] Horatius Cocles,[41] Mucius,[42] and Cloelia.[43] We

---

35 Zevi 2005.30, cf. 31 on 'the historical truth of the regal foundation of Ostia'.
36 Zevi 2005.32: 'Since [the tradition about Aristodemus] concerns a highly polemical contest
    against the patricians responsible for driving out the Tarquins, it is more than probable that
    it would have mentioned the name of the king of Rome by whom Tarquin was kindly
    received and introduced into the highest social levels of the day, that is to say that same
    Ancus Marcius, along with perhaps mention of his military endeavours and conquests made
    by or with him.' More than probable?
37 Cassius Dio 43.45.4 (seven plus Brutus), Plutarch *Brutus* 1.1 (drawn sword); Brutus statue
    also mentioned by Pliny *Nat. Hist.* 34.23.
38 Asconius 29C, Pliny *Nat. Hist.* 34.23.
39 See Hölscher 1978.328–31, Coarelli 1999b.369.
40 Plutarch *Publicola* 19.6, 'near the Senate-house, of simple and archaic workmanship'.
41 Livy 2.10.12 (*in comitio*), Dionysius of Halicarnassus 5.25.2, Plutarch *Publicola* 16.7 ('in the
    temple of Vulcan'), Aulus Gellius 4.5.1–6 (*in comitio* 5.1, *in area Volcani* 5.4), *De uiris illus-
    tribus* 11.2 (*in Volcanali*).
42 *De uiris illustribus* 12.7, site not given.
43 Livy 2.13.11 (*in summa sacra uia*), Dionysius of Halicarnassus 5.35.2 (on Sacra Via), Seneca
    Consolatio ad Marciam 16.2 (*in sacra uia*), Pliny *Nat. Hist.* 34.29 (*contra Iouis Statoris aedem in
    uestibulo Superbi domus*), Plutarch *Publicola* 19.5 (on Sacra Via as you go to the Palatine),
    Plutarch *Moralia* 250f (on Sacra Via), Servius on *Aeneid* 8.646 (*in sacra uia*).

know that the identity of the bronze girl on a horse was disputed (Cloelia or Valeria?),[44] and it seems that the 'Horatius Cocles' statue at the Volcanal could also be identified as Romulus, or as a play-actor struck by lightning, whose remains were buried there.[45] What seemed to the historians to be evidence for their history of early Rome was probably nothing of the kind.

Two items on Porsenna preserved in the literary sources are interestingly inconsistent with the historians' bland portrait of the chivalrous king. The first is the elder Pliny's quotation from a treaty between Porsenna and the Roman People; since it forbade the Romans the use of iron except for agricultural purposes, it was evidently a treaty of surrender.[46] It is impossible to know how authentic the supposed document was, but Pliny goes on to quote 'very ancient writers' (*uetustissimi auctores*), from whom he may have got the information, and Tacitus too takes it for granted that the city was surrendered to Porsenna.[47]

The other item was an old custom still in use in Livy's time: whenever the quaestors carried out an auction of public property, the first business was always a symbolic 'sale of the goods of king Porsenna'.[48] That would seem to commemorate the sale of booty from a defeated enemy,[49] in this case an unwelcome master who has been forced to withdraw. Livy, to his credit, is aware of the inconsistency of this ritual with the tale of goodwill and mutual admiration he has just narrated, but in the end he is happy to find a 'probable explanation', that the departing Porsenna generously left his headquarters fully stocked for the Romans' benefit; Dionysius and Plutarch report this version as accepted fact.[50]

This episode offers a glimpse into what may lie behind *any* item in the smooth and plausible narrative of early Rome that is offered by Livy, Dionysius and Plutarch. It so happens that in this case we can detect a rival version, possibly based on documentary evidence, in the inconspicuous allusions of Pliny and Tacitus, and a contradictory oral tradition, embedded in the

---

44 See p. 289 above.

45 Romulus: Dionysius of Halicarnassus 2.54.2, with p. 10 above on rival interpretations of the Volcanal complex. *Ludius*: Festus 370L.

46 Pliny *Nat. Hist.* 34.139: *in foedere quod expulsis regibus populo Romano dedit Porsina, nominatim comprehensum inuenimus ne ferro nisi in agri cultu uteretur.*

47 Tacitus *Histories* 3.72.1 on the Capitoline temple of Jupiter, *quam non Porsenna dedita urbe neque Galli capta temerare potuissent.*

48 Livy 2.14.1: *mos traditus ab antiquis usque ad nostram aetatem inter cetera sollemnia manet, bona Porsennae regis uendendi.* Cf. Dionysius of Halicarnassus 5.34.4 (quaestors), Plutarch *Publicola* 19.6 (auction).

49 So Ogilvie 1965.268 ('it will have been a semi-religious commemoration of a Roman success'), who notes the parallel with the *auctio Veientium* (Festus 430L, cf. Plutarch *Romulus* 25.5, *Moralia* 277c–d).

50 Livy 2.14.1 (*huic tam pacatae profectioni ab urbe Regis Etrusci abhorrens mos...*), 2.14.3 (*proximum uero est...*); Dionysius of Halicarnassus 5.34.4, Plutarch *Publicola* 19.5–6.

quaestors' symbolic ritual at auctions. Without the fortuitous survival of that
counter-evidence, we might have been tempted to say 'As is well known,
there is an ancient and uncontested tradition' that the Romans of the new
Republic successfully persuaded Porsenna to abandon his alliance with the
Tarquins.

In fact, what Livy offers is not ancient tradition at all, but a literary narrative
progressively created by his predecessors and elaborated by himself. If the terms
of 'Porsenna's treaty with the Roman People' were available to Pliny, they
were surely available equally to Livy. But he ignores them, just as he ignored
the evidence for the *praetor maximus*.[51] The reason is obvious: to try to take
account of the implications of such data would have made it impossible for
Livy to write his sort of history at all. He wanted to present a morally exemplary narrative which would be like a monument for his readers to
contemplate.[52] The story was something he had inherited from his predecessors; odd bits of evidence that were incompatible with it just had to be passed
over.

What would Livy have made of the 'companions of Poplios Valesios', if he
had known about the Satricum inscription? He might perhaps have identified
them as the friends who warned Publius Valerius that his house on the Velia
was making him unpopular with the citizens,[53] but he could not do what the
modern historian does, and take them as evidence for a quasi-Homeric archaic
society.[54] That would have made nonsense of his whole narrative. Using such
'indications' to make inferences about an impenetrably distant past is what
Thucydides thought a historian ought to do,[55] but neither Livy nor Dionysius
nor Plutarch was interested in following his example.

Even so, there is material in their narratives that can be exploited. Livy did
mention the 'sale of the goods of king Porsenna', even if he had to explain it
away; Plutarch did report the summoning of Jupiter by magical means, even
though he regarded the story as 'fabulous and ridiculous';[56] and when we infer
a traditional performance genre that kept old tales of Roman heroism alive, it
is Livy himself who unwittingly provides the evidence,[57] with his repeated

---

51 Livy 7.3.5; pp. 10–11 above.
52 Livy preface 10: *hoc illud est praecipue in cognitione rerum salubre ac frugiferum, omnis te exempli
    documenta in inlustri posita monumento intueri.*
53 Livy 2.7.6–7, cf. Plutarch *Publicola* 10.3 (τῶν φίλων διεξιόντων).
54 E.g. Cornell 1995.144: 'The otherwise rather unusual word *sodales* seems to have a particular
    social significance in this context and to refer to the armed followers of an independent
    warlord. The most obvious comparison is with the Homeric *hetairoi*, and it is no accident
    that this is exactly how Dionysius of Halicarnassus translates it (9.15.3).'
55 Thucydides 1.20.1–21.1 (p. 8 above).
56 Plutarch *Numa* 15.6 (ταῦτα μὲν οὖν τὰ μυθώδη καὶ γελοῖα. . .); see pp. 162–6 above.
57 See chapter 2 above.

reports of soldiers singing at triumphs. More often it is what the poets say—
Ennius on 'Fauns and prophets', Ovid on the Kalends of April—that enables us
to get an insight into unwritten Rome. Such insights are very uncertain, quite
different from the confident narrative of the historians, and they are often very
surprising, because the past is a foreign country where they do things differently. But I hope this book has shown that they are worth seeking out.

Bibliography

Adam and Briquel 1982: Richard Adam and Dominique Briquel, 'Le miroir prénestin de l'antiquario comunale de Rome et la légende des jumeaux divins en milieu latin à la fin du IVe siècle av. J.C.', *Mélanges de l'École française de Rome (Antiquité)* 94: 33–65.

Adams 1982: J.N. Adams, *The Latin Sexual Vocabulary*. London: Duckworth.

Alföldi 1965: Andrew Alföldi, *Early Rome and the Latins* (Jerome Lectures series 7). Ann Arbor: University of Michigan Press.

Alföldi 1974: Andreas Alföldi, *Die Struktur des voretruskischen Römerstaates*. Heidelberg: Winter.

Ammerman 1990: A. Ammerman, 'On the Origins of the Roman Forum', *American Journal of Archaeology* 94: 627–46.

Ammerman 1998: Albert J. Ammerman, 'Environmental Archaeology in the Velabrum, Rome: Interim Report', *Journal of Roman Archaeology* 11: 213–23.

Ammerman 2006: Albert Ammerman, 'Adding Time to Rome's *imago*', in Lothar Haselberger and John Humphrey (eds), *Imaging Ancient Rome: Documentation—Visualization—Imagination* (JRA Supplement 61, Portsmouth RI): 297–308.

Anderson 1992: William S. Anderson, 'The Limits of Genre: Response to Francis Cairns', in Karl Galinsky (ed.), *The Interpretation of Roman Poetry: Empiricism or Hermeneutics?* (Studien zur klassischen Philologie 67, Frankfurt: Peter Lang): 96–103.

Ando 2000: Clifford Ando, *Imperial Ideology and Provincial Loyalty in the Roman Empire*. Berkeley: University of California Press.

Ankarloo and Clark 1999: Bengt Ankarloo and Stuart Clark, 'Introduction', in Valerie Flint *et al.*, *Witchcraft and Magic in Europe: Ancient Greece and Rome* (London: Athlone Press): xi–xvi.

Arcella 1985: Luciano Arcella, 'Il mito di Cloelia e i Valerii', *Studi e materiali di storia delle religioni* 9: 21–42.

Aronen 1999: Jaakko Aronen, 'Perché il verso saturnio fu chiamato "saturnio"?', in Nicole Blanc and André Buisson (eds), *Imago antiquitatis: religions et iconographie du monde romaine* (Paris: de Boccard): 53–72.

Astin 1967: A.E. Astin, *Scipio Aemilianus*. Oxford: Clarendon Press.

Badian 1966: E. Badian, 'The Early Historians', in T.A. Dorey (ed.), *Latin Historians* (London: Routledge and Kegan Paul): 1–38.

Badian 1984: E. Badian, 'The House of the Servilii Gemini: A Study in the Misuse of Occam's Razor' , *Papers of the British School at Rome* 52: 49–71.

Bagnasco Gianni 1996: Giovanna Bagnasco Gianni, *Oggetti iscritti di epoca orientalizzante in Etruria* (Biblioteca di Studi Etruschi 30). Florence: Olschki.

Barchiesi 1994: Alessandro Barchiesi, *Il poeta e il principe: Ovidio e il discorso augusteo*. Bari: Laterza

Barchiesi 1997: Alessandro Barchiesi, *The Poet and the Prince: Ovid and Augustan Discourse*. Berkeley: University of California Press.

Barnes 1982: Timothy D. Barnes, 'The date of the *Octavia*', *Museum Helveticum* 39: 215–17.

Baroni 2001: Irene Baroni, 'Livelli di occupazione dell'età del Bronzo nel Giardino Romano: il Bronzo recente', *Bullettino della commissione archeologica comunale di Roma* 102: 291–8.

Barr 1962: W. Barr, 'Horace *Odes* I, 4', *Classical Review* 12: 5–11.

Barré 1840: L. Barré, *Herculaneum et Pompei* vol. 8 (*Museé Secret*). Paris.

Battaglia and Emiliozzi 1979: Gabriella Bordenache Battaglia and Adriana Emiliozzi, *Le ciste prenestine*, I Corpus: 1.1. Rome: Consiglio nazionale delle ricerche.

Battaglia and Emiliozzi 1990: Gabriella Bordenache Battaglia and Adriana Emiliozzi, *Le ciste prenestine*, I Corpus: 1.2. Rome: Consiglio nazionale delle ricerche.

Beacham 1991: Richard C. Beacham, *The Roman Theatre and its Audience*. London: Routledge.

Beard 1986: Mary Beard, 'Cicero and Divination', *Journal of Roman Studies* 76: 33–46.

Beard, North and Price 1998: Mary Beard, John North and Simon Price, *Religions of Rome*, two volumes: 1 *A History*, 2 *A Sourcebook*. Cambridge University Press.

Beazley 1947: J.D. Beazley, *Etruscan Vase-Painting*. Oxford: Clarendon Press.

Beazley 1963: J.D. Beazley, *Attic Red-Figure Vase-Painters*, ed. 2. Oxford: Clarendon Press.

Belier 1991: Wouter W. Belier, *Decayed Gods: Origin and Development of Georges Dumézil's 'Idéologie Tripartie'* (Studies in Greek and Roman Religion 7). Leiden: Brill.

Beness and Hillard 2001: J.L. Beness and T.W. Hillard, 'The Theatricality of the Deaths of C. Gracchus and Friends', *Classical Quarterly* 51: 135–40.

Bernheimer 1952: Richard Bernheimer, *Wild Men in the Middle Ages: a Study in Art, Sentiment and Demonology*. Cambridge MA: Harvard University Press.

Bernstein 1998: Frank Bernstein, *Ludi publici: Untersuchungen zur Entstehung und Entwicklung der öffentlichen Spiele im republikanischen Rom* (*Historia* Einzelschrift 119). Stuttgart: Franz Steiner.

Bettelli 1997: Marco Bettelli, *Roma, la città prima della città: i tempi di una nascita* (Studia archeologica 86). Rome: L'Erma di Bretschneider.

Bevington and Rasmussen 1993: David Bevington and Eric Rasmussen (eds), *Doctor Faustus A- and B-Texts (1604, 1616)*. Manchester University Press.

Binder 1964: Gerhard Binder, *Die Aussetzung des Königskindes* (Beiträge zur klassischen Philologie 10). Meisenheim am Glan: Hain.

Bloomer 1992: W. Martin Bloomer, *Valerius Maximus and the Rhetoric of the New Nobility*. London: Duckworth.

Boardman 1997: John Boardman, *The Great God Pan: The Survival of an Image* (Walter Neurath Memorial Lecture 29). London: Thames and Hudson.

Bodel 1994: John Bodel, 'Graveyards and Groves: A Study of the *Lex Lucerina*', *American Journal of Ancient History* 11: 1–133.

Boëls-Janssen 1993: Nicole Boëls-Janssen, *La vie religieuse des matrones dans la Rome archaïque* (Collection de l'École française de Rome 176). Rome: École française de Rome.

Boissier 1893: Gaston Boissier, 'Les *fabulae praetextae*', *Revue de philologie* 17: 101–8.

Bömer 1958: Franz Bömer, *P. Ovidius Naso: Die Fasten*, vol. 2. Heidelberg: Carl Winter.

Borgeaud 1988: Philippe Borgeaud, *The Cult of Pan in Ancient Greece* (trans. Kathleen Atlass and James Redfield, orig. edition Rome 1979). University of Chicago Press.

Bowersock 1990: G.W. Bowersock, 'The Pontificate of Augustus', in Kurt A. Raaflaub and Mark Toher (eds), *Between Republic and Empire: Interpretations of Augustus and his Principate* (Berkeley: University of California Press): 380–94.

Bowie 2000: Angus Bowie, 'Myth and Ritual in the Rivals of Aristophanes', in David Harvey and John Wilkins (eds), *The Rivals of Aristophanes: Studies in Athenian Old Comedy* (London: Duckworth and Classical Press of Wales): 317–39.

Bremer 1975: J.M. Bremer, 'The Meadow of Love and Two Passages in Euripides' *Hippolytus*', *Mnemosyne* 28: 268–80.

Bremmer 1987a: J.N. Bremmer, 'Romulus, Remus and the Foundation of Rome', in J.N. Bremmer and N.M. Horsfall, *Roman Myth and Mythography* (*BICS* Supplement 52, London: Institute of Classical Studies): 25–48.

Bremmer 1987b: J.N. Bremmer, 'Slow Cybele's Arrival', in J.N. Bremmer and N.M. Horsfall, *Roman Myth and Mythography* (*BICS* Supplement 52, London: Institute of Classical Studies): 105–12.

Brenk 1986: F.E. Brenk, 'In the Light of the Moon: Demonology in the Early Imperial Period', in H. Temporini and W. Haase (eds), *Aufstieg und Niedergang der römischen Welt* 2.16.3 (Berlin: De Gruyter): 2068–2145.

Brink 1971: C.O. Brink, *Horace on Poetry: The Ars Poetica*. Cambridge University Press.

Brink 1982: C.O. Brink, *Horace on Poetry: Epistles Book II*. Cambridge University Press.

Briquel 1974: Dominique Briquel, 'Le problème des Dauniens', *Mélanges de l'École française de Rome: Antiquité* 86: 7–40.

Briscoe 1971: J. Briscoe, 'The First Decade', in T.A. Dorey (ed.), *Livy* (London: Routledge and Kegan Paul): 1–20.

Brommer 1944: Frank Brommer, *Satyrspiele: Bilder griechischer Vasen*. Berlin: De Gruyter.

Brommer 1949–50: Frank Brommer, 'Pan im 5. und 4. Jahrhundert v. Chr.', *Marburger Jahrbuch für Kunstwissenschaft* 15: 5–42.

Broughton 1951: T. Robert S. Broughton, *The Magistrates of the Roman Republic*, vol. 1. New York: American Philological Association.

Bruckmann 1893: *Epitheta deorum quae apud poetas Graecos leguntur* (Roscher Suppl. 1). Leipzig: Teubner.

Burkert 1983: Walter Burkert, *Home Necans: The Anthropology of Ancient Greek Sacrificial Ritual and Myth* (trans. Peter Bing, orig. edition Berlin 1972). Berkeley: University of California Press.

Buxton 1994: Richard Buxton, *Imaginary Greece: The Contexts of Mythology*. Cambridge University Press.

Cairns 1992: Francis Cairns, 'Propertius 4.9: "Hercules Exclusus" and the Dimensions of Genre', in Karl Galinsky (ed.), *The Interpretation of Roman Poetry: Empiricism or*

Hermeneutics? (Studien zur klassischen Philologie 67, Frankfurt: Peter Lang): 65–95.

Calvino 1988: Italo Calvino, *Lezioni americane: Sei proposte per il prossimo millennio.* Milan: Garzanti.

Cameron 1976: Alan Cameron, *Circus Factions: Blues and Greens at Rome and Byzantium.* Oxford: Clarendon Press.

Cameron 2004a: Alan Cameron, *Greek Mythology in the Roman World* (American Classical Studies 48). New York: Oxford University Press.

Cameron 2004b: Alan Cameron, 'Vergil Illustrated between Pagans and Christians: Reconsidering "the late-4th c. Classical Revival", the dates of the manuscripts, and the places of production of the Latin Classics', *Journal of Roman Archaeology* 17.502–25.

Campbell 2000: Brian Campbell, *The Writings of the Roman Land Surveyors* (JRS Monographs 9). London: Society for the Promotion of Roman Studies.

Carandini 1990: A(ndrea) C(arandini), 'Domus aristocratiche sopra le mura e il pomerio del Palatino', in Mauro Cristofani (ed.), *La grande Roma dei Tarquini: catalogo della mostra* (Rome: L'Erma di Bretschneider): 97–9.

Carandini 1995: Andrea Carandini, 'Racconto breve dello scavo con disegni', in *Palatium e Sacra Via I: Tavole = Bollettino di archeologia* 34: 1–75.

Carandini 1997: Andrea Carandini, *La nascita di Roma: Dèi, Lari, eroi e uomini all'alba di una civiltà.* Turin: Einaudi.

Carandini 2000: Andrea Carandini, *Giornale di scavo: Pensieri sparsi di un archeologo.* Turin: Einaudi.

Carandini 2003: Andrea Carandini, 'Il mito romuleo e le origini di Roma', in Mario Citroni (ed.), *Memoria e identità: La cultura romana costruisce la sua imagine* (Studi e testi 21, Florence: Università degli Studi di Firenze): 3–19.

Carandini 2004: Andrea Carandini, *Palatino, Velia e Sacra Via: Paessaggi urbani attraverso il tempo* (Workshop di archeologia classica, Quaderni 1). Rome: Edizioni dell'Ateneo.

Carandini 2006: Andrea Carandini, *Remo e Romolo: Dai rioni dei Quiriti alla città dei Romani (775/750–700/675 a.C.).* Turin: Einaudi.

Carandini *et alii* 1997: A. Carandini, G. Ricci, M.T. D'Alessio, C. De Davide, N. Terrenato, 'La villa dell'Auditorium dall'età arcaica all'età imperiale', *Römische Mitteilungen* 104: 117–148.

Carandini and Cappelli 2000: Andrea Carandini and Rosanna Capelli (eds), *Roma: Romolo, Remo e la fondazione della città.* Milan: Electa.

Carandini and Carafa 1995: Andrea Carandini and Paolo Carafa, *Palatium e Sacra Via I: Prima delle mura, l'età delle mura e l'età case arcaiche = Bollettino di archeologia* 31–3.

Carandini, Carafa and Filippi forthcoming: Andrea Carandini, Paolo Carafa, Dunia Filippi, *Palatium e Sacra Via III.*

Carpenter 1997: Thomas H. Carpenter, *Dionysian Imagery in Fifth-Century Athens.* Oxford: Clarendon Press.

Cazenove 1983: Olivier de Cazenove, 'Lucus Stimulae: les aiguillons des Bacchanales', *Mélanges de l'École française de Rome (Antiquité)* 95: 55–113.

Cazenove 1986: Olivier de Cazanove, 'Le thiase et son double: Images, statuts, functions du cortège divin de Dionysos en Italie centrale', in *L'association dionysiaque dans les sociétés anciennes* (Collection de l'EFR 89). Rome: École française de Rome.

Champeaux 1982: Jacqueline Champeaux, *Fortuna: Le culte de la Fortune à Rome et dans le monde romain des origins à la mort de César*, vol. 1. Rome: École française de Rome.

Champeaux 1987: Jacqueline Champeaux, *Fortuna: Le culte de la Fortune à Rome et dans le monde romain des origins à la mort de César*, vol. 2. Rome: École française de Rome.

Chassignet 1996: Martine Chassignet, *L'annalistique romaine*, vol. 1. Paris: Les Belles Lettres.

Christenson 2000: David M. Christenson, *Plautus: Amphitruo* (Cambridge Greek and Latin Classics). Cambridge University Press.

Cichorius 1922: Conrad Cichorius, *Römische Studien: Historisches, Epigraphisches, Literaturgeschichtliches aus vier Jahrhunderten Roms*. Leipzig: Teubner.

Coarelli 1983: Filippo Coarelli, *Il foro romano: periodo archaico*. Rome: Quasar.

Coarelli 1985: Filippo Coarelli, *Il foro romano: periodo repubblicano e augusteo*. Rome: Quasar.

Coarelli 1987: Filippo Coarelli, *I santuari del Lazio in età repubblicana* (Studi NIS archeologia 7). Rome: Nuova Italia Scientifica.

Coarelli 1988: Filippo Coarelli, *Il foro boario dalle origini alle fine della repubblica*. Rome: Quasar.

Coarelli 1995: F. Coarelli, 'Flora, templum (in Colle)', in Eva Margareta Steinby (ed.), *Lexicon Topographicum Urbis Romae* 2, D–G (Rome: Quasar): 254.

Coarelli 1996: Filippo Coarelli, *Revixit ars: arte e ideologia a Roma dai modelli ellenistici alla tradizione repubblicana*. Rome: Quasar.

Coarelli 1997: Filippo Coarelli, *Il Campo Marzio dalle origini alla fine della repubblica*. Rome: Quasar.

Coarelli 1999a: Filippo Coarelli, 'Sacra Via', in Eva Margareta Steinby (ed.), *Lexicon Topographicum Urbis Romae* vol. IV (Rome: Quasar): 223–8.

Coarelli 1999b: Filippo Coarelli, 'Statuae regum Romanorum', in Eva Margareta Steinby (ed.), *Lexicon Topographicum Urbis Romae* vol. IV (Rome: Quasar): 368–9.

Coarelli 2005: Filippo Coarelli, 'I percorsi cerimoniali a Roma in età regia', in Emanuele Greco (ed.), *Teseo e Romolo: Le origini di Atene e Roma a confronto* (Tripodes 1, Athens: Scuola archaeologica italiana): 29–42.

Cole 1993: Susan Guettel Cole, 'Procession and Celebration at the Dionysia', in R. Scodel (ed.), *Theatre and Society in the Classical World* (Ann Arbor: University of Michigan Press): 25–38.

Cole 2006: Spencer Cole, 'Cicero, Ennius, and the Concept of Apotheosis at Rome', *Arethusa* 39.3: 531–48.

Collingwood 1946: R.G. Collingwood, *The Idea of History*. Oxford: Clarendon Press.

Colonna 1976: Giovanni Colonna, '"Scriba cum rege sedens"', in *Mélanges offerts à Jacques Heurgon: L'Italie préromaine et la Rome républicaine* (Collection de l'École française de Rome 27, Rome): 187–95.

Colonna 1987: Giovanni Colonna, 'Etruria e Lazio nell'età dei Tarquini', in Mauro Cristofani (ed.), *Etruria e Lazio arcaico: Atti dell'incontro di studio* (Quaderni del Centro di studio per l'archeologia etrusco-italica 15, Rome: CNR): 55–66.

Connor 1989: W.R. Connor, 'City Dionysia and Athenian Democracy', *Classica et Mediaevalia* 40: 7–32.

Cornell 1986: Timothy J. Cornell, 'The Value of the Literary Tradition Concerning Archaic Rome', in Kurt A. Raaflaub (ed.), *Social Struggles in Archaic Rome: New Perspectives on the Conflict of the Orders* (Berkeley: University of California Press): 52–76.

Cornell 1991: Tim Cornell, 'The Tyranny of the Evidence: A Discussion of the Possible Uses of Literacy in Etruria and Latium in the Archaic Age', in *Literacy in the Roman World* (*JRA* Supplement 3, Ann Arbor): 7–33.

Cornell 1995: T.J. Cornell, *The Beginnings of Rome: Italy and Rome from the Bronze Age to the Punic Wars (c.1000–264 BC)*. London: Routledge.

Courtney 1993: Edward Courtney (ed.), *The Fragmentary Latin Poets*. Oxford: Clarendon Press.

Courtney 1995: E. Cortney (ed.), *Musa Lapidaria: A Selection of Latin Verse Inscriptions* (American Classical Studies 36). Atlanta GA: Scholars Press.

Crawford 1974: Michael H. Crawford, *Roman Republican Coinage*. Cambridge University Press.

Crawford 1996: M.H. Crawford (ed.), *Roman Statutes* (*BICS* Supplement 64), two volumes. London: Institute of Classical Studies.

Crawford 1998: M.H. Crawford, 'Numa and the Antiquarians', *Faventia* 20/1: 37–8.

Cristofani 1990: Mauro Cristofani (ed.), *La grande Roma dei Tarquinii: catalogo della mostra*. Rome: L'Erma di Bretschneider.

Crook, Lintott and Rawson 1994: J.A. Crook, Andrew Lintott and the late Elizabeth Rawson (eds), *Cambridge Ancient History*, second edition, vol. 9, *The Last Age of the Roman Republic, 146–43 BC*. Cambridge University Press.

Csapo and Slater 1994: Eric Csapo and William J. Slater, *The Context of Ancient Drama*. Ann Arbor: University of Michigan Press.

Culham 1991: Phyllis Culham, 'Documents and *Domus* in Republican Rome', *Libraries and Culture* 26: 119–34.

Curti 1993: Emmanuele Curti, 'The Use of Myth in Roman Propaganda', unpublished paper given at a conference in London, 23 November 1993.

Daremberg and Saglio 1896: Ch. Daremberg and Edm. Saglio (eds), *Dictionnaire des antiquités grecques et romaines*, vol. 2.2. Paris: Hachette.

Dark 2000: Ken Dark, *Britain and the End of the Roman Empire*. Stroud: Tempus.

Davidson 2000: James Davidson, '*Gnesippos paigniagraphos*: the Comic Poets and the Erotic Mime', in David Harvey and John Wilkins (eds), *The Rivals of Aristophanes: Studies in Athenian Old Comedy* (London: Duckworth and Classical Press of Wales): 41–64.

Davies 1984: J.K. Davies, 'The Reliability of the Oral Tradition', in Lin Foxhall and John K. Davies (eds), *The Trojan War: Its Historicity and Context* (Bristol Classical Press): 87–110.

Dearden 1995: C.W. Dearden, 'Pots, Tumblers and Phlyax Vases', in Alan Griffiths (ed.), *Stage Directions: Essays in Ancient Drama in Honour of E.W. Handley* (*BICS* Supplement 66, London: Institute of Classical Studies): 81–6.

Degrassi 1947: Atilius Degrassi (ed.), *Inscriptiones Italiae*, XIII *Fasti et elogia*, fasc. 1 *Fasti consulares et triumphales*. Rome: Libreria dello stato.

Degrassi 1963: Atilius Degrassi (ed.), *Inscriptiones Italiae*, XIII *Fasti et elogia*, fasc. 2 *Fasti anni Numani et Iuliani*. Rome: Istituto poligrafico dello stato.

De Puma 1987: Richard Daniel De Puma, *Etruscan Tomb-Groups: Ancient Pottery and Bronzes in Chicago's Field Museum of Natural History*. Mainz: von Zabern.

De Simone 1981: Carlo De Simone, 'Gli Etruschi a Roma: evidenza linguistica e problemi metodologici', in *Gli Etruschi e Roma: Atti dell'incontro di studio in onore di Massimo Pallottino* (Rome: Giorgio Bretschneider): 94–103.

Dickie 2001: Matthew W. Dickie, *Magic and Magicians in the Greco-Roman World*. London: Routledge.

Dierichs 1997: Angelika Dierichs, *Erotik in der Römischen Kunst*. Mainz: von Zabern.

Dorcey 1992: Peter F. Dorcey, *The Cult of Silvanus: a Study in Roman Folk Religion* (Columbia Studies in the Classical Tradition 20). Leiden: Brill.

Drossart 1974: P. Drossart, 'Le theatre aux nones caprotines (à propos de Varron, *De lingua Latina* 6,18)', *Revue de philologie* 48: 54–64.

Drummond 1989: A. Drummond, 'Rome in the Fifth Century II: the Citizen Community', in F.W. Walbank *et alii* (eds), *The Cambridge Ancient History* (ed. 2) VII.2: *The Rise of Rome to 220 BC* (Cambridge University Press): 172–242.

Duff and Duff 1934: John W. Duff and Arnold M. Duff (eds), *Minor Latin Poets* (Loeb Classical Library 284). Cambridge MA: Harvard University Press.

Dulière 1979: Cécile Dulière, *Lupa Romana: recherches d'iconographie et essai d'interprétation* (Études de philologie, d'archéologie et d'histoire 18). Brussels: Institut historique Belge de Rome.

Dumézil 1929: Georges Dumézil, *Le problème des centaures: étude de mythologie comparée indo-européenne*. Paris: Geuthner.

Dumézil 1970: Georges Dumézil, *Archaic Roman Religion* (trans. Philip Krapp, orig. edition Paris 1966). University of Chicago Press.

Dumézil 1973: Georges Dumézil, *Mythe et épopée* III, *Histoires romaines*. Paris: Gallimard.

Dumézil 1988: Georges Dumézil, *Mitra-Varuna: An Essay on Two Indo-European Representations of Sovereignty* (trans. Derek Coltman, orig. edition Paris 1940). New York: Zone Books.

Duval 1976: Yves-Marie Duval, 'Les Lupercales, Junon et le printemps', *Annales de Bretagne et des pays de l'Ouest* 83: 253–72.

Duval 1977: Yves-Marie Duval, 'Des Lupercales de Constantinople aux Lupercales de Rome', *Revue des études latines* 55: 222–70.

Enea 1981: *Enea nel Lazio: archeologia e mito* (exhibition catalogue). Rome: Palombi.

Engelmann 1975: Helmut Engelmann, *The Delian Aretalogy of Sarapis* (Études préliminaires aux religions orientales dans l'Empire romain 44). Leiden: Brill.

England 1921: E.B. England, *The Laws of Plato*, vol. 2. Manchester University Press.

Fantham 1983: Elaine Fantham, 'Sexual Comedy in Ovid's *Fasti*: Sources and Motivation', *Harvard Studies in Classical Philology* 87: 185–216.

Fantham 1989: R. Elaine Fantham, 'Mime: the Missing Link in Roman Literary History', *Classical World* 82: 153–63.

Fantham 1992: Elaine Fantham, 'Ceres, Liber and Flora: Georgic and Anti-Georgic Elements in Ovid's *Fasti*', *Proceedings of the Cambridge Philological Society* 38: 39–56.

Fantham 1996: Elaine Fantham, *Roman Literary Culture from Cicero to Apuleius*. Baltimore: Johns Hopkins University Press.

Fantham 1998: Elaine Fantham, *Ovid: Fasti Book IV* (Cambridge Greek and Latin Classics). Cambridge University Press.

Faranda 1971: R. Faranda (trans.), *Detti e fatti memorabili di Valerio Massimo*. Turin: Utet.

Feeney 1991: D.C. Feeney, *The Gods in Epic: Poets and Critics of the Classical Tradition*. Oxford: Clarendon Press.

Feeney 2005: Denis Feeney, 'The Beginnings of a Literature in Latin', *Journal of Roman Studies* 95: 226–40.

Feldherr 1998: Andrew Feldherr, *Spectacle and Society in Livy's History*. Berkeley: University of California Press.

Finley 1964: M.I. Finley, 'The Trojan War', *Journal of Hellenic Studies* 84: 1–9.

Fishwick 1967: Duncan Fishwick, 'Hastiferi', *Journal of Roman Studies* 57: 142–160.

Flower 1995: Harriet I. Flower, '*Fabulae Praetextae* in Context: When Were Plays on Contemporary Subjects Performed in Republican Rome?', *Classical Quarterly* 45: 170–190.

Forsythe 1994: Gary Forsythe, *The Historian L. Calpurnius Piso Frugi and the Roman Annalistic Tradition*. Lanham MD: University Press of America.

Forsythe 1999: Gary Forsythe, *Livy and Early Rome: A Study in Historical Method and Judgment* (*Historia* Einzelschrift 132). Stuttgart: Franz Steiner.

Forsythe 2002: Gary Forsythe, 'Dating and Arranging the Roman History of Valerius Antias', in Vanessa R. Gordon and Eric W. Robinson (eds), *Oikistes: Studies in Constitutions, Colonies, and Military Power in the Ancient World, Offered in Honor of A.J. Graham* (Leiden: Brill): 99–112.

Foucher 1976: L. Foucher, 'Flagellation et rites de fécondité aux Lupercales', *Annales de Bretagne et des pays de l'Ouest* 83: 273.

Fox 1993: Matthew Fox, 'History and Rhetoric in Dionysius of Halicarnassus', *Journal of Roman Studies* 83: 31–47.

Fox 1996: Matthew Fox, *Roman Historical Myths: The Regal Period in Augustan Literature*. Oxford: Clarendon Press.

Fraccaro 1907: Plinio Fraccaro, *Studi Varroniani: De gente populi Romani libri IV*. Padua: Draghi.

Fraschetti 2002: Augusto Fraschetti, *Romolo il fondatore* (Quadrante Laterza 112). Rome: Laterza.

Frier 1979 (= 1999): Bruce W. Frier, *Libri annales pontificum maximorum: The Origins of the Annalistic Tradition* (Papers and Monographs of the American Academy in Rome 27). Rome: American Academy (ed. 2 1999, Ann Arbor: University of Michigan Press).

Gabba 1991: Emilio Gabba, *Dionysius and the History of Archaic Rome* (Sather Classical Lectures 56). Berkeley: University of California Press.

Gabba 2000: Emilio Gabba, *Roma arcaica: storia e storiografia* (Storia e letteratura 205). Rome: Edizioni di storia e letteratura.

Gallia 2007: Andrew B. Gallia, 'Reassessing the "Cumaean Chronicle": Greek Chronology and Roman History in Dionysius of Halicarnassus', *Journal of Roman Studies* 97: 50–67.

Gantz 1993: Timothy Gantz, *Early Greek Myth: a Guide to Literary and Artistic Sources*, two volumes. Baltimore: Johns Hopkins University Press.

Garland 1992: Robert Garland, *Introducing New Gods: The Politics of Athenian Religion*. London: Duckworth.

Gerhard 1868: E. Gerhard, *Gesammelte akademische Abhandlungen und kleine Schriften*. Berlin.

Gerhard *et al.* 1897: E. Gerhard et al., *Etruskische Spiegel* 5. Berlin: Georg Reimer.

Giancotti 1967: Francesco Giancotti, *Mimo e gnome: studio su Decimo Laberio e Publilio Siro* (Biblioteca di cultura contemporanea 98). Messina: G. D'Anna.

Gidlow 2004: Christopher Gidlow, *The Reign of Arthur: From History to Legend*. Stroud: Sutton.

Giglioli 1935: G.Q. Giglioli, *L'arte etrusca*. Milan: Fratelli Treves.

Gjerstad 1969: E. Gjerstad, 'Porsenna and Rome', *Opuscula Romana* 7: 149–61.

Goldberg 1995: Sander M. Goldberg, *Epic in Republican Rome*. New York: Oxford University Press.

Goldberg 2006: Sander Goldberg, 'Ennius after the Banquet', *Arethusa* 39.3: 427–47.

Gordon 1999: Richard Gordon, 'Imagining Greek and Roman Magic', in Valerie Flint *et al.*, *Witchcraft and Magic in Europe: Ancient Greece and Rome* (London: Athlone Press): 159–275.

Graham 1998: A.J. Graham, 'The Woman at the Window: Observations on the "Stele from the Harbour" of Thasos', *Journal of Hellenic Studies* 118: 22–40.

Grandazzi 1991: Alexandre Grandazzi, *La fondation de Rome: Réflexion sur l'histoire*. Paris: Les Belles Lettres.

Grant 1971: Michael Grant, *Roman Myths*. New York: Scribners.

Greco 1985: Emanuele Greco, 'Un santuario di età repubblicana presso il foro di Paestum', *La parola del passato* 40: 223–32.

Green 1994: J.R. Green, *Theatre in Ancient Greek Society*. London: Routledge.

Green 1995: J.R. Green, 'Theatrical Motifs in Non-Theatrical Contexts on Vases of the Later Fifth and Fourth Centuries', in Alan Griffiths (ed.), *Stage Directions: Essays in Ancient Drama in Honour of E.W. Handley* (*BICS* Supplement 66, London: Institute of Classical Studies): 93–121.

Greene 1938: G.C. Greene, *Scholia Platonica* (Philological Monographs 8). Haverfordiae: American Philological Association.

Griffin 1976: Miriam T. Griffin, *Seneca: a Philosopher in Politics*. Oxford: Clarendon Press.

Griffin 1985: Jasper Griffin, *Latin Poets and Roman Life*. London: Duckworth.

Griffin 1994: Miriam Griffin, 'The Intellectual Developments of the Ciceronian Age', in J.A. Crook, Andrew Lintott and Elizabeth Rawson (eds), *The Cambridge Ancient History*, IX (ed. 2) *The Last Age of the Roman Republic, 146–43 BC* (Cambridge University Press): 689–728.

Griffin 1997: A.H.F. Griffin, *A Commentary on Ovid* Metamorphoses *Book XI* (*Hermathena* 162–3). University of Dublin.

Griffiths 1998: Alan Griffiths, 'Where Did Early Roman History Come From?', unpublished paper given at a conference in Bristol, 15 July 1998.

Gruen 1990: Erich S. Gruen, *Studies in Greek Culture and Roman Policy* (Cincinnati

Classical Studies n.s. 7). Leiden: E.J. Brill.

Gruen 1992: Erich S. Gruen, *Culture and National Identity in Republican Rome* (Cornell Studies in Classical Philology 52). Ithaca, N.Y.: Cornell University Press.

Guerrini 1981: Roberto Guerrini, *Studi su Valerio Massimo* (Biblioteca di studi antichi 28). Pisa: Giardini.

Gurval 1995: Robert Alan Gurval, *Actium and Augustus: The Politics and Emotions of Civil War*. Ann Arbor: University of Michigan Press.

Gury 1998: Françoise Gury, 'À propos de l'image des incubes latins', *Mélanges de l'École française de Rome (Antiquité)* 110: 995–1021.

Guthrie 1962: W.K.C. Guthrie, *A History of Greek Philosophy*, I *The Earlier Presocratics and the Pythagoreans*. Cambridge University Press.

Habinek 2005: Thomas Habinek, *The World of Roman Song: From Ritualized Speech to Social Order*. Baltimore: Johns Hopkins University Press.

Hanson 1959: John A. Hanson, *Roman Theater-Temples* (Princeton Monographs in Art and Archaeology 33). Princeton University Press.

Hardie 1996: Alex Hardie, 'Pindar, Castalia and the Muses of Delphi (the *Sixth Paean*)', in Francis Cairns and Malcolm Heath (eds.), *Papers of the Leeds International Seminar, Ninth Volume* (Leeds: Francis Cairns): 219–57.

Harries 2006: Jill Harries, *Cicero and the Jurists: From Citizens' Law to the Lawful State*. London: Duckworth.

Harris 1989: William V. Harris, *Ancient Literacy*. Cambridge MA: Harvard University Press.

Harrison 2000: George W.M. Harrison (ed.), *Seneca in Performance*. London: Duckworth and Classical Press of Wales.

Harvey 2004: David Harvey, 'Herodotus Mythistoricus: Arion and the Liar? (1.23–4)', in Vassos Karageorghis and Ioannis Taifacos (eds), *The World of Herodotus* (Nicosia: University of Cyprus): 287–305.

Head 1911: B.V. Head, *Historia Numorum* (second edition). Oxford: Clarendon Press.

Hedreen 1992: Guy Hedreen, *Silens in Attic Black-Figure Vase-Painting: Myth and Performance*. Ann Arbor: University of Michigan Press.

Hedreen 1994: Guy Hedreen, 'Silens, Nymphs and Maenads', *Journal of Hellenic Studies* 114: 47–69.

Hellegouarc'h 1963: J. Hellegouarc'h, *Le vocabulaire latin des relations et des partis politiques sous la république* (Publications de la Faculté des Lettres et Sciences Humaines de l'Université de Lille, 11). Paris: Les Belles Lettres.

Henderson 1979: A.A.R. Henderson, *P. Ovidi Nasonis Remedia Amoris*. Edinburgh: Scottish Academic Press.

Henderson 2001: John Henderson, *Telling Tales on Caesar: Roman Stories from Phaedrus*. Oxford University Press.

Herkommer 1968: E. Herkommer, *Die Topoi in den Proömien der römischen Geschichtswerke* (diss.). Tübingen.

Hodgkinson 1997: M.J. Hodgkinson, *C. Licinius Macer and the Historiography of the Early Republic*. University of Exeter PhD thesis.

Holleman 1974: A.W.J. Holleman, *Pope Gelasius I and the Lupercalia*. Amsterdam: Hakkert.

Hollis 1998: A.S. Hollis, 'A Tragic Fragment in Cicero, *Pro Caelio* 67?', *Classical Quarterly* 48: 561–4.

Holloway 1994: R. Ross Holloway, *The Archaeology of Early Rome and Latium*. London: Routledge.

Hölscher 1978: Tonio Hölscher, 'Die Anfänge römischer Repräsentationskunst', *Mitteilungen des Deutschen Archaeologischen Instituts, Roemische Abteil* 85: 315–57.

Horsfall 1972: Nicholas Horsfall, 'Varro and Caesar: Three Chronological Problems', *Bulletin of the Institute of Classical Studies* 19: 120–8.

Horsfall 1979a: Nicholas Horsfall, 'Stesichorus at Bovillae?', *Journal of Hellenic Studies* 99: 26–48.

Horsfall 1979b: Nicholas Horsfall, 'Epic and Burlesque in Ovid, *Met.* VIII.260ff', *Classical Journal* 74: 319–32.

Horsfall 1985: Nicholas Horsfall, 'CIL VI 37965 = CLE 1988 (Epitaph of Allia Potestas): a commentary', *Zeitschrift für Papyrologie und Epigraphik* 61: 251–72.

Horsfall 1994: Nicholas Horsfall, 'The Prehistory of Latin Poetry: Some Problems of Method', *Rivista di filologia* 122: 50–75.

Horsfall 2003: Nicholas Horsfall, *The Culture of the Roman Plebs*. London: Duckworth.

Hubaux 1958: Jean Hubaux, *Rome et Véies: Recherches sur la chronologie légendaire du moyen âge romain*. Paris: Les Belles Lettres.

Hübinger 1992: Ulrich Hübinger, 'On Pan's Iconography and the Cult in the Sanctuary of Pan on the Slopes of Mount Lykaion', in Robin Hägg (ed.), *The Iconography of Greek Cult in the Archaic and Classical Periods* (*Kernos* Supplement 1, Liège: Centre d'Étude de la Religion Grecque Antique): 189–212.

Hughes 1997: Alan Hughes, 'KONNAKIS: A Scene from the Comic Theatre', *Echos du monde classique* 41: 237–46.

Humm 2000: Michel Humm, 'Spazio e tempo civici: riforma delle tribù e riforma del calendario alla fine del quarto secolo a.C.', in Christer Bruun (ed.), *The Roman Middle Republic: Politics, Religion and Historiography c.400–133 BC* (Acta Instituti Romani Finlandiae 23, Rome): 91–119.

Humphrey 1986: John H. Humphrey, *Roman Circuses: Arenas for Chariot Racing*. London: B.T. Batsford.

Hutton 2003: Ronald Hutton, *Witches, Druids and King Arthur*. London: Hambledon and London.

Jacoby 1962: Felix Jacoby, *Die Fragmente der griechischen Historiker: Zweiter Teil B, Kommentar*. Leiden: Brill.

Jocelyn 1971: H.D. Jocelyn, 'VRBS AVGVRIO AVGVSTO CONDITA: Ennius ap. Cic. *Div.* 1.107 (= *Ann.* 77–96 V^2)', *Proceedings of the Cambridge Philological Society* 17: 44–74.

Johns 1986: Catherine Johns, 'Faunus at Thetford: an Early Latian Deity in Late-Roman Britain', in Martin Henig and Anthony King (eds), *Pagan Gods and Shrines of the Roman Empire* (Monograph 8, Oxford Committee for Archaeology): 93–103.

Jurgeit 1992: Fritzi Jurgeit, 'Interventi ottocenteschi sulla cista di Karlsruhe', *Bollettino d'arte* 74–75: 85–94.

Jurgeit 1999: Fritzi Jurgeit, *Die etruskischen und italischen Bronzen im Badischen Landesmuseum Karlsruhe* (Terra Italia 5), two volumes. Rome: Gruppo editoriale internazionale.

Kaibel 1899: Georgius Kaibel (ed.), *Comicorum Graecorum fragmenta*, I fasc. 1. Berlin: Weidmann.

Keaveney 2003: Arthur Keaveney, 'The Tragedy of Gaius Gracchus: Ancient Melodrama or Modern Farce?', *Klio* 85: 322–32.

Keaveney 2005: Arthur Keaveney, 'Sulla and the Games of Hercules', *L'Antiquité Classique* 74: 217–23.

Keaveney 2006: Arthur Keaveney, 'Livy and the Theatre: Reflections on the Theory of Peter Wiseman', *Klio* 88: 510–15.

Klotz 1953: Alfredus Klotz, *Tragicorum fragmenta* (*Scaenicorum Romanorum fragmenta* I). Munich: Oldenbourg.

Kraay and Hirmer 1966: C.M. Kraay and M. Hirmer, *Greek Coins*. London: Thames and Hudson.

Kragelund 1982: Patrick Kragelund, *Prophecy, Populism, and Propaganda in the 'Octavia'* (Opuscula Graecolatina 25). Copenhagen: Museum Tusculanum.

Kragelund 1999: Patrick Kragelund, 'Senecan Tragedy: Back on Stage?', *Classica et Mediaevalia* 50: 235–47.

Kragelund et al. 2002: Patrick Kragelund *et alii*, 'Historical Drama in Ancient Rome: Republican Flourishing and Imperial Decline?', *Symbolae Osloenses* 77: 5–105.

Kraus 1994: Christina S. Kraus, '"No Second Troy": Topoi and Refoundation in Livy, Book V', *Transactions of the American Philological Association* 124: 267–89.

Kumaniecki 1970: K. Kumaniecki, 'Les discours égarés de Cicéron Pro Cornelio', *Mededelingen van de Koninklijke Academie voor Wetenschappen, Letteren en Schone Kunsten van Belgie, Kl. Lett.* 32.4: 3–36.

Laird 1993: Andrew Laird, 'Sounding Out Ecphrasis: Art and Text in Catullus 64', *Journal of Roman Studies* 83: 18–30.

Lanciani 1891: Rodolfo Lanciani, 'Miscellanea topografica: insigne Larario del Vico Patrizio', *Bullettino della commissione archeologica comunale di Roma* 19: 305–11.

Lanciani 1990: Rodolfo Lanciani, *Storia degli scavi di Roma*, vol. 2. Rome: Quasar.

Latacz 2004: Joachim Latacz, *Troy and Homer: Towards a Solution of an Old Mystery*. Oxford University Press.

Leach 1993: E.W. Leach, 'The entrance room in the House of Iulius Polybius and the nature of the Roman vestibulum', in Eric M. Moormann (ed.), *Functional and Spatial Analysis of Wall Painting* (Annual Papers on Classical Archaeology, Supplement 3, Leiden: Babesch): 23–8.

Le Gall 1953: Joël Le Gall, *Le Tibre fleuve de Rome dans l'antiquité*. Paris: Presses universitaires de France.

Leigh 1996: Matthew Leigh, 'Varius Rufus, Thyestes and the Appetites of Antony', *Proceedings of the Cambridge Philological Association* 42: 171–97.

Liebeschuetz 1979: J.H.W.G. Liebeschuetz, *Continuity and Change in Roman Religion*. Oxford: Clarendon Press.

Lepper and Frere 1988: Frank Lepper and Sheppard Frere, *Trajan's Column: a New Edition of the Cichorius Plates*. Gloucester: Alan Sutton.

Levene 1993: D.S. Levene, *Religion in Livy* (*Mnemosyne* Supplement 127). Leiden: Brill.

Liberatore 1995: Daniela Liberatore, 'Un Marsia nel Foro di Alba Fucens? Una proposta di identificazione', *Ostraka* 4: 249–55.

Lintott 1968: A. W. Lintott, *Violence in Republican Rome*. Oxford: Clarendon Press.

Littlewood 1975: R.J. Littlewood, 'Ovid's Lupercalia (*Fasti* 2.267–452): a Study in the Artistry of the *Fasti*', *Latomus* 34: 1060–72.

Littlewood 1980: R.J. Littlewood, 'Ovid and the Ides of March (*Fasti* 3.523–710); a Further Study in the Artistry of the *Fasti*', in Carl Deroux (ed.), *Studies in Latin Literature* 2 (Collection Latomus 168, Brussels): 301–21.

Littlewood 1981: R.J. Littlewood, 'Poetic Artistry and Dynastic Politics: Ovid at the *Ludi Megalenses* (*Fasti* 4.179–372), *Classical Quarterly* 31: 381–95.

Liverani 1996: P. Liverani, 'Ianiculum', in Eva Margareta Steinby (ed.), *Lexicon Topographicum Urbis Romae* vol. IV (Rome: Quasar): 89–90.

Luce 1930: Stephen Bleecker Luce, 'Attic Red-Figured Vases and Fragments at Corinth', *American Journal of Archaeology* 34: 334–43.

Luck 1999: Georg Luck, 'Witches and Sorcerers in Classical Literature', in Valerie Flint *et al.*, *Witchcraft and Magic in Europe: Ancient Greece and Rome* (London: Athlone Press): 91–158.

Lugli and Rosa 2001: Francesca Lugli and Carlo Rosa, 'Prime evidenze di opere di terrazzamento del Capitolium nell'età del Bronzo recente', *Bullettino della commissione archeologica comunale di Roma* 102: 281–90.

Lulof 1996: Patricia S. Lulof, *The Ridge-Pole Statues from the Late Archaic Temple at Satricum* (Scrinium 9, Satricum 5). Amsterdam: Thesis publishers.

Mace 1996: Sarah Mace, 'Utopian and Erotic Fusion in a New Elegy by Simonides (22 West^2)', *Zeitschrift für Papyrologie und Epigraphik* 113: 233–47.

MacLachlan 1992: Bonnie MacLachlan, 'Sacred Prostitution and Aphrodite', *Studies in Religion/Sciences Religieuses* 21/2: 145–62.

MacMullen 1966: Ramsay MacMullen, *Enemies of the Roman Order: Treason, Unrest, and Alienation in the Empire*. Cambridge, MA: Harvard University Press.

Malkin 1998: Irad Malkin, *The Returns of Odysseus: Colonization and Ethnicity*. Berkeley: University of California Press.

Maltby 1991: Robert Maltby, *A Lexicon of Ancient Latin Etymologies* (Arca 25). Leeds: Francis Cairns.

Mannhardt 1904: Wilhelm Mannhardt, *Wald- und Feldkulte*, vol. 1, 2nd ed. Berlin: Borntraeger.

Mantuanus 1481: Fratris Baptistae Mantuani vatis et theologi profundissimi opus absolutissimum de sacris diebus. . . Pictavis [Poitiers] in edibus Iacobi Boucheti.

Manuwald 2001: Gesine Manuwald, *Fabulae praetextae: Spuren einer literarischen Gattung der Römer* (Zetemata 108). München: C.H. Beck.

Marincola 1997: John Marincola, *Authority and Tradition in Ancient Historiography*. Cambridge University Press.

Markus 1990: Robert Markus, *The End of Ancient Christianity*. Cambridge University Press.

Marquadt 1886: Joachim Marquadt, *Das Privatleben der Römer* (Handbuch der römischen Alterthumer VII). Leipzig: Hirzel.

Martelli 1987: Marina Martelli, *La ceramica degli Etruschi*. Novara: Istituto geografico De Agostini.

Mastrocinque 1983: Attilio Mastrocinque, 'La cacciata di Tarquinio il Superbo: tradizione romana e letteratura greca', *Athenaeum* 61: 457–80.

Mastrocinque 1988: Attilio Mastrocinque, *Lucio Giunio Bruto: Ricerche di storia, religione e diritto sulle origini della repubblica romana.* Trento: edizioni La Reclame.

Mazzarino 1966: Santo Mazzarino, *Il pensiero storico classico*, II.1. Bari: Laterza.

McKay 1975: A.G. McKay, *Houses, Villas and Palaces in the Roman World.* London: Thames and Hudson.

McKeown 1979: J.C. McKeown, 'Augustan Elegy and Mime', *Proceedings of the Cambridge Philological Society* 25: 71–84.

Menichetti 1995: Mauro Menichetti, *Quoius forma virtutei parisuma fuit... Ciste prenestine e cultura di Roma medio-repubblicana* (Archeologia Perusina 12), Rome: Giorgio Bretschneider.

Merivale 1969: Patricia Merivale, *Pan the Goat-God: His Myth in Modern Times.* Cambridge MA: Harvard University Press.

Michelini 1987: Ann Norris Michelini, *Euripides and the Tragic Tradition* (Wisconsin Studies in Classics). Madison: University of Wisconsin Press.

Michels 1951: Agnes Kirsopp Michels, 'The Drama of the Tarquins', *Latomus* 10: 13–24.

Michels 1967: Agnes Kirsopp Michels, *The Calendar of the Roman Republic.* Princeton University Press.

Millar 1964: Fergus Millar, *A Study of Cassius Dio.* Oxford: Clarendon Press.

Millar 1998: Fergus Millar, *The Crowd in Rome in the Late Republic* (Jerome Lectures 22). Ann Arbor: University of Michigan Press.

Miller 1916: Konrad Miller, *Itineraria Romana: römische Reisewege an der Hand der tabula Peutingeriana dargestellt.* Stuttgart: Strecker.

Moles 1993: John Moles, 'Livy's Preface', *Proceedings of the Cambridge Philological Association* 39: 141–68.

Momigliano 1957: Arnaldo Momigliano, 'Perizonius, Niebuhr and the Character of Early Roman Tradition', *Journal of Roman Studies* 47: 104–14.

Momigliano 1984: Arnaldo Momigliano, 'Georges Dumézil and the Trifunctional Approach to Roman Civilization', *History and Theory* 23: 312–30.

Momigliano 1987: Arnaldo Momigliano, *Ottavo contributo alla storia degli studi classici e del mondo antico* (Raccolta di studi e testi 161). Rome: Edizioni di storia e letteratura.

Momigliano 1989: A. Momigliano, 'The Origins of Rome', in F.W. Walbank *et alii* (eds), *The Cambridge Ancient History* (ed. 2) VII.2: *The Rise of Rome to 220 BC* (Cambridge University Press): 52–112.

Momigliano 1990: Arnaldo Momigliano, *The Classical Foundations of Modern Historiography* (Sather Classical Lectures 54). Berkeley: University of California Press.

Mommsen 1860: Theodor Mommsen, *Geschichte des römischen Münzwesens.* Berlin: Weidmann.

Mommsen 1864: Theodor Mommsen, *Römische Forschungen*, vol. 1. Berlin: Weidmann.

Mommsen 1887: Theodor Mommsen, *Römische Staatsrecht* (ed. 3), vol. 2.1. Leipzig: Hirzel.

Mommsen 1893: Theodor Mommsen (ed.), *Corpus Inscriptionum Latinarum* vol. 1 part 1 (ed.2). Berlin: Reimer.

Montanari 1976: Enrico Montanari, *Roma: momenti di una presa di coscienza sociale* (Chi siamo 3). Rome: Bulzoni.

Moorton 1988: R.F. Moorton, 'The Genealogy of Latinus in Virgil's *Aeneid*', *Transactions of the American Philological Association* 118: 253–9.

Morrow 1960: Glenn Raymond Morrow, *Plato's Cretan City: A Historical Interpretation of the* Laws. Princeton University Press.

Mueller 2002: Hans-Friedrich Mueller, *Roman Religion in Valerius Maximus*. London: Routledge.

Münzer 1897: Friedrich Münzer, *Beiträge zur Quellenkritik der Naturgeschichte des Plinius*. Berlin: Weidmann.

Münzer 1920: Friedrich Münzer, *Römische Adelsparteien und Adelsfamilien*. Stuttgart: Metzler.

Münzer 1932: F. Münzer, 'Memmius (1)', *Paulys Real-Encyclopädie* 15: 603–4.

Münzer 1937: Friedrich Münzer, 'Die römischen Vestalinnen bis zur Kaiserzeit', *Philologus* 92: 47–67 and 199–222.

Münzer 1939: F. Münzer, 'Tuccia (12)', *Paulys Real-Encyclopädie* 7A: 768–70.

Nijboer *et al.* 1999/2000: A.J. Nijboer, J. van der Plicht, A.M. Bietti Sestieri, A. De Santis, 'A High Chronology for the Early Iron Age in Central Italy', *Palaeohistoria* 41/42: 163–76.

Nock 1972: Arthur Darby Nock, *Essays on Religion and the Ancient World*. Oxford: Clarendon Press.

North 1989: J.A. North, 'Religion in Republican Rome', in F.W. Walbank *et al.* (eds), *The Cambridge Ancient History*, VII part 2 (ed. 2) *The Rise of Rome to 220 BC* (Cambridge University Press): 573–624.

North 1992: J.A. North, 'Deconstructing Stone Theatres', in *Apodosis: Essays presented to Dr. W.W. Cruickshank to mark his Eightieth Birthday* (London, St Paul's School): 75–83.

North 2000a: J.A. North, *Roman Religion* (New Surveys in the Classics 30). Oxford University Press.

North 2000b: J.A. North, 'Prophet and Text in the Third Century BC', in Edward Bispham and Christopher Smith (eds), *Religion in Archaic and Republican Rome and Italy: Evidence and Experience* (Edinburgh University Press): 92–107.

Oakley 1997: J.H. Oakley, 'Hesione', *Lexicon Iconographicum Mythologiae Classicae* 8.1: 623–9 and 8.2: 386–9.

Oakley 1997: S.P. Oakley, *A Commentary on Livy Books VI–X*, vol. I. Oxford: Clarendon Press.

Oakley 1998: S.P. Oakley, *A Commentary on Livy Books VI–X*, vol. II. Oxford: Clarendon Press.

Oakley 2005: S.P. Oakley, *A Commentary on Livy Books VI–X*, vol. IV. Oxford: Clarendon Press.

Ogden 1999: Daniel Ogden, 'Binding Spells: Curse Tablets and Voodoo Dolls in the Greek and Roman Worlds', in Valerie Flint *et al.*, *Witchcraft and Magic in Europe: Ancient Greece and Rome* (London: Athlone Press): 1–90.

Ogden 2001: Daniel Ogden, *Greek and Roman Necromancy*. Princeton University Press.

Ogden 2002: Daniel Ogden, *Magic, Witchcraft and Ghosts in the Greek and Roman Worlds*. New York: Oxford University Press.

Ogilvie 1965: R.M. Ogilvie, *A Commentary on Livy Books 1–5*. Oxford: Clarendon Press.

Otis 1966: Brooks Otis, *Ovid as an Epic Poet*. Cambridge University Press.

Otto 1890: August Otto, *Die Sprichwörter und sprichwörtlichen Redensarten der Römer*. Leipzig.

Otto 1913: W.F. Otto, 'Die Luperci und die Feier der Lupercalien', *Philologus* 72:161–95

Page 1941: D.L. Page, *Select Papyri* 3 (Loeb Classical Library). London: Heinemann.

Page 1973: Denys Page, 'Stesichorus: the *Geryoneïs*', *Journal of Hellenic Studies* 93: 138–54.

Pailler 1988: Jean-Marie Pailler, *Bacchanalia: La repression de 186 av. J.-C. à Rome et en Italie* (BEFAR 270). Rome: École française de Rome.

Pairault Massa 1992: Françoise-Hélène Pairault Massa, *Iconologia e politica nell'Italia antica: Roma, Lazio, Etruria dal VII al I secolo a.C.* (Biblioteca di archeologia 18). Milan: Longanesi.

Pallottino 1981: Massimo Pallottino, *Genti e culture dell'Italia preromana* (Guide allo studio della civiltà romana 1.2). Rome: Jouvence.

Palombi 1997: Domenico Palombi, *Tra Palatino ed Esquilino: Velia, Carinae, Fagutal* (*RINASA* Supplement 1). Rome: Istituto nazionale d'archeologia e storia dell'arte.

Panayotakis 1995: Costas Panayotakis, *Theatrum Arbitri: Theatrical Elements in the Satyrica of Petronius* (*Mnemosyne* Supplement 146). Leiden: Brill.

Panciera 1986: Silvio Panciera, 'Ancora sull'iscrizione di Cornelius Surus magister scribarum poetarum', *Bullettino della commissione archeologica comunale di Roma* 91: 35–44.

Parke 1988: H.W. Parke, *Sibyls and Sibylline Prophecy in Classical Antiquity*. London: Routledge.

Parker 1993: Hugh C. Parker, '*Romani numen soli*: Faunus in Ovid's *Fasti*', *Transactions of the American Philological Association* 123: 199–217.

Pasco-Pranger 2002: Molly Pasco-Pranger, 'A Varronian Vatic Numa? Ovid's *Fasti* and Plutarch's *Life of Numa*', in D.S. Levene and D.P. Nelis (eds), *Clio and the Poets: Augustan Poetry and the Traditions of Ancient Historiography* (*Mnemosyne* Supplement 224, Leiden: Brill): 291–312.

Pasco-Pranger 2006: Molly Pasco-Pranger, *Founding the Year: Ovid's* Fasti *and the Poetics of the Roman Calendar* (*Mnemosyne* Supplement 276). Leiden: Brill.

Pelling 1985: C.B.R. Pelling, 'Plutarch and Catiline', *Hermes* 113: 311–29.

Pelling 2002: Christopher Pelling, *Plutarch and History: Eighteen Studies*. London: Classical Press of Wales and Duckworth.

Pensabene 1998: Patrizio Pensabene, 'Vent'anni di studi e scavi dell'Università di Roma "La Sapienza" nell'area sud-ovest del palatino (1977–1997)', in Carlo Giavarini (ed.), *Il Palatino: area sacra sud-ovest e Domus Tiberiana* (Studia archaeologica 95, Rome: L'Erma di Bretschneider): 1–154.

Peruzzi 1998: Emilio Peruzzi, *Civiltà greca nel Lazio preromano* (Studi dell'Accademia Toscana 'La Columbaria' 165). Florence: Leo S. Olschki.

Peter 1906: Hermann Peter, *Historicorum Romanorum reliquiae* vol. 2. Leipzig: Teubner.

Phillips 1968: Kyle M. Phillips, jr, 'Perseus and Andromeda', *American Journal of Archaeology* 72: 1–23.

Pick 1917: Behrendt Pick, 'Ein Vorlaufer des Mephistopheles auf antiken Münzen', *Jahrbuch der Goethe-Gesellschaft* 4: 153–64.

Pick 1931: Behrendt Pick, *Aufsätze zur Numismatik und Archäologie*. Jena: Frommann.

Pickard-Cambridge 1968: A.W. Pickard-Cambridge, *The Dramatic Festivals of Athens* (rev. ed.). Oxford: Clarendon Press.

Piranomonte 2001: M. Piranomonte, 'Annae Perennae nemus', in Adriano La Regina (ed.), *Lexicon Topographicum Urbis Romae: Suburbium* I, A–B (Rome: Quasar): 59–63.

Piranomonte 2002: Marina Piranomonte (ed.), *Il santuario della musica e il bosco sacro di Anna Perenna*. Milan: Electa.

Pontrandolfo 2000: Angela Pontrandolfo, 'Dioniso e personaggi fliacici nelle imagini pestane', *Ostraka* 9.1: 117–34.

Porte 1985: Danielle Porte, *L'étiologie religieuse dans les Fastes d'Ovide* (Collection d'études anciennes). Paris: Les Belles Lettres.

Pötscher 1984: Walter Pötscher, 'Die Lupercalia—eine Strukturanalyse', *Grazer Beiträge* 11: 221–49.

Poucet 1989: Jacques Poucet, 'Réflexions sur l'écrit et l'écriture dans le Rome des premiers siècles', *Latomus* 48: 285–311.

Poucet 2000: Jacques Poucet, *Les Rois de Rome: tradition et histoire*. Louvain: Académie royale de Belgique 2000).

Purcell 2003: Nicholas Purcell, 'Becoming Historical: The Roman Case', in David Braund and Christopher Gill (eds), *Myth, History and Culture in Republican Rome* (University of Exeter Press): 12–40.

Ramsey 1980: J. T. Ramsey, 'A Reconstruction of Q. Gallius' Trial for Ambitus: One Less Reason for Doubting the Authenticity of the *Commentariolum Petitionis'*, *Historia* 29: 402–21.

Rawson 1971: Elizabeth Rawson, 'The Literary Sources for the Pre-Marian Army', *Papers of the British School at Rome* 39: 13–31.

Rawson 1985: Elizabeth Rawson: *Intellectual Life in the Late Roman Republic*. London: Duckworth.

Rawson 1991: Elizabeth Rawson, *Roman Culture and Society: Collected Papers*. Oxford: Clarendon Press.

Rawson 1993: Elizabeth Rawson, 'The Vulgarity of the Roman Mime', in H.D. Jocelyn and H.V. Hurt (eds), *Tria Lustra: Essays and Notes Presented to John Pinsent* (Liverpool: LCM): 255–60.

Reynolds 1982: Joyce Reynolds, *Aphrodisias and Rome: Documents from the Excavation of the Theatre at Aphrodisias* (*JRS* Monograph 1). London: Society for the Promotion of Roman Studies.

Rhodes 1981: P.J. Rhodes, *A Commentary on the Aristotelian* Athenaion Politeia. Oxford: Clarendon Press.

Ribbeck 1881: Otto Ribbeck, 'Ein historisches Drama', *Rheinisches Museum* 36: 321–2.

Ribbeck 1887: Otto Ribbeck, *Tragicorum Romanorum fragmenta*, ed. 3. Leipzig: Teubner.

Richard 1983: Jean-Claude Richard, *Pseudo-Aurélius Victor, Les origines du peuple romain*. Paris: Les Belles Lettres.

Richter 1901: Otto Richter, *Topographie der Stadt Rom* (Handbuch der klassischen Altertums-Wissenschaft 3.3.2). Munich: Beck.

Ridgway 1988: David Ridgway, 'The Etruscans', in *The Cambridge Ancient History* (ed. 2), vol. IV *Persia, Greece and the Western Mediterranean c. 525–479 B.C.* (Cambridge University Press): 634–75.

Ridgway 1992: David Ridgway, *The First Western Greeks*. Cambridge University Press.

Ridgway 1996: David Ridgway, 'Greek Letters at Osteria dell'Osa', *Opuscula Romana* 20: 87–97.

Ritschl 1862: Fridericus Ritschelius (ed.), *Priscae Latinitatis monumenta epigraphica ad archetyporum fidem exemplis lithographis repraesentata*. Berlin: Reimer.

Rose 1928: H.J. Rose, *A Handbook of Greek Mythology, Including its Extension to Rome*. London: Methuen.

Rose and Price 1996: H.J. R(ose) and S.R.F. P(rice), 'Calendar, Roman', in Simon Hornblower and Anthony Spawforth (eds), *The Oxford Classical Dictionary* (ed. 3, Oxford University Press): 274.

Rösler 1990: Wolfgang Rösler, '*Mnemosyne* in the *Symposion*', in Oswyn Murray (ed.), *Sympotica: a Symposium on the Symposion* (Oxford: Clarendon Press): 230–7.

Säflund 1932: Gösta Säflund, *Le mura di Roma repubblicana: Saggio di archeologia romana* (Acta Instituti Romani Regni Sueciae 1). Lund: Gleerup.

Santangeli Valenziani and Volpe 1996: R. Santangeli Valenzani and R. Volpe, 'Nova Via', in E.M. Steinby (ed.), *Lexicon Topographicum Urbis Romae* 3, H–O (Rome: Quasar): 346–9.

Schauenberg 1981: Konrad Schauenberg, 'Andromeda', *Lexicon Iconographicum Mythologiae Classicae* 1.1: 774–90 and 1.2: 622–42.

Schmidt 1989: Peter Lebrecht Schmidt, 'Postquam ludus in artem paulatim verterat: Varro und die Frügeschichte des römischen Theaters', in Gregor Vogt-Spira (ed.), *Studien zur vorliterarien Periode im frühen Rom* (ScriptOralia 12, Tübingen: Gunter Narr): 77–133.

Schofield 1986: Malcolm Schofield, 'Cicero For and Against Divination', *Journal of Roman Studies* 76: 47–65.

Schultz 2006: Celia E. Schultz, *Women's Religious Activity in the Roman Republic*. Chapel Hill: University of North Carolina Press.

Schumacher 1968–9: W.W. Schumacher, 'Antikes und Christliches zur Auspeitschung der Elia Afanacia', *Jahrbuch für Antike und Christentum* 11–12: 65–75.

Schweitzer 1955: B. Schweitzer, 'Zum Krater des Aristonothos', *Römische Mitteilungen* 62: 78–106.

Sciarrino 2006: Enrica Sciarrino, 'The Introduction of Epic in Rome: Cultural Thefts and Social Contexts', *Arethusa* 39.3: 449–69.

Seaford 1984: Richard Seaford, *Euripides Cyclops, with Introduction and Commentary*. Oxford: Clarendon Press.

Seaford 1994: Richard Seaford, *Reciprocity and Ritual: Homer and Tragedy in the Developing City-State*. Oxford: Clarendon Press.

Segal 1968: Charles P. Segal, 'Circean Temptations: Homer, Vergil, Ovid', *Transactions of the American Philological Association* 99: 419–42.

Serrati 2006: John Serrati, 'Neptune's Altars: The Treaties between Rome and Carthage (509–226 BC)', *Classical Quarterly* 56: 113–34.

Sherk 1969: Robert K. Sherk, *Roman Documents from the Greek East: Senatus consulta and epistulae to the Age of Augustus*. Baltimore: Johns Hopkins University Press.

Silk 2000: M.S. Silk, *Aristophanes and the Definition of Comedy*. Oxford University Press.

Simon 1982: Erika Simon, *The Ancient Theatre* (trans. C.E. Vafopoulou-Richardson). London: Methuen.

Simon 1997: Erika Simon, 'Silenoi', *Lexicon Iconographicum Mythologiae Classicae* 8.1: 1108–1133.

Skidmore 1996: Clive Skidmore, *Practical Ethics for Roman Gentlemen: the Work of Valerius Maximus*. University of Exeter Press.

Skutsch 1968: Otto Skutsch, *Studia Enniana*. London: Athlone Press.

Skutsch 1985: Otto Skutsch, *The Annals of Quintus Ennius*. Oxford: Clarendon Press.

Slater 2005: W.J. Slater, 'Mimes and *Mancipes*', *Phoenix* 59: 316–23.

Smith 1996: Christopher John Smith, *Early Rome and Latium: Economy and Society c.1000 to 500 BC*. Oxford: Clarendon Press.

Smith 2003: Joseph A. Smith, 'Flavian Drama: Looking Back with Octavia', in A.J. Boyle and W.J. Dominik (eds), *Flavian Rome: Culture, Image, Text* (Leiden: Brill): 391–430.

Smits 1946: Elisabeth Clementine Henriette Smits, *Faunus*. Leiden: Leidsche Uitgeversmaatschappij.

Solin 1983: Heikki Solin, 'Varia onomastica: V. Κλεῖκλος', *Zeitschrift für Papyrologie und Epigraphik* 51: 180–2.

Solin and Brandenburg 1980: H. Solin and H. Brandenburg, 'Paganer Fruchtbarkeitsritus und Martyriumsdarstellung?: zum Grabrelief der Elia Afanacia im Museum der Prätextat-Katakombe zu Rom', *Archäologische Anzeiger* 1980: 271–84.

Soltau 1909: Wilhelm Soltau, *Die Anfänge der roemischen Geschichtschreibung*. Leipzig.

Spaeth 1996: Barbette Stanley Spaeth, *The Roman Goddess Ceres*. Austin: University of Texas Press.

Steffen 1952: Victor Steffen, *Satyrographorum Graecorum fragmenta*. Poznań: Poznańskie Towarzystwo Przyjaciół Nauk.

Stern 1968: H. Stern, 'Un calendrier romain illustré de Thysdrus', in *Tardo antico e alto medioevo: la forma artistica nel passaggio dall'antichità al medioevo* (Rome: Accademia dei Lincei): 177–200.

Stibbe et al. 1980: C.M. Stibbe, G. Colonna, C. De Simone, H. Versnel, *Lapis Satricanus: Archaeological, epigraphical, linguistic and historical aspects of the new inscription from Satricum* (Archeologische Studiën van het Nederlands Instituut te Rome, Scripta Minora 5). The Hague: Ministerie van Cultuur, Recreatie en Maatschappelijk Werk.

Storchi Marino 1999: Alfredina Storchi Marino, *Numa e Pitagora: sapientia constituendae civitatis*. Naples: Liguori Editore.

Sumner 1973: G.V. Sumner, *The Orators in Cicero's* Brutus: *Prosopography and Chronology* (*Phoenix* Supplementary volume 11). University of Toronto Press.

Syme 1939: Ronald Syme, *The Roman Revolution*. Oxford: Clarendon Press.

Syme 1958: Ronald Syme, *Tacitus*. Oxford: Clarendon Press.

Szilágyi 1981: J.C. Szilágyi, 'Impletae modis saturae', *Prospettiva* 24: 2–23.

Taplin 1993: Oliver Taplin, *Comic Angels, and Other Approaches to Greek Drama through Vase-Paintings*. Oxford: Clarendon Press.

Taplin 2000: Oliver Taplin, 'The Spring of the Muses: Homer and Related Poetry', in Oliver Taplin (ed.), *Literature in the Greek World* (New York: Oxford University Press): 4–39.

Taylor 1939: Lily Ross Taylor, 'Cicero's Aedileship', *American Journal of Philology* 60: 194–202.

Taylor 1960: Lily Ross Taylor, *The Voting Districts of the Roman Republic* (Papers and Monographs of the American Academy in Rome 20). Rome: American Academy.

Taylor 1962: Lily Ross Taylor, 'Forerunners of the Gracchi', *Journal of Roman Studies* 52: 19–27.

Timpe 1988: Dieter Timpe, 'Mündlichkeit und Schriftlichkeit als Basis der frührömischen überlieferung', in Jürgen von Ungern-Sternberg and Hansjörg Reinau (eds), *Vergangenheit in mündlicher Überlieferung* (Colloquium Rauricum 1, Stuttgart: Teubner): 266–86.

Tomasetti 1910: Giuseppe Tomasetti, *La campagna di Roma antica, medioevale e moderna*, vol. 2. Rome.

Torelli 1982: Mario Torelli, *Typography and Structure of Roman Historical Reliefs* (Jerome Lectures 14). Ann Arbor: University of Michigan Press.

Torelli 1984: Mario Torelli, *Lavinio e Roma: riti iniziatrici e matrimonio tra archeologia e storia*. Rome: Quasar.

Torelli 1993: Mario Torelli, 'Gli aromi e il sale: Afrodite ed Eracle nell'*emporia* arcaica dell'Italia', in Attilio Mastrocinque (ed.), *Ercole in occidente* (Labirinti 2, Università degli studi di Trento): 91–117.

Torelli 1996: Mario Torelli, 'Riflessioni sulle registrazioni storiche in Etruria', *Eutopia* 5: 13–22.

Torelli 1997: *Il rango, il rito e l'immagine: alle origini della rappresentazione storica romana*. Milan: Electa.

Torelli 1999: *Tota Italia: Essays in the Cultural Foundation of Roman Italy*. Oxford: Clarendon Press.

Tortorella 2000: Stefano Tortorella, 'L'adolescenza dei gemelli, la festa dei *Lupercalia* e l'uccisione di Amulio', in Andrea Carandini and Rosanna Cappelli (eds), *Roma: Romolo, Remo e la fondazione della città* (Milan: Electa): 244–55.

Traversari 1960: Gustavo Traversari, *Gli spettacoli in acqua nel teatro tardo-antico*. Rome: L'Erma di Bretschneider.

Travlos 1971: *A Pictorial Dictionary of Ancient Athens*. London: Thames and Hudson.

Trendall 1959: A.D. Trendall, *Phlyax Vases* (*BICS* Supplement 8). London: Institute of Classical Studies.

Trendall 1967: A.D. Trendall, *The Red-Figured Vases of Lucania, Campania and Sicily*. Oxford: Clarendon Press.

Trendall 1987: A.D. Trendall, *The Red-Figured Vases of Paestum*. London: British School at Rome.

Trendall 1989: A.D. Trendall, *Red-Figure Vases of South Italy and Sicily: a Handbook*. London: Thames and Hudson.

Trendall and Cambitoglou 1982: A.D. Trendall and A. Cambitoglou, *The Red-Figured Vases of Apulia*, vol. 2. Oxford: Clarendon Press.

Ulf 1982: Christoph Ulf, *Das römische Lupercalienfest* (Impulse der Forschung 38). Darmstadt: Wissenschaftliche Buchgesellschaft.

Ungern-Sternberg 1986: Jürgen von Ungern-Sternberg, 'The Formation of the "Annalistic Tradition"; the Example of the Decemvirate', in Kurt A. Raaflaub (ed.), *Social Struggles in Archaic Rome: New Perspectives on the Conflict of the Orders* (Berkeley: University of California Press): 77–104.

Ungern-Sternberg 1988: Jürgen von Ungern-Sternberg, 'Überlegungen zur frühen römischen überlieferung im Lichte der Oral-Tradition-Forschung', in Jürgen von Ungern-Sternberg and Hansjörg Reinau (eds), *Vergangenheit in mündlicher Überlieferung* (Colloquium Rauricum 1, Stuttgart: Teubner): 237–65.

Vaahtera 1993: Jyri Vaahtera, 'On the Religious Nature of the Place of Assembly', in Unto Paananen et al. (eds), *Senatus Populusque Romanus: Studies in Roman Republican Legislation* (Acta Instituti Romani Finlandiae 13, Helsinki University Press): 97–116.

Vanggaard 1988: Jens H. Vanggaard, *The Flamen: A Study in the History and Sociology of Roman Religion*. Copenhagen: Museum Tusculanum.

Van Sickle 1986: John Van Sickle, *Poesia e potere: il mito Virgilio*. Bari: Laterza.

Versnel 1976: H.S. Versnel, review of Alföldi 1974, *Bibliotheca Orientalis* 33: 391–401.

Versnel 1993: H.S. Versnel, *Transition and Reversal in Myth and Ritual* (Studies in Greek and Roman Religion 6.2). Leiden: Brill.

Veyne 1960: Paul Veyne, 'Iconographie de la "transvectio equitum" et des Lupercales', *Revue des études anciennes* 62: 100–10.

Veyne 1961: Paul Veyne, 'Le Marsyas "colonial" et l'indépendance des cités', *Revue de philologie* 35: 87–98.

Viscogliosi 1993: A. Viscogliosi, 'Circus Flaminius', in Eva Margareta Steinby (ed.), *Lexicon Topographicum Urbis Romae* I (Rome: Quasar): 269–72.

Von Staden 1989: Heinrich von Staden, *Herophilus: The Art of Medicine in Early Alexandria*. Cambridge University Press.

Wachter 1987: Rudolf Wachter, *Altlateinischer Inschriften: sprachliche und epigraphische Untersuchungen zu den Documenten bis etwa 150 v.Chr.* Bern: Peter Lang.

Walbank 1957: F.W. Walbank, *A Historical Commentary on Polybius*, vol. I. Oxford: Clarendon Press.

Walker 1993: Andrew D. Walker, '*Enargeia* and the Spectator in Greek Historiography', *Transactions of the American Philological Association* 123: 353–77.

Wallace-Hadrill 1997: Andrew Wallace-Hadrill, 'Mutatio morum: The Idea of a Cultural Revolution', in T. Habinek and A. Schiesaro (eds), *The Roman Cultural Revolution* (Cambridge University Press): 3–22.

Wardle 1998: D. Wardle, *Valerius Maximus: Memorable Deeds and Sayings Book 1*. Oxford: Clarendon Press.

Wardman 1974: Alan Wardman, *Plutarch's Lives*. London: Elek.

Watson 1974: Alan Watson, *Law Making in the Later Roman Republic*. Oxford: Clarendon Press.

Weinstock 1971: Stefan Weinstock, *Divus Julius*. Oxford: Clarendon Press.

Weis 1992: Anne Weis, 'Marsyas I', *Lexicon Iconographicum Mythologiae Classicae* 6.1: 366–78.

Welwei 1967: Karl-Wilhelm Welwei, 'Das Angebot des Diadems an Caesar und das Luperkalienproblem', *Historia* 16: 44–69.

Welwei 2000: Karl-Wilhelm Welwei, 'Lucius Iunius Brutus—ein fictiver Revolutionsheld', in Karl-Joachim Hölkeskamp and Elke Stein-Hölkeskamp (eds), *Von Romulus zu Augustus: grosse Gestalten der römischen Republik* (Munich: 2000): 48–57.

West 1966: M.L. West, *Hesiod: Theogony*. Oxford: Clarendon Press.

West 1978: M.L. West, *Hesiod: Works and Days*. Oxford: Clarendon Press.

West 1989: M.L. West, 'The Early Chronology of Attic Tragedy', *Classical Quarterly* 39: 251–4.

Wirszubski 1950: Ch. Wirszubski, *Libertas as a Political Idea at Rome During the Late Republic and Early Empire*. Cambridge University Press.

Wiseman 1974: T.P. Wiseman, *Cinna the Poet and Other Roman Essays*. Leicester University Press.

Wiseman 1976: T.P. Wiseman, 'Two Questions on the Circus Flaminius', *Papers of the British School at Rome* 44: 44–7.

Wiseman 1979: T.P. Wiseman, *Clio's Cosmetics: Three Studies in Greco-Roman Literature*. Leicester University Press.

Wiseman 1981: T.P. Wiseman, 'The Temple of Victory on the Palatine', *Antiquaries Journal* 61: 35–52.

Wiseman 1983: T.P. Wiseman, 'The Wife and Children of Romulus', *Classical Quarterly* 33: 445–52.

Wiseman 1985: T.P. Wiseman, *Catullus and His World: A Reappraisal*. Cambridge University Press.

Wiseman 1987a: T.P. Wiseman, *Roman Studies Literary and Historical*. Liverpool: Francis Cairns.

Wiseman 1987b: T.P. Wiseman, 'Con Boni nel foro: I diari romani di W. St. Clair Baddeley', *Rivista dell'Istituto Nazionale d'Archeologia e Storia dell'Arte* serie 3, 8–9: 119–49.

Wiseman 1988: T.P. Wiseman, 'Satyrs in Rome?: The Background to Horace's *Ars poetica*', *Journal of Roman Studies* 78: 1–13.

Wiseman 1991: T.P. Wiseman, *Flavius Josephus: Death of an Emperor* (Exeter Studies in History 30). University of Exeter Press.

Wiseman 1993a: T.P. Wiseman, 'Lying Historians: Seven Types of Mendacity', in C. Gill and T.P. Wiseman (eds), *Lies and Fiction in the Ancient World* (University of Exeter Press): 122–46.

Wiseman 1993b: T.P. Wiseman, 'The She-Wolf Mirror: an Interpretation', *Papers of the British School at Rome* 61: 1–6.

Wiseman 1994: T.P. Wiseman, *Historiography and Imagination: Eight Essays on Roman Culture*. University of Exeter Press.

Wiseman 1995: T.P. Wiseman, *Remus: a Roman Myth*. Cambridge University Press.

Wiseman 1996: T.P. Wiseman, 'What Do We Know About Early Rome?', *Journal of Roman Archaeology* 9: 310–15.

Wiseman 1998: T.P. Wiseman, *Roman Drama and Roman History*. University of Exeter Press.

Wiseman 2004a: T.P. Wiseman, *The Myths of Rome*. University of Exeter Press.

Wiseman 2004b: T.P. Wiseman, 'Where was the Nova Via?', *Papers of the British School at Rome* 62: 167–83.

Wiseman 2006a: T.P. Wiseman, 'Andrea Carandini and *Roma Quadrata*', *Accordia Research Papers* 10: 103–26.

Wiseman 2006b: T.P. Wiseman, 'The Cult Site of Anna Perenna: Documentation, Visualization, Imagination', in Lothar Haselberger and John Humphrey (eds), *Imaging Ancient Rome: Documentation—Visualization—Imagination* (*JRA* Supplement 61, Portsmouth RI): 51–61.

Wright 2005: Matthew Wright, *Euripides' Escape-Tragedies: A Study of Helen, Andromeda, and Iphigeneia among the Taurians*. Oxford University Press.

Zetzel 1995: James E.G. Zetzel, *Cicero De re publica: Selections*. Cambridge University Press.

Zevi 1968: Fausto Zevi, 'Considerazioni sull'elogio di Scipione Barbato', *Studi miscellanei* 15: 69–73.

Zevi 1993: Fausto Zevi, 'Per l'identificazione della Porticus Minucia Frumentaria', *Mélanges de l'École française de Rome (Antiquité)* 105: 661–708.

Zevi 1995: Fausto Zevi, 'Demarato e i re "corinzi" di Roma', in A. Storchi Marino (ed.), *L'incidenza dell'antico: studi in memoria di Ettore Lepore*, I (Naples: Luciano editore): 291–314.

Zevi 2005: Fausto Zevi, 'From Ancus Marcius to Apollodorus of Damascus: Notes on the Port Area of Ostia', in Simon Keay, Martin Millett, Lidia Paroli and Kristian Strutt (eds), *Portus* (Archaeological Monographs 15, London: British School at Rome): 30–42.

Ziołkowski 1989: Adam Ziołkowski, 'The *Sacra Via* and the Temple of Jupiter Stator', *Opuscula Romana* 17: 225–39.

Ziołkowski 2004: Adam Ziółkowski, *Sacra Via Twenty Years After* (Journal of Juristic Papyrology, Supplement 3). Warsaw: Raphael Taubenschlag Foundation.

Zorzetti 1980: Nevio Zorzetti, *La pretesta e il teatro latino arcaico* (Forme materiali e ideologie del mondo antico 14). Naples: Liguori.

Zorzetti 1990: Nevio Zorzetti, 'The *Carmina Convivalia*', in Oswyn Murray (ed.), *Sympotica: a Symposium on the Symposion* (Oxford: Clarendon Press): 289–307.

Zwierlein 1966: Otto Zwierlein, *Die Rezitationsdramen Senecas* (Beiträge zur klassischen Philologie 20). Meisenheim am Glan: Hain.

Illustration Credits

Fig. 1   De Simone 1981 tav. III(a): Giorgio Bretschneider editore, Rome.
Fig. 2   Rome, Antiquarium forense, inv. 1918: Soprintendenza per i Beni Archeo-
         logici di Roma.
Fig. 3   Richter 1901.364 (Abb. 32).
Fig. 4   Richter 1901, Taf. 5 (opposite p. 42).
Fig. 5   Ritschl 1862, pl. I (a).
Fig. 7   Piranomonte 2002.18: Soprintendenza per i Beni Archeologici di Roma.
Fig. 8   Piranomonte 2002.26: Soprintendenza per i Beni Archeologici di Roma.
Fig. 9   Barré 1840, fig. 27b: British Library.
Fig. 10 Gerhard et al. 1897.54.
Fig. 11 Gerhard et al. 1897.172.
Fig. 12 © The Trustees of the British Museum.
Fig. 14 Gerhard et al. 1897.52–3.
Fig. 15 Gerhard et al. 1897.51–2.
Fig. 16 German Archaeological Institute, Rome: Felbermeyer, Neg. D-DAI-Rom
         1932.0120.
Fig. 17 *Monumenti dell'Instituto* 9, tav. LVIII.
Fig. 18 *Monumenti dell'Instituto*, Supplement, tav. XIX.
Fig. 19 Drawing by Dr F. Jurgeit Blanck (Jurgeit 1999.1.528–33, 2.254–5).
Fig. 20 *Monumenti dell'Instituto* 10, tav. XLVI.
Fig. 21 Istituto di Studi sulle Civiltà Italiche e del Mediterraneo Antico, Rome.
Fig. 22 *Monumenti dell'Instituto* 9, tav. XXIII.
Fig. 23 *Monumenti dell'Instituto* 9, tav. XXII.
Fig. 24 Gerhard et al. 1897, no. 120.
Fig. 25 The Walters Art Museum, Baltimore (54.136).
Fig. 26 Istituto di Studi sulle Civiltà Italiche e del Mediterraneo Antico, Rome.
Fig. 27 Gerhard et al. 1879, no. 44.
Fig. 28 Soprintendenza per i Beni Archeologici dell'Etruria Meridionale (foto n.
         224535).
Fig. 29 Soprintendenza archeologica per le province di Salerno, Avellino e
         Benevento.
Figs 30–31   Istituto di Studi sulle Civiltà Italiche e del Mediterraneo Antico, Rome.
Fig. 32 Soprintendenza per i Beni Archeologici di Puglia, inv. 8154.
Fig. 33 Soprintendenza per i Beni Archeologici dell'Etruria Meridionale (foto n.
         4559).
Fig. 34 Soprintendenza per i Beni Archeologici dell'Etruria Meridionale (foto n.
         117795).

Fig. 35   © The Trustees of the British Museum.

Fig. 36   © The Cleveland Museum of Art, 1999. John L. Severance Fund, 1989.73.

Fig. 37   © Monumenti musei e gallerie ponteficie (Museo Gregoriano, foto n. XXXV.31.16).

Fig. 38   Musée d'art et d'histoire, Geneva (inv. 23471): photo Yves Siza.

Fig.s 39–42   Istituto di Studi sulle Civiltà Italiche e del Mediterraneo Antico, Rome (fig. 42 redrawn by Sean Goddard).

Fig. 43   *Monumenti dell'Instituto*, Supplement, tav. XV.

Fig. 44   Soprintendenza per i Beni Archeologici delle province di Napoli e Caserta.

Fig. 46   © The Trustees of the British Museum.

Fig.s 47–54   Drawn by Sean Goddard.

Index of Passages

General Index